International Perspectives on Child & Adolescent Mental Health

Volume 2

Selected Proceedings of the Second International Conference on Child & Adolescent Mental Health, Kuala Lumpur, Malaysia, June 2000

International Perspectives on Child & Adolescent Mental Health

Volume 2

Selected Proceedings of the Second International
Conference on Child & Adolescent Mental Health,
Kuala Lumpur, Malaysia, June 2000

Edited by

Nirbhay N. Singh
Virginia Commonwealth University, USA

Thomas H. Ollendick
Virginia Polytechnic Institute and State University, USA

Ashvind N. Singh
Virginia Commonwealth University, USA

2002

ELSEVIER
Amsterdam - Boston - Londen - New York - Oxford - Paris
San Diego - San Francisco - Singapore - Sydney - Tokyo

ELSEVIER SCIENCE Ltd
The Boulevard, Langford Lane
Kidlington, Oxford OX5 1GB, UK

First edition 2002

Library of Congress Cataloging in Publication Data
A catalog record from the Library of Congress has been applied for.

British Library Cataloguing in Publication Data
A catalogue record from the British Library has been applied for.

ISBN: 0 08 044105 X

♾ The paper used in this publication meets the requirements of ANSI/NISO Z39.48-1992 (Permanence of Paper).
Printed in The Netherlands.

PREFACE

The biennial Elsevier conference on Child and Adolescent Mental Health is designed to provide a forum for mental health experts from various disciplines and countries to discuss and evaluate the current status of our knowledge in this field. The Second International Conference on Child and Adolescent Mental Health was held in Kuala Lumpur, Malaysia, on June 6-10, 2000, and was attended by scientists and practitioners from 28 countries.

The conference included a wide-ranging, worldwide program covering major aspects of child and adolescent mental health. The conference began with workshops by international scholars on topics of far-reaching significance. This was followed by keynote presentations and concurrent scientific sessions on wide ranging topics, each chosen on the basis of its relevance to current mental health issues in terms of both research and practice. The keynote presentations by Dr. John R. Weisz from the University of California, Los Angeles, USA, Dr. Matthew R. Sanders from the University of Queensland, Australia, and Patricia Howlin from the University of London, UK, were intellectually exciting, clinically relevant, and of immediate practical significance. Further, there were poster presentations and networking sessions for participants from all countries.

This volume presents a selection of papers presented at the conference. These papers highlight research and practice in child and adolescent mental health from around the world.

CONTENTS

PART 7
CULTURAL MENTAL HEALTH

Mental Health of Children and Adolescents

Ramasammy Manikam
Maryland Hospital for Children

Ramasammy Manikam · Maryland Hospital for Children · Department of Pediatrics · Division of
Gastroenterology · 22 South Greene Street N5E7 · Baltimore · Maryland 21201 · United States.

*International Perspectives on Child and Adolescent Mental Health. Volume 2: Proceedings of the Second International
Conference*, edited by N. N. Singh, T. H. Ollendick, and A. N. Singh. © 2002 Elsevier Science Ltd. All rights reserved.

Most persons are better able to define mental illness than mental health. Mental health issues are seen as a dichotomy: mentally sane or mentally ill. However, there is a temperate zone between mental health and mental illness. Many levels of mental health states, containing a majority of children with mental health problems, lie in this zone. Children in this zone do not meet the diagnostic criteria for any mental disorder or illness, and fall through the cracks until their problems become severe to fall within the diagnostic criteria. Apathy, stress, low self-esteem, and other mental distress in children may be ignored or misinterpreted. They are then left to suffer the indignation of being labeled as bad or crazy; and seen as lacking willpower and character. Such dismissive labels harm children and their families.

Childhood mental health problems have negative human and economic consequences not only for the children but also their families and their community. Children's mental health is everyone's business. Children's mental health affects everyone directly or indirectly. A troubled child adversely affects the family, the neighborhood, the school, the society; and even the world now brought closer together in time and space with improved travel, the media, and the internet. Adults have to realize that taking care of children's mental health benefits them as well.

Many definitions of mental health have been offered. The World Health Organization (1999) defines mental health as a state of emotional and social wellbeing; realizes his or her abilities, copes with the normal stresses of life, woks productively or fruitfully, and contributes to his or her community. The World Federation for Mental Health, a citizen-based mental health organization defined mental health as a condition that permits the optimal physical, intellectual, and emotional development of the individual, and compatible with that of other individuals' (Brody, 1987). The bottom line is good health in children, physical and mental, is a fundamental requirement for growth and development, learning, happiness, and to become productive citizens.

What is a Mental Health Problem

Mental health problem in children is the destabilization of their mental health, causing an imbalance in mental homeostasis marked by alterations in thought, behavior, and feelings. Their cognitive, emotional and social capacities are interfered with. Such imbalances can arise out of their daily living challenges, unmet needs, and unfulfilled goals. The symptom complex at the low end of severity may not meet the diagnostic criteria for classification as a mental disorder or illness.

A mental disorder or illness, on the other hand, is noted when the symptom complex is severe enough to meet the criteria set forth in ICD10 and DSM-IV. The DSM-IV defines mental health disorder 'as a clinically significant behavioral and psychological syndrome or pattern, that occurs in an individual associated with distress (e.g., a painful symptom) or disability (i.e., impairment in one of more important areas of functioning), with risk of suffering death, pain, disability, or loss of freedom'. Stated simply, a mental health disorder is a problem that affects children's ability to think, feel and act in an adaptive manner that promotes positive health and welfare for themselves and others around them.

Children across the world experience similar circumstances such as stress and poverty, and poor mental health. However, the construction of mental health issues varies across families, cultures and nations. Their unique construction and understanding of mental health affects their response to the mental health issues of children. Problems in children can be exaggerations of normal developmental trends or disturbed family interactions; and not necessarily that of a disordered pathology. The threshold for identification of these range of behaviors of mental health problems differ as a function of cultural norms. Numerous cross-national, cross-cultural, and cross-ethnic studies conducted in Australia (Achenbach, et al., 1990), Holland (Achenbach, et al., 1987), Puerto Rico (Achenbach, et al., 1990), Thailand (Weisz, et al., 1993), and Denmark (Arnett & Balle-Jensen, 1993) support the hypothesis.

In some ways Szasz (1974), and others with similar views, may be right in the argument that problems and conflicts of living should not be considered as mental illness. There are many instances in the DSM series where a disorder in one version is erased in the next, confirming Szasz's view that mental health labels are subjective assignments confined to cultural norms.

Scope of the Problem

Mental Health is a major public health challenge around the world. The rate of mental health problems in children continues to rise. The Global Burden of Disease study (Murray & Lopez, 1996) revealed that mental health problems are responsible for as much as 11 per cent of the disease burden worldwide. Mental health problems are identified as the top five leading conditions causing disability, and contribute the most to the global burden of disease and disability. Measured by the Disability Adjusted Life Years (DALY) instrument, depression alone accounted for 36.5% of the global burden of disease. Children and adolescents were reported to be at special risk of being affected by the burden of mental health problems especially those experiencing disrupted nurturing and extreme poverty.

On the average, fifteen to twenty percent of children and adolescents suffer from mental health problems (Zubrick, Silburn, Burton, & Blair, 2000). It is reasonable to assume that the current epidemiological data do not represent the real scope of the problem. Children kept hidden out of shame and stigma by their families, children experiencing subclinical symptoms or disturbance, children seeking healing from alternative therapeutic settings and local traditions and systems, and children with mental deficiency do not participate in epidemiological studies.

The exact number of children with mental health problems and their relative severity is unknown. But it is obvious that the problem is substantial and much more severe than acknowledged. According to the United States Surgeon General, mental disorders account for 4 of the 10 leading causes of disability for individuals five years and older (U.S. Department of Health and Human Services, 1999). Mental health disorders rank second only to cardiovascular illnesses in the United States; depression is the leading cause of disability and suicide the leading preventable causes of death. One in five children have a diagnosable mental disorder with 11% experiencing functional impairment (Levin & Hanson, 2001).

Status of Children's Mental Health

Today's generation of children confront risks unheard of a few decades ago. Young children are exposed to high rates of violence, from a variety of sources, including domestic violence, live war coverage and reports of violence in television. Exposure to violence at a young age is very costly to long-term mental health including anxiety, depression, aggression, sleep problems, and delinquency (Fantuzzo, Depalo, Lambert, Martion, Anderson, & Sutton, 1991; Schwab-Stone, Ayers, & Kasparov, et al., 1995).

Travel, television, and the internet expose children to information outside their religion, culture, and social behaviors at an age when their intellectual capacity is immature to assess and evaluate such information. Parents do not have full control of the information flow. In many cases, parents themselves are swept away by the strong information current.

Child and adolescent life spans roughly 20 years (0-19 years of age). Great changes take place in their physical, cognitive, social, and emotional domains during these youthful years. In addition, as the children mature their physical and social world expands to include the extended family members, teachers, and friends. These expanded domains of the physical and social world exert their influence on the children. Children with positive nurturing, guidance, and love from their parents can be expected to traverse positively the many challenges during their growing years. However, urbanization and industrialization has changed the developmental milieu of today's adolescent. Young people, in most cases, are forced by necessity of education and job, to migrate from their indigenous neighborhood to major cities. In doing so, they lose their extended families, their peer group, and social support systems. They lose the traditional 'hand holding' methods of initiation and guidance of the rights of passage into adulthood.

Rather, the adolescent is left to his/her own biological strengths and social history to negotiate the ever-changing ecological milieu.

Children form the largest segment of the poor. They live in unsafe neighborhoods, uncaring communities, and in many cases in dysfunctional families. The physical environment of poor children including the neighborhood and schools are breeding grounds for emotional and psychological trauma. Children's mental health is inexorably linked with that of their immediate family. These children suffer, grow up angry and bitter, and when they perceive life as unforgiving without hope lash out at others with devastating consequences for all concerned. The number of runaways, throwaways, and giveaways are on the rise. Children's mental health is in immediate need of global attention.

Mental health needs of children are not the priority in most countries. However, increase in children's mental health problems and its pervasive social, and health and economic costs has brought mental health problems in children to the forefront in many countries. Further, the recent, spate of high profile school shooting cases in America has brought urgency to this matter. Children's mental health, in many countries, is considered a public health crisis, and a call has gone out for action. Perhaps the loudest call for action has come from the World Health Organization (WHO) and the National Institute of Health (NIH) in the United States of America. The WHO is actively addressing mental health issues of children primarily through funding school programs in various countries. Some of the projects include: 'life skills' education, psychosocial competency training, child-friendly schools development, reduce bullying, social climate improvement, and connect families and schools to work in cooperation

Childhood adverse experiences can derail the normal developmental processes to produce a wide variety of disruptions in physical, social, emotional, and cognitive development (Cicchetti & Toth, 1998). Such derailment can interfere with information processing, affect regulation, and social relation building, all of which are essential towards positive development. Children are almost always considered the problem when a referral is made to a service provider. Very little investigation is conducted to evaluate the role of the adults and the environment to determine the owner of the problem. Behavior is reciprocal and contextual and to ignore this fact makes the child a victim of circumstances. The child's problematic behavior could well be an adaptive response to an unloving parents, uncaring teachers, or uncouth peers.

Manifestations of psychological dysfunction are indications of problems in living not symptoms of disease process. We need to reconceptualize and delineate psychopathology from psychosocial stresses of daily hassles of living. Simply fitting a child's living problems into the more than three hundred DSM-IV categories does the child and the family a disservice, especially in the face of stigma and the long-term negative consequences of such labels.

The Goal

Children live in an uncertain, unpredictable and unstable world. Children and adolescents have unique developmental and social needs. Their life situation and problems are superimposed upon their changing growth and development. It is a wonder most of our children do well in the face of such adversity.

The questions are simple and straightforward. How to raise mentally healthy and happy children? Why do some children succumb to mental health problems? What factors make some children thrive despite experiencing severe negative life experience? Answers to these simple questions are, however, complex. Phylogenic, ontogenic, and socio-cultural factors are implicated in the growth and development of children. These factors are interrelated and interlocked. Children are biologically wired to grow, while they are socially structured to acquire life skills. Positive and successful development depends on repeated and varied interactions between the child's biological structure and social demands. Synergy between these two factors results in successful growth with good mental health of the child. Interruption at any stage is a risk for failure, the consequences of which may have far reaching effects. Children born healthy, cared for by loving parents, served by adequate resources, attend good schools, and reside in a safe and secure neighborhood will in all probability lead a happy and productive life. The goal then should be to foster normal growth and development and promote resilience to mental health problems. Achieving these goals require understanding of the mechanism of mental health and pathways to mental health problems.

Mechanism of Mental Health Problems

The mechanism of mental health in children can be understood from biology, personal characteristics, and environmental factors. Genetic, biological, neurological, and hormonal studies point to the impact early experiences on emotional development. High levels of stress in the formative years have negative brain development (Shore, 1997), and lasts long (Kazdin, 1993) with high cost to society. There is strong scientific evidence of the interplay between biology and the environment (Bronfenbrenner, 1994) in mental health. Yet, most studies oversimplify behaviors and offer single causative explanations.

A number of central concepts and assumptions underlie our current understanding of children's mental health and mental disorders. These concepts have been variously defined

(Cicchetti & Cohen, 1995; Jensen, 1998; Sroufe & Rutter, 1984). But, by and large these concepts are based on the premise that psychopathology in childhood arises through a complex multi-layered interaction of the child characteristics (including biological, psychological, and genetic factors), the environment (including parent, sibling, and family relations, peer and neighborhood factors, school and community factors, and the larger social-cultural context). There is strong evidence to suggest that genetic, biological, neurological, and hormonal factors impact on children's emotional development. Therefore, understanding of children's history and past experiences is essential to unraveling the 'why's' and 'how's' of children's mental status, both normal and abnormal.

The medical model has tended to minimize the social context as a significant factor in mental health issues. This view still persists with many schools of thoughts vociferously defending their paradigm from within their self-prescribed prism, despite strong evidence from the more psychosocial or psycho-spiritual perspectives (Boyle, 1990; Breggin, 1993). The reliance on a medical model for the explanation for mental health and mental illness may have contributed to the current state of how persons view mental illness and how health policies are made and services delivered

Biology

The human brain is a complex and dynamic organ, not easily explained. Evidence shows that stressful social environments activate hormones that influence neuron distribution. High levels of stress in the earliest years can undermine brain development, and permanent effects on the neurobiological systems in the brain Shore, 1997). Children who experience extreme stress in their early years are at greater risk for developing cognitive, behavioral and emotional difficulties.

The recent cracking of the human genetic code has brought high hopes in the identification and treatment of mental illness. There is increasing consensus that biologic factors exert pronounced influences on several disorders such as pervasive developmental disorder and autism (Piven, 1997) and social phobia (Pine, 1997)

Genetic abnormalities are not the only form of biological influences. Abnormalities of the central nervous system caused by injury, infection, poor nutrition, or environmental toxins may also influence behavior, thinking, or feeling. Behavioral disorders like conduct disorder appear to have predisposing causes of perinatal factors of prematurity, birth trauma, and low birthweight (McGee, Silva & Willimans, 1984).

Though subtle influences of biology may lie behind patterns of behaviors not all mental health problems and mental illness are solely due to biology. Biological precipitates alone cannot be expected to cause mental problems, in the absence of environmental coupling.

Personal Factors

In most cases, children's mental health problems do not dwell in them, but as a consequence of disrupted attachment, inappropriate parenting, unsavory peers, and unmet goals. However, with their birth children bring the ingredients that absorb, interpret, and translate life's experiences and interactions in unique ways, different in kind and degree from others. These genetic contributions include negative dispositions and temperament. Strong negative dispositions and temperaments have the capacity to derail positive care in parents, especially vulnerable parents who experience severe stresses and have mental health problems of their own.

Strong positive relationship exists between deviant temperamental patterns in early infancy and later misconduct (Carey & McDevitt, 1973). Heightened behavioral responses in play behavior, exaggerated response to mild provocation, aggression, and impulsiveness are seen as signs of later difficulty. Temperamentally difficult infants exhibit a threefold greater rate of conduct disorder in later life than do temperamentally easy infants (Thomas & Chess, 1977). Destructiveness and non-submissiveness at age three are listed as significant predictors of delinquency in adolescence (Glueck & Glueck, 1950). Serious emotional deviance increases as misbehaving youth grow into adulthood. Long term follow up studies (Offord, Sullivan, Allen, & Abrams, 1979) of 20- and 30- years showed increased rate in psychiatric hospitalization of aggressive youth 9-11%, and alcoholism 8%. These rates are two to three times that of the population as a whole (Robins, 1966).

Children's ability to pursue goals, control behaviors in socially acceptable forms, and to secure wants and needs requires emotional regulation. Emotional regulation and behavior control occurs within a social context. Children in toxic environments fail to develop such regulations and suffer negative consequences of their faulty emotions and behaviors. In the absence of a match between children's predisposition, caregiver capabilities, and community support children's emotional and mental health development is adversely affected. The child's positive self-esteem, perceived autonomy, easy temperament, internal locus of control, adequate perceptual and communication skills and accurate cognitive appraisal of the situation, along with environmental and family support increase the child's therapeutic effect (Carey, 1992).

Adolescence is a unique phase in the continuum of human growth and development. It is exciting, challenging, confusing, frustrating, and even frightening. Parents find difficulty in handling adolescents; but adolescents find it equally difficult to deal with their experiences, the adults around them, and the complex environment they live in. Children, especially adolescents, succumb to 'optimistic bias', a form of thinking error through which they have a tendency to view themselves invulnerable to negative life events. This error in thinking causes them to take up health compromising 'thrill seeking' behaviors rather easily. Adults tend to label these behaviors as 'risk taking' behaviors. Most adolescents tend to correct themselves after the 'experimental' phase of the thrill seeking behaviors. However, some persist in such health-threatening patterns of behaviors for prolonged periods leading them to severe mental health problems.

Environment

The environment of children expands through their developing years. The environment, initially limited to the home, expands to include the extended family, neighborhood, and schools. All these domains exert their influence upon the developing child. It is doubtful that effective interventions that promote good mental health will persist without attention to these environmental influences. The physical environment itself is as important as the socio-cultural environment in explaining differences in psychosocial health (Brogan & James, 1980).

Adults and peers outside the home influence and subject children to their power of influence. Children who failed to receive strong attachment and nurturance with inept , neglectful, and uninvolved parents will have little resource to fight off the power of these outside influences. Children in poverty with resulting deprivation of basic needs, even with the best of parents, are also vulnerable to outside influence.

Peer group influence is a strong factor in children's behaviors. Children tend to 'follow' peers with whom they identify with in many areas of life including violence, sex, drugs, alcohol and others (Brookes-Gunn, & Paikoff, 199; Smith, Udry, & Moris, 1985). Therefore, interventions must pay attention to the peer group, a key factor influencing whether a young person will lead a young adulthood characterized by violent and aggressive behaviors. Prevention, parent supervision, healthy neighborhoods and communities; and early interventions are important to stem the unhealthy influence of outsiders on children.

Family

Children are products of their biology and families, until they engage with the outside world. The family environment into which children are born will have the greatest impact. Parents are children's first peers, teachers, and therapists. The attachment they form and the nurturance they receive from their parents will have life long influence. Early disruptions in emotional development and care giving relationships can have lasting negative consequences. Many problems evident in older children and adolescents are believed to originate in early childhood. Children growing out of poor attachment experience disturbed development in love, self-esteem, security, trust, recklessness, vigilance, and even aggression (Cristtenden & Ainsworth, 1989); and exhibit poor language, cognition, and general health (Schaefer, 1989). These children may fail to learn empathy, and understand others view point and affective states. Many parents fail to socialize and direct their children's positive behaviors. Many health damaging behaviors of children are at least in part attributable to inadequate parenting.

Children's difficult behaviors are a source of irritation, resentment and hostility with parents who are unhappy and poor. Families with troubled children have a tendency to become overly intrusive and limit their children's independence and creativity, subjugating them to a life of dependency and unhappiness. Caring for a child with mental health problems may cause the family stigma and isolation. Further, they may also exhaust their financial and emotional capital. Such stress on the parents may lead to the child being resented and even rejected.

Healthy families stride to provide love and emotional support, safe environment, security, training, and basic care and nurturance. They direct the child in socially acceptable behaviors with opportunities for experience, acceptance and satisfaction (Talbot, 1976). Dysfunctional families on the other hand are inflexible and ineffective in meeting life's challenges and solving their children's problems. They are too strict or too permissive with their children, and the family atmosphere one of chaos, frustration and pain, and stagnation (Stierlin, Wirshing, & Knauss, 1977).

The physical and emotional health of parents is a critical variable in the mental and physical health of their children. Preventive services should aim at fostering mentally and physically healthy parents. Poor parental mental health in a deprived environment is a stamp for stress, poor self-esteem, poor achievement and subsequent delinquent behaviors and mental illness of their children Basic needs of children and their families are of utmost importance. Inadequate basic needs stunt the potential growth and development of families and their children. Poverty, lack of food, shelter, clothing, sanitation, and health amenities affect both physical and mental health of individuals.

Family construction varies among communities and nations. The two parent heterosexual family is on the decline. Today's families include single parent, same-sex parents, foster parents, adoptive parents, divorced parents, and third-generation parents. Mental health development of children from these non-traditional families is yet to be fully studied. In the past, parents were naturally guided through modeling, teaching, training and support by their nuclear families, extended families, and the 'village'. Industrialization and social development has changed the family structure. In many countries, children are rarely cared for by parents. Rather, the children are taken care by nannies, baby sitters, and day care staff. Others grow up with foster parents, orphanages, and third generation relatives. Children from these reconstituted families are deprived of the opportunities to grow up observing their mothers care for their health during pregnancy, watch their mothers care for their infant siblings, participate in the care of their baby siblings, and learn how their mothers nurture their babies.

Research suggests that caregiver behaviors profoundly influence infants in language, cognition, and general health (Schaefer, 1989). Parent child interaction is an important contributor to the development of the child. Rutter (1977), for example, found that an average of 61% of the children of hostile or neurotic parents were deviant on teacher rating scales compared with only 10% of the children of non-symptomatic parents. Quinton, Rutter, and Rowlands (1976) in their study found that an average of 46% of children with 'very poor marriages' exhibited behavioral deviance, compared to an average of 28% for the 'poor' marriage, and only 13% for the 'good ' marriage population. Miller, Court, Knox, and Brandon (1974) based on their study concluded that problematic children in school nearly always are maladjusted at home.

There is unanimous agreement on the importance of parents and good parenting and children's mental health. However, there is little agreement on what is 'good parenting'. Effective parenting is not static and does not reside within the parents. Social, legal, cultural, and immediate neighborhood practices impact parent view on parenting. 'Good and bad parenting', for the most part is determined by children's behaviors and not necessarily on what the parent does. However, it can't be denied that harsh, punitive, and abusive parenting makes resilient children 'unhappy' and vulnerable children 'mentally ill'. Families of children referred for externalizing disorders are reported to experience socio economic disadvantage, high levels of stress, diminished support network, family dysfunction, and parent psychopathology (Kazdin, 1995). Caregivers with psychopathology, alcohol and drug use, and domestic violence make incompetent parents and lack the capacity to prioritize family needs or resources to their children's well being.

Almost all families experience crisis at some point in time. Yet, just like resilient children, most families overcome adversities and demands and perform their parenting roles effectively, promoting the child's positive mental health development. For others, however, the crisis touches their vulnerability threshold sending them spiraling down to persistent mental health problems unless timely support and intervention is afforded.

Saving our Children's Mental Health

Knowledge of childhood mental health has expanded over the years. A lot is known about precipitates of children's mental health problems, and what works in limiting the negative consequences of their inherited and acquired aspects of poor mental health. Our knowledge is incomplete and imprecise. We may never achieve the statistical specificity and clinical sensitivity we seek for confidence and reassurance, given the multi-complex interplay of the domains and variables that influence mental health of children, as discussed under the 'mechanisms of mental health' section. Despite the limitations, informed application of what we know can help millions of children and their families to maintain good mental health, to solve practical problems, and to avoid the downward spiral into persistent mental health disorders

A number of factors from multiple domains contribute to poor mental health of children. There is a need for programs and services to adequately address these factors and domains. Programs should be planned, coordinated and integrated. Properly designed and executed mental health programs can reduce the percentage of children with poor mental health. Poorly designed and executed mental health programs on the other hand are a waste at great cost.

Given the multi-faceted nature of mental health problems, a number of programs should be simultaneously put in force to address mental health problems of children. These programs can be classified as prevention, protection and prescription.

Prevention

Prevention is the first link in the chain of programs outlined above. The purpose of prevention is to arrest problems from occurring. There are three major categories in prevention: primary, secondary and tertiary. Primary prevention is designed to preempt and interrupt the emergence of a condition even before it's early stages, secondary prevention to halt the continuation after a problem has been identified, and tertiary prevention to arrest further worsening of a problem.

Many countries now have focused on prevention of mental health. In the United States, the Department of Health and Human Services has mandated specific prevention programs. The European Network on Mental Health promotion has been set up to identify and disseminate good practice in mental health promotion and prevention. The World Health Organization has produced a manifesto on 'Primary Prevention of Mental, Neurological and Psychosocial Disorders' (WHO, 1998).

Current focus on prevention is essential, but still a step too late. The first stage of prevention should begin with services to would be parents. Constitutional and environmental influences begin long before the birth of a child (Eyberg, 1998). All possible steps should be taken to ensure that would be parents are educated, trained, and given adequate resources before they become parents. High school curriculums should include education and training in mental and physical health. Sexually active individuals should be targeted for ongoing services. Those who are poor, smoke, do drugs, engage in promiscuous sexuality, have poor emotional regulation, and susceptible to mental illness should be targeted for prevention services, before they become pregnant

Risk Factors

Prevention requires targeting vulnerable at risk children. There are numerous risk factors that impact children's development. A number of key risk factors were reported in the Newcastle Study (Kolvin, Miller, Fleeting, & Kolvin, 1988) and are similar with that of Rutter's (1987) findings. Identified risk factors include poverty, marital disruption, overcrowding, large family, caregiver criminality, maternal psychiatric disorder, low social status, and care of the child placed outside the home. Further, both studies concluded that the weight of cumulative risk factors contributed to the probability of psychiatric disorders in children; independent of any single or type of risk factors.

Economic hardship can indirectly increase a child's risk of developing a behavioral disorder because it may cause behavioral problems in the parents and increase the risk of child abuse (Dutton, 1986). The relationship between stressful life events and risk for child mental disorders are well established (Hammen, 1988; Jensen, 1988). This relationship is complicated, perhaps reflecting the impact of individual differences and developmental changes. Risk factors are correlated and interactive, making the developing and testing models of the impact of risk factors on childhood mental health difficult. Patterson (1966), however, suggested that combining the measurable risk factors into a single model to assess their cumulative effects might be productive. Research using a combined risk model may reveal clusters of risk variables in a hierarchical fashion.

Risk factors can have direct and indirect effects on children's mental health, and are unique to each individual. A risk factor for one child may not have the same effect or to the same degree in another child. Nevertheless, there is strong research evidence that some risk factors are more salient than others.

Poverty (code Z59.5, International Classification of Diseases) is one such salient risk factor, and is considered a primary cause of poor mental health in children and adolescents; who comprise about 40% of the world's total population. Poverty adversely affects physical needs, safety and security; emotional stress, and social isolation and drift. Chronic adversity of moderate to severe intensity over a long duration is the main conduit for poverty and subsequent mental health problems and disorders. The parent's physical and mental health is influenced by their socioeconomic status. The poor living under adverse socio-economic and unsafe environmental conditions suffer from poor housing and sanitation, diseases, inadequate health care, and nutritional deficiencies. Schoenthaler (1983) identified six deficiencies accruing out of poor diet. These include hypoglycemia, vitamin and mineral deficiencies, cerebral allergies, environmental contaminants, minimal brain dysfunction, and neuro-regulator imbalances. Schauss (1980) further stated that dietary deficiencies account for a large proportion of antisocial behavior.

Severe deprivation affects children's overall health including brain development, cognition, and emotional regulation. Poor families are usually of low occupational status, and their children attend poor school systems. Poor neighborhoods have high rates of suicide, depression, anxiety states and schizophrenia (Gomm, 1996; Brandon, 1991; Davis & Wainwright, 1996). Poverty affects the quality of parenting behaviors and early home learning environment (Shaw & Vondara, 1995). The findings of poverty as a salient risk factor on children's poor mental health support Maslow's (1970) theory that financial assistance to meet the minimum subsistence level of an individual or family is the prerequisite to address all other problems. As such, programs focused entirely on the individual is set up for failure, if the family and socio-environmental community is not included in the master plan for prevention and treatment

There is substantial evidence that problem behaviors in children takes place in the home with family members serving as the initial trainers. Ineffective parents set the stage for coercive interaction between the child and the family members (Patterson, 1982). Parental stress and illness is a strong risk factor on children. Intra-family disruption and disturbance by way of conflict, violence, and abusive behaviors towards their children would result in 'emotional wounding' and poor mental health. The lack of positive attachment and social development with caregivers and immediate family members should be considered a strong marker and risk factor of poor development in children.

The number of adolescent mother's are on the rise. Studies have repeatedly shown that young mothers are restrictive and punitive in discipline, are emotionally distant, and express greater negativity towards their children (Bolton, 1990; Nitz, Ketterlinus, & Brandt, 1995). There is evidence to suggest that insecure attachment is a risk factor in maltreatment and its harmful consequences (Crittendon, & Ainsworth, 1989). Attachment is critical in a child's life

(Bowlby, 1969). Poor attachment can lead to increased vulnerability and maladaptive behaviors. Children without an attachment figure may fail to trust others, feel threatened, and fear relationships and abandonment (Byng-Hall, 1995). Children with medical risk, developmental delays, or difficult temperament are set up for higher risk for further injury from their adolescent parents who do not have the emotional stamina to deal with such child deficits. Positive attachment creates healthy bonds and feelings of safety and security, and allows the child to feel confident and to explore the world developing positive self-esteem and survival skills. Therefore, the need for positive attachment in children cannot be overemphasized.

In a world of two-parent working families children receive less attention from their parents opening up to greater influence from their peers. The influence of maladaptive peers is a strong risk factor and can be very damaging to a child. Children with degraded attachment, multiple stresses, and in the company of maladaptive peers is a volatile combustive mixture for the likelihood of adverse outcomes, such as delinquency (Loeber & Farrington, 2000). Urbanization and industrialization has changed the developmental milieu of today's adolescent. Young people, in most cases, are forced by necessity of education and job, to migrate from their indigenous neighborhood to major cities. In doing so, they lose their extended families, their peer group, and social support systems; and the traditional 'hand holding' methods of initiation and guidance of the rights of passage into adulthood. Rather, the adolescent is left to his own biological strengths and social history to negotiate the changing ecological milieu.

Prevention targeting risk factors is difficult. The expression of children's mental health problems can vary as a function of their biological vulnerability, personal, and socio-cultural factors. Such variations demand further studies to specify their pathways. Prevention through general population activities and focused work with at risk individuals at many levels will reach the largest population reducing the number that eventually may need interventions. A broad approach, one that considers biology, sociology, and personal regulation; along with risk factors, protective factors, and mediating and moderating factors are most likely to succeed. Education currently is used as a main source of prevention. Education is necessary but insufficient. Knowledge does not automatically translate into practice. Community reorganization and competency promotion aspects along with other aids and assistance are essential for families to apply their knowledge.

Prevention and intervention programs in child and adolescent mental health are effective (Durlak & Wells, 1997). Rickel and Lampi's (1981) study is one such example. Results of their two-year follow up study of a preventive mental health program for preschoolers evidenced that high-risk children's performance was comparable to those who had not experienced behavioral or learning difficulties. Skeels (1966) took infants lacking in emotional care in orphanages and placed them in wards of mentally retarded adolescents and adults. These children reportedly received lots of love and social interaction. The infants made strong progress socially and cognitively, and were attractive enough to be adopted. They grew up to lead normal adult lives. Their cohorts left in the orphanages did not fare as well

Prevention can reduce the incidence and prevalence of mental health problems with significant benefits to the individual and society in general. Prevention works, is important and can be cost effective. Yet, prevention cannot eliminate all mental health problems in all persons for all times. As such, mental health protection, the next link in the chain of programs is necessary.

Protection

Epidemiological studies report 15 to 20 per cent of children experience mental health problems. Thus, between 85 and 80 per cent of children adapt to life's stressors without undue difficulty. Determining why some children collapse under the weight of life's stressors while others under similar condition function relatively unscarred is important. Factors such as the caregiver internal resources, emotional health, social competence, intelligence, external circumstances of their lives, social support, financial security, stable job, and stigma have been postulated as reasons for their resiliency and subsequent ability to nurture the growth and development of the child (Baldwin, Baldwin, & Cole, 1990). Rutter (1990) mentioned of a "risk trajectory", certain turning points in life, unless modified by a protective factor could lead to negative outcomes. A better knowledge of those who cope successfully can assist our understanding in helping those who are coping less well (Ricciuti, 1981).

Protective factors may promote resiliency and reduce the likelihood of mental health problems. A number of protective factors have been advanced by Rutter (1990) and Garmezy (1985), they include: parental mental health, positive marital relationship, parenting skills; adequate resources, safe and healthy neighborhood; positive peer group, and positive educational experience. Rutter (1987) cited minimizing risk conditions, arresting negative chain reactions after exposure to a risk, strengthening self-esteem and self-efficacy of individuals, and opportunities for alternate choices and actions as primary protective processes.

Social support is a strong protective factor. Extended families can act as buffers during times of crisis in the family. Nuclear families can take advantage of extended families for support. The support of alternative caregivers and extended family members including grandparents can act as protective factors and strengthen the family (Werner & Smith, 1992).

Participation in healthy adaptive social activities can be protective against risks. Varon and Riley (1999) found adolescents full of well being and good mental health when the mothers participated in frequent religious services.

Early experiences are critical for the building of strong stable mental health. Later adolescent and adult problems are evident in early childhood. This continuity from children to adolescence to adulthood does not hold true for all children under all circumstances. A number of factors including changes in family, support systems, peer relationships and others moderate the nature and severity of such mental health problems (Patterson, DeVaryshe, & Ramsey, 1989). However, isolated problematic behaviors do exist in children and adolescents, and most do not develop a rigid fixed pattern of such behaviors across their lives (Kazdin, 1995).

Resilience

Many children are not vulnerable to their negative experiences, including those with multiple severe risks are known to live productive happy lives (Garmenzy, 1991). A majority of children growing up in families who are mentally ill, alcoholic, abusive, criminally involved, poverty-stricken, or war-torn turn their negative life trajectory into "resilience," (Werner & Smith, 1992). Cumulative evidence from similar studies (Comer, 1984; Edmonds, 1986; Heath & McLaughlin, 1993; Rutter, Maughan, Mortimore, Ouston, & Smith, 1979; Weis & Fine, 1993) very strongly indicate that individuals who do well despite their adversity possess resilience.

Resilience, also considered as protective factors, falls into three categories: relationships, expectations, and participation. Children with caring and supportive adults, positive expectations, with meaningful participation in activities rise above their negative experiences. Meaningful school activities with responsibility for each child in those activities should become part of high expectations for children. Through these meaningful activities children can learn many of life's skills including respect, work ethics, compassion, failure, problem solving, resilience, and critical thinking, and cooperation and many other positive life skills that will serve them well in their future. Werner and Smith's (1989) forty-year longitudinal study found that resilient children encountered teachers as positive role models and confidants. This should not come as a surprise given that children mandated to spend nearly half their day in school spend more time with their teachers than their caregivers. Caring teachers with a positive attitude may easily become mentors to children, especially to those children who are poor and unhappy. This evidence is both positive and negative. Positive because there is a mechanism by which children's mental health can be saved; at the same time, negative because currently schools fail to function as good social agents for children. In fact, many studies suggest that schools are not caring, nurturing, or positive institutions for the majority of school children (Sarason, 1990).

Early intervention is critical to helping children and their families with mental health problems. Conflicts and problems need to be identified early, assessed thoroughly, and treated appropriately. Children's early behaviors and attitudes are easily molded when they are young and still impressionable and amenable to persuasive social influences. Failure to take the initiative by parents and responsible adults would deliver the children to their reference group, their peers, to be influential forces (Langer & Warheit, 1992). Early intervention can be very effective in protecting children from risk factors and strengthening their resilience. However, resilience is not a static factor. It is rather a dynamic multidimensional process (Garmezy, 1993). Protection can reduce the number of children with mental health problems. However, there will always be those who are vulnerable to biopsychosocial influences despite good prevention and protection. These children would benefit from early prescription of interventions and management.

Prescription

There is strong evidence that treatment of mental disorders is possible, effective, at low cost (Setorius, deGirolanno, Andrews, German, & Eisenberg, 1993). Despite the strong evidence of efficacious interventions, little is put into practice, and there is a wide gap between people's mental health needs and access to services (Waxman, Weist & Benson, 1999). Scarcity of funding and competent professionals, unavailable and inaccessible services, and inhibition by consumers to seek services due to mistrust and the stigma attached act as barriers to service utilization.

Inner city families are generally unaware of the many programs available to them or how to access those available services; while outer village families do not have adequate services and the available few are not always located within easy reach. As a consequence millions of children with serious emotional disturbances do not get the services they need (Stephenson, 2000).

Accessing mental health services requires understanding the pathway to effective care. This involves among others, recognizing mental health problems, identifying appropriate service systems, and seeking individual providers. There are scores of disciplines and hundreds of 'therapies', not counting the army of voluble charlatans making loud claims about their competency and effectiveness. Each practitioner in advertising for dollars claims efficacy. Traversing the professional maze is not an easy task even for non-mental health professionals, let alone the less informed and the poor. Non-mental health professionals tend to refer children to whom they know and are available rather than choice based on competency of the provider. Consumers are not equipped to evaluate the scientific practitioner, the pseudo-scientist, and the snake-oil salesman. Good providers are few, not easily accessible, and are costly. There is little 'true' accountability or quality assurance worldwide for children's mental health services.

Children generally have multiple problems across settings; making recognition and treatment complicated. Prompt identification of at risk children prevents a spiral of adverse events. Mental health problems once entrenched affect multiple systems and domains, increase in severity and negatively impact therapy at immense cost and time. Brief education and short-term therapy is insufficient to change longstanding inappropriate behaviors, dysfunctional communication patterns, deep-rooted negative feelings and thinking, and patterned hostile behaviors towards each other. Long term education and collaborative problem solving strategies with practice and training is required.

Development of a good intervention does not guarantee effectiveness. Rather, a good treatment needs to be broad-based with the right program, personnel, and resources. Interventions should be provided within the context of a coherent organized seamless system of services, from molecular clinical treatment to molar community based services. In addition, children and families may need assistance with housing, childcare, respite care, health care, material assistance, parent training, crisis intervention, and even job placement. Along with the development, implementation, and monitoring of interventions close communication, co-operation and collaboration among the various systems and providers is a must. Sustained treatment effectiveness cannot be achieved without such broad-based treatment and support.

Good examples of broad-based programs exist. The Family Research Consortium III (FRCIII), centered in Pennsylvania State University is based on such a broad based agenda. The FRCIII aims to promote intellectual exchange and collaborative research and training in the study of diversity, family process, and child and adolescent mental health. The Child and Adolescent Directorate of the south London, Maudsley also offers a broad-based program. This program has set up four levels or tiers of interlocking network of services. The tiers are matched to the increasing severity of the child's mental health problem. The goal of the comprehensive program is to promote parenting and child well-being, prevent childhood and parenting problems, identify and intervene as soon as possible, provide non-stigmatized access to specialists care, and where warranted refer to more specialized services (Cox, Davis, & Wiseman, 1995). It is reported that the program has had many successes including 'significant beneficial changes in parenting and childhood difficulties, and a very high levels of satisfaction with the service' (Davis, & Spurr, 1998). Longitudinal data should provide insight into the programs strength and weakness. Broad-based programs such as the above should be conducted with children and families with mental health problems.

Policies

It is important to recognize that mental health activities are subject to policies that prioritize and regulate health matters and appropriate funding. Published literature on public policies and their effects on children's mental health are sparse. Nations formulate policies that directly and indirectly affect children's growth and development. Policy effects on children can be direct (child abuse laws, labor laws, school lunch), indirect (housing and tax laws), or by omission (non-availability of health care, insurance, neighborhood schools), and by commission (child welfare laws, environmental laws, scholarships).

Work place policies also impact children's mental health status. Childcare facilities on site, flexible work hours, flexible leave options to coincide with children's school holidays and vacations, parenting leave for illness and care-giving responsibilities, and availability of low cost comprehensive medical and mental health insurance coverage are some of the ways work place policies impact children's mental health.

Children's mental health should be considered a public health issue. Eradication of poverty and hunger should be a top priority of all nations. The poor living under adverse socio economic and unsafe environmental conditions suffer the most, and cannot be expected to lead mentally healthy and happy lives. Poor housing and sanitation, diseases, inadequate health-care, and nutritional deficiencies have a strong influence in physical and mental health. Public mental health policies should aim at improving children's living standards and their social and physical environment. Policies should target infrastructure to enable decentralizing care and to make services available at the local level. Existing services should be integrated and coordinated and barriers broken to make mental health services available and accessible to all.

Services

The current medicalization and therapy based approach to mental health of children should be reassessed. Supportive care in a social milieu needs strengthening. Mosher and Burti's (1994) call for emphasis on identifying needs as opposed to understanding the psychological mechanism of symptom formation as the center of community mental health service should be heeded and further studied. It is time to stop thinking of 'treatment' and 'intervention' and consider 'programs' and 'services'. Interventions when necessary should be provided as a component of a comprehensive program of services.

Services for children's mental health is much more than intervention of target behaviors of interest. Many of the mechanisms and change process of behavior change has been identified by research, and treatment effectiveness documented (Banks, Patterson, & Reid, 1987). Yet the overall outcome of children's mental health problems is less than satisfactory. The problem lies in the philosophy and conceptualization of the mental health problem, and the models of services delivered in addressing these problems. Powerful treatments delivered through a poor modality will fail to sustain improvement over a period of time. Mental health work with children should always include their families, and where appropriate the environment. Treating only the child without simultaneously educating and training their families and readjusting their environment is like debugging a floppy disk without cleaning the virus in the hard drive. The floppy gets infected each time it is placed into the same computer.

Children with mental health problems have unmet needs, be it physical, material, social, or psychosocial. A primary need of most families is emotional support and practical help (Holaday, 1984). As Maslow (1954) asserted, cure and skill based approaches in dealing with children's mental health will seldom succeed if their needs are not met. Social capital is especially important for those who are at the low end of the social strata. Practical support can mediate children's emotional distress, while improved social support benefits the entire family (Wallander and Varni, 1989). Strengthening a family's social capital in the community in which they carry out their daily activities may be a prudent prevention and intervention strategy (Runyan, et al., 1998). Social capital benefits children receive from their immediate community relationship strengthen children's self-esteem and provide lasting hope

Children with mental health problems are usually served through the emergency departments, mental health clinics, hospitals, and public and private clinics. Such services will always be necessary as no amount of mental health prevention and promotion will eliminate mental health problems in all children. Yet, waiting till the children's mental health problems become severe is inappropriate, inefficient, and costly. Addressing problems at the point of emergence is less complex, reduces escalating treatments, and produces efficacious results at reduced cost. Main (1946), proposed that every sector of the population should have an organized 'therapeutic community' He envisioned the therapeutic community as one in which hospitals use the community to re-socialize the neurotic individual for life in the natural society. There are many existing avenues that should be fully explored to provide preventive, protective, and prescriptive services to children. These avenues are underutilized with their full potential untapped. Three such avenues are the primary care provider, the schools, and the modern technology.

Primary-Care Services

Most families visit or are visited by their primary care providers, and therefore, primary care providers have access to families and their children for assessment and interventions. Primary care providers are also the most likely to be the first to observe children's emerging problem behaviors. They are in a unique position to handle infant mental health. Mental health services accessed through primary care providers are not stigmatized and therefore bound to be more readily acceptable to the families. However, most primary care providers are not conducting screening, assessment, or treatment of mental health matters in their pediatric patients. There are many reasons for such apathy including a dualistic view of the mind and body and lack of knowledge and interest.

A large percentage of families visiting primary care providers exhibit mental health problems (Mauksch, 2001). However, mental health issues of these families are not being addressed adequately. Primary care providers' attitude towards pediatric mental health is changing. Pediatric residents are now receiving education and training in developmental health and behavioral issues, and their contextual implications on health and development of children in general. Primary care providers are beginning to show interest in the area of family mental health as they recognize the influence of the children's cognitive, social, and emotional development has on their understanding and cooperation in their medical care. Children's mental health cannot and should not be separated from their physical health. The two act in concert and are inextricably linked.

Mental health professionals have not taken the lead in educating or working with primary care physicians. Mental health professionals should be teaching at every medical school and work with interns. Workshops should be offered to practicing primary care physicians to equip them with tools to serve mental health issues of the families they serve. Primary care providers should be encouraged to work with mental health professionals in a multidisciplinary service. There is great scope to merge mental and physical health services for children in a primary care service provider.

School-Based Services

Schools remain the most powerful setting available to educate and treat children in mental health issues. Children from as early as 5 years up to 17 years of age spend nearly two-thirds of their life in school or school-related activities. School based mental health services are accessible, convenient, affordable, can be delivered without a stigma in a comprehensive manner. There is no place like schools to prime children for their good mental health. According to the United States Department of Health and Human Services, a large portion of its health objectives can be attained directly or indirectly through schools (Vernon-Smiley, & Wooley, 1996). Yet, schools as a setting for mental health service delivery are ignored in most countries, underutilized in many, and inappropriately used in others.

Children from inner cities and outer villages are generally poor and usually not school-ready. Nearly 29 percent of Head Start children are found to have serious emotional and behavioral problems (Knitzer, 1996). These children lack academic stimulation, structure, routine, and schedules at home. They also lack self-esteem, social skills, transportation, proper clothing, and means to purchase necessary material for class projects. These children are avoided by well-behaved peers and often ignored by teachers, eliminating the opportunity for role-play and learning of appropriate behaviors. Head Start and similar educational programs are worthy and should be encouraged. However, these programs will fail if they are not given a healthy start and their needs unmet.

School children in increasing numbers are exhibiting poor mental health. Yet, there is not a proper system in place for assessing and preventing children's mental health problems. The physical environment of the school, teachers and other school personnel, and the school policies and procedures are known to cause problem behaviors in children. In fact, it has been posited that some of these schools are not only poor socializing agents but are even training grounds for antisocial behaviors. School children's problems range from poor academic performance, disruptiveness, truancy, delinquency, inattentiveness, poor attendance, and poor task completion. Peer victimization and low social support by school personnel, further, adds to the problem (Ken Rigby, 2000).

In the absence of a system to proactively address children's mental health problems, problem children are tested, labeled and shuffled into various compartments including special education, and emotional and behavior disordered classes. Special education classes have a poor track record of a therapeutic environment and academic achievement. The emotional and behavior disordered classes are often under the care of 'tough' classroom teachers; who often display the very behaviors that the children placed under their care exhibit. In many schools, these classrooms resemble correctional facilities and function like one.

Problem children are regularly suspended. Two-parent working families cannot supervise their children who are sent home or suspended. These children are usually home alone, opening themselves to observing and adapting the many unhealthy behaviors they may come across through the television, internet, and maladaptive peers. For many inner city adolescents time alone at home is a privilege to experiment with drugs, smoking, living dangerously, violence, delinquency, and sexual exploration.

There is a deep disconnect between schools and parents, especially parents from inner cities and outer villages. These parents are poor, lack higher education, and have poor verbal and social skills. They feel uncomfortable meeting with their children's teachers or participating in their children's school activities. They have a sense of low self-esteem especially when they are poor, unable to present a picture of sophistication unlike the more affluent parents.

A wide chasm exists between schools and outside specialists and agencies. Very few schools collaborate with neighborhood universities and mental health facilities. In many cases, an unwilling partnership is forged through research projects funded by the outside researchers'. This partnership is temporary with little carry over effect at the completion of the research project. School personnel rarely, unless under the direction of a strong administrator, cooperate with outside professional to collect data or implement protocols, resulting in poor treatment integrity and insignificant improvement in the child.

Public policies and priorities to children's education and children's mental health is partly the cause for the disconnection. Many schools are severely under funded. Teachers are poorly paid, overworked, and made to instruct under very difficult circumstances. Under these circumstances schools find it hard to attract good teachers or keep them. No one is minding the teachers stress and mental health, which invariably affects their functioning and the mental health of the children under their care. To the children some of the teachers are but images of their difficult parents.

Mental health difficulties experienced by poor and vulnerable at risk children can be mitigated by the quality of schools and teachers, especially in the early grades. As such resources to correct the deficits, and school based mental health programs are critical. School based mental health service is a growing concept in many countries. These programs should be adequately funded, monitored, and evaluated for their effectiveness.

Technology-Based Services

Many developing countries and rural parts of developed countries have an acute shortage of mental health professionals and services. Information technology may offer some solutions to this scarcity of resources, services, and personnel. Systematic effort should be made to exploit the advances of information and communication technologies to deliver mental health services to underserved population, especially rural schools. The technology is being heavily promoted with success in physical medicine.

Technological application in mental health services can have other benefits besides reaching the underserved: minimize travel, cost-effective, reduced threat and stigma, and improved participation. Technologies currently in use include telephone, email, e-health, tele-health, and interactive audio-video systems. Applications of these systems are still in its infancy, and fraught with difficulties including power shortage, software glitches, and maintenance staff. There are still many nagging issues to be solved in utilizing this medium for mental health services. Issues of confidentiality and liability being the most important. Mental health governing bodies should formulate consensus statements and position papers to guide practitioners.

There are few controlled studies comparing technological services with traditional modalities. However, initial findings are encouraging. Oakley-Browne and Toole (1994) had compared therapy via computer system and therapy from general practitioners. Majority of their study subjects preferred therapy via computer rather than therapy from their general practitioners. Elford, White, St John, Maddigan, Ghandi, and Bowering (2001) evaluated user satisfaction with a PC-based videoconferencing system with 30 children. The providing psychiatrists expressed great satisfaction with the information they got through the tele-assessment. Ninety three percent of the parents gave the highest rating of satisfaction with the services. Ninety sever percent indicated they would prefer to use the tele-psychiatry system to traveling to see a child psychiatrist in person. All the children showed preference to using the tele-psychiatry system, and 56% of them stated they liked the 'television doctor' better than the 'real' doctor. Children seem to find remote tele-service less threatening than the white-coated or tie strung doctor.

This new technology has a great future if well planned and utilized. The needs of poor countries and poor parts of developed countries can be met to a large degree with advanced technology. Providing tele-mental health service requires robust clinical, technical, and managerial considerations. Further, the major challenge to tele-mental health becoming widespread in use is for practitioners and patients to successfully adapt to the system.

Advocacy

Advocacy is neither a major activity nor a priority with mental health professionals. Advocacy is critical to address the many problems faced by researcher, practitioners, and consumers in the mental health field. Mental health professionals should be in the frontline of advocacy. Mental health professionals have the knowledge and expertise to make them effective advocates for children who are powerless, parents who are helpless, and leaders who are clueless. In a world of competing priorities and finite health care dollars, advocacy for best practices, efficacious interventions, effective programs, ineffective policies, and priorities of research dollars become paramount. Professionals in the front line of service and research should lead this fight.

Policy makers seldom realize or pay attention to the indirect effects their policies may have on children's mental health. Policies can negatively impact family preservation. Mental health professionals have the duty to study, advocate for, and inform policy makers on the potential effects a law may have on children and their caregivers social and mental health. Associations such as the American Psychological Association have taken on this task. But state, local, and community level actions are equally important, and very much lacking. Consumer advocacy groups are growing rapidly. Professionals should join forces with consumer advocacy groups to strengthen their cause. Health of the population should mean mental and physical health. Both are interrelated and affect each other. Medical practitioners and mental health professionals should jointly work to improve the total health of children.

Advocacy groups across national borders are also growing. Worldwide Consumer and professional chat rooms on the internet, teleconferences, international meetings such as the International Conference on Child and Adolescent Mental Health (ICCMH) bring together professionals and consumers across the world to focus on children's mental health issues. Such movements can be expected to keep children's mental health issues active and not allow it to be ignored or neglected.

Summary and Implications

Mental health in children is a serious problem and on the rise. Biological, personal, and social factors influence children's mental health. Early childhood is the critical period of neurological and social development with lasting effects. Quality of physical and emotional development in children profoundly influences adult life. Maternal health and proactive parenting guidance are necessary to give children a healthy start. Most studies have concluded that problem behaviors in children and adolescents are predictive of poor mental health in adults.

The prevention literature has highlighted resilience that place children at risk and protective factors that protect mental health in children. Informed application of the knowledge at an early stage can be efficacious and cost-effective in the long run, even if they seem expensive in the short-term. Tightly controlled prevention studies consistently show significant results. However, implementing these controlled studies in field work is very difficult. Future studies should attempt to conduct research in the natural setting.

Children's mental health is intricately tied to their parent's mental health and status. It makes implicit logic that preventive efforts be directed towards would be parents, expectant mothers, and at risk families. Early assessment in parent child attachment is immensely valuable especially among at risk families. All services with children should include the family in the overall plan. Families should be empowered, and made to feel that things are done with them rather than that things are done to them. Children's mental health services that fail to address the children's family and environmental issues are doomed to failure.

Children's early inappropriate behaviors are strong indicators of later problems, and in many cases these same problems manifest in more severe forms in adulthood. Thus, early intervention could reduce both short and long-term mortality and morbidity.

Children's physical environment is very important. The environment can be a risk or protective factor. Inner city and outer village families are known to engage in high rates of addictive and abusive behaviors. When environments are highly toxic or pathologic, children's behaviors in such settings may also be pathologic. Yet, children and families under negative or difficult circumstances may find the use of these behaviors to be adaptive responses. Thus, it is important that children's environment is safe, healthy, and nurturing. Federal, state, and local policies along with caregiver, community, and school personnel should cooperate and collaborate in serving the mental health of children.

Children are mandated to spend a large part of their life in schools, away from home and their parents. Schools should be transformed into positive educational and therapeutic environments, with curriculums that stress all the elements children need, to grow to be healthy and happy adults. Such a school focus can enhance children's mental health and build resilience. Schools should build stronger partnership with the parents and also with specialists and resources in the community.

Most children with mental health problems do not receive services. The poor bear the brunt of the inequity and inequality of mental health services. Service to children should be considered from a program perspective rather as intervention and treatment. Programs should be organized in a coherent manner provided across settings and maintained long after the target behavior is suppressed or enhanced.

Social and material support is key to preventing stress, building resilience, and promoting mental health. Basic needs of children and their families are of utmost importance. Unmet needs are sure to stunt the potential growth and development of families and their children.

Poverty, lack of food, shelter, clothing, and sanitation and health amenities affect both physical and mental health of individuals. Unless this cycle of disadvantage is broken social problems and mental heath issues in children will become epidemic, contributing to intergenerational mental health problems. Nations should place eradicating poverty and hunger as their number one task in addressing children's mental health and social problems. Families should be encouraged to stay engaged with their community and not isolated. Families should have opportunities to attend faith centers and participate in community activities. Each community should have 'therapeutic community centers' to assist families with such opportunities.

Families fear visiting mental health centers for fear of stigma, cost, additional travel and burden, and even fear of involuntary admission. In many cases families also fail to notice their poor parenting styles or their children's emerging mental health problems. Primary care physicians regularly see these families and their children. Mental health screening should be a routine practice at the primary physician's office as part of an overall health service. They can work with mental health professionals onsite, as a multidisciplinary team, or on a consultation basis. Physicians should receive education and training in mental health assessment. Mental health professionals should engage in such collaborative work with schools and pastoral counselors where families can receive services without stigma, at reduced cost, and in their neighborhood.

Effective treatment of mental health problems at low cost is possible. However, the overall results are not encouraging. This is so because mental health care systems are complex, uncoordinated, and fragmented. In many cases programs and delivery systems are difficult to access and families strain to get in them. Continuum of care as opposed to episodic service provision is needed. Recovery is not a linear process and children need support systems to hold them up when progress falters. A systematic follow up post treatment in preventing risk factors that gave rise to the condition should be in place. Strength based services should be offered using children's own resources, coping strategies, and family and social support systems.

Each person has a very different combination of background, biology, environment, expectations, motivations, health beliefs, culture, learning style, and goals. Prevention, protection, and prescription should be addressed within the family cultural norms and children's individual characteristics.

Severely dysfunctional families and children with severe mental health problems cannot be expected to execute the care plan to manage their condition. Multi-dysfunctional families and inner city and outer village families should be assigned case-management staff to negotiate care and set up a system of care for the children.

Certain aspects in a child's life act as key risk factors. Poverty, single parent, marital discord, overcrowding, paternal criminality, maternal psychiatric disorder, and poor parenting have been repeatedly identified as core risks. The accumulation of risk factors negatively influence children's development, especially when there are no social and material support systems to weigh against the risk factors.

There is a paucity of applied research in children's mental health. Field based research should be actively pursued. Researchers should work with clinicians in translating clinical findings into community practice. Firm answers are lacking in keystone risk and protective factors; or when single risk factors and rare events in a child's life hold its pattern causing children to become inflexible to change.

REFERENCES

Achenbach, T.M., Bird, H.R., Canino, G., Phares, V., Gould, M.S., & Rubio-Stipec, M. (1990). Epidemiological comparisons of Puerto Rican and U.S. mainland children: parent, teacher and self-reports. *Journal of American Academy of Child and Adolescent Psychiatry, 29,* 84-93.

Achenbach, T.M., Hensley V.R., Phares, V., Grayson, D. (1990). Problems and competencies reported by parents of Australian and American Children. *Journal of Child Psychological Psychiatry, 31,* 265-286.

Achenbach, T.M., Verhulst, F.C., Baron, G.D., Akkerhuis, G.W. (1987). Epidemiological comparisons of Dutch and American children: Behavioral/emotional problems and competencies reported by parents for ages 4 to 16. *Journal of American Academy of Psychiatry, 26,* 326-332.

American Psychiatric Association (1994), *Diagnostic and Statistical Manual of Mental Disorders* (4th ed.). Washington, DC: American Psychiatric Association

Arnett H., Balle-Jensen, L. (1993). Cultural bases of risk behavior: Danish adolescents. *Child Development, 64,* 1842-1855.

Baldwin, A., Baldwin, C., & Cole, R. (1990). Stress-resistant families and stress-resistant children. In J. Rolf, A. Masten, D. Cicchetti, K. Nuechterlein, & S. Weintraub (Eds.), *Risk and protective factors in the development of psychopathology* (pp. 257-280). Cambridge, England: Cambridge University Press.

Bank, L., Patterson, G.R., & Reid, J.B. (1987). Delinquency prevention through training parents in family management. *Journal of Applied Behavior Analysis, 10,* 75-82.

Bolton, F. (1990). The risk of child maltreatment in adolescent parenting. In A. Stiffman & R. Feildman (Eds.), *Contraception, pregnancy and parenting* (pp 223-247). London: England Kingsley.

Bowlby, J. (1969). *Attachment and loss*, Vol. 1. *Attachment.,* New York: Basic Books.

Boyle, M. (1990). *Schizophrenia. A Scientific Delusion?* London: Routledge.

Brandon, D.(1991). Innovation without Change? *Consumer Power in Psychiatric Services.* London: Macmillan.

Breggin, P. (1993). *Toxic psychiatry.* London: Harper Collins.

Brody, E.B. (1987). *Mental health and world citizenship: The view from an international, nongovernmental organization.* Austin, Texas: Hogg Foundation for Mental Health.

Brogan, D.R., & James, L.D. (1980). Physical environment correlates of psychosocial health among urban residents. *American Journal of Community Psychology, 8*(5), 507-522

Bronfenbrenner, U. (1994). Nature-nurture reconceptualized in developmental perspective: a bioecological model. *Psychological Review, 101(4)*, 568-586.

Brookes-Gunm, J., & Paikoff, R.L, (1991). Promoting healthy behavior in adolescences: The case of sexuality and pregnancy. *Bulletin of the New York Academic Medicine, 67,* 527-547.

Bying-Hall, J. (1995). Creating a secure family base: some implications of attachment theory for family therapy. *Family Process, 34*(1), 45-58.

Carey, W.B. (1992). Early health crises and vulnerable children. In M.D. Levine, W.G. Carey, & A.C.Crocker (Eds.). *Developmental behavioral pediatrics* (2nd ed.). Philadelphia: W.B.Saunders.

Carey, W.B., & McDevitt, S.C. (1973). Stability and change in individual temperament diagnoses from infancy to early childhood. *Journal of the American Academy of Child Psychiatry, 17,* 331-337.

Cicchetti, D., & Cohen, D. J. (1995). *Developmental psychopathology.* New York: John Wiley.

Cicchetti, D., & Toth, S. L. (1998). The development of depression in children and adolescents. *American Psychologist, 53,* 221–241.

Comer, J. (1984). Home-school relationships as they affect the academic success of children. *Education and Urban Society, 16,* 323-337.

Cox, A., Davis, H., & Wiseman, M. (1995). *Proposal for a model child mental health service.* London: Lewisham & Guy's Mental Health NHS Trust.

Crittendon, P.M. & Ainsworth, M.D.S.(1989). Child maltreatment and attachment theory. In D.Cicchetti & V.Carlson (Eds.), *Child maltreatment theory and research on the causes and consequences of child abuse and neglect,* (pp. 432-463). New York:Cambridge University Press.

Davis, A. & Wainwright, H. (1996). Poverty, work and the mental health services. *Breakthrough, 1*(1), 47-55.

Davis, H. & Spurr, P. (1998). Parent counseling: An evaluation of a community child mental health service. *Journal of Child Psychology and Psychiatry, 39*(3), 365-376.

Durlak, J.A. & Wells, A.M. (1997). Evaluation of indicated preventive intervention: Mental health program for children and adolescents. *American Journal of Community Psychology, 26,* 775-802.

Dutton, D. (1986). Financial, organizational and professional factors affecting health care utilization. *Society in Scientific Medicine, 23*(7), 721-735.

Edmonds, R. (1986). Characteristics of Effective Schools. In U. Neisser, (Ed). *The school achievement of minority children: New perspectives* (pp. 93-104). Hillsdale, NJ: Lawrence Erlbaum.

Elford D.R., White, H., St John, K., Maddigan, B., Ghandi, M., & Bowering, R. (2001). A prospective satisfaction study and cost analysis of a pilot child telepsychiatry service in *Newfoundland Journal of Telemedicine and Telecare,7* (2), 73-81.

Eyberg, S.M. (1998). Child and adolescent psychotherapy research: developmental issues. *Journal of Abnormal child Psychology 21,* 306-311.

Fantuzzo, J.W., DePaola, L.M., Lambert, L., Martino, T., Anderson, G., & Sutton, S. (1991). Effects of Interparental violence on the psychological adjustment and competencies and young children. *Journal of Consulting Clinical Psychology, 59,* 258-265.

Gamrezy, N. (1993). Children in poverty: Resilience despite risk. *Psychiatry, 56*(1), 127-136.

Garmenzy, N. (1994). Resiliency and vulnerability to adverse developmental outcomes associated with poverty. *American Behavioral Scientist, 34,* 416-430.

Garmezy, N. (1985). Stress-resistant children: the search for protective factors. *Journal of Child Psychology and Psychiatry, 4,* 213-233.

Garmezy, N. (1991). Resiliency and Vulnerability to Adverse Developmental Outcomes Associated with Poverty. *American Behavioral Scientist, 34,* 416-430.

Glueck, S.,& Glueck, E. (1950). *Unraveling juvenile delinquency.* New York: Commonwealth Fund.

Gomm R.(1996). Mental health and inequality. In T. Heller (Ed.). *Mental health matters.* Basingstoke: Macmillan.

Hammen, C. (1988). Self-cognitions, stressful events, and the prediction of depression in children of depressed mothers. *Journal of Abnormal Child Psychology, 16*(3), 347-360.

Heath, S.B., & M.W. McLaughlin, Eds. (1993). *Identity and inner-city youth: Beyond ethnicity and gender.* New York: Teachers College Press.

Holaday, B.(1984). Challenges of rearing a chronically ill child. *Nursing Clinic of North America, 19,* 361-368.

Jensen, J.M. (1998). Factors protecting children living in disharmonious homes: Maternal reports. *Journal of the American Academy of Child and Adolescent Psychiatry, 29,* 60-69.

Kazdin, A.E. (1993). Adolescent mental health: Prevention and treatment programs. *American Psychologist, 48*(2), 127-141.

Kazdin, A.E. (1995). *Conduct disorders in childhood.*(2nd ed.). Thousand Oaks, CA: Sage.

Knitzer, J. (1996). *Map and track: Initiatives for young children and families.* New York: National Centre for Children in Poverty.

Kolvin, I., Miller,F.J.W., Fleeting, M. & Kolvin, P.A. (1988). Risk/protective factors for offending with particular reference to deprivation. In: Rutter, M. (Ed.). *Studies of psychosocial risk: The power of longitudinal data* (pp.77-95). Cambridge: Cambridge University Press.

Langer, L.M., & Warheit, G.J. (1992). The Pre-adult health decision-making model: Linking decision-making directness/orientation to adolescent health related attitudes and behaviors. *Adolescence, 27,* 108.

Leckman, J.F., Ruchinkin, V., Vermeiren, R., & Schwab-stone, M. (2000). Cultural considerations in the treatment of children and adolescent: Operationalizing the importance of culture in treatment. *Child and Adolescent Psychiatry in Clinical North America, 10*(4), 729-743.

Levin, B.L., & Hanson, A. (2001). Rural mental health services. In S. Loue & B.E. Quill (Eds.), *Handbook of rural health.* New York: Plenum Publishers.

Loeber, R., & Farrington, D.P. (2000). Young children who commit crime: Epidemiology, developmental origins, risk factors, early interventions, and policy implications. *Developmental Psychopathology, 12*(4), 737-762.

Main, T. (1946). The hospital as a therapeutic institution. *Bulletin of the Menninger Clinic, 10*, 66-68.

Marks, I.M., Baer, L., & Greist, J.H.(1998). Home self-assessment of obsessive—compulsive disorder: use of a manual and a computer-conducted telephone interview: two UK-US studies. *British Journal of Psychiatry, 172*, 406-412.

Maslow, A.(1970). *The assessment of need.* London: Viking.

Maslow, A.(1954). *Motivation and personality.* New York: Harper and Row.

Mauksch, L.B. (2001). Mental illness, functional impairment, and patient preferences for collaborative care in an uninsured, primary care population. *Journal of Family Practice.*

McGee, R., Silva, P.A., & Williams, S. (1984). Perinatal, neurological, environmental and developmental characteristics of seven with stable behavior problems. *Journal of Child Psychological Psychiatry, 25*(4), 573-586.

Miller, F.J., Court, S.D., Knox, E.G., & Brandon, S. (1974). *The school years in Newcastle upon Tyne: 1952-1962.* London: Oxford University Press.

Mosher, B. & Bruti, L. (1994). *Community mental health.* London: W.W. Norton.

Murray, C.J., & Lopez, A.D. (1996). Evidence-based health policy-lessons from the Global Burden of Disease Study. *Science, 274*, 740-743.

Nitz, K., Ketterlinus, R. & Brandt, L. (1995). The role of stress, social support, and family environment in adolescent mothers parenting. *Journal of Adolescent Research, 10*, 358-392.

Offord, D.R., Sullivan, K., Allen, N. & Abrams, N. (1979). Delinquency and hyperactivity. *Journal of Nervous and Mental Disorders, 167*(12), 734-741.

Patterson, G.R. (1982). *Coercive family process*. Eugene, OR: Castalia.

Patterson, G.R., DeVaryshe, B.D., & Ramsey, E. (1989). A developmental perspective on antisocial behavior. *American Psychologist 44,* 329-335.

Piven, J. (1997). The biological basis of autism. *Current Opinions in Neurobiology, 7*(5), 708-712.

Quiton, D., Rutter, M., & Rowlands, O. (1976) An evaluation of in interview assessment of marriage. *Psychological Medicine 6,* 577-586

Ricciuti, H.N. (1981). Adverse environmental and nutritional influences on mental development: A perspective. *Journal of the American Dietetic Association 49,* 115-120.

Rickel, A.U., & Lampi, L. (1981), A two-year follow-up study of a preventive mental health program for preschoolers. *Journal of Abnormal Child Psychology, 9*(4), 455-464.

Ring-Kurtz, S. E., Sonnichsen, S., & Hoover-Dempsey, K. V. (1995). School-based mental health services for children. In L. Bickman & D. Rogers (Eds.), *Children's mental health services: Research, policy, and evaluation* (Vol. 1, pp. 117-144). Thousand Oaks, CA: Sage.

Robins, I.N. (1966). *Deviant children grown up*. Baltimore: Williams & Wilkins.

Runyan, D.K., Hunter, W.M., Socolar, R.R. Amaya-Jackson, L., English, D., & Landsverk, J. (1998). Children who prosper in unfavorable environments: the relationship to social capital. *Pediatrics 101*(1), 12-18.

Rutter, M. (1990). Psychosocial resilience and protective mechanism. In J. Rolf, A.S. Masten, D. Cicchetti, K.H. Neuchterlein, S. Weintraub (Eds.). *Risk and protective factors in the development of psychopathology,* (pp. 181-214). Cambridge: Cambridge University Press.

Rutter, M. (1987). Psychosocial resilience and protective mechanisms. *American Journal of Orthopsychiatry 57,* 316-331.

Rutter, M., Maughan, P., Mortimore, J., Ouston, A., & Smith,. B. (1979). *Fifteen thousand hours*. Cambridge, MA: Harvard University Press.

Sarason, S. (1990). *The predictable failure of educational reform.* San Francisco: Jossey-Bass.

Sartorius, N., DeGirolanno, G., Andrews, G., Gorman, A., & Eisenberg, L. (1993). In N. Sartorius, G. DeGilolamo, G. Andrew, A. Gorman, & L. Eisenberg (Eds.). *Treatment of mental disorder: A review of effectiveness.* Washington: American Psychiatric Press.

Schauss, A.G. (1980). *Diet, crime, and delinquency.* Berkeley: Parker House.

Schoenthaler, S.J. (1983). Diet and crime: an empirical examination of the value of nutrition in the control and treatment of incarcerated juvenile offenders. *International Journal of Biosocial Research, 4,* 25-39.

Shore, A.N. (1997). Early organization of the nonlinear right brain and development of a predisposition to psychiatric disorders. *Developmental Psychopathology, 9*(4), 595-631.

Schwab-Stone, M.E., Ayers, T.S., & Kasparov, W. (1995). No safe haven: A study of violence exposure in an urban community. *Journal of American Child and Adolescent Psychiatry, 34,* 1343-1352.

Shaefer, E.S. (1989). Dimensions of mother-infant interaction: Measurement stability, and predictive validity. *Infant Behavior and Development 12,* 379-393.

Shaw, D.S., & Vondara, J.L. (1995). Infant attachment security and maternal prediction of early behavior problems: A longitudinal study of low-income families. *Journal of Abnormal Child Psychology, 23,* 335-337.

Skeels, H.M. (1996). Adult status of children with contrasting early life experience. *Monographs of the Society for Research in Child Development, 31,*1-65.

Smith, E.A., Udry, J.R., & Morris, N.M. (1985). Pubertal development and friends: A biosocial explanation of adolescent sexual behavior. *Journal of Health and Social Behavior, 26,* 183-192.

Sroufe, L.A., & Rutter, M. (1984). The domain of developmental psychopathology. *Child Development, 55*(1), 17-29.

Stephenson, J. (2000). Children with mental problems not getting the care they need. *Journal of the American Medical Association, 285,* 2043-2044.

Stierlin, H., Wirshing, M., & Knauss, W. (1977). Family dynamics and psychosomatic disorders in adolescence. *Psychotherapy and Psychosomatics, 28*(14), 243-251.

Szasz, T.S. (1974). The myth of psychotherapy. *American Journal of Psychotherapy, 28*(4), 517-526.

Talbot, S.(1976). Concepts which influence health and health care. *Jamaican Nurse, 16*(3), 234-256.

Thomas, A., & Chess, S. (1977). *Temperament and development.* New York: Brunner/Mazel.

36

U. S. Department of Health and Human Services. (1999). *Mental health: A report of the surgeon general.* Rockville, MD: U. S. Department of Health and Human Services, Substance Abuse and Mental Health Services Administration, Center for Mental Health Services, National Institutes of Health, National Institute of Mental Health.

Varon, S.R., & Riley, A.W. (1999). Relationship between maternal church attendance and adolescent mental health and social functioning. *Psychiatric Services, 50,* 799-805.

Vernon-Smiley, M.E., & Wooley, S.F. (1996). Comprehensive school health- adolescent medicine. *State of the Art Reviews, 7,* 261-271.

Vitaro, F., Brendgen, M., Pagani, L., Tremblay, R. E., & McDuff, P. (1999). Disruptive behavior, peer association, and conduct disorder: Testing the developmental links through early intervention. *Development and Psychopathology, 11,* 287-304.

Wallander, J.A., & Varni, J.W. (1989). Social support and adjustment in chronically ill and handicapped children. *American Journal of Community Psychology, 17,* 185-201.

Waxman, R.P., Weist, M.D., & Benson, D.M. (1999). Toward collaboration in the growing education-mental health interface. *Clinical Psychology Review, 19*(2), 239-253.

Werner, E., & Smith, R. (1989). *Vulnerable but invincible: A longitudinal study of resilient children and youth.* New York: Adams, Bannister, and Cox.

Werner, E., & Smith, R. (1992). *Overcoming the odds: High-risk children from birth to adulthood.* New York: Cornell University Press.

WHO (1999). *Constitution.* The World Health Organization. Geneva: WHO.

2

Challenges and New Directions in Developing Effective Empirically Validated Parenting and Family Intervention Programs

Matthew R. Sanders
The University of Queensland

Matthew R. Sanders · Parenting and Family Support Centre · School of Psychology · The University of Queensland · Brisbane QLD 4702 · Australia.

International Perspectives on Child and Adolescent Mental Health. Volume 2: Proceedings of the Second International Conference, edited by N. N. Singh, T. H. Ollendick, and A. N. Singh. © 2002 Elsevier Science Ltd. All rights reserved.

The quality of family life is fundamental to the health and well-being of children. At the most basic level, families ensure the survival of children by providing food, shelter, nurturance, supervision, and protective clothing, while the family's financial resources influence a child's health status and access to adequate health care. Families also have a primary role in a child's education and provide the first and most important social context for human development. Other important aspects of the family include the provision of care for those who are unable to fend for themselves, and protection against mental illness through warm, stable, supportive family relationships and effective interpersonal communication (Pratt, Kerig, Cowan, & Cowan, 1988). They are gatekeepers to family members' access to health services, and they can be the agents of change to produce improvements in the psychological well-being of family members, particularly children (Sanders, 1995).

There is widespread concern about the behavioral and emotional problems of children and youth. Australian prevalence surveys shows between 14-18% of children and adolescents show significant behavioral and emotional problems (Sawyer, et al., 2000; Zubrick, et al., 1995). The Queensland Health 1996 survey of 1218 parents revealed that 25% of parents reported that their child's behavior was moderately to extremely difficult and 28% perceived that their eldest child less than 12 years of age had an emotional or behavioral problem in the last 6 months (Sanders, Tully, et al., 1999).

Epidemiological studies indicate that family risk factors such as poor parenting, family conflict, and marital breakdown are powerful early predictors for the development and maintenance of behavioral and emotional problems in children and adolescents (e.g., Cummings & Davies, 1994; Dryfoos, 1990; Robins & Price, 1991). Specifically, the lack of a warm, positive relationship with parents; insecure attachment; harsh, inflexible, rigid, or inconsistent discipline practices; inadequate supervision of and involvement with children; marital conflict and breakdown; and parental psychopathology (particularly maternal depression and high levels of parenting stress), increase the risk that children develop major behavioral and emotional problems, including conduct problems, substance abuse, antisocial behavior, and participate in delinquent activities (e.g., Coie, 1996; Loeber & Farrington, 1998; Patterson, 1982).

In contrast, supportive family relationships have been shown to be a significant predictor of positive adjustment in childhood and adolescence, and indirect evidence suggests that supportive family relationships are a protective factor for conduct problems and adolescent adjustment problems (Cauce, Reid, Landesman, & Gonzales, 1990; Cohen & Wills, 1985; Rutter, 1979; Wills, Vaccaro, & McNamara, 1992).

THE NEED FOR PARENTING INTERVENTIONS

Partly in response to this concern about children and the prevalence of various family risk factors in the community, greater attention is being given to the importance of better preparation for parents to undertake their role in raising children. Unfortunately, parents generally receive little preparation beyond the experience of having been parented themselves, with most learning on the job through trial and error (Risley, Clark, & Cataldo, 1976; Sanders, Tully, et al., 1999). The changing social ecology of parenthood is also complicating the task of raising children. The already demanding role of parenthood is further complicated when parents do not have access to extended family support networks (such as grandparents, trusted family friends) for advice on child-rearing, or when they experience the stress of separation, divorce, or repartnering (Lawton & Sanders, 1994; Sanders, Nicholson, & Floyd, 1997). The high rate of divorce contributes to more children being raised in single parenthood households.

THE CONTRIBUTION OF FAMILY INTERVENTION

Behavioral Family Intervention (BFI) based on social learning models has the strongest empirical support of any form of child psychotherapy or approaches to family intervention (Brestan & Eyberg, 1998; Kazdin, 1998; Sanders, 1995, 1996, 1999). There have been several recent comprehensive reviews that have documented the efficacy of BFI as an approach to helping children and their families (Lochman, 1990; McMahon, 1999; Sanders, 1996, 1998; Taylor & Biglan, 1998). The following conclusions summarise the state of the evidence concerning the effects of parenting interventions.

Parenting Interventions Produce Clinically Meaningful Changes in Children's Behavior and Adjustment

There is clear evidence that BFI can benefit children with disruptive behavior disorders, particularly children with oppositional defiant disorders (ODD) and their parents (Forehand & Long, 1988; McMahon & Wells, 1998; Webster-Stratton, 1994). The empirical basis of BFI is strengthened by evidence that the approach can be successfully applied to many other clinical problems and disorders including attention deficit hyperactivity disorder (ADHD) (Barkley, Guevremont, Anastopoulos, & Fletcher, 1992), persistent feeding difficulties (Turner, Sanders, & Wall, 1994), pain syndromes (Sanders, Shepherd, Cleghorn, & Woolford, 1994), anxiety disorders (Barrett, Dadds, & Rapee, 1996), autism and developmental disabilities (Schreibman,

Kaneko, & Koegel, 1991), achievement problems, and habit disorders and well as everyday problems of normal children (see Sanders, 1996; Taylor & Biglan, 1998 for reviews of this literature). Meta analyses of treatment outcome studies often report large effect sizes (Serketich & Dumas, 1996), with good maintenance of treatment gains (Forehand & Long, 1988). Treatment effects have been shown to generalize to school settings (McNeil, Eyberg, Eisenstadt, Necomb, & Funderbunk, 1991) and to various community settings outside the home (Sanders & Glynn, 1981). Parents participating in these programs are generally satisfied consumers (Webster-Stratton, 1989).

Parenting Interventions Reduce Parental Emotional Distress

It is also becoming increasingly evident that the benefits of BFI are not restricted to children, with several studies now showing effects on other areas of family functioning, including reduced maternal depression and stress (Sanders & McFarland, 2000), increases in parental satisfaction and efficacy (Connell, Sanders, & Markie-Dadds, 1997); and reduced levels of parental anger (Sanders, Gravestock, Pidgeon, Connors, & Brown, 2000). Parent training appears to be an effective treatment in its own right for certain types of adult distress.

Parenting Interventions Can Reduce Marital Distress

Several studies have shown that parenting interventions can also improve marital relationships and reduce marital conflict over parenting issues (e.g., Nicholson & Sanders, 1999; Sanders, Markie-Dadds, Tully, & Bor, 2000; Sanders & Shallcross, in prep; Webster-Stratton, 1998). Other evidence shows that the effects of parenting interventions can be enhanced with the provision of brief marital counseling for martially discordant couples who have children with oppositional behavior problems (Dadds, Schwartz, & Sanders, 1987).

Summary of Evidence

BFI's have met a number of important scientific and clinical criteria that strengthen confidence in the intervention approach. These include the following:

Pervasive effects on the quality of family life: Clinically meaningful outcomes have been demonstrated by applying rigorous criteria for clinical improvement such as the clinical reliable change index (Jacobson & Truax, 1991) for child outcomes. These have shown that as many as 75% of children evidence clinically reliable change. Furthermore there is little evidence that parenting interventions produce negative side effects, symptom substitution, or other adverse family outcomes. Research findings demonstrating that children show fewer behavioral problems after their parents participate in BFI programs, coupled with findings that parents are less stressed, angry, and depressed, more confident, and experience less relationship conflict with partners indicate that BFI has powerful intervention effects within the entire family system. The considerably reduced conflict in the homes of participating parents and the greater sense of personal efficacy in the parenting role means a higher quality of life for adults and children alike. Preventive and treatment effects: BFI has been successfully used both as a treatment for established cases of children with severe conduct problems and also as a preventive intervention for children at risk of developing disorders (e.g., Sanders, et al., 2000).

Replication of key findings across multiple sites and investigators: The primary treatment effects which have shown that decreases in parental negative disciplinary behavior and increases in parents' use of a variety of positive attending and other relationship enhancing skills lead to improved child behavior have been replicated many times in different studies, involving different investigators in several different countries (United States, Great Britain, Australia, New Zealand, Canada, and Hong Kong), with a wide variety of client populations (Sanders, 1999). The effectiveness of different delivery modalities: There is increasing evidence showing that a variety of delivery modalities can produce similar positive outcomes for children including individual, group, telephone assisted and self-directed variants of parenting programs (e.g., Connell, Sanders, & Markie-Dadds, 1997; O'Dell, 1974; Sanders, et al., 2000).

Effectiveness with a range of family types: In the area where the strongest support for BFI is evident, namely for disruptive behavior problems in preadolescent children, interventions have been successfully used with two parent families, single parents, and step families (Nicholson & Sanders, 1999).

High levels of consumer acceptability: High levels of consumer satisfaction have been repeatedly demonstrated in different controlled evaluations of BFI and for specific parenting techniques advocated (see McMahon, 1999; Webster-Stratton, 1989). In sum, these findings confirm that BFI is a powerful clinical resource for effecting change in family relationships for a wide range of behavioral and emotional problems in children.

LIMITATIONS OF CURRENT APPROACHES TO FAMILY INTERVENTION

Despite the evidence supporting the efficacy and effectiveness of BFI, there is little room for complacency. There are a several significant limitations with current approaches that must be addressed by researchers and practitioners if these interventions are to have a significant impact on family relationships at a population level. A major concern for the family intervention field in general is that empirically supported interventions are underutilized by professionals and are not readily accessible to families who might benefit from them (Taylor & Biglan, 1998). Most children with behavioral problems receive no professional assistance from mental health professionals (Zubrick, et al., 1995). For example, in a large sample of 4-16 year old children, only 2% of children with an identifiable mental health problem had received any specialist mental health assistance. Furthermore, there is low participation rates in parent education particularly in families who are considered most at risk for the development of serious problems (Sanders, Tully, et al, 1999). Non-evaluated parent education and family support programs continue to dominate the field, where programs are offered to the public with little or no known effects. In the absence of any meaningful form of accountability or quality control to ensure evidence based family interventions are promoted, the public is exposed to a diverse range of untested and in some instances even potentially harmful interventions.

Empirically supported family intervention programs generally have limited reach. It is also of continuing concern that indigenous and ethnic minority groups have low representation in clinical outcome trials. These groups are amongst the most disadvantaged sectors of the community and are more likely to dropout from intervention (Kazdin, 1998). Access problems are compounded by the relative inflexibility of delivery formats required by most interventions, particularly the requirement for face-to-face session attendance during regular working hours. For families with both parents working or families living in rural, remote, or otherwise isolated areas meeting this attendance requirement can be an insurmountable problem.

Another criticism of family intervention as a risk reduction approach is that it may simply be insufficient as an intervention on its own, particularly for complex problems such as conduct disorder, ADHD, and drug abuse where there are multiple interacting risk factors. Some researchers have argued from epidemiological evidence that longer more intensive multi-risk factor interventions covering home, school, peer groups, and the children themselves are required to prevent conduct disorders (McMahon, Slough, & Conduct Problems Prevention Research Group, 1996; Kazdin, 1997). However, it has still yet to be demonstrated convincingly through long term outcome studies that such an approach will be more effective than targeting a more limited subset of risk and protective factors such as parenting skills, maternal depression, or marital discord. Receiving multiple interventions can be problematic for families with limited resources, as they may add to the burden of care already experienced by the family (e.g., additional appointments, more professionals to deal with, extra costs). This is particularly the case if the child has special needs such as a chronic disability.

TOWARDS A CONTEXTUAL APPROACH TO FAMILY INTERVENTION

To achieve a significant improvement in parenting competence, a population health perspective is needed. The concept of designing "family friendly" environments to support and empower parents requires interventions that target social contexts that, in turn, influence parents on a day to day basis including (the mass media, primary health care services, child care and school systems, religious organizations, worksites, and the political system).

In an effort to address some of the above limitations and to develop a contextually meaningful approach to supporting parents, the Triple P-Positive Parenting Program, a multi-level, preventively oriented, parenting and family support strategy has been developed by the author and his colleagues at the University of Queensland in Brisbane, Australia. The program aims to prevent severe behavioral, emotional and developmental problems in children by enhancing the knowledge, skills, confidence, and teamwork of parents. The program has five levels of intervention on a tiered continuum of increasing strength (see Table 1) for parents of preadolescent children from birth to 12 years of age, although a version of parents of teenagers is also under development.

The rationale for this tiered multilevel strategy is that there are differing levels of dysfunction and behavioral disturbance in children, and parents have differing needs and desires regarding the type, intensity, and mode of assistance they require. The multilevel strategy is designed to maximize efficiency, contain costs, avoid waste and over servicing, and to ensure the program has wide reach in the community. Also, the multidisciplinary nature of the program ensures the better utilization of the existing professional workforce in the task of promoting competent parenting.

The program targets four different developmental periods from infancy to preadolescence. Within each developmental period, the reach of the intervention can vary from being very broad (targeting an entire population) or quite narrow (targeting only high risk children). This flexibility enables individual practitioners to determine the scope of the intervention given their own service priorities and funding. Alternatively, the program can be delivered as a government funded service provided on a free to consumer basis.

Theoretical Basis of Triple P

Triple P is a form of behavioral family intervention based on social learning principles (e.g., Patterson, 1982). Triple P aims to enhance family protective factors and to reduce risk factors associated with severe behavioral and emotional problems in preadolescent children.

Specifically the program aims to: 1) enhance the knowledge, skills, confidence, self sufficiency, and resourcefulness of parents of preadolescent children; 2) promote nurturing, safe, engaging, non-violent, and low conflict environments for children; and 3) promote children's social, emotional, language, intellectual, and behavioral competencies through positive parenting practices.

The program content draws on: (1) Social learning models of parent-child interaction that highlight the reciprocal and bidirectional nature of parent-child interactions (e.g., Patterson, 1982). This model identifies learning mechanisms, which maintain coercive and dysfunctional patterns of family interaction, and predicts future antisocial behavior in children (Patterson, Reid, & Dishion, 1992). As a consequence the program specifically teaches parents positive child management skills as an alternative to coercive parenting practices. (2) Research in child and family behavior therapy and applied behavior analysis which has developed many useful behavior change strategies, particularly research which focuses on rearranging antecedents of problem behavior through designing more positive engaging environments for children (Risley, et al., 1976; Sanders, 1992; 1996). (3) Developmental research on parenting in everyday contexts such that the program targets children's competencies in naturally occurring everyday contexts, drawing heavily on work which traces the origins of social and intellectual competence to early parent-child

Table 1. The Triple P Model of Parenting and Family Support

Level of Intervention	Target Population	Intervention Methods	Program Materials	Possible Target Behaviors
1. Universal Triple P	All parents interested in information about promoting their child's development.	Anticipatory well child care involving the provision of brief information on how to solve developmental and minor behavior problems. May involve self-directed resources, brief consultation, group presentations and mass media strategies.	Positive Parenting booklet Positive Parenting tip sheet series Families video series Every Parent Triple P Program Guide	Common every day behavior difficulties
2. Selective Triple P	Parents with a specific concern about their child's behavior or development.	Provision of specific advice for a discrete child problem behavior. May be self-directed or involve telephone or face-to-face clinician contact or group sessions.	Level 1 materials Primary Care Triple P Practitioner's Manual Developmental wall chart Consultation flip chart	Bedtime routine difficulties Temper tantrums Meal time behavior problems Toilet training
3. Primary Care Triple P	Parents with specific concerns about their child's behavior or development that require active skills training.	Brief therapy program (1 to 4 clinic sessions) combining advice, rehearsal and self-evaluation to teach parents to manage a discrete child problem behavior.	Level 1 and 2 materials	As for Level 2 Persistent eating problems Pain management

Table 1. continued

Level of Intervention	Target population	Intervention Methods	Program Materials	Possible Target Behaviors
4. Standard Triple P	Parents of children with more severe behavior problems. Parents wanting intensive training in positive parenting skills.	Intensive program focussing on parent-child interaction and the application of parenting skills to a broad range of target behaviors. Includes generalisation enhancement strategies. May be self-directed or involve telephone or face-to-face clinician contact or group sessions.	Level 1 to 3 materials Every Parent's Self-Help Workbook Standard Triple P Practitioner's Manual and Every Parent's Family Workbook Group Triple P Facilitator's Manual and Every Parent's Group Workbook	General behavior management concerns Aggressive behavior Oppositional Defiant Disorder Conduct Disorder Learning difficulties
5. Enhanced Triple P	Parents of children with concurrent child behavior problems and family dysfunction	Intensive program with modules including home visits to enhance parenting skills, mood management strategies and stress coping skills, and partner support skills.	Levels 1 to 4 materials Enhanced Triple P Practitioner's Manual and Every Parent's Supplementary Workbook	Persistent conduct problems Concurrent child behavior problems and parent problems (such as relationship conflict, depression). Child maltreatment

relationships (e.g., Hart & Risley, 1995; White, 1990). Children's risk of developing severe behavioral and emotional problems is reduced by instructing parents to use naturally occurring daily interactions to teach children language, social skills and developmental competencies, and problem solving skills in an emotionally supportive context. Particular emphasis is placed on using child-initiated interactions as a context for the use of incidental teaching (Hart & Risley, 1975). Children are at greater risk for adverse developmental outcomes, including behavioral problems, if they fail to acquire core language competencies and impulse control during early childhood (Hart & Risley, 1995). (4) Social information processing models which highlight the important role of parental cognitions such as attributions, expectancies, and beliefs as factors which contribute to parental self-efficacy, decision making, and behavioral intentions (e.g., Bandura, 1977, 1995). Parent's attributions are specifically targeted in the intervention by encouraging parents to identify alternative social interactional explanations for their child's behavior. (5) Research from the field of developmental psychopathology has identified specific risk and protective factors which are linked to adverse developmental outcomes in children (e.g., Emery, 1982; Grych & Fincham, 1990; Hart & Risley, 1995; Rutter, 1985). Specifically the risk factors of poor parent management practices, marital family conflict, and parental distress are targeted risk factors.

As parental discord is a specific risk factor for many forms of child and adolescent psychopathology (Grych & Fincham, 1990; Rutter, 1985; Sanders & Markie-Dadds, 1997), the program fosters collaboration and teamwork between caregivers in raising children. Improving couples' communication is an important vehicle to reduce marital conflict over child rearing issues, and to reduce personal distress of parents and children in conflictual relationships (Sanders, Markie-Dadds, & Turner, 1998).

Triple P also targets distressing emotional reactions of parents including depression, anger, anxiety and high levels of stress especially with the parenting role (Sanders, Markie-Dadds, & Turner, 1999). Distress can be alleviated through parents developing better parenting skills, which reduces feelings of helplessness, depression, and stress. Enhanced levels of the intervention use cognitive-behavior therapy techniques of mood monitoring, challenging dysfunctional cognitions and attributions, and by teaching parents specific coping skills for high risk parenting situations. (6) A population health perspective to family intervention involves the explicit recognition of the role of the broader ecological context for human development (e.g., Biglan, 1995; Mrazek & Haggerty, 1994; National Institute of Mental Health, 1998). As pointed out by Biglan (1995) the reduction of antisocial behavior in children requires a community context for parenting to truly change. Triple P's media and promotional strategy, as part of a larger system of intervention, aims to change this broader ecological context of parenting. It does this by normalizing parenting experiences (particularly the process of participating in parent education), by breaking down parents' sense of social isolation, increasing social and emotional support from others in the community, and by validating and acknowledging publicly the importance and difficulties of parenting. It also involves actively seeking community involvement and support in the program by the engagement of key community stakeholders (e.g., community leaders, businesses, schools, and voluntary organizations).

Self Regulation and Parental Competence

The approach to promoting parental competence views the development of a parent's capacity for self-regulation as a central skill. This involves teaching parents skills that enable them to become independent problem solvers. Karoly (1993) defined self regulation as follows: " Self-regulation refers to those processes, internal and or transactional, that enable an individual to guide his/her goal directed activities over time and across changing circumstances (contexts). Regulation implies modulation of thought, affect, behavior, and attention via deliberate or automated use of specific mechanisms and supportive metaskills. The processes of self-regulation are initiated when routinized activity is impeded or when goal directedness is otherwise made salient (e.g., The appearance of a challenge, the failure of habitual patterns; etc)..." (p. 25). This definition emphasizes that self-regulatory processes are embedded in a social context that not only provides opportunities and limitations for individual self-directedness, but also implies a dynamic reciprocal interchange between the internal and external determinants of human motivation. From a therapeutic perspective, self-regulation is a process whereby individuals are taught skills to modify their own behavior. These skills include how to select developmentally appropriate goals, monitor a child's or a parent's own behavior, choose an appropriate method of intervention for a particular problem, implement the solution, self monitor their implementation of solutions via checklists relating to the areas of concern, and to identify strengths or limitations in their performance and set future goals for action.

This self-regulatory framework is operationalized to include:

Self-sufficiency: As a parenting program is time limited, parents need to become independent problem solvers so they can begin to trust their own judgment and become less reliant on others in carrying out basic parenting responsibilities. Self-sufficient parents have the resilience, resourcefulness, knowledge, and skills to parent with confidence.

Self-efficacy: This refers to a parent's belief that they can overcome or solve a parenting or child management problem. Parents with high self-efficacy have more positive expectations about the possibility of change.

Self-management: The tools or skills that parents use to become more self-sufficient include self-monitoring, self-determination of performance goals and standards, self evaluation against some performance criterion, and self-selection of change strategies. As each parent is responsible for the way they choose to raise their children, parents select which aspects of their own and their child's behavior they wish to work on, to set goals for themselves, to choose specific parenting and child management techniques they wish to implement, and to self evaluate their success with their chosen goals against self determined criteria. Triple P aims to help parents make informed decisions by sharing knowledge and skills derived from contemporary research into effective child rearing practices. An active skills training process is incorporated into Triple P to enable skills to be modeled and practiced. Parents receive feedback regarding their implementation of skills learned in a supportive context, using a self-regulatory framework (see Sanders & Dadds, 1993).

Personal agency: Here the parent increasingly attributes changes or improvements in their situation to their own or their child's efforts rather than to chance, age, maturational factors or other uncontrollable events (e.g., spouses' bad parenting or genes). This outcome is achieved by prompting parents to identify causes or explanations for their child's or their own behavior.

Encouraging parents to become self-sufficient means that parents become more connected to social support networks (partners, extended family, friends, child care supports). However, the broader ecological context within which a family lives cannot be ignored (poverty, dangerous neighborhoods, community, ethnicity, culture). It is hypothesized that the more self-sufficient parents become the more likely they are to seek appropriate support when they need it, to advocate for children, become involved in their child's schooling, and to protect children from harm (e.g., by managing conflict with partners, and creating a secure low conflict environment).

Core Features of Triple P

There are several other key distinctive features of Triple P as a family intervention that are discussed below.

Principle of program sufficiency. This concept refers to the notion that parents differ in the strength of intervention they may require to enable them to independently manage a problem.

Triple P aims to provide the minimally sufficient level of support parents require to do their job. For example, parents seeking advice on a specific topic (e.g., tantrums) can receive clear high quality, behaviorally specific advice in the form of a parenting tip sheet on how to manage or prevent a specific problem. For such a parent, levels 1 or 2 of Triple P would constitute a sufficient intervention.

Flexible tailoring to identified risk and protective factors. The program enables parents to receive parenting support in the most cost-effective way possible. Within this context, a number of different programs of varying intensity have been developed. For example, Level 5 provides intervention for additional family risk factors, such as marital conflict, mood disturbance, and high levels of stress.

Varied delivery modalities. Several of the levels of intervention in Triple P can be delivered in a variety of formats, including individual face to face, group, telephone assisted or self-directed programs, or a combination of these formats. This flexibility enables parents to participate in ways that suit their individual circumstances and allows participation from families in rural and remote areas who typically have less access to professional services.

Wide potential reach. Triple P is designed to be implemented as an entire integrated system at a population level. However, the multi-level nature of the program enables various combinations of the intervention levels and modalities within levels to be used flexibly as either universal, indicated, or selective prevention strategies depending on local priorities, staffing, and budget constraints. Some communities using Triple P will use the entire multilevel system, while others may focus on getting the Level 4 group program implemented at a population level, while seeking funding support for the other levels of intervention.

A multi-disciplinary approach. Many different professional groups provide counsel and advice to parents. Triple P was developed as a professional resource that can be used by a range of helping professionals. These professionals include community nurses, family doctors, pediatricians, teachers, social workers, psychologists, psychiatrists, and police officers among others. At a community level rigid professional boundaries are discouraged and an emphasis is placed on providing training and support to a variety of professionals to become more effective in their parent consultation skills. Exclusive reliance on a single discipline such as clinical psychology will almost surely guarantee that there will be little or no impact on family relationships at a population level.

CONTEXTS FOR EFFECTIVE PARENTING INTERVENTION

A comprehensive approach to the provision of parent education requires a targeted focus from a variety of social contexts that influence parents. These include the media, primary care, school, worksite and the political context.

Mass Media

One way to disseminate effective parenting interventions more widely is by using the mass media. The mass media play an important role in providing health information for the general public (Egger, Donovan, & Spark, 1993), and television acts as the primary vehicle for mass media in today's society. Television has been shown to have the capacity to influence awareness and to change attitudes, beliefs, and behaviors, making it one of the most powerful educational resources available at the present time (Hofstetter, Schultze, & Mulvihill, 1992; Zimmerman, 1996). For example, evidence from the public health field has shown that televised media strategies can successfully increase community awareness of the risk and protective factors impacting upon health and well-being, promote health preserving behaviors such as abstaining from drinking alcohol when driving, and be instrumental in modifying potentially harmful behaviors such as cigarette smoking, poor diet and lack of exercise (Biglan, 1995; Sorenson, Emmons, Hunt, & Johnston, 1998).

Although the mass media have been used widely in the health promotion field, little is known about resulting effectiveness in the field of family intervention. There are several potential advantages of using media strategies such as television as an information source for parenting and family issues. Television has a pervasive influence on modern families: adults watch approximately 3 hours of television per day (Nielson, 1998); 47% of adults rate television as the best medium for accurate and reliable news; 61.8% choose to obtain news and information from television; and 79.6% report it to be the most influential advertising source for them (Federation of Australian Commercial Television Stations, 1995).

A televised parent education program has the advantage of being able to be accessed in the privacy of the home by a large proportion of the population, some of whom, such as parents living in rural and remote locations, may otherwise be difficult to reach. As an early intervention / prevention strategy, it has the potential to significantly decrease costs associated with accessing professional services. Alternatively, it may assist parents to recognize early warning signs of behavioral and emotional problems in children and encourage them to seek professional advice early when a minimal level of intervention may be sufficient to address recent onset, discrete, child behavior problems (Sanders & Markie-Dadds, 1996). Moreover, a televised parent education program could promote and increase community awareness of effective parenting strategies and understanding of the role family relationships play in the health and well-being of young children (Sanders, 1999). Media interventions of this type have the capacity to create a social milieu that is supportive of parent education and family change (Flay, 1987) that can be used to counter alarmist, sensationalized, or parent blaming messages (Sanders, 1999). An added advantage of a televised parent education program is that any behavioral change achieved by watching the program is likely to be attributed to one's own efforts (Flay 1987), thus increasing parents' feelings of personal competence and self-efficacy.

To be most effective as a mechanism of behavior change, rather than operating purely as a strategy for raising public awareness, a media intervention needs to not only provide information about the problem behavior but also provide practical advice about how to deal with it effectively (Andrews, McLeese, & Curran, 1995; Flay & Burton, 1990, Owen, Bauman, Booth, Oldenburg, & Magnus, 1995). For example, Parloto, Green, and Fishman (1992) found that efforts to teach mothers about the general principles of nutrition were less successful in changing infant feeding patterns than programs that pinpointed food-related behaviors and gave specific skills-based information, such as teaching mothers how to adequately prepare their infant's food. Similarly, for the mass media to be a successful vehicle for the promotion of effective parenting skills and the modification of parental behavior, information about functional strategies for promoting competence in children and for dealing with problem behavior need to be provided. Behavior change then requires parents to adopt a self-regulatory approach that involves self-monitoring, self-identification of personal strengths and weaknesses, and personal goal setting (Halford, Sanders, & Behrens, 1994; Webster-Stratton, 1992).

A Universal Triple P prevention strategy was recently developed to include a media campaign on parenting based around a television series, Families, which was shown in prime time on a commercial television network in New Zealand. The 13, 30-minute episode series was in an "infotainment" style to ensure the widest reach possible for Triple P. Such programs are very popular and according to ratings data, frequently attract around 20-35% of the viewing audience (Neilson, 1997). The series used an entertaining format to provide practical information and advice to parents on a variety of common behavioral and developmental problems in children as well as other parenting issues. The main segments were: a feature story, which presented brief discussions on a number of family issues (e.g., school involvement and the role of fathers); a segment in which a celebrity family discussed a range of issues about their family; family health care tips; animal care and integrating the pet into family life; interesting facts about the current state of families in society; and a brief Triple P segment.

The 5–7 minute Triple P segment each week enabled parents to complete a 13-session Triple P intervention at home. The Triple P segments provided brief examples of the causes of child behavior problems from a social learning perspective, provided information on how to monitor child behavior, and presented clear guidelines for using a range of parenting strategies designed to encourage desirable behavior in children (e.g., descriptive praise, positive attention), prevent problems from occurring (e.g., providing engaging activities), and manage difficult behavior (e.g., rule setting, directed discussion, planned ignoring, and the provision of clear instructions backed up by logical consequences, quiet time or time-out). These strategies were integrated into parenting plans for common problems (e.g., whining, disobedience, aggression, and temper tantrums), for promoting children's development (e.g., encouraging creativity and involvement in sport, and helping with homework), and for managing developmental issues (e.g., cooperative play; sleeping difficulties and eating difficulties). In addition, each Triple P segment presented a modeled demonstration of the suggested strategies.

A cross promotional strategy using radio and the print media was also used to prompt parents to watch the program and inform them of how to contact a Triple P telephone information line for more information about parenting. The Families fact sheets (specifically designed parenting tip sheets providing a written version of the information from the Triple P segment) were also available by writing to a Triple P Centre, calling the Triple P information line, or through a retail chain store.

To evaluate whether this form of media intervention could significantly impact on family functioning, Sanders, Montgomery, and Brechman-Toussaint (2000) randomly assigned mothers with children aged between 2 and 8 years either to a media intervention or control group. Mothers in the intervention group were given the television series, in the format of videos and tip sheets. These mothers watched two episodes of the series (in their own home) each week, at a time convenient to them, and read the relevant tip sheets. Mothers in the control group received no intervention for 6 weeks. As predicted, mothers in the media condition reported significant reductions in child behavior problems post-treatment in comparison to the control group. Reductions occurred in both the intensity of problem behavior and the number of problems that mothers were experiencing with their child. The percentage of children from the control condition falling in the clinical range for problem behavior did not change from pre- to post-intervention, yet there was a significant decrease in the percentage of children from the media condition who fell in the clinical range — from 46% prior to the intervention (over twice the national average) to 14% remaining in the clinical range following the intervention. Mothers in the media condition also reported an increased sense of competence and satisfaction in their parenting abilities relative to mothers in the control group. Anecdotally, many mothers reported that the realization they were doing some things "the right way" was one of the most salient outcomes of the program. A strong trend was also indicated for mothers in the media condition to demonstrate a reduction in dysfunctional parenting styles (e.g., laxness, overly harsh discipline, nagging) relative to the mothers in the waitlist condition.

Although the up-front costs of establishing a media-based intervention program such as Families is substantial, the reach may be wide and the long-term benefits to individuals and the community may far outweigh these initial costs.

As Triple P has been disseminated more widely in the community, different kinds of media activities have been used to promote the program in the community. These activities have included the broadcast of Triple P positive parenting tips (approximately 60 seconds each) on community radio stations, a weekly newspaper column on positive parenting, editorial and feature articles on the program, 30-second television commercials promoting the five key principles of positive parenting (a safe engaging environment, a positive learning environment, assertive discipline, reasonable expectations, and taking care of ourselves as parents), positive parenting inserts in school newsletters, public lectures and presentations, news and current affairs stories on network television. Triple P has been featured on the Australian version of 60 Minutes as well as on numerous other current affairs programs. These treatments have generally tracked one or more children through the intervention and have promoted strong public interest in the program.

These activities provide examples of ways in which the media can be used to promote program awareness, which in turn can create demand for evidence-based programs. Our experience has been that it is important to develop appropriate referral networks and back-up services for more intensive interventions when required. For some families this is the only participation they will have in a parenting program. Hence, designing a media campaign to ensure that messages are thematically consistent, culturally appropriate, and practical is critical to ensure that messages are acceptable and have appropriate impact. This level of intervention may be particularly useful for parents who have sufficient personal resources (i.e., motivation, literacy skills, commitment, time and support) to implement suggested strategies with only brief parenting advice. However, a media strategy is unlikely to be effective on its own for parents who have a child with a severe behavioral disorder or where a parent has few of the resources listed above, is depressed, is in a conflictual relationship, or suffering from major psychopathology. In these instances a more intensive form of intervention is indicated (e.g., Level 4, Level 5).

Primary Care as a Setting for Parenting Interventions

The last decade has seen an increasing emphasis on treating mental health problems at the primary care level (Giel, Koeter, & Ormel, 1990). The family doctor or child health nurse is often the first point of contact for parents experiencing behavioral difficulties with their young children. A large number of pediatric consultations deal with parental concerns about their child's behavior, development or school achievement (Christopherson, 1982, 1983; Oberklaid, Dworkin, & Levine, 1979; Taylor & Biglan, 1998; Triggs & Perrin, 1989). Primary care professionals are well positioned to provide parenting support and yet are commonly under-resourced and under-trained for the provision of effective mental health programs for children and families.

A recent parenting survey showed that doctors were the professionals most frequently consulted by caregivers of children with an emotional or behavioral problem (Sanders, Tully, et al., 1999). The Western Australian Child Health Survey showed that 65% of parents of children with behavioral and emotional problems consulted a doctor during a 6-month period. Only 2% saw a mental health specialist (Zubrick, et al., 1995). However, anecdotal evidence suggests that pediatric physicians and nurses receive little training in the detection and management of child behavior problems or in counseling parents about their child's behavior.

In a national U.S. survey of over 2000 parents with children under 3 years of age, Young and colleagues (Young, Davis, Schoen, & Parker, 1998) highlighted parents' concerns and the information they would like to receive from their pediatric physician or nurse. The majority of parents reported having a regular source of pediatric health care, which met their child's health needs, yet many were not satisfied with the help they received with regard to understanding their child's growth, development or care. Less than one quarter had talked with their pediatric clinician about discipline or promoting their child's development. However, parents who received this type of information were significantly more satisfied with their pediatric clinician than those who had not. A majority of parents (79%) reported a desire for more information from their pediatric clinician in at least one of six areas of child rearing (i.e., newborn care, sleep patterns, crying, toilet training, discipline, and encouraging early learning) and 53% wanted information in at least three of these areas. These data suggest that personalized advice, in the context of an ongoing supportive relationship, is the need being expressed by parents.

As they have regular contact with young families, primary care services can undertake several important tasks to promote children's mental health. Early detection of significant deviations from normal development and provision of advice to parents seeking information about developmental issues should become part of routine well-child care. Provision of brief behavioral counseling for child behavior problems and increased access to early intervention on dysfunctional family interaction patterns could help to prevent later, more serious problems. Primary care service providers can perform a triage function for the appropriate referral of moderate to severe child behavior problems to specialized services. This would help match intervention strength to individual family needs and ensure that the limited funds available for specialist mental health services are directed where they are most needed. In the long term, widespread implementation of such preventive primary care interventions could function to decrease the number of children requiring specialist health services. Through this type of primary care strategy, parenting support would become an integral part of family health care provision.

Two recent independent trials have assessed the impact of Triple P interventions in primary care settings. The first (Williams, Zubrick, Silburn, & Sanders, 1997) examined the effectiveness of specialized training and implementation of a group format intensive parenting skills training program (Markie-Dadds, Turner, & Sanders, 1997; Turner, Markie-Dadds, & Sanders, 1998) by primary care staff. The program was administered as a selective prevention demonstration project to reduce the prevalence of conduct problems at a population level. The target population was all parents of 3–4 year old children living in a metropolitan area with high socioeconomic disadvantage and high child abuse notification rates. The intervention was relatively brief — four 2-hour group sessions and four 15–30 minute individual telephone consultations. Groups were facilitated by community health nurses. Three in five eligible families attended the program and 85% of families completed at least 7 of the 8 program sessions. The program was successful in reducing dysfunctional parenting from twice the population average to general population levels and significantly reduced disruptive behavior problems in the children of participating families. This trial has shown not only extremely high community support for parenting programs offered through primary care settings, it has also demonstrated positive outcomes for parents and children.

The second study (Sultana, Matthews, De Bortoli, & Cann, 2000) involved a randomized controlled trial comparing two brief parenting interventions (Level 2 and 3 Triple P; Turner, Sanders, & Markie-Dadds, 1999) implemented by maternal and child health nurses, in comparison to a waitlist control condition. The study aimed to evaluate the impact of the Level 2 intervention (involving self-administration of written parenting advice following a 15 minute consultation) in comparison to the Level 3 intervention (involving four brief consultations supported by written and videotape parenting advice). Participants were 50 families of children aged between 18 months and 6 years with a recent onset, mild to moderate, behavior problem. Results showed the Level 3 intervention to produce significant reductions in child behavior problems and more appropriate discipline practices in comparison to the waitlist control condition. Moderate positive parent and child outcomes were achieved by families in the Level 2 intervention, however results did not differ significantly from the waitlist control condition. The Level 3 intervention proved superior to Level 2 on one measure of child behavior problems (Parent Daily Report Checklist; Chamberlain & Reid, 1987), and in reducing conflict between parents over parenting. These results provide further support for the efficacy of primary care staff in offering brief, early parenting support, resulting in reduced child problem behavior and improved parenting practices.

The School as a Setting for Parenting Interventions

Triple P has also been used as a transitional program targeting the parents of children in their first year of school. McTaggert and Sanders (2000) evaluated the effects of Triple P as a transition to primary school program. They randomly assigned 25 schools to receive either Group Triple P and an information campaign or to a control group. At the end of grade 1, there were fewer children reported by teachers in Triple P schools to have behavior problems and a significant increase in self-report measures of parenting skills than in schools where parents had not participated in Group Triple P. A similar project using the adolescent version of Group Triple P is currently being trialed in 4 Queensland state high schools. The encouraging preliminary finding from these studies suggested that the school could be used as a community context to support the needs of parents.

The Worksite as a Setting For Parenting Intervention

Another important area of intervention involves the development of parenting interventions as an employee assistance scheme to enable workers who are parents to more effectively balance work and home responsibilities. There is increasing evidence that family conflict contributes to work stress, low motivation, accidents at work, and low productivity. Conflict with children before and immediately after work is a source of considerable stress for many parents. We have recently been involved in developing and evaluating Triple P parenting strategies as a worksite intervention where the effects of intervention are assessed at both the family and worksite level. Ultimately programs tailored to the needs of working parents and delivered at work may put flesh on "family friendly" employment policies increasingly advocated for within business organizations.

The Political Context

Parenting interventions occur within a sociopolitical context. Family intervention researchers need to hone their skills of political advocacy, so that more resources go to funding the dissemination of evidence based parenting and family intervention programs. One concern is that many governments do not see parenting interventions as part of main stream clinical services delivered through health or mental health services. Rather parenting interventions are often funded in the welfare sector with non-government organizations being funded to deliver parenting programs. These funding mechanisms often occur with minimal accountability requirements and little insistence that evidence based parenting interventions be used. Moreover, little systematic effort is devoted to providing adequate professional training to practitioners to deliver parenting intervention.

New Directions

As there is increasing recognition of the important role of the family in influencing the lives of both children and adults, there are several ways in which this already important area can be further strengthened.

Continuing push for funding of evidence-based parenting interventions. Skillful political advocacy is needed to shift the importance and priority given to programs to support families and children. Within an Australian context there has been considerable improvement both at a state and federal level to providing funding to strategies to strengthen families. Unfortunately the level of funding provided often does not match the apparent importance given to the area by the political rhetoric.

Provision of incentives for parents to undertake properly evaluated parenting programs. If we are serious about providing adequate parent education and training to parents to undertake their parenting role there is merit in providing proper incentives to parents to undertake such training. Just as churches increasingly insist on a marriage preparation course as a requirement before being able to get married in a church, consideration needs to be given to the development of a range of incentives to encourage participation. These range from tax credits to direct payments to families who have completed a course.

Moving away from a skills deficit model. Much of the outcome literature attesting to the efficacy of BFI has used measures of child negative or problem behavior (e.g., disruptive, non-compliant, or aggressive behavior) as the primary index of success. While this emphasis is understandable given the priorities of funding agencies to treat or reduce distress or dysfunction, the relative absence of well validated measures of prosocial or adaptive functioning has inadvertently contributed to perception of the approach being negative rather than focusing on the healthy adaptive and positive effects of the interventions on children's sociability, empathy, and self esteem. While a skills deficit approach to identifying parental behaviors that are associated with poor child outcomes has enabled key parenting behaviors such as negative reinforcement traps to be pin pointed, many families engaging in problematic parenting practices may show a number of strengths which are not well represented in characterizations of family functioning.

Highlighting the "human" face of BFI. To counter perceptions that BFI is rigid, inflexible, and "cold" it is important that promoting professional training programs and in the actual training programs themselves that efforts are made to underscore the true complexity, skillfulness, concern for therapeutic process, and flexibility of the approach. This means being more explicit about how issues such as client resistance, homework compliance problems, within session parental conflict, and active skills training procedures such as behavioral rehearsal are used. High quality professionally produced videotapes are important tools to achieve these ends.

Research into additional areas of application. Although much progress has been made, there are many areas where good quality parenting interventions need to be developed and evaluated. These include programs for drug abusing parents, parents of children with life threatening illness (e.g., cystic fibrosis), parents with severe mental illness, parents with disabilities, and parents in prison.

Research into the dissemination process itself. An important challenge for funding organizations is to redirect some of its resources to fund research into the dissemination process. While considerable clinical research funding has been devoted to developing evidence-based approaches, very little has been devoted to the dissemination of these programs. Research is needed to gain a better understanding of the psychological and organizational variables which influence practitioners and agencies to adopt, implement and maintain their use of evidence-based parenting programs is required.

CONCLUSIONS

Raising competent, well-adjusted children is a community responsibility. Parenting and family interventions based on social learning theory are a powerful and underutilized resource. Empirically supported parenting and family intervention strategies arguably should be the centerpiece of public health efforts to prevent family, relationship distress and mental health problems. While it is undoubtedly true that healthy families lead to healthy, well adjusted children, in order to achieve this ideal, family practitioners need to break away from a traditional delivery paradigm and adopt a far more contextual perspective in understanding and ameliorating parenting and other family difficulties in the community.

REFERENCES

Andrews, A. B., McLeese, D. G., & Curran, S. (1995). The impact of a media campaign on public action to help maltreated children in addictive families. *Child Abuse and Neglect, 19*, 921-932.

Bandura, A. (1977). Self-efficacy: Toward a unifying theory of behavioral change. *Psychological Review, 84*, 191-215.

Bandura, A. (1995). *Self-efficacy in changing societies.* New York: Cambridge University Press.

Barkley, R. A., Guevremont, D. C., Anastopoulos, A. D., & Fletcher, K. E. (1992). A comparison of three family therapy programs for treating family conflicts in adolescents with attention-deficit hyperactivity disorder. *Journal of Consulting and Clinical Psychology, 60*, 450-462.

Barrett, P.M., Dadds, M.R. & Rapee, R.M. (1996). Family treatment of childhood anxiety: A controlled trial. *Journal of Consulting and Clinical Psychology, 65*, 627-635.

Biglan, A. (1995). Translating what we know about the context of antisocial behavior into a lower prevalence of such behavior. *Journal of Applied Behavior Analysis, 28*, 479-492.

Brestan, E. V., & Eyberg, S. M. (1998). Effective psychosocial treatments of conduct-disordered children and adolescents: 29 years, 82 studies, and 5,272 kids. *Journal of Clinical Child Psychology, 27*, 180-189.

Cauce, A. M., Reid, M., Landesman, S., & Gonzales, N. (1990). Social support in young children: Measurement, structure, and behavioral impact. In B. R. Sarason, I. G. Sarason, & G. R. Pierce (Eds.), *Social support: An interactional view* (pp. 64-94). New York: Wiley.

Chamberlain, P., & Reid, J.B. (1987). Parent observation and report of child symptoms. *Behavioral Assessment, 9*, 97-109.

Christopherson, E. R. (1982). Incorporating behavioral pediatrics into primary care. *Pediatric Clinics of North America, 29*, 261-295.

Christopherson, E.R. (1983). Behavioral pediatrics: An overview. In P.J. McGrath & P. Firestone (Eds.), *Pediatric and adolescent behavioral medicine: Issues in treatment* (pp. 1 -12). New York: Springer.

Coie, J.D. (1996). Prevention of violence and antisocial behavior. In R.D. Peters, & R.J. McMahon (Eds.), *Preventing childhood disorders, substance abuse, and delinquency* (pp. 1-18). Thousand Oaks, CA: Sage.

Connell, S., Sanders, M. R., & Markie-Dadds, C. (1997). Self-directed behavioral family intervention for parents of oppositional children in rural and remote areas. *Behavior Modification, 21*, 379-408.

Cohen, S., & Wills, T. A. (1985). Stress, social support, and the buffering hypothesis. *Psychological Bulletin, 98*, 310-357.

Cummings, E.M., & Davies, P. (1994). *Children and marital conflict: The impact of family dispute and resolution.* New York: Guildford.

Dadds, M. R., Schwartz, S. & Sanders, M. R. (1987). Marital discord and treatment outcome in the treatment of childhood conduct disorders. *Journal of Consulting & Clinical Psychology, 55*, 396-403.

Dryfoos, J. G. (1990). *Adolescents at risk: Prevalence and prevention.* New York: Oxford University Press.

Egger, G., Donovan, R., & Spark, R. (1993). *Health and the media.* Sydney: McGraw-Hill Book Company.

Emery, R. E. (1982). Interparental conflict and the children of discord and divorce. *Psychological Bulletin, 92*, 310-330.

Federation of Australian Commercial Television Stations. (1995). Attitudes to the media. Sydney: Author.

Flay, B. R. (1987). Mass media and smoking cessation: A critical review. *American Journal of Public Health, 77*, 153-160.

Flay, B. R., & Burton, C. (1990). Effective mass communication strategies for public health campaigns. In C. Atkin & L. Wallack (Eds.), *Mass communication and public health: Complexities and conflicts* (pp. 129-146). Newbury Park, CA: Sage.

Forehand, R. L., & Long, N. (1988). Outpatient treatment of the acting out child: Procedures, long term follow-up data, and clinical problems. *Advances in Behavior Research and Therapy, 10*, 129-177.

Giel, R., Koeter, M.W.J., & Ormel, J. (1990). Detection and referral of primary-care patients with mental health problems: The second and third filter. In D. Goldberg & D. Tantam (Eds.), *The public health impact of mental disorder* (pp. 25-34). Toronto, Canada: Hogrefe and Huber.

Grych, J. H., & Fincham, F. D. (1990). Marital conflict and children's adjustment: A cognitive-contextual framework. *Psychological Bulletin, 108*, 267-290.

Halford, W. K., Sanders, M. R., & Behrens, B. C. (1994). Self-regulation in behavioral couples' therapy. *Behavior Therapy, 25*, 431-452.

Hart, B., & Risley, T. R. (1975). Incidental teaching of language in the preschool. *Journal of Applied Behavior Analysis, 8,* 411-420.

Hart, B., & Risley, T. R. (1995). *Meaningful differences in the everyday experience of young American children.* Baltimore: Paul H. Brookes.

Hofstetter, C. R., Schultze, W. A., & Mulvihill, M. M. (1992). Communications media, public health, and public affairs: Exposure in a multimedia community. *Health Communication, 4,* 259-271.

Jacobson, N. S., & Traux, P. (1991). Clinical significance: A statistical approach to defining meaningful change in psychotherapy research. *Journal of Consulting and Clinical Psychology, 59,* 12-19.

Karoly, P. (1993). Mechanisms of self-regulation: A systems view. *Annual Review of Psychology, 44,* 23-52.

Kazdin, A. E. (1997). A model for developing effective treatments: Progression and interplay of theory, research, and practice. *Journal of Clinical Child Psychology, 26,* 114-129.

Kazdin, A. E. (1998). Psychosocial treatments for conduct disorder in children. In P. E. Nathan & J. M. Gordon (Eds.), *A guide to treatments that work* (pp. 65-89). new York: Oxford University Press.

Lawton, J. M., & Sanders, M. R. (1994). Designing effective behavioral family interventions for stepfamilies. *Clinical Psychology Review, 14,* 463-496.

Lochman, J. E. (1990). Modification of childhood aggression. In M. Hersen, R. M. Eisler, & P. M. Miller (Eds.), *Progress in behavior modification* (Vol. 25, pp. 47-85). New York: Academic Press.

Loeber, R., & Farrington, D. P. (1998). Never too early, never too late: Risk factors and successful interventions for serious and violent juvenile offenders. *Studies on Crime and Crime Prevention, 7,* 7-30.

Markie-Dadds, C., Sanders, M. R., & Turner, K. M. T. (1999). Every parent's self-help workbook. Brisbane, Australia: Families International Publishing.

McMahon, R.J. (1999). Parent Training. In S.W. Russ & T. Ollendick (Eds.) *Handbook of psychotherapies with children and families* (pp. 153-180). New York: Plenum Press.

McMahon, R. J., Slough, N. M., & Conduct Problems Prevention Research Group. (1996). Family-based intervention in the fast track program. In R. D. Peters & R. J. McMahon (Eds.), *Preventing childhood disorders, substance abuse, and delinquency.* Thousand Oaks, CA: Sage.

McMahon, R. J., & Wells, K. C. (1998). Conduct problems. In E. J. Mash & R. A. Barkley (Eds.), *Treatment of childhood disorders* (2nd ed.; pp. 111-207). New York: Guilford.

McNeil, C.B., Eyberg, S., Eisenstadt, T.H., Newcomb, K., & Funderbunk. (1991). Parent child interaction therapy with behavior problem children: Generalization of treatment effects to the school setting. *Journal of Clinical Child Psychology, 20*, 140-151.

McTaggart, P., & Sanders, M. R. (2000). *An evaluation of a universal training program for parents of children starting school.* Manuscript in preparation.

Mrazek, P., & Haggerty, R. J. (1994). *Reducing the risks for mental disorders.* Washington: National Academy Press.

National Institute of Mental Health. (1998). *Priorities for prevention research at NIMH: A report by the national advisory mental health council workgroup on mental disorders prevention research* (NIH Publication No. 98-4321). Washington, DC: U. S. Government Printing Office.

Neilson, A. C. (1997). *People meter rating analysis.* Sydney, Australia: Author.

Nicholson, J.M., & Sanders, M.R. (1999). Randomized controlled trial of behavioral family intervention for the treatment of child behavior problems in stepfamilies. *Journal of Divorce and Remarriage, 30*, 1-23.

Nielson, A. C. (1998). *Average amount of time spent exposed to television by age group.* Sydney: Author.

Oberklaid, F., Dworkin, P.H., & Levine, M.D. (1979). Developmental-behavioral dysfunction in preschool children: Descriptive analysis of a pediatric consultative model. *American Journal of Diseases of Children, 133*, 1126-1131.

O'Dell, S. (1974). *Training parents in behavior modification: A review.* Psychological Bulletin, 81, 418-433.

Owen, N., Bauman, A., Booth, M., Oldenburg, B., & Magnus, P. (1995). Serial mass media campaigns to promote physical activity: Reinforcing or redundant? *American Journal of Public Health, 85*, 244-248.

Parloto, I, Green, S. H., & Fishman, H. (1992). *Communicating to improve nutrition behavior: The challenge of motivating the audience to act.* Washington DC: Academy for Educational Development for the International Conference on Nutrition.

Patterson, G. R. (1982). *Coercive family process.* Eugene, OR: Castalia Press.

Patterson, G.R., Reid, J.B. & Dishion, T.J. (1992). *Antisocial boys.* Eugene, OR: Castalia.

Pratt, M. W., Kerig, P., Cowan, P. A., & Cowan, C. P. (1988). Mothers and fathers teaching 3-year-olds: Authoritative parenting and adult scaffolding of young children's learning. *Developmental Psychology, 24*, 832-839.

Risley, T. R., Clark, H. B., & Cataldo, M. F. (1976). Behavioral technology for the normal middle class family. In E. J. Mash, L. A. Hamerlynck, & L. C. Handy. (Eds.), *Behavior modification and families* (pp. 34-60). New York: Brunner/Mazel.

Robins, L. N., & Price, R. K. (1991). Adult disorders predicted by childhood conduct problems: Results from NIMH epidemiological catchment area project. *Psychiatry, 54*, 116-132.

Rutter, B. M. (1979). The prognostic significance of psychological factors in the management of chronic bronchitis. *Psychological Medicine, 9*, 63-70.

Rutter, M. (1985). Family and school influences on behavioral development. *Journal of Child Psychology and Psychiatry, 26*, 349-368.

Sanders, M. R. (1992). Enhancing the impact of behavioral family intervention with children: Emerging perspectives. *Behavior Change, 9*, 115-119.

Sanders, M. R. (Ed.). (1995). *Healthy families, healthy nation: Strategies for promoting family mental health in Australia*. Australia: Australian Academic Press.

Sanders, M. R. (1996). New directions in behavioral family intervention with children. In T. H. Ollendick & R. J. Prinz, (Eds.), *Advances in clinical child psychology* (Vol. 18, pp. 283-330). New York: Plenum Press.

Sanders, M.R. (1998). The empirical status of psychological interventions with families of children and adolescents. In L. L'Abate (Ed.). *Family psychopathology: The relational roots of dysfunctional behavior*. New York: Guildford.

Sanders, M.R. (1999). The Triple P-Positive Parenting Program: Towards an empirically validated multilevel parenting and family support strategy for the prevention of behavior and emotional problems in children. *Clinical Child and Family Psychology Review, 2*, 71–90.

Sanders, M. R., & Glynn, E. L. (1981). Training parents in behavioral self-management: An analysis of generalization and maintenance effects. *Journal of Applied Behavior Analysis, 14*, 223-237.

Sanders, M. R., Gravestock, F., Pidgeon, A., Connors, M. D., & Brown, S. (2000, October). *Pathways Positive Parenting Program: Enhanced behavioral intervention for families at-risk of child maltreatment*. Paper presented at the 8th Annual Queensland Child Health Conference, Brisbane, QLD, Australia.

Sanders, M. R., & Markie Dadds, C. (1996). Triple P: A multilevel family intervention program for children with disruptive behavior disorders. In P. Cotton, H. Jackson, (Eds.), *Early intervention and prevention in mental health* (pp. 59-85). Melbourne, Australia: Australian Psychological Society Ltd.

Sanders, M. R., & Markie-Dadds, C. (1997). Managing common child behavior problems. In M. R. Sanders, C. Mitchell, & G. J. A. Byrne (Eds.), *Medical consultation skills: Behavioral and interpersonal dimensions of health care* (pp. 356–402). Melbourne, Australia: Addison-Wesley-Longman.

Sanders, M.R., Markie-Dadds, C., Tully, L., & Bor, B. (2000). The Triple P - Positive Parenting Program: A comparison of enhanced, standard and self-directed behavioral family intervention for parents of children with early onset conduct problems. *Journal of Consulting and Clinical Psychology, 68*, 624-640.

Sanders, M. R., Markie-Dadds, C., & Turner, K. M. T. (1998). *Practitioner's manual for Enhanced Triple P*. Brisbane: Families International.

Sanders, M. R., Markie-Dadds, C., & Turner, K. M. T. (1999). *Practitioner's manual for Enhanced Triple P*. Brisbane, Australia: Families International Publishing.

Sanders, M. R., & McFarland, M. L. (2000). The treatment of depressed mothers with disruptive children: A controlled evaluation of cognitive behavioral family intervention. *Behavior Therapy, 31*, 89-112.

Sanders, M. R., Montgomery, D. T., & Brechman-Toussaint, M. L.(2000). The mass media and the prevention of child behavior problems: The evaluation of a television series to promote positive outcomes for parents and their children. *Journal of Child Psychology and Psychiatry, 41*, 939-948.

Sanders, M. R., Nicholson, J. M., & Floyd, F. J. (1997). Couples' relationships and children. In W. K. Halford, & H. J. Markman (Eds.), *Clinical handbook of marriage and couples interventions* (pp. 225-253). Chichester, England UK: John Wiley.

Sanders, M. R., & Shallcross, E. (2000). *Effects of a television series on parenting and family survival skills on parent-child interactions.* Manuscript submitted for publication.

Sanders, M. R., Shepherd, R. W., Cleghorn, G., & Woolford, H. (1994). The treatment of recurrent abdominal pain in children. A controlled comparison of cognitive-behavioral family intervention and standard pediatric care. *Journal of Consulting and Clinical Psychology, 62*, 306-314.

Sanders, M. R., Tully, L. A., Baade, P., Lynch, M. E., Heywood, A., Pollard, G., & Youlden, D. (1999). A survey of parenting practices in Queensland: Implications for mental health promotion. *Health Promotion Journal of Australia, 9*, 105-114.

Sawyer, M. G., Arney, F. M., Baghurst, P. A., Clark, J. J., Graetz, B. W., Kosky, R. J., Nurcombe, B., Patton, G. C., Prior, M. R., Raphael, B., Rey, J., Whaites, L. C., & Zubrick, S. R. (2000). *The mental health of young people in Australia: The child and adolescent component of the national survey of mental health and well-being.* Canberra: Australian Government Printing Service.

Schreibman, L., Kaneko, W. M., & Koegel, R. L. (1991). Positive affect of parents of autistic children: A comparison across two teaching techniques. *Behavior Therapy, 22*, 479-490.

Serketich, W.J., & Dumas, J.E. (1996). The effectiveness of behavioral parent training to modify antisocial behavior in children: A meta-analysis. *Behavior Therapy, 27*, 171-186

Sorensen, G., Emmons, K., Hunt, M., & Johnston, D. (1998). Implications of the results of community intervention trials. *Annual Review of Public Health, 19*, 379-416.

Sultana, C.R., Matthews, J., De Bortoli, D., & Cann, W. (2000). *An evaluation of two levels of the Positive Parenting Program (TRIPLE P) delivered by primary care practitioners.* Unpublished manuscript, RMIT University, Melbourne, VIC, Australia.

Taylor, T. K., & Biglan, A. (1998). Behavioral family interventions for improving child-rearing: A review of the literature for clinicians and policy makers. *Clinical Child and Family Psychology, 1*, 41-60.

Triggs, E. G., & Perrin, E. C. (1989). Listening carefully: Improving communication about behavior and development: Recognizing parental concerns. *Clinical Pediatrics, 28*, 185-192.

Turner, K.M.T., Markie-Dadds, C, & Sanders, M.R. (1998). *Facilitator's manual for Group Triple P.* Brisbane, QLD, Australia: Families International.

Turner, K.M.T., Sanders, M.R., & Markie-Dadds, C. (1999). *Practitioner's manual for Primary Care Triple P.* Brisbane, QLD, Australia: Families International.

Turner, K. M. T., Sanders, M. R., & Wall, C. R. (1994). Behavioral parent training versus dietary education in the treatment of children with persistent feeding difficulties. *Behavior Change, 11*, 242-258.

Turner, K. M. T., Markie-Dadds, C., & Sanders, M. R. (1996). *Triple P tip sheet series for toddlers.* Brisbane, Australia: Families International Publishing.

Turner, K. M. T., Sanders, M. R., & Markie-Dadds, C. (1996). *Triple P tip sheet series for preschoolers.* Brisbane, Australia: Families International Publishing.

68

Turner, K. M. T., Sanders, M. R., & Wall, C. (1994). A comparison of behavioral parent training and standard education in the treatment of persistent feeding difficulties in children. *Behavior Change, 11*, 105-111.

Webster Stratton, C. (1989). Systematic comparison of consumer satisfaction of three cost effective parent training programs for conduct problem children. *Behavior Therapy, 20*, 103-115.

Webster-Stratton, C. (1992). Individually administered video-tape parent training: "Who benefits?" *Cognitive Therapy and Research, 16*, 31-65.

Webster Stratton, C. (1994). Advancing videotape parent training: A comparison study. *Journal of Consulting and Clinical Psychology, 62*, 583-593.

Webster-Stratton, C. (1998). Preventing conduct problems in Head Start children: Strengthening parenting competencies. *Journal of Consulting and Clinical Psychology, 66*, 715-730.

White, B. L. (1990). *The first three years of life*. New York: Prentice Hall Press.

Williams, A., Zubrick, S., Silburn, S., & Sanders, M. (1997). *A population based intervention to prevent childhood conduct disorder: The Perth Positive Parenting Program demonstration project*. Paper presented at the 9th National Health Promotion Conference, Darwin, Northern Territory, Australia.

Wills, T. A., Vaccaro, D., & McNamara, G. (1992). The role of life events, family support, and competence in adolescent substance use: A test of vulnerability and protective factors. *American Journal of Community Psychology, 20*, 349-374.

Young, K.T., Davis, K., Schoen, C., & Parker, S. (1998). Listening to parents: A national survey of parents with young children. *Archives of Pediatrics and Adolescent Medicine, 152*, 255-262.

Zubrick, S.R., Silburn, S.R., Garton, A., Burton, P., Dalby, R., Carlton, J., Shepherd, C., & Lawrence, D. (1995). *Western Australia Child Health Survey: Developing health and well-being in the nineties*. Perth, Western Australia: Australian Bureau of Statistics and the Institute for Child Health Research.

Zubrick, S.R., Silburn, S.R., Burton, P., & Blair, E. (2000). Mental health disorders in children and young people: Scope, cause and prevention. *Australian and New Zealand Journal of Psychiatry, 34*(4), 570-578.

3

Interventions and Outcome in Autism

Patricia Howlin
Saint George's Hospital Medical School

Patricia Howlin · St. George's Hospital Medical School · Department of Psychology · Cranmer Terrace · London SW17 ORE · United Kingdom.

International Perspectives on Child and Adolescent Mental Health. Volume 2: Proceedings of the Second International Conference, edited by N. N. Singh, T. H. Ollendick, and A. N. Singh. © 2002 Elsevier Science Ltd. All rights reserved.

Estimates of the prevalence of autism and related disorders vary widely but it is clear that the rates are considerably higher than the 4-5 per 10,000 typically cited in early reports (e.g., Lotter, 1978). A recent review by Fombonne (1999) of 23 epidemiological studies conducted between 1966 and 1998 indicates that the combined rate for autism and autism spectrum disorders (not including Asperger syndrome) is around 18.7 per 10,000. Figures from the National Autistic Society in the UK (1997) are even higher, with prevalence rates for all autism related disorders, including Asperger syndrome, being given as 91 per 10,000. Although these statistics need to be viewed with some caution (they are based on small samples, which tend to yield higher prevalence rates and far wider confidence limits), it is evident that the number of individuals who fall within the "autistic spectrum" is far greater than once thought.

Understanding of the fundamental cause (or causes) of autism still has far to go but it is now well established that genetic factors are implicated in a substantial proportion of cases (Rutter, 1999; Szatmari, Jones, Zwaigenbaum, & Maclean, 1999). It is likely that research in the 21st century will focus on issues related to genetic mechanisms. However, as Rutter (1999) notes, it will probably be many years before such research has any practical implications in terms of more effective intervention strategies.

INTERVENTIONS FOR AUTISM

Almost three decades ago, Kanner (1973) commented that in the 30 years since he had first described the condition: "There has been a hodge-podge of theories, hypotheses and explanations . . . yet no-one has succeeded in finding a therapeutic setting, drug, method or technique that has yielded the same or lasting results for all children. It is expected that a next 30 or 20 year follow-up will be able to present a report of ... more hopeful prognosis." Unfortunately, much therapeutic research in this area has continued to be characterized by controversy and unsubstantiated claims, and randomized control trials of even the most widely used interventions are virtually non-existent.

The first published accounts of treatments for autism began to appear in the 1950's, when the condition was viewed primarily as a psychiatric disorder with a psychogenic cause. Kanner (1951), for example, although initially suggesting that autism was a developmental disorder ("We must assume that these children come into the world with an innate inability to form the usual biologically provided affective contact with people") was later influenced by contemporary views of the link between autism and schizophrenia. He also commented on the lack of warmth shown by many parents and their tendency towards a "mechanization of human contacts"

(Kanner, 1943). Throughout the 1950's and 60's, therefore, as awareness of autism continued to grow, psychoanalysis, together with drugs and other treatments (including ECT) used for schizophrenia tended to be the treatments of choice for children with autism (Campbell, 1978).

In the mid to late 1960's autism began to be viewed as a behavioral disorder, with many studies demonstrating the effectiveness of operant approaches (Bandura, 1969; Ullman & Krasner, 1965). Such interventions were generally clinic based, with children frequently being treated as long-term inpatients. Parents were only minimally, if at all, involved in treatment, and the focus of therapy tended to be on the elimination of "undesirable" behaviors, notably tantrums, aggression or self injury. The procedures used to increase skills such as social interactions or communication were often highly prescriptive and inflexible, and took little note of individual factors such as the child's developmental level, or the family situation. There was heavy reliance on food based rewards and frequent use of aversive procedures, including electric shock (see Howlin & Rutter, 1987)

During the 1970's, largely due to the influential work of Rutter (1972), recognition of the fundamental cognitive, social and communication deficits underlying the disorder led to a shift to more individually based treatment programs; acknowledgement of the importance of structured educational approaches and of the crucial role of parents in therapy. As problems of generalization and maintenance became evident, home based interventions began to replace inpatient programs and there was much wider use of naturalistic teaching and reinforcement strategies.

The 1980's witnessed increasing integration of home and school based programs, greater involvement of typically developing peers in therapy and a steady movement towards more inclusive education. There was growing recognition, too, of the need for early intervention and of the role played by communication deficits in causing many of the "challenging behaviors" frequently associated with autism. Reactions against abuses arising from the uncontrolled use of aversive procedures led to a focus on the development of more positive treatment strategies. However, in some quarters, the use of any form of behavioral intervention (including extinction or time out procedures) was condemned (McGee, Menolascino, Hobbs, & Menousek, 1987), with the result that care staff were sometimes deprived of some of their most effective management techniques.

It was in the 1980's, too, that the needs of more able people with autism and Asperger syndrome began to be better understood. Wing (1981) was responsible for first bringing Asperger's (1944) original writings to the attention of clinicians and the syndrome now appears in both DSM-IV and ICD-10 diagnostic systems. Generally the term is used for individuals who show the same types of social-communication deficits and stereotyped and repetitive behaviors found in autism, but who have an IQ within the normal range (i.e., 70+), and whose early language development was not significantly delayed. However, there is considerable disagreement about the validity of the diagnostic criteria used to distinguish between autism and Asperger syndrome (Kim, Szatmari, Bryson, & Wilson, 2000; Leekham, Libby, Wing, Gould, & Gillberg., 2000; Manjiviona & Prior, 1999). Wing (2000) herself expressed concern that she may unwittingly have opened a "Pandora's box" and research evidence increasingly indicates that there are no consistent empirical grounds on which to distinguish between high functioning individuals with autism and those with Asperger syndrome (Howlin, 2001).

In the last decade, therapeutic work in the field of autism has been characterized by a number of both positive and less positive trends. On the positive side there were extensive attempts to extend functional analytic approaches to intervention, based on an awareness of the role of communication deficits in causing many problem behaviors (Durand & Carr, 1991; Greenspan & Wieder, 1999). However, much of this work has been experimentally based and has not always proved easy to adapt to naturalistic and less well-staffed environments. Indeed, Fisher, Piazza, Cataldo, Harrell, Jefferson, and Connor (1993) have suggested that, because of the difficulties of implementing functional analysis strategies in homes or schools, a return to the use of a "combination of training plus punishment (may produce) the largest and most consistent results."

Other positive trends have included the increased focus on developmental approaches to enhance generalized communication skills in young children (Prizant, Schuler, & Wetherby, 1997); the emphasis on teaching "pivotal" responses related to social and communicative interactions (Koegel & Koegel, 1995; Koegel, Koegel, Harrower, & Carter, 1999); greater reliance on naturalistic reinforcers, and recognition of the need to encourage self initiation and self motivation (Prizant & Rubin, 1999). There have also been a number of attempts to improve the fundamental deficits associated with autism such as impairments in "Theory of Mind" or social understanding more generally. Whilst such programs have their limitations (Howlin, Baron-Cohen, Hadwin, & Swettenham, 1998) they do provide teachers, parents and others with strategies and guidelines that can be adapted for use in many different settings

Nevertheless, there is still, particularly in the US, considerable use of medication even for very young children (see Gringras, 2000; McDougle, 1997 for reviews). Among the many different pharmacological agents used are the "one size fits all" type (such as fenfluramine) that have been claimed to have a positive impact on almost all aspects of children's functioning. Then there are more specific agents including SSRI'S (fluoxetine; fluvoxamine); other antidepressants, such as clomipramine; stimulants (mainly methylphenidate); anti-hypertensive agents (clonidine); anti-psychotics (haloperidol); opioid antagonists (naltrexone) to treat self injurious behavior; mood stabilizers, such as lithium; anti-convulsants, and other agents including melatonin and megavitamins (c.f. Rimland, 2000). Such treatments are not limited to children with more severe behavioral problems and rates of medication, even amongst more able individuals with autism are considerable. For example, in a sample of 109 high functioning patients (both adult and child), Martin, Scahill, Lawrence Klin and Volkmar (1999) found that 32 % had been prescribed anti-depressant medication (mostly SSRI's); 20% had taken some form of neuroleptic and the same proportion had received stimulant medication. Over half the sample was currently receiving psychotropic treatment- 26% were on 1 drug, 23% on 2 and 6% were on 3 or more. Over two-thirds (69%) had received psychotropic medication at some time in their lives. Despite such high rates of prescribing there are few adequate randomized control trials of the use of psychotropic medications in autism and little if any information about the long-term effects, especially when given to young children. However, Fenfluramine, which, throughout much of the 1980's, was widely used as a treatment of choice for many children with autism in the US has now been largely withdrawn because of concerns about serious side effects and potential long-term damage (see Cambell, Schopler, Cueva, & Hallin, 1996 for review). Another recent treatment, extensively publicized by the media, involves injections with Secretin (a gastro-intestinal peptide hormone). This has been claimed to have almost "miraculous" effects (Horvath 1998; Rimland, 1998), with rapid improvements in behavior and language being cited. Nevertheless, an increasing number of parents are now beginning to report severe, adverse side-effects, and initial control trials indicate no advantages over placebo injections (Sandler, et al., 1999).

There is no shortage of claims for other therapies that are said significantly to improve outcome, some even resulting in cures or "recovery". Among such interventions are Holding therapy, music therapy, scotopic sensitivity training, Facilitated Communication, Auditory Integration Training, Conductive Education, Daily Life Therapy, Gentle Teaching, the Options method, and the Waldon approach (see Howlin, 1998 for review). Reports on the dramatic (and always positive) effects of other therapies, from swimming with dolphins, cranial osteopathy, or being swung around in nets, also make regular appearances in the press (Muller, 1993). Unfortunately, few of these methods have been subject to any form of experimental investigation; there are no randomized comparison trials or even well controlled single case or small group studies. Thus, for most there is neither any evidence that the treatment is effective…nor that it is not!

Facilitated Communication (FC) and Auditory Integration Training (AIT) are amongst the very few therapies that have been subject to detailed evaluation. FC involves a facilitator who supports the client's hand, wrist or arm whilst he or she uses a keyboard, or letter board, to spell out words, phrases or sentences. Its use with people with autism is based on the theory that many of their difficulties result from a movement disorder, rather than social or communication deficits. The facilitator should presume that the client possesses unrecognized literacy skills and the provision of physical support can then lead to "Communication Unbound" (Biklen, 1990). The therapy has been the focus of around 50 studies involving at least 300 subjects. These have demonstrated conclusively that there is virtually no evidence of independent communication (c.f. Bebko, Perry & Bryson, 1996). Moreover, so extensive have been the concerns over abuses arising from this technique that, the American Psychological Association (1994) adopted the resolution that: "Facilitated Communication is a controversial and unproved procedure with no scientifically demonstrated support for its efficacy". However, although the method is now generally discredited it continues to be used (The Times, 2000).

Auditory Integration Therapy, which involves listening to electronically processed music through headphones for a total of 10 hours, (usually in 2 x 30 minute sessions over a 10 day period) is another treatment that has proved popular in Europe, the US and Australia. Despite early, positive reports (Rimland & Edelson, 1994, 1995) recent research suggests that the effects are no greater than with a placebo treatment (Dawson & Watling, 2000; Mudford, et al., 2000).

Pre-School Intervention Programs

Of the many different interventions claiming to have a positive impact on outcome, those with an emphasis on the early development of cognitive, play, social and communication skills are better supported by empirical evidence. Home based interventions, specifically designed for children with autism (Howlin & Rutter, 1987; Lovaas, 1987) indicate that if parents can be helped to develop appropriately structured and consistent management strategies during the child's early years, this can enhance social, cognitive and linguistic development and minimize later behavioral problems. Early specialist educational programs also have positive effects (see Rogers, 1996) The most successful programs appear to involve intensive support (of 15 or more hours per week); tend to last at least 6 months, and require a high adult: child ratio. However, because of problems in methodology and research design, conclusions about their effectiveness, especially in the longer term, remain limited. Progress appears to be enhanced if children begin intervention before 5 years, but there is no information on exactly how early programs should begin. Similarly, although some research indicates that IQ and language levels are important predictive variables, with the most handicapped children making least progress other studies have found no relationship between pre-treatment level and outcome (Smith, Groen, & Wynn, 2000).

There is a variety of other early intervention programs, such as Hanen (Manolson, 1992) and Early Bird (Shields 2001), that focus specifically on improving the interaction (verbal and non-verbal) between parents and very young children with autism. Involvement in such programs is generally highly valued by families (Shields 2001) but again there are no well-controlled evaluative studies.

Many other questions remain to be answered concerning the specific effects of early intervention. These include the relative importance of the different components of treatment and of the treatment variables responsible for change, the roles of parents and other professionals, and the comparative merits of one-to-one versus group teaching, or home-based versus school based programs. There is an urgent need, too, for the development of standardized protocols to assess functioning before and after treatment in order to make valid and reliable comparisons between different interventions (Rogers, 1998).

Intensive Home Based Behavioral Programs

Probably the most controversial approach to early intervention has been the intensive home-based "Applied Behavioral Analysis" (ABA) program widely promoted by Lovaas and his colleagues. Therapy, which is provided on a 1:1 basis for 40 or more hours a week and lasts for at least two years, is claimed to bring about "recovery" from autism (Perry, Cohen, & DeCarlo, 1995). The children involved are reported to have shown large and significant gains in IQ (of 30 points or more), rates of integration into mainstream school are high and around 40% are said to have achieved "normal functioning", with the gains persisting into adolescence. (Lovaas, 1993; McEachin, Smith, & Lovaas, 1993). Although methodologically stronger than other early intervention projects, there have been criticisms concerning the experimental design and particular controversy over the use of terms such as "recovery" or "normal functioning" (see Gresham & MacMillan, 1998; Mesibov, 1993). The intensity of involvement required also limits opportunities for replication studies and the few that have been conducted have generally used a modified design, with smaller numbers of children (e.g. Sheinkopf & Siegel, 1998; Smith, Groen & Wynn, 2000). Although progress is generally enhanced following ABA based interventions, recent studies have suggested more modest gains, and do not describe participants as achieving normal functioning. It is also evident that not all children respond equally favorably to intervention (Smith, et al., 2000). Progress is generally more limited among those with an IQ in the severe-profound range, or those who fail to acquire verbal imitation within the first 4-6 months (Smith & Lovaas, 1997).

A further problem concerns the psychometric assessments used to monitor change over time as there are no single, well-standardized assessments that are suitable for use with both young non-verbal infants and older children. A recent study by Magiati and Howlin (2001, in press) indicates that the tests used at initial diagnosis and later follow-up can significantly influence conclusions about the extent of change. Certain instruments (such as the Bayley Scales, Bayley, 1993) when used with non-speaking children with autism tend to provide lower estimates of initial functioning than tests that focus more on the child's non-verbal ability (e.g. The Merrill Palmer scales, Stutsman, 1948). A child who is initially tested on the latter test (which is likely to produce a relatively high estimate of cognitive level) and then re-assessed some years later on a different measure may show less apparent change over time than one who is first tested on the Bayley. These authors suggest that, in any investigation of treatment effectiveness over time, it is essential to take account of the nature of the original assessment and to be aware of whether the particular tests used produce higher or lower estimates of early levels of functioning. In addition, given the problems associated with early testing, it is important that pre-and post intervention assessments should not rely on a single IQ measure. A combination of measures is likely to provide a more reliable and valid picture of the child's abilities. Moreover, in order to assess the real extent of change, the same measures should be used pre- and post intervention and, when comparing outcome in intervention and non-intervention groups, the same tests (before and after treatment) must be used for both groups. Only in this way is it possible to draw valid conclusions about the comparative effects of treatment.

Many other problems related to the assessment of treatment effects are discussed by Prizant and Rubin (1999; see also Lord, 2000). Anderson and Romanczyk (1999) conclude "ABA includes a large number of conceptually consistent techniques that can, and should, be used in various combinations across many different contexts". However, whilst it is generally accepted that home-based behavioral therapy is a good option for children with autism there is still no evidence that such treatment approaches are more effective, especially in the longer term than other treatments of similar intensity or structure (Sheinkopf & Siegel, 1998).

Longer-term evaluations, covering many different aspects of functioning are required if the true cost-effectiveness of the time, effort and energy expended by families in these programs is to be adequately assessed. Future research also needs to concentrate on developing appropriate strategies to compare different intervention models, and to examine more closely the differential effects of treatment techniques, intensity, structure and setting on different subgroups of children with the autistic spectrum. The important question is not so much "does this or that technique work?" but rather "which approaches offer most to which types of children? "

The Importance Of Appropriate Education

Whatever the controversy over other forms of treatment, the importance of specialized educational programs for children with autism is extensively documented (Burack, Root, & Zigler, 1997; Howlin, 2001). The TEACCH program, (Schopler, Mesibov, & Hearsey, 1995) developed in North Carolina, but now widely used in many parts of the world, is an educational approach that is founded on the need for structure. In particular it emphasizes the need for appropriate environmental organization and the use of clear visual cues to circumvent communication difficulties. The program takes account of developmental levels and the importance of individually based teaching, as well as incorporating behavioral and cognitive approaches. However, although there have been many anecdotal reports of its effectiveness (Campbell, et al., 1996), there is relatively little in the way of independent evaluations

Many other approaches to education, focusing specifically on strategies to overcome the fundamental impairments in autism have been reported, although again, evaluative studies are sparse. Quill (1995) provides detailed information on programs designed to improve social and communication functioning. The Picture Exchange Communication System, (PECS; Bondy & Frost, 1996) uses symbols, pictures or objects to enhance communication skills in the classroom. The "Bright Start Programme" (Butera & Haywood; 1995) focuses on the development of cognitive and meta-cognitive abilities. Koegel and Koegel (1995) illustrate how traditional behavioral techniques can be successfully adapted for use in more naturalistic school settings. There is also an increasing number of studies documenting the potential value of computer based teaching (Chen & Bernard-Opitz, 1993; Powell & Jordan, 1997; Tjuus, Heimann, & Nelson, 2001).

RESEARCH BASED EVIDENCE FOR EFFECTIVE APPROACHES TO INTERVENTION

It is evident, given the current state of research in the field of autism, that no one approach has been demonstrated to be superior to all others or to be equally effective for all children. Prizant and Rubin (1999) note that the knowledge base for intervention programs should derive from a combination of different sources, including theory (developmental, learning, family systems etc); clinical and educational data, knowledge about best practice, and empirical data from well designed small group and single case studies. Such information can then be used to indicate *components* of treatment (both home and school based) that are likely to be beneficial for the majority of children.

There is evidence of the need for individually designed intervention programs (Anderson & Romanczyk, 1999; Prizant & Rubin, 1999). These will need to take account of the child's cognitive level, the severity of autistic symptomatology, and overall developmental level. Although behaviorally oriented strategies have been shown to be effective in very many studies these seem to be more generally effective if combined with educational approaches that are relevant to the individual's pattern of skills and deficits (Howlin, 1998; Koegel & Koegel, 1995; Schopler, et al., 1995). The application of findings from research with typically developing young children, particularly in the areas of social engagement and communication (c.f. Wetherby, Schuler, & Prizant, 1997) has also been shown to be important in developing individually tailored interventions of an appropriate level.

Many studies attest to the importance of structured educational/daily living programs, with a particular emphasis on visually based cues. These provide the individual with autism with a predictable and readily understandable environment, which helps to minimize confusion and distress (Jordan & Powell, 1995; Quill, 1995; Schopler & Mesibov, 1995; Wetherby & Prizant, 1999)

Beneficial effects have been demonstrated for interventions that focus on the development of social-communication and play activities, especially with peers (Lord, 1995; Quill, 1995; Wolfberg & Schuler, 1993). The implementation of specialist training programs, for example to improve "Mind-reading" skills (Howlin, et al., 1998; Ozonoff & Miller, 1995, Swettenham, 1995) or social understanding (Gray, 1995; Mesibov, 1984; Williams, 1989) may also prove of value for many children.

It is now well established that many so-called undesirable or challenging behaviors are frequently a reflection of limited behavioral repertoires or poor communication skills. A focus on skill enhancement, and the establishment of more effective communication strategies is, therefore, often the most successful means of reducing difficult or disruptive behaviors (Durand & Carr, 1991; Prizant, et al., 1997; Schuler, Peck, Willard, & Theimer, 1989).

Effective treatments must also specifically address the core deficits of autism (i.e., social, communication and behavioral).

The profound communication deficits, which are found at all levels of intellectual ability, may never be fundamentally altered but much can be done by ensuring that the communication used by parents and other care staff is appropriate for the individual's *comprehension* level and that verbal messages are augmented as much as possible by visual or other means (Howlin, 1998).

Impairments in social understanding can give rise to behaviors that are unacceptable or offensive to other people, especially as individuals grow older. Behaviors that are perfectly acceptable in a three year old (close body contact, removal of clothing, talk about intimate topics etc) can, if not modified, result in major problems in adulthood. The establishment of simple, but invariable rules from an early age can help to minimize, if not entirely avoid such difficulties.

Stereotyped and ritualistic tendencies, too, may often be the underlying cause of many behavior problems and, again, frequently become progressively more unacceptable with age (Howlin, 1998; Howlin & Rutter, 1987; Schopler, 1995). From early childhood, it is important to set clear limits on when, where, with whom, and how often these behaviors are allowed, so disruption to other activities is minimized. However, rituals, routines, or special interests can also play a vital role in therapy; they may be helpful in reducing anxiety or distress; they are powerful sources of motivation and reinforcement, and may also open the door to later social contacts.

The implementation of treatment approaches that are family centered, rather than exclusively child oriented appears to ensure effective generalization and maintenance of skills (Marcus, Kunce, & Schopler, 1997). The development of management strategies, which can be implemented consistently but in ways that do not demand extensive sacrifice in terms of time, money or other aspects of family life, seems most likely to offer benefits for all involved.

HOW CAN PROFESSIONALS OFFER PARENTS PRACTICAL HELP

Interpreting Treatment Claims

Whist professional researchers in this area bemoan the lack of randomized control treatment trials, parents themselves may find it almost impossible to make sense of the many claims and counter claims with which they are continually bombarded. After all, who can easily turn their back on a treatment that could change the course of their child's life forever? As one parent with a 22-year-old son writes:

"Nobody wants to give up without a good fight ...We weren't so much searching for a miracle. Really, we were just looking for something- anything- because to do nothing had become intolerable. Perhaps that is the case for all parents. If you had a child like this you would try everything. For one mother 'everything' means to go into debt, fly to a foreign country, put her child into a tank with dolphins....

For our family it meant different things at different times: pounds of bitter tasting vitamins, rigid behavior modification, spinning in a suspended net, doing what the doctor didn't say, traveling 2,500 miles across the country to a new home, keeping him at home, giving him over into the care of others.

I try not to think too much about what would or would not have happened had we tried or not tried a particular treatment. But each time I hear of something new- often a therapy we could not even have imagined- a little spark inside my brain briefly ignites and I wonder once again, what if. . . . ?" (Muller, 1993).

Professional criticisms of unproven treatments as "garbage science" (Rimland, 2000), although possibly quite correct, may simply provoke parents into seeking alternative therapies. Instead, it may prove more productive to encourage families to seek basic information on the results of therapy for themselves. Any effective program should be able to provide some information on longer-term outcome (not just immediately after intervention). It should be made clear what assessments are carried out on individual children prior to treatment and what are the criteria for acceptance into treatment and what are the exclusion criteria. Information should also be provided on the types of children or families for whom the program is most effective (is it more successful, for example, for those of high or low ability; for those with good language or poor communication skills; does it work better with younger or older children; are there any family factors that seem to be related to outcome?). If possible, parents should also try to establish whether any independent evaluation methods have been used to assess the outcome of treatment and whether evidence exists to demonstrate its superiority over other programs. Media reports of the latest miracle cure, or glowing testimonials on office walls do not constitute satisfactory evidence of treatment effectiveness. Parents also need to be clear about the economic and other hidden costs of treatment. How much time will be involved? What is likely to be the impact on impact on siblings and family relationships generally and can it be fitted into regular family/ school/ social life? Moreover, parents are more likely to treat claims for the latest "miracle therapy" with greater skepticism if they are provided with practical advice, from the outset, on ways of dealing with difficulties at home.

Practical Management Strategies
Provide parents with a detailed individual assessment of their child

Autism is recognized as being a "spectrum" disorder, in that profiles of skills and deficits will differ from child to child. The severity of communication and social impairments will vary as will the extent and pervasiveness of ritualistic and obsess ional behaviors. There may be changes with chronological age and cognitive abilities can range from profound retardation to superior intelligence. An intervention program that is appropriate for a 3-year-old, severely mentally retarded, non verbal child of three will need to be very different from one that is suitable for 13-year-old, verbally fluent child with IQ of 130. Thus, for most children a detailed cognitive, linguistic and behavioral assessment – which is fully communicated to parents- will be the first essential step in ensuring suitable treatment

Recognition that apparently similar behaviors may have different causes for the same child at different times (and for different children)

So called "challenging behaviors" may arise because the child lacks the ability to communicate his or her needs, distress, anxiety or confusion in any other way; because of the response such behaviors receive from others, or simply because they are the most effective way of controlling his /her environment. Before any attempt to intervene takes place, it is essential to try to determine: why the behavior occurs; what it achieves for the child; how others respond to it, and what might be done to replace it? In other words the focus of intervention should be on the underlying cause, not on the surface behavior.

Understanding the role of the fundamental deficits associated with autism

Communication difficulties. As noted earlier, many behavioral problems arise because the child's has little or no ability to control the environment by verbal means. Similarly, anxiety, confusion or distress may occur because of failure to understand what is happening, or why. Hence, apparently inappropriate behaviors may be the child's only effective means of communication. It is crucial, therefore, to try to establish the purpose of problem behavior (to avoid/escape situations; gain objects/food attention) and to teach child equally effective ways to communicate his or her needs e.g., by pictures, objects, symbols or simple gestures.

It is equally essential to focus on the need to improve *other's* communication and to ensure that speech to the child is simple, concrete and concise, and that the words used actually mean what the adult wants them to mean. Asking a child with autism "Can you hang up your coat?" may meet with an affirmative reply, but is unlikely to result in any action, as none has been directly specified. Sarcasm and metaphor (he lost his head; its raining buckets; I could kill for a cup of tea) are equally likely to be misunderstood. Whenever possible, especially when dealing with more abstract concepts, sequences of activities or hypothetical events, speech should be augmented by visual cues (pictures, written lists, symbols) appropriate to the child's level of understanding.

Social impairments. Deficits in this area may also be at the root of many inappropriate behaviors. Children with autism may be unaware of how to share, how to take part in joint play activities, or how to approach other people in an acceptable way. Impairments in "Theory of mind" will also affect their ability to consider others' point of view, or respond appropriately to other people's emotions. Whist the pervasiveness of the social impairment means that certain aspects of social understanding will remain throughout life many unacceptable behaviors can be minimized if attention is paid to ensuring that even the very young child is taught simple invariable rules. (For example, never take off your clothes in public - except at the beach or at the doctors; don't approach strangers; don't touch things in shops; don't talk about certain topics). For more able children it is also important to teach basic social skills, such as how to approach others, give your name, join in (structured) games with peers, as well as ensuring that the basic rules of hygiene and self care are established from an early age.

Ritualistic and stereotyped behaviors. These, too, may be at the root of many other unacceptable or "challenging " behaviors. Disruption of routines, or unpredictable change, frequently result in distress, anxiety and aggression, whilst the pursuit of obsessional interests and behaviors may both limit acquisition of other skills and interfere with other activities

The solutions generally are to try gradually to reduce the amount of time the child spends in a particular ritualistic activity, or to limit the number of places/people where it is allowed. Resistance to change is often best dealt with by helping the child to predict change and by gradually introducing planned change into the daily routine. Similarly the problems caused by attachments to specific objects can be reduced by gradually reducing the amount of time spent with the object; the number of places where the object is allowed; or even the size of object (Howlin, 1998). However, it is important, when dealing with ritualistic behaviors that the aim of intervention should be to modify not necessarily to eliminate them. This is because routines and special interests etc can be used as very effective rewards and, just as importantly, may be a major source of comfort for the child in times of stress.

Environmental restructuring. It is also essential to encourage parents, teachers and others to focus their intervention efforts as much on changing the environment as the child. Many problems can be minimized if care is taken simply to avoid situations that trigger problems (e.g., play times or games lessons at school can be replaced by time in the library or computer room). Much can also be achieved by efforts to improve others' awareness of the needs of someone with autism, and to understand the need for a *consistent* approach to management. Many problems can be reduced, or even eliminated, by ensuring that the child's environment and daily routine are as predictable and as controllable as possible. This does not mean that the same regime must be followed everyday, but that the child should be forewarned of any necessary alterations to the routine or environment.

Early identification. Finally, and perhaps most importantly, there is a crucial need for early diagnosis and the provision of appropriate advice and support for parents. This can do much to help minimize or avoid later problems but, unfortunately, delays in diagnosis are still common. Howlin and Asgharian (1999) in a large scale survey found that despite the fact that the majority of parents became concerned in the first months or year of their child's life, they faced many delays and frustrations in obtaining a diagnosis. Many children were not diagnosed until the age of 5 or later, well after the optimal period for the onset of intervention. In the case of more able children, and for those with Asperger syndrome, the average age of diagnosis was around 11 years! It is also the case that, even after diagnosis, families can experience considerable difficulties in obtaining information about local facilities or schools. It may be easier for parents to learn (via the media or the Internet) about "exotic" therapies, such as swimming with dolphins, than it is to access information about appropriate nursery provision in their own neighborhood. Better documented and more readily available information about the benefits that local schools or units may be able to offer, could well prevent parents wasting time and money on treatments from another continent.

OUTCOMES AND INTERVENTIONS IN ADOLESCENCE AND ADULTHOOD

Follow-Up Studies Into Adulthood

There have been a number of follow-up studies of individuals with autism as they move into adulthood. Many are predominantly anecdotal (e.g., Kanner, 1973) and the different measures used to assess outcome in others makes it difficult to reach clear conclusions about long-term prognosis. The first systematic follow-up study of adults with autism was conducted by Rutter and his colleagues towards the end of the 1960's. Although many individuals remained dependent on others for support, most showed some positive behavioral changes as they grew older (see Lockyer & Rutter, 1969, 1970; Rutter, Greenfield, & Lockyer, 1967; Rutter & Lockyer, 1967). Subsequent follow-up reports (e.g. Gillberg & Steffenberg, 1987; Kobayashi, Murata & Yashinaga, 1992; Lotter, 1974a, 1974b) also noted improvements in behavior around mid adolescence. It appears, too, that the general outcome for adults has improved somewhat over time (Howlin & Goode, 1998) although relatively few individuals are able to live independently or develop close friendships, and rates of employment remain low.

In the most detailed of these recent studies, Goode, Howlin and Rutter (in preparation) followed up 76 individuals, (65 males and 11 females) all aged 21 or over, who had originally been diagnosed in childhood. Although the average performance IQ of the group at follow-up was in the mid 70's, language abilities remained at a low level and only seven individuals were living independently or semi-independently. Over a third still lived with their parents and just over half were in residential accommodation, mostly specifically for people with autism; 10 individuals were in long-stay hospital care. Only seven people were in regular, paid employment; one was self-employed; four others worked in a voluntary capacity and 10 were in some form of sheltered or supported employment. Over two thirds attended day or residential centers. Few individuals had close friends and although 2 men had married, one had later divorced. A composite rating of independence and social performance indicated that around 15% could be described as having a "good" or "very good" outcome and 23% were rated as functioning "fairly well". The remainder of the group was highly dependent, living either in special residential units or long-term hospital care.

Even amongst studies of more able individuals (i.e., those with Asperger syndrome or high functioning autism: Howlin, Mawhood & Rutter, 2000; Lord & Venter; 1992; Mawhood, Howlin, & Rutter, 2000; Rumsey, Rapoport & Sceery, 1985; Szatmari, Bartolucci, Bremner, Bond &Rich, 1989) most of the people involved remained socially isolated and continued to show some communication problems. Only a tiny minority had married or entered into a sexual relationship, and close, intimate friendships were rare. Relatively few were in regular employment and those jobs that did exist were generally low level and poorly paid. Amongst all the participants in these studies, the majority were still living with their parents, and almost none lived entirely independently. Despite the relatively high IQ levels of the cases involved, attainments generally were poor (Ramsey, et al; 1985). Mawhood, et al. (2000) also found that obsessional and ritualistic tendencies continued to give rise to problems. Lord and Venter (1992) comment on the very variable outcome between individuals and suggest that, although generally prognosis in autism is determined by innate cognitive and linguistic abilities, for adults of this level, outcome may be influenced more by the availability of adequate support networks than by individual skills.

Factors Related to Outcome

In almost all follow-up studies, two variables have been consistently associated with later prognosis. The first is the level of language attained by the age of 5-6 years; very few of those who remain without speech after this age are reported to have a positive outcome. The second important prognostic indicator is IQ. Individuals who are either untestable as children, or who have non-verbal I.Q. scores within or below the moderately retarded range, almost invariably remain highly dependent. However, relatively good cognitive and communication skills do not necessarily guarantee a successful outcome (Howlin, et al., 2000). The presence of *additional* skills or interests (such as specialized knowledge in particular areas, or competence in mathematics, music or computing) which allow individuals to find their own "niche" in life, and which may enable them to be more easily integrated into society, also seems to be of prognostic importance (Kanner, 1973)

The prognostic implications of many other variables, including the severity of early childhood symptoms (De Meyer, et al., 1973; Lord & Venter (1992) or social and family factors remains uncertain. In almost every follow-up study outcome has been poorer for females than males but the number of women involved is generally very small and differences rarely reach significance (Goode, et al., in preparation); the lower mean IQ of females further complicates the issue (Lord & Schopler, 1985). The development of epilepsy also seems to correlate with a poorer outcome, but again this is associated, at least to some extent, with low IQ.

Interventions in Adulthood

In comparison with the vast amount of research on interventions for children with autism, there are very few studies of special therapeutic programs for older individuals. Much of the literature pertaining to this age group focuses on the modification of very challenging behaviors or the acquisition of basic life skills by those with severe or profound intellectual disabilities. However, outcome studies suggest that most individuals tend to improve with age and for some (particularly those who become more aware of their difficulties) adolescence can often be a period of remarkable improvement and change (Kanner, 1973). Programs to enhance social understanding and improve interpersonal behaviors have been found to have positive, if somewhat circumscribed effects (Attwood, 2000; Howlin & Yates, 1999; Mesibov, 1984) and wider provision of social skills programs for adolescents and young adults could perhaps help to minimize their social difficulties. Others might profit from cognitive- behavioral programs, to help them cope more effectively with emotional or practical difficulties (c.f., Hare, Jones, & Paine, 1999, Stoddart, 1999). Success in the job market can also be significantly improved by supported employment schemes that focus on teaching appropriate work and social skills. Even individuals with moderate to severe intellectual impairments have been helped to find and maintain employment by these means (Keel, Mesibov & Woods, 1997; Smith, Belcher & Juhrs, 1995). For those who are more able such schemes can significantly increase the chances of clients finding employment, and lead to much higher and better paid levels of work (Mawhood & Howlin, 1999).

Psychiatric Difficulties in Adulthood

Kanner's (1949) early views on the relationship between autism and schizophrenia were unequivocal: "I do not believe that there is any likelihood that early infantile autism will at any future time have to be separated from the schizophrenias." Nevertheless, Rutter (1972) and Wing (1986) have documented many crucial differences between the two conditions. And although some researchers (e.g., Wolff & McGuire, 1995) have suggested an association between Asperger syndrome and schizoid disorders, this view is largely unsupported (Wing, 1986).

That is not to say, of course, that autism and schizophrenia never co-exist and there is a number of single case reports on the co-morbidity of the two conditions (see review by Clarke, Baxter, Perry, & Brasher, 1999). However, larger scale studies of children and adults with autism have failed to find any evidence of increased rates of schizophrenia. (Chung, Luk, & Lee, 1990; Ghaziuddin, Weidmer-Mikhail & Ghaziuddin, 1998). None of the cases followed up by Kanner, over a period of 40 years, was reported as showing positive psychiatric symptoms (delusions or hallucinations). Rumsey, et al. (1985), in a detailed psychiatric study of 14 young adults found no evidence of schizophrenia and Volkmar and Cohen (1991) found only one individual with an unequivocal diagnosis of schizophrenia in a sample of 163 cases. In Goode's study of 76 adults with autism, all over the age of twenty-one, none had developed a schizophrenic illness (Goode, et al., in preparation).

Schizophrenia also appears to be uncommon amongst more able individuals or those with Asperger syndrome. Asperger (1944) noted that only 1 out of his 200 cases developed schizophrenia. Tantam (1991) diagnosed 3 cases of schizophrenia in 83 individuals with Asperger syndrome, but these were all psychiatric referrals. None of the 19 relatively able subjects in the study by Mawhood and colleagues (2000) had developed a schizophrenic disorder and only one individual in a similar group studied by Szatmari, et al. (1989) had been treated for chronic schizophrenia.

Nevertheless, although the presence of first rank schizophrenic symptoms is relatively unusual, there are reports of individuals who show isolated psychotic symptoms, including delusional thoughts. A number of other authors have described cases of delusional disorder, various unspecified psychoses, paranoid ideation, catatonia and hallucinations (Clarke, Littlejophns, Corbett, & Joseph, 1989; Rumsey, et al., 1985; Szatmari, et al., 1989; Tantam,

1991, 2000; Wing & Shah, 2000). Obsessional compulsive disorders have also been reported although it can often prove very difficult to distinguish between these and the ritualistic and stereotyped behaviors that are characteristic of autism (Szatmari, et al.,1989).

By far the most prevalent psychiatric disturbances reported are those related to anxiety and depression. (see Clarke, et al., 1999; Lainhart & Folstein, 1994; Tantam, 2000.) Tantam (1991) comments that in several cases the illness incorporated a delusional content, often linked with the individual's autistic preoccupations. One patient of the author's, for example, had threatened to shoot himself because he believed the American and British Air Control authorities had conspired to prevent him from qualifying as an airline pilot.

In Rumsey's follow-up of 14 relatively high functioning individuals, generalized anxiety problems were found in half the sample. Wing, (1981) also found that just under a quarter of her group of 18 individuals with Asperger syndrome showed signs of an affective disorder. Three had attempted suicide or talked about doing so. Wolff (2000) noted that death from suicide in her cohort of "schizoid" individuals (several of whom probably had Asperger syndrome) was 4.0%, compared with the same age population prevalence of 0.002%. Attempted suicide was also common.

In a recent review of case studies of psychiatric illness in autism by far the most common psychiatric diagnosis reported was psychotic depression (Howlin, 2000). This accounted for over a quarter of diagnoses in the studies reviewed and a further 16% were non-specific affective disorders mostly related to anxiety and depression. Bipolar disorders and mania were the next most common types of disorder, occurring in about 20% of the cases. In the autistic population as a whole, Abramson, et al. (1992) suggested that the overall risk of affective disorders is around 33%, a figure similar to that reached by Tantam (1991). Schizophrenic type diagnoses in the case reports reviewed by Howlin (2000) were much less frequent, representing around 12% of all psychiatric diagnoses. Volkmar and Cohen (1991) suggested that the frequency of schizophrenia in individuals with autism is around 0.6%, which is roughly comparable to that in the general population. They concludes that: "it does not appear that the two conditions are more commonly observed together than would be expected on a chance basis" and there is certainly little evidence to support claims of "an excess of schizophrenia in later life" (c.f. Wolff & McGuire, 1995).

Although few hard data are available it is often suggested that the risk of psychiatric disturbance, especially related to depression and anxiety, is high amongst individuals with Asperger syndrome (or high functioning autism). Although sometimes (wrongly) described as being a "mild" form of autism, Asperger syndrome may be just as disabling. Moreover, because of individuals' relatively high cognitive ability and *apparently* competent use of language, they frequently fail to receive the level of support they need. Many have extensive linguistic and comprehension difficulties (especially involving abstract or complex concepts); their understanding of the more subtle aspects of social interaction is often profoundly limited, and their obsessional interests and behaviors may also prove a barrier to social integration. Others' expectations of their social and academic potential are often unrealistically high and there may be constant pressure for them to "fit in" to "normal society". This can lead to enormous pressure and sometimes intolerable levels of anxiety and stress.

Finding the appropriate treatment for depression and anxiety related disorders can also prove difficult and although medication can be helpful this rarely works in isolation. Psychoanalytically based interventions may be considered (Maratos, 1996) but there is little evidence of their effectiveness (Campbell, et al., 1996). Individual psychotherapy or counseling may assist higher functioning people to deal with anxiety or depression, and the pain that comes from recognizing their difficulties and differences. However, clinical experience suggests that this *must* be combined with direct practical advice on how to deal with problems, otherwise many individuals become obsessed with the past, or with other possible explanations for their difficulties, making it almost impossible for them to "move on" in a positive way. If appropriately adapted, cognitive behavioral approaches seem to be of potential benefit (Hare, et al., 1999; Stoddart, 1999) although there is very little systematic research in this area, and even single case studies are rare. The difficulties inherent in diagnosing mental health problems in people with autism also need to be recognized. Impoverished language, literal interpretation of questions, concrete thinking and obsessionality can all give rise to misunderstandings, and possible misdiagnosis, even the case of individuals who appear relatively able. For those with more severe intellectual disabilities and little or no speech, the danger is that psychiatric illness will go undiagnosed, even when serious problems arise.

More research into psychiatric conditions in adulthood is badly needed, not only to identify the true level of risk, but also to improve knowledge amongst clinicians about how psychiatric disorders in this group are manifest. It is particularly important for clinicians working in adult services to be aware that autism and psychiatric illnesses can co-exist. However, differential diagnosis cannot be made on the basis of a single face-to face interview, and a detailed developmental history from parents (or someone who has known the individual well since childhood) will be required in order to distinguish between behaviors caused by the autism and those caused by the additional psychiatric disorder.   Better understanding of appropriate intervention strategies, both pharmacological and psychological, is also required. Clinical experience suggests that delays in diagnosing and treating psychiatric disorders in this group are particularly undesirable as behavior patterns that are established during the course of the illness (e.g., disturbed waking and sleeping patterns) can then be very difficult to alter, even when the patients condition generally has improved (Howlin, 1997)

CONCLUSIONS

There is no evidence that long-term outcome in autism can be significantly affected by the implementation of any one particular intervention method (Howlin, 1998; Prizant & Rubin, 1999). Although it is evident that the provision of early intervention and specialist educational programs has enabled many children with autism to attain a level of functioning that would never have been envisaged 50 years ago, there remains a pressing need to improve the age at which the diagnosis is first made. Adequately controlled trials of some of the most widely used educational and therapeutic programs are also essential. Finally, the improvements in educational provision and family support programs that have occurred over the last 4 decades must now be followed up by improvements in supported employment and living schemes, and in social and mental health provision for adults. In particular, the needs of those who are more able need to be more widely recognized.

REFERENCES

Abramson, R. K., Wright H. H, Cuccara, M. L., Lawrence L.G., Babb S., Pencarinha, D., Marstellar, F., & Harris E.C. (1992). Biological liability in families with autism. *Journal of the American Academy of Child and Adolescent Psychiatry, 31,* 370-371.

American Psychological Association. (1994, August). *Resolution on Facilitated Communication.* Author.

Anderson, S. R. & Romanczyk, R.G. (1999). Continuum-based behavioral models *Journal of the Association for Persons with Severe Handicaps, 24,* 162-173

Asperger, H. (1944). Autistic psychopathy in childhood. Translated and annotated by U. Frith (Ed.), *Autism and Asperger Syndrome.* (1991). Cambridge: Cambridge University Press.

Attwood, T. (2000) Strategies for improving the social integration of children with Asperger syndrome. *Autism; International Journal of Research and Practice 4,* 85-100.

Bandura, A. (1969) *Principles of behavior modification.* New York: Holt, Rinehart and Winston.

Baron-Cohen, S. (1988). Assessment of violence in a young man with Asperger's Syndrome. *Journal of Child Psychology and Psychiatry, 29,* 351-360.

Bayley, N. (1993). *Bayley Scales of Infant Development, Second edition.* San Antonio, TX: The Psychological Corporation.

Bebko, J.M., Perry, A., & Bryson, S. (1996). Multiple method validation study of facilitated communication: II Individual differences and subgroup results. *Journal of Autism and Developmental Disorders, 26,* 19-42.

Biklen, D. (1990). Communication unbound: autism and praxis. *Harvard Educational Review, 60,* 291-315.

Bondy, A., & Frost, L. (1996). Educational approaches in pre-school: behavior techniques in a public school setting. In E. Schopler & G. B. Mesibov (Eds.), *Learning and cognition in Autism* (pp.311-334). New York: Plenum Press.

Burack, J.A., Root, R., & Zigler, E. (1997). Inclusive education for children with autism: reviewing ideological, empirical and community considerations. In D. Cohen & F. Volkmar (Eds.), *Handbook of Autism and Pervasive Developmental Disorders* (2nd Edition, pp 796-807). New York: Wiley.

Butera, G., & Haywood, H.C. (1995). Cognitive education of young children with autism: an application of Bright Start. In E. Schopler, & G. Mesibov. (Ed.), *Learning and cognition in Autism.* New York. Plenum Press.

Campbell, M. (1978). Pharmacotherapy. In M Rutter & E Schopler (Eds.), *Autism: A reappraisal of concepts and treatment* (pp. 337-355). New York: Plenum.

Campbell, M., Schopler, E. Cueva, J.E., & Hallin, A. (1996). Treatment of Autistic Disorder. *Journal of the American Academy of Child and Adolescent Psychiatry. 35, 134*-143.

Chen, S., & Bernard-Opitz V. (1993). Comparison of personal and computer assisted instruction for children with autism. *Mental Retardation 31*, 368-376

Chung, S. Y., Luk, F. L., & Lee E. W. H. (1990). A follow-up study of infantile autism in Hong Kong. *Journal of Autism and Developmental Disorders, 20*, 221-232.

Clarke, D. J., Baxter, M., Perry, D., & Prasher, V. (1999). The diagnosis of affective and psychotic disorders in adults with autism. *Autism: International Journal of Research and Practice, 3*, 149-164.

Clarke, D. J., Littlejohns, C. S., Corbett, J. A., & Joseph, S. (1989). Pervasive developmental disorders and psychoses in adult life. *British Journal of Psychiatry, 155*, 692-699.

Dawson, G., & Watling, R. (2000). Interventions to facilitate auditory, visual and motor integration in autism: a review of the evidence. *Journal of Autism and Developmental Disorders, 30*, 415-422.

DeMyer, M. K., Barton, S., DeMyer, W. E., Norton, J. A., Allan, J., & Steele, R. (1973). Prognosis in autism: A follow-up study. *Journal of Autism and Childhood Schizophrenia, 3*, 199-246.

Durand, M. B, & Carr, E.G. (1991). Functional communication training to reduce challenging behavior: Maintenance and application in new settings. *Journal of Applied Behavior Analysis, 24*, 251-254.

Fisher, W., Piazza, C., Cataldo, M., Harrell, R., Jefferson, G., & Connor, R. (1993). Functional Communication training with and without extinction and punishment. *Journal of Applied Behavior Analysis, 26*, 23-36.

Fombonne, E. (1999). The epidemiology of autism: a review. *Psychological Medicine, 29*, 769-786

Ghaziuddin, M., Weidmer-Mikhail, E., & Ghaziuddin, N. (1998). Comorbidity in Asperger Syndrome: A preliminary report. *Journal of Intellectual Disability Research, 42*, 279-283.

Gillberg, C., & Steffenberg, S. (1987). Outcome and prognostic factors in infantile autism and similar conditions: a population-based study of 46 cases followed through puberty. *Journal of Autism and Developmental Disorders, 17*, 272-288.

Goode, S., Howlin, P., & Rutter, M. (in preparation). A cognitive and behavioral study of outcome in young adults with autism

Gray, C.A. (1995). Teaching children with autism to "read" social situations. In A. Quill (Ed.), *Teaching children with Autism: Strategies to enhance communication and socialization* (pp. 219-242). New York: Delmar.

Greenspan, S.J., & Wieder, S. (1999). A functional developmental approach to autism spectrum disorders. *Journal of the Association for Persons with Severe Handicap*, 3, 147-161.

Gresham, F. M., & Macmillan, D.L. (1998). Early Intervention Project: can its claims be substantiated and replicated. *Journal of Autism and Developmental Disorders*, 28, 5-13.

Gringras, P. (2000). Practical pediatric psychopharmacological prescribing in autism: The potential and the pitfalls. *Autism: International Journal of Research and Practice, 4*, 229-243.

Hare, D., Jones, J. P.R., & Paine, C. (1999). Approaching reality: The use of personal construct assessment in working with people with Asperger syndrome. *Autism; International Journal of Research and Practice, 3*, 165-176.

Horvath, K. (1998). Improved social and language skills after Secretin administration in patients with autistic spectrum disorders. *Journal of the Association of the Academy of Minority Physicians, 9*, 1-15.

Howlin P. (1997). *Autism: Preparing for adulthood.* London: Routledge.

Howlin, P. (1998). Treating children with Autism and Asperger Syndrome: A guide for parents and professionals. Chichester: Wiley.

Howlin, P. (2000). Outcome in adult life for more able individuals with autism or Asperger syndrome. *Autism: International Journal of Research and Practice, 4*, 63-84.

Howlin, P. (submitted). Language ability and other behaviors in high functioning individuals with autism spectrum disorders: a comparison of adults with autism and Asperger syndrome matched for non-verbal IQ.

Howlin P., & Asgharian, A. (1999). The diagnosis of autism and Asperger syndrome: findings from a survey of 770 families. *Developmental Medicine and Child Neurology, 41*, 834-839.

Howlin, P., Baron-Cohen, S., Hadwin, J., & Swettenham, J. (1998). *Teaching children with Autism to mindread: A practical manual for parents and teachers.* Chichester: Wiley.

Howlin P., & Goode, S. (1998). Outcome in adult life for individuals with autism. In F. Volkmar (Ed.), *Autism and developmental disorders.* New York: Cambridge University Press.

Howlin, P., & Rutter, M. (1987). *Treatment of autistic children.* Chichester: Wiley.

Howlin, P., Mawhood, L.M., & Rutter M. (2000). Autism and developmental receptive language disorder - a follow-up comparison in early adult life. II. Social, behavioral and psychiatric outcomes. Journal of Child Psychology and Psychiatry, 41, 561-578.

Howlin, P., & Yates P. (1999). The effectiveness of a social skills group for adults with autism: Information update. *Autism: International Journal of Research and Practice, 3,* 299-308

Jordan, R., & Powell, S. (1995). *Understanding and teaching children with Autism.* Chichester: Wiley.

Kanner, L. (1943). Autistic disturbances of affective contact. *Nervous Child, 2,* 217-250.

Kanner, L. (1949). Problems of nosology and psychodynamics of early infantile autism. *American Journal of Orthopsychiatry, 19,* 416-426.

Kanner, L. (1951). The conception of wholes and parts in early infantile autism. *American Journal of Psychiatry, 108,* 23-26.

Kanner, L. (1973). Childhood psychosis: Initial studies and new insights. New York: Winston/Wiley.

Keel, J.H., Mesibov, G., & Woods, A.V. (1997). TEACCH- Supported employment program. *Journal of Autism and Developmental Disorders, 27,* 3-10.

Kim, J.A., Szatmari, P., Bryson, S., Streiner, D.L., & Wilson, F. (2000). The prevalence of anxiety and mood problems among children with autism and Asperger syndrome. *Autism: International Journal of Research and Practice, 4,* 117-132.

Kobayashi, R., Murata, T., & Yashinaga, K. (1992). A follow-up study of 201 children with autism in Kyushu and Yamaguchi, Japan. *Journal of Autism and Developmental Disorders, 22,* 395-411.

Koegel, L.K., Koegel, R. L., Harrower, J.K. & Carter, C.M. (1999). Pivotal response intervention I: Overview of approach. *Journal of the Association for Persons with Severe Handicaps, 24,* 174-185.

Koegel, R.L., & Koegel, L.K. (1995). Teaching children with Autism: Strategies for initiating positive interactions and improving learning opportunities. Baltimore: Brookes.

Lainhart, J. E., & Folstein, S. E. (1994). Affective disorders in people with autism: A review of published cases. *Journal of Autism and Developmental Disorders, 24,* 587-601.

Leekham, S., Libby, S., Wing, L., Gould, J., & Gillberg, C. (2000). Comparison of ICD-10 and Gillberg's criteria for Asperger syndrome. *Autism: International Journal of Research and Practice, 4,* 11-28.

Lockyer, L., & Rutter, M. (1969). A five to fifteen year follow-up study of infantile psychosis: III. Psychological Aspects. *British Journal of Psychiatry, 115,* 865-882.

Lockyer, L., & Rutter, M. (1970). A five to fifteen year follow-up study of infantile psychosis: IV Patterns of cognitive abilities. *British Journal of Social and Clinical Psychology, 9,* 152-163.

Lord, C. (1995). Facilitating social inclusion: Examples from peer intervention programs. In E, Schopler & G, Mesibov (Eds.), *Learning and cognition in Autism* (pp. 221-239). New York: Plenum Press.

Lord, C. (2000). Achievements and future directions for intervention research in communication and autism spectrum disorders. *Journal of Autism and Developmental Disorders, 30,* 393-398.

Lord, C., & Schopler E. (1985). Differences in sex ratios in autism as a function of measured intelligence. *Journal of Autism and Development Disorders, 15,* 185-193.

Lord, C., & Venter A. (1992). Outcome and follow-up studies of high functioning autistic individuals. In E. Schopler & G.B. Mesibov (Eds.), *High functioning individuals with Autism* (pp.187-200). New York: Plenum.

Lotter, B. (1974a). Factors related to outcome in autistic children. *Journal of Autism and Childhood Schizophrenia, 4,* 263-277.

Lotter, B. (1974b). Social adjustment and placement of autistic children in Middlesex: a follow-up study. *Journal of Autism and Childhood Schizophrenia, 4,* 11-32.

Lotter, V. (1978). Follow-up studies. In Rutter, M., & Schopler, E. (Eds.), Autism: A reappraisal of concepts and treatment (pp. 475-95). New York: Plenum·

Lovaas, O.I. (1987). Behavioral treatment and normal educational and intellectual functioning in young autistic children. *Journal of Consulting and Clinical Psychology, 55,* 3-9.

Lovaas, O.I. (1993). The development of a treatment - research project for developmentally disabled and autistic children. *Journal of Applied Behavior Analysis, 26,* 617-630.

Magiati, I., & Howlin, P. (2001). Evaluating the long-term effectiveness of early intervention for young children with autism: preliminary baseline data and methodological difficulties. *Autism: International Journal of Research and Practice (in press).*

Manjiviona, J., & Prior M. (1999). Neuropsychological profiles of children with Asperger syndrome and autism. *Autism: International Journal of Research and Practice, 3,* 27-354.

Manolson, A. (1992). *It takes two to talk.* Hanen Center.

Maratos, O. (1996). Psychoanalysis and the management of pervasive developmental disorders, including autism. In: C. Trevarthen, K. Aitken, D. Papoudi, & J. Robarts (Eds.),

Children with Autism: Diagnosis and interventions to meet their needs. New York: Wiley.

Marcus, L.M., Kunce, L. J., & Schopler, E. (1997). Working with families. In D. Cohen, & F. Volkmar (Eds.), *Handbook of Autism and Pervasive Developmental Disorders* (2nd Edition, pp. 631-649). New York: Wiley.

Martin, M., Scahill, L., Lawrence, M.S.N., Klin, A.M., & Volkmar, F.R. (1999). Higher functioning pervasive developmental disorders: rates and patterns of psychotropic drug use. *Journal of the American Academy of Child and Adolescent Psychiatry, 38,* 923-931.

Mawhood, L., & Howlin P. (1999). The outcome of a supported employment scheme for high functioning adults with autism or Asperger syndrome. *Autism: International Journal of Research and Practice, 3,* 229-254.

Mawhood, L.M., Howlin, P., & Rutter M. (2000). Autism and developmental receptive language disorder - a follow-up comparison in early adult life. I: Cognitive and language outcomes. Journal of Child Psychology and Psychiatry, 41, 547-559.

McDougle, C.J. (1997). Psychopharmacology. In D. J. Cohen, & F.R. Volkmar (Eds.), *Handbook of Autism and Pervasive Developmental Disorders (2nd ed.; pp. 707-729).* New York: John Wiley.

McEachin, J.J., Smith, T., & Lovaas, O.I. (1993). Long-term outcome for children with autism who received early intensive behavioral treatment. *American Journal on Mental Retardation, 97,* 359-372.

McGee, J.J., Menolascino, P.E., Hobbs D.C., & Menousek, P.E. (1987). *Gentle teaching: A non-aversive approach to helping persons with mental retardation.* New York: Human Sciences Press.

Mesibov, G.B. (1984). Social skills training with verbal autistic adolescents and adults: A treatment model. *Journal of Autism and Developmental Disorders, 14,* 395-404.

Mesibov, G.B. (1993). Treatment outcome is encouraging: Comments on McEachin, et al. *American Journal of Mental Retardation, 97,* 379-380.

Mudford, O.C., Cross, B.A., Breen, S., Cullen, C., Reeves, D., Gould, J., & Douglas, J. (2000). Auditory integration training for children with autism: No behavioral benefits detected. *American Journal of Mental Retardation, 105,* 118-129.

Muller, J. (1993). Swimming against the tide. *Communication* 27,6.

National Autistic Society. (1997). *Statistics Sheet 1. How many people have autistic spectrum disorders?* London: National Autistic Society Publications.

Ozonoff, S., & Miller J.N. (1995). Teaching theory of mind: A new approach to social skills training for individuals with autism. *Journal of Autism and Developmental Disorders, 25,* 415-433.

Perry, R., Cohen, I., & DeCarlo, R. (1995). Deterioration, autism and recovery in two siblings. *Journal of the American Academy of Child and Adolescent Psychiatry. 34,* 233-237.

Powell, S., & Jordan, R. (1997). Autism *and learning: A guide to good practice.* London: David Fulton.

Prizant, B.M., & Rubin, E. (1999). Contemporary issues in interventions for autism spectrum disorders: A commentary. *Journal of the Association for Persons with Severe Handicaps, 24,* 199-208.

Prizant, B., Schuler A., Wetherby A., & Rydell, P. (1997). Enhancing language and communication development: Language approaches. In D. Cohen & F. Volkmar (Eds.), *Handbook of Autism and Pervasive Developmental Disorders* (2nd ed.; pp. 572-605). New York: Wiley.

Quill, K. A. (1995). Teaching children with autism: Strategies to enhance communication and socialization. New York: Delmar.

Rimland, B., & Edelson, S.M. (1994). The effects of Auditory Integration Training on autism. *American Journal of Speech-Language Pathology, 5,* 16-24.

Rimland, B., & Edelson S.M. (1995). A pilot study of auditory integration training in autism. *Journal of Autism and Developmental Disorders, 25,* 61-70.

Rimland, B. (1998). The use of secretin in autism: some preliminary answers. *Autism Research Review International, 12(4),* 3.

Rimland, B (2000) "Garbage science", brick walls, crossword puzzles, and mercury. *Autism Research Review International, 14 (4),* 3.

Rogers, S.J. (1996). Early intervention in autism. *Journal of Autism and Developmental Disorders, 26,* 243-246.

Rogers, S.J. (1998). Empirically supported comprehensive treatments for young children with autism. *Journal of Clinical Child Psychology, 27,* 168-179.

Rumsey, J. M., Rapoport, J. L., & Sceery, W. R. (1985). Autistic children as adults: psychiatric social and behavioral outcomes. *Journal of the American Academy of Child Psychiatry, 24,* 465-473.

Rutter, M. (1972). Childhood schizophrenia reconsidered. *Journal of Autism and Childhood Schizophrenia, 2,* 315-337.

Rutter, M. (1999). Autism: Two way interplay between research and clinical work. *Journal of Child Psychology and Psychiatry, 40*, 169-188.

Rutter, M. & Lockyer L. (1967). A five to fifteen year follow-up study of infantile psychosis: I. Description of sample. *British Journal of Psychiatry, 113,* 1169-1182.

Rutter, M., Greenfield, D., & Lockyer, L. (1967). A five to fifteen year follow-up study of infantile psychosis: II. Social and behavioral outcome. *British Journal of Psychiatry, 113*, 1183-1199.

Sandler, A.D., Sutton, K., De Weese, J., Girardi, M.A., Sheppard, V., & Bodfish, J.W. (1999). A double blind placebo controlled trial of synthetic human secretin in the treatment of autism and pervasive developmental disorder. *Journal of Developmental and Behavioral Pediatrics, 20*, 400.

Sheinkopf, S.J., & Siegel, B. (1998). Home-based behavioral treatment of young children with autism. *Journal of Autism and Developmental Disorders, 28*, 15-23.

Schopler, E., & Mesibov G.B. (1995). *Learning and cognition in Autism.* New York: Plenum Press.

Schopler, E. (1995). Parent survival manual: A guide to crisis resolution in Autism and related developmental disorders. New York: Plenum.

Schopler, E., Mesibov, G.B., & Hearsey, K. (1995). Structured teaching in the TEACCH system. In E. Schopler, & G. Mesibov (Eds.), *Learning and cognition in Autism* (pp. 243-267). New York: Plenum Press.

Schuler, A.L., Peck, C.A., Willard, C. & Theimer K. (1989). Assessment of communicative means and functions through interview: Assessing the communicative capabilities of individuals with limited language. *Seminars in Speech and Language, 10*, 51-61.

Shields, J (2001). The NAS Early Bird Programme: Partnership with parents in early intervention. *Autism: International Journal of Research and Practice, 5*, 49-56.

Sheinkopf, S.J., & Siegel, B. (1998). Home-based behavioral treatment for young children with autism. *Journal of Autism and Developmental Disorders, 28*, 15-23.

Smith, M., Belcher, R., & Juhrs, P. (1995). *A guide to successful employment for individuals with Autism.* Baltimore, MD: Paul H. Brookes.

Smith, T., Groen, A.D., & Wynn, J.W (2000). Randomized trial of intensive early intervention for children with Pervasive Developmental Disorder. *American Journal on Mental Retardation, 4*, 269-285.

Smith, T., & Lovaas, O.I. (1997). The UCLA young autism project: A reply to Gresham and McMillan. *Behavioral Disorders, 22*, 203-215.

Stoddart, K. (1999). Adolescents with Asperger syndrome: Three cases studies of individual and family therapy. *Autism: International Journal of Research and Practice, 3*, 255-272.

Stutsman, R. (1948). *Merrill-Palmer Scale of Mental Tests.* Los Angeles: Western Psychological Services.

Swettenham, J. (1995). Can children with autism be taught to understand false beliefs using computers? *Journal of Child Psychology and Psychiatry, 37*, 157-166.

Szatmari, P., Bartolucci, G., Bremner, R. S., Bond, S., & Rich, S. (1989). A follow-up study of high functioning autistic children. *Journal of Autism and Developmental Disorders, 19,* 213-226.

Szatmari, P., Jones, M.B., Zwaigenbaum, L., & Maclean, J.E. (1999). Genetics of autism: Overview and new directions. *Journal of Autism and Developmental Disorders, 28*, 351-368.

The Times. (2000, July 26th). Law report: The family division. *In re D (a child) Evidence: Facilitated Communication.*

Tjuus, T., Heimann, M., & Nelson, K.E. (2001). Interaction patterns between children and their teachers when using a specific multimedia and communication strategy: observations from children with autism and mixed handicaps. *Autism: International Journal of Research and Practice, 5*, (in press).

Tantam D. (1991). Asperger's Syndrome in adulthood. In U. Frith (Ed.), *Autism and Asperger Syndrome* (pp. 147-183). Cambridge: Cambridge University Press.

Tantam, D. (2000). Psychological disorder in adolescents and adults with Asperger's Syndrome. *Autism: International Journal of Research and Practice, 4*, 47-62.

Ullman, L.P., & Krasner, L. (1961). *Case studies in behavior modification.* New York: Holt, Rinehart and Winston

Volkmar, F. R., & Cohen D. J. (1991). Comorbid association of autism and schizophrenia. *American Journal of Psychiatry 148*, 1705-1707.

Wetherby, A., & Prizant, B. (1999). Profiles of communicative and cognitive-social abilities in autistic children. *Journal of Speech and Hearing Research, 27*, 364-377.

Williams, T.I. (1989). A social skills group for autistic children. *Journal of Autism and Developmental Disorders, 19*, 143-156.

Wing, L. (1981). Asperger's syndrome: A clinical account. *Psychological Medicine, 11*, 115-129.

Wing, L. (1986). Clarification on Asperger's syndrome: Letter to the Editor. *Journal of Autism and Developmental Disorders, 16*, 513-515.

Wing, L (2000). Past and future of research on Asperger syndrome. In A. Klin, F.R. Volkmar, & S.S. Sparrow (Eds.), *Asperger Syndrome* (pp. 418-432). New York: Guildford Press.

Wing, L., & Shah, A. (2000). Catatonia in autistic spectrum disorders. *British Journal of Psychiatry, 176,* 357-362.

Wolfberg, P.J., & Schuler A.L. (1993). Integrated playgroups: A model for promoting the social and cognitive dimensions of play. *Journal of Autism and Developmental Disorders, 23,* 1-23.

Wolff, S (2000). Schizoid personality in childhood and Asperger syndrome. In A. Klin, F.R. Volkmar, & S.S. Sparrow (Eds.), *Asperger Syndrome* (pp. 278-308). New York: Guildford Press.

Wolff, S., & McGuire, R. J. (1995). Schizoid personality in girls: A follow-up study. What are the links with Asperger's syndrome? *Journal of Child Psychology and Psychiatry, 36,* 793-818.

4

The Positive Parenting Program: An Early Intervention to Improve Personal Relationships Between Teenagers and their Parents

Alan Ralph
University of Queensland

Matthew R. Sanders
University of Queensland

Alan Ralph · Director, Training and Standards APS · School of Psychology · University of Queensland · Brisbane 4072 · Queensland · Australia.

International Perspectives on Child and Adolescent Mental Health. Volume 2: Proceedings of the Second International Conference, edited by N. N. Singh, T. H. Ollendick, and A. N. Singh. © 2002 Elsevier Science Ltd. All rights reserved.

In ideal circumstances a major goal for parents is to provide a context where children develop gradually over time along a continuum from dependence as infants to independence as socially responsible well-functioning adults. One area along this continuum that often causes apprehension for parents is the period when children approach and enter their teenage years. A significant reason for this concern is the increasing demands for greater freedom, particularly in relation to engaging in activities or events that parents consider risky or unnecessary. Often these activities will be counter to the parents' values and beliefs. Parents are only too aware that the consequences of increased freedom by teenagers, or excessive restrictions, can be highly problematic. These include academic failure, which can lead to drop out and unemployment; family conflict, which can lead to homelessness, depression and suicide; substance abuse, which can lead to addiction; drunkenness, which can lead to physical injury; delinquency, which can lead to serious crime; and high-risk sexual behavior, which can lead to early pregnancy or sexually transmitted diseases. Parents typically attempt to regulate access to events and activities based on their own values and beliefs, including notions of age-appropriateness, risk, relevance, and cost. Often these events or activities will be attractive to teenagers because they are more readily available to older children, or to children of parents with different values or beliefs.

The transitions that mark changes in access typically occur as a series of small incremental steps rather than as a smooth line. Undoubtedly there is variation among families and cultural groups concerning how, and at what age, these transitions are accomplished and there is no clear set of rules to guide parents when to grant increased access to specific events or activities. As teenagers increasingly attempt to establish their own identities, independent of their parents, conflicts will inevitably arise about whether or when they are allowed to participate in a broad range of activities and events. The way in which these conflicts are dealt with can have a major impact on the relationship between a teenager and his or her parents, and this in turn can impact on other issues such as academic achievement, self-esteem, vocational success, and the teenager's future marital and parenting behavior.

The behavior of young children is for the most part, influenced by consequences in their immediate environment. However, natural reinforcers for adaptive prosocial behaviors are often weak, delayed, uncertain, and difficult to discriminate, and typically produce a gradual, cumulative effect over time. It is often necessary to invest considerable amounts of time practicing prosocial behavior to bring it to the level where natural reinforcement is available, e.g., music rehearsal, sports practice, school homework, arts and craftwork. By contrast, many potent reinforcers are available that immediately and consistently strengthen behavior that has little adaptive function, and may even be maladaptive. For example, television strengthens inactivity and passivity, added food flavoring strengthens consumption of junk food, and viewing computer games strengthens button pressing. In addition, avoidance of the effort required to practice skills is often strengthened by easy access to alternative, more immediate reinforcers, such as watching TV, hanging out with peers, or fantasizing. Many parents intuitively understand these contingencies and attempt to arrange home routines to minimize avoidance of essential skills building, and to limit access to powerful reinforcers of non-adaptive behavior. Thus, in well-functioning families with young children, parents control access to desirable activities and events, often by setting appropriate contingencies (e.g., when you can ride your bike without training wheels, then you can ride outside the garden). As time goes by and a child's behavior becomes increasingly skilful and responsible, parents adjust the contingencies, and start to include children more in the process of negotiation to determine access to new activities and events. As children grow older still and their adaptive prosocial behavioral repertoire becomes firmly established, parents encourage them to take an increasingly active role in family and personal contingency planning, including the selection of consequences for following or breaking family rules.

When faced with a growing child's demands for increased freedom, some parents are unwilling or ignorant of the need to establish and maintain rules or contingencies in the home, resulting in their children's early and unrestricted access to desired activities. Although some children in these circumstances may develop a socially and personally adaptive behavioral repertoire, this is likely to occur only where some other agency creates an environment that shapes and maintains such a repertoire by arranging appropriate contingent relations. For example, a boarding school, religious community, sports coach, or prosocial peer group can have such an effect independent of parental inaction. For the majority of children who are not in contact with such agencies, a more likely outcome is for socially maladaptive behavior to be strengthened in preference to socially adaptive behavior. Problems then occur for parents if they endeavor to establish contingent reinforcement, following an incident where their child's maladaptive behavior brings them into conflict with other figures in authority who may have attempted to establish their own contingencies to shape adaptive behavior (e.g., teachers, police). This is particularly problematic if parents and children have a weak history of contingency management. Parents often find they no longer have control of the reinforcers necessary to strengthen adaptive behavior or weaken maladaptive behavior. In addition, the aversive consequences of the child's behavior when parents attempt to establish contingency management are often so powerful for the parent that they overwhelm the more minimal positive consequences that might otherwise maintain the parent's new behaviors.

Other parents respond to teenagers' demands for increased freedom by continuing to impose rules and contingencies that fail to acknowledge their increasing competence, and resist their teenager's attempts to renegotiate the contingencies and gain increased access to restricted activities. Teenagers in this situation often have difficulties interacting with their peers due to restrictions placed on them by their parents. Problems occur for parents as the teenager endeavors to challenge or subvert parental authority. This often leads to frequent and increasingly violent arguments and deception, or more internalized but equally serious problems such as psychological or physical withdrawal, reductions in eating or speaking, and self-harm or even suicide attempts. Other consequences may include parents separating, or a teenager leaving home, either of their own volition, or being evicted by parents.

As children become older, their peers, the media, and adults other than their parents increasingly come to influence their behavior, including their verbal behavior. The move into high school brings increasing demands for independence and responsibility. Teenagers are expected to make more decisions for themselves. This includes being more self-directed with schoolwork, and working out their own beliefs about whom they are and what they want to do with their lives. As opportunities for greater access to a wider range of activities increase, teenagers may be tempted to experiment in ways that might put their health or future prospects at risk, in return for access to powerful immediate gratification and peer approval. Some risk-taking is normal or short-lived, but it can be very worrying for parents and may lead to serious or long-term problems.

Sexual maturation occurs at different times for different teenagers and this can make them very self-conscious and sensitive to comments. Puberty produces powerful biochemical changes that prepare individuals for adulthood, including changes in sexual awareness and related behaviors that are often the product of evolutionary determinants. Boys become physically stronger and increasingly compete with each other for access to reinforcement available from girls. Girls become capable of childbearing, and develop characteristics and behaviors that communicate this change to boys, increasing girls' competitiveness for access to reinforcers available from boys. Although these are a direct legacy of our early evolutionary history, social and cultural rules and customs have overlaid them, mediating them in different ways in different cultures. In many cultures social contingencies are arranged in an attempt to delay access to sexual activity and child rearing for several years while enforcing social contingencies reinforcing further education or vocational training. In Western cultures, these contingencies operate alongside a plethora of socially approved explicit and covert sexual stimuli that provide a competing context. This has the potential to increase family conflict as parents try to manage increasing demands by their teenagers for access to the powerful reinforcers that adults typically restrict for themselves, e.g., sexual activity, freedom of association, and access to alcohol and other recreational drugs. Parents who fail to manage these demands well find the contingencies they are attempting to maintain increasingly irrelevant.

A further complication is that the gradual trend of transitions during childhood seems to change gear in adolescence and the demands for increased freedom seem to become more like a cascade. In a well-functioning family, where the child has acquired a prosocial behavioral repertoire, this will correspond with increased participation by the teenager in determining contingencies related to restricted activities, and the maintenance and further development of adaptive behavior in relation to the particular challenges of their move toward adulthood. It is important to look more closely at some of the salient features of this process.

A crucial part of providing a secure environment that promotes children's development and psychological growth is parental attention and affection. Most parents find this comes fairly naturally with young children, although some have temperaments that make this more difficult. However, as well as having a general strengthening effect on family attachment, attention and affection also have more specific contingent strengthening effects on the particular behaviors they follow. Thus parents are able to strengthen prosocial adaptive behavior in their children by providing contingent attention and approval. However, as teenagers spend increasing amounts of time away from home or engaged in individual activities in the home (doing homework, on the phone to friends, listening to music in their room), opportunities for parents to provide positive attention and affection for behavior they approve of will decrease. In addition, teenagers will increasingly have their behavior strengthened by attention and approval from their peers.

The behavior that is strengthened by peers may not be strengthened by parents, and of course vice versa. However, most teenagers learn the discriminant stimuli that help them behave differentially in a range of settings, so they will typically behave in parent-approved ways at home in order to obtain positive reinforcement available there, and in peer-approved ways in peer settings in order to obtain positive reinforcement available there. There are of course occasions in each setting when the discrimination process breaks down and produces the 'wrong' behavior. For example, swearing may be commonly reinforced by peers, but disapproved of by parents at home. A teenager will generally manage to maintain different verbal repertoires under the control of the different reinforcement contingencies operating in the two settings. Most well functioning socialized adults learn this discrimination and behave differently at sporting events, at church, and at work. Occasionally however, a situation at home may be almost identical to a situation with peers, or a teenager may be tired or irritable, and swearing behavior may occur at home "by accident." These are usually relatively minor problems that cause most well adjusted families few lasting difficulties, providing there is still a regular and reliable source of parental approval and positive attention for appropriate teenager behavior. The medium-term outcome in such families is for parents to continue as an important source of positive reinforcement for their teenagers (and vice versa) in addition to the positive reinforcement provided by peers, and other people in their lives.

As children mature physically, psychologically, intellectually, and socially, a natural increase in separation occurs between them and their parents. This is a normative gradual process with adjustments required on both sides. When teenagers finally leave home to lead a more independent existence from a family of this description, it can be accomplished without major family disruption, and family members are able to maintain regular contact and support to varying degrees.

However, in families where the amount of positive reinforcement provided by parents to a teenager is low, or declining, this can create a situation where a teenager is receiving most positive reinforcement from their peers. Behavior that is dependent upon parent reinforcement (e.g., speaking without swearing, wearing parent-favored clothes) will therefore become gradually weakened, and peer-approved behavior (e.g., swearing, wearing parent-aversive clothes) may become more common, even at home. This is likely to prove increasingly aversive for parents who may themselves respond with even fewer positive consequences for their teenager's behavior, and opportunities for positive reinforcement may cease altogether. The result is not only a decline in contingent reinforcement, but also in noncontingent reinforcement.

In this model, what leads to the reduction in the rate of parent-provided positive consequences is either (1) parental unwillingness to provide changes to contingent relations that could bring gradually increased access to restricted activities as children demonstrate increasing competence and responsibility, or (2) the child's noncontingent and unrestricted access to such activities independent of any increase in competence and responsibility. This problem is compounded, particularly for the latter group, if the peers that the teenager is associating with are engaging in deviant or antisocial behavior. If parents permit their children to associate with deviant peers (either knowingly or unknowingly) their acquisition of undesirable behavior will escalate. This is likely to lead to a rapidly increasing gap between parents and their teenagers.

In a home environment lacking in positive consequences for teenager behavior, it is hardly surprising that teenagers withdraw into their own rooms, spend as little time at home as possible, and reduce their interactions with parents to a minimum. Although this low-positive environment may not be a fun place to be, for some teenagers, being left alone often may have some short-term benefits. In such an environment we might expect that the teenager and parents are maintaining a relationship that while it may have occasional aversive exchanges, is predominantly neutral.

However, in other families we see not only a rapid reduction in positive reinforcement, but also an accompanying increase in the use of aversive consequences. In such family settings, we might expect that what interactions do occur tend to be conflictual and unpleasant. Any behavior by the teenager that leads to escape from or avoidance of these aversive arguments is likely to be strengthened, and will thus lead to further avoidance and escape by the teenager in the future. The logical endpoint of this process is complete separation, sometimes leading to the teenager leaving home at an available opportunity, or after a particularly violent confrontation. The prospects for further positive engagement between teenager and parent(s) are poor. Some families never recover from splits of this sort, whereas in others, covert communication between the teenager and another family member (e.g., mother, younger sibling) is sometimes used to maintain contact of sorts.

It is therefore important for parents to accept the idea of gradual separation with their teenager as being normative. The main issue concerns the speed at which it is appropriate for this separation to occur and whether the separation allows continuation of the parent-child (now parent-teenager) bond. Separation need not be sudden, conflictual, or final. Parents who can maintain (or increase) the level of contingent and noncontingent positive reinforcers for desirable teenage behavior are better able to deal with undesirable events when they occur. This can be achieved by gradually providing increased access to restricted activities contingent upon parallel increases in prosocial, responsible behavior on the part of the teenager. Some undesirable events may be unavoidable, but it is important that they not lead to a downward spiral whereby parent-teenager interactions become increasingly aversive, and positive reinforcement opportunities become scarcer and scarcer.

EMPIRICAL SUPPORT FOR THE MODEL

It has been known for some time that adolescents who exhibit behavior problems typically have difficulty with communication, problem-solving, and interpersonal relationships (Alexander, 1973; Prinz, Rosenblum, & O'Leary, 1978). Poor parent-adolescent communication has been frequently linked to delinquency (Henggeler, 1989), and general deviance (Stewart & Zaenglein-Senger, 1984). In a sample of almost 1000 children studied longitudinally in Dunedin, results showed a strong relationship between DSM-III disorders and social competence in both pre-adolescents and adolescents (McGee & Williams, 1991). There are also significant cross sectional and longitudinal correlations between serious conduct problems and self reported polysubstance abuse (Hawkins, et al., 1992; Van Kammen, Loeber, & Stouthamer-Loeber, 1991). Conduct-problem behavior is more likely to begin before drug abuse than vice versa; and an escalation of delinquent or antisocial acts is often accompanied by substance abuse (Elliott, Huizinga, & Ageton, 1985; Prinz, 1998). Biglan, et al. (1990) examined high-risk sexual behavior among adolescents in grades 8 though 12 and observed high correlations with other problem behaviors such as antisocial behavior, academic difficulties, smoking, alcohol and other drug use. This suggests that it is typically the same young people engaging in a wide range of problem behaviors.

Where children display non-compliant and antisocial behavior, parents are often poorly equipped to provide consistent affection and discipline to their children (Greenwood, Model, Rydell, & Chisea, 1997). Family support is a significant predictor of positive adjustment in childhood and adolescence and indirect evidence suggests that family support is a protective factor for adolescent substance abuse and conduct problems (Cauce, Reid, Landesman, & Gonzales, 1990; Cohen & Wills, 1985; Wills, Vaccaro, & McNamara, 1992).
There is good evidence that the onset and maintenance of adolescent substance abuse and conduct disorders are associated with a number of family practices (Block, Block, & Keyes, 1988; Farrington, et al., 1990; Hawkins, Catalano, & Miller, 1992; Loeber & Stouthamer-Loeber, 1986; Steinberg, Fletcher, & Darling, 1994). These include poor family management; disrupted, coercive, or non-existent parenting; inappropriate discipline; inadequate parent monitoring; and parent irritability.

Parenting variables related to adolescent high-risk sexual behavior include limited parental availability, low levels of parent monitoring and support, and coercive family exchanges (Biglan, et al., 1990). Also implicated were friends who engaged in problem behavior and alcohol use. Specifically, the authors call for prevention strategies that modify or compensate for the peer and familial context that appear to contribute to the spectrum of adolescent problem behaviors.

Poor parental monitoring in middle childhood has also been shown to be a significant factor in children's movement into a deviant peer network in early adolescence (Dishion, Patterson, Stoolmiller, & Skinner, 1991), and higher levels of monitoring have been associated with lower levels of adolescent deviance (Lamborn, Dornbusch, & Steinberg, 1996). Parental monitoring is a strong predictor of male adolescent delinquency (Loeber & Dishion, 1983; Loeber & Stouthamer-Loeber, 1987), and differences in parents' monitoring practices correlated directly with levels of antisocial behavior in boys (Patterson & Dishion, 1985), and indirectly via increased contact with delinquent peers. There is also evidence that inadequate parental monitoring has been implicated in fire-setting (Kolko & Kazdin, 1986; 1990), as well as early substance use (Baumrind, Moselle, & Martin, 1985; Brown, Mounts, Lamborn, & Steinberg, 1993; Dishion, & Loeber, 1985; Dishion, Reid, & Patterson, 1988; Fletcher, Darling, & Steinberg, 1995).

Several studies have investigated the relative roles of parental monitoring and family communication on adolescent deviance. While all have found high correlations for both, regression analyses differ as to the primary variable. Weintraub and Gold (1991) reported an additive and interactive relationship, while Patterson and Stouthamer-Loeber (1984) identified monitoring as the primary parenting variable in a sample of white Caucasian males. For African-American male adolescents, Gray-Ray and Ray (1990) reported communication as the primary variable, while Smith and Krohn (1995), in a study of Hispanic and African-American adolescents found the two variables differed as a function of the adolescent's ethnic background. However, monitoring was firmly associated with reductions in deviant behavior for African American and Latino families in studies by Gorman-Smith, Tolan, Zelli, and Huesmann (1996), and Lamborn, et al., (1996). In an attempt to provide a definitive answer, Forehand, Miller, Dutra, and Chance (1997) studied a community sample of 907 Black American and Hispanic adolescents and their mothers. As with the previous studies, there were significant correlations between both parenting variables and adolescent deviance. However, results supported the primacy of the monitoring variable for both ethnic groups.

Two more recent studies have provided perhaps the clearest picture yet of the parenting constructs that could be targeted when developing early interventions to prevent severe adolescent problems. Metzler, Biglan, Ary, and Li (1998) built on work by Dishion, Li, Spracklen, Brown, and Haas (in press) to investigate the association between six parenting constructs (positive family relations, parent-child conflict, parental rule-making, consistent enforcement of rules, positive reinforcement for desirable behavior, and parental monitoring), and three adolescent criterion variables (association with deviant peers, antisocial behavior, substance use). Results showed that parent-child conflict, positive family relations, and parental monitoring were most highly related to the criterion variables. Conflict with parents was strongly associated with contact with deviant peers, substance use, and engaging in antisocial behavior. High levels of positive family relations, parental monitoring, rule setting, and positive reinforcement were associated with less contact with deviant peers, less engagement in antisocial behavior, and less substance use.

INTERVENTION RESEARCH

There are four main treatment approaches that aim to reduce problem behavior once it appears in adolescence. These can be divided into: (1) treat the adolescent; (2) treat the parents; (3) treat the adolescent and the parent; and (4) treat the broader family system.

Treat the Adolescent

Attempts to provide interventions to adolescents without addressing other aspects of their environment have generally been less than successful when subjected to rigorous experimental investigation (Kazdin, 1987, 1991, 1995; Mann & Borduin, 1991). However, one approach that has had some success has involved removing the adolescents from their natural home, and placing them in a specially designed setting, sometimes referred to as a halfway house. Perhaps the best known of these, and certainly one of the best documented in terms of evaluation, is the Teaching Family Model (TFM) developed by Wolf and colleagues, and implemented at Achievement Place during the 1970s (Phillips, Phillips, Fixsen, & Wolf, 1973; Wolf, Phillips, Fixsen, Braukman, Kirigin, Willner, & Shumaker, 1976). Substantial improvements in prosocial behavior and reductions in delinquent behavior were demonstrated using contingency management (Kirigin, Braukman, Atwater, & Wolf, 1982), but gains were lost when the youths returned to their home settings (Jones, Weinrott, & Howard, 1981).

Controlled group outcome studies have shown that cognitive-behavioral therapies can produce significant reductions in adolescent depression (Kahn, Kehle, Jenson, & Clark, 1990; Lewinsohn, Clarke, Hops, & Andrews, 1990). However, one-third to one-half of adolescents treated in these studies showed little improvement.

Treat the Parents

Parent Management Training (PMT), often conducted in groups, has been promoted as a cost-effective treatment strategy and has a relatively long and well-documented history, and research attests to its efficacy with young children (Dumas, 1989; Graziano & Diament, 1992; Kazdin, 1987, 1991). A small number of programs have also reported good results with parents of middle-school children. Preparing for the Drug-Free Years (Hawkins, Catalano, & Kent, 1991) is a five-session universal intervention that has been shown to be efficacious in improving parental monitoring, involvement with their children, and rule enforcement (Catalano, Kosterman, Haggerty, Hawkins, & Spoth, 1998; Kosterman, Hawkins, Spoth, Haggerty, & Zhu, 1997).

The Adolescent Transition Program (ATP; Dishion, Kavanagh, & Kiesner, in press) has reportedly produced significant effects on parents' skill and on youth behavior in a randomized controlled trial with parents of adolescents at-risk for substance use, academic failure and antisocial behavior (Dishion & Andrews, 1995). The program focused on helping parents increase their positive reinforcement of appropriate behavior, while at the same time setting limits and developing consistent, noncoercive discipline practices. Dishion and Andrews (1995) used highly trained research staff to deliver the parenting program, and Irvine, Biglan, Smolkowski, Metzler, and Ary (1999) replicated the research, this time using group leaders who were not mental health practitioners to deliver the parenting skills classes to 303 parents of at risk middle school children in small communities. Using randomized allocation to immediate treatment or wait-list conditions, Irvine, et al. (1999) reported reductions in coercive parenting practices, together with improved reinforcement of appropriate behavior, limit setting, remaining calm, and problem solving. They also reported improvements on some but not all adolescent indicators, and wait-list families did not always improve after receiving the intervention.

A study by Dishion and Patterson (1992) who reported a decrease in behavior problems with children aged up to 12.5 years was extended by Ruma, Burke, and Thompson (1996) who delivered the same standardized, manualized program of between 12 and 16 hours of parent training in weekly 2 hour blocks, to a group of parents with adolescents. There were reductions in problem behavior post-treatment for the adolescent group, but less than for the younger groups, and the adolescent post-treatment mean was still in the clinical range on the Achenbach Child Behavior Checklist (CBCL). Using the Reliable Change Index (Jacobson & Revenstorf, 1988; Jacobson and Truax, 1991) the authors investigated how many of those originally in the clinical range of the CBCL improved by at least 8 points and moved out of the clinical range. Only 6% of the adolescents in this subset met the strictest criterion for improvement, with a further 15% showing improvement, but not moving out of the clinical range. It is also worth noting that of the 304 mothers who commenced the group parenting sessions, 98 failed to complete, giving a retention rate of only 65%.

In another study that utilized an intensive PMT with parents of chronic adolescent offenders by pairs of highly experienced therapists, significant reductions were reported in police-recorded offences. Although the results persisted during a 3-year follow-up, offending gradually increased to the point where it was not significantly different from that of a control group (Bank, Marlowe, Reid, Patterson, & Weinrott, 1991). The high level of training and experience necessary to implement these procedures militate against their widespread adoption for handling community-level problems.

Treat the Family

Variants of family therapy have long been employed to target child and adolescent behavior problems and reviews by Hazelrigg, Cooper, and Borduin (1987), and Alexander, Holtzworth-Munroe, and Jameson (1994) has identified those for which there is credible support. Many interventions aimed at improving family functioning include components that successfully enhance family communication and problem solving skills (Alexander & Parsons, 1973; Gordon, Arbuthnot, Gustafson, & McGreen, 1988; Kifer, Lewis, Green, & Phillips, 1974; Robin, Kent, O'Leary, Foster, & Prinz, 1977; Serna, Schumaker, Hazel, & Sheldon, 1986). However, in the few studies that measured in-home interactions to investigate whether the acquired improvements generalized from the clinic-based training setting using in-home, results were mixed (Foster, Prinz, & O'Leary, 1983; Robin, 1981). In an attempt to examine this issue more closely, Serna, Schumaker, Sherman, and Sheldon (1991) taught improved communication and problem-solving skills to three families with adolescent children between the ages of 12 and 16, and then studied audiotapes of naturalistic family interactions to assess whether the skills were used. In-home taped interactions were either directed or non-directed. Directed interactions featured the teacher prompting parents and adolescents to use the previously trained skills in discussions of real-life problem situations. Non-directed interactions were unprompted and free ranging. Results replicated the findings of previous studies in showing that skills teaching was effective in producing increased use of the skills in the training setting. During directed interactions there was some generalization of skills, but not during non-directed interactions, and additional in-home skills review and practice had little effect on this. However, the addition of weekly in-home family conferences produced high levels of skills generalization in both directed and nondirected interactions. Family conferences featured in-home training in family problem-solving discussions moderated by a trainer. The conferences were highly structured with the teacher providing modeling, prompts, corrective feedback, and praise.

The authors speculate that the family conferences may tap in to several of the generalization-inducing methods described by Stokes and Baer (1977). These include the use of common stimuli (home setting and real-life problems); naturally occurring maintaining contingencies (solving real-life problems); the selection and labeling of problem situations and specific skills required to solve the problems outside the family conference; and regular practice at solving multiple exemplars of family problems over a period of weeks.

Greater parental involvement in treatment has been shown to predict greater improvement during treatment for adolescent depression (Clarke, Hops, Lewinsohn, Andrews, Seeley, & Williams, 1992) and three other studies have shown that family intervention strategies are effective in the treatment of adolescents with eating disorders (Russell, et al., 1987; Le Grange, Eisler, Dare, & Russell, 1992; Robin, Siegel, Koepke, Moye, & Tice, 1994). Russell, et al. (1987) compared the effects of family therapy and individual supportive psychotherapy after a period of inpatient treatment. For patients with an onset prior to 19 years of age and duration of less than three years family therapy was superior in terms of weight gain. A subsequent report from the same trial (Dare, et al., 1990) revealed that engagement of families in therapy is a significant problem with quite high levels of drop out in both family therapy (36%) and individual therapy (33%). Robin, et al. (1994) found that behavioral family systems therapy which emphasized parental influences over eating and weight gain, coupled with communication skills training and cognitive restructuring, was more effective than psychodynamically oriented individual therapy in changing measures of body-mass index. The two programs were comparable on measures of psychopathology and eating-related family conflict. It is important to note that the individual therapy program involved some collateral parent sessions.

Treating the Broader Family System

Weissberg, Caplan, and Harwood (1991) have argued for multilevel, multicomponent prevention programs conducted in collaboration with families, schools, and communities to promote competence in children.

Treatment Foster Care (TFC). TFC was developed at the Oregon Social Learning Center and has shown good results (Chamberlain, 1990; Chamberlain & Reid, 1991). This package included PMT for the biological family, home contingency management by trained foster parents, a school program monitored by teachers and foster parents, and close monitoring and supervision of peer relationships. Other components for such problems as substance abuse are added as needed. Typical placement length is 6 months, after which adolescents return to their biological parents. Evaluations of this intervention have shown that adolescents receiving TFC compared to controls (treatment as usual) have lower rates of subsequent institutionalization, display fewer daily problem behaviors, and cost the state significantly less.

Multi-Dimensional Family Therapy (MDFT). MDFT is based on the premise that change in an individual adolescent results from change in the broader family system. MDFT typically includes four major areas of intervention: (1) the adolescent's intrapersonal and interpersonal functioning (e.g., with parents and peers); (2) the parent's intrapersonal and interpersonal functioning (i.e., parenting practices and general adult functioning); (3) parent-adolescent interactions; and (4) family members' interactions with persons outside the family (e.g., school and welfare personnel, probation officers). Treatment typically requires from between 14 and 16 sessions and spans up to 6 months duration in total.

A controlled clinical trial reported by Liddle and Dakof (1995a,1995b) showed reductions in drug use post-treatment and at 12 month follow-up, when compared with adolescent group therapy, and multifamily educational intervention. There were also moderate gains in academic grades for those receiving MDFT. A further study by Schmidt, Liddle, and Dakof (1996) in which 29 families received MDFT, clearly linked improvements in parenting practices with changes in adolescent symptoms – something rarely examined before. Despite these promising findings, only 59% of families (17/29) showed such dual improvements. A further 21% of families (6/29) showed a reduction in adolescent drug abuse despite there being no measurable improvement in parenting practices, and 10% (3/39) showed improved parenting practices but no reduction in adolescent drug abuse. The remaining 10% showed no improvements on either parent or adolescent measures. The authors acknowledge the possibility that for some adolescents, it may be too late to challenge well-established, often peer-supported antisocial behavior patterns that have replaced more prosocial behaviors that require ongoing parental maintenance and support.

Multi-Systemic Therapy (MST). MST is a comprehensive multi-setting intervention for adolescent offenders. The approach uses present-focused, action-oriented, individually tailored strategies targeting intrapersonal (e.g., cognitive), family, peer, and school factors associated with antisocial behavior. Treatment is usually held in a family's home and in the local community (schools, recreation centers). The program has a strong emphasis on teaching skilling parents so they can independently tackle their concerns in raising adolescents. The results from this research have been impressive, given the severity of the conduct problems experienced by participating families. Borduin, Mann, Cone, Henggeler, Fucci, Blaske, and Williams (1995) compared MST and individual therapy in a study involving 176 juvenile offenders. Results showed that MST was more effective in preventing future offending and in reducing family correlates of disturbance (i.e., more cohesion and adaptability and increased supportiveness and less observed conflict hostility during family interactions).

COMPARISON STUDIES

Barkley, Guevremont, Anastopoulos, and Fletcher (1992) examined three different types of family interventions for adolescents with attention deficit disorders. They compared behavioral parent training, based on Forehand and Barkley's work; family problem solving and communication training based on Patterson and Forgatch's work; and structural family therapy based on Minuchin's work. All three therapies reduced negative communication, anger during conflicts, maternal depression, and the number of internalizing and externalizing symptoms. All three therapies also improved ratings of school adjustment. Despite these improvements, most of the adolescents (70-95%) in each group showed no clinically significant change in the number or intensity of family conflicts. The authors highlighted the importance of long-term, multimodal, joint pharmacological-psychological interventions.

Kazdin, Siegel, and Bass (1992) compared child-focused Problem-Solving Skills Training (PSST), with Parent Management Training (PMT), and a combined PSST/PMT condition. Results showed that all conditions produced significant improvements in child dysfunction, prosocial competence, and aggressive, antisocial, and delinquent behavior, that were evident at home, school, and in the community that were maintained at 1–year follow-up. Although the combined condition appeared to have a greater impact, the children in the sample were aged from 7 to 13 years, and there is no indication as to whether there were any variations in treatment effect due to age. Dishion and Andrews (1995) compared the effects of a group parent training intervention; a group adolescent intervention; a combined parent and adolescent group program; a self directed intervention involving information, but no face-to-face therapy contact; and a no-treatment control group. Results showed that although both the parent-only and adolescent-only group programs produced greater short term improvements in observed and reported family conflict, only the parent condition reduced subsequent tobacco use at follow up, and long term effects on problem behavior were minimal overall. An interesting finding was that the adolescent-only group program resulted in higher rates of tobacco use and problem behavior than the control condition, pointing to the dangers of peer interventions with high-risk adolescent samples.

Robin (1981) compared "behavioral-systems" family therapy for parent adolescent conflict with alternative treatments that included a mixture of systemic, eclectic, and psychodynamic family therapies. Both groups showed reductions in parent adolescent conflict immediately post treatment on the self-report measures. However, the behavioral systems therapy showed superior outcome on measures of problem solving, communication and self-reported satisfaction with therapy.

COMBINATION STUDIES

A combination of PMT and Family Systems Therapy has been reported to be successful with adolescent offenders (Alexander & Parsons, 1973). However, the results of this research were difficult to interpret due to methodological problems, and no replication has yet succeeded in producing similar results, although current research is underway and results are awaited with interest. Some classroom-based interventions have also reduced anti-social behavior, but there has been no study that combines PMT with a systematic classroom management program.

However, to date there have been no controlled evaluations of programs for parents of adolescents that have been shown to be effective in reducing these risks, and the few treatment interventions that have produced replicable reductions in antisocial behavior or substance abuse (Bank, et al., 1991; Chamberlain, 1990; Henggeler, et al., 1998), are intensive and difficult to reproduce at the level required to impact on the large numbers of adolescents known to be at risk in the community.

Dishion and McMahon (1998) have also suggested several implications of monitoring for the prevention of child problem behavior. These include targeting what they refer to as parental motivation to monitor. This can be achieved in various ways such as using motivational interviewing to list strengths and weaknesses and identify family change options (Dishion, Kavanagh, & Kiesner, in press); addressing dysfunctional marital relationships that disrupt parents' tendencies to take on family leadership roles (e.g., Liddle & Dakof, 1995a); or via universal strategies that provide parents with information about community norms regarding children's unsupervised time (e.g., Biglan, 1995). They also identify parents' lack of knowledge or skills in effectively monitoring their children as a potential target for intervention, as well as ecological changes that facilitate such monitoring, such as dedicated telephone lines at school that encourage parents to maintain regular contact to provide them with daily information about school attendance, disciplinary infractions, or conflicts (Bry & Canby, 1986; Reid, 1993).

Another key issue is the difficulty encountered in engaging and retaining parents in treatment programs. A recent review of relevant research suggests these might be successfully addressed by means of letter writing, intensive telephone contact, and parent orientation meetings that form part of an ecological, multilevel approach involving contact with children, parents, school personnel, and local social and community networks (Morrissey-Kane & Prinz, 1999).

Spoth and Redmond (1995) recently applied the Health Belief Model to this question of parent's intentions to attend and participate in parenting programs. They recommend reducing or removing potential barriers to attendance, particularly for parents with low income, by carefully scheduling and locating program settings. They also suggest it may be necessary to provide transport, and tangible rewards for initial and continued participation. One possible factor in discouraging parental participation is that parents may underestimate the relationship between actual problem prevalence and their own child's risk – this is hypothesized to cause parents to perceive higher levels of future child risk, but then minimize the severity of the problem, with the result that a program may be perceived as less beneficial. The authors recommend the use of media campaigns and educational programs to better inform parents of the child risk factors, the severity of risk-related problems (e.g., substance abuse), and the related benefits of prevention programs. Another important predictor was prior parenting resource use. This may mean that parents should be engaged in lower level activities during targeted school promotions prior to attempts to engage them in attending more intensive parenting sessions.

SUMMARY

In summary, relative to other interventions with adolescents, Behavioral Family Interventions (BFI) delivered to parents have shown promise that warrants further development and evaluation. However, for BFIs to be efficacious there are several key issues to be addressed. First, they must be deliverable to large numbers of parents – this means training large numbers of practitioners to accomplish this. Programs must therefore be robust, coherent, and standardized with well-designed manuals and other resources. Second, in order to engage parents, an intervention should aim to create a maximally conducive environment in the community prior to offering parenting programs, reduce or remove deterrents for attendance, and feature direct invitations to parents to attend with reinforcement for attendance. Third, it must foster positive family environments where there is an effective but non-coercive disciplinary strategy, increase parental monitoring of teenager behavior, actively promote routines for risk reduction and avoidance, and incorporate family meetings to maximize maintenance and generalizability.

THE TRIPLE P: POSITIVE PARENTING PROGRAM FOR PARENTS WITH TEENAGERS

The Triple P-Positive Parenting Program is a multi-level, parenting and family support strategy originally developed by Matt Sanders and his colleagues at the University of

Queensland in Brisbane, Australia. The program was designed to prevent severe behavioral, emotional and developmental problems in children from birth to age 12 by enhancing the knowledge, skills, and confidence of parents.

The program described here is an upward extension that aims to address the concerns of parents of teenagers aged 12-16. There are five levels of intervention on a tiered continuum of increasing strength. Level 1, a universal parent information strategy, provides all interested parents with access to useful information about parenting through a coordinated media and promotional campaign using print and electronic media, as well as user-friendly parenting tip sheets and videotapes which demonstrate specific parenting strategies. This level of intervention aims to increase community awareness of parenting resources, receptivity of parents to participating in programs, and to create a sense of optimism by depicting solutions to common behavioral and developmental concerns. Level 2 is a selective, one- to two- session primary health care intervention providing anticipatory developmental guidance to parents of children and teenagers with mild behavior difficulties. Level 3 is a four-session selective intervention that targets children and teenagers with mild to moderate behavior difficulties and includes active skills training for parents. Level 4 is an indicated intervention aimed at managing more severe behavioral difficulties and is delivered to families either individually in a standard 8- to 10- session version, as a group parent training program, or in a telephone-assisted self-directed format. Level 5 is an enhanced behavioral family intervention program for families where parenting difficulties are complicated by other sources of family distress (e.g., marital conflict, parental depression or high levels of stress, or teenager difficulties outside the family).

This tiered multilevel strategy recognizes that there are differing levels of dysfunction and behavioral disturbance in children and adolescents, and parents have differing needs and desires regarding the type, intensity and mode of assistance they may require. The multilevel strategy is designed to maximize efficiency, contain costs, avoid waste and over servicing, and ensure the program has wide reach in the community. Also the multidisciplinary nature of the program involves the better utilization of the existing professional workforce in the task of promoting competent parenting. For a more thorough description of the theoretical basis of Triple P, see Sanders (1996, 1999).

Biglan (1995) maintains that the reduction of antisocial behavior in children and adolescents requires the community context for parenting to change. Triple P has an explicit public health perspective on family intervention that involves a tacit recognition of the role of the broader ecological context for human development, and incorporates a media and promotional strategy as part of a larger system of intervention (e.g., Biglan, 1995; Mrazek & Haggerty, 1994;

National Institute of Mental Health, 1998). It does this by normalizing parenting experiences (particularly the process of participating in parent education), by breaking down parents' sense of social isolation, increasing social and emotional support from others in the community, validating and acknowledging publicly the importance and difficulties of parenting, and by teaching parents skills that enable them to become independent problem solvers (Karoly, 1993) as well as specific coping skills for high risk parenting situations.

Principles of Positive Parenting

Five core positive parenting principles form the basis of the program and address specific risk and protective factors known to predict positive developmental and mental health outcomes in children and adolescents. These core principles are: (1) ensuring a safe and engaging environment; (2) creating a positive learning environment; (3) using assertive discipline; (4) having realistic expectations; and (5) taking care of oneself as a parent. These translate into a range of specific parenting strategies, which are outlined in Table 1.

Table 1.   Parenting Skills Promoted Through Triple P

STRATEGY	DESCRIPTION	APPLICATIONS
Developing Positive Relationships		
Spending time with a teenager	Spending frequent, small amounts of time when there is no pressure to get other things done	Opportunities for teenagers to enjoy parent contact and maintain a positive relationship
Talking to a teenager	Having brief conversations about topics that are of interest to them	Promoting opportunity to voice opinions and to discuss issues important to them
Showing affection	Adult-to-teenager displays of affection that don't cause public embarrassment	Demonstrate appropriate ways of showing affection and maintaining parent-teenager relationship
Increasing Desirable Behavior		
Using descriptive praise	Providing encouragement and approval by describing the behavior that is appreciated	Encouraging appropriate behavior (e.g., being responsible, doing chores, helping others)
Giving attention	Providing positive non-verbal approval	As above
Providing opportunities for engaging activities	Creating opportunities for teenagers to explore and try out new social and recreational activities	Encouraging independence; identifying activities that teenagers can participate in and develop new skills and interests

Table 1 continued

STRATEGY	DESCRIPTION	APPLICATIONS
Teaching New Skills and Behaviors		
Setting a good example	Demonstrating desirable behavior by parental modeling	Showing teenagers how to behave appropriately, especially in relation to interpersonal interactions and moral issues
Coaching problem-solving	Helping teenagers to deal with a problem in a constructive and effective way	Promoting independence; assisting with difficult decisions, dilemmas, and challenges
Using behavior contracts	Negotiating an agreement to deal with an issue which is causing dispute or distress	Assisting a teenager to develop personal responsibility
Holding a family meeting	Organizing a set time for family members to work together to set goals for change	Teaching compromise, decision making, and personal responsibility
Managing Problem Behavior		
Establishing family rules	Negotiating in advance a set of fair, specific, and enforceable rules	Clarifying expectations and avoiding casual conflict
Using directed discussion	The identification and rehearsal of the correct behavior following occasional rule breaking	Correcting occasional rule breaking, or initial violations following a new rule being applied
Making clear, calm requests	Making a specific request to start a new task, or stop a problem behavior and start a preferred alternative behavior	Initiating an activity, or terminating a problem behavior and saying what is required instead
Backing up requests with logical consequences	The provision of a specific consequence which involves the removal of an activity or privilege from the teenager for a set time	Dealing with noncompliance, mild problem behaviors that do not occur often
Dealing with emotional behavior	Helping a teenager to deal with unpleasant or intense emotional responses that interfere with effective problem-solving or cause increased conflict and/or distress	Promoting emotional management; assisting a teenager to cope with events that cause distress; modeling arousal-reduction techniques to avoid unpleasant conflict
Using behavior contracts	Negotiating an agreement to deal with an issue which is causing dispute or distress	Assisting a teenager to develop personal responsibility for their actions
Holding a family meeting	Organizing a set time for family members to work together to set goals for change	Teaching compromise, decision making, and personal responsibility

Table 1 continued

STRATEGY	DESCRIPTION	APPLICATIONS
Dealing with Risky Behavior		
Identifying risky situations in advance	Anticipating events a teenager is likely to want to engage in that may be risky	Preventing unexpected demands from leading to conflict or decision-making under pressure
Obtaining accurate information	Ensuring important decisions are not taken on the basis of emotive or inaccurate beliefs	Demonstrates information seeking to reduce the risk of undesirable outcomes
Explaining concerns and risks	Share concerns with teenager and explain nature of perceived risk	Explains parents' concerns and motivation for rules; identifies the nature of the risk;
Selecting risk-reduction strategies	Problem-solving and negotiating in advance a set of fair, specific, and enforceable rules	Establishing the best possible plan to reduce or avoid risky situations while still participating in peer activities
Holding a review session	Organizing a set time to review how well the strategies worked	Teaching compromise, decision making, and personal responsibility
Monitoring teenagers	Establish a parent or community network	Establish communal responsibility to share load among parents
Using behavior contracts	Negotiating an agreement to deal with an issue that is causing dispute/distress	Teaching compromise, decision making, and responsibility

Level 4 Intervention

As mentioned above, the Triple P Program has five levels of intervention. There is not sufficient space here to detail all levels but an outline of the Level 4 intensive parenting skills training program is now provided to illustrate the program. This indicated preventive intervention targets families where detectable problems are identified, but diagnostic criteria for a behavioral disorder are not yet met. This can be offered to families individually, or as a group version of the program with the goal of identifying and engaging parents of teenagers with severe disruptive and aggressive behavior. Although delivery of the program in a group setting may mean parents receive less individual attention, there are several benefits of group participation for parents. These benefits include support, friendship, and constructive feedback from other parents as well as opportunities for parents to normalize their parenting experience through peer interactions.

In the self-directed delivery mode, detailed information is provided in a parenting workbook, which outlines a 10-week self-help program for parents. Each weekly session contains a series of set readings and suggested homework tasks for parents to complete. Some parents require and seek more support in managing their children than simply having access to information. Hence, the self-help program may be augmented by weekly 15-30 minute telephone consultations. This consultation model aims to provide brief, minimal support to parents as a means of keeping them focused and motivated while they work through the program and assists in tailoring the program to the specific needs of the family. Rather than introducing new strategies, these telephone consultations direct parents to those sections of the written materials that may be appropriate to their current situation.

Irrespective of the mode of delivery, parents are sequentially introduced to four major areas: (1) factors that influence teenagers' behavior; (2) strategies for encouraging teenagers' development, (3) strategies for managing misbehavior; and (4) routines for dealing with risky behavior (see Table 1). Throughout the program parents are encouraged to examine their expectations, assumptions, and beliefs about the influences on teenagers' behavior and to choose goals that are developmentally appropriate for the teenager and realistic for the parent. Developmentally appropriate expectations are taught in the context of parents' specific expectations concerning difficult and prosocial behaviors rather than through the more traditional age and stages approach to teaching about teenager development. Parents are encouraged to discuss these issues with their teenage children, and to talk regularly with other parents to establish support networks and to assist in monitoring their teenagers' behavior when they are away from home or school.

Parents are taught a variety of behavior management skills including providing brief contingent attention following desirable behavior, and how to encourage and promote participation in engaging activities. A strong emphasis is placed on the importance of engaging teenagers in stimulating activities and ensuring adequate supervision and monitoring in an appropriate developmental context (Dishion & McMahon, 1998; Forehand, Miller, Dutra, & Chance, 1997; Risley, Clark & Cataldo, 1976). The program also provides parents with strategies to respond positively and constructively to teenager-initiated interactions (e.g., requests for help, information, advice, attention) that encourage them to participate more in family decision making, learn more advanced skills, and solve increasingly complex social and interpersonal problems for themselves (Hart & Risley, 1975, 1995). Specific behavior management strategies are taught as alternatives to coercive and ineffective discipline practices, such as shouting, threatening or using physical punishment. These include: negotiating and implementing family rules; making clear, calm requests; providing logical consequences; how to deal calmly with emotional behavior; and the use of behavior contracts where less structured strategies are ineffective. Parents are also encouraged to plan ahead to deal with behavior that has the potential to put a teenager's health or future prospects at risk.

Segments from the videotape *Every Parent's Guide to Teenagers* (Ralph & Sanders, in press) are used to demonstrate positive parenting skills, and parents are provided with workbooks to assist them to utilize the strategies as they are introduced. Active skills training methods are employed that include modeling, rehearsal, feedback, and homework tasks. Several generalization enhancement strategies are incorporated (e.g., training with sufficient exemplars, training loosely by varying the stimulus condition for training) to promote the transfer of parenting skills across settings, siblings and time, and the use of family meetings between sessions to discuss and plan how to implement the changes that the parents have identified as important for their family.

All levels of Triple P specifically encourage parents to view parenting as part of a larger context of personal self-care, resourcefulness, and well being, by teaching parents practical parenting skills that both parents (where appropriate) are able to implement. In the more intensive level of intervention (Level 5) couples are also taught effective marital communication skills and are encouraged to explore how their own emotional state affects their parenting, and consequently their teenager's behavior. Parents develop specific coping strategies for managing difficult emotions including depression, anger, anxiety, and high levels of parenting stress at high risk times.

The Level 4 group program is currently being evaluated as part of a transition to high-school program where it is offered to all parents of students entering their first year of high school. Preliminary data are currently being evaluated and follow-up data collection is planned. An experimental trial of the Level 4 standard intervention is also underway with the program being delivered to individual families with teenagers aged between 12 and 14 years of age who are displaying severe problem behaviors. General practitioners are also being trained to deliver the Level 3 primary care program to parents of teenagers who present at their practices. Triple P, which has proven successful with children aged 12 years and under, is now being complemented by a new version for parents with teenagers aged between 12 and 16, in what will become a comprehensive multi-tiered, community-based preventive intervention for conduct disorders for children of all ages.

REFERENCES

Alexander, J.F. (1973). Defensive and supportive communications in normal and deviant families. *Journal of Consulting and Clinical Psychology, 40,* 223-231.

Alexander, J.F., & Parsons, B.V. (1973). Short-term behavioral intervention and delinquent families: Impact on family process and recidivism. *Journal of Abnormal Psychology, 81,* 219-225.

Alexander, J.F., Holtzworth-Munroe, A., & Jameson, P. (1994). The process and outcome of marital family therapy: Research review and evaluation. In A.E. Bergin & S.L. Garfield (Eds.), *Handbook of psychotherapy and behavior change* (4th ed., pp. 595-630). New York: Wiley.

Bank, L., Marlowe, J.H., Reid, J.B., Patterson, G.R., & Weinrott, M.R. (1991). Comparative evaluation of parent-training interventions for families of chronic delinquents. *Journal of Abnormal Child Psychology, 19,* 15-33.

Barkley, R.A., Guevremont, D.C., Anastopoulis, A. D., & Fletcher, K.E. (1992). A comparison of three family therapy programs for treating family conflicts of chronic delinquents. *Journal of Consulting and Clinical Psychology, 60,* 450-462.

Baumrind, D., Moselle, K., & Martin, J.A. (1985). Adolescent drug abuse research: A critical examination from a developmental perspective. *Advances in Alcohol Substance Abuse, 4,* 4-67.

Biglan, A. (1995). Translating what we know about the context of antisocial behavior into a lower prevalence of such behavior. *Journal of Applied Behavior Analysis, 28,* 479-492.

Biglan, A., Metzler, C. W., Wirt, R., Ary, D., Noell, J., Ochs, L., French, C., & Hood, D. (1990). Social and behavioral factors associated with high-risk sexual behavior among adolescents. *Journal of Behavioral Medicine, 13,* 245-261.

Block, J., Block, J.H., & Keyes, S. (1988). Longitudinally foretelling drug usage in adolescence: Early childhood personality and environmental precursors. *Child Development, 59,* 336-355.

Borduin, C.M., Mann, B.J., Cone, L.T., Heggeler, S.W., Fucci, D., Blaske, D.M., & Williams, J.R. (1995). Multisystemic treatment of serious juvenile offenders: Long term prevention of criminality and violence. *Journal of Consulting and Clinical Psychology, 63,* 569-575.

Brown, B.B., Mounts, N., Lamborn, S.D., & Steinberg, L. (1993). Parenting practices and peer group affiliation in adolescence. *Child Development, 64,* 467-482.

Cauce, A., Reid, M. Kandesmann, S. & Gonzales, N. (1990). Social support in young children: Measurement, structure, and behavioral impact. In B.R. Sarason, & I.R. Sarason (Eds.) *Social support: An interactional view* (pp. 64-94). New York, NY: John Wiley & Sons.

Chamberlain, P. (1990). Comparative evaluation of Specialized Foster Care for seriously delinquent youths: A first step. *Community Alternatives: International Journal of Family Care, 2,* 21-36.

Chamberlain, P., & Reid, J. (1991). Using a specialized foster care treatment model for children and adolescents leaving the state mental hospital. *Journal of Community Psychology, 19,* 266-276.

Clarke, G., Hops, H., Lewinsohn, P.M., Andrews, J., Seeley, J.R., & Williams, J. (1992). Cognitive-behavioral group treatment of adolescent depression: Prediction of outcome. *Behavior Therapy, 23,* 341-352.

Cohen, S. & Wills, T.A. (1985). Stress, social support, and the buffering hypothesis. *Psychological Bulletin, 98,* 310-357.

Coie, J.D. (1996). Prevention of violence and antisocial behavior. In R.S. Peters & R.J. McMahon (Eds.), *Preventing childhood disorders, substance abuse, and delinquency* (pp. 1-18). Thousand Oaks: Sage.

Dare, C., Eisler, I., Russel, G.F.M., & Szmuckler, G.I. (1990). The clinical and theoretical impact of a controlled trial of family therapy in anorexia nervosa. *Journal of Marital and Family Therapy, 16,* 39-57.

Dishion, T.J., & Andrews, D.W. (1995). Preventing escalation in problem behavior with high-risk young adolescents: Immediate and 1-year outcomes. *Journal of Consulting and Clinical Psychology, 63,* 538-548.

Dishion, T.J., & Loeber, R. (1985). Male adolescent marijuana and adolescent use: The role of parents revisited. *American Journal of Drug and Alcohol Abuse, 11,* 11-25.

Dishion, T.J., & McMahon, R.J. (1998). Parental monitoring and the prevention of child and adolescent problem behavior: A conceptual and empirical formulation. *Clinical Child and Family Psychology Review, 1,* 61-75.

Dishion, T.J., & Patterson, G.R. (1992). Age-effects in parent training outcome. *Behavior Therapy, 23,* 719-729.

Dishion, T.J., Reid, J.B., & Patterson, G.R. (1988). Empirical guidelines for a family intervention for adolescent drug use. *Journal of Chemical Dependency Treatment, 1,* 189-222.

Dishion, T.J., Patterson, G.R., Stoolmiller, M., & Skinner, M.L. (1991). Family, school, and behavioral antecedents to early adolescent involvement with antisocial peers. *Developmental Psychology, 27,* 172-180.

Dishion, T.J., Li, F., Spracklen, K., Brown, G., & Haas, E. (in press). The measurement of parenting practices in research on adolescent problem behavior: A multimethod and multitrait analysis. In R.S. Ashery (Ed.), *Research meeting on drug abuse prevention through family interventions.* (NIDA Research Monograph). Washington, DC: National Institute on Drug Abuse.

Dumas, J.E. (1989). Treating antisocial behavior in children: Child and family approaches. *Clinical Psychology Review, 1,* 197-222.

Elliott, D.S., Huizinga, D., & Ageton, S.S. (1985). *Explaining delinquency and drug use.* Beverly Hills, CA: Sage Publications.

Farrington, D.P., Loeber, R., Elliott, D.S., Hawkins, J.D., Kandel, D.B., Klein, M.W., McCord, J., Rowe, D.C., & Tremblay, R.E. (1990). Advancing knowledge about the onset of delinquency and crime. In B.B. Lahey & A.E. Kazdin (Eds.), *Clinical child psychology* (Vol. 13; pp. 283-342.). New York: Plenum.

Fletcher, A.C., Darling, N., & Steinberg, L. (1995). Parental monitoring and peer influences on adolescent substance use. In J. McCord (Ed.), *Coercion and punishment in long-term perspectives* (pp. 259-271). New York: Cambridge University Press.

Forehand, R., Miller, K.S., Dutra, R., & Chance, M.W. (1997). Role of parenting in adolescent deviant behavior: Replication across and within two ethnic groups. *Journal of Consulting and Clinical Psychology, 65,* 1036-1041.

Foster, S.L., Prinz., R.J., & O'Leary. K.D. (1983). Impact of problem-solving communication training and generalization procedures on family conflict. *Child and Family Behavior Therapy, 5,* 1-23.

Gordon, D.A., Arbuthnot, J., Gustafson, K.E., & McGreen, P. (1988). Home-based behavioral systems family therapy with disadvantaged juvenile delinquents. *The American Journal of Family Therapy, 16,* 243-255.

Gorman-Smith, D., Tolan, P.H., Zelli, A., & Huesmann, L.R. (1996). The relation of family functioning to violence among inner-city youths. *Journal of Family Psychology, 10,* 115-129.

Gray-Ray, P., & Ray, M.C. (1990). Juvenile delinquency in the black community. *Youth and Society, 22,* 67-84.

Graziano, A.M., & Diament, D.M. (1992). Parent behavioral training: An examination of the paradigm. *Behavior Modification, 16*, 13-38.

Greenwood, P.W., Model, K.E., Rydell, C.P., & Chisea, J. (1997). *Diverting children from a life of crime: Measuring costs and benefits.* Santa Monica, CA: RAND.

Hart, B. & Risley, T.R. (1975). Incidental teaching of language in the pre-school. *Journal of Applied Behavior Analysis, 8,* 411-420.

Hart, B. & Risley, T.R. (1995). *Meaningful differences in the everyday experiences of young American children.* Baltimore: Paul H. Brookes Publishing Co.

Hawkins, J.D., Catalano, R.F., & Kent L.A. (1991). Combining broadcast media and parent education to prevent teenage drug abuse. In L. Donohew, H.E. Sypher, & W.J. Bukowski (Eds.), *Persuasive communication and drug abuse prevention* (pp 283-294). Hillsdale, NJ: Erlbaum.

Hawkins, J.D., Catalano, R.F, & Miller, J.Y. (1992). Risk and protective factors for alcohol and other drug problems in adolescence and early adulthood: Implications for substance abuse prevention. *Psychological Bulletin, 112,* 64-105.

Hazelrigg, M.D., Cooper, H.M., & Borduin, C.M. (1987). Evaluating the effectiveness of family therapies: An integrative review and analysis. *Psychological Bulletin, 101,* 428-442.

Henggeler, S.W. (1989). *Delinquency in adolescence.* Newbury Park, CA: Sage.

Henggeler, S.W., Borduin, C.M, & Mann, B.J. (1993). Advances in family therapy: Empirical foundations. *Advances in Clinical Child Psychology, 15,* 207-241.

Henggler, S. W. , Schoenwald, S.K., Borduin, C.M., Rowland, M.D., & Cunningham, P.B. (1998). *Multisystemic treatment of antisocial behavior in children and adolescents.* New York: Guilford.

Irvine, A.B., Biglan, A., Smolkowski, K., Metzler, C.W. & Ary, D.V. (1999). The effectiveness of a parenting skills program for parents of middle school students in small communities. *Journal of Consulting and Clinical Psychology, 67,* 811-825.

Jacobson, N.S., & Revenstorf, D. (1988). Statistics for assessing the clinical significance of psychotherapy techniques: Issues, problems, and new developments. *Behavioral Assessment, 10,* 133-145.

Jacobson, N.S., & Truax, P. (1991). Clinical significance: A statistical approach to defining meaningful change in psychotherapy research. *Journal of Consulting and Clinical Psychology, 59,* 12-19.

Jones, R.C., Weinrott, M.R., & Howard, J.R. (1981). *The national evaluation of the Teaching Family model. Final report to the Center for Studies of Antisocial and Violent Behavior.* Bethesda, MD: National Institute of Mental Health

Kahn, J.S., Kehle, T.J., Jenson, W.R., & Clarke, E. (1990). Comparison or cognitive-behavioral relaxation, and self-monitoring interventions for depression among middle-school students. *School Psychology Review, 19,* 196-210.

Karoly, P. (1993). Mechanisms of self-regulation: A systems view. *Annual Review of Psychology, 44,* 23-52.

Kazdin, A.E. (1987). Treatment of antisocial behavior in children: Current status and future directions. *Psychological Bulletin, 102,* 187-203.

Kazdin, A.E. (1991). Effectiveness of psychotherapy with children and adolescents. *Journal of Consulting and Clinical Psychology, 59,* 785-798.

Kazdin, A.E. (1995). *Conduct disorders in childhood and adolescence* (2nd ed.). Newbury Park, CA: Sage.

Kazdin, A.E., Siegel, T.C., & Bass, D. (1992). Cognitive problem-solving skills training and parent management training in the treatment of antisocial behavior in children. *Journal of Consulting and Clinical Psychology, 60,* 733-747.

Kifer, R.E., Lewis, M.A., Green, D.R., & Phillips, E.L. (1974). Teaching predelinquent youths and their parents to negotiate conflict situations. *Journal of Applied Behavior Analysis, 7,* 357-364.

Kirigin, K.A., Braukman, C.J., Atwater, J.D., & Wolf, M.M. (1982). An evaluation of teaching (Family Achievement Place) group homes for juvenile offenders. *Journal of Applied Behavior Analysis, 15,* 11-16.

Kolko, D.J., & Kazdin, A.E. (1986). A conceptualization of fire setting in children and adolescents. *Journal of Abnormal Child Psychology, 14,* 49-61.

Kolko, D.J., & Kazdin, A.E. (1990). Matchplay and firesetting in children: Relationship to parent, marital, and family dysfunction. *Journal of Clinical Child Psychology, 19,* 229-238.

Kosterman, R., Hawkins, J.D., Spoth, R., Haggerty, K.P., & Zhu, K. (1997). Effects of a preventive parent-training intervention on observed family interactions: Proximal outcomes from Preparing for the Drug Free Years. *Journal of Community Psychology, 25,* 337-352.

Lamborn, S.D., Dornbusch, S.M., & Steinberg, L. (1996). Ethnicity and community context as moderators of the relations between family decision-making and adolescent adjustment. *Child Development, 67,* 283-301.

Lebow, J.L., & Gurman, A.S. (1995). Research assessing couple and family therapy. *Annual Review of Psychology, 46,* 27-57.

LeGrange, D., Eisler, I., Dare, C. & Russell, G.F.M. (1992). Evaluation of family treatments in adolescent anorexia nervosa: A pilot study. *International Journal of Eating Disorders, 12, 347-357.*

Lewinsohn, P.M., Clarke, G.N., Hops, H., & Andrews, J. (1990). Cognitive-behavioral treatment for depressed adolescent. *Behavior Therapy, 21,* 385-401.

Liddle, H.A., & Dakof, G.A. (1995a). Family-based treatment for adolescent drug use: State of the science. In E. Rahdert & D. Czechowicz (Eds.), *Adolescent drug abuse: Clinical assessment and therapeutic interventions* (pp. 218-254). Rockville, MD: National Institute on Drug Abuse.

Liddle, H.A., & Dakof, G.A. (1995b). Family therapy for drug abuse: Promising but not definitive efficacy evidence. *Journal of Marital and Family Therapy, 21,* 511-544.

Loeber, R., & Dishion, T.J. (1983). Early predictors of male delinquency: A review. *Psychological Bulletin, 94,* 68-99.

Loeber, R., & Stouthamer-Loeber, M. (1986). Family factors as correlates and predictors of juvenile conduct problems and delinquency. In M. Tonry & N. Morris (Eds.) *Crime and justice: An annual review of research. Vol.7.* Chicago: Chicago University Press.

Loeber, R., & Stouthamer-Loeber, M. (1987). Family interaction as antecedent to the direction of male aggressiveness. *Journal of Abnormal Social Psychology, 66,* 239-242.

Mann, B.J. & Borduin, C.M. (1991). A critical review of psychotherapy outcome studies with adolescents: 1978-1988. *Adolescence, 26,* 505-541.

McGee, R., & Williams, S. (1991). Social competence in adolescence: Preliminary findings from a longitudinal study of New Zealand 15-year-olds. *Psychiatry, 54,* 281-291.

Metzler, C.W., Biglan, A., Ary, D.V., & Li, F. (1998). The stability and validity of early adolescents' reports of parenting constructs. *Journal of Family Psychology, 12,* 600-619.

Morrissey-Kane, E. & Prinz, R.J. (1999). Engagement in child and adolescent treatment: The role of parental cognitions and attributions. *Clinical Child and Family Psychology, 3,* 183-198.

Mrazek, P.J., & Haggerty, R.J. (1994). *Reducing risks for mental disorders: Frontiers for preventive intervention research.* Washington, DC: National Academy Press.

National Institute of Mental Health. (1998). *Priorities for prevention research at NIMH.* Washington, DC: US Government Printing Office.

Patterson, G.R., & Dishion, T.J. (1985). Contributions of families and peers to delinquency. *Criminology, 23,* 63-79.

Patterson, G.R., & Stouthamer-Loeber, M. (1984). The correlation of family management practices and delinquency. *Child Development, 55,* 1299-1307.

Phillips, E.L., Phillips, E.A., Fixsen, D.L., & Wolf, M.M. (1973, June). Achievement Place: Behavior shaping works for delinquents. *Psychology Today, 7,* 75-79.

Prinz, R. (1998). Conduct disorders. In A. Bellack, & M. Hersen (Eds.), *Comprehensive clinical psychology.* London: Elsevier.

Prinz, R.J., Rosenblum, R.S., & O'Leary, K.D. (1978). Affective communication differences between distressed and non-distressed mother-adolescent dyads. *Journal of Abnormal Child Psychology, 3, 373-*383.

Ralph, A. & Sanders, M.R. (in press). *Every parents' guide to teenagers* [videotape]. Brisbane, Australia: Families International Publishing,

Reid, J.B. (1993). Prevention of conduct disorder before and after school entry: Relating interventions to developmental findings. *Development and Psychopathology, 5,* 243-262.

Risley, T.R., Clark, H.B., & Cataldo, M.F. (1976). Behavioral technology for the normal middle class family. In E.J. Mash, L.A. Hamerlynck, & L.C. Handy. (Eds.). *Behavior modification and families.* New York: Brunner/Mazel.

Robin, A.L. (1981). A controlled evaluation of problem-solving communication training with parent-adolescent conflict. *Behavior Therapy, 12,* 593-609.

Robin, A.L., Siegel, P.T., Koepke, T., Moye, A.W., & Tice, S. (1994). Family therapy versus individual therapy for adolescent females with anorexia nervosa. *Developmental and Behavioral Pediatrics, 15, 111-*116.

Robin, A.L., Kent, R., O'Leary, K.D., Foster, S.L., & Prinz, R.J. (1977). An approach to teaching parents and adolescents problem-solving communication skills: A preliminary report. *Behavior Therapy, 8,* 639-643.

Ruma, P.R., Burke, R.V., & Thompson, R.W. (1996). Group parent training: Is it effective for children of all ages? *Behavior Therapy, 27,* 159-169.

Russell, G.F.M., Szmukler, G.I., Dare, C., & Eisler, I. (1987). An evaluation of family therapy in anorexia nervosa and bulimia nervosa. *Archives of General Psychiatry, 44,* 1047-1056.

Sanders, M.R. (1996). New directions in behavioral family interventions with children. In T.H. Ollendick, & R.J. Prinz (Eds.). *Advances in Clinical Child Psychology, Vol.18.* (pp. 283-330). New York: Plenum Press.

Sanders, M.R. (1999). Triple P – Positive Parenting Program: Towards an empirically validated multi-level parenting and family support strategy for the prevention of behavior and emotional problems in children. *Clinical Child and Family Psychology Review, 2, 71-90.*

Sanders, M.R., & Dadds, M.R. (1993). *Behavioral family intervention.* Boston: Allyn & Bacon.

Schmidt, S. E., Liddle, H.A., & Dakof, G.A. (1996). Changes in parenting practices and adolescent drug abuse during multidimensional family therapy. *Journal of Family Psychology, 10,* 12-27.

Serna, L.A., Schumaker, J.B., Sherman, J.A., & Sheldon, J.B. (1991). In-home generalization of social interactions in families of adolescents with behavior problems. *Journal of Applied Behavior Analysis, 24,* 733-746.

Smith, C., & Krohn, M.D. (1995). Delinquency and family life among male adolescents: The role of ethnicity. *Journal of Youth and Adolescence, 24,* 69-93.

Steinberg, L., Fletcher, A., & Darling, N. (1994). Parental monitoring and peer influences on adolescent substance abuse. *Pediatrics, 93,* 1-5.

Stewart, C.S., & Zaenglein-Senger, M.M. (1984). Female delinquency, family problems, and parental interactions. *Social Casework: The Journal of Contemporary Social Work, 9,* 428-432.

Stokes, T.F., & Baer, D.M. (1977). An implicit technology of generalization. *Journal of Applied Behavior Analysis, 10,* 349-368.

Weintraub, K.J., & Gold, M. (1991). Monitoring and delinquency. *Criminal Behavior and Mental Health, 1,* 268-281.

Weissberg, R.P., Caplan, M., & Harwood, R.L. (1991). Promoting competent young people in competence-enhancing environments: A systems-based perspective on primary prevention. *Journal of Consulting and Clinical Psychology, 59,* 830-841.

Wills, T.A., Vaccaro, D., & McNamara, . (1992). The role of life events, family support, and competence in adolescent substance use: A test of vulnerability and protective factors. *American Journal of Community Psychology, 20,* 349-374.

Wolf, M.M., Phillips, E.L., Fixsen, D.L., Braukman, C.J., Kirigin, K.A., Willner, A.G., & Shumaker, J. (1976). Achievement Place: The teaching family model. *Child Care Quarterly, 5,* 92-103.

5

Reorientation of Service Delivery in Australia to an Early Intervention Approach

Anne O'Hanlon
Flinders University of South Australia

Robert Kosky
Adelaide University

Graham Martin
Flinders University of South Australia

Pauline Dundas
Adelaide University

Cathy Davis
Flinders University of South Australia

Anne O'Hanlon · University of Adelaide · c/o 4/86 Osmond Terrace · Norwood· South Australia 5067 · Australia.

International Perspectives on Child and Adolescent Mental Health. Volume 2: Proceedings of the Second International Conference, edited by N. N. Singh, T. H. Ollendick, and A. N. Singh. © 2002 Elsevier Science Ltd. All rights reserved.

Over a $2 billion is spent each year in Australia for mental health services (Commonwealth Department of Health and Aged Care, 2000a) and most of our current services are orientated to mature adults. However, most serious chronic psychiatric illnesses have their onset in the teenage and early adult years of life (Rey, 1992) and are often the precursor to life-long difficulties in mental health and social wellbeing. Each year in Australia, about 100,000 children and young people aged 5 to 25 years develop crippling emotional disorders and about a million more young people are seriously affected by emotional problems (Zubrick, et al., 1995). The futures of the young people affected by such conditions are placed in jeopardy, their families are stressed and there are ramifications at every level of society (Kosky & Hardy, 1992).

In 1992, the Health Ministers of the Commonwealth of Australia and the State and Territory governments recognized the need to improve conditions and services for people with mental illnesses. Together, they set up the National Mental Health Strategy as a collaborative framework for the reform of Australia's mental health services. The strategy had as its objective improvements in a number of areas. These included recognition of consumer rights, the relationship between mental health and general health sectors, the mix between hospital and community services and between preventive and curative services, the roles of primary care and non-government organizations, and the monitoring of the quality of the help provided to those in need.

One aspect of reform to claim the attention of the health ministers was the potential benefits that might come from intervening in the natural history of mental disorders as early as possible. For some authorities, an early intervention approach seemed to be a realistic way to reduce the tragic disablement so often associated with mental disorders and yet to utilize precious resources effectively (Kosky & Hardy, 1992; McGorry, et al., 1996).

However, few mental health services across Australia were geared to early intervention. In 1995-6, the Mental Health Branch, on advice from the Early Intervention Working Party of the National Strategy, established three major national projects in early intervention. These projects were: early intervention in psychotic illnesses (Early Psychosis Prevention and Intervention Centre - EPPIC), early intervention in anxiety disorders (Griffith Early Intervention Project - GEIP), and early intervention for the mental health of young people (The Australian Early Intervention Network for Mental Health in Young People -Auseinet). These projects were not entirely separate, but overlapped in various areas.

More recently, the Commonwealth Department of Health and Aged Care has developed a national action plan which outlines the policy and conceptual framework for promotion, prevention and early intervention for mental health in Australia (Commonwealth Department of

Health and Aged Care, 2000b). A companion monograph provides the theoretical and conceptual framework for the plan (Commonwealth Department of Health and Aged Care, 2000c).

As soon as an early intervention approach is adopted, it becomes apparent that more than just traditional mental health services need to be involved. General health providers, education, welfare, justice, pastoral care services and so on, are in early contact with people who are becoming unwell. These services also involve workers from many fields and professions, not just doctors and nurses. Most importantly, early intervention means a realistic and open exchange with those who are becoming ill and their carers. To develop ways to link these diverse groups and agencies was one of the challenges for Auseinet.

AUSEINET

The Australian Early Intervention Network for Mental Health in Young People (Auseinet) was originally established in 1997 to coordinate a national approach to early intervention for mental health in young people. Auseinet was jointly developed at Flinders University of South Australia and the University of Adelaide in South Australia and funded by the Commonwealth Department of Health and Aged Care under the National Mental Health Strategy and the National Youth Suicide Prevention Strategy. The Auseinet project has recently expanded to include mental health promotion and prevention, as well as early intervention, and to cover the entire lifespan. It is now known as The Australian Network for Promotion, Prevention and Early Intervention for Mental Health.

Auseinet sought to raise awareness of early intervention in a broad audience of consumers, carers and service providers and to develop and promote methods for putting early intervention principles into practice. The project had three interrelated streams: the development and maintenance of a national early intervention network; the identification and promotion of good practice in early intervention; and the reorientation of service delivery towards an early intervention approach.

The national early intervention network began in July 1997 and by December 2000 included more than 4000 individuals, agencies and organizations. The network comprises carer and consumer groups, child and adolescent mental health workers and primary health providers, as well as education, juvenile justice, family and youth services. A variety of strategies were used to develop and expand the network. Workshops were conducted in Australian states and the northern territory in order to inform people about early intervention in mental health, promote the Auseinet project and showcase local early intervention programs. Information about early intervention was also disseminated at other meetings and conferences and via media interviews.

The network was further extended by liaising with other early intervention projects and working groups and through Auseinet's function as a national clearinghouse on early intervention. Information, discussion and debate about early intervention were maintained through the Auseinet website http://auseinet.flinders.edu.au, a quarterly newsletter (Auseinetter: Auseinet 1997 - 2000) and an email discussion group einet@flinders.edu.au.

All outputs of the project can be viewed on the Auseinet website. To date, Auseinet has produced a range of books:

1. National stocktake of early intervention programs (Davis, Martin, Kosky, & O'Hanlon, 1998).
2. National stocktake of prevention and early intervention programs (Davis, Martin, Kosky, & O'Hanlon, 1999).
3. Model projects for early intervention in the mental health of young people: Reorientation of services (O'Hanlon, Kosky, Martin, Dundas, & Davis, 2000).
4. Early intervention in the mental health of young people: A literature review (Davis, Martin, Kosky & O'Hanlon, 2000).

It has also edited a series entitled Clinical approaches to early intervention in child and adolescent mental health which includes:

1. Attention deficit hyperactivity disorder in preschool aged children (Hazell, 2000).
2. Early intervention for anxiety disorders in children and adolescents (Dadds, Seinen, Roth,& Harnett, 2000).
3. Early intervention in conduct problems in children (Sanders, Gooley, & Nicholson, 2000).
4. The perinatal period: Early interventions for mental health (Kowalenko, Barnett, Fowler, & Matthey, 2000).
5. The psychological adjustment of children with chronic conditions (Swanston, Williams, & Nunn, 2000).

In this chapter, we focus on the reorientation stream of the Auseinet project by presenting an overview of some practical models for the reorientation of service delivery to early intervention. This involved reorienting a range of agencies so that they developed a deeper awareness of the natural history of symptoms over the life span and of the early onset of many emotional problems. We wanted to demonstrate how reorientation to early intervention could prevent long-term disability and ease the burdens of suffering for children, adolescents and their families. The reorientation process outlined in this chapter has been fully documented in O'Hanlon, et al. (2000).

DEFINITIONS

Early intervention

For the purposes of the Auseinet project, we drew upon Mrazek and Haggerty's (1994) mental health intervention spectrum for mental disorders. In Figure 1, the shaded segments of the spectrum indicate Auseinet's focus.

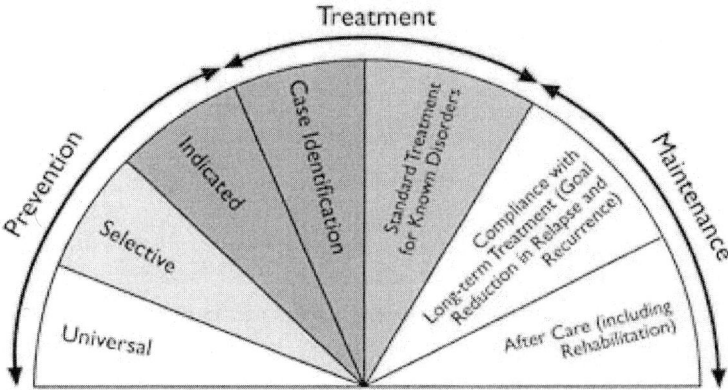

Figure 1. The mental health intervention spectrum for mental disorders (adapted from Mrazek & Haggerty, 1994).

We were interested in interventions for individuals or subgroups in the population known to be at higher than average risk of developing a mental disorder, that is, selective interventions. Examples include children of parents with a mental illness or a problem with substance abuse, children with certain medical illnesses, or young people who have been abused. They may not show signs of problems, symptoms or illnesses at the point of intervention, but are considered to be at risk.

We were also interested in indicated interventions. These are aimed at individuals known to be at high risk because they have early signs and symptoms of mental disorder, but do not meet the diagnostic criteria of a disorder. They may have a high number of risk factors for a given illness, or biological markers known to predispose to mental illness.

Finally, we were interested in case identification. This is probably the area that makes most sense to clinicians. It seems obvious to state that we should be able to identify illness at the earliest possible time. We should know what the best treatment and support programs are, and we should be clear about how to reach out and maintain access for those experiencing a first clearly defined episode of illness. We know in practice, however, that the whole area is much more complex.

During the timeframe of the Auseinet project, the definition of early intervention used by the Commonwealth Mental Health Branch and some other groups in Australia was redefined to include only indicated interventions, case identification and treatment for known disorders (i.e., where signs and symptoms of a disorder are present). Selective interventions were considered to be 'prevention' given the absence of signs and symptoms (Commonwealth Department of Health and Aged Care, 2000c).

Capacity Building

Capacity building is central to the process of reorientation. It refers to the implementation of integrated sets of strategies to enhance an organization's capacity to achieve health gains. It is most often used to refer to gains in health promotion, but we believe it can also be applied to early intervention. Ideally, capacity will be potentially sustainable in the longer term.

Agencies

The agencies described in this chapter include small support groups, community projects, non-government organizations and government departments of education, health and community services. The agencies were not necessarily primarily mental health focused, but they all provided services to a significant number of children or young people who had, or were at risk of developing, mental health problems.

REORIENTING SERVICES

Capacity Building

The reorientation of services is essentially a process of organizational change (Gray & Casey, 1995). To bring about change, an organization can build its capacity to achieve clearly specified health gains. While most of the work on 'capacity building' is found in the health promotion literature, the general principles can be applied to early intervention.

The term "capacity building" is used in different ways in the literature (Hawe, Noort, King, & Jordens, 1997). It is sometimes used simply to refer to the capacity of an organization to build an infrastructure to support particular programs, and other times to the capacity for a program to be sustained after an initial demonstration phase. It can also be used more broadly to refer to enhancing the problem solving capability of individuals, organizations and communities (Hawe, et al., 1998). It would seem that all are points on a continuum of capacity building. The first is mostly limited to immediate gains, the second relates to longer-term maintenance and sustainability, while the third is a higher order outcome in which a community develops generalized skills to tackle a range of health issues.

Given that health organizations often have scarce resources, it makes sense to build mechanisms that have the potential to be sustained in the longer-term (Hawe, et al., 1997). Health gains are more likely to be sustained if capacity building strategies involve a range of individuals and groups. These can include key staff within the organization that are responsible for keeping the health issue on the agenda, as well as senior managers, middle managers and service providers. The strategies should also involve key individuals and groups in other organizations and in the community (Gray & Casey, 1995; Lefebvre, 1992).

Sustainability is also more likely to be achieved if individuals and organizations are encouraged to take responsibility for identifying, planning and implementing their own initiatives. This may involve giving people information, training them to work differently and supporting new practices at the organizational level. In this way, the initiatives can be maintained after the removal of dedicated funding and personnel (Radoslovich & Barnett, 1998).

Strategies For Building And Sustaining Capacity

New South Wales Department of Health (1998) developed a strategic framework for building capacity within an organization. It was intended to guide health promotion activities, but we believe that it can also be applied to early intervention. The framework delineates three key components for effective capacity building and proposes strategies for each. Capacity can best be sustained by developing integrated sets of strategies across the three components.

Workforce development focuses on improving the skills and knowledge of the staff within the organization. Strategies can include continuing education, professional development and training opportunities for staff, as well as professional support and supervision. While workforce development is a vital component for building capacity, on its own it is unlikely to bring about sustainable change.

Organizational development focuses on strengthening organizational support for building capacity. Strategies include developing strategic plans and policies, ensuring management support and commitment (e.g., by involving senior managers in steering committees) and developing recognition and reward systems.

Resource allocation is listed as a separate component to organizational development in order to emphasize its importance. The organization's chances of building capacity are likely to be increased if sufficient financial and human resources and administrative support are made available and if staff members have access to information and specialist advice when required.

This framework is useful for planning and assessing capacity building within an organization. However, it is also important to develop strategies for building capacity across organizations and within the broader community (Hawe, et al., 1998). It would seem fruitful to expand each of the three components to encourage cooperation and collaboration with other organizations e.g. by combining resources to train staff, developing interagency plans and policies and pooling resources to support these endeavors.

The development of partnerships and networks, sometimes called 'healthy alliances', are vital for building and sustaining capacity (Hawe, et al., 1997; Kickbusch, 1997; Nutbeam, 1997; Radoslovich & Barnett, 1998; Scriven, 1998). Healthy alliances are driven by the needs of the health agenda and a belief that these are better achieved through joint agency activity (Douglas, 1998). There is ample evidence in the health promotion literature that partnerships between agencies, and with the community, are effective in bringing about health gains (Gillies, 1998).

Partnerships can be informal or formal. Strategies for developing informal partnerships include networking with other organizations, sharing information and working together to develop training programs. Partnerships can be formalized through strategies such as the development of shared plans, agreements and policies. A successful collaboration does not necessarily require that the parties share the same paradigm; they must, however, have a clearly defined common purpose and a shared language (Seaburn, et al., 1996). It is important to have a commitment between the leaders in both services as well as liaison individuals in each setting to provide a conduit for information and ideas (Seaburn, et al., 1996).

Measuring Capacity

Measuring the extent to which capacity has been built and sustained is particularly challenging. Reorientation is a lengthy process and many positive outcomes may not be apparent in the short term. Some modest immediate gains may have great potential to be sustained, while other promising immediate gains may not be sustained in the longer term (Hawe, et al., 1997). A long-term commitment of resources is needed to allow changes and results to become evident (Guldan, 1996). In reality, many programs are judged on their immediate outcomes rather than allowed time for their strengths to emerge.

It is therefore important to differentiate between 'output indicators' which can be assessed in the short-term and 'outcomes' which may only be apparent in the much longer term (Hawe, et al., 1997). In a relatively short reorientation phase such as ours, it was more realistic to focus on output indicators.

Gray and Casey (1995) identified a range of interrelated measures to determine the success of capacity building strategies within an organization. These include the commitment of senior management, the allocation of resources, coordination to ensure a solid infrastructure to support initiatives, increased skills across the whole organization and working with other sectors to achieve sustainable health gains. Funnell and Oldfield (1998) identified output indicators to determine the success of alliances. These include knowledge and attitude change, skill development, policy change and service and environment change.

THE REORIENTATION PROCESS

Selecting the Projects

Auseinet funded a variety of model projects in the reorientation of service delivery towards early intervention for the mental health of children and young people. Tenders were invited from agencies that wished to reorient their service but needed assistance to do so. Two hundred and thirty three agencies requested information and seventy-nine tenders were received from a diverse range of agencies from around Australia. They included mental health services, family and community services, primary health services, aboriginal services, education departments and support groups. We aimed to select a range of agencies that reflected the cultural, geographic and functional diversity of service providers across Australia.

There were several selection criteria. The agencies had to provide services to a significant number of children or young people in distress, but did not have to be primarily mental health focused. They had to demonstrate an understanding of early intervention in mental health issues and be able to show how it related to their work. It was also important that the staff of the agencies were receptive to the early intervention approach and that the agencies intended to continue to use the approach after the conclusion of the project. At a more practical level, the agencies had to demonstrate that the objectives of the project would be an effective and efficient use of resources and that they had set realistic and achievable timelines to undertake the work.

Developing the Projects

The time frame for bringing about reorientation was limited to less than one year, so we had to be realistic about the amount of change that could be achieved in that time. The overarching goal of the projects was to implement reorientation strategies that had potential to be sustained after the Auseinet project was completed.

The reorientation officers were asked to work with agency staff to maximize opportunities for and overcome barriers to reorientation and implement a tailored training program to help staff develop knowledge and skills in early intervention. They were to suggest modifications to existing policies and procedures where necessary and promote a collaborative approach to early intervention by establishing and strengthening links with other agencies. A final requirement was to evaluate the outcomes of the project in terms of staff satisfaction and increased knowledge about the mental health of the young people involved with the agency.

We put considerable energy into overseeing, supporting and guiding the reorientation process but did not want to be overly prescriptive about the methods used to achieve objectives. It was important that management and staff saw the objectives of the project as relevant to their own needs and, ultimately, the needs of their clients. Therefore, we adopted a principle throughout of collaboration and cooperation with the agencies. We believed that reorientation had to be largely self-directed if it was to succeed in the short term and be sustained beyond the timeframe of our funding.

We were also keen to foster a coordinated, team approach with the reorientation officers. For most of them, early intervention and reorientation were new concepts, so it was essential to provide support and guidance as needed. We also wanted to promote a sense of cohesion and common purpose amongst them in order to encourage the sharing of ideas and experiences, to provide support against difficulties and to counter the potential problem of geographical distance.

THE REORIENTATION PROJECTS

Model projects were established in four government agencies and four non-government agencies across Australia. Figure 2 shows the location of the eight agencies involved in the reorientation process and Table 1 shows a summary of the eight model projects. The first three columns indicate the location of the agency, the target age groups and the mental health issues addressed by the agency, and the broad outcomes that each project hoped to achieve. (The remaining three columns summarize the reorientation strategies developed by the agencies and are addressed in the discussion.)

The agencies represented a range of service types and cultures in urban and rural locations. They included a mental health service, two educational services, a primary health unit, an Aboriginal service, several community-based services and state government departments providing family and children's services. Two of the projects were collaborations between two state government departments.

Six of the agencies were regional centers, with either a rural catchment area or a rural-remote catchment area. Only two agencies were located in a capital city; one providing a statewide service and the other providing services to a small, disadvantaged community. The preponderance of rural/regional locations was largely the result of these agencies being able to demonstrate significant unmet mental health needs.

Auseinet provided funds to each agency to employ a part-time reorientation officer from late July 1998 to the end of May 1999. The first three of the agencies listed in Table 1 contributed their own funds to employ the reorientation officer full time, and therefore the projects tended to have broader objectives. The reorientation officers were all experienced in mental health work but varied in their professional backgrounds (e.g., psychology, social work, mental health nursing, education, counseling).

Early Intervention In A School Setting
Barrington Support Service, Devonport, Tasmania

The Barrington District is located on the north west coast of Tasmania. It covers an area of 3,000 square kilometres and has a population of approximately 56,000 people. The district has 19 primary schools, 7 secondary schools, a special school and an early special education center, with a total of 9,000 students. The Barrington Support Service provides resource, teaching and learning support to the schools, along with professional development programs that address the needs of school communities.

Table 1. Agency characteristics and summary of the strategies used to build capacity

Agency name and location	Mental health issues addressed by agency (target age range)	Desired outcomes	Reorientation strategies		
			Workforce development	Organizational development	Resource allocation
Government agencies					
Barrington Support Service Devonport, Tasmania	Suicide, attempted suicide and severe psychiatric disorders (5 to 18 years)	More effective ways for teachers and support staff to respond to serious mental health issues	Staff training	Policy development Formal partnerships	Position continued (in modified form)
Lower Great Southern Primary Health Service & Albany District Education Office Albany, Western Australia	Depression, anxiety and conduct problems (5 to 18 years)	Early intervention training for staff and development of a district wide interagency policy	Staff training	Policy development Formal partnerships Agency plans	Position continued
Hunter Mental Health Services & Department of Community Services Newcastle and the Lake Macquarie area, New South Wales	Children at risk because their primary care giver has a mental illness (0 to 10 years)	An effective early intervention approach for maintaining positive family environments and better outcomes for young children at risk	Staff training Resource folder Conjoint placements	Policy development Formal partnerships	Position continued (in modified form)
Child and Family Services Launceston and northern area of Tasmania	Challenging behavior among state wards and repeat offenders (10 to 18 years)	Use of early intervention to avoid admission to juvenile detention centres	Staff training Service map	Informal partnerships developed through Umbrella Group	Position not continued

Table 1 continued.

Agency name and location	Mental health issues addressed by agency (target age range)	Desired outcomes	Workforce development	Reorientation strategies	
				Organizational development	Resource allocation
Non-government Agencies					
Children of Prisoners' Support Group Sydney, New South Wales (statewide service)	Anxiety, depression, disruptive behavior in children who have a caregiver in custody (0 to 18 years)	Achievement of a positive impact on the mental health of a specific 'at risk' group	Staff training Training manual Referral list	Policy development Informal partnerships developed through Steering Committee	Funding sought for position to continue
Mildura Aboriginal Corporation Mildura and Sunraysia district, Victoria	Antisocial behavior, violence, drug and alcohol use, teenage pregnancy among at risk indigenous youth (13 to 24 years)	'From Shame to Pride' workshop developed as a culturally acceptable program to address indigenous mental health issues	Staff training Training manual	Informal partnerships through networking Commitment to further training	Funding sought for further training sessions
Karawara Community Project Perth, Western Australia	Serious conduct disorders, drug use and emotional problems (0 to 18 years)	Application of early intervention within a small community organization dealing with a multicultural and socially disadvantaged population	Staff training Management seminar Training kit	Informal partnerships developed through policy and management seminar	Position continued (in modified form)

This project was chosen to determine whether reorientation could be achieved in schools in an area where mental health services were meager. Four primary schools and two secondary schools were involved in the reorientation process. The overall objective was to help teachers and school support staff to develop the skills they needed to identify and address serious mental health issues experienced by the students.

The FRIENDS program for anxiety (Barrett, Lowry-Webster & Holmes, 1998) was run in three of the primary schools and the Resourceful Adolescent Program (RAP; Schochet, Whitefield & Holland, 1998) was run in the two secondary schools. Several other schools expressed an interest in becoming involved and additional funds were subsequently secured for this purpose.

There were significant indications of change within the Barrington Support Service and the broader educational district. Workforce development was achieved through training the teaching and specialist support staff to enhance their mental health literacy. Senior managers, teaching staff and specialist support staff demonstrated a high level of commitment to the reorientation process and a readiness to adopt early intervention principles to enhance the mental health of the young people in their schools.

Informal and formal partnerships were established. For example, Barrington Support Service and a Child and Adolescent Mental Health Service held a combined forum to examine effective interagency work practices. The forum resulted in nine recommendations, including organizational and policy changes and the Child and Adolescent Mental Health Services team made a commitment to provide ongoing access and training for Barrington Support Service personnel.

Early intervention approaches in the education sector have great potential. We consider that this project provided a useful model for applying early interventions in a school setting. It focused on training staff to be alert for signs of mental health problems and also implemented programs for two of the problems most commonly seen in young people (anxiety and depression). It was achieved at low cost and was an effective use of resources. The project has potential to be developed within the pilot schools and applied in other schools.

A Collaboration Between Health And Education Departments
Lower Great Southern Primary Health Service and Albany District Education Office
Albany, Western Australia

During 1998/99 the Lower Great Southern Primary Health Service provided public health programs in the South West and Great Southern Regions of Western Australia. These regions have a population of approximately 230,000 people and cover an area half the size of Victoria. Albany Education District is located in the Great Southern region of Western Australia, with the City of Albany at its southern-most point. The District Office in Albany provides support to the 27 Education Department schools in the district. This project was chosen because it brought together two influential government departments that were capable of having a substantial positive impact on the mental health of children and young people. The main objective of the project was to realign policies and practices in order to deliver early intervention programs for school-aged children and adolescents.

A series of Interagency Managers' Forums was convened, during which a district wide interagency policy and an implementation plan were formulated. Fourteen agencies, including Health and Education Departments of Western Australia, Ministry of Justice, Aboriginal Affairs Department, Albany Consumers Team and the Police Department, made a commitment to the policy. The project brought about a positive shift in the way the agencies thought about the services they provided to the young people of the Albany district and helped them to identify areas where they could enhance or create services. The process of collaboration highlighted that many of the agencies, although not primarily mental health focused, dealt with mental health issues on a regular basis. The project will be replicated in the Central and Upper Great Southern regions, culminating in a policy that will incorporate early intervention as a priority in all major agencies across the entire Great Southern region.

Staff of the participating agencies, as well as teachers, parents and community members, were trained in a range of topics related to mental health. They included early intervention, youth suicide prevention, depression, anxiety, early psychosis, eating disorders, attention deficit hyperactivity disorder, post-natal depression and bereavement. The training sessions were subsequently replicated with the Central Great Southern and the Upper Great Southern Health Services.

We found this to be a successful model of interagency collaboration. It brought together a broad range of services, each of which had a commitment to enhancing the mental health of young people, but in which there was previously little intercommunication. The project generated a great deal of interest not only in the Albany district but also across a large region of south Western Australia.

A Collaboration Between Mental Health And Community Services
Hunter Mental Health Services and NSW Department of Community Services
Newcastle, New South Wales

Two groups of welfare and health care professionals were involved in the project; community mental health workers from the Lake Macquarie Mental Health Service (which is part of Hunter Mental Health Service) and child protection workers from the Department of Community Services. The Lake Macquarie City Council local government area has a population of 185,000. The district incorporates the southern suburbs of the city of Newcastle as well as high growth suburbs on the eastern and western shores of Lake Macquarie.

This project was chosen because it presented an opportunity for two agencies to work together towards the common goal of providing better services for children whose primary carer has a mental illness. A systematic interagency approach had been lacking because the two agencies have different cultures, histories, professional backgrounds and a limited understanding of each other's legislative base, policies and programs. The project sought to reorient child protection casework and community mental health clinical intervention into a collaborative program in which knowledge, skills and resources were shared.

Staff from both agencies were trained in a broad range of early intervention issues. These included an overview of adult and pediatric mental illnesses, the effects of parental mental illness on parenting capacity and family functioning, methods for enhancing resilience in children in affected families, recognizing child maltreatment and intervening to protect children and principles of child protection casework using a risk assessment model. In order to correct misconceptions, information about the other agency's policies and practices was presented and discussed.

A Memorandum of Understanding was developed to facilitate collaborative casework between the Department of Community Services and the Hunter Mental Health Service. The Memorandum delineated the basis on which case coordination between the agencies would occur, the criteria for the referral of clients to the program and the respective casework responsibilities of the two agencies.

The main achievement of the project was the implementation of conjoint field placements. Child Protection Officers each spent two days on placement with the Lakes Mental Health Team and the Lakes Mental Health workers spent two days on placement in Toronto and Charlestown Community Services Centres. The placements allowed staff from the two agencies to observe everyday procedures in the other's agency, establish working relationships, and gain insight into the need for interagency collaboration. Throughout the three months of the placement process, there were numerous instances of conjoint assessments and cooperative case planning. The foundation was laid for ongoing collaboration between the Department of Community Services' Charlestown and Toronto child protection teams and Lake Macquarie Mental Health Service.

We consider that this was a good model for aligning the work practices of two services with formal, traditional structures, in which there are different philosophical bases. The conjoint placement scheme is an effective model for informing staff of the workings of other agencies. It requires commitment from managers and staff and a substantial coordination effort, but is likely to yield benefits. The initiatives have a high probability of being sustained.

Early Intervention For Children With Challenging Behaviors
Child And Family Services, Launceston, Tasmania

Child and Family Services provides protection services to children and young people who have experienced or are at risk of harm, maltreatment or neglect. In 1996-97, approximately 800 notifications were received, of which 150 were classified as "child harm and maltreatment." In the same period, the Youth Justice Services in the area worked with over 150 young people charged with offending. Many of them had been subjected to maltreatment or neglect and a significant number had mental health related problems. While many of the young people needed help to address the problems they were facing, there were no mental health services in the Northern Tasmanian region specifically to assist them. This project was chosen because it provided an opportunity to intervene in antisocial behaviors which were developing on a trajectory to detention, and therefore to avoid a lengthy, more costly and frequently less successful rehabilitation after the offending behaviors became established.

The overall objective of the project was to assist staff to address the needs of children and young people with challenging behaviors. Staff of the agency nominated the issues in which they most wanted training. These included an overview of early intervention for mental health, anger management, anxiety and depression. Information packages containing materials from the training sessions, along with resources for parents and information on good practice in early intervention, were developed as an ongoing resource.

The main product of the project was a map of services for young people in the Launceston area. These included aboriginal, migrant, health, drug and alcohol, sexual assault and student support services. The services were grouped to indicate those most relevant for problems faced by children, adolescents and parents. The map was made available to all service providers in the community sector in the region and was considered to be an invaluable resource.

An Umbrella Group was formed to sustain the momentum of the project and to further develop strategies for early intervention in mental health. It had representatives from several agencies in Launceston who made a commitment to continue promoting early intervention by involving senior management, creating protocols for early intervention referrals and providing ongoing training opportunities.

Children With A Parent In Prison
Children Of Prisoners' Support Group, Sydney, New South Wales

Children of Prisoners' Support Group is a state-wide, non-government organization located just outside the gates of the Silverwater Correctional Complex in Sydney. The organization assists children from five hundred families per year. It provides a range of direct services to children of prisoners, outside carers and imprisoned parents. These include support groups for children and carers, casework for children of imprisoned parents and their families, pre and post release service for families, and transport to take children to visit an imprisoned parent.

This agency was chosen to be part of the Auseinet project because it was a grassroots self-help organization whose staff members were in a position to identify young people at risk of developing mental health problems, but did not have any formal training in mental health issues. The overall objective of the project was to inform staff and volunteers about the mental health issues often experienced by children who have a caregiver on remand or in custody.

Training sessions were attended by staff, volunteers and transport workers from Children of Prisoners' Support Group, as well as several other organizations involved in the care of children and young people. The topics included an overview of early intervention, attention deficit hyperactivity disorder, anxiety, marijuana use, depression, sexual abuse, psychosis and postnatal depression.

Extensive networking with other services, in particular mental health services, provided an opportunity to develop referral links and resulted in greater community awareness about children of imprisoned parents and the Children of Prisoners' Support Group itself. A Steering Committee was formed with representation from Children of Prisoners' Support Group, Mulawa Welfare, Life After Prison Ministries (Anglicare), CRC Justice Support, Department of Community Services, Corrections Health Service and Department of Corrective Services.

A "Mental Health Early Intervention Policy" was designed to minimize the psychological and emotional impacts of having a parent in prison. The focus of the policy was the identification of early signs of mental health problems and strategies for effective referral and support. The policy has the potential to guide the agency in considering mental health issues in all areas of its service delivery.

A resource manual was compiled from information sheets from New South Wales Health, New South Wales Mental Health Information Service and from guest speakers and also included the mental health intervention policy. A referral list was compiled to provide details of appropriate referral services, particularly within the Western Sydney Area Health Service.

We consider that this project was a realistic approach to early intervention for a special group of children who are at risk of developing mental health problems. The agency itself does not have the resources to provide mental health services directly to the children. Instead, staff and volunteers of the agency have been skilled to identify potential problems and to refer to other services where appropriate.

A Culturally Determined Training Program
Mildura Aboriginal Corporation, Mildura, Victoria

Mildura Aboriginal Corporation is a non-government agency that was established in Mildura, Victoria approximately twelve years ago. It provides services to the Aboriginal Community in the Sunraysia District, and transient Aboriginal people from other areas. The immediate service area of Mildura Aboriginal Corporation has a population of approximately 3000 people (in New South Wales and Victoria) that increases by up to 800 people during periods of seasonal work in the district. The corporation provides a range of services to Aboriginal families, sole parents, elderly and young people. They include Health Services, Welfare Services, Family Group Home, "Warrakoo" Life Skills Rehabilitation Program, Women's Program, and Cultural Heritage Awareness Program.

The most enduring problems experienced by the indigenous community are mental health related, yet non-indigenous mental health workers typically have a very limited understanding of indigenous cultural issues. People in the local Aboriginal community have believed for some time that the criteria used to diagnose mental disorders are not sufficiently sensitive to the local indigenous culture. Mildura Aboriginal Corporation believed it was time to reframe the issue of distress among the community in terms of 'mental well-being'.

The objective of the project was to develop a training program called 'From Shame to Pride' to enhance the skills of staff and ultimately empower children and young people to cope with the social problems they face every day. The content of the workshops was determined by the needs of the community and the participants. The most pressing needs identified by the community were anger management, conflict resolution, family counseling and family mediation. The participants requested training in the assessment and support of young people and skills to deal with young people presenting with violent or challenging behaviors. Grief, suicide, racism and drug and alcohol issues were also explored during the course of the program.

Four intensive workshops each of three days duration were conducted over a 10-month period. A key feature of the program was its flexibility to allow other issues to be addressed as they arose. Issues were explored through a range of techniques such as role-play, meditation, sharing of stories, and the discussion of real life scenarios. The participants felt very strongly that future training programs should be 'owned' by them as an indigenous group. They wanted training programs to be tailored to the needs of the group, to be 'hands on' and practical and conducted in small groups over a number of short training periods.

The group demonstrated a high level of commitment to the program right through to the final session. Previous training programs undertaken by the Mildura Aboriginal Corporation (and many other indigenous organizations) had an anticipated attendance of 40% for the first day, and 10% for the second day. Very few programs would be attempted over a three-day period. The 'From Shame to Pride' program appears to have overcome the problem of attrition by providing an interesting and culturally appropriate program which allowed the participants to develop skills, confidence and self esteem.

We consider that this project can be viewed as a culturally appropriate, alternative model for this specific community. The project was an effective use of resources and achieved impressive results within a short timeframe and with limited funds. The strength of the project was the consultation with the community to find an appropriate training program and the flexibility to respond to the ongoing needs of the participants. It is an example of what can be achieved within an indigenous community but, given their heterogeneity, should not be viewed as a model which can necessarily be replicated in other communities.

A Multicultural Community Project
Karawara Community Project, Perth, Western Australia

Karawara Community Project is a non-government community agency situated in the last large housing development in Perth. This community has a large indigenous population and a transient population of migrant people, many of whom have recently arrived from places where they have experienced war or privation. The Karawara district has a high level of poverty and many families and individuals who struggle against disadvantage. Many of the young people who make use of Karawara Community Project facilities are reluctant to use the public system because of previous bad experiences, cultural and language barriers and suspicion of authority.

Karawara Community Project is run by a committee of community representatives and has a staff of about 16 people, most of whom are part time or volunteer.

Karawara Community Project was chosen because it was a community-based organization working in an area of severe disadvantage with a multicultural population. It had developed a safe haven in which children and families could develop better interpersonal and social skills. Through this project, Karawara Community Project hoped to enrich their work by concentrating on mental health issues. They sought to raising awareness of early intervention, extend networks and provide training in early intervention to staff and volunteers.

Raising awareness of early intervention was achieved through presentations to the staff at the Karawara Community Project, the Rotary Club and the Western Australian Welfare Association and site visits to other agencies. Education on early intervention was targeted at managers of other agencies via a "Policy and Management Seminar." It included a discussion of current practice, early intervention programs and strategies for accessing funds and developing special interest groups.

Informal partnerships were strengthened with Disability Services Commission, Family and Children's Services, Aboriginal Medical Service, Clontarf Aboriginal College, Marmooditj Aboriginal Service and Lady Gowrie Community Centre. A Steering Committee was formed to support the project and facilitate the spread of information through the network. It had representatives from Juvenile Justice, Community Health (including the Bentley Mental Health Unit) Education Department, Family and Children's Services, Southcare, Lady Gowrie Community House, Uniting Church, Youth Affairs Council and Karawara Community Project.

A training kit entitled 'Early Intervention Assessment Schedule for Young People' (EiASY-P) was developed for staff and volunteers with no formal mental health training. The kit was designed to guide the recognition of young people who might be at risk of developing, or already displayed signs of, mental health problems. The kit contained background information on early intervention in mental health and an assessment proforma covering normal development, psychosocial problems, internalizing/externalizing disorders and psychotic disorders. It also contained information on what to do after assessment (e.g. monitoring, referral and emergency response).

The project was conducted under challenging circumstances. We consider that this project has a valuable lesson for what can be achieved in a small community setting with limited resources, i.e. that reorientation needs time to develop. Interest in the project, outside the host agency, was initially slow but gathered momentum and credibility when the EiASY-P kit was developed.

A Rural And Remote Welfare Organization
Anglicare CQ, Rockhampton, Central Queensland

Anglicare was established in 1983 as a non-government family welfare agency auspiced under the Anglican Church. The agency provides individual and group support and intervention services for families at risk of social disintegration and family breakdown. Since 1989, Anglicare has established a network of centers and services in Central Queensland, covering a geographical region of 600,000 square kilometres with approximately 250,000 residents. Anglicare provides a range of services across Central Queensland. These included rural and isolated accommodation services, family and adolescent counseling and support services, foster care provider services, childcare services, youth information and referral services, mental health information and referral services, Aboriginal welfare and mental health community development.

This agency was chosen because it was part of a large, stable non-government organization with a rural and remote focus. It afforded an opportunity to determine whether reorientation to early intervention could be achieved across a vast geographical area. The overall objective of the project was to reorient Anglicare staff and key personnel in other agencies to an early intervention approach to mental health.

A two-stage training program was developed through consultation with the Child and Youth Mental Health Service, Rockhampton District Mental Health Service, Central Queensland University and the Rural Health Training Unit. The participants were assisted to develop an awareness of their role in mental health and to develop an understanding of early intervention. The session covered information on mental illness and the identification of early warning signs in young people. The participants identified depression, anxiety and suicide as the most pressing issues for further training and these became the key focus for the next stage of training.

The second stage of training was presented in two regional locations (Gladstone and Rockhampton). The aim was to build upon the skills and knowledge developed in the first stage, with particular emphasis on responding to depression, anxiety and suicide. Techniques used in the training session included intensive small group discussions of each of these mental health issues, large group discussion to clarify facts and in-depth analysis using case scenarios. Training manuals were developed for both stages of the training program and provided a detailed record for future use. An information kit was designed to assist workers to understand and respond to young people with mental health problems. The kit contained information sheets on a range of disorders, service brochures and a list of resources and internet sites.

We consider that this was an appropriate model for reorienting services in a large organization spanning a vast geographical area. The project was realistically limited to improving the mental health literacy of staff who have contact with young people.

DISCUSSION

Overview of strategies

An overview of the model projects, including a summary of the strategies used by each of the agencies to build capacity is shown in Table 1. The summary of strategies follows the framework developed by the New South Wales Department of Health (1998) that was outlined earlier.

All agencies made workforce development, in the form of staff training and development, the foundation of their reorientation process. As most of the agencies were not primarily mental health focused, enhancing the mental health literacy of staff was a vital first step in reorientation. The smaller agencies in particular were less likely to have staff with the qualifications needed to conduct early interventions directly with young people. These projects more realistically aimed to inform staff about the mental health issues faced by the young people who used their service, gave them the skills to recognize risk factors and early warning signs and established procedures for appropriate referral.

For most of the projects, a record of the training program and a resource package were prepared. These should be valuable reference sources for staff and a useful guide for future training programs. Several of the projects also prepared practical documents for future use in the agency, including referral procedures (e.g., Children of Prisoners' Support Group and Karawara Community Project) and a map of local services for young people (Child and Family Services).

All of the projects showed evidence of organizational development in the form of management commitment, informal partnerships, formal partnerships and policy development. Management support was demonstrated by the formation of steering committees (e.g., Children of Prisoners' Support Group) and reference groups (e.g., Anglicare CQ) to guide the progress of the projects and the formation of an umbrella group to continue the work in early intervention (Child and Family Services).

The development of partnerships was one of the most successful aspects of the model projects. All of the agencies successfully established informal partnerships with others in the local area. The training sessions were an important strategy for developing informal partnerships and networks. Most of the agencies included guest speakers and staff from other agencies in their training programs, thereby establishing new networks or strengthening existing ones. Some of the smaller agencies (e.g., Children of Prisoners' Support Group and Karawara Community Project) found this had the added benefit of raising their profile in the community. Some of the agencies (e.g., Mildura Aboriginal Corporation and the Primary Health and Education Department collaboration) actively sought to promote their projects by informing the broader community about the initiatives they were developing.

Several of the projects developed successful formal partnerships. Two of the larger projects were collaborations between influential agencies. Both had the resources to allow the projects to expand beyond their original scope. For example, the Primary Health and Education Department collaboration in Albany expanded to include more agencies in the interagency agreement than had originally been planned and several other groups were included in the training program. The Hunter Mental Health and Department of Community Services project was able to cement its collaboration by developing the conjoint field placement program. This was an unplanned initiative, but became one of most significant achievements of the project. Barrington Support Service also developed partnerships with its six pilot schools and was flexible enough to be able to respond to the unexpected number of young people identified in the screenings for anxiety or depression.

Policy development occurred within individual agencies as well as between agencies. The two collaborative projects (Primary Health and Education Department, Albany; Hunter Mental Health and Department of Community Services, Newcastle) formalized their working relationships and future directions by developing interagency agreements and policies. Children of Prisoners' Support Group developed an early intervention policy outlining referral and support mechanisms and two other agencies developed recommendations for incorporating early intervention into new policies (Barrington Support Service and Anglicare).

All of the agencies allocated resources to the projects and several of the larger agencies contributed additional funds to employ the reorientation officer full time. After our funding phase had finished, most of the agencies had allocated funds to maintain the reorientation position. Several of the agencies continued the position in much the same form so that training programs can be completed or replicated (e.g. Barrington Support Service and the Primary Health and Education Department collaboration). Others modified the position to take the reorientation process in a new direction, such as combining staff training with direct intervention work with young people (e.g. the Hunter Mental Health and Department of Community Services collaboration and Karawara Community Project).

In summary, there were many indicators of change within the agencies, including the commitment of management and staff, the allocation of resources and the skilling of staff in early intervention approaches to mental health. There were also indicators of successful alliances, including informal networking, formal partnerships and policy development.

Commonalities

We consider that the projects we have described have certain elements in common. They shared a sense of being at the edge of the developments in the provision of mental health services to young people. There was an excitement generated by this knowledge that transcended the different styles and objectives of the agencies and which brought the reorientation workers together. All of the projects were multidisciplinary in approach and expertise, and they all involved close collaborations between the mental health disciplines. Clear targets and objectives helped this collaboration.

The projects all took an ecological view of mental health, that is, they all considered the real life circumstances of the young person. All attempted to link with other human services in the public and private sector and thereby to diminish the barriers to access that are sometimes encountered by people in the early stages of mental health problems. This overall approach seems to us to contrast with most traditional styles of mental health service delivery, which often seem to be developed in isolation. We think that the way forward in mental health service delivery may be through the development of partnerships with the many people who are concerned about children and young people. We do recognize that curative, personal treatment approaches and rehabilitation would continue to play an important role.

There were also differences between the agencies that participated in the reorientation process. The larger agencies, which were supported by government departments (e.g. the Hunter Mental Health and Department of Community Services collaboration) or by non-government organizations (e.g., Anglicare CQ), were able to provide more infrastructure support for the reorientation officer, and most of them contributed additional funds to employ the reorientation officer on a full time basis. The smaller agencies (e.g., Children of Prisoners' Support Group) typically could not provide this extra support and the reorientation officer was usually employed just over half time.

The projects that were conducted in the larger, government agencies typically had a broader range of objectives than did those in the smaller, non-government agencies. This is not to denigrate the achievements of the smaller projects; we believe that the scope of each project represented a realistic appraisal of what could be achieved with the resources available to the agency. It is worth noting, however, that most of the projects achieved more than was originally envisaged.

Opportunities For And Barriers To Early Intervention

The most commonly identified opportunity for reorientation was the positive commitment of the managers and staff of the agencies. Some of the reorientation officers in the non-government agencies saw the opportunity to increase the skill levels of staff as an essential component of the reorientation process. Several of the reorientation officers in the government agencies felt that they were able to capitalize upon a burgeoning climate of acceptance of early intervention in their region. Overall, the reorientation officers in the government agencies identified more opportunities than those in the non-government agencies.

We consider that there were many other opportunities for reorientation to an early intervention approach. The early intervention approach may give professionals who are enthusiastic and knowledgeable about the mental health of young people the opportunity to be innovative in their approach to clinical work. The early intervention approach also has the potential to involve consumers and carers in the development, running and evaluation of projects. In doing so, some practical matters relating to access can be addressed (e.g. transportation and childcare, cultural sensitivity and language barriers).

The early intervention approach tends to include people who are sometimes overlooked, for example the families of people who have a mental illness or children who have a parent in prison. The approach may present an opportunity to define more clearly what target areas are important in the public health approach to mental health. The early intervention approach may also play a role in destigmatizing mental health problems. This could be achieved by incorporating mental health issues into ordinary community services (e.g., Karawara Community Project has early intervention programs housed together with childcare and playgroup facilities).

There were opportunities to strengthen links with other agencies and groups, for example by departments working together to achieve commonly agreed objectives and to develop protocols with wide acceptance. There were indications of public support for the projects and some of the models (e.g. the Primary Health and Education Department collaboration in Albany) have already been taken up by other groups.

The biggest barrier to reorientation was the heavy workloads of mental health professionals in the host agency and in the other collaborating agencies. Despite these being discreet projects, it seemed that it was often impossible to prevent the demands on the staff's time and attention coming from many other sources. Several of the reorientation officers found that some staff were initially reluctant to be involved in the reorientation projects because of their already heavy workloads. Generally, the reluctance was short-lived; as staff became involved in the training they tended to become enthusiastic about the project and prioritized their time to enable greater involvement in the project.

The reorientation officers also commented on the demands of their own workloads. Most felt that they had insufficient time in which to achieve the objectives of the project. Several of the reorientation officers in the non-government agencies especially found their workload demanding because they were generally employed on a part-time basis. Most commented that they thought that the resources devoted to the project by the organization were insufficient.

One of the difficulties that we faced was that our central aim was to train staff and not to provide direct clinical services. However, when knowledge of the early intervention objectives of the projects became known throughout the community, often through newspaper, radio and television, unrealistic expectations were inadvertently developed. Some of those in the government agencies felt that as the projects became more widely known in the community, there was a strong tendency for greater demands to be put on the project staff. Not all these demands could be met, which sometimes was a source of frustration to the agency staff.

FUTURE DIRECTIONS

Evaluation

At the time of writing, the projects have not yet been fully evaluated for their effectiveness. However, the projects have been well documented by the groups involved and they have been highly accountable to their parent organizations and to Auseinet. The reorientation officers evaluated staff attitudes and knowledge about early intervention and mental health issues, as well as the process and content of the training sessions (see O'Hanlon, et al., 2000). In all cases, there were encouraging signs of effectively achieving their objectives. External evaluators, who spoke with the reorientation officers and their agency supervisors on several occasions during the project, also evaluated the projects, again with promising results.

We believe that there is potential to replicate and extend the projects, and to develop better forms of evaluation that could, for example, more fully address the needs of consumers and carers. Evaluations of this type have the potential to produce accountable programs that, in turn, could give administrators flexibility in their service delivery, (e.g. by moving scarce resources to programs in which effectiveness can be demonstrated).

Sustainability

Various strategies were used to enhance the likelihood of sustainability. These included establishing umbrella groups, developing formal and informal partnerships, developing new or modifying existing early intervention policies and replicating the project in other regions. Most of the reorientation officers left detailed records of the strategies developed throughout the process (e.g., final reports, training manuals, resource folders and referral lists).

We are not yet in a position to determine the extent to which the strategies for change have been sustained. Hawe, et al., (1997) describe two broad indicators of sustainability. The first is the extent to which initiatives and programs have been absorbed into the everyday practice of the organization, after dedicated funding has ceased. The second indicator is the extent to which initiatives and programs have been adopted by other organizations. Both of these indicators are difficult to measure in the short term. While we were able to make an objective judgment of the potential of the different strategies to be sustained (see O'Hanlon, et al., 2000 for details), longer-term outcomes need to be assessed. In December 2000, the Auseinet project received substantial funding to continue for a further two years. Follow up measurement of the reorientation projects is scheduled to commence in mid 2001.

REFERENCES

Auseinet (1997-2000). *Auseinetter, Issues 1-11.* Adelaide: The Australian Early Intervention for Mental Health in Young People.

Barrett, P., Lowry-Webster, H., & Holmes, J. (1998). *The FRIENDS programme.* Brisbane: Australian Academic Press.

Commonwealth Department of Health and Family Services. (1997). *Fourth annual report: Changes in Australia's mental health services under the National Mental Health Strategy 1995-96.* Canberra: Commonwealth Department of Health and Family Services.

Commonwealth Department of Health and Aged Care. (2000a). National Mental Health Report 2000: Sixth annual report: Changes in Australia's mental health services under the First Mental Health Plan of the National Mental Health Strategy 1993-98. Canberra: Commonwealth Department of Health and Aged Care.

Commonwealth Department of Health and Aged Care. (2000b). *National action plan for promotion, prevention and early intervention for mental health.* Canberra: Mental Health and Special Programs Branch, Commonwealth Department of Health and Aged Care.

Commonwealth Department of Health and Aged Care. (2000c). *Promotion, prevention and early intervention for mental health: A monograph.* Canberra: Mental Health and Special Programs Branch, Commonwealth Department of Health and Aged Care.

Dadds, M., Seinen, A., Roth, J. & Harnett, P. (2000). Early intervention for anxiety disorders in children and adolescents. In R. Kosky, A. O'Hanlon, G. Martin, & C. Davis (Series Eds.), *Clinical approaches to early intervention in child and adolescent mental health.* Adelaide: Australian Early Intervention Network for Mental Health in Young People.

Davis, C., Martin, G., Kosky, R., & O'Hanlon, A. (1998). *National stocktake of early intervention programs.* Adelaide: The Australian Early Intervention for Mental Health in Young People.

Davis, C., Martin, G., Kosky, R., & O'Hanlon, A. (1999). *National stocktake of prevention and early intervention programs.* Adelaide: The Australian Early Intervention for Mental Health in Young People.

Davis, C., Martin, G., Kosky, R., & O'Hanlon, A. (2000). *Early intervention in the mental health of young people: A literature review.* Adelaide: The Australian Early Intervention Network for Mental Health in Young People.

Douglas, R. (1998). A framework for health alliances. In A. Sriven (Ed.), *Alliances in health promotion.* London: Macmillan.

Funnell, R & Oldfield, K. (1998). An evaluation tool for the self-assessment of healthy alliances. In A. Scriven (Ed.), *Alliances in health promotion.* London: Macmillan.

Gillies, P. (1998). Effectiveness of alliances and partnerships for health promotion. Health *Promotion International, 13,* 99-120.

Gray, E., & Casey, L. (1995, June). *Building capacity for health gains in two Australian settings.* Paper presented to 3rd International Health Promoting Hospitals Conference, Linkoping, Sweden.

Guldan, G. (1996). Obstacles to community health promotion. *Social Science and Medicine, 43,* 689-695.

Hawe, P., King, L., Noort, M., Gifford, S., & Lloyd, B. (1998). Working invisibly: health workers talk about capacity building in health promotion. *Health Promotion International, 13,* 285-295.

Hawe, P., Noort, M., King, L., & Jordens, C. (1997). Multiplying health gains: the critical role of capacity building within health promotion programs. *Health Policy, 39,* 29-42.

Hazell, P. (2000). Attention deficit hyperactivity disorder in preschool aged children. In R. Kosky, A. O'Hanlon, G. Martin, & C. Davis (Series Eds.), *Clinical approaches to early intervention in child and adolescent mental health (Vol. 1).* Adelaide: Australian Early Intervention Network for Mental Health in Young People.

Kickbusch, I. (1997). Health promoting environments: the next steps. *Australian and New Zealand Journal of Public Health, 21,* 431-434.

Kosky, R., & Hardy, J. (1992). Mental health: Is early intervention the key? *The Medical Journal of Australia, 156,* 147-8.

Kowalenko, N., Barnett, B., Fowler, C., & Matthey, S. (2000). The perinatal period: early interventions for mental health. In R. Kosky, A. O'Hanlon, G. Martin, & C. Davis (Series Eds.), *Clinical approaches to early intervention in child and adolescent mental health (Vol. 4).* Adelaide: Australian Early Intervention Network for Mental Health in Young People.

Lefebvre, R. C. (1992). Sustainability of health promotion programs. *Health Promotion International, 7,* 239-240.

McGorry, P.D., Edwards, J., Mihalopoulos, C., Harrigan, S.M. & Jackson, H.J. (1996). EPPIC: An evolving system of early detection and optimal management. *Schizophrenia Bulletin, 22,* 305-326.

Mrazek, P.J., & Haggerty, R.J. (1994). *Reducing risks for mental disorders: Frontiers for intervention research.* Washington: National Academy Press.

New South Wales Department of Health (1998). How to apply capacity building to health promotion action: A framework for the development of strategies. *The Health Promotion Strategies Unit.*

Nutbeam, D. (1997). Creating health promoting environments: overcoming barriers to action. *Australian and New Zealand Journal of Public Health, 21,* 355-359.

O'Hanlon, A., Kosky, R., Martin, G., Dundas, P., & Davis, C. (2000). *Model projects for early intervention in the mental health of young people: Reorientation of services.* Adelaide: The Australian Early Intervention Network for Children and Young People.

Radoslovich, H. & Barnett, K. (1998). *Making the move.* Adelaide: South Australian Department of Human Services.

Rey, J. (1992). The Epidemiologic Catchment Area (ECA) study: Implications for Australia. *Medical Journal of Australia, 156,* 200-203.

Schochet, I., Whitefield, K. & Holland, D. (1998). *The resourceful adolescent programme.* Brisbane: Griffith University.

Scriven, A. (1998). *Alliances in health promotion.* London: Macmillan Press Ltd.

Seaburn, D., Lorenz, A, Gunn, B., Gawinski, B. & Mauksch, L. (1996). Models of collaboration: A guide for mental health professionals working with health care practitioners. New York: BasicBooks.

Sanders, M.R., Gooley, S., & Nicholson, J. (2000). Early intervention in conduct problems in children. Vol. 3 in R. Kosky, A. O'Hanlon, G. Martin, & C. Davis (Series Eds.), *Clinical approaches to early intervention in child and adolescent mental health (Vol. 3).* Adelaide: Australian Early Intervention Network for Mental Health in Young People.

Swanston, H., Williams, K. & Nunn, K. (2000). The psychological adjustment of children with chronic conditions. Vol. 5 in R. Kosky, A. O'Hanlon, G. Martin & C. Davis (Series Eds.), *Clinical approaches to early intervention in child and adolescent mental health (Vol. 5).* Adelaide: Australian Early Intervention Network for Mental Health in Young People.

Zubrick S.R., Silburn S.R., Garton A., Burton, P., Dalby, R., Carlton, J., Shepherd, C. & Lawrence, D. (1995). *Western Australian child health survey: Developing health and well being in the nineties.* Perth, Western Australia: Australian Bureau of Statistics and Institute for Child Health Research.

6

Mitigating the Effects of War and Displacement on Children

William Yule
University of London Institute of Psychiatry

William Yule · University of London Institute of Psychiatry · Institute of Psychiatry de Crespigny Park · London SE5 8AF· United Kingdom

International Perspectives on Child and Adolescent Mental Health. Volume 2: Proceedings of the Second International Conference, edited by N. N. Singh, T. H. Ollendick, and A. N. Singh. © 2002 Elsevier Science Ltd. All rights reserved.

Since the end of World War II in 1945, it has been estimated that there have been more than 127 other wars with between 21.8 million and 40 million deaths.   In addition to this slaughter, such conflicts have resulted in many refugees and displaced people worldwide. Since the ending of the "cold war" between the superpowers, the world is now realizing that there are many local wars that give rise to real misery.   The rise in nationalism and the civil wars associated with tribalism throughout the world are characterized by vicious targeting of the civilian population. UNICEF recently estimated that over 80% of the victims of today's warfare are women and children.   Civilian populations are deliberately targeted; "ethnic cleansing" and massacres are almost commonplace; populations are held hostage and under siege; even international economic sanctions are used as weapons in the struggles.

Whether it is in Vietnam, Cambodia, Rwanda or Bosnia, these modern wars result in many families with young children fleeing for safety.   "Ethnic cleansing" in Yugoslavia deliberately caused hundreds of thousands of people to leave the places they grew up in and try to get refuge elsewhere. Simply to escape the fighting and risk of reprisal, people uproot and seek safety in other countries. The result is that it has been estimated that there are over 19 million people who are refugees (within the formal meaning of the term as defined by the 1951 UN Convention) with a further 27 million people living in refugee-like situations and 25 million being internally displaced but not having crossed any international border (Rutter, 1994). It does not take much imagination to think of the experiences children may have had in fleeing from their homes under threat, witnessing fighting and destruction, seeing violent acts directed at their loved ones, leaving their friends and possessions behind, marching or being transported in crowded vehicles, spending months in transit camps and eventually finding temporary respite in a country at peace while the authorities decide whether the family can be granted permission to remain legally and indefinitely.

Put this way, it can be seen that the experiences that many refugee children have faced are contrary to what most people consider to be the basic needs of every child: the need for continuity of care by a loved one; the need for shelter and food; the need for safety and security; the need for good schooling. All these are compromised. One has only to read the Declaration of Amsterdam - The Declaration and Recommendations on the Rights of Children in Armed Conflict adopted by consensus at a meeting in Amsterdam on 21 June 1994 (Aldrich & van Baarda, 1994) to appreciate how difficult it becomes to meet the needs of children displaced in such dreadful circumstances.

At present, there seems to be no end to the number of bitter local wars that result in children being displaced from their homes, with or without their families. Despite the apparent hardening of attitudes in many western countries towards refugees and asylum seekers, 50% of refugees are to be found in the Middle East and South Asia, 30% in Africa, 10% in North America and only 4% in Europe.

Even so, this means that most Western European countries have a sizeable number of refugee children living within them, and the United Kingdom is no exception. Most large cities have known refugee communities within them, and in London, there can be scarcely a school that does not have some refugee children on roll. The educational needs of these children have been recognized for a long time (Rutter, 1994), even if they are not always adequately met. Meeting the child's educational needs and providing a semblance of stability into part of their daily life is an important aspect of meeting their overall mental health needs.

In addition to the duties laid on member states by the United Nations in relation to refugees, the UN Convention on the Rights of Children specifically recognizes that a child has a right not to be separated from its parents (Article 9); a right of access to healthcare (Article 24); a right to education (Article 28). Article 38 states inter alia that "States parties shall take all feasible measures to ensure protection and care of children affected by armed conflict". More specifically, Article 39 states:

> "States parties shall take all appropriate measures to promote physical and psychological recovery and social reintegration of a child victim of any form of neglect, exploitation or abuse; torture or any other form of cruel, inhuman, or degrading treatment or punishment; or armed conflict. Such recovery and reintegration shall take place in an environment which fosters the health, self-respect and dignity of the child".

In 1996, the report of the UN Secretary General on the Impact of Armed Conflict on Children (The Machel Report) took evidence from many war-affected countries around the world. It reiterated strongly that psychological recovery and social reintegration must be a central feature of all humanitarian programs. It acknowledged that all such programs that aim to alleviate psychological suffering must take into account the social and cultural context of the children and their families (Report of Programme Workshop in the Area of Psychosocial Care and Protection, Nyeri, Kenya: 2-6 September 1998: UNICEF).

Currently, there is increased interest in ensuring that such psychosocial programs delivered as part of humanitarian responses to war and natural disasters should be based on evidence based practice. A joint working party between the International Society for Traumatic

Stress Studies and the United Nations will shortly report on current views on the best ways to mitigate the effects of war and disasters on all those affected – adults, UN personnel, and children.

This chapter will examine some of the responses of refugee children to their losses and the traumatic events that have befallen them, and examines some of the ways that education, health and social services can work with other community based agencies to provide emotional support to refugee children.

Stress Reactions in Children

Given the sorts of frightening experiences that children may experience during war and migration, one can expect to find a wide range of psychopathological reactions among them. Many of these will be normal reactions that respond to reassurance and a return to normal living conditions. But other reactions will be associated with considerable, disabling and chronic distress.

I have described in detail elsewhere the reactions of children and adolescents surviving life-threatening disasters (Yule, 1992; Yule & Williams, 1990). They show a wide range of symptoms which tend to cluster around signs of re-experiencing the traumatic event, trying to avoid dealing with the emotions that this gives rise to, and a range of signs of increased physiological arousal. There may be considerable co-morbidity with depression, generalized anxiety or pathological grief reactions. Some of the reactions are summarized in Table 1.

Table 1.   Stress Reactions in Children

- Sleep Disturbance
- Separation Difficulties
- Concentration Difficulties
- Memory Problems
- Intrusive Thoughts
- Difficulties Talking with Parents and /or Friends
- Heightened Alertness to Dangers
- Premature Awareness of Mortality
- Fears
- Irritability
- Anxiety and Panic
- Depression
- Bereavement

It was not until the persisting problems of Vietnam veterans were better documented that it was realized that three major groups of symptoms – distressing recurring recollections of the traumatic event; avoidance of stimuli associated with the trauma; and a range of signs of increased physiological arousal – formed a coherent syndrome that came to be labeled Post Traumatic Stress Disorder (PTSD)(APA, 1980; Horowitz, 1976).   PTSD is classified in formal psychiatric diagnostic schemes as an anxiety disorder.   It was increasingly described as "a normal reaction to an abnormal situation," and so, logically, it was queried whether it should be regarded as a psychiatric disorder at all (O'Donohue & Eliot, 1992).   Indeed, debate still rages as to whether such a "disorder" can legitimately be diagnosed in people from different cultures.   However, for present purposes, it provides a useful framework within which to examine children's reactions to major stressors.

It is, of course, not only the "objective" nature of the stressful experience that matters, but also how the child subjectively interprets that experience.   There can be wide individual differences in reactions to what, to the outsider, may appear to be very similar experiences.   There have been relatively few studies of the effects of major trauma on children so that the full range of post-traumatic symptoms and their prevalence at different ages are not clearly established.   The Psychiatric classificatory systems of the American Psychiatric Association (1994; The Diagnostic and Statistical Manual or DSM) and the World Health Organization's International Classification of Diseases (1994, ICD) both provide diagnostic criteria that have been valuable in focusing the attention of researchers and clinicians on the disorder, but there is still a need for careful descriptive studies of representative groups of traumatized children to establish the natural history of the disorder in children.   In particular, there is a need to examine the ways in which major stress reactions manifest in young, pre-school children (Almqvist & Brandell-Forsberg, 1997; Scheeringa, Zeanah, Drell, & Larrieu, 1995).

Incidence of PTSD in Children

When PTSD was first recognized among adults, there was considerable skepticism as to whether such a disorder could be said to exist in children and adolescents.   However, once the children themselves were asked about their subjective reactions to major stressors, it was soon apparent that PTSD could be a significant outcome in a sizeable minority of children.

We are now beginning to get better estimates of the incidence of PTSD in children and adolescents following specific events as the ways of assessing and diagnosing are improving.   Pynoos, et al. (1987) examined the occurrence of PTSD in 159 children one month after an attack by a sniper on their school playground.   77% of the children in the directly threatened group developed moderate to severe PTSD. Following the sinking of the cruise ship, "Jupiter", half the adolescents developed PTSD with many more having sub-threshold disorders (Yule, et al., 2000).

Following our pilot study of the incidence of PTSD among children presenting at Accident & Emergency following road traffic accidents (Canterbury, Yule, & Glucksman, 1993), there have been five other British studies that have closely followed our methodology (Yule, 2000). Overall, they report that around 33% of children who experience an RTA but who are not so seriously ill as to have lost consciousness go on to develop PTSD -- a sizeable and previously unrecognized pool of psychopathology.

In addition, there is now good evidence from both civilian and war studies for a strong exposure - effect relationship (Yule, 1998). There is also cumulative evidence that different types of traumatic event have different potential for causing PTSD. Thus, overall we now know that PTSD can be a common reaction after a life-threatening event. But what of its' natural history?

Natural History

There are very few longitudinal studies that indicate the natural history of PTSD in children and adolescents. Our seven years follow-up study of adolescents who survived the sinking of the cruise ship Jupiter in 1988 compared approximately 200 of the survivors with about 100 controls (Bolton, et al, 2000). We found that 52% of the survivors developed PTSD, mainly in the first 4-6 weeks after the sinking. A few developed it later - often on the anniversary - but these were mainly just sub-threshold earlier. So we can agree with the adult literature in finding that in civilian disasters (as opposed to the Vietnam War) delayed onset PTSD is rare.

Fifteen percent of the survivors still met criteria for a diagnosis of PTSD at the end of the 7 years and so PTSD is neither a rare nor a minor consequence of a single acute traumatic event. And, PTSD was not the only symptom; significant depressions were also sparked off by the trauma.

While an increasing number of cross-sectional studies of children and war are beginning to be published, there are scarcely any longitudinal studies that address the question of how the sort of chronic, repeated trauma associated with war affect children long term. Again, such studies are badly needed.

Treatment of Stress Reactions in Children

Enough is known about the effects of war and disasters on children to know that the total needs for psychosocial assistance will far exceed the normally available resources. In major disasters, the physical and social infrastructure may be destroyed. In the aftermath of war, there may be few if any child mental health professionals left to deliver services. Ways need to be found to deliver low-cost but effective interventions to many children. This, of course, lies behind the philosophy of the World Health Organization when it advises that good mental health services should be community based, accessible and non-stigmatizing. Ideally, there should be community-based services promoting good mental health and so there should be less need of expensive (in terms of human resources needed for delivery) individual therapies.

It needs to be said that whatever services are developed, they should be evidence based – even where the evidence base is far from complete. Thus, ironically, we know a great deal more about treating stress reactions in individuals and in small groups and so it is not surprising that when clinicians ventured out to advise on helping children affected by war that they should draw on this experience and literature. Unfortunately, that gave the impression that such clinicians saw all children's distress as indicating major psychiatric problems. Equally unfortunately, there is an even greater dearth of examples of community-based interventions that have been properly evaluated. Thus, at the present time, mental health professionals working in war-affected areas are trying to implement programs that are based on good research evidence but are adapted for delivery to large numbers.

Against this background, let us briefly consider some of the evidence for the effectiveness of treatments for stress reactions in children.

Crisis Intervention: Critical Incident Stress Debriefing

Debriefing was originally developed to assist emergency personnel adjust to their emotional reactions to events encountered in the course of their rescue work. It makes use of group support techniques within a predominantly male, macho culture where expressing and sharing feelings is not the norm. The technique has now been adapted for use with children following a wide variety of traumas (Dyregrov, 1991). However, the very nature of refugee children's experiences means that it is unlikely that classical debriefing techniques will be used in the place of sanctuary. Even so, the technique is nowadays so wisely discussed following a major incident that for the sake of completeness it is described here.

Within a few days of an incident, the survivors are brought together in a group with an outside leader. During the introductory phase, the leader sets the rules for the meeting emphasizing that they are there to share feelings and help each other, and that what goes on in the meeting is private. The information should not be used to tease other children. No one has to talk, although all are encouraged to do so. They then go on to clarify the facts of what actually happened in the incident. This permits the nailing of any rumors. They are asked about what they thought when they realized something was wrong, and this leads naturally into discussions of how they felt and of their current emotional reactions. In this way, children share the various reactions they have experienced and usually learn that others feel similarly. The leader labels their responses as normal (understandable) reactions to an abnormal situation. Many children are relieved to learn they are not the only ones experiencing strange feelings and so are relieved that there is an explanation and that they are not going mad. The leader summarizes the information arising in the group, and educates the children into what simple steps they can take to control some of their reactions. They are also told of other help available should their distress persist.

There is evidence that this structured crisis intervention is helpful in preventing later distress in adults (Canterbury & Yule, 1999; Duckworth, 1986; Dyregrov, 1988; Robinson & Mitchell, 1993). However, recent criticisms have been raised about the lack of proper randomized control trials. Some studies which have not used the CISD model but have rather used individualized crisis interventions have not only failed to find evidence in favor of early intervention with adults but even claim that some people are made worse by early intervention (Wessely, Rose & Bisson, 1997; Rose & Bisson, 1998). Indeed, a three year follow up of 30 RTA survivors given a one hour "debriefing" by a researcher within 24-48 hours of the accident found them to have more problems than 31 survivors not given the intervention (Mayou, Ehlers & Hobbs, 2000). Thus, both the nature of the crisis intervention and its timing are crucial issues that require further careful study.

Fortunately, the situation with children is a little more optimistic. Yule and Udwin (1991) describe their use of critical incident stress debriefing with girls who survived the sinking of the Jupiter. Self-report data 5 months after the incident suggest that this reduced levels of stress, particularly those manifested in intrusive thoughts (Yule, 1992). Stallard and Law (1993) show more convincing evidence that debriefing greatly reduced the distress of girls who survived a school bus crash. However, we still do not know when best to offer such debriefing to survivors of a disaster, nor indeed whether all survivors benefit.

Group Treatment

Where natural groupings exist in communities and schools, it makes sense to direct some therapeutic support through such groups (Ayalon, 1988; Farberow & Gordon, 1981; Galante &

Foa, 1986; Yule & Udwin, 1991; Yule & Williams, 1990). The aims of such therapeutic groups should include the sharing of feelings, boosting children's sense of coping and mastery, sharing ways of solving common problems. Although no examples have been published to date, it would seem appropriate to offer group treatment to refugees who have experienced broadly similar events.

Gillis (1993) suggests that it is optimal to work with groups of 6 to 8 children. His experience following a school sniper attack was that it was better to run separate groups for boys and girls because of the different reactions they had to the attack. Boys showed more externalizing problems and girls showed more internalizing ones.

Different authors have imposed varying degrees of structure on their groups, with Galante and Foa (1986) adopting a fairly structured approach where different topics were tackled at each meeting, while Yule and Williams (1990) describe not only a very unstructured, problem-solving approach but also ran a parallel group for the parents. Different incidents will require different approaches.

Group approaches seem to be very therapeutic for many children but not all problems can be solved in the group. Gillis (1993) suggests that high risk children--those whose lives were directly threatened, who directly witnessed death, who were physically injured, who had pre-existing problems 'or who lack family support--should be offered individual help. More generally, children whose problems persist despite group help should be treated individually.

Individual Treatment

To date, there is little evidence that drug treatments have a central role, so the focus has been mainly on cognitive behavioral treatments that aim both to help the survivor make sense of what happened and to master their feelings of anxiety and helplessness.

Asking children to draw their experience often assists recall of both the event and the emotions (Blom, 1982; Galante & Foa, 1986; Newman, 1976; Pynoos & Eth, 1986). Drawings were not used as "projective" techniques, but as ways of assisting talking about the experience. However, there is evidence from a large study of 600 primary school children in Bosnia that structured art therapy does not help reduce the symptoms of distress (Bunjevac & Kuterovac, 1994).

Most survivors recognize that sooner or later "they must face up to the traumatic event". The problem for the therapist is how to help the survivor re-experience the event and the emotions that it engenders in such a way that the distress can be mastered rather than magnified. Therapeutic exposure sessions that are too brief may sensitize rather than desensitize (Rachman,

1980) so therapist may need to use much longer exposure sessions than normal (Saigh, 1986). Fuller suggestions of useful techniques to promote emotional processing are given elsewhere (Perrin, Smith & Yule, 2000; Rachman, 1980; Saigh, 1992; Smith, Perrin & Yule, 1999; Yule, 1991).

Exposure under supportive circumstances seems to deal well with both intrusive thoughts and behavioral avoidance. The other major symptom of child PTSD that requires attention is sleep disorder. A careful analysis will reveal whether the problem is mainly one of getting off to sleep or in waking because of intrusive nightmares related to the disaster. In the former case, implementing relaxing routines before bed and masking thoughts with music may help. In the latter, there are now some promising cognitive behavioral techniques for alleviating nightmares (Halliday, 1987; Marks, 1978; Palace & Johnston, 1989; Seligman & Yellen, 1987).

Ayalon (1983) suggests the use of stress-inoculation techniques (Meichenbaum, 1975; Meichenbaum & Cameron, 1983), among many others, to prepare Israeli children to cope with the effects of "terrorist" attacks. These ideas seem eminently sensible, but their implementation awaits systematic evaluation.

Prevention

Most would agree that prevention is better than cure and so more emphasis on preventing accidents (and war) would help put many of us out of business. In the meantime, we can at least help key institutions - notably schools - prepare for how they may respond to the sorts of crises that hit them.

Anne Gold and I counsel schools to be "Wise Before the Event" (Yule & Gold, 1993). Head Teachers and senior staff should develop contingency plans to deal with the aftermath of possible disasters. I am proud to say that this booklet was presented to every school in the UK by the Calouste Gulbenkian Foundation and we have had very positive feedback on its usefulness.

Working with Children in War: Experiences in Bosnia

Since July 1993, I have been working with UNICEF and other agencies in Bosnia to alleviate the distress caused by the war to children and their families. With advice from Rune Stuvland, Psychosocial Advisor to UNICEF in former Yugoslavia, and together with my colleagues Patrick Smith, Sean Perrin, Berima Hacam and David Schwartz, we developed a public health model for intervention using the school system as the vector for delivery. Our remit was to help build local capacity to meet the mental health needs of children, and to do it in such a way that the developments were sustainable. That essentially meant that we had to identify and train suitable local people to deliver mental health services.

Our hierarchical model of service delivery was founded on providing all primary school teachers with some understanding of the needs of children affected by war and of first aid measures they could take to help. The syllabus of the Level I training was developed with local teaching staff and they delivered it, first to all teachers in and around Mostar and later, Sean Perrin took an elaborated version and delivered it to over 2,000 teachers in Zenica and central Bosnia.

This first level training consisted of four seminars whose content was worked out with local educationalists. The seminars covered "The role of the school in difficult circumstances," "Working with parents," "Burnout and prevention," and "Identifying and helping children." It must be remembered that Yugoslavia had previously had a communist regime with the educational syllabus being tightly controlled centrally. Over half the people who were acting as teachers had had other professions prior to the war and all had lived through the horrors of the war, many being badly affected by their experiences. Hence the need to consider how best schools could respond to local needs, how they could collaborate on an equal footing with parents and how the teachers could look after themselves. This was not just another program on PTSD being imposed insensitively from outside.

We provided some selected teachers with more advanced training. This covered such topics as: working with parents, CBT treatments, bereavement in children, anger management, classroom management, needs of pre-school children, special educational needs, and speech difficulties. We also trained staff of some NGOs in basic counseling skills so they could work with adolescents presenting at youth clubs. Finally, we set up a resource and counseling center attached to a mother and child out-patient clinic to which children could be referred for small group and individual work.

To give some idea of the problems the children presented, we undertook a survey of nearly 3,000 primary school children, completed after the Dayton Peace Accord. The children reported very high levels of stressful experiences during the war. They also report high levels of intrusive thoughts and avoidance behaviors, but somewhat surprisingly, their levels of anxiety and depression were not elevated compared to British normative data, possibly because of the cessation of hostilities (Smith, et al, 2001).

The Need for Evaluation

We can only report these findings because we worked on a battery of instruments that indicate both the levels of exposure to war trauma and the subjective reactions the children experienced. It was part of UNICEF and our remit to develop such a battery that could be used both to estimate the level of need within a population and also monitor the effects of planned interventions. There was little to guide us when we started in 1993 and there was no time to wait while ideal instruments were developed. This was action research in the raw!

Following a number of seminars organized by UNICEF in Bosnia and Norway in 1993 and 1994, a strategy was developed and implemented whereby in collaboration with the Center for Crisis Psychology in Bergen, our group would take the lead in developing a suitable battery. We aimed to develop a brief battery that could be used in mass screening, would be sufficiently comprehensive to cover most of the major reactions expected, and yet would be easily understood and acceptable to children, parents, teachers and government officials. UNICEF encouraged all NGOs it sponsored to use the core battery and we hoped that different groups would add other measures as they chose so as to add to knowledge while still permitting comparison across different interventions.

The core group of measures consisted of a version of the War Trauma Questionnaire adapted for the Bosnian experience; a revised version of the Impact of Event Scale for children, including items on arousal; the Birleson Depression Scale; the Children's Manifest Anxiety Scale; and brief Grief Inventory. Our studies in Bosnia indicated that these aims were mainly achieved. The battery has been used in subsequent studies by different investigators and in different languages (e.g., Papageorgiou, et al. [2000] with Serbian refugees in Greek Macedonia; Giannopolou, et al [in press] with Greek children following the Athens earthquake; many colleagues in Turkey following the recent earthquake there; Yule, et al. [2001] with Albanian refugees from Kosovo). Whilst improvements are constantly being made, this battery seems to be serving many useful purposes and illustrates the need to have good measures to guide better practice.

Particular Needs of Refugee Children

So far, the discussion has focused on stress reactions in children with only passing acknowledgement that refugees will probably have experienced an unusual number or degree of stressful experiences. Some people may well protest that it is "pathologizing" or "medicalizing" these experiences to be talking about stress reactions at all, let alone talking about PTSD. It has already been noted that there are wide individual differences in response to stress and by no means all children exposed to a life threatening experience go on to develop PTSD. But many do show other stress reactions and, of course, children who have been uprooted from their homes and who may have lost a parent or other loved one during the turmoil may also have unresolved grief reactions. While recognizing that most of these reactions are "normal" in the sense of being understandable, they still require that action be taken by those in authority to alleviate the children's distress. Diagnosis and labeling are but means to mobilizing the needed resources.

It is also true that children can be resilient. As noted earlier, half the adolescents who survived the sinking of the cruise ship, "Jupiter," went on to develop a full-blown PTSD. Among the others, many showed a number of stress symptoms that interfered with daily life but fell short of a diagnosable condition. While it is true that from the point of view of understanding development it is good to focus more on invulnerable and resilient children, it remains the case that vulnerable ones require help.

These stress reactions are not merely transient phenomena that settle down quickly once a child feels safe and secure. That may happen, but in the case of children exposed to war, the long-term effects can continue for many years (Elbedour, Bensel, & Bastien, 1993). Even in the case of civilian disasters, the effects can be long lasting, so that the seven year follow-up of survivors of the "Jupiter" sinking is currently reporting that half those who had PTSD within the first year still have it seven years later. Many others experienced other anxiety states and depression in the interim.

So what can and should we do? The first thing is to note that refugee children are at high risk of having mental health problems. It follows, therefore, that the school and other public health services should ensure that proper monitoring procedures are in force to ensure that help is given when required. This may mean having consultations and discussions with local child guidance, school psychological services and other mental health services, as well as contact with appropriate refugee advocacy groups.

The best thing the school can then do is to provide a secure and predictable environment in which the child can settle and learn. (See examples of good practice in Rutter & Jones, 1998). Education is even more highly prized among many refugees as that leads on to skills that can be taken with the child whatever the outcome of applications for citizenship. Within the pastoral care system, those teachers who will be caring for the refugee need to be alerted to some of the issues discussed above. They need to develop good, trusting relationships with the child in the hope that worries and concerns may be shared.

But this is where a particular problem in working with refugees comes to the fore. As van der Veer (1992) points out, many refugees will have gone to great lengths to escape the country where they felt threatened and may have been involved in illegal activities to get to their country of refuge. They may be suspicious of all people in authority and adults may have told children never to tell outsiders anything. They may have to conceal things they did while fleeing. Until decisions are taken about their future legal status, they will be reticent to share all the truth. Thus, teachers and other adults should not expect children to be totally frank about what happened to them, and this may hinder the process of helping children come to terms with their experiences.

A further complication arises when the fate of those left behind is unclear. Adults try to protect children from the worst, and this may be counterproductive. Discussing the needs of refugee children in Slovenia, a number of teachers told me that the worst thing they had to deal with was when they knew that a child's father had been killed in the war in Bosnia, but the mother had forbidden them to tell the child. A brief discussion confirmed that the teachers agreed that it was by far the best policy to be honest and truthful with the children as otherwise when they did discover that the father was dead, they would be angry with mother and teacher and find it harder to trust adults in the future. In any case, the child surely had a right to grieve. In that instance, what started out as a series of crises could be resolved by developing a school policy of openness. Parents would be told that the school would help them to tell children any bad news and would be on hand to support them through the difficult time. Again, teachers helping refugee children need to be aware of any family left behind who are seen as being at risk from the authorities and need to allow children to share their worries as far as is possible.

In the early days when a child joins a school, the help of an interpreter may be necessary. Here, a further possible complication may have to be considered. Many modern conflagrations are civil wars, often of complex natures and divided along religious or ethnic lines. It is vital to check that any interpreter that one involves is acceptable to the child and family. Families are understandably nervous that émigrés of different groupings may be spies or may feed information back to their original country. Considerable sensitivity is required. To say to a child, "Oh, you are from Iran [or Iraq, or Rwanda or Bosnia] Come and meet another child from there...." without knowing that both children are from compatible subgroups, may be less than helpful! Issues to do with interpreters are fully discussed by van der Veer (1995).

Refugee children will probably have experienced stresses that most of us hope never to face. Many of them will cope reasonably well. Others will cope better of their mental health needs are recognized and appropriate help offered. Schools are in a vital position to ensure that such help is offered. Both in the provision of a good caring atmosphere and in seeking appropriate outside support, schools can make an enormous difference to the future adjustment of children who have been the unwitting victims of adults' failures to resolve differences other than by force.

Large Scale Interventions

Ten years on from the genocide in Rwanda and there have been many other wars and massive natural disasters. Hundreds of thousand of children have been made homeless and had to flee their birthplaces following tragedies like the earthquakes in Turkey, Greece, Taiwan, El Salvador and India or the floods in Mozambique and Bangladesh or the political upheavals in Kosovo or the fighting in Afghanistan, Chechnya, Sri Lanka or Algeria – to name but a few. What can be done to alleviate suffering on such a large scale?

Obviously, the first need is to ensure the safety of the children and to meet their physical needs – food, shelter, clean water and sanitation – while making sure they are in contact with their families. Then there is the need to provide some form of schooling both to continue to improve the skills of the children and to provide a much needed predictability and routine to their unsettled lives. When these basic requirements are met, then one can help to bring relief to their psychological distress.

As mentioned earlier, meeting the psychological needs of the children should be built in to all emergency and rebuilding initiatives. Staff setting up tent cities – be they civilian or military – can be advised about the importance of play and education, as well as finding ways to reunite children with their families as they get lost in the vast impersonal rows of canvas. Those providing education need to have the sort of preparation and support we developed in Bosnia in order that they can provide some emotional first aid to children in their care.

Having had experience of working in such emergency situations, six of us (Atle Dyregrov, Rolf Gjestad, Leila Gupta, Patrick Smith, Sean Perrin, and I) met in Norway in the summer of 1998 and discussed what we would recommend to those responding to another major disaster. From that brain storming session, we developed a manual for "Teaching Recovery Techniques" (Smith, et al., 1999). We wanted to develop flexible materials that could address common early distressing reactions that would help children on the road to recovery. The intervention should be capable of being delivered by sensitive people who get on well with children but who probably would have little or now child mental health experience. We strongly suggest that they organize so that there are two group leaders to a group of 10 children. The intervention consists of three half -day modules for all children followed by a fourth meeting for those who have been bereaved. A one-session meeting for parents to explain the intervention and give them suggestions on helping their children is an essential element of the package.

The philosophy behind the manual is that wherever possible, the advice should be based on good empirical evidence. However, we recognize that children cannot wait while all the evidence piles up. Therefore, some of the suggestions are drawn from our own and others' clinical experience. Because of this, we see it as vital that whoever uses the manual must evaluate its effects. To that end, we provide the latest version of our core battery of screening and outcome measures and insist that those who use the package under license (from the Foundation for Children and War which owns the copyright) send us their outcome data so we can adapt the package in the light of experience.

We had intended evaluating the package ourselves before releasing it to colleagues. However, the spate of natural disasters and wars at the end of the century forced us to license some colleagues to use it first. At the time of writing in early 2001, impressions and results are just being fed back to us. There is considerable enthusiasm and many positive comments from workers who have used it in Turkey. But cynics, including us, may worry that anything seems better than nothing when chaos reigns. The specter of possible harm arising from inappropriate applications still hangs over the enterprise. Thus, it was exciting to get the preliminary results from a study in Athens where the manual was implemented by mental health professionals who were largely unfamiliar with cognitive behavioral techniques. They found the suggestions and exercises brought immediate relief to children in the groups they ran and this was confirmed in the self-report questionnaire data from the children themselves (Giannopolou, 2000).

The three main sessions concentrate on helping children deal with the troubling symptoms of intrusion, arousal and avoidance. Children are taken through various warm-up exercises and helped to adopt a problem-solving and group-sharing approach to the difficulties. With regard to intrusion, they are taught about how traumatic reminders can upset them. They practice various imagery techniques to demonstrate to themselves that they can gain some control over the intrusive images that have troubled them. They are introduced to distraction techniques, dual attention techniques (similar to some of the EMDR techniques) and dream work – how to manage frightening, repetitive dreams. To reduce arousal, they are first helped to identify their reactions and then to be able to relax at will, using their own techniques where possible bolstered by breathing exercised and muscle relaxation. They are helped to schedule their activities, to look at better sleep hygiene and to develop and practice coping self-statements. With respect to avoidance, the exercises introduce them to the concept of graded exposure, giving short practice in imaginal exposure followed by self-reinforcement. They are encouraged to draw, write and talk about the incidents and above all to look to the future rather than the past.

In other words, this is a psycho-social-educational program. It is designed to be delivered by people with a minimum of experience, but who are supervised by someone with more mental health expertise. Under the auspices of the Foundation for Children and War we intend developing and refining the package, as there is clearly a great demand for effective, low-cost interventions that can be used with large numbers of children following catastrophes of all sorts.

CONCLUSIONS

Most countries in the world - with the notable exceptions of Somalia and the United States of America - have endorsed the UN Convention on the Rights of the Child. And yet, until recently, UNICEF's charter proscribed it from working with boys aged over 14 years as they were deemed to be of fighting age. There has been great concern raised about the effects of bearing arms and of killing people on "boy soldiers" - but where are the empirical studies on how best to re-educate and rehabilitate such victims of war? As the Machel report (1996) pointed out, modern day rapid-fire weapons are so light that children can readily use them and we need to have a better understanding how to help such victims as long as war exists.

I have indicated earlier how some of us are advising local agencies on how to intervene on a large enough scale to make a significant improvement to the lives of the displaced children. All too often, well meaning individuals and NGOs respond to perceived needs during emergencies and do so ignorant of previous work and without evaluating what they are doing. There is a great need for further studies of the immediate and long-term effects of all such interventions. I have tried to show in this chapter how applying the findings and lessons of clinical research can benefit those affected by wars and disasters. Action research in the real world can be exciting but need not be any less rigorous than that undertaken in the luxury of research clinics.

It would be lovely to think that children's right to develop peacefully will be better respected in this new millennium. But if that is not immediately achievable, at least we are a lot closer than we were 10 years ago to making a significant contribution to improving their adjustment and their happiness.

ACKNOWLEDGMENTS

Much of the work referred to in this chapter was supported by grants from UNICEF, the European Union Administration in Mostar, and the Institute of Psychiatry. I am grateful to Dr Patrick Smith who spent 15 months in Mostar working on the project, to Drs Orlee Udwin, Sean Perrin and David Schwartz who also spent time in Bosnia; to Mrs. Berima Hacam and the volunteer teachers in Mostar who have helped so many children her; to Mr. Rune Stuvland, UNICEF's Psychosocial advisor in the former Yugoslavia with whom we worked closely; and to Dr Atle Dyregrov of the Centre for Crisis Psychology in Bergen, Norway, from whom I have learned so much. Earlier versions of this chapter were presented at meetings of the British Psychological Society and the Association for Child Psychology and Psychiatry.

REFERENCES

Aldrich, G.H. & van Baarda, T.A. (1994). *Declaration of Amsterdam - The Declaration and Recommendations on the Rights of Children in Armed Conflict.* The Hague: International Dialogues Foundation.

Almqvist, K. & Brandell-Forsberg, M. (1997). Refugee children in Sweden: Post-traumatic stress disorder in Iranian preschool children exposed to organized violence. *Child Abuse and Neglect, 21,* 351-366.

American Psychiatric Association. (1980). *Diagnostic and Statistical Manual of Mental Disorders (3rd Ed.).* Washington, DC: APA

American Psychiatric Association. (1994). *Diagnostic and Statistical Manual of Mental Disorders (4th Ed.).* Washington, DC: APA

Ayalon, O. (1983). Coping with terrorism: The Israeli case. In D Meichenbaum & M.E. Jaremko (Eds.), *Stress reduction and prevention* (pp. 293-339). New York: Plenum.

Ayalon, O. (1988). *Rescue! Community oriented preventive education for coping with stress.* Haifa: Nord Publications

Bolton, D., O'Ryan, D., Udwin, O., Boyle, S., & Yule, W. (2000). The long-term psychological effects of a disaster experienced in adolescence: II. General psychopathology. *Journal of Clinical Child Psychology and Psychiatry, 41,* 513-523.

Blom, G.E. (1986). A school disaster - intervention and research aspects. *Journal of the American Academy of Child Psychiatry, 25,* 336-345.

Bunjevac, T. & Kuterovac, G. (1994). *Report on the results of psychological evaluation of the art therapy program in schools in Herzegovina.* Zagreb: UNICEF.

Canterbury, R. & Yule, W. (1999) Debriefing and crisis intervention. In W. Yule (Ed), *Post Traumatic Stress Disorder: Concepts and therapy* (pp. 221-238). Chichester: Wiley.

Canterbury, R., Yule, W., & Glucksman, E. (1993, June). *PTSD in child survivors of road traffic accidents.* Paper presented to Third European Conference on Traumatic Stress, Bergen, Norway.

Duckworth, D. (1986). Psychological problems arising from disaster work. *Stress Medicine,* 315-323.

Dyregrov, A. (1988). *Critical incident stress debriefings.* Unpublished manuscript, Research Center for Occupational Health and Safety, University of Bergen, Norway.

Dyregrov, A. (1991). *Grief in children: A handbook for adults.* London: Jessica Kingsley Publishers.

Elbedour, S., ten Bensel, R., & Bastien, D.T. (1993). Ecological integrated model of children of war: Individual and social psychology. *Child Abuse & Neglect, 17*, 805-819.

Farberow, N.L., & Gordon, N.S. (1981). *Manual for child health workers in major disasters.* Washington, DC: U.S. Government Printing Office.

Galante, R., & Foa, D. (1986). An epidemiological study of psychic trauma and treatment effectiveness after a natural disaster. *Journal of the American Academy of Child Psychiatry, 25*, 357 – 363.

Giannopolou, I. (2000). Personal communication.

Gillis, H. M. (1993). Individual and small-group psychotherapy for children involved in trauma and disaster. In C.F. Saylor (Ed.), *Children and disasters* (pp. 165-186). New York: Plenum.

Halliday, G. (1987). Direct psychological therapies for nightmares: A review. *Clinical Psychology Review, 7*, 501-523.

Horowitz, M.J. (1976). *Stress-response syndromes.* New York: Jason Aronson.

Keppel-Benson, J.M., & Ollendick, T.H. (1993). Posttraumatic stress disorders in children and adolescents. In C.F. Saylor (Ed.), *Children and disasters* (pp. 29-43). New York: Plenum.

Marks, I. (1978). Rehearsal relief of a nightmare. *British Journal of Psychiatry, 133*, 461-465.

Mayou, R., Ehlers, A., & Hobbs, M. (2000). Psychological debriefing for road traffic accident victims. *British Journal of Psychiatry, 176*, 589-593.

Meichenbaum, D. (1975). Self instructional methods. In F. Kanfer & A. Goldstein (Eds.), *Helping people change* (pp 357-391). New York: Pergamon.

Meichenbaum, D., & Cameron, R. (1983). Stress inoculation training: toward a general paradigm for training coping skills. In D. Meichenbaum & M.E. Jaremko (Eds.), *Stress reduction and prevention* (pp. 115-154). New York: Plenum.

Newman, C.J. (1976). Children of disaster: Clinical observation at Buffalo Creek. *American Journal of Psychiatry, 133*, 306-312.

O'Donohue, W. & Eliot, A. (1992.) The current status of post traumatic stress syndrome as a diagnostic category: Problems and proposals. *Journal of Traumatic Stress, 5*, 421- 439.

Palace, E.M. & Johnston, C. (1989.) Treatment of recurrent nightmares by the dream reorganization approach. *Journal of Behavior Therapy and Experimental Psychiatry, 20*, 219-226.

Papageorgiou, V., Frangou-Garunovic, A., Iordanidou, R., Yule, W., Smith, P., & Vostanis, P. (2000). War trauma and psychopathology in Bosnian refugee children. *European Child and Adolescent Psychiatry, 9,* 84-90.

Perrin, S., Smith, P., & Yule, W.(2000). The assessment and treatment of posttraumatic stress disorder in children and adolescents. *Journal of Child Psychology and Psychiatry, 41,* 277-289.

Pynoos, R.S., & Eth, S. (1986). Witness to violence: The child interview. *Journal of the American Academy of Child Psychiatry, 25,* 306-319.

Pynoos, R.S., Frederick, C., Nader, K., Arroyo, W., Steinberg, A., Eth, S., Nunez, F., & Fairbanks, L. (1987). Life threat and posttraumatic stress in school-age children. *Archives of General Psychiatry, 44,* 1057 - 1063.

Rachman, S. (1980). Emotional processing. *Behavior Research and Therapy, 18,* 51-60

Robinson, R.C., & Mitchell, J.T. (1993). Evaluation of psychological debriefings. *Journal of Traumatic Stress, 6,* 367-382.

Rose, S., & Bisson, J. (1998). Brief early psychological intervention following trauma: a systematic review of the evidence. *Journal of Traumatic Stress, 11,* 697-710.

Rutter, J. (1994). *Refugee children in the classroom.* Stoke-on-Trent: Trentham Books.

Rutter, J. & Jones, C. (1998). *Mapping the field: Initiatives in refugee education.* Stoke-on-Trent: Trentham Books.

Saigh, P. A. (1986). In vitro flooding in the treatment of a 6-yr-old boy's posttraumatic stress disorder. *Behavior Research and Therapy, 24,* 685-688.

Saigh, P.A. (1992). The behavioral treatment of child and adolescent posttraumatic stress disorder. *Advances in Behavior Research and Therapy, 14,* 247-275.

Scheeringa, M.S., Zeanah, C.H., Drell, M.J., & Larrieu, J.A. (1995). Two approaches to the diagnosis of Posttraumatic Stress Disorder in infancy and early childhood. *Journal of the American Academy of Child and Adolescent Psychiatry, 34,* 191-200.

Seligman, M. E., & Yellen, A. (1987). What is a dream? *Behavior Research and Therapy, 25,* 1-24.

Smith, P., Dyregrov, A., Yule, W., Gupta, L., Perrin, S., & Gjestad, R. (1999). *Children and disaster: Teaching recovery techniques.* Bergen, Norway: Foundation for Children and War.

Smith, P., Perrin, S., & Yule, W. (1999). Therapy matters: Cognitive behavior therapy for post traumatic stress disorder. *Child Psychology and Psychiatry Review, 4,* 177-182.

Smith, P., Perrin, S., Yule, W., Hacam, B. & Stuvland, R. (in press). *War exposure and children from Bosnia-Herzegovina: Psychological adjustment in a community sample.*

Stallard, P., & Law, F. (1993). Screening and psychological debriefing of adolescent survivors of life-threatening events. *British Journal of Psychiatry, 163,* 660-665.

United Nations. (1987). *Convention on the rights of the child.* New York: Author.

United Nations. (1996). *Report of the UN Secretary General on the Impact of Armed Conflict on Children (The Machel Report).* New York: Author.

Van der Veer, G. (1992). *Counseling and therapy with refugees: Psychological problems of victims of war, torture and repression.* Chichester: John Wiley.

Wessely, S., Rose, S., & Bisson, J. (1997). *A systematic review of brief psychological interventions (debriefing) for the treatment of immediate trauma-related symptoms and the prevention of posttraumatic stress disorder (protocol).* The Cochrane Library (CD-ROM) Oxford: Update Software Inc.

World Health Organization. (1994). *International Classification of Diseases: 10th Edition (ICD-10).* WHO: Geneva.

Yule, W. (1991) Work with children following disasters. In M. Herbert (Ed.), *Clinical child psychology: Social learning, development and behavior* (pp. 349-363). Chichester: John Wiley.

Yule, W. (1992). Post traumatic stress disorder in child survivors of shipping disasters: The sinking of the "Jupiter". *Psychotherapy and Psychosomatics, 57,* 200-205.

Yule, W. (1998). Psychological adaptation of refugee children. In J. Rutter & C. Jones (1998). *Mapping the field: initiatives in refugee education.* Stoke-on-Trent: Trentham Books.

Yule, W. (2000). Emmanuel Miller Lecture: From pogroms to "ethnic cleansing": Meeting the needs of war affected children. *Journal of Child Psychology and Psychiatry, 41,* 695-702.

Yule, W., Bolton, D., Udwin, O., Boyle, S., O'Ryan, D. & Nurrish, J. (2000). The long-term psychological effects of a disaster experienced in adolescence: I. The incidence and course of post-traumatic stress disorder. *Journal of Clinical Child Psychology and Psychiatry, 41,* 503-511.

Yule, W. & Gold, A. (1993). *Wise before the event: Coping with crises in schools.* London: Calouste Gulbenkian Foundation.

Yule, W., Turner, S., Bowie, C., Shapo, L., Dunn, G., Smith, P. & Perrin, S. (2001). *The mental health needs of Kosovo child refugees.* Unpublished Manuscript.

Yule, W., & Udwin, O. (1991). Screening child survivors for post-traumatic stress disorders: Experiences from the "Jupiter" sinking. *British Journal of Clinical Psychology, 30,* 131-138.

Yule, W., & Williams, R. (1990). Post traumatic stress reactions in children. *Journal of Traumatic Stress, 3,* 279-295.

7

Preventing Depression in Adolescence: Short Term Results from the Problem Solving for Life Program

Susan H. Spence
University of Queensland

Caroline L. Donovan
University of Queensland

Susan H. Spence · School of Psychology · University of Queensland · St. Lucia · QLD 4072 · Australia.

International Perspectives on Child and Adolescent Mental Health. Volume 2: Proceedings of the Second International Conference, edited by N. N. Singh, T. H. Ollendick, and A. N. Singh. © 2002 Elsevier Science Ltd. All rights reserved.

While prevention has been a primary focus of the medical profession for some time, the mental health sector has been somewhat slow to follow suit. While the prevalence rates of mental health problems are large and there are enormous economic, personal and social costs associated with them, the mental health sector has continued to focus upon treatment rather than prevention. A number of academic psychological journal articles discussing the theory of prevention strategies for mental health problems have emerged recently. However, substantially fewer controlled trials examining the efficacy of prevention programs targeting psychological disorders have been conducted to date. As governments and funding bodies are becoming aware of the potential financial and social benefits of preventing psychological disorders, funds and incentives for prevention research are becoming more accessible.

Prevention has been defined as intervention that occurs before the onset of a clinically diagnosable disorder that aims to reduce the number of new cases of that disorder (Munoz, Mrazek, & Haggerty, 1996). Preventative methods therefore, may be viewed as any attempt to prevent entry to, or progression along, the trajectory towards a severe, debilitating psychological disorder (Mrazek & Haggerty, 1994). While depression is only one of many psychological disorders with which adolescents may be afflicted, there are many important reasons why the disorder should be the focus of preventative efforts. This chapter examines these reasons, and details the prevention programs to date that have targeted adolescent depression. The chapter concludes with a brief outline of the Problem Solving For Life Program (PSFL; Spence, Sheffield, & Donovan, in submission), a universal program aimed at preventing adolescent depression.

Numerous treatment studies report the efficacious results of interventions such as cognitive therapy (see Lewinsohn & Clarke, 1999) and interpersonal psychotherapy (e.g., Mufson, Weissman, Moreau, & Garfinkel, 1999) in the treatment of adolescent depression. However, there are a number of reasons why prevention of the disorder is preferable to treatment.

Prevalence and Consequences

Depression is a common and extremely debilitating disorder. In adolescence it has a point-prevalence rate of approximately 2-5% (Anderson, Williams, McGee, & Silva, 1987; Kashani, Carlson, & Beck, 1987; Lewinsohn, Clarke, & Rohde, 1994), and a cumulative percentage rate by age 18 years of approximately 20-28% (Feehan, McGee, Raja, & Williams, 1994; Lewinsohn, Rohde, Seeley, Klein, & Gotlib, in press). It would appear that while depression is extremely infrequent in preschool children (less than 1%; Kashani, et al., 1987;

Kashani, Holcomb, & Orvaschel, 1986) and primary school children (less than 2%; Anderson, Williams, McGee, & Silva, 1987; Costello, Costello, Edelbrock, & Bums, 1988), an increase in the prevalence of the disorder occurs during mid-adolescence (Rehm & Sharp, 1996). By the age of 13 years, a gender bias has emerged with more females than males experiencing depression (Hankin & Abramson, 1999). The mean age of onset of depression has been found to be 14.9 years of age, with females demonstrating slightly earlier onset than males (Lewinsohn, et al., 1994).

Not only is adolescent depression relatively common, but also there are also many negative consequences associated with it. Depression is an extremely debilitating disorder that invokes severe distress amongst its sufferers and their families. There is evidence that childhood and adolescent depression is disruptive to both school performance and interpersonal relationships (Kellam & Rebok, 1992; Zubrick, et al., 1997), with longer term negative consequences including poor family relationships, an increased risk of substance abuse, and conduct disorder (Harrington, Fudge, Rutter, Pickles, & Hill, 1990; Lewinsohn, Rohde, Seeley, Klein, & Gotlib, 2000; Poznanski & Mokros, 1994; Rohde, Lewinsohn, & Seeley, 1991). In short, adolescent depression is common and results in many negative outcomes for the afflicted individual. Prevention programs may reduce the prevalence rates of the disorder and thus the aversive consequences associated with it.

Unrecognized Symptoms & Chronic Course

A second reason why prevention of adolescent depression is preferential to treatment is that adolescent depression is frequently left undiagnosed and untreated. Teachers and parents often misinterpret the disorder as a transient and normal phase of adolescence. As a result, depression tends to be ignored or punished, and many adolescents do not receive the psychological treatment they require. This consequence represents a serious issue, as empirical research suggests that clinical levels of many cases of adolescent depression do not in fact remit if left untreated. Furthermore, episodes tend to reoccur, and many cases of adult depression are found to originate during adolescence (Kovacs & Gatsonis, 1989; Oldehinkel, Wittchen, & Schuster, 1999). Evidence suggests that depressive episodes in adolescence are predictive of future depressive episodes in early adulthood (Kovacs, et al., 1984). Programs aimed at preventing adolescent depression therefore, have the potential to alleviate a lifetime of human suffering.

Ineffectiveness of Treatment for Some Sufferers

While effective treatments for depression exist, there is a percentage of young people for whom neither medication nor current psychological therapies are successful. For example, Clarke, Rohde, Lewinsohn, Hops, and Seeley (1999) found that 33% of depressed adolescents remained depressed at completion of CBT therapy. Similarly, in a meta-analysis, Lewinsohn & Clarke (1999) found that only 63% of depressed adolescents showed clinically significant improvement at the end of treatment. Furthermore, antidepressant treatment for depression has been found to have a much weaker effect for children and adolescents compared to adult sufferers (e.g., Birmaher, Ryan, Williamson, Brent, & Kaufman, 1996). Clearly, it would be preferable to prevent the development of depression, rather than waiting until such problems are well established and potentially difficult and costly to treat.

Economic Perspective

From an economic point of view, there are many costs associated with depression. These costs include the expense of unemployment, days lost from work, hospitalization, psychotherapy, 'medication and pension payments. Major depression is expected to produce one of the greatest levels of global burden of disease within the next 30 years (Murray & Lopez, 1996). Add to this the problem that the demand for mental health services already exceeds supply (Winett, 1998), and it becomes apparent that community mental health services will be increasingly overburdened and unable to provide the necessary assistance for an ever-increasing demand. Unfortunately, alternative private mental health facilities are frequently too expensive for those most in need. From a purely economic and practical perspective therefore, prevention programs targeting adolescent depression are a more viable option that treatment.

Association Between Depression and Suicide

One of the most serious arguments for the prevention of adolescent depression is the established link between depression and suicide. Research has demonstrated that depression and hopelessness are key factors in the prediction of adolescent suicide (Grilo, et al., 1999) and that most young people who attempt or commit suicide are depressed in the weeks leading up to the attempt (Dori & Overholser, 1999; Reynolds & Mazza, 1994). A very important consequence of depression prevention therefore, may be a reduction in the suicide rate.

Summary

In summary, there are a number of important reasons for favoring prevention of adolescent depression over treatment. Depression in adolescence is common and has many serious consequences associated with it, not the least of which is an increased risk of suicide. Due to its manifestation in adolescence, depression is often unrecognized and is therefore likely to mark the beginning of a chronic course. In addition, treatment is expensive, not readily available, and ineffective for a proportion of sufferers.

From the above discussion, it is clear that prevention of adolescent depression is necessary and timely. However, prevention requires a thorough understanding of the risk and protective factors associated with the disorder of concern. The following section outlines some of the many risk and protective factors associated with depression and ways in which they may be modified in prevention programs.

RISK & PROTECTIVE FACTORS

Depression is a complex problem resulting from an inter-play between many biological, psychological and environmental factors. Risk factors refer to variables, the presence of which increase the chance of onset of the psychopathology (Coie, et al., 1993). They may be biological, environmental, or psychological in nature. Risk factors for adolescent depression have been found to include:

- a family history of depression (Reinherz, Giaconia, Hauf, Wasserman, & Paradis, 2000)
- being female (e.g., Greenberger, Chen, Tally, & Dong, 2000)
- elevated exposure to negative life events and daily hassles (Adams & Adams, 1993; Lewinsohn, et al., 1994)
- relationship difficulties with peers, parents and other family members; interpersonal skills deficits (Faust, Baum, & Forehand, 1985; Puig-Antich, et al., 1993; Puig-Antich, et al., 1985a; Puig-Antich, et al., 1985b)
- cognitive distortions (Beck, 1976; Garber, Weiss, & Shanley, 1993)
- pessimistic attributional style involving negative interpretation and expectations of events relating to the self, the world and the future (Kazdin, Rodgers, & Colbus, 1986; Lewinsohn, et al., 1994; Nolen Hoeksema, Girgus, & Seligman, 1992)

- self-control skill deficits (Rehm, Fuchs, Roth, Kornblith, & Romano, 1979)
- parental divorce (Lustig, Wolchik, & Weiss, 1999)
- attention deficit hyperactivity disorder (Mick, Santangelo, Wypij, & Biederman, 2000)
- poor body image (Stice, Haywood, Cameron, Killen, & Taylor, 2000)
- subclinical Axis II disorders (Daley, Hammen, Burge, Davila, & Paley, 1999)
- stress (Schraedley, Gotlib, & Hayward, 1999)
- physical and sexual abuse (Shraedley, et al., 1999)
- recent relationship break-up (Monroe, Rohde, Seeley, & Lewinsohn, 1999)
- substance use disorders (Reinherz, et al., 2000)
- eating disorders (Lewinsohn, Striegel-Moore, & Seeley, 2000), and
- conflict with parents (e.g., Greenberger,et al., 2000).

In contrast to risk factors, protective factors improve resilience to both risk factors and psychological disorder (Coie, et al., 1993; Cowen, 1985; Garmezy, 1985; Rutter, 1985). There are a number of mechanisms through which protective factors may operate. For example, they may protect against a disorder by directly affecting the disorder or by decreasing the likelihood of negative chain reactions. Alternatively, protective factors may prevent a risk factor from occurring altogether or may provide a protective buffer against a risk factor. Protective factors may also act by affecting the mediational link through which a risk factor operates (Coie, et al., 1993; Dignam & West, 1988; Wheaton, 1986). Protective factors associated with depression have been found to include:

- enhanced problem solving skills and problem solving orientation (Nezu, Nezu, & Perri, 1989)
- positive self-esteem (Lewinsohn, et al., 1994)
- enhanced coping skills (Lewinsohn, et al., 1994), and
- family and peer support (Lewinsohn, et al., 1994).

When designing prevention strategies, knowledge of risk and protective factors is essential. An understanding of the risk factors associated with a particular disorder is important in the identification of potential participants for a prevention program. In contrast, knowledge concerning the protective factors associated with a disorder may form the basis of the prevention program itself The lists of risk and protective factors presented above are in no way exhaustive, but illustrate the substantial knowledge base we have at our disposal for the development and implementation of preventative strategies for adolescent depression. Drawing on this knowledge, researchers and practitioners have started to examine the effectiveness of programs designed to prevent adolescent depression. The following section describes some of this research, and simultaneously highlights both the infancy of the area and its enormous potential.

EMPIRICAL STUDIES

It is possible to distinguish between three levels of prevention that differ in terms of their target population: indicated, selective and universal. Below is a review of the major prevention 'studies to date that have evaluated the effectiveness of programs designed to prevent the development of depression in young people. They are categorized in terms of the population targeted in the particular study, so that the usefulness of each approach to the prevention of adolescent depression may be assessed.

Indicated Prevention

Indicated prevention strategies focus on high-risk individuals who demonstrate minimal but detectable symptoms of a mental disorder, or biological markers suggestive of a predisposition towards the development of a clinical-level mental disorder (Mrazek & Haggerty, 1994). These studies are based on evidence indicating that elevated depressive symptoms increase the risk of future depressive episodes (Dohrenwend, Shrout, Egri, & Mendelsohn, 1980; Roberts & Gotlib, 1997; Weissman, Fendrich, Wamer, & Wickramaratne, 1992).

Two innovative, indicated prevention programs have focused on adolescent depression. The first, the Penn Prevention Program (Jaycox, Reivich, Gillham, & Seligman, 1994), was delivered by doctoral psychology students to groups of students aged 10-13 years during twelve, 1-hour after-school sessions. Participants were identified as being "high-risk" on the basis of self-report measures of depressive symptoms and level of family conflict. The intervention consisted of instruction about the relationships between events, thoughts and feelings, challenging negative beliefs and negative explanatory style, social problem solving, and coping skills.

Results indicated that participants in the intervention group demonstrated significantly lower levels of depressive symptoms both immediately following intervention and at 6-month follow-up. While intervention did not reduce conduct problems at home, those in the prevention group showed a significant reduction in conduct problems at school compared to controls.

Furthermore, compared to controls, attribution of negative events to negative, stable and enduring causes was significantly reduced for those in the prevention group. At 2-year follow up, the benefits of the prevention program appeared to be maintained. Compared to the control group, the prevention group demonstrated fewer depressive symptoms (with moderate to severe symptoms being reduced by half) and a more positive explanatory style (Gillham, Reivich, Jaycox, & Seligman, 1995). A more recent follow-up however, suggested that while the intervention group retained their enhanced positive explanatory style, the effects on depressive symptoms had faded (Gillham & Reivich, 1999). Overall however, the results of the (Jaycox, et al., 1994) study are extremely encouraging for indicated depression prevention programs.

The second study investigating the efficacy of indicated prevention for adolescent depression was conducted by Clarke, et al. (1995). This study was the first to evaluate the effectiveness of a program for preventing depressive <u>disorder</u> rather than depressive <u>symptoms</u>. The "Coping With Stress" course was delivered to 9th and 10th graders by Masters level psychologists and counselors during fifteen, 45-minute group sessions at the rate of three sessions per week for five weeks. The course comprised cognitive techniques aimed at identifying and challenging negative and irrational thoughts. While depressive symptoms and global functioning improved from pre- to post-intervention for the prevention group compared to the control group, the improvements were not retained at 12-month follow-up. However, using survival analyses of diagnostic interview at 6 and 12-month follow-up, the results indicated significantly fewer new cases of Major Depressive Disorder and Dysthymia over the follow up period for the intervention group compared to the control group.

In summary, the outcome of indicated programs for the prevention of adolescent depression is encouraging, but by no means can we conclude that they are effective in the long-term. In addition to the impact upon depression, it is important to consider the costs compared to the benefits of indicated prevention programs. Given that only a sub-sample of the population are involved, such programs do not involve such high staffing and resource costs as those involving complete populations. However, there are also a number of difficulties associated with indicated prevention. While many measures of childhood depressive symptoms exist, it is important to demonstrate their specificity and sensitivity in detecting sub-clinical levels of adolescent depression and to confirm the validity of cut-off scores as being indicative of high-risk status. A further issue concerns the "singling out" of particular children from their peer group for participation in such programs. Such labeling may lead to self and other perceptions of being "different" at an age when fitting in with one's peers is of utmost importance.

Selective Prevention

Selective prevention strategies are targeted towards subgroups or individuals who are assumed to have a high lifetime or imminent risk of developing a problem as the result of exposure to some biological, psychological, or social risk factor(s). For the majority of selective prevention studies, depression is but one outcome of interest. That is, most selective prevention programs identify participants based on a particular risk factor (e.g., bereavement, parental psychopathology, parental divorce or experience of trauma). The intervention is designed to bring about some change in the risk factor of concern or to enhance protective factors, with evaluation including a range of potential positive effects including reductions in depressive symptoms (e.g., Gross & McCaul, 1992; Hains, 1992; Hains & Ellmann, 1994). Given that most risk factors are common to several forms of psychopathology, in most instances, selective prevention is not targeting depression specifically, but rather the prevention of mental health problems more generally. A detailed review of the selective prevention literature is beyond the scope of this paper, and a more extensive discussion can be found in (Spence, 1996). Briefly, it can be said that the research has produced mixed findings with respect to the effectiveness of selective prevention.

Encouraging short-term results have been found for programs designed to assist children to cope with difficult life circumstances. Short-term beneficial effects have been found from several programs designed to help children to cope with the effects of parental divorce (e.g., Hodges, 1991; Perry, et al., 1989; Short, 1998). Positive short-term effects have also been reported for preventive interventions for children and adolescents who have been recently bereaved (Sandier, West, Baca, Pillow, et al., 1992) or whose parents have a mental disorder such as depression (Beardslee, Salt, Porterfield, & Rothberg, 1993; Beardslee, Wright, Salt, & Drezner, 1997). Unfortunately, follow-up periods tend to be relatively short, making it difficult to determine whether preventive interventions have a benefit in the long-term, over and above the effects of passage of time and normal youth developmental changes. Where follow-up has been conducted over several years, the evidence of long-term benefit of selective prevention has been mixed. For example, (Pedro-Carroll & Cowen, 1985) found that the benefits of a program to assist children to cope with divorce were reduced at 3-year follow-up, despite still being strong at 2-year follow-up. Beardslee, et al. (1997) showed better adaptive functioning at 1.5-year follow-up for children of depressed parents who attended a clinician-facilitated psycho-educational program compared to those who were enrolled in a lecture discussion group.

It is also important to consider the costs and benefits of selective prevention, in comparison to other approaches. As for indicated prevention strategies, selective prevention strategies are restricted to sub-samples of the population and in some respects should be cheaper to administer than programs targeting whole populations. However, there are also disadvantages inherent in selective strategies. Such approaches assume that we have the knowledge, techniques and opportunities to identify and access children who experience specific risk factors. The potential negative impact of being identified and labeled as being "at risk" also exists. Furthermore, most research into risk factors for mental health problems has shown that many children do not experience adverse outcomes as a consequence of exposure to the risk factor. The term "risk" is a statistical one, meaning that the presence of the variable increases the probability of some adverse outcome. Thus, selective prevention includes many young people who would not have progressed to an adverse outcome if left alone. One of the challenges for researchers in the future is to identify more accurately those at greatest risk, perhaps as a consequence of exposure to various combinations and permutations of risk factors.

Universal Prevention Studies

"Universal" prevention targets entire populations that are not selected on the basis of any associated risk factors. Three studies that examined the effectiveness of universal programs to prevent adolescent depression warrant discussion. Clarke, Hawkins, Murphy, and Sheeber (1993) provided data on two studies of 9th and 10th grade adolescents. The first study consisted of three, 50-minute primary prevention sessions comprising three lectures and two, 20-minute videotapes. Teachers were trained to deliver the material comprising information on depression, encouragement for adolescents to seek help when necessary, and to increase their daily pleasant activities. Results indicated that a decrease in depressive symptoms was not evident for girls at either post-intervention or 12-week follow-up. For boys, there was a trend for the program to produce positive effects in the short-term, but these had disappeared by 12-week follow-up. When high-risk participants were examined separately, a positive effect on depressive symptoms was found at post-intervention for boys only, but had again disappeared by 12-week follow-up.

The second study by Clarke, et al. (1993) again employed 9th and 10th graders. However, the curriculum was modified so that students were exposed to five consecutive 50-minute sessions conducted by trained teachers. The first session comprised a shortened lecture and 20-minute videotape concerning depression. The remaining four sessions focused upon skills-based strategies for increasing pleasant events. There were no significant intervention effects for either girls or boys at post-intervention or 12-week follow-up, even when high-risk participants were examined separately.

More recently, Shochet, et al. (in press) reported a universal prevention study focusing on adolescent depression. The study examined the effectiveness of the Resourceful Adolescent Program (with and without parental participation), compared to a monitoring only control group. The RAP program was conducted by psychologists with groups of 8-12 participants over 11 weekly, 40-5 0 minute sessions. The program comprised affirmation of existing strengths, skills for coping with stress, building and accessing psychological support networks, interpersonal skills, and conflict resolution training. The parent sessions comprised stress management, identification of parental strengths, information on adolescent development, strategies for promoting their child's self-esteem, independence and attachment issues, and interpersonal and conflict resolution skills. Results of the study were extremely encouraging. The adolescents in both RAP groups demonstrated a small but significant reduction in depressive symptoms compared to the control group at both post-intervention and 10-month follow-up on one of two measures of depression. The involvement of parents in the program did not add significantly to its effect, although there was a low rate of attendance by parents at the sessions. Rice and Meyer (1994) reported the process results of a psycho-educational intervention program aimed at preventing depression in young adolescents. Unfortunately, measures of pre-intervention levels of depressive symptoms were not taken, and hence the effectiveness of the study cannot be determined. Nevertheless, the paper provides some useful description of the practicalities of a school-based universal prevention program.

Again, it is important to examine the costs and benefits associated with this particular type of prevention strategy. Universal prevention involves large populations and substantial funding and resources. School represents an obvious setting in which large numbers of young people are a relatively captive audience. The challenge is to develop mechanisms and systems through which preventive interventions can be applied in a relatively cheap but effective manner.

Despite the many and varied practical and financial difficulties, universal prevention research has the potential to be of enormous benefit in reducing the prevalence of mental disorders. Given that all children receive the intervention, the problem of "missing" some students at risk is avoided. It also avoids problems associated with labeling or selection of specific individuals. However, for 'such programs to become widespread, we need to identify cost-effective methods of delivery. Those programs that require intensive training of staff, and implementation by mental health professionals or small-group delivery (e.g., Shochet, et al., in press) are extremely expensive. For example, Shochet, et al. (in press) reported 143 hours of therapist time for 125 adolescents. A more economical option would be for the program to be run by teachers within the normal school curriculum. If the materials were self explanatory and self-contained, and an adequate amount of teacher training was provided, teacher delivery of the program may be feasible.

The present study reports the short-term findings of a classroom-based, teacher delivered universal prevention program. The study includes a large sample size and random assignment of schools to experimental conditions. The Problem Solving For Life project (PSFL; Spence, et al., in submission) represents a universal prevention program developed to prevent adolescent depression. Teachers deliver the program on a whole-class basis as part of the school curriculum.

Methodology

The PSFL study employed 1500 Year 8 students ranging in age from 12-14 years (at commencement of the study), who attended one of 16 secondary schools. Schools were matched in pairs on the basis of size and State versus private funding and then randomly assigned to either PSFL or to a control condition. This chapter reports the short-term outcome of the program. Full details of the study can be found in Spence, et al. (in submission).

Participants were assessed prior to intervention (pre-intervention), and again immediately after completion of the PSFL course (post-intervention). The study will evaluate outcome on an annual basis over the next 3 years, but only the short-term results are reported here. Evaluation included the Beck Depression Inventory (BDI; Beck, Ward, Mendelson, Mock, & Erbaugh, 1961) and the Social Problem-Solving Inventory-Revised Short Form (SPSI-R; D'Zurilla & Maydeu-Olivares, 1995). Future long-term follow-up evaluation will include a range of additional measures relating to diagnostic status, attributional style, general psychopathology, and social functioning.

While the project was essentially universal, separate analyses were conducted for "high risk" participants. As such, a sub-component of the study was representative of a selective prevention paradigm. High-risk participants were identified through their scores on the BDI and Dysthymia questions. All high-risk participants received the mood disorders sections of the Anxiety Disorders Schedule for Children (ADIS-C; Silverman & Albano, 1996) in order for diagnostic status to be assessed. Any participants receiving a clinical diagnosis from this interview were referred to the school counselor or guidance officer and excluded from the analyses of high-risk participants.

The PSFL course was conducted as an 8-session program delivered by teachers through subjects such as Religious Education, Home Economics, Health and Physical Education and Personal Development. Each fully self contained session required approximately 45-50 minutes for delivery, and thus fined into a single school period. Teachers were trained for a minimum of

6 hours to ensure adequate delivery of the program. They were provided with pre-prepared program materials that required minimal preparation and included supporting materials such as resource books, overheads, background notes, handouts, cartoons, puzzle pieces and posters. In this way, the course was fully manualized and self-contained in order to ensure consistency across teachers and schools.

The Problem Solving For Life Curriculum

The PSFL curriculum was an amalgamation of both social problem-solving techniques and cognitive restructuring techniques. The social problem solving component was based on the work of D'Zurilla and Nezu (1980) and has been described as a) making available a variety of alternative responses to a problem situation and b) increasing the probability of selecting the most appropriate and useful response among those alternatives (D'Zurilla & Goldfried, 1971). As adequate social problem-solving ability has been found to be a protective factor in the development of adolescent depression, and training in social problem-solving has been shown to be an effective treatment for depression (Nezu, et al., 1989), enhancement of an adolescent's problem-solving skills is likely to provide a buffer against depression.

Recent problem-solving theorists have emphasized the importance of "problem orientation" (Haaga, et al., 1995) that refers to the cognitive set an Individual takes with them to a problem situation. While some individuals approach problems with a constructive cognitive set (or positive problem orientation), others approach them with a dysfunctional cognitive set (or negative problem orientation). A positive problem orientation is necessary before effective problem-solving skills (e.g., generating alternative solutions, choosing the best solution etc.) can be accomplished. In order to increase an individual's propensity for a positive problem orientation, cognitive restructuring principals become very important.

The cognitive restructuring component of the PSFL program was based on the cognitive theory and associated techniques of (Ellis, 1958). Ellis' (1958) ABC model suggests that beliefs or thoughts (B) concerning activating events (A) lead to certain emotional and behavioral consequences (C). Hence, it is the thoughts and beliefs that a person has about a particular event that lead them to feel depressed or anxious rather than the event per se. In order to change how an individual feels therefore, it is necessary to identify and challenge their maladaptive thoughts or beliefs, and replace them with more adaptive thoughts or beliefs. The use of cognitive restructuring as a treatment for depressed adolescents has been shown to be extremely beneficial in a number of empirical studies (see Harrington, Whittaker, & Shoebridge, 1998).

As described above, the PSFL course incorporated cognitive restructuring methods and social problem solving techniques. Specifically, the 8-session program involved the following:

Session 1. Introduction of the aims and goals of the program, identification of thoughts, feelings and activating events, discussion of different types of problems, identifying ones own problems (large and daily hassles)

Session 2. The link between problems, thoughts, feelings and actions; cognitive challenging and changing unhelpful thoughts to helpful thoughts

Session 3. Discussion of characteristics of positive and negative problems solvers; use of the Think-Feel-Do model

Session 4. Personal problem identification, definition and goal setting (gathering facts and understanding the problem)

Session 5. Generation of solutions and evaluation of consequences

Session 6. Decision-making and the prediction of consequences

Session 7. Putting solutions into action and the identification of social support sources and help

Session 8. Integration of all cognitive and problem solving skills and use of rapid problem solving methods

RESULTS

High-Risk Group

About 27% of intervention subjects and 26% of control subjects were categorized as high-risk. The classification of high- versus low-risk subjects was validated by significant differences between groups on key dimensions. Specifically, the high-risk group reported significantly lower problem-solving skills and social functioning compared to the low-risk group. In addition, the high-risk subjects demonstrated a more negative explanatory style and higher internalizing and externalizing scores compared to the low-risk group. Finally, the high-risk group reported a significantly greater number of family problems and negative life events compared to the low risk group.

Analyses revealed that while both control and experimental high-risk groups declined in depressive symptoms from pre- to post-intervention, the PSFL group declined significantly more so (see Figure 1). Importantly, while the BDI scores for the intervention group declined to sub-clinical levels of depressive symptoms, this did not occur for the control group.

Similarly, analyses for total problem-solving ability revealed that, while both control and intervention groups increased in problem-solving ability over time, the intervention group improved significantly more so (see Figure 2). In addition, the intervention group demonstrated significant reductions in negative problem-solving orientation and avoidant problem solving, whereas the control group did not.

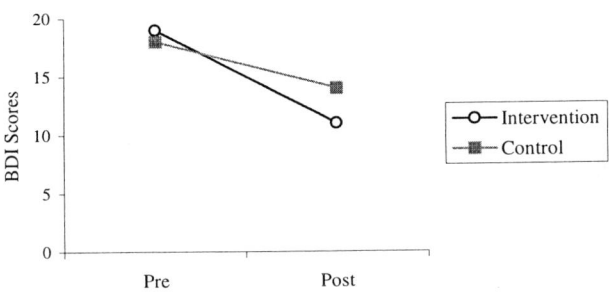

Figure 1.   Scores for the High-Risk Group

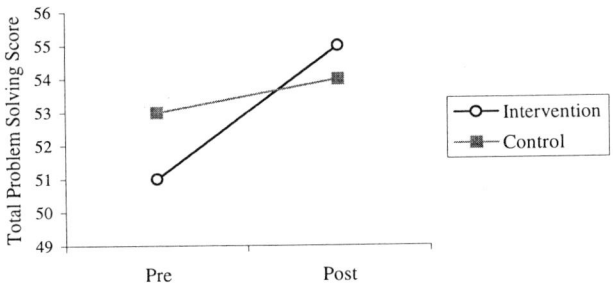

Figure 2.   Total Problem Solving Scores for the High-Risk Group

Low-Risk Sample

Similar results were evident for the low-risk sample. While the control group evidenced an increase in BDI scores and a slight reduction of problem-solving scores from pre to post-intervention, the PSFL group demonstrated a slight decline in BDI scores and an increase in problem-solving ability over time (see Figures 3 & 4). In addition, compared to the control group, the intervention group demonstrated greater reductions in negative problem orientation, impulsive problem solving and avoidant problem solving.

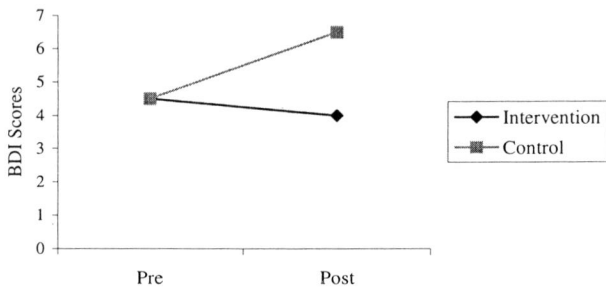

Figure 3. BDI Scores for the Low-Risk Group

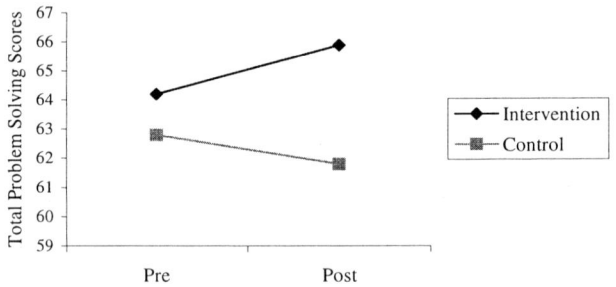

Figure 4. Total Problem Solving Scores for the Low-Risk Group

SUMMARY

In summary, the PSFL course was associated with increased social problem-solving

SUMMARY

In summary, the PSFL course was associated with increased social problem-solving ability, and decreased depressive symptoms in both high- and low-risk intervention groups from pre- to post-intervention. That such effects were found in such a large sample and with both high and low-risk subjects is very encouraging for universal prevention research. The project will now progress to examine the longer-term impact of PSFL over the next few years in order to determine whether the positive benefits are maintained.

This chapter has illustrated the debilitating consequences of adolescent depression and the potential advantages of its prevention. As many studies have been conducted to identify risk and protective factors associated with adolescent depression, we are now in a position to use this information to develop preventative interventions for the disorder. While the prevention of adolescent depression as an area of empirical enquiry is in its infancy, a number of studies have already produced encouraging results. Governments, communities, funding bodies, clinicians and the general public must embrace the concept of prevention of mental health problems with enthusiasm and support. If effective methods of prevention of depression in adolescence can be identified, the cost-savings to individuals and the community will be considerable.

REFERENCES

Adams, J., & Adams, M. (1993). Effects of a negative life event and negative perceived problem-solving alternatives on depression in adolescents: A prospective study. *Journal of Child Psychology and Psychiatry and Allied Disciplines, 34,* 743-747.

Anderson, J. C., Williams, S., McGee, R., & Silva, P. A. (1987). DSM-III disorders in preadolescent children: Prevalence in a large sample from the general population. *Archives of General Psychiatry, 44,* 69-76.

Beardslee, W. R., Salt, P., Porterfield, K., & Rothberg, P. C. (1993). Comparison of preventive interventions for families with parental affective disorder. *Journal of the American Academy of Child and Adolescent Psychiatry, 32,* 254-263.

Beardslee, W. R., Wright, E. J., Salt, P., & Drezner, K. (1997). Examination of children's responses to two preventive intervention strategies over time. *Journal of the American Academy of Child and Adolescent Psychiatry, 36,* 196-204.

Beck, A. T. (1976). *Cognitive therapy and the emotional disorders.* New York: International Universities Press.

Beck, A. T., Ward, C. H., Mendelson, M., Mock, J., & Erbaugh, J. (1961). An inventory for measuring depression. *Archives of General Psychiatry, 4, 53-63.*

Birmaher, B., Ryan, N. D., Williamson, D. E., Brent, D. A., & Kaufman, J. (1996). Childhood and adolescent depression: A review of the past 10 years. Part II. *Journal of the American Academy of Child and Adolescent Psychiatry 35,* 1575-1583.

Clarke, G. N., Hawkins, W., Murphy, M., & Sheeber, L. (1993). School-based primary prevention of depressive symptomatology in adolescents: Findings from two studies. *Journal of Adolescent Research, 8,* 183-204.

Clarke, G. N., Hawkins, W., Murphy, M., & Sheeber, L. B. (1995). Targeted prevention of univocal depressive disorder in an at-risk sample of high school adolescents: A randomized trial of group cognitive intervention. *Journal of the American Academy of Child and Adolescent Psychiatry, 34,* 3 12-321.

Clarke, G. N., Rohde, P., Lewinsohn, P. M., Hops, H., & Seeley, J. R. (1999). Efficacy of acute group treatment and booster sessions. *Journal of the American Academy of Child and Adolescent Psychiatry 38,* 272-279.

Coie, J. D., Watt, N. F., West, S. G., Hawkins, J. D., Asarnow, J. R., Markman, H. J., Ramey, S. L., Shure, M. B., & Long, B. (1993). The science of prevention: A conceptual framework and some directions for a National Research Program. *American Psychologist, 48,* 1013-

1022.

Costello, E. J., Costello, A. J., Edelbrock, C., & Bums, B. J. (1988). Psychiatric disorders in pediatric primary care: Prevalence and risk factors. *Archives of General Psychiatry, 45,* 1107-1116.

Cowen, E. L. (1985). Person-centered approaches to primary prevention in mental health: Situation focused and competence enhancement. *American Journal of Community Psychology, 13,* 3 1-49.

Daley, S. E., Hammen, C., Burge, D., Davila, J., & Paley, B. (1999). Depression in Axis II symptomatology in an adolescent community sample: Concurrent and longitudinal associations. *Journal of Personality Disorders, 13, 47-59.*

Dignam, J. T., & West, S. G. (1988). Social support in the workplace: Tests of six theoretical models. *American Journal of Community Psychology, 16,* 70 1-724.

Dohrenwend, B. P., Shrout, P. E., Egri, G., & Mendelsohn, F. S. (1980). Nonspecific psychological distress and other dimensions of psychopathology. *Archives of General Psychiatry, 37,* 1229-1236.

Dori, G. A., & Overholser, J. C. (1999). Depression, hopelessness, and self-esteem: Accounting for suicidality in adolescent psychiatric inpatients. *Suicide and Life Threatening Behavior 29,* 309-318.

D'Zunilla, T. J., & Goldfried, M. R. (1971). Problem solving and behavior modification. *Journal of Abnormal Psychology, 78,* 107-126.

D'Zurilla, T. J., & Maydeu-Olivares, A. (1995). Conceptual and methodological issues in social problem-solving assessment. *Behavior Therapy, 26,* 409-432.

D'Zunilla, T. J., & Nezu, A. (1980). A study of the generation-of-alternatives process in social problem solving. *Cognitive Therapy and Research, 4,* 67-72.

Ellis, A. (1958). Rational psychotherapy. *Journal of General Psychology, 59,* 35-49.

Faust, J., Baum, C. G., & Forehand, R. *(1985).* An examination of the association between social relationships and depression in early adolescence. *Journal of Applied Developmental Psychology, 6,* 29 1-297.

Feehan, M., McGee, R., Raja, S., & Williams, S. M. (1994). DSM-III-R disorders in New Zealand 1 8-year-olds. *Australian and New Zealand Journal of Psychiatry, 28,* 87-99.

Garber, J., Weiss, B., & Shanley, N. (1993). Cognitions, depressive symptoms and development in adolescents. *Journal of Abnormal Psychology, 102, 47-57.*

Garmezy, N. (1985). Stress resistant children: The search for protective factors. In J. Stevenson (Ed.), *Recent research in developmental psychopathology.* Oxford: Pergamon Press.

Gillham, J. E., & Reivich, K. J. (1999). Prevention of depressive symptoms in school children: A research update. *Psychological Science, 10,* 46 1-462.

Gillham, J. E., Reivich, K. J., Jaycox, L. H., & Seligman, M. E. P. (1995). Prevention of depressive symptoms in schoolchildren: Two-year follow-up. *Psychological Science, 6,* 343-*351.*

Greenberger, E., Chen, C., Tally, S. R., & Dong, Q. (2000). Family, peer, and individual correlates of depressive symptomatology among and Chinese adolescents. *Journal of Consulting and Clinical Psychology, 68,* 209-219.

Grilo, C. M., Sanislow, C. A., Fehon, D. C., Lipschitz, D. S., Martino, S., & McGlashan, T. H. (1999). Correlates of suicide risk in adolescent inpatients who report a history of childhood abuse. *Comprehensive Psychiatry 40,* 422-428.

Gross, J., & McCaul, E. (1992). An evaluation of a psychoeducational and substance abuse risk reduction intervention for children of substance abusers. *Journal of Community Psychology, 75-87.*

Haaga, D. A. F., Fine, J. A., Terrill, D. R., Stewart, B. L. (1995). Social problem-solving deficits, dependency, and depressive symptoms. *Cognitive Therapy and Research, 19,* 147-158.

Hains, A., & Ellmann, S. W. (1994). Stress inoculation straining as a preventative intervention for high school students. *Journal of Cognitive Psychology, 8,* 2 19-232.

Hains, A. A. (1992). A stress inoculation training program for adolescents in a high school setting: A multiple baseline approach. *Journal of Adolescence, 15, 163-175.*

Hankin, B. L., & Abramson, L. Y. (1999). Development of gender differences in depression: Description and possible explanations. *Annals of Medicine, 31,* 372-379.

Harrington, R., Fudge, H., Rutter, M., Pickles, A., & Hill, J. (1990). Adult outcomes of childhood and adolescent depression. *Archives General Psychiatry, 47,* 465-473.

Harrington, R., Whittaker, J., & Shoebridge, P. (1998). Psychological treatment of depression in children and adolescents. *British Journal of Psychiatry, 173,* 29 1-282.

Hodges, W. F. (1991). *Intervention for children of divorce.* New York: John Wiley.

Jaycox, L. H., Reivich, K. J., Gillham, J., & Seligman, M. E. P. (1994). Prevention of depressive symptoms in school children. *Behavior Research and Therapy 32,* 801-8 16.

Kashani, J., H. , Carlson, G. A., & Beck, N. C. e. a. (1987). Depression, depressive symptoms, and depressed mood among a community sample of adolescents. *American Journal of Psychiatry 144,* 931-934.

Kashani, J. H., Holcomb, W. R., & Orvaschel, H. (1986). Depression and depressive symptoms in preschool children from the general population. *American Journal of Psychiatry, 143,*

1138-1 143.

Kazdin, A. E., Rodgers, A., & Colbus, D. (1986). The Hopelessness Scale for Children: Psychometric characteristics and concurrent validity. *Journal of Consulting and Clinical Psychology, 54,* 24 1-245.

Kellam, S. G., & Rebok, G. W. (1992). Building developmental and etiological theory through epidemiologically based preventive intervention trials. In J. McCord & R. E. Tremblay (Eds.), *Preventing antisocial behavior: interventions from birth through adolescence* (pp. 162-195). New York: Guilford Press.

Kovacs, M., & Gatsonis, C. (1989). Stability and changes in childhood-onset depressive disorders: Longitudinal course as a diagnostic validator. In L. Robins, J. L. Fleiss, & J. Barrett (Eds.), *The validation of psychiatric disorders* (pp. 5 7-75). New York: Raven Press.

Lewinsohn, P. M., & Clarke, G. N. (1999). Psychosocial treatments for adolescent depression. *Clinical Psychology Review, 19,* 329-342.

Lewinsohn, P. M., Clarke, G. N., & Rohde, P. (1994). Psychological approaches to the treatment of depression in adolescents. In W. M. Reynolds & H. E. Johnston (Eds.), *Handbook of depression in children and adolescents.* New York: Plenum Press.

Lewinsohn, P. M., Rohde, P., Seeley, J. R., Klein, D. N., & Gotlib, I. H. (2000). Natural course of adolescent major depressive disorder in a community sample: Predictors of recurrence in young adults. *American Journal of Psychiatry 157(10),* 1584-1591.

Lewinsohn, P. M., Striegel-Moore, R. H., & Seeley, J. H. (2000). Epidemiology and natural course of eating disorders in young women from adolescence to young adulthood. *Journal of the American Academy of Child and Adolescent Psychiatry 39,* 1284-1292.

Mick, E., Santangelo, S. L., Wypij, D., & Biederman, J. (2000). Impact of maternal depression on ratings of comorbid depression in adolescents with attention-deficit/hyperactivity disorder. *Journal of the American Academy of Child and Adolescent Psychiatry, 39,* 314-319.

Monroe, S. M., Rohde, P., Seeley, J. R., & Lewinsohn, P. M. (1999). Life events and depression in adolescence: Relationship loss as a prospective risk factor for first onset of major depressive disorder. *Journal of Abnormal Psychology, 108,* 606-614.

Mrazek, P. J., & Haggerty, R. J. (Eds.). (1994). *Reducing the risks for mental disorders: Frontiers for preventive intervention research.* Washington DC: National Academy Press.

Mufson, L., Weissman, M. M., Moreau, D., & Garfinkel, R. (1999). Efficacy of interpersonal psychotherapy for depressed adolescents. *Archives of General Psychiatry, 56,* 573-579.

Munoz, R. F., Mrazek, P. J., & Haggerty, R. J. (1996). Institute of Medicine report on prevention of mental disorders: Summary and commentary. *American Psychologist, 51,* 1116-1122.

Murray, C. J. C., & Lopez, A. D. (Eds.). (1996). *The global burden of disease.* Harvard: WHO, World Bank, & Harvard School of Public Health.

New, A. M., New, C. M., & Perri, M. G. (1989). *Problem-solving therapy for depression: Theory, research, and clinical guidelines.* New York, NY: John Wiley and Sons.

Nolen Hoeksema, S., Girgus, J. S., & Seligman, M. E. (1992). Predictors and consequences of childhood depressive symptoms: A 5-year longitudinal study. *Journal of Abnormal Psychology, 101,* 405-422.

Oldehinkel, A. J., Wittchen, H. U., & Schuster, P. (1999). Prevalence, 20-month incidence and outcome of unipolar depressive disorders in a community sample of adolescents. *Psychological Medicine, 29,* 655-668.

Pedro-Carroll, J. L., & Cowen, E. L. (1985). The Children of Divorce Intervention Project: An investigation of the efficacy of a school-based prevention program. *Journal of Consulting and Clinical Psychology, 53,* 603-611.

Perry, C. L., Grant, M., Embeng, G., Florenzano, R. U., Langdon, M. C., Myeni, A. D., Waahlberg, R., Berg, S., Anderson, K., Fisher, K. J., Blaze-Temple, D., Cross, D., Saunders, B., Jacobs, D. R., & Schmid, T. (1989). WHO collaborative study on alcohol education and young people: Outcomes of a four-country pilot study. *The international Journal of the Addictions, 24,* 1145-1171.

Poznanski, E. O., & Mokros, H. B. (1994). Phenomenology and epidemiology of mood disorders in children and adolescents. In W. M. Reynolds & H. E. Johnston (Eds.), *Handbook of depression in children and adolescents.* New York: Plenum Press.

Puig-Antich, J., Kaufman, J., Ryan, D., Williamson, D. E., Dahl, R. E., Lukens, E., Todak, G., Ambrosini, P., Rabinovich, H., & Nelson, B. (1993). The psychosocial functioning and family environment of depressed adolescents. *Journal of American Academy of Child and Adolescent Psychiatry, 32,* 244-253.

Puig-Antich, J., Lukens, E., Davies, M., Goetz, D., Brennan-Quattrock, J., & Todak, G. (1 985a). Psychosocial functioning in prepubertal major depressive disorders: I. Interpersonal relationships during the depressive episode. *Archives of General Psychiatry 42,* 500-507.

Puig-Antich, J., Lukens, E., Davies, M., Goetz, D., Brennan-Quattrock, J., & Todak, G. (1985b). Psychosocial functioning in prepubertal major depressive disorders: II. Interpersonal relationships after sustained recovery from affective episode. *Archives of General*

Psychiatry, 42, 511-517.

Rehm, L. P., Fuchs, C. Z., Roth, D. M., Komblith, S. J., & Romano, J. M. (1979). A comparison of self-control and assertion skills treatments of depression. *Behavior Therapy, 10,* 429-442.

Reinherz, H. Z. , Giaconia, R. M., Hauf, A. M. C., Wasserman, M. S., & Paradis, A. D. (2000). General and specific childhood risk factors for depression and drug disorders by early adulthood. *Journal of the American Academy of Child and Adolescent Psychiatry, 39,* 223-231.

Reynolds, W., & Mazza, J. J. (1994). Suicide and suicidal behaviors in children and adolescents. In W. M. Reynolds & H. E. Johnston (Eds.), *Handbook of depression in children and adolescents.* New York: Plenum Press.

Rice, K. G., & Meyer, A. L. (1994). Preventing depression among young adolescents: Preliminary process results of a psycho-educational intervention program. *Journal of Counseling and Development, 73,* 145-152.

Roberts, J. E., & Gotlib, I. H. (1997). Temporal variability in global self-esteem and specific self-evaluation as prospective predictors of emotional distress: Specificity in predictors and outcome. *Journal of Abnormal Psychology, 106,* 521-529.

Rohde, P., Lewinsohn, P. M., & Seeley, J. R. (1991). Comorbidity of unipolar depression: II. Comorbidity with other mental disorders in adolescents and adults. *Journal of Abnormal Psychology, 100,* 214-222.

Rutter, M. (1985). Resilience in the face of adversity: Protective factors and resistance to psychiatric disorder. *British Journal of Psychiatry, 147,* 598-611.

Sandler, I. N., West, S. G., Baca, L., Pillow, D. R., & al., e. (1992). Linking empirically based theory and evaluation: The Family Bereavement Program. *American Journal of Community Psychology, 20,* 491-52 1.

Schraedley, P. K., Gotlib, I. H., & Hayward, C. (1999). Gender differences in correlates of depressive symptoms in adolescents. *Journal of Adolescent Health, 25,* 98-108.

Shochet, I. M., Dadds, M. R., Holland, D., Whitefield, K., Hamett, P. H., & Osgarby, S. (in press). The efficacy of a universal school-based program to prevent adolescent depression. *Journal of Clinical Child Psychology.*

Shod, J. L. (1998). Evaluation of a substance abuse prevention and mental health promotion program for children of divorce. *Journal of Divorce and Remarriage, 28,* 139-155.

Silverman, W. K., & Albano, A. M. (1996). *Anxiety Disorders Interview schedule for DSM-IV - Child Version: Parent Interview Schedule.* San Antonio: The Psychological Corporation

Harcourt, Brace & Company.

Spence, S. H. (1996). A case for prevention. In P. Cotton & H. Jackson (Eds.), *Early intervention and prevention in mental health* (pp. 1-19). Melbourne: The Australian Psychological Society.

Spence, S. H., Sheffield, J., & Donovan, C. L. (in submission). Preventing adolescent depression. Unpublished manuscript.

Stice, E., Haywood, C., Cameron, R. P., Killen, H. D., & Taylor, C. B. (2000). Body image and eating disturbances predict onset of depression among female adolescents: A longitudinal study. *Journal of Abnormal Psychology, 109,* 43 8-444.

Weissman, M. M., Fendrich, M., Warner, V., & Wickramaratne, P. (1992). Incidence of psychiatric disorder in offspring at high and low risk for depression. *Journal of the American Academy of Child and Adolescent Psychiatry, 3 1,* 640-648.

Wheaton, B. (1986). Models for the stress-buffering functions of coping resources. *Journal of Health and Social Behavior, 26,* 3 52-365.

Winett, R. A. (1998). Prevention: A proactive developmental-ecological perspective. In T. H. Ollendick & M. Hersen (Eds.), *Handbook of child psychopathology* (3rd ed., pp. 637-671). New York: Plenum Press.

Zubrick, S. R., Silburn, S. R., Teoh, H. J., Carlton, J., Shepherd, C., & Lawrence, D. (1997). *Western Australian child health survey: Education, health and competency catalogue 4305.5.* Perth, WA: Australian Bureau of Statistics.

8

The Resourceful Adolescent Program:
A Universal Approach to the Prevention of
Depression in Adolescents

Ian M. Shochet
Griffith University

Roslyn Montague
New South Wales Institute of Psychiatry

David Ham
Griffith University

Ian M. Shochet · School of Applied Psychology · Griffith University · Nathan 4111 · Australia.

International Perspectives on Child and Adolescent Mental Health. Volume 2: Proceedings of the Second International Conference, edited by N. N. Singh, T. H. Ollendick, and A. N. Singh. © 2002 Elsevier Science Ltd. All rights reserved.

Adolescent depression is currently recognized as a major mental health problem. There are compelling reasons to focus our attention on approaches to prevent adolescent depression. Emerging evidence of the effectiveness of prevention intervention would suggest that the allocation of mental heath resources toward depression prevention programs might prove to be highly beneficial. This chapter describes the nature and severity of the problem of adolescent depression, examines existing approaches to the prevention of adolescent depression, and argues for the value of a universal approach to prevent depression among this population. We describe a school-based depression prevention program, the Resourceful Adolescent Program (RAP) that has been specifically designed to be conducted as a routine part of the school curriculum. A number of controlled trials of this program are described. These provide very encouraging early evidence for the value of this approach to the prevention of adolescent depression and also provide directions for future research in this area.

Adolescent Depression

Depression was the second greatest contributor to death or disability in established market economies and the fourth greatest in the world in 1990 (Murray & Lopez, 1996a), and is predicted to become the second greatest contributor in both established market economies and the world by the year 2010 (Murray & Lopez, 1996b), making it a major cause for concern. In the past, research on depression has focused on the adult population. However, there is now a strong focus on depression in adolescents, partly arising from indications that adolescent depression is a strong predictor of depression in adult life (Birmaher, et al., 1996).

It has been estimated that between 15% and 20% of adolescents will have suffered from depression before the end of adolescence, with point prevalence for depression estimated at up to 8.4% (Anderson & McGee, 1994; Fleming & Offord, 1990; National Health and Medical Research Council [NH&MRC], 1996). Although the results of the first major national survey of child and adolescent mental health in Australia are yet to be released (Sawyer, et al., 2000; Zubrick, Silburn, Burton, & Blair, 2000), the point prevalence of adolescent depressive disorders in Australia is estimated at approximately 5% while the point prevalence of major depressive disorder in adolescents is estimated to be approximately 2.7% (Commonwealth Department of Health and Aged Care [DHAC], 1998). In one Australian study, 12% of adolescents reported feeling depressed for most of the time (DHAC, 1998), while in another study 43% of youth in a community sample reported feeling sad for at least two weeks during the past year (NH&MRC, 1996).

Depression in adolescents has been associated with a range of negative outcomes including social deficits, poor academic performance, physical ill-health and substance abuse, and with increased prevalence of self-harming and suicidal behavior (Birmaher, at al., 1996; DHAC, 2000). One Australian study found that up to half of the youths who died by suicide in Queensland were depressed (DHAC, 1998). Depressed adolescents are, in later life, less likely to complete tertiary education and more likely to experience negative life events and earn lower incomes than those who did not suffer adolescent depression (Lewinsohn & Clarke, 1999).

Given this evidence (e.g. Keller, Lavori, Beardslee, Wunder, & Ryan, 1991; Peterson, et al., 1993) of the prevalence and negative consequences of adolescent depression, there is justification for attempts to minimize the incidence of depression in adolescents and to prevent the development of depressive symptoms when they occur. In Australia, under the current National Mental Health Plan, there is a strong emphasis on the development, evaluation, and implementation of evidence-based preventive interventions targeting adolescent depression (Australian Health Ministers [AHM], 1998; DHAC, 1999). We shall now examine the current status of preventive research and the Resourceful Adolescent Program (Shochet, Holland, & Whitefield, 1997) as one example of the evidence-based preventive implementations targeting adolescent depression.

Principles of Prevention

While the emphasis of treatment interventions is on the reduction of existing symptoms of a disorder after the disorder has been identified, the emphasis of preventive interventions is on reducing the incidence of a disorder in the general population or to prevent the further development of minimal identifiable symptoms of the disorder. Preventive interventions target populations rather than individuals and aim to reduce the potency of the risk factors that increase the probability of development of the disorder and to strengthen the protective factors that act as buffers against the development of the disorder. Theory-based knowledge of the ways in which the risk and protective factors influence the development of the disorder allows the optimal timing of the intervention to maximize its effect on the trajectory of the disorder (Mrazek & Haggerty, 1994; Tolan, Quintana, & Gorman-Smith, 1998).

As preventive interventions focus on the long-term reduction in the incidence of the disorder, the evaluation of the efficacy of these interventions could be expected to focus on reductions in the number of cases of the disorder, with fewer cases expected to occur in groups exposed to the preventive interventions than in the general population. However such reductions may not be evident for several years after the intervention. As preventive interventions often target factors or moderating variables that are in turn predicted on the basis of theory to influence the development of the disorder, it is likely that changes may be observed in these factors shortly after the intervention or at follow-up testing several months later. Changes in these factors may provide a means of evaluation of the intervention, well before long-term changes in prevalence or severity of the disorder become apparent (Tolan, et al., 1998).

Preventive interventions are classified with reference to the population to which the intervention is addressed. Universal preventive interventions aim to reduce the incidence of new cases of a disorder in a whole population, for example, all families with adolescents or all adolescents in a particular school. Selective interventions aim to reduce the incidence of new cases in a group or part of the population that is considered to be at elevated risk for the disorder because of the presence of certain risk factors that predispose individuals in that group to the disorder. Indicated preventive interventions aim to minimize or prevent the further development of the disorder in individuals who already display early or minimal symptoms of the disorder and are considered at risk of further development of the disorder but do not meet the criteria to be diagnosed with the disorder (Mrazek & Haggerty, 1994).

Universal, selective, and indicated preventive interventions each have advantages and disadvantages that need to be considered in determining which type of intervention is to be developed and implemented. Indicated interventions require some screening process to determine which individuals display the early symptoms required to meet the criteria for this type of intervention. The intervention is then limited to this target group, so can be made more intensive and involve greater cost per person, with significant change expected in each participant. Selective interventions also require the identification of those individuals at heightened risk who are to be included, although the method of selection is not required to be as accurate as for indicated interventions. Again the intervention is limited to the selected group, although this target group will usually be larger than for an indicated intervention. The expected outcome is a reduction in risk to approximate normal levels of risk. Hence the intensity and cost per person of the intervention may be lower than for an indicated intervention. For a universal intervention there is no selection process, and the group of potential participants is thus very large, including all members of the targeted population; this limits the possible intensity of the intervention and the cost per participant. Universal interventions have the added advantage of impacting on persons who for some reason may not be identified as "at risk" and thus not be involved in a selective or indicated intervention but may later develop the disorder without any intervention (Tolan, et al., 1998).

Both selective and indicated interventions thus require the identification of potential participants and their involvement in the intervention which could easily lead to their being stigmatized or seen as "different" to non-participants by themselves or others. For adolescents, for whom peer group acceptance is critical, this may be a very strong impediment to involvement in an indicated or selective preventive program. This problem of stigmatization does not arise with universal interventions and in the case of interventions with adolescents may be avoided by offering the intervention as an all-inclusive part of the normal school program.

Preventive Interventions for Adolescent Depression

Prior to discussion of the current state of prevention research related to adolescent depression, it is necessary to identify the risk and protective factors on which preventive interventions would be based. Individual risk factors include prior subclinical levels of depression, previous history of depressive disorders, stressful life events, poor problem-solving skills, use of ineffective coping strategies, negative body image, low self-esteem, and lack of social support (Lewinsohn, Roberts, et al., 1994). Negatively distorted self-evaluations (Stark, et al., 1998) and a cognitive style that attributes failure or negative occurrences to global, stable, internal factors (Lewinsohn, Roberts, et al., 1994) also predict future depression, while this negative cognitive style is also influenced by current or previous depression (Nolen-Hoeksema, Girgus, & Seligman, 1986).

Environmental risk factors for adolescent depression include many related to the family environment (Kaslow, Deering, & Racusin, 1994; Lewinsohn, Clarke, Seeley, & Rohde, 1994; Shochet & Dadds, 1997) with family conflict, especially escalating parent-adolescent conflict, and expression of parental over-control considered to be major risk factors for depression and other problems during adolescence (Burbach, Kashani, & Rosenberg, 1994; Lewinsohn, Roberts, et al., 1994). Severe parent-adolescent conflict is also associated with elevated risk for chronicity and relapse in depressed adolescents (Birmaher, et al., 2000). Parental psychopathology is another potent risk factor for adolescent depression (Kaslow, et al., 1994).

There are also potent family-based protective factors against adolescent depression. Age-appropriate secure attachment to parents negatively correlates with adolescent depressive symptomatology (Papini, Roggman, & Anderson, 1991), while adolescents who develop appropriately increasing autonomy alongside continuing close relationships with their parents are at reduced risk of depression (Kaslow, et al., 1994). Secure parental attachment in adolescence has been found to be related to positive self-perceptions leading to resilience to stress (Kenny, Moilanen, Lomax, & Brabeck, 1993).

To date, the literature reveals few adequately evaluated preventive interventions for adolescent depression (Durlak & Wells, 1997, 1998). There is evidence for the efficacy of indicated and selective preventive interventions. In an indicated preventive intervention, Jaycox, Reivich, Gillham, and Seligman (1994) provided training in cognitive skills, social problem solving, negotiation, coping skills and assertiveness to 10 - 13 year old adolescents, and found that participants displayed significant reductions in symptoms of depression compared with controls at post-intervention and at 2-year follow-up (Gillham, Reivich, Jaycox, & Seligman, 1995). Another successful trial of an indicated preventive intervention (Clarke, et al., 1995) was based on a program developed by Lewinsohn, Clarke, Hops, and Andrews (1990) for treating adolescent major depression and included cognitive restructuring and training in developing and using improved coping skills. The intervention was offered to 14 - 15 year old boys who displayed elevated levels of depressive symptomatology but did not meet diagnostic criteria for any depressive disorder. Clarke, et al. (1995) found that trial participants displayed significant improvements in depressive symptoms after the intervention and at follow-up compared with wait-list controls. Both of these indicated prevention studies reported poor recruitment rates of less than 20% and less than 50%, respectively, and high attrition rates of 30% and 27%, respectively, indicating possible problems with a self-selection bias.

These studies have addressed the individual risk factors for depression but not the family-based risk factors. With strong evidence for the very important role of the family in adolescent development and in the development of adolescent depression, there is also a place for interventions that address the family based risk and protective factors for depression. There has been very little research into the efficacy of interventions to address these family-based risk factors (see Diamond, Serrano, Dickey, and Sonis [1997], and Lewinsohn and Clarke [1999], for reviews). In one trial of selective preventive interventions to reduce the incidence of depression in adolescents who as the children of depressed parents were at elevated risk of depression, Beardlsee and his colleagues compared a clinician-based family intervention focusing on the family's experience of the parents' depression with a lecture-based psychoeducational intervention (Beardslee, 1989; Beardslee, et al., 1992, 1993; Bearedslee & MacMillan, 1993). Parents in the family intervention condition reported greater changes in behaviors and attitudes and subsequently reduction in risk factors for adolescent depression than those in the lecture condition, although no information about changes in adolescents' depression or recruitment rates was reported.

Several family based interventions have included parent skills training to improve parents' communication and conflict resolution skills and to help parents reinforce cognitive-behavioral skills taught to their adolescents. This approach has not resulted in significant improvements attributable to the parent interventions (Brent, et al., 1997; Lewinsohn, et al.,

1990), possibly because conflict management approaches focus on and bring into salience existing conflicts (Brent, et al., 1997). The literature provides little indication of how preventive family based interventions can effectively reduce the incidence of adolescent depression.

The research discussed here provides some support for the development and implementation of indicated and selective preventive interventions for adolescent depression, but also demonstrates the limitations on recruitment for these programs. The possible stigmatization of participants in indicated and selective interventions may be a factor in the poor recruitment rates for these programs. The implementation of universal intervention programs as part of school activities, if necessary in addition to indicated programs, would allow the interventions to reach a greater number of participants including those not identified for indicated programs. However there are very few such universal programs that address adolescent depression either for adolescents or for their families.

The Resourceful Adolescent Programs

The Resourceful Adolescent Programs were developed to fill the need for universal interventions against adolescent depression. The Resourceful Adolescent Program for Adolescents (RAP-A) is an 11-session program designed to be implemented as part of the school curriculum in the classroom. It addresses the individual risk factors for depression of stress, low self-esteem, negative cognitive styles, poor problem-solving skills and poor social support. The Resourceful Adolescent Program for Parents (RAP-P) is a three-session program offered to parents; it addresses some of the family-based risk and protective factors for adolescent depression. These programs will now be discussed in some detail, followed by a discussion of the evaluations of the interventions.

The Resourceful Adolescent Program for Adolescents (RAP-A)

RAP-A was developed for 12 - 15 year old adolescents (Year 8 and Year 9 students) as part of the school curriculum. It was implemented during one 45-minute period per week for one school term. Year 8 and Year 9 students were selected as the target group on the basis of evidence that the incidence of depression increases sharply after age 15 years (Burke, Burke, Regier, & Rae, 1990; Lewinsohn, Clarke, et al., 1994). The program is designed to forestall this acceleration in the development of depression. To avoid the possibility of stigmatization that may be associated with selective or indicated interventions, RAP-A was offered as a universal intervention to all students in the cohort. RAP-A sessions were conducted by trained facilitators, usually school teachers, guidance officers and other professionals who have undertaken an approved training course. A Group Leaders' Manual outlined the content and process for each session, while each student received a Participant Workbook (Shochet, Whitefield, & Holland, 1997).

Rather than focus on deficits and symptoms, RAP-A focuses on the recognition and reinforcement of existing personal strengths and the development of additional skills and psychological resources. The overall aim of the program is to promote positive coping strategies and to enable participants to maintain a sense of self in difficult and stressful situations.

RAP-A includes several of the proven cognitive-behavioral elements of the interventions discussed above. These include stress management using self-management and self-relaxation strategies; cognitive restructuring; helping adolescents to identify and challenge negative or distorted thinking and develop positive self-talk; and problem solving strategies based on defining problems, identifying and evaluating solutions and implementing the chosen solution step by step. RAP-A also includes interpersonal components such as establishing and drawing on support networks, applying understanding of others' perspectives in maintaining peace, and promoting harmony. These components are drawn from Interpersonal Psychotherapy for depression (Klerman & Weissman, 1993; Mufson, Moreau, Weissman, & Klerman, 1993); they address known predictors of depression such as interpersonal conflict (Harter & Jackson, 1993; Lewinsohn, Roberts, et al., 1994).

The theme throughout the program is one of resourcefulness metaphorically based on the children's story of "The Three Little Pigs." In this nursery tale one little pig built a house of straw and another built a house of sticks but when adversity struck in the form of the big bad wolf these houses collapsed allowing the little pigs to be eaten. However the third and most resourceful little pig built a house of bricks that was strong and resilient and protected the pig from the wolf. As the program proceeds participants build their own personal "RAP-A house" using personal resource bricks such as "Personal Strength Bricks," "Keeping Calm Bricks," or "Problem Solving Bricks." In each session, participants engage in group activities that enable them to practice the skills being taught and experience how these skills can help them, and to relate each new skill to building their level of self-esteem as they respond to different situations.

RAP-A commences with a "getting to know you" session in which the facilitator and participants engage in activities to encourage them to get to know each other. In the second session the RAP program is outlined, group rules are developed and participants explore the concept of self-esteem and identify personal strengths. They are introduced to a method of self-assessment of self-esteem that is used through the course. In Session 3, participants are introduced to the RAP Model which helps them understand how their physical, behavioral, cognitive and emotional responses to situations relate to each other and influence how they react in different situations. Session 4 focuses on identifying body clues related to stress, and ways of managing stress and remaining calm. Session 5 examines self-talk and its influence on emotions and behavior, and Session 6 introduces participants to ways of challenging faulty self-talk and cognitive errors and substituting "resourceful" thoughts, and the positive effects of resourceful thinking on self-esteem. In Session 7, participants examine problem solving methods, the evaluation of different solutions and the selection and implementation of appropriate solutions. Session 8 focuses on identifying and accessing personal support networks. In Session 9, participants are encouraged to see situations from the perspective of others, and to use this skill to reduce and manage conflict. Session 10 continues to address conflict and the ways in which participants can "make the peace" and "keep the peace," particularly in the family environment, and demonstrates how doing this makes for a happier environment and builds self-esteem. In Session 11 participants review the program, complete an evaluation of the program, engage in activities that apply the course material to different situations, and celebrate with a party. There is scope for combining a limited number of sessions if necessary to fit the program into a term shorter than 11 weeks.

The Resourceful Adolescent Program for Parents (RAP-P)

RAP-P was developed as a universal preventive intervention for adolescent depression and addresses the family-based risk factor of parent-adolescent conflict and the protective factors of developing independence coupled with strong parental attachment. It is intended for use with parents of Year 8 and Year 9 (12 - 14 years old) adolescents. RAP-P is a positively focused resilience building program based on identifying and building on parents' competencies and strengths. The aims of RAP-P are: to help parents boost their own self-esteem, differentiation and self-management skills; reduce their own negative emotional reactivity to their adolescents; boost their adolescents' self-esteem; and reduce and manage their adolescents' negative emotional reactivity to them.

In RAP-P, systems theory is integrated with cognitive-behavioral theory and strategies and a knowledge of normal adolescent development (Bowen, 1976, 1978; Kerr & Bowen, 1988). From the family systems perspective, RAP-P focuses on the inter-generational effects of the parents' levels of differentiation of self on their adolescents and the inter-relationships between differentiation, stress, and conflict. A person displaying good differentiation of self is able to separate their rational and emotional functioning on the intrapersonal level and, on the inter-personal level, to maintain both a sense of belonging to their family and a sense of separateness and individuality. With these characteristics, a person is able to maintain a healthy self-esteem in the face of conflict and stress. An undifferentiated person becomes highly anxious and emotionally reactive both intrapersonally and in relationships and is less able to soothe themselves in times of conflict and stress. Poor differentiation arises from early life experiences of failed attempts in their family of origin either to develop closeness to others or to maintain separation from others; these experiences result in a high level of anxiety and overly critical perceptions of the behavior of others. During adolescence, children make constant adjustments in their relationships with their parents, particularly with respect to their developing independence and the changing nature of their closeness to their parents. Well-differentiated parents are able to perceive these changes as part of the normal cycle of adolescent development and are not threatened by them. However, undifferentiated parents see such changes as threats to themselves and react with struggles for control that exacerbate any conflict with their adolescents. The children of poorly differentiated parents are likely to reproduce the poor differentiation of their parents so differentiation has intergenerational effects.

RAP-P draws on cognitive behavioral strategies for stress management, cognitive restructuring, and management and prevention of conflict, and introduces parents to cognitive-behavioral principles related to self-managed change in behaviors and emotions. RAP-P also applies social learning theory in that group facilitators model to participants those interpersonal processes such as active listening, validating, positive reinforcement and showing empathy that are central to good family relationships. A psychoeducational approach is adopted to assist parents to be aware of and understand the normal developmental needs of early adolescents. With the understanding that what is happening is part of the normal development of their adolescents, the parents are less likely to react emotionally and more likely to provide support to their adolescents.

A Group Leaders' Manual (Shochet, Osgarby, Holland, & Whitefield, 1998) defines the course content and process while parents receive a Participant's Workbook (Shochet, Osgarby & Dyer, 1999). The program is presented by trained facilitators in three sessions each of which is 2-3 hours. Session 1 focuses on identifying what parents are doing well, understanding how stress affects parents, and managing stress. In Session 2 parents are encouraged to understand their teenager better by reflecting on their own adolescence and to identify and develop ways of enhancing their teenager's self-esteem and supporting their adolescent's independence. Session 3 focuses on promoting harmony in families, reducing and managing conflict between teenagers and parents, and looking forward to a positive future with the teenagers. The format of the program includes presentation of material by facilitators, small group discussions, and large group summary sessions.

Evaluation of the Resourceful Adolescent Programs

Although there are many different programs being used to improve the well being of adolescents, many of these have not been adequately evaluated in controlled trials and many have no evidence for their efficacy (Kazdin, 1993). With an increasing emphasis on the use of only evidence-based interventions in Australian Mental Health programs (DHAC, 1998; Mitchell, 2000) the proper evaluation of the Resourceful Adolescent Programs has been a priority, with a number of controlled trials in various stages of completion. These trials will now be examined.

Initial trial of RAP-A and RAP-P

The initial trial of the Resourceful Adolescent Programs evaluated RAP-A and RAP-P as universal school-based preventive interventions (Shochet, et al., in press). Participating Year 9 students were allocated to one of three conditions: RAP-A, with students receiving RAP-A only; RAP-F, with students receiving RAP-A while their parents were invited to participate in RAP-P workshops; and a no-intervention comparative group. RAP-A was implemented in classrooms as part of the school curriculum while RAP-P was provided to participating parents as three three-hour workshops at night, during the 11-week duration of RAP-A. It was predicted that students in the intervention groups would show fewer depressive symptoms than those in the comparative group at post-intervention and at 10-month follow-up, with greater reductions in symptoms in the RAP-F group.

Recruitment and attrition rates for students showed the anticipated improvement over those found in the indicated trials reviewed previously (Clarke, et al., 1995; Gillham, Reivich, Jaycox, & Seligman, 1995). Participation was 88% and attrition was 5.8% between pre- and post- testing, and 19.8% from pre-testing to follow-up. Much of this later attrition was due to absences on the day of testing and to relocations from the school. Ninety-eight percent of students who started RAP-A completed it. These improved recruitment and attrition rates provide support for the implementation of universal school-based preventive programs for adolescent depression.

Outcome measures were three self-report measures of depression: the Children's Depression Inventory (CDI; Kovacs, 1992), the Reynolds Adolescent Depression Scale (RADS; Reynolds, 1987), and the Beck Hopelessness Scale (BHS; Beck & Steer, 1988; Beck, Weissman, Lester, & Trexler, 1974). Both RAP-A and RAP-F intervention groups showed statistically and clinically significant improvements on these measures compared to the comparison group. At post-test and follow-up, students in the intervention groups recorded significantly lower mean levels of depressive and hopelessness symptoms than those in the comparative group. The RAP-F group did not show the predicted improvement over the RAP-A group; this may have been attributable to the disappointingly low recruitment rate for RAP-P with only 36% of students in this condition having a parent who attended any RAP-P workshops and only 10% having a parent who attended all workshops. As a result, this trial provided no evidence that RAP-P has any effect on adolescent depression.

This trial provided evidence that RAP-A can benefit both sub-clinically depressed and healthy participants. Students with elevated depression and hopelessness pre-test scores in the intervention groups were significantly more likely to record scores in the healthy range and less likely to fall in the clinical range than no-intervention students. At follow-up, there was a significant difference between the intervention and comparison groups in the clinical status of students who at pre-test recorded levels of depressive and hopelessness symptoms in the healthy range. No initially healthy students in the intervention groups showed sub-clinical symptoms at follow-up, compared to 10.1% of initially healthy students in the comparison group. Thus by being offered as a universal intervention to all students, RAP-A provided a benefit to students would not normally have been recruited into an indicated program.

One limitation of the trial described above was that the intervention and control conditions ran with different cohorts of year nine students at different times of the year. It is possible that cohort or seasonal effects influenced the results of this trial. We are currently conducting a large multi-site national trial (described below) in which we will attempt to replicate the above trial while controlling for seasonal and cohort effects.

New South Wales Effectiveness Trial

One of the issues that surfaced soon after the initial trial, was the importance of sustainability. In the initial trial the RAP-A, facilitators were trained personnel provided by the research grant. This level of resource would not be sustainable in the long term. The question arose as to whether resources from within the school or allied health support systems (i.e., teachers, school psychologists, guidance officers, nurses) could effectively implement the program. An additional question was whether the program could be implemented over a shorter more intensive period, for example, two hours per week for five weeks. The schools indicated that, because of the timetable structure, this would greatly improve the capacity for the implementation of the RAP-A program as a routine part of the school curriculum.

Under the direction of the second author of this chapter, a trial is currently being completed in Sydney to investigate this form of implementation of the RAP-A program. In addition to the outcome on depressive symptoms, this trial has also gathered both qualitative and quantitative responses regarding the program from the adolescents. A total of 1,006 ninth grade adolescents from five different schools were allocated by school to either a RAP-A ($\underline{N}$=525) or control condition ($\underline{N}$=481). Scores on depressive symptoms as measured by the CDI, the RADS, and the BHS were collected at pre-test post-test and six month follow-up. Preliminary analysis indicates a statistically significant intervention effect in favor of the RAP-A program. There do not appear to be any statistically significant differences in the effects of the program as a result of teachers versus health professionals implementing the program. This suggests that the use of teachers as a resource would seem appropriate. The effect size was not as strong as in the initial trial, which raises some concern about whether the program effect is diluted when the program is implemented for two hours per week for five weeks rather than for 50-60 minutes for 11 weeks. There may be more opportunity for transfer and generalization of skills when the program content is more spread out.

The students' perceptions of the program were generally positive. A random selection of adolescents were interviewed four months after the completion of the program and asked whether they could recall the program content and whether they could provide any specific examples about how the program had helped them. To minimize the possibility of positive response bias, the interviewer was an outside person not previously known to the students. Below we list some of the responses provided by the students to the question "Can you give me some specific examples of when you used skills from the RAP program?"

When we play football, if someone starts swearing, I think don't worry, don't hit him yet - work things out first. Before I would have started punching way before.

With your parents and stuff, you should see their side of the story more.

Yes I was pretty stressed one night and I put on some really calm music and relaxed. Before I wouldn't have done anything.

Like not thinking negatively, like if someone stands you up, don't think they don't like you, just think they missed the bus or something. Don't blame them.

Someone stood me up twice. Before the program I would have been pissed and called her and just kept yelling at her. So it's a good program because it changed my life a bit.

I wouldn't use it every day, but I've used it before. At my best friends party there was a bit of drug use there, it got offered to me but I just passed it along and nothing was said. Before I would have probably used it if I didn't do RAP because I probably wasn't thinking, then, like afterwards it made me think about a lot of things like that.

I get into a lot of arguments with my brother and sister and sometimes my friends, but now I look to what will benefit me and I say, 'okay what are they going through' so I don't get so upset as much. Before it always used to be my way.

The New South Wales trial provides strong encouragement to continue with a universal approach to the prevention of adolescent depression. For many participants, the program is perceived as making very salient changes to their coping ability. The program would appear to be sustainable in the school system, and teachers seem to be effective deliverers of the program. It might be preferable to incubate the program content over a longer period of time. Future research should focus on the value of providing revision or booster sessions in subsequent years.

RAP-P Trial

A trial of the Resourceful Adolescent Parent Program as a stand-alone universal preventive intervention is currently in progress. As mentioned in the initial trial, the recruitment rate was too low for us to draw any conclusions about the value of the RAP-P program. This trial is designed to evaluate the effectiveness of two forms of RAP-P, as three workshops or as a videotaped program with workbook and telephone facilitation, in preventing adolescent depression. A video program was well received in an earlier pilot trial but participant feedback indicated that telephone facilitation would be an essential part of the intervention. It was expected that the video format in which parents could access information in their own home and at their convenience would greatly improve recruitment. It was predicted that parents' involvement in either format of RAP-P would result in lower levels of parent-adolescent conflict and improved parental attachment in their adolescents. These variables are both theoretically and empirically linked to the reduction in adolescent depression (Kaslow, et al., 1994). We have predicted that reductions in adolescents' depressive symptoms would also result from parents' involvement in RAP-P. We have also predicted reductions in parents' stress levels and in their emotional reactivity, with consequent improvements in parent-adolescent conflict and in parent-child interactions.

Six state schools and five non-government schools with a total Year 8 population of 1612 were involved in this study. Schools were randomly allocated to one of three conditions: RAP-P workshops, RAP-P videotaped program with workbooks and telephone facilitation, and wait-list control condition in which parents will be offered the program after final testing.

Despite a recruitment process including strong endorsement from the schools, recruitment for the parent programs was again poor, with parents of 15% of the Year 8 students taking part. The increased parent participation which was the goal of the development of the videotaped program was not realized; the video program attracted the lowest recruitment rate at 11.6%, with recruitment for the workshop program the highest at 19.4% and the control condition attracting 13.7% of the families. The video condition not only did not bring about an increase in recruitment, as initially anticipated, but there was also a low rate of completion of the intervention. Six months after the commencement of the video program, just over a quarter of the video condition participants had completed the program and the post-intervention questionnaires. In the workshop condition, close to two thirds of the parents completed the program and the post-intervention questionnaires. It is interesting to note that in the workshop condition there was a 95% retention rate after parents attended the first session. In other words most of the participants that were lost to that condition were lost before the first face-to-face contact.

Early data analysis of participants' reactions to the program showed that both the workshops and the video program were well received, although the workshop program received significantly more positive ratings than the video program. Mean scores on a five-point scale for satisfaction with the program, helpfulness of the program, and how encouraging and how enjoyable participants found the programs to be were 4.45, 4.10, 4.41 and 4.43, respectively, for the workshops and 3.94, 3.57, 3.89, and 3.57, respectively, for the video program. Thus the participants certainly valued the program, particularly in the workshop condition, but only at the follow-up will we have the data to evaluate whether we have altered the trajectory of those risk and protective factors in parent-adolescent relationship to prevent adolescent depression. The available data indicate that the theoretical model on which the intervention is based is appropriate, with the predicted relationships being found between the parent-adolescent risk and protective factors and adolescent depression.

National Trial of RAP-A and RAP-P

With a grant from the Australian National Health and Medical Research Council, a multi-site national trial of RAP-A and RAP-P began in 2001 and will be completed in 2003. This trial will involve 10 pairs of schools, generally with a cohort of 100-200 grade eight students from lower to middle socioeconomic areas in southeast Queensland, New South Wales, Tasmania, and Western Australia. The schools in each pair are closely matched on socioeconomic status and size. Pairs of schools are randomly allocated to either the RAP-A condition in which students receive RAP-A, or the RAP-F condition in which students receive RAP-A and parents receive RAP-P. In each pair one school is randomly allocated to the intervention condition in 2001, with the other school being in the no-intervention control condition in 2001. In 2002 the allocation to intervention and control conditions within pairs will be reversed.

This trial project has been designed to avoid the methodological problems of the initial trial. School effects will be controlled by having the intervention and control conditions in the same school in sequential cohorts. Cohort and seasonal effects will be controlled by having the intervention and control conditions in the same school at the same time in two different years and in matched schools at the same time.

Participation in the trial will be offered to all Year 8 students in participating schools. RAP-A will be offered as part of the school curriculum and facilitated predominantly by school teachers and support staff trained as RAP-A facilitators. The New South Wales effectiveness trial has provided encouragement for us to use teachers as facilitators. Adolescent participants will complete similar measures at pre-intervention, post-intervention and 12-month follow-up. These measures will include self-report measures of depression and anxiety, problem solving skills, cognitive explanatory style, attachment to parents, self-esteem, major life events and school culture. Parents and adolescents will complete parallel versions of measures of parent-adolescent conflict, and a behavioral questionnaire related to the adolescents. A structured clinical interview will be administered to selected students to provide convergent data on depressive symptoms. Schools will provide academic, attendance and discipline data on participating students to provide convergent information about the adolescents' wellbeing. Treatment integrity will be assessed by three convergent means: facilitator self-reports, participant reports, and observation of randomly selected groups in each school. It is hoped that this trial will provide extensive data on the proximal and distal effects of universal prevention programs for adolescent depression. It is also hoped that the added benefit of intervening with parents will be adequately assessed.

CONCLUSION

Given the incidents and problems associated with adolescent depression there is compelling evidence of the need for a prevention approach that can engage and recruit adolescents on a wide scale. A school-based universal approach to prevention of adolescent depression would seem to offer the opportunity to overcome problems of recruitment and engagement often encountered in indicated or selective approaches to prevention and even in the treatment of clinical cases of adolescent depression. The Resourceful Adolescent Program (RAP-A) was developed with a view to implementing routine stress reduction programs within the classroom curriculum, and targeting adolescents at an age just before the incidents of depression begin to increase quite sharply. A parallel parent program was developed with the view to enhancing maintenance of the intervention by optimizing the family risk and protective factors towards healthy development.

The trials and evaluations that have been conducted have provided support for most of the premises on which the Resourceful Adolescent Programs are based. With the universal approach, the rates of recruitment and engagement of adolescents have met or exceeded our expectations. Excellent support from the schools, education authorities, and parents has assisted in this regard. The trials have also demonstrated that the program has been able to be implemented with fidelity to program protocol. While more research needs to be done, it would seem, at this point, that educators are not less effective than health workers in the delivery of the program. The program is generally valued by the adolescents and there is evidence that the program is effective in preventing symptoms of depression on a population prevention basis.

The trials have shown that some adolescents benefit more extensively than others. Some adolescents report that the program had a major positive impact on psychological and behavioral wellbeing, others were indifferent to the program. The future challenge would be to understand the variables that predict the variation in effectiveness of the program. These could be contextual factors, like family, school-based, or facilitator variables or intra-psychic factors. As in the treatment literature this will be a difficult search but an important endeavor.

More research to find a program that will encourage a larger percentage of parents to participate will need to be conducted. Parent involvement is crucial given the relationship between family risk and protective factors and adolescent depression, suicide, or psychopathology in general. To date, we have not been able to provide evidence for the feasibility or value of the universal approach with parents. The multi-site trial and the stand alone parent trial should provide a realistic opportunity to assess the value of the parent program either as an adjunctive or stand alone program. It may be that the intense relationship building required to engage parents is not sustainable on a universal basis, but it would be premature to conclude that this would never be feasible.

It is very encouraging, however, that a positively oriented strength-based (rather than pathology-based) universal approach, targeting adolescents in the schools, can be used to enhance psychological health. Careful and systematic research is required to test the generalizability of these early findings and the factors that enhance the possibility of continued effective implementation in the real world context.

REFERENCES

Anderson, C.A., & McGee, R. (1994). Comorbidity of depression in children and adolescents. In W. M. Reynolds & H. F. Johnson (Eds.), *Handbook of depression in children and adolescents*. New York: Plenum.

Australian Health Ministers (1998). *Second national mental health plan*. Canberra: Australian Government Publishing Service.

Beardslee, W. R. (1989). The role of self-understanding in resilient individuals: The development of a perspective. *American Journal of Orthopsychiatry, 59* , 266 - 278.

Beardslee, W. R., Hoke, L., Wheelock, I., Rothberg, P. C., van der Velde, P., & Swatling, S. (1992). Initial findings on preventive interventions for families with parental affective disorders. *American Journal of Psychiatry, 149*, 1335-1340.

Beardslee, W. R., & MacMillan, H. L. (1993). Preventive intervention with the children of depressed parents: A case study. *Psychoanalytic Study of the Child, 48*, 249-276.

Beardslee, W. R., Salt, P., Porterfield, K., Rothberg, P. C., van der Velde, P., Swatling, S., Hoke, L., Moilanen, D., & Wheelock, I. (1993). Comparison of preventive interventions for families with parental affective disorder. *Journal of the American Academy of Child Psychiatry, 32*, 254-263.

Beck, A. T., & Steer, R. A. (1988). *Beck Hopelessness Scale*. New York: The Psychological Corporation.

Beck, A. T., Weissman, A., Lester, D., & Trexler, L. (1974). The measurement of pessimism: The Hopelessness Scale. *Journal of Consulting and Clinical Psychology, 42*, 861 - 865.

Birmaher, B., Brent, D. A., Kolko, D., Baugher, M., Bridge, J., Holder, D., Iyenger, S., & Ulloa, R. E. (2000). Clinical outcome after short-term psychotherapy for adolescents with major depressive disorder. *Archives of General Psychiatry, 57*, 29-36.

Birmaher, B., Ryan, N.D., Williamson, D. E., Brent, D. A., Kaufman, J., Dahl, R.E., Perel, J., & Nelson, B. (1996). Childhood and adolescent depression: A review of the past 10 years. Part 1. *Journal of the American Academy of Child and Adolescent Psychiatry, 35*, 1427-1439.

Bowen, M. (1976). Theory in the practice of psychotherapy. In P. J. Guerin (Ed.), *Family therapy: Theory and practice* (pp. 42-90). New York: Gardner Press.

Bowen, M. (1978). *Family therapy in clinical practice*. New York: Jason Aronson.

Brent, D. A., Holder, D., Kolko, D., Birmaher, B., Baugher, M., Roth, C., Iyengar, S., & Johnson, B. A. (1997). A clinical psychotherapy trial for adolescent depression comparing cognitive, family, and supportive therapy. *Archives of General psychiatry, 54,* 877-885.

Burbach, D. J., Kashani, J. H., & Rosenberg, T. K. *(1989). Parental bonding and depressive disorders in adolescents.* Journal of Child Psychology and Psychiatry and Allied Disciplines, 30, *183 - 204.*

Burke, K. C., Burke, J. D., Regier, D. A., & Rae, D. S. (1990). *Age at onset of selected mental disorders in five community populations.* Archives of General Psychiatry, 47, *511-518.*

Clarke, G. N., Hawkins, W., Murphy, M., Sheeber, L. B., Lewinson, P. M., & Seeley, J. R. (1995). Targeted prevention of unipolar depressive disorder in an at-risk sample of high school adolescents: A randomized trial of a group cognitive intervention. *Journal of the American Academy of Child Adolescent Psychiatry, 34,* 312 - 321.

Commonwealth Department of Health and Aged Care. (1998). *National health priority areas report: Mental health.* Canberra: Australian Government Publishing Service.

Commonwealth Department of Health and Aged Care. (1999). *Mental health promotion and prevention national action plan.* Canberra: Australian Government Publishing Service.

Commonwealth Department of Health and Aged Care. (2000). *National youth suicide prevention strategy: Setting the evidence-based research agenda for Australia (A literature review).* Canberra: Commonwealth of Australia.

Diamond, G. S., Serrano, A. C., Dickey, M., & Sonis, W. A. (1996). Current status of family-based outcome and process research. *_Journal of the American Academy of Child and Adolescent Psychiatry, 35,* 6-16.

Durlak, J. A., & Wells, A. M. (1997). Primary prevention mental health programs for children and adolescents: a meta-analytic review. *American Journal of Community Psychology, 25,* 115-152.

Durlak, J. A., & Wells, A. M. (1998). Evaluation of indicated preventive intervention (secondary prevention) mental health programs for children and adolescents. *American Journal of Community Psychology, 26,* 775-802.

Fleming, J. E., & Offord, D. R. (1990). Epidemiology of childhood depressive disorders: A critical review. *Journal of the American Academy of Child and Adolescent Psychiatry, 29,* 571 - 580.

Gillham, J. E., Reivich, K. J., Jaycox, L. H., & Seligman, M. E. (1995). Prevention of depressive symptoms in school children: Two year follow-up. *Psychological Science, 6,* 343 - 350.

Harter, S., & Jackson, B. K. (1993). Young adolescents' perceptions of the link between low self-worth and depressed affect. *Journal of Early Adolescence, 13,* 383 - 407.

Jaycox, L. H., Reivich, K. J., Gillham, J., & Seligman, M. E. P. (1994). Prevention of depressive symptoms in school children. *Behavior Research and Therapy, 32*, 801-816.

Kaslow, N. J., Deering, C. G., & Racusin, G. R. (1994). Depressed children and their families. *Clinical Psychology Review, 14*, 39 - 59.

Kazdin, A. E. (1993). Adolescent mental health: prevention and treatment programs. *American Psychologist, 48*, 127-141.

Keller, M., Lavori, P. W., Beardslee, W. R., Wunder, J., & Ryan, N. (1991). Depression in children and adolescents: New data on "undertreatment" and a literature review on the efficacy of available treatments. *Journal of Affective Disorders, 21*, 163 - 171.

Kenny, M. E., Moilanen, D. L., Lomax, R., & Brabeck, M. M. (1993). Contributions of parental attachments to view of self and depressive symptoms among early adolescents. *Journal of Early Adolescence, 13*, 408-430.

Kerr, M. E., & Bowen, M. (1988). *Family evaluation: An approach based on Bowen theory.* New York: Norton.

Klerman, G. L., & Weissman, M. M. (1993). The place of psychotherapy in the treatment of depression. In G. L. Klerman & M. M. Weissman (Eds.), *New applications of interpersonal psychotherapy* (pp. 51 – 71). Washington, DC: American Psychiatric Press.

Kovacs, M. (1992). *The Children's Depression Inventory manual.* North Tonawanda: Multi-Health Systems.

Lewinsohn, P. M., & Clarke, G. N. (1999). Psychosocial treatments for adolescent depression. *Clinical Psychology Review, 19*, 329-342.

Lewinsohn, P. M., Clarke, G. N., Hops, H., & Andrews, J. (1990). Cognitive-behavioral treatment for depressed adolescents. *Behavior Therapy, 21*, 385-401.

Lewinsohn, P. M., Clarke, G. N., Seeley, J. R., & Rohde, P. (1994). Major depression in community adolescents: Age at onset, episode duration, and time to recurrence. *Journal of the American Academy of Child and Adolescent Psychiatry, 33*, 714 - 722.

Lewinsohn, P. M., Roberts, R. E., Seeley, J. R., Rhode, P., Gotlib, I. H., & Hops, H. (1994). Adolescent psychopathology II: Psychosocial risk factors for depression. *Journal of Abnormal Psychology, 103*, 302-315.

Mitchell, P. (2000). *Valuing young lives: evaluation of the National Youth Suicide Prevention Strategy.* Melbourne: Australian Institute of Family Studies.

Mrazek, P. J., & Haggerty, R.J. (Eds.). (1994). <u>Reducing risks for mental disorders:</u> *Frontiers for preventive intervention research.* Washington DC: National Academy Press.

Mufson, L., Moreau, D., Weissman, M. M., & Klerman, G. L. (1993). Interpersonal psychotherapy for adolescent depression. In G. L. Klerman & M. M. Weissman (Eds.), *New applications of interpersonal psychotherapy* (pp. 130-166). Washington DC: American Psychiatric Association Press.

Murray, C. J. L., & Lopez, A. D. (1996a). The global burden of disease in 1990: final results and their sensitivity to alternative epidemiological perspectives, discount rates, age-weights and disability weights. In C. J. L. Murray & A. D. Lopez (Eds.), *The global burden of disease: A comprehensive assessment of mortality and disability from diseases, injuries, and risk factors in 1990 and projected to 2020* (pp. 247-293). Cambridge, MA: Harvard School of Public Health, World Health Organization and World Bank.

Murray, C. J. L., & Lopez, A. D. (1996b). Alternative visions of the future: projecting mortality and disability, 1990-2020. In C. J. L. Murray & A. D. Lopez (Eds.), *The global burden of disease: a comprehensive assessment of mortality and disability from diseases, injuries, and risk factors in 1990 and projected to 2020* (pp. 325-395). Cambridge, MA: Harvard School of Public Health, World Health Organization and World Bank.

National Health and Medical Research Council. (1996). *Clinical Practice guidelines: Depression in young people.* Canberra: NHMRC.

Nolen-Hoeksema, S., Girgus, J. S., & Seligman, M. E. P. (1986). Learned helplessness in children: A longitudinal study of depression, achievement, and explanatory style. *Journal of Personality and Social Psychology, 51,* 435-442.

Papini, D. R., Roggman, L. A., & Anderson, J. (1991). Early adolescent perceptions of attachment to mother and father: a test of the emotional buffering hypothesis. *Journal of Early Adolescence, 11,* 258-275.

Peterson, A. C., Compas, B. E., Brooks-Gunn, J., Stemmler, M., Ey, S., & Grant, K. E. (1993). Depression in adolescence. *American Psychologist, 48,* 155 - 168.

Reynolds, W. M. (1987). *Reynolds Adolescent Depression Scale.* Odessa, FL: Psychological Assessment Resources Inc.

Sawyer, M. G., Kosky, R. J., Graetz, B. W., Arney, F., Zubrick, S. R., & Baghurst, P. (2000). The National Survey of Mental Health and Wellbeing: The child and adolescent component. *Australian and New Zealand Journal of Psychiatry, 34,* 214-220.

Shochet, I., & Dadds, M. (1997). Adolescent depression and the family: A paradox. *Clinical Child Psychology and Psychiatry, 2,* 307 - 312.

Shochet, I. M., Dadds, M. R., Holland, D., Whitefield, K., Harnett, P. H., & Osgarby, S. M. (in press). The efficacy of a school-based program to prevent adolescent depression. *Journal of Clinical Child Psychology.*

Shochet, I., Holland, D., & Whitefield, K. (1997). *The Griffith Early Intervention Depression Project: Group Leader's Manual.* Brisbane: Griffith Early Intervention Project.

Shochet, I., Osgarby, S., & Dyer, C. (1999). *Resourceful Adolescent Parent Program: Participant's Workbook.* Brisbane: Resourceful Adolescent Program.

Shochet, I., Osgarby, S., Holland, D., & Whitefield, K. (1998). *Resourceful Adolescent Parent Program: Group Leader's Manual.* Brisbane: Resourceful Adolescent Program.

Shochet, I., Whitefield, K., & Holland, D. (1997). *The Griffith Early Intervention Depression Project: Participant's Workbook.* Brisbane: Griffith Early Intervention Project.

Stark, K. D., Swearer, S., Sommer, D., Hickey, B. B., Napolitano, S., Kurowskki, C., & Dempsey, M. (1998). School-based treatment for depressive disorders in children. In K. C. Stoiber & T. R. Kratochwill (Eds.), *Handbook of group interventions for children and families* (pp. 68-99). Boston: Allyn & Bacon.

Tolan, P. H., Quintana, E., & Gorman-Smith, D. (1998). Prevention approaches for families. In L. L'Abate (Ed.), *Family psychopathology: the relational roots of dysfunctional behavior* (pp. 379-400). New York: Guilford.

Zubrick, S. R., Silburn, S. R., Burton, P., & Blair, E. (2000). Mental health disorders in children and young people: Scope, cause and prevention. *Australian and New Zealand Journal of Psychiatry, 34,* 570-578.

9

A Community Service Model for Delivery of Early Childhood Mental Illness Prevention Programs

Amanda Wheeler
Central Coast Mental Health Service

Paul Riviere
Central Coast Mental Health Center

Amanda Wheeler · Central Coast Mental Health Service · Early Childhood Mental Illness Prevention Workers · Mandala Clinic · P.O. Box 361 · Gosford · NSW 2250 · Australia.

International Perspectives on Child and Adolescent Mental Health. Volume 2: Proceedings of the Second International Conference, edited by N. N. Singh, T. H. Ollendick, and A. N. Singh. © 2002 Elsevier Science Ltd. All rights reserved.

The National Mental Health Plan is the overall broad plan of national significance that mental health services operate under in Australia. It has as its aims to build on the achievements of the following: (a) improved linkages between sectors, government and external stakeholders; (b) improved understanding of mental illness, its prevention and mental health promotion; and (c) identification, development and field-testing of innovative service and funding models. Further priority areas for reform include: (a) promotion and prevention; (b) development of partnerships in service reform; and (c) quality and effectiveness of service delivery.

There is an obligation to develop plans for a comprehensive mix of mental health services, including the establishment of service delivery systems which ensure effective service networks and coordination of care are fostered, especially between public, private and non government sectors. Partnerships and strategic alliances are to be developed with the wider health sector (e.g., child and family health, community health, health promotion) and community support services (e.g., family support, education both government and non government sectors).

In determining how to go about preventing childhood disorders, the system of service delivery was influenced by research in Canada from the *Better Beginnings Better Future* project. They noted that for the project to be successful the model must have these characteristics:

Be based on known effective prevention programs. The Positive Parenting Program (Triple P) is an evidence-based parenting program with over 15 years of research and a sound theoretical framework.

Be ecological. Successful prevention programs understand that the child lives in the family and the family in the community, so components of successful programs address the wholeness of the child and environment (Bronfenbrenner 1979,1987). Therefore strategies that improve each part of the environment within which the children spend their time (e.g., homes, childcare centers) need to be put in place. Triple P is a parenting program that impacts on the child's home environment and childcare environment if carers jointly participate in the program. This was encouraged on the Central Coast, for example, by training family day care staff in the Triple P program, who then ran the Triple P program for family day carers and parents.

Be tailored to meet local needs and desires as risk factors vary from community to community. The Triple P program is multilevel and can be used from universal to targeted prevention strategies depending on the community's needs. Consultation was held with key community stakeholders through involving them in a Mental Illness Prevention Steering Committee and a Triple P sub-committee. This allowed it to be responsive to the community's needs.

Be comprehensive. Triple P is a multilevel prevention program so that services could be tailored to families needs and referrals made if appropriate. It can be applied on a universal to targeted basis and has a range of delivery modes e.g. individual to group to meet a range of different needs. It also covers a range of topics that impact on families such as family survival tips as well as behavior management strategies.

Have high quality management and administrative approaches in place along with adequate resources. On the Central Coast two professional staff were appointed to coordinate and resource the delivery of the Triple P program.

Integrated with other programs and community activities. Preschool, family day care and family support services staff was trained in Triple P so that they could provide these services to their clients and complement their existing service delivery.

Be meaningful, having significant parent and community involvement (i.e., concept of community, family and parent empowerment). The Triple P program is designed to support families, parents and community groups to skill themselves and develop their support networks in the community. This is demonstrated by bringing parents together in a community venue and in a group program run by workers in the community. The principles of the Triple P program involve parent empowerment and the self-regulatory model. Evaluations are done on the program both from facilitators and parents to get feedback from the community on the Triple P program. Community representation on both the MIPT Steering Committee and the Triple P sub-committee also demonstrated this characteristic.

These characteristics are continuing to be shown in research to be important in implementing successful prevention programs (e.g., Ounce of Prevention Fund, 1994). Mrazek and Haggerty (1994) in looking at prevention research further emphasize that you need to involve the community in the program for it to be successful. They state that the community's functions include the following: helping to define the problem and accessing the needs of the community; ensure the readiness of the host organization (i.e., organization is acceptable and able to reach the community); helping to select a model program (i.e., evidenced-based and aims to meet the needs identified by the community); balancing fidelity and adaptability while implementing the program; evaluate the program's effectiveness; and provide feedback to the researchers.

The area of health promotion and prevention is also important to consider when choosing a service delivery system. The key concepts in it that were considered on the Central Coast were:

1. Mental health promotion operates in a public health framework and focuses on settings (such as family, schools) and on life stages. Strategies aim at building resilience and enhancing coping mechanisms for dealing with stresses across the lifespan, especially at points of transition. This would include projects in education settings such as schools and life-stage programs aimed at improving parenting skills.
2. Community education about mental illness to be done in key settings e.g. family and childcare.
3. Key groups of workers to be targeted for mental health promotion and education are teachers and workers in government and non-government services.

The population health model for provision of mental health is a useful tool that acts as a broad framework. This model has various domains that it explores from level of focus, spectrum of interventions, whole of life span target groups and level of service. The level of focus ranges from the whole population to an individual. The spectrum of interventions ranges from prevention to maintenance interventions. The whole of life span means that all age groups are to be considered from infancy to old age when developing interventions. The level of services available to people need to include some from all the service levels (i.e., primary, secondary and tertiary). The service of system delivery in the Central Coast fitted into the whole population focus, is used as a prevention intervention, and concentrates on the early childhood end of the lifespan.

In the context of a population health model there is a process that includes the assessment, morbidity, interventions and outcomes as determined and reported in populations. It also implies an understanding of the social systems influencing health and their environments and institutions. It will include prevention activities directed to populations that are vulnerable. It will also include population approaches such as education that may be dealt with through personal health services e.g. early childhood nurses, social workers at family care cottages. These services or programs will require appropriately skilled workforce and infrastructure. Therefore training in the Triple P program is given to staff to enhance their skills and coordinators appointed to provide the administration and support structures.

Population health assessments are often carried out to set the baseline in determining broad community needs and also the health impact or health burden in the community. Relevant population based demographic data for example was collected to assist in ascertaining the communities needs and where in the community it was strongest. The data assessed by the above and/or other measures are the basis for defining the problem or issues that will be dealt with, and whether or not appropriate responses or interventions can be provided. Population health assessments contribute by establishing the problem at a population level, for instance, the extent of the need, the health burden and contributing factors. Health assessments provide the basis for interventions targeted at the population or those at risk, through relevant educational and preventive strategies, as well as through personal health services.

Mental health promotion applies to those interventions, which would promote positive mental health, either through social or other interventions that may enhance factors contributing to positive mental health, for instance personal resiliency and social disadvantage. It tends to be used for broadly based population, environmental or setting interventions.

Interventions offered as prevention can be viewed in the mental health intervention spectrum for mental disorders model as developed by Mrazek and Haggerty (1994). A population health model starting at universal interventions directed towards a whole population would include universal preventive interventions aimed at improving the mental health of the population, for instance education of the community to enhance resilience or to lessen risk factors associated with mental illnesses. These may also include interventions to strengthen or develop communities, to improve social capital, through acting on variables that are negative for mental health. In this case study this variable was parenting skills and it was offered to the whole community within community organizations with the objective of increasing social capital. They may overlap significantly with concepts of mental health promotion. An example of this in our case study is the preschool awards that were developed and set up for all pre schools in the Central Coast.

Selective interventions focus on sub-populations at higher risk of mental health problems and disorders and provide interventions to individuals, groups or these populations to diminish risk. They would include the offering of parenting programs to disadvantaged populations as we did in family support clients, pre schools in certain disadvantaged areas.

Indicated interventions are aimed at populations and individuals at very high risk of disorder onset, for instance with incipient symptoms. Programs of early intervention sit across indicated interventions and early case identification and treatment focused on the earliest stages of illness. On the Central Coast Triple P was offered to parents of children who had been diagnosed as having ADHD or identified behavioral difficulties, parents diagnosed as having a mental illness (e.g., post-natal depression and clients of child protection services who had been notified as families at risk with children being removed from their care).

The importance of the development and evaluation of programs with demonstrated efficacy in the prevention of mental health problems in infancy, childhood and adolescence are noted. This includes programs targeting children vulnerable through parenting difficulties, family discord, and family disruption.

The review, *Healthy Families, Healthy Nations* by Sanders (1995) states that the period of early childhood from age 3 to the commencement of formal schooling is a significant stage of development. In Prevention Initiatives for Child and Adolescent Mental Health (NSW Health 2000), Hawkins and Catalano (1990) are cited as having identified two important developmental tasks that must be achieved to lower risk for adverse mental health outcomes: acquisition of language skills to prepare the child to read and write, and development of impulse control.

Mzarek and Haggerty (1994) cite risk factors that may hinder the acquisition of these tasks and which need to be addressed in a prevention intervention. These risk factors include: economic deprivation; poor family management or parenting practices; cognitive or developmental delays; pre school difficulties; and early behavioral problems.

These principles, framework and research interacted together and determined how the Triple P model was set up and implemented in the Central Coast. It is also against this background that lead to the choice of service system delivery and the program that was implemented in the CCAHS.

The Triple P program fulfilled the criteria indicated by the Second National Mental Health Plan (1998-2003). Triple P is a multilevel intervention developed for parents and carers of children aged 2 - 10 years. It can be used at various levels of the prevention spectrum (i.e., universal, indicated and targeted. It can also be used by professionals from a broad range of disciplines e.g. psychologists, social workers, nurses, GPs and allied health professionals, and teachers). Information from the Standing Committee in Social Issues Report Working For Children: Communities Supporting Families indicates that, currently, parenting education programs are being run by a range of professionals and sectors. This therefore highlighted the possibility of creating strategic alliances with these groups by supporting them in what they were doing and preventing duplication of service provision.

PUTTING THEORY INTO PRACTICE

The National Mental Health Strategy (Australian Department of Health and Family Services, 1992-1997) identified mental health as a priority area requiring whole of government, non-government and community attention. The Second National Mental Health Plan (1998 - 2003) builds on this to consolidate the areas of prevention, early intervention and mental health promotion. It emphasizes the importance of developing interagency partnerships and of improving the quality and effectiveness of service delivery. As part of their response to this plan the Central Coast Mental Health Service established an Early Childhood Mental Illness Prevention Team.

In 1997, funding was made available to the Central Coast Mental Health Service to employ three project workers to implement and evaluate health promotion and mental illness prevention programs for the reduction of conduct and emotional disorders in children. Jointly these workers formed the Mental Illness Prevention Team (MIPT). Two of these positions were to develop and implement community based programs for the prevention of conduct and behavioral disorders in early childhood. As part of their responsibility they were to coordinate the Triple P program.

An interagency approach was adopted to promote this program across the community. This approach aimed to widely disseminate the program, increase program accessibility, encourage community adoption of the program, and streamline service provision by avoiding duplication of services.

Planning

In 1998, MIPT commenced by selecting membership for a steering committee which would ratify direction of their activities. This committee agreed to meet monthly for the first 12 months of the project, then review its role. It was made up of departmental managers from the Central Coast Mental Health Service, Youth Health Service, Child and Family Health, Department of Community Services and the Department of Education and Training. Since there was a significant amount of work to be done in establishing Triple P, a sub-committee was recruited by the coordinator. This was comprised of key clinical personnel from participating agencies and met fortnightly for 18 months. In planning how to introduce the program, the Coordinator and committee had to take into account the needs of the rapidly growing population.

Demographics of Central Coast

In 1998, the Central Coast had an estimated population of 281,251 (ABS, 1998), representing 4.4% of the NSW population. The resident population for Gosford and Wyong, the Coast's neighboring shires was 155,144 and 126,107 respectively. Although the population growth for both the Central Coast and NSW is expected to slow over the next ten years, it is anticipated that the Coast will remain a relatively high growth area. Based on Department of Health projections (November 1997), the Central Coast population is expected to increase by 9%

between 1996-2001 and 8% between 2001-2006, while NSW is expected to grow at a rate of 5% and 4.5%, respectively.

There is also likely to be a significant difference in the rate of growth between the two local government areas. Gosford's growth rate is projected to decline from 7% to 4% over the next decade while Wyong's growth rate is expected to remain constant at approximately 12%. The principal reason for the difference between the shires, is the lack of land suitable for housing development in the Gosford Local Government Area as opposed to Wyong Local Government Area where there is ongoing development potential.

Children

The proportion of 0-14 year olds is higher than the state average, which has implications for service delivery in the future (see Table 1).

Table 1.   Children on the Central Coast Compared to NSW (June 1998)

Age	Male	Female	CC Total	% of CC Population	NSW Total	% of NSW Population
0 – 4	10 228	9 940	20 168	7.2	435 170	6.9
5 – 9	11 094	10 455	21 549	7.7	444 653	7.0
10 -14	10 368	9 874	20 242	7.2	436 414	6.9
Total	31 690	30 269	61 959	22.1	1316 237	21.8

Prevalence Rates of Mental Health Problems and Disorders of Children

The NSW Strategy: Making Mental Health Better for Children and Adolescents (1999) suggests that at any one time, one in five children aged 4 to 16 will experience mental health problems (see Table 2).   Until recent epidemiological studies in Western Australia and nationally, identifying the extent of mental health problems in children and young people has been complex. Recent international studies have found the prevalence of mental health disorders in children in the order of 16-20% between the ages of 4 and 11. With 5.6 million children and young people under the age of 25 living in Australia (1996 Census), it has been estimated that at any one time, 393,000 4-11 year old children have an identifiable mental health disorder.

Table 2.   Prevalence of Mental Health Problems in 4-16 year olds

Mental Health Problem	Prevalence (%)
Delinquent problems	9.5%
Thought problems	8.6%
Attention problems	6.3%
Social problems	5.9%
Somatic complaints	5.0%
Aggressive behaviors	3.7%
Anxiety/depression	3.6%
Withdrawn	2.6%
Overall prevalence	18.0%

Setting Objectives of Triple-P on the Central Coast

Impact objectives included:

- Increase parental knowledge and skills in effective behavior management strategies.
- Improve early detection, referral and clinical management of children with more severe behavioral and emotional disorders.
- Improve children's' developmental readiness for school.   Mental health promotion is to operate in a public health framework and focus on settings (such as preschools, family and schools) and on life stages.
- To increase the level of parental satisfaction in the community.

Outcome objectives included:

- reducing the use of aversive parenting methods
- increasing the use of positive parenting behaviors
- increasing parents sense of self-efficacy in parenting
- reducing parental depression, anxiety and stress

- reducing the level of marital problems
- decrease behavioral problems in children through reducing the levels disruptive, aggressive and oppositional behavior.

Refining the Role of the Triple P Coordinator

The role of the Triple P coordinator involved the following:
- Coordinate the implementation of Triple P on the Central Coast of NSW
- Provide training and support to professionals to facilitate Triple P
- Evaluate the effectiveness of Triple P
- Generate promotional resources such as brochures and posters
- Distribute Triple P resources – videos, facilitator manuals, participant workbooks, registration and evaluation packs, brochures and posters.
- Plan pilot programs
- Identify avenues for delivery of Level 5 Triple P

Training of Group Facilitators

Three rounds of Triple P Training were conducted. The first training was conducted in November 1997 with 12 participants from the Department of Education and Training, and the Area Health Service. The second round of training (July 1998) included 16 staff from the Child and Family Health Service and a further 9 staff from non-government services. Further training was conducted in 1999 as well an accreditation program.

Organization and Administrative Supports to Sustain the Program

In promoting the program to be taken up by an interagency network it was agreed to offer them a proven strategy that would augment and improve the effectiveness of their service provision. To coincide with the introduction of the program a set of standardized forms were developed to facilitate application, placement and evaluation of the program for participating agencies. Complimenting this, a manual of policies and procedures relating to program delivery were developed and sent to all facilitators. This ensured a consistent standard of service delivery by all facilitators and agencies involved. The Coordinator maintained a central database of those applying to do the program and could refer applicants to the suburb nearest to them where a group was being conducted. Applicants would be contacted by telephone and screened for suitability to participate. Criteria for inclusion in groups were that the parent/carer have a child/children aged 2-10 in their care and that the participant does not have an acute mental illness.

Strategies for Promoting the Program

Incentives for participating agencies included the provision of assistance in locating and subsidizing venue hire, organizing and subsidizing child care arrangements, offering subsidized facilitator training, providing co-facilitator support to conduct groups and program evaluation support.

All agencies providing a service to children and families were targeted with promotional materials. Included were early childhood services, primary schools, general medical practitioners and community support agencies, government and non-government. A health promotion campaign was conducted with the child-care centers. The Triple P coordinator offered free training to services that could demonstrate practice that promoted positive mental health in children.

The Mental Illness Prevention Team participated in various early childhood interagency meetings to promote the activities of the team.

The Area Health Design and Art department developed posters for display in services and brochures giving a brief explanation of the program as well as having an inclusive application coupon. An information package for service providers and Triple P facilitators was developed to accompany the posters and brochures.

Media releases were organized through the local radio station and community newspaper advertising a Triple P promotional week to be conducted at a local primary school that had a parent-support centre on-site. Staff members from participating agencies were available to answer parents' questions about parenting and childhood behavior problems. The promotion was also conducted during the evening to ensure access for working parents. Parent tip sheets were distributed free of charge and parents were informed about the availability of the Triple P program

After six months, two extra promotional activities were commenced. A quarterly Newsletter was developed to update and inform all agencies about our mental illness prevention activities. This was used to provide ongoing promotion of the project. It also advertised the Quarterly Interest Group *Promoting Positive Mental Health in Families* that was convened by the team. This consisted of team members and guest speakers providing information forums to service providers on current issues relating to child and family mental health.

Pilot Groups

Two Pilot groups were run to assist in evaluating preliminary organizational structures. One was conducted at the school based parent-support centre, in a suburb recognized as having a significant level of socio-economic disadvantage. Staff from two non-government services collaborated to conduct this group. The second pilot group was conducted in a Family Care Cottage staffed by Area Health Staff. Parents and carers attending these groups were recruited from the promotional week, held one-month prior.

Policy and Procedure Manual

The coordinator developed a Policy and Procedure Manual for facilitators to use when running Triple P groups. This provided clear guidelines for organizing and running groups, how to utilize the support of the coordinator along an interagency model, child protection procedures, roles and responsibilities. Standards of professional behavior expected from facilitators were also addressed. This will be updated on a regular basis as required.

Pre- and Post-Assessment

Seven measures were administered before and after program participation. These included:

Family Background Questionnaire. Much of this measure is adapted from the Western Australian Child Health Survey. Essential biographical data includes contact details, the child's detail, parents' marital status, relationship to the child, current employment status and educational background. It also includes family background details such as the names an ages of all family members, information on family composition, parent's income and level of government support, parent's use of other health services, and the child's health and development. Changes were made to the questionnaire that applied to questions that identified cultural and socio-economic variations of participants accessing the program.

Eyberg Child Behavior Inventory. This inventory by Eyberg and Pincus measures parental perceptions of disruptive behavior in children aged 2-16 years of age. It incorporates a measure of frequency of disruptive behaviors that are a problem for parents.

Parenting Scale

This scale by Arnold, O'Leary, Wolff and Acker (1993) is a 30-item questionnaire measuring three dysfunctional discipline styles in parents. It yields scores relating to three factors, laxness, over reactivity and verbosity.

Parenting Sense of Competence Scale. This is a 17-item questionnaire, which assesses parents' views of their competence as parents on two dimensions, satisfaction with their parenting role, and feelings of efficacy as a parent.

<u>Parent Problem Checklist</u>. This is a 1-item questionnaire that measures inter-parental conflict over child rearing. It rates parents' ability to cooperate and work together in family management.

<u>Abbreviated Dyadic Adjustment Scale</u>. This scale distinguishes between distressed and non-distressed couples on relationship satisfaction, drawing upon aspects of communication, intimacy, cohesion and disagreement.

<u>Depression and Anxiety Stress Scale</u>. This is a 42-item questionnaire that assesses symptoms of depression, anxiety and stress in adults.

<u>Client Satisfaction Questionnaire</u>. This measure was specifically designed to measure consumer satisfaction with parent training programs. The CSQ asks the following questions:

> How would you rate the quality of service provided?
>
> How well the program met the parents/carers needs?
>
> How well the program increased the parent's skill?
>
> Was there a decrease in the child's problem behaviors?
>
> Would the parent recommend the program to others?

Evaluating Interagency Implementation Process

The following measures were used to evaluate the program implementation:

- Facilitator evaluation form
- Record and monitor group numbers and attendance
- Questionnaire for consumers who do not complete program
- Tip sheet evaluation form for Level 1,2 & 3
- Uptake of child care subsidy
- Uptake of refreshment subsidy
- Monitoring the number of agencies participating in the program
- Level 5 referrals - time frame and service provider

Identify Avenues of Ongoing Support for Parents Completing the Program

For those participants who had clinically significant post-assessment results, it was necessary to identify avenues for delivery of the Level 5 program or other generic service options. Clients meeting the criteria were sent a letter offering discussion of assessment results and referral options. Most common referrals were to Child and Family Health staffed by social workers, nurses, and psychologists, Family Support Services, Services, School based Community Interagency Support Service, Department of Community Services and The Department of Education and Training counseling and home-school liaison team.

Program Impact

The coordinators completed an evaluation report after 12 months of the Triple P program commencing. The evaluation looked at both the impact of the Triple P program and its impact on the Central Coast. Some of the data from this report is covered below.

The general trend appears positive for the program, such that the vast majority of parents have more favorable scores on each of the questionnaires at the post-assessment stage.

The Client Satisfaction Questionnaire indicates there was a positive response and a high level of satisfaction to all aspects of the program.

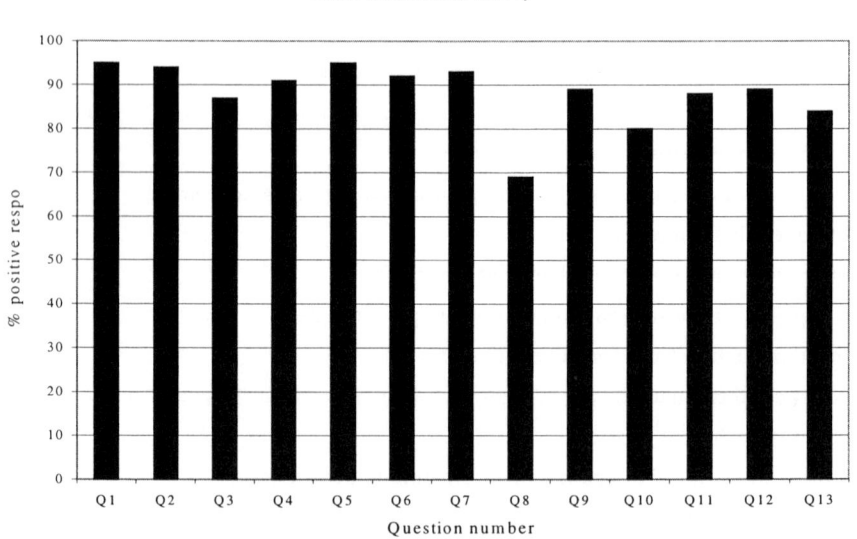

On all aspects of the program, participants recorded a positive to very positive response. For question 8, participants were not as positive about the impact the program had on their relationship with their partner as for other aspects.

A frequent comment received was that "it should be compulsory for all parents to attend this program." Another finding was that only a small number of people dropped out of the course once they had commenced it. These people on being surveyed also indicated a high level of satisfaction with the program but unforeseen circumstances prevented them from completing the course.

Groups ideally cater for 10 participants, but often there were two or three non-starters per group. This resulted in groups being under-utilized and further extending our waiting lists. This problem has been overcome by allocating up to 12 participants per group instead of 10 per group as recommended. There is usually a 3-month waiting list to access groups, indicating there is a continuing high level of demand for the Triple P program. An increasing number of referrals appear to be coming via word of mouth from those who have completed the group program, indicating that participants are finding the program helpful.

Discussion of Implementation Process

Two years after the introduction of the program there are 60 facilitators trained in Triple P from a wide range of organizations. These facilitators have conducted 45 groups in the first 12 months and nearly 60 in the second. This has been achieved by acquiring the commitment of the facilitators to run two groups in their first year. This has allowed the facilitators to develop their skills, as well as confidence, in running the groups and to go on to consider accreditation. Another aspect that has aided this process has been the availability of the Coordinator to organize the groups and provide any necessary support that the facilitators might need. By encouraging the co-facilitation of groups, facilitators are able to offer each other support and debriefing. Co-facilitation also eases the workload for the facilitator during the program especially in regard to the 4 weekly telephone calls that follow on from the group sessions. Networking across agencies has improved interagency co-operation and community adoption of the program.

There has been some attrition amongst facilitators, particularly those trained in the first 12 months, prior to our stipulation that those privy to training would be obliged to conduct at least 2 groups within a year. Two reasons would appear to account for this. First, although some of the early childhood nurses from the Child & Family Health Service expressed interest in participating, they found it difficult to reschedule existing work practice to run groups during their working day. They felt it unfair that time-in-lieu would be the only remuneration for conducting groups of an evening and negotiation did not proceed further. Other disciplines appeared to have more flexibility in scheduling their work and therefore were more available and willing to run evening groups. Second, a small number of facilitators recruited from non-government services expressed apprehension about their confidence and ability to conduct groups. Despite encouragement from the Coordinator and offers of co-facilitation, it was difficult to recruit the services of these facilitators. Nevertheless, the vast majority who trained were impressed with the program content and resources and were able to utilize the Triple P resources for one on one work with parents and carers.

The two Family Care Cottages ran and evaluated information sessions on Triple P and found this to be an effective way for the staff to deal with clients who presented with behavioral management issues. It also acted as a feeder into the group program, therefore streamlining the provision of services to their clients.

Group Evaluations Completed by Triple P Facilitators

Twenty-one facilitator evaluation sheets were returned from a possible 45 over a 12-month period. The majority of facilitators reported that the sequence of the program content ran logically and smoothly. Session 3 was singled out for the large amount of content to be covered and that it frequently ran overtime. Facilitators thought group process and program content was very difficult to balance. Most facilitators commented that group participants were supportive of each other and seemed to benefit from sharing their parenting experiences.

No changes were made to the sequence of the program, however some sections were condensed, or, group exercises deleted if time was short. This was frequently reported for Session 3. Some facilitators extended the two-hour sessions by up to an hour.

Facilitators reported that the following worked well: co-facilitation of groups, positive feedback from participants' homework tasks, coordination and administration of the program. Facilitators reported a variety of responses to the follow-up telephone calls, sessions 5-8. This component of the program was sometimes not completed for a range of reasons e.g. participants not available to receive the telephone call; participants not wishing to receive the full complement of telephone calls. The other difficulties they reported were related to Session 3 not being completed in the time allocated, overall, too much content in the program.

Tip Sheet Evaluation

The Child and Family Health Service was provided with a 12 month supply of Triple P tip sheets at no cost. 11,000 mixed tip sheets have been distributed via the 6 sector community health centers across the Central Coast. All facilitators, from both government and non-government agencies, were provided at the time of training with a complimentary sample pack of tip sheets. An evaluation form was issued and distributed to 24 facilitators. As only 9 survey forms were returned the response rate is too small to make any reliable assessments.

Uptake of Child-Care Subsidy

The organization and subsidization of child-care has been offered for every group. This was a free service to all participants. Of the 45 groups conducted 5 did not require child-care. A problematic issue was that occasionally parents changed their child-care arrangements without informing the facilitator, but child carers still required payment for that particular session. Subsequent child-care was then cancelled or the number of carers adjusted for these groups.

Uptake of Refreshment Subsidy

A maximum of $40 was available to organizations to subsidies the provision of refreshments at the four sessions per group. Most facilitators chose to provide refreshments via their own alternative funding arrangements. This was ceased in the second year due to budget constraints.

Level 5 Referrals

From the post assessments we have had indications of 41 who met the criteria for Level 5 follow up. Of the letters of offer sent to those who met these criteria, 14 responded and were given referrals to Level 5 providers or other appropriate services.

Profile of Participants

Generally, the program has been attended by parents of children who do not have multiple risk factors that predispose for the development of conduct and behavior disorders. This is an area that needs to be examined in the future; that is, the marketing and program applicability for families with multiple risk factors. Possible target groups in the community indicated for prevention programs would include clients of DCS, parents of children who have a developmental disability, parents affected by a mental illness, parents who have drug & alcohol issues, parents affected by severe socio-economic disadvantage.

RECOMMENDATIONS OF IMPLEMENTATION EVALUATION

Our recommendations include:

1. Continue to employ the services of a Coordinator to assist in the ongoing dissemination and promotion of the Triple P program, and to offer support and

assistance to facilitators in running the groups.

2. Continue to provide the Positive Parenting Program to families on the Central Coast with an ongoing evaluation process in collaboration with the University of Newcastle.

3. Continue to provide child-care to participants in some form to maintain accessibility to the program. Explore alternative options for the provision of childcare (e.g., Occasional Childcare, Family Daycare) by charging a nominal fee for childcare. Funding options for the provision of childcare should also be investigated.

4. Continue to provide Triple P tip sheets to organizations on the Central Coast at a discount price. The use and effectiveness of L1, 2 and 3 of the program should continue to be monitored and evaluated. The evaluation tools used to accomplish this need to be reviewed to ensure a greater response rate than that received in the first year of the program.

5. Continue to provide Triple P Training programs to organizations on the Central Coast under the current guidelines (i.e., user pays and commitment to run 2 groups in the first 12 months after completion of training).

6. Continue to develop and encourage the interagency and community development focus of the project. Children's Services such as preschools, long day care and occasional day care should be targeted to further the availability of the program to the community.

7. Explore the option of providing refresher courses on a regular basis to facilitators and participants of the program.

8. Continue to monitor the effectiveness of the program.

9. Conduct a 12-month follow up evaluation of those who participated in the program to assess the maintenance of initial impact of the program.

10. Test and evaluate adaptation of the program for specific target groups with multiple risk factors and presently not accessing services (e.g., young parents, parents/carers with a mental health problem, parents of children with disabilities and the hearing impaired.

11. Revise the content of the pre-assessment and post-assessments in order to facilitate ease of completion, and increase return rate.

12. Continue to monitor the dissemination of the program and effectiveness of marketing strategies and referral sources to the program to be noted. This

information can be gathered in the telephone interview prior to commencing the program.

13. Cease provision of refreshment subsidy and encourage organizations to provide it for their clients if they wish to.

14. Investigate funding options for provision of sessional payments to Tripe P facilitators in order to provide more evening and weekend groups for partners wishing to do the program together.

Despite the intentions of the coordinators for implementing the program, it is has not always been possible to follow strategies and time frames. In process evaluation the need has arisen for flexibility and it has proved advantageous to review the implementation strategies regularly.

REFERENCES

Australian Department of Health and Family Services. (1992). *National Mental Health Strategy: 1992-1997.* Australia: Author.

Australian Health Ministers. (1998). *Second national mental health plan.* Canberra, Australia: Commonwealth Department of Health and Family Services.

Centre for Mental Health (2000). *Prevention initiatives for child and adolescent mental health.* Sydney, Australia: NSW Health Department.

Mrazek, P.J. & Haggerty, R.J. (1994). *Reducing risks for mental disorders: Frontiers for preventive intervention research.* Washington, DC: National Academy Press.

National Mental Health Promotion and Prevention Working Party 1998–2003. *Mental Health Promotion and Prevention National Plan.* Australia: Commonwealth Department of Health and Aged Care.

Sanders, M.R. (1995). *Healthy families, healthy nation: Strategies for promoting family mental health in Australia.* Australian Academic Press.

Standing Committee on Social Issues. (1998). *Working for children: supporting families: Inquiry into parent education and support programs.* New South Wales: Parliament of NSW Legislative Council.

10

The Revised Version of the Screen for Anxiety Related Emotional Disorders (SCARED-R): A New Scale for Measuring Childhood Anxiety

Peter Muris
Maastricht University

Peter Muris · Maastricht University · Department of Medical, Clinical, and Experimental Psychology · P.O. Box 361 · Maastricht 6200 MD · The Netherlands.

International Perspectives on Child and Adolescent Mental Health. Volume 2: Proceedings of the Second International Conference, edited by N. N. Singh, T. H. Ollendick, and A. N. Singh. © 2002 Elsevier Science Ltd. All rights reserved.

Anxiety disorders are among the most prevalent psychiatric problems in children and adolescents. Epidemiological research shows that between 8 and 12% of youths suffer from anxiety complaints that are severe enough to interfere with daily life and functioning (see for a review see Bernstein, Borchardt, & Perwien, 1996). According to the latest edition of the Diagnostic and Statistical Manual of Mental Disorders (DSM-IV; American Psychiatric Association [APA], 1994), the following anxiety disorders can be distinguished in children and adolescents: separation anxiety disorder, generalized anxiety disorder, panic disorder, social phobia, specific phobia, obsessive-compulsive disorder, and post-traumatic or acute stress disorder (the essential features of these anxiety disorders are summarized in Table 1). A recent factor analytic study by Spence (1997) provided empirical support for the DSM-IV classification of anxiety disorders in children. In that study, anxiety symptoms were found to cluster into anxiety categories that are in keeping with the anxiety disorders as listed in the DSM-IV.

In both research and clinical practice, self-report questionnaires for measuring childhood anxiety symptoms are frequently used. This type of measure is easy-to-administer, requires a minimum of time, and captures information about anxiety symptoms from the child's point of view (Strauss, 1993). The three most widely used questionnaires for assessing anxiety in children and adolescents are the State-Trait Anxiety Inventory for Children (STAIC; Spielberger, 1973), the Revised Children's Manifest Anxiety Scale (RCMAS; Reynolds & Richmond, 1978), and the Fear Survey Schedule for Children — Revised (FSSC—R; Ollendick, 1983). Although these scales are reliable and provide usable information on childhood anxiety symptoms, their most important shortcoming is that scores on these scales are difficult to relate to the separate anxiety disorders as described in clinical classification systems such the DSM. As a result, the clinical utility of these measures is restricted.

In the past years, various attempts have been made to develop questionnaires for measuring various aspects of anxiety in terms of the nosologic constructs that are currently employed by researchers and clinicians. One example is the Spence Children's Anxiety Scale (SCAS; Spence, 1998) that maps symptoms of panic disorder, separation anxiety disorder, social phobia, obsessive-compulsive disorder, generalized anxiety disorder, and specific phobias. Another questionnaire that closely follows the DSM taxonomy of anxiety disorders is the Screen for Child Anxiety Related Emotional Disorders (SCARED).

This chapter provides a description of the Revised version of the SCARED (SCARED-R), summarizes its psychometric properties, and then illustrates the practical value of the scale in an early intervention frail for anxiety disordered children.

Table 1. DSM-IV Defined Anxiety Disorders in Children and Adolescents: Essential Features and SCARED-R

Anxiety disorder	Essential Feature	Item (number in questionnaire)
Separation Anxiety Disorder (including School Phobia)	Excessive anxiety concerning separation from the home or from significant attachment figures	I get scared when I sleep away from home (7) I follow my parents wherever they go (13) I worry about sleeping alone (19) I have nightmares about my parents (29) I have nightmares about bad happening to me (36) I am afraid to be alone at home (45) I don't like being away from my family (50) I worry that bad happens to my parents (52) I get headaches or stomach aches when I am at school (3) I don't like going to school (17) I worry about going to school (30) I am scared to go to school (58)
Generalized Anxiety Disorder	Persistent and excessive anxiety and worry	I worry about others not liking me (8) I am nervous (11) I worry about being as good as other kids (21) I worry about things working out for me (38) I am a worrier (41) People tell me I worry too much (49) I worry about the future (55) I worry about how well I do things (57) I worry about things that happened in the past (59)

Table 1 continued.

Anxiety disorder	Essential Feature	Item (number in questionnaire)
Panic Disorder	Panic attacks, i.e., discrete periods of intense fear that are accompanied by somatic and cognitive symptoms	When frightened, it is hard to breath (1)
		When frightened, I feel like passing out (9)
		People tell me that I look nervous (14)
		When frightened, I feel like going crazy (18)
		When frightened, I feel that things are not real (27)
		I feel weak and shaky (35)
		When frightened, I sweat a lot (40)
		I get really scared for no reason (44)
		When frightened, I feel like I am choking (48)
		I am afraid of having anxiety attacks (51)
		When frightened, I feel like throwing up (56)
		When frightened, I feel dizzy (60)
Social Phobia	Marked fear of social situations	I don't like to be with people I don't know (4)
		I feel nervous with people I don't know well (15)
		I find it hard with people I don't know (47)
		I am shy with people I don't know well (53)
Specific Phobias (including animal, Blood-Injection-Injury, and Situational-Environmental Phobias)	Marked and persistent anxiety provoked by exposure to a specific feared object or situation	I am afraid of an animal that is not really dangerous (22)
		I am so scared of a harmless animal that I do not dare to touch it (37)
		I am afraid of an animal that most people do not fear (65)

Table 1 continued.

Anxiety disorder	Essential Feature	Item (number in questionnaire)
Specific Phobias (contd.)		When I see blood, I get dizzy (5)
		I am afraid to visit the doctor (16)
		I am afraid to visit the dentist (20)
		I am scared when I get an injection (33)
		I am afraid to get a serious disease (34)
		I feel scared when I watch an operation (42)
		I don't like being in a hospital (66)
		I am afraid of heights (2)
		I get scared when there is thunder in the air (23)
		I feel scared when I have to fly in an airplane (28)
		I get scared in small, closed places (61)
		I am afraid of the dark (63)
Obsessive-Compulsive Disorder	The occurrence of obsessions, i.e., intrusive thoughts that cause marked anxiety, and compulsions, repetitive behaviors that serve to neutralize anxiety	I want that things are fixed in order (6)
		I think that I will be contaminated with a serious i.e.,disease (10)
		I have thoughts that frighten me (12)
		I do things more than twice in order to check whether I did it right (24)
		I want things to be clean and tidy (26)
		I do things to get less scared of my thoughts (31)
		I doubt whether I really did something (39)
		I fantasize about hurting other people (54)
		I have thoughts that I prefer not to have (62)

Table 1 continued.

Anxiety disorder	Essential Feature	Item (number in questionnaire)
Post-Traumatic or Acute Stress Disorder	The re-experience on an extremely traumatic event accompanied by increased arousal and avoidance of stimuli associated with the trauma	I have frightening dreams about a very aversive event I once experienced (25) I try not to think about a very aversive experience I once had (43) I get scared when I think back of a very aversive experience I once had (46) I have unwanted thoughts about a very aversive event I once experienced (64)

Note: DSM-IV=Diagnostic and Statistical Manual of Mental Disorders, fourth edition, SCARED-R=Screen for Child Anxiety Related Emotional Disorders-Revised. Items of the Separation Anxiety Disorder, Generalized Anxiety Disorder, Panic Disorder, and Social Phobia scales were taken from the original 38 items SCARED (Birmaher, et al., 1997).

DESCRIPTION OF THE REVISED SCARED (SCARED-R)

The original SCARED (Birmaher, Khetarpal, Brent, et al., 1997) consists of 38 items that can be allocated to five anxiety subscales. Four of these subscales represent anxiety disorders as classified in the DSM, namely panic disorder, social phobia, generalized anxiety disorder, and separation anxiety disorder. The fifth subscale is school phobia, which according to Birmaher, et al. (1997), can best be considered as a separate anxiety disorder in children and adolescents. To cover the anxiety disorders listed in the DSM more fully, Muris, et al. (1999b) revised the SCARED in three ways. First, school phobia items were added to the separation anxiety disorder subscale. This was done because, in the DSM-IV (APA, 1994), school phobia is considered as a potential symptom of separation anxiety disorder. Second, 15 new items were created and added in an attempt to assess the three most important types of specific phobias, i.e., animal phobia, blood-injection-injury phobia, and situational/environmental phobia. Finally, although post-traumatic stress disorder and obsessive-compulsive disorder are relatively rare among children and adolescents, 13 additional items were added in order to measure symptoms of these anxiety disorders. In total, the revised SCARED (SCARED-R) consists of 66 items that measure symptoms of the entire spectrum of anxiety disorders that according to the DSM may occur in children and adolescents.

Thus, the SCARED-R measures symptoms of separation anxiety disorder (12 items including 4 items measuring school phobia), generalized anxiety disorder (9 items), panic disorder (13 items), social phobia (4 items), specific phobias (15 items representing the three main types of specific phobia: animal phobia, blood-injection-injury phobia, and situational-environmental phobia), obsessive-compulsive disorder (9 items), and post-traumatic or acute stress disorder (4 items) (the exact items of the SCARED-R are shown in Table 1). Children and adolescents rate how frequently they experience each symptom on a 3-point Likert scale: almost never, sometimes, or often. These are scored 0, 1, and 2, respectively. SCARED-R total and subscale scores can be computed by summing across relevant items.

PSYCHOMETRIC PROPERTIES OF THE SCARED-R

Reliability

Various studies (Muris, et al., 1999b; Muris, Merckelbach, Van Brakel, & Mayer, 1999c) have shown that the internal consistency of the SCARED-R is satisfactory. Cronbach's alpha values are generally higher than 0.90 for the total score of the SCARED-R and higher than 0.60

for the separate subscales. In agreement with these results, it has been reported that more than 90% of item-total and item-subscale correlations are well above 0.30. The test-retest stability of the SCARED-R is also acceptable: the test-retest correlation coefficient is 0.81 and varies between 0.40 and 0.78 for the various subscales (Muris, et al., 1999c).

Factor Structure

Factor analysis of the original 38-item SCARED in samples of clinically referred and normal children has yielded the predicted five-factor structure that is in keeping with the subscales of separation anxiety disorder, generalized anxiety disorder, social phobia, panic disorder, and school phobia (Birmaher, et al., 1997; Muris, et al., 1999b).

In should be acknowledged that the extension and revision of the SCARED (see supra) has negatively affected the factor structure of the scale. Muris, et al. (1 999b) failed to find a satisfactory factor structure for the 66-item SCARED-R. More specifically, both exploratory and confirmatory factor analyses did not yield the expected factors representing the anxiety disorders as defined in the DSM. This negative result might be due to the fact that Muris, et al. (1999b) relied on a sample of normal children. It may well be the case that in samples of clinically referred children, the hypothesized DSM-like factor structure of the SCARED-R would emerge. However, it is more plausible to assume that the construction of a scale that assesses the entire spectrum of anxiety disorders symptoms while possessing a satisfactory factor structure is an impracticable enterprise. Spence (1997; p.282), for example, noted that "it is not meaningful to search for a specific phobia factor" as the criteria for this anxiety disorder focus on a single stimulus. Nevertheless, specific phobias certainly are one of the most prevalent anxiety disorders in children and adolescents (Muris & Merckelbach, in press) and so it seems useful for clinicians to have this disorder included in the scale. In a similar vein, although symptoms of obsessive-compulsive disorder and post-traumatic or acute stress disorder are relatively rare and hence may have a detrimental influence on the factor structure of the SCARED-R, inclusion of such symptoms enhances the clinical utility of the questionnaire.

Parent-Child Agreement

The correspondence between child and parent report of the SCARED-R was examined in a sample of 71 normal primary school children (Muris, et al., 1999c). Children completed the SCARED-R in their classrooms. Parents were visited at home and asked to fill in the parent version of the scale. This parent version *is* identical to the child version, except that items are rephrased in terms of the parents' perspective. Examples are 'When my child is frightened, his/her heart beats fast', 'My child worries about things working out for him/her', and 'My child does not like to be with people he/she does not know'). Parent-child agreement appeared to be very modest: the parent-child correlation was 0.30 for the SCARED-R total score, was lowest for generalized anxiety disorder (r = 0.03), and highest for situational-environmental phobias (r = 0.56). In addition, *it* was found that parents rated the frequency of children's anxiety symptoms as significantly lower than children themselves. All in all, these results are in keeping with previous research showing that parents generally underestimate the frequency and severity of their children's anxiety complaints (see Rapee, Barrett, Dadds, & Evans, 1994).

Convergent and Divergent Validity

A series of studies in samples of normal children has indicated that the SCARED-R possesses good convergent validity. To begin with, the total score of the SCARED-R correlates substantially with scores on the aforementioned 'traditional' childhood anxiety scales such as the FSSC-R (r = 0.67), the RCMAS (r = 0.86), and the state anxiety (~ = 0.65) and trait anxiety r = 0.73) scales of the STAIC (Muris, Merekelbach, Mayer, et al., 1998b; Muris, Merekelbach, Mayer, & Van Dongen, 1998c). It is noteworthy that two recent studies in clinically referred children have yielded highly similar results. That is, in a mixed sample of children with anxiety disorders and disruptive disorders, the SCARED-R total score correlated 0.64 with the FSSC-R (Muris & Steerneman, in press).

Similarly, in a group of children suffering from various anxiety disorders, the SCARED-R correlated 0.69 with the trait anxiety version of the STAIC (Muris, Mayer, Bartelds, Tiemey, & Bogie, in press a). Furthermore, positive associations were found between SCARED-R scores and scales measuring depression (g = 0.62), negative self-statements (rs between *0.57* and 0.72), and internalizing problem behavior (r = 0.77; Muris, Merekelbach, Mayer, & Snieder, 1998a; Muris, et al., 1998c; Muris, Merckelbach, Moulaert, & Gadet, 2000c). Finally, it should be mentioned that the SCARED-R correlated in the predicted way with an alternative scale that can be used to assess childhood anxiety symptoms as defined in the DSM (the aforementioned SCAS). The total scores of SCARED-R and SCAS were strongly correlated (rs of 0.89 and 0.88). Most importantly, however, SCARED-R subscales were most substantially connected to their SCAS counterparts. Thus, SCARED-R generalized anxiety disorder was strongly associated with SCAS generalized anxiety disorder, SCARED-R separation anxiety disorder with SCAS separation anxiety disorder, and so on (Muris, et al., 1999c; Muris, Schmidt, & Merckelbach, 2000d).

Evidence for the divergent validity of the SCARED-R has also emerged. For example,

Muris, et al. (1998a) found SCARED-R scores to correlate more convincingly with anxious self-statements (rs of 0.60 and 0.70) than with depressive self-statements (rs of 0.36 and *0.54*). In addition, SCARED-R scores are more substantially associated with the internalizing scale of the Youth Self-Report (Achenbach, 1991) than with the externalizing scale (rs being 0.77 and 0.49, respectively; Muris, et al., 2000c).

Concurrent and Discriminant Validity

In a sample of 290 randomly selected primary school children, the connection between SCARED-R scores and DSM-defined anxiety disorders was examined. Children not only completed the SCARED-R, but were also administered a standardized clinical interview (the Diagnostic Interview Schedule for Children [DISC]; National Institute of Mental Health, 1992) in order to systematically investigate whether they fulfilled DSM-criteria for common childhood anxiety disorders, viz, generalized anxiety disorder, separation anxiety disorders, and specific phobia. Results showed that children with subclinical symptoms of an anxiety disorder (as measured by means of the DISC) scored significantly higher on the corresponding SCARED-R subscale than children without such symptoms (Muris, Merckelbach, Mayer, & Prins, 2000b).

Muris, et al. (in press b) explored the utility of the SCARED-R as a screening tool for the identification of children at high risk for prevalent anxiety disorders. More than 500 children aged 7-14 years completed the SCARED-R. From this sample, high and low anxious children were selected. High anxious children scored in the highest decile of the subscales generalized anxiety disorder, separation anxiety disorder, and/or social phobia. Low anxious children scored in the lowest decile. Both groups then received a semi-structured interview (the child version of the Structured Clinical Interview for DSM-IV; Hien, Matzner, First, et al., 1994) to assess to what extent they fulfilled the DSM-IV criteria for the relevant anxiety disorders. Results provided support for the predictive validity of the SCARED-R. That is, children who scored high on the SCARED-R total score had a 9 times higher risk of suffering from a DSM-IV anxiety disorder diagnosis than children who scored low on the SCARED-R total score. In particular, the separation anxiety disorder subscale appeared to be a good predictor of diagnosis: children who scored high on this subscale had a 19 times higher risk of meeting the full criteria for separation anxiety disorder than children who scored low on this subscale.

In a further study, Muris and Steerneman (in press) compared SCARED-R scores of clinically referred children with anxiety disorders and disruptive disorders (e.g., oppositional-defiant disorder, conduct disorder). Results showed that anxiety disordered children displayed higher scores on most of the SCARED-R scales than children with disruptive disorders, thus supporting the discriminant validity of the scale.

Validity of Specific SCARED-R Subscales

While the above described studies have yielded evidence for the validity of the more common childhood anxiety disorders (e.g., separation anxiety disorder, generalized anxiety disorder), further research will be necessary to examine the utility of SCARED-R subscales which assess less prevalent anxiety problems. A first attempt was made by Muris, Merckelbach, Korver, and Meesters (2000a) who investigated the validity of the SCARED post-traumatic or acute stress disorder subscale. More specifically, children who scored high on this subscale (i.e., 'trauma group') and control children (matched on school, gender, and age) were interviewed about their most aversive life event. In addition, children completed self-report questionnaires of traumatic experiences and PTSD symptomatology. Results showed that children in the trauma group more frequently reported life events that independent judges considered to be 'potentially traumatic' than did control children. Furthermore, children in the trauma group reported having experienced more traumatic incidents and had higher scores on PTSD-related questionnaires compared with control children. All in all, these results support the validity of the post-traumatic or acute stress disorder subscale of the SCARED-R.

The Clinical Utility of the SCARED-R

An illustration of the clinical utility of the SCARED-R can be found in a recent study by Muris, et al. (in press a). In that study, an intervention protocol for anxiety disorders was carried out in a large sample of unselected primary school children aged 8 to 13 years. All children (*N* = 425) from grades 5 to 8 of four primary schools in the southern part of The Netherlands completed the SCARED-R and the trait version of the STAIC during regular classes. Forty-two children were selected because they had high anxiety scores. More precisely, according to the normative means as provided by Muris, et al. (2000d), these children scored in the top 10% of SCARED-R subscales separation anxiety disorder, generalized anxiety disorder, and/or social phobia, and had a SCARED-R total scores that was at least 1 $\underline{SD}$ above the age- and gender appropriate mean.

Six months later, selected children were interviewed by a child psychologist using the Anxiety Disorders section of the DISC (see supra). Thirty-six children *(85.7%)* were found to meet the full criteria for at least one of the major anxiety disorders and were invited to participate in the treatment program. The primary DSM-III-R anxiety disorder diagnosis of the 36 children were generalized anxiety disorder (n = 14), separation anxiety disorder (n = 14), social phobia (n

= 7), and obsessive-compulsive disorder (n = 1). In 16 children (44.4%), there was comorbidity with at least one other anxiety disorder, i.e., specific phobia (n = 11), generalized anxiety disorder (n = 6), social phobia (n = 4), and separation anxiety disorder (n = 2). Seven of the children were diagnosed with three anxiety disorders

The Coping Koala Cognitive-Behavioral Treatment (see Barrett, Dadds, & Rapee, 1996) is a manualized program consisting of 12 sessions of about 30-40 minutes which focus on recognizing anxious feelings and somatic reactions to anxiety, cognitive restructuring in anxiety-provoking situations, coping self-talk, exposure to feared stimuli, evaluating performance, and administering self reinforcement. During the first four sessions, anxiety management procedures are introduced, role-played by the therapist, and practiced by the children. Throughout the remaining eight sessions children applied the newly learned coping skills in real-life situations, starting with low-stress situations and gradually increasing to high-stress situations (see Table 2). Children were treated at their schools and received 2 weekly sessions of the CBT program. Therapists were clinical psychology students who were trained to work with the program. Each week, therapists were supervised by an experienced clinical child psychologist. During this supervision, upcoming sessions were prepared and specific treatment issues were discussed.

To examine its treatment sensitivity, SCARED-R scores as well as scores on a traditional measure of childhood anxiety, i.e., the STAIC, were not only obtained at baseline (i.e., 6 months before treatment), but also at pre- and post-treatment. It was hypothesized that SCARED-R and STAIC scores would remain relatively stable from baseline to pre-treatment, but then show significant decreases from pre- to post-treatment.

Results confirmed our hypothesis, that is, children's anxiety levels did not show noticeable changes in the half-year preceding the CBT intervention (i.e., from screening to pre-treatment). However, after treatment, children's anxiety levels as indexed by the SCARED-R and the STAIC decreased substantially (see Figure 1). In 75.0% of the children, clinically significant improvement was observed. That is, their post-treatment anxiety scores were within the normal range. In terms of Jacobson and Truax's (1991) "reliable change index," 77.8% of the children improved on both anxiety scales.

From this study, two important conclusions regarding the clinical utility of the SCARED-R can be drawn. First of all, the SCARED-R proved to be a sensitive instrument for detecting anxiety disordered children: almost 90% of the children with high scores indeed appeared to fulfill the DSM-criteria for one or more anxiety disorders. Additional analyses provided evidence for the idea that the SCARED-R is sensitive to tap symptoms of specific anxiety disorders. Stepwise logistic regression analyses were carried out in which SCARED-R total and subscale scores were the predictors, whereas the most prevalent anxiety disorder diagnosis (i.e., generalized anxiety disorder, separation anxiety disorder, and social phobia) was the dependent variables. In all analyses, pertinent subscale scores appeared to be a better predictor of diagnosis than the total anxiety score. As an illustration, correlations between SCARED-R generalized anxiety disorder, separation anxiety disorder, and social phobia, on the one hand, and their corresponding anxiety disorder diagnosis, on the other hand, were 0.50, 0.67, and 0.62. Correlations between the SCARED-R total score and these anxiety disorder diagnoses were remarkably smaller: 0.32, 0.10, and 0.52, respectively.

Second, the data indicated that the SCARED-R reliably taps treatment effects (see also Muris, Merckelbach, Gadet, Moulaert, & Tierney, 1999a). That is, scores on this measure remained stable from baseline to pre-treatment and then declined significantly from pre- to post-treatment. Additional analyses even showed that the SCARED-R explained variance in treatment effect over and above the STAIC. Furthermore, some support was found for the idea that the SCARED-R can be used to tap specific changes in children's anxiety symptoms: the largest effect sizes were found for those SCARED-R subscales that covered the anxiety disorders that were the most important targets for treatment.

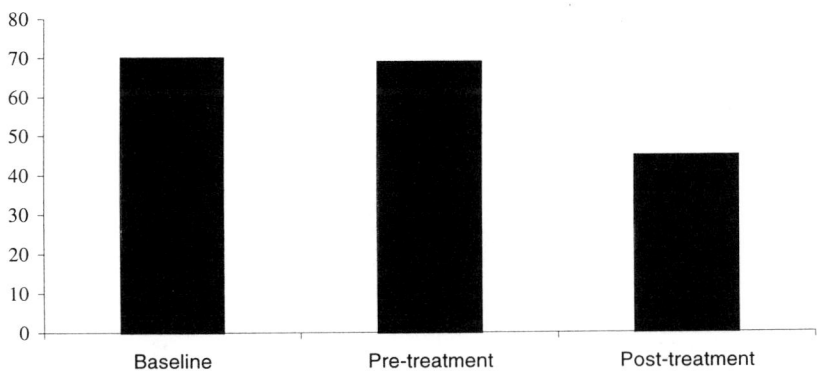

Figure 1.   Mean SCARED-R total score of the 36 anxiety disordered children at baseline, pre-treatment, and post-treatment.   SCARED-R = Screen for child Anxiety Related Emotional Disorders – Revised.

Table 2. The 12 Sessions of the "Coping Koala," a Cognitive-Behavioral Treatment Program for Anxiety Disordered Children

Session 1	Introduction	Acquaintance and introduction
Session 2	How do I feel?	Recognition of emotions
Session 3	How does my body react?	Recognition of physical sensations that accompany anxiety and fear
Session 4	Let's relax	Teaching the child how to relax by means of progressive relaxation
Session 5	What do I think?	Giving the child insight into the relation between situation, thoughts, and feelings Giving the child insight into the fact that thoughts to a large extent determine Whether he/she becomes anxious or not
Session 6	What should I do?	Teaching the child to choose new (non-anxious) behavior in anxiety-provoking situations
Session 7	How are we doing so far?	Teaching the child to evaluate his/her own behavior and to reinforce himself/herself for new (non-anxious) behavior
Session 8	FEAR-plan	Teaching the child to cope effectively with anxiety-provoking situations by Means of the FEAR-plan
Session 9	Start to exercise	Applying the FEAR-plan to a relatively easy anxiety-provoking situation
Session 10	It becomes harder	Applying the FEAR-plan to a moderately anxiety-provoking situation
Session 11	Guess what we are doing?	Applying the FEAR-plan to a situation that provokes a lot of anxiety
Session 12	You did it!	Termination of treatment

CONCLUSION

In their comprehensive review of childhood anxiety measures, Stallings and March (1995, p. 127) noted that "Ideally, instruments to assess anxiety in young persons should: (1) provide reliable and valid ascertainment of symptoms across multiple symptom domains; (2) discriminate symptom clusters; (3) evaluate severity; (4) incorporate and reconcile multiple observations, such as parent and child ratings; and *(5)* sensitive to treatment-induced change in symptoms." The present overview seems to indicate that the SCARED-R possesses most of these properties and hence suggests that this scale is a useful self report instrument of childhood anxiety in both clinical and research settings.

Three critical remarks should be made to qualify this conclusion. First of all, the attempt to fully cover the anxiety disorders as defined in the DSM has obscured the structure of the SCARED-R. Although a good factor structure is not a <u>condition sine qua non</u> of a measure's validity, this certainly is a minus point of the scale. Second, the SCARED-R is useful as an initial screening of anxiety symptoms, but it should be kept in mind that a diagnostic interview is necessary to establish whether a child really suffers from an anxiety disorder. More precisely, in most cases, SCARED-R subscales only (to some extent) tap the main feature (in the DSM: criterion A) of various anxiety disorders. Third, just like any other measure of childhood anxiety, the SCARED-R wrestles with the 'problem' of comorbidity among anxiety disorders (see Costello & Angold, 1995). For example, worry is not an exclusive symptom of generalized anxiety disorder, but also figures in social phobia and separation anxiety disorder (APA, 1994). Furthermore, it is evident that physical symptoms are not exclusively present in panic disorder but also play a role in other anxiety disorders (Sallee & Greenawald, 1995). As a result, some of the previous studies have failed to document specific connections between SCARED-R subscales and anxiety disorders (Muris, et al., in press b).

A key advantage of the SCARED-R is that the scale is closely connected to current classification systems such as the DSM and thus facilitates communication about the various types of childhood anxiety symptoms and related diagnostic categories. The past decade has seen a steady increase of research on fear and anxiety in children (e.g., Bernstein, et al., 1996). Reliable, valid, and up-to-date instruments such as the SCARED-R will further stimulate systematic research in this important area.

REFERENCES

Achenbach, T.M. (1991). *Manual for the Youth Self-Report and 1991 Profile.* Burlington, VT: University of Vermont, Department of Psychiatry.

American Psychiatric Association. (1994). *Diagnostic and Statistical Manual of Mental Disorders* (4th edition). Washington, DC: Author.

Barrett, P.M., Dadds, M.R., & Rapee, R.M. (1996). Family treatment of childhood anxiety: A controlled trial. *Journal of Consulting and Clinical Psychology 64,* 333-342.

Bernstein, G.A., Borchardt, C.M., & Perwien, A.R. (1996). Anxiety disorders in children and adolescents: A review of the past 10 years. *Journal of the American Academy of Child and Adolescent Psychiatry, 35* 1110-1119.

Birmaher, B., Khetarpal, S., Brent, D., Cully, M., Balach, L., Kaufffian, J., & McKenzie Neer, S. (1997). The Screen for Child Anxiety Related Emotional Disorders (SCARED): Scale construction and psychometric characteristics. *Journal of the American Academy of Child and Adolescent Psychiatry, 36,* 545-553.

Costello, E.J., & Angold, A. *(1995).* Epidemiology. In J.S. March (Ed.), *Anxiety disorders in children and adolescents* (pp.109-124). New York: Guilford Press.

Hien, D., Matzner, F. J., First, M. B., Spitzer, R. L., Gibbon, M., & Williams, J. B. W (1994). *Structured Clinical Interview for DSM-IV-Child Edition (Version 1.0).* Columbia University, New York: Author.

Jacobson, N.S., & Truax, P. (1991). Clinical significance: A statistical approach to defining meaningful change in psychotherapy research. *Journal of Consulting and Clinical Psychology, 59,* 12-19.

Muris, P., Mayer, B., Bartelds, E., Tierney, S., & Bogie, N. (in press a). The revised version of the Screen for Child Anxiety Related Emotional Disorders (SCAREDR): Treatment sensitivity in an early intervention trial for childhood anxiety disorders. *British Journal of Clinical Psychology.*

Muris, P. & Merckelbach, H. (in press). The etiology of childhood specific phobia: A multifactorial model. In M.W. Vasey & M.R. Dadds (Eds.), *The developmental psychopathology of anxiety.* New York: Oxford Press.

Muris, P., Merckelbach, H., Gadet, B., Moulaert, V., & Tierney, S. (1999a). Sensitivity for treatment effects of the Screen for Child Anxiety Related Emotional Disorders. *Journal of Psychopathology and Behavioral Assessment, 21, 323-335.*

Muris, P., Merckelbach, H., Kindt, M., Bagels, S., Dreessen, L., Van Dorp, C., Habets, A.,

Rosmuller, S., & Snieder, N. (in press b). The utility of the Screen for Child Anxiety Related Emotional Disorders (SCARED) as a tool for identifying children at high risk for prevalent anxiety disorders. *Anxiety Stress and Coping.*

Muris, P., Merckelbach, H., Ktirver, P. & Meesters, C. (2000a). Screening for trauma in children and adolescents: The validity of the Traumatic Stress Disorder scale of the Screen for Child Anxiety Related Emotional Disorders. *Journal of Clinical Child Psychology, 29,* 406-413.

Muris, P., Merckelbach, H., Mayer, B., & Prins, E. (2000b). How serious are common childhood fears? *Behavior Research and Therapy, 38,* 2 17-228

Muris, P., Merckelbach, H., Mayer, B. & Snieder, N. (1998a). The relationship between anxiety disorders symptoms and negative self-statements in children. *Social Behavior and Personality, 26,* 307-316.

Muris, P., Merckelbach, H., Mayer, B., Van Brakel, A., Thissen, S., Moulaert, V., & Gadet, B. (1998b). The Screen for Child Anxiety Related Emotional Disorders and its relationship to traditional childhood anxiety measures. *Journal of Behavior Therapy and Experimental Psychiatry, 29,* 327-339

Muris, P., Merckelbach, H., Moulaert, V., & Gadet, B. (2000c). Associations of symptoms of anxiety disorders and self-reported behavior problems in normal children. *Psychological Reports, 86,* 157-162.

Muris, P., Merckelbach, H., Schmidt, H., & Mayer, B. (1999b). The revised version of the Screen for Child Anxiety Related Emotional Disorders (SCARED-R): Factor structure in normal children. *Personality and Individual Differences, 26,_99-112.*

Muris, P., Merckelbach, H., Van Brakel, A. & Mayer, B. (1999c). The Screen for Child Anxiety Related Emotional Disorders (SCARED): Further evidence for its reliability and validity. *Anxiety Stress and Coping, 12,* 411-425.

Muris, P., Merckelbach, H., Van Brakel, A., Mayer, B., & Van Dongen, L. (1998c). The Screen for Child Anxiety Related Emotional Disorders: Relationship with anxiety and depression in normal children. *Personality and Individual Differences, 24,* 451-456.

Muris, P., Schmidt, H. & Merckelbach, H. (2000d). Correlations between two self-report questionnaires for measuring DSM-defined anxiety disorder symptoms in children: The Screen for Child Anxiety Related Emotional Disorders and the Spence Children's Anxiety Scale. *Personality and Individual Differences, 28,* 333-346.

Muris, P., & Steerneman, P. (in press). The Revised version of the Screen for Child Anxiety Related Emotional Disorders (SCARED-R): First evidence for its reliability and validity in a clinical sample. *British Journal of Clinical Psychology.*

National Institute of Mental Health (NIMH; 1992). *Diagnostic Interview Schedule for Children (DISC). Version 2.3.* New York: New York State Psychiatric Institute, Division of Child and Adolescent Psychiatry.

Ollendick, T.H. (1983). Reliability and validity of the Revised Fear Survey Schedule for Children (FSSC-R). *Behavior Research and Therapy, 21,* 685-692.

Rapee, R.M., Barrett, P.M., Dadds, M.R. & Evans, I. (1994). Reliability of the DSMIII-R childhood anxiety disorders using structured interview: Interrater and parent-child agreement. *Journal of the American Academy of Child and Adolescent Psychiatry, 33,* 984-992.

Reynolds, C.R., & Richmond, B.O. (1978). What I think and feel: A revised measure of children's manifest anxiety. *Journal of Abnormal Child Psychology, 6,* 271-280.

Sallee, R., & Greenawald, J. *(1995).* Neurobiology. In J.S. March (Ed.), *Anxiety disorders in children and adolescents* (pp. 3-34). New York: Guilford Press.

Spence, S.H. (1997). Structure of anxiety symptoms among children: A confirmatory factor-analytic study. *Journal of Abnormal Psychology, 106,* 280-297.

Spence, S.H. (1998). A measure of anxiety symptoms among children. *Behavior Research and Therapy, 36,* 545-566.

Spielberger, C.D. (1973). *Manual for the State-Trait Anxiety Inventory for Children.* Palo Alto, CA: Consulting Psychologists Press.

Stallings, P., & March, J.S. *(1995).* Assessment. In J.S. March (Ed.), *Anxiety disorders in children and adolescents* (pp.125-147). New York: Guilford Press.

Strauss, C.C. (1993). Anxiety disorders. In T.H. Ollendick & M. Hersen (Eds.), *Handbook of child and adolescent assessment* (pp.239-250). Boston: Allyn & Bacon.

11

Preliminary Development of a Culturally Appropriate Measure for Asian Children's Depression

Jessie B. Koh
The National University of Singapore

Weining C. Chang
The National University of Singapore

Daniel S.S. Fung
Woodbridge Hospital

Carolyn Kee
Woodbridge Hospital

Jessie B. Koh · The National University of Singapore · Department of Social Work and Psychology · Blk AS6 Level 4 · 11 Lawlink · Republic of Singapore 117570.

International Perspectives on Child and Adolescent Mental Health. Volume 2: Proceedings of the Second International Conference, edited by N. N. Singh, T. H. Ollendick, and A. N. Singh. © 2002 Elsevier Science Ltd. All rights reserved.

Depression has been a well-researched construct in psychology, psychiatry, and medical anthropology. While a rich body of literature on depression has been accumulated, much remains to be explored, especially when it is studied in cross-cultural contexts. A major issue has been the universality or cultural specificity of the phenomenological experiences and manifestations of depression across cultures. This leads to a more urgent issue concerning the validity of applying Western developed instruments to populations of different cultures. The present study aimed at exploring the daily experiences of depression in Asian children with which to develop a culturally appropriate measure of depression for these children.

Kleinman (1977) in advocating for a "new cross-cultural psychiatry," cautioned against the dangers of "category fallacy," that is, Western derived psychiatric diagnostic categories may not necessarily be directly applicable in another cultural context, where the same or similar categories may not be found, hence resulting in a categorization fallacy. Along a similar line of concern, variations in the phenomenology of depression across cultures suggested caution against the direct application of Western developed measures in different cultural contexts for assessment purposes. Specifically, two issues could be raised: (1) Is the coverage of depressive symptoms in these Western developed assessment measures cross-culturally applicable and relevant? (2) Will there be culture-specific symptoms that these assessment measures fail to tap?

The research literature on cross cultural psychology and psychiatry has suggested differences in the manifestations of depression by populations of different cultures. Notable differences have been found in symptom presentations. Kraepelin (1904) reported the presence of psychiatric syndromes in Algeria and Indonesia that were radically different from those he had observed in Germany. Mason, Shore, and Bloom (1985) reported that the Hopi identified five syndromes of depression, of which only one shares significant parameters with Western depressive disorders. As a matter of fact, Kleinman and Good (1985) have dedicated a whole volume, Culture and depression, to the research and discussion on the conceptualization and manifestations of depression in different cultures. A closer examination of the research literature revealed that the Western populations have a higher tendency to report symptoms in affective terms while the non-Western populations, in particular, the Asians have a higher tendency to report symptoms in somatic terms (e.g., Chang, 1985; Kleinman, 1977; Pfeiffer, 1967; Shinfuku, et al., 1973).

Most commonly known and widely used assessment measures for children's depression have been developed in the West, based on observations made in, and empirical data collected from, Western populations. Some examples of these assessment measures are Kovacs' (1980/1981) Children Depression Inventory, Centre for Epidemiological Studies Depression

Scale (Radloff, 1977), and the Mood and Feelings Questionnaire (Angold, et al., 1987). With the available evidence suggesting cultural variations in depressive experiences, the validity of direct application of these Western instruments in non-Western cultures is questionable.

A set of "core depressive symptoms" that included "sadness, joylessness, anxiety, tension, lack of energy, loss of interest, loss of ability to concentration, and ideas of insufficiency" (p. 61) was identified in an international study conducted by the World Health Organization (1983). This study included countries with as varied cultural backgrounds as Canada, Switzerland, Japan, and Iran. Cross-cultural variations in the presentation and expression of symptoms, where "other symptoms" were reported, were also found in the same study. In a more recent review, Matsumoto (2000) concluded that there are both universal and culture-specific ways of symptom presentations of depression. Similar conclusions have been reached by researchers such as Al-Issa (1995) and Tanaka-Matsumi and Draguns (1997). Most researchers agree that the symptoms of depression are multi-faceted (for instance, see Chang, 1985), and there are symptoms that are commonly shared by people of different cultures (Zung, 1977), considered "core symptoms." Nonetheless, there have also been advocates urging for the need to look for culture-specific symptoms. It is generally recognized that the specific cultural environment in which the individual operates may shape the perception, expression and understanding of depression (e.g., Marsella, 1980; Weiss & Kleinman, 1988).

Recognizing the universality and culture-specificity of depressive experiences, the direct transfer of Western developed assessment measures for use with populations of different cultural backgrounds may warrant caution. These measures may contain culturally inappropriate symptoms, that is, symptoms that are specific to the Western population that might not be present in other cultures. More importantly, these Western measures do not include depressive symptoms specific to the culture in question. One way to address this issue of acquiring valid assessment measures is to take the cultural psychologists' approach (Cole, 1996), that is, to observe depression within the context of culture with which to produce assessment instruments for the particular culture. This involves (1) identification of culture-specific symptoms and (2) examination of the relevance of core symptoms found in established measures as part of the phenomenology of depression to the population of the culture of interest.

Emotions are socially construed and, therefore, inherently cultural (Geertz, 1973; Lutz, 1985). Emotions "may be seen as an assortment of socially shared scripts composed of physiological, subjective and behavioral processes" (Kitayama & Markus, 1994, p. 5). The phenomenological experiences of emotions and their communications are intimately influenced by such processes as the concept of self and the language used in the culture (Jenkins, 1994).

Via these processes the phenomenological world and one's emotional experiences interact with each other. The entire process of emotion takes place within the framework of culture, which gives meanings to the antecedents, subjective experiences and socially appropriate expressions. To look for culture-specific experiences and expressions of emotions, an understanding of the local social world is critical.

The daily life of Asians is characterized by a salient emphasis on interpersonal relationships. Adaptation to this environment requires skillful management to maintain a complex web of close and long-term relationships. Enmeshed in this rich cultural tradition, the Asian self is constructed via and within the context of social interactions with others (Chang, Lee, & Koh, 1996) — an interdependent self as Markus and Kitayama (1991) put it. In this collectivist context, the Asians are socialized to accept and accommodate to the social reality that others are part of their life (Chang, Chua, & Toh, 1996).

Anthropological literature has found that interpersonal processes bridge the social world and the body-self (Lewis-Fernandes & Kleinman, 1994). Embedded within a close-knit, highly interdependent social context, Asians regard the potential loss of these relationships a great source of distress. Concerns over interpersonal relationships thus naturally constitute an essential part of one's emotional experiences.

Taking the cultural psychology approach, the present study attempted to develop a culturally appropriate measure of depression for Asian children. An interpersonal dimension, with items generated on the basis of Asian children's everyday expressions of depression, was postulated to be a culture-specific facet of depression to these children. This dimension was added to the internationally identified core symptoms of depression, whose validity was also investigated in the study.

METHOD

Item Generation

A review of literature on children's depression revealed seven dimensions, namely, affective manifestations, loss of interest, cognitive dysfunctioning, behavioral manifestations, depressed cognition, existential concern, and psychosomatic manifestations. With the newly postulated interpersonal dimension, eight dimensions were included in the Asian Children Depression Scale (ACDS) at this initial phase.

Items of the established dimensions were adopted with modification. Items for the interpersonal dimension were generated, based on a theoretical conceptualization of the dimension. Before writing the items, observations were carried out with target-aged, six to twelve year old children in order to gather culture-specific expressions of depression. These children's normal everyday expressions of depression were used as items in the scale. Careful attention was paid to the wording and length of each item. Wordings used were kept simple to reflect the nature of children's speech, and each item was kept short to avoid children finding them overwhelmingly lengthy. An initial pool of 56 items distributed across the eight dimensions was generated. A primary school teacher was asked to serve as an expert informer, who provided feedback and suggestions as to the pool of items to ensure comprehensibility by children, especially by the 6-year-olds. Revisions on item wordings were made accordingly.

After completing the above steps, 10 clinicians from the Child Guidance Clinic of Singapore composed of child psychologists and child psychiatrists were asked to assess the face validity of the items and to provide feedback and suggestions on the item wordings. They identified the items that they thought best described depressive symptoms for Asian children and changed any item wording to what they thought would be more comprehensible to children.

Concurrently, 44 Chinese children of the target age range from the community were asked to assess the face validity of the items. They were first asked to (i) identify items from the scales that they thought describe depression and (ii) indicate any word that they did not understand. Following that, they were asked to respond to the scale with the actual test presentation format. The former exercise was to assess their concepts of depression and their understanding of the item wordings. The latter was to gather feedback with regards to the presentation format of the scale, which included the comprehensibility of the instructions and the ease of responding to the 5-point scale.

With the data obtained from the clinicians and children, initial elimination of the items was carried out. The following criterion was adopted: Items that were not identified by either at least 50% of the professionals or at least 50% of the children as depressive symptoms were discarded. Six items were eliminated from the initial pool of items as a result, with 50 items remaining, which were distributed across eight factors. From the feedback and suggestions gathered, certain item wordings were further amended. No changes were made to the presentation format of the measure.

VALIDATION

Participants

Four hundred and seventy four Chinese community school-going children, age 6 to 12 participated in the present study. There was a good mix of boys (n = 239, 50.4%) and girls (n = 235, 49.6%). These children were mainly drawn from the Primary One (6-7 years old), Primary Three (8-10 years old) and Primary Six (11-12 years old) classes.

Instruments

Items generated in the item-generation phase were incorporated into a scale —Asian Children Depression Scale (ACDS) for further tests. Together with two established scales (see below), the ACDS was administered in the present phase.

Asian Children Depression Scale (ACDS). The ACDS was the measure under construction. It was designed to assess symptoms of depression for use with Asian children age 6 to 12. It is to be a self-report measure with a 5-point response scale, ranging from "strongly disagree" (1) to "strongly agree" (5). In this validation phase, it was comprised of 50 items that were distributed across eight dimensions, i.e., the newly postulated interpersonal dimension and the seven established dimensions of depression.

Children Depression Inventory (CDI) (Kovacs, 1980/1981). The CDI is a widely used 27-item self-rated measure that assesses depressive symptoms in children and adolescents. Each CDI item is comprised of three statements, where respondents are asked to pick the one that best describes them. The three statements reflect the severity of each symptom, with 1 indicating "absence of symptom," 2 indicating "mild symptom," and 3 indicating "definite symptom." Internal consistency of the CDI has been reported to be satisfactory, with Cronbach alphas ranging from .71 to .89 (Kovacs, 1980/1981). In the present study, a Cronbach alpha of .87 was obtained. This measure was used to assess convergent validity of the ACDS.

State Trait Anxiety Inventory for Children (STAIC) (Spielberger, 1973). The STAIC is a widely used 40-item self-rated measure that is comprised of two separate sections, assessing state (20 items) and trait (20 items) anxious symptoms in children and adolescents. Each STAIC item is scored on a 3-point response scale. Internal consistency of the STAIC has been reported to be satisfactory. For the state anxiety measure, Cronbach alphas of .82 for males and .87 for females have been reported; for the trait anxiety measure, Cronbach alphas of .78 for males and .81 for females have been found (Spielberger, 1973). In the present study, Cronbach alphas of .87 and

.88 were obtained for state and trait anxiety, respectively. This measure was used to assess discriminant validity of the ACDS.

Procedure

The scales were administered during the children's classes. During the scale administration process, the Primary Three and Six students worked on the scales by themselves, as it was found from the item-generation phase that children with at least Primary Three level were able to handle the questions independently. They were allowed to ask questions when needed. For the Primary One students, items were read out to them as they may have yet acquired adequate reading skills.

RESULTS

Factor Structure

Confirmatory factor analysis (CFA) was used to develop and cross-validate the factor structure of the ACDS. To carry out these analyses, particularly to allow for cross-validation of the factor structure, two samples were required. The entire sample was randomly split into two unequal groups. The first group, i.e., the development group ($\underline{n} = 324$) was used to develop the factor structure. The second group, i.e., the validation group ($\underline{n} = 150$) was used for cross-validation purpose.

Identifying Internal Factor Structure

The factor structure was developed and confirmed through a series of model assessments of fit, item trimming, model re-specification and testing of alternative model processes using the LISREL 8 program (Jöreskog & Sörbom, 1993).

In the present study, model fit was assessed following conventional criteria, i.e., using the chi-square statistic and a number of goodness of fit indices. The chi-square is a widely used index for assessing goodness of fit; however, one disadvantage of its usage is that it is overly sensitive to sample size. In studies with large sample sizes, chi-square statistic tends to be significant, leading to rejection of models even when they are theoretically plausible. Recognizing this and to correct for it, other goodness of fit indices that are less sensitive to sample size are often relied upon in addition to the chi-square statistic. Multiple fit indices are necessary to provide convergent evidence of model fit. The other fit indices included in the present study were: Jöreskog and Sörbom's (1989) adjusted goodness of fit index (AGFI),

Bentler and Bonett's (1980) non-norm fit index (NNFI), Bentler's (1990) comparative fit index (CFI), Steiger's (1990) root mean square error of approximation (RMSEA) and Jöreskog and Sörbom's (1986) the standardized root mean square residual (SRMR). The values of AGFI, NNFI and CFI range from .00 to 1.00, and conventionally, values of .90 and above indicate a good model-data fit. The value of RMSEA ranges from .00 to 1.00, and as recommended by Brown and Cudeck (1993), a value of .05 and below indicates a good model-data fit. The value of SRMR ranges from .00 to 1.00, and conventionally, a value of .10 and below indicates a good model-data fit.

The chi-square statistic was used to compare relative fit between nested models in the present study. Specifically, the chi-square difference test was used to choose between models with nested relationships in the model re-specification and testing of alternative model processes. A more parsimonious model (i.e., more constrained) is nested under a more complex model (less constrained). Statistically, a non-significant chi-square difference value between models indicates that the more parsimonious model is preferred; where a significant chi-square difference value is obtained, the more complex model is preferred.

The initial model of the ACDS consisted of 50 items distributed across eight factors. This model was tested, it did not fit the data well, χ^2 (1147, $\underline{n}$ = 324) = 2127.24, $\underline{p}$ < .05, AGFI = .76, NNFI = .79, CFI = .80, RMSEA = .05, SRMR = .06.

Item trimming was carried out. Two criteria were adopted: (1) multiple loadings, i.e., items that loaded on two or more factors were discarded, and (2) low factor loadings, i.e., items with loading less than 0.35 were eliminated. A total of 27 items were discarded. The remaining 23 items were distributed across seven factors. All the items in the existential concern factor were discarded. After item trimming, the inter-correlations among the seven factors were assessed. It was found that the correlations between the factors of behavioral manifestations and loss of interest ($\underline{r}$ = 1.00, $\underline{p}$ < .05), between depressed cognition and the interpersonal dimension ($\underline{r}$ = 1.00, $\underline{p}$ < .05), as well as between the affective manifestations and cognitive dysfunctioning ($\underline{r}$ = .88, $\underline{p}$ < .05) were high, suggesting that each pair of the factors could possibly be a single, unitary construct. A series of model re-specification were carried out.

Starting with the pair having the highest correlation coefficient, the first re-specification combined the factors of behavioral manifestations with loss of interest, resulting in a six-factor model, which was nested under the seven-factor model. The chi-square difference test between the two models revealed a non-significant change in chi-square, $\Delta\chi^2$ (6, $\underline{n}$ = 324) = 8.07, indicating the six-factor model as the preferred model.

The second re-specification combined the factors of depressed cognition and the interpersonal dimension, resulting in a five-factor model, which was nested under the six-factor model. The chi-square difference test between the two models revealed a non-significant change in chi-square, $\Delta\chi^2$ (5, $\underline{n}$ = 324) = 11.02, indicating the five-factor model as the preferred model.

The last re-specification combined the factors of affective manifestations and cognitive dysfunctioning, resulting in a four-factor model, which was nested under the five-factor model. The chi-square difference test between the two models revealed a non-significant change in chi-square, $\Delta\chi^2$ (4, $\underline{n}$ = 324) = 2.13, indicating the four-factor model as the preferred model.

The resulting four-factor model was found to have a good fit, χ^2 (224, $\underline{n}$ = 324) = 340.09, $\underline{p}$ < .05, AGFI = .90, NNFI = .94, CFI = .94, RMSEA = .04, SRMR = .04. The factors were Negative Affect and Cognitive Dysfunction (4 items), Loss of Interest (5 items), Psychosomatic Manifestations (4 items), and the interpersonal dimension: Self and Relationship Esteem (10 items) (see Appendix 1 for sample items).

Two plausible alternative models were tested; the purpose was to rule out the possibility of these models, which would establish the four-factor model as the best-fit model. One reasonable alternative model was the loading of all the 23 items on one single factor, presumably depression. This one-factor model was tested, and a moderate fit was obtained, χ^2 (230, $\underline{n}$ = 324) = 498.31, $\underline{p}$ < .05, AGFI = .84, NNFI = .85, CFI = .87, RMSEA = .06, SRMR = .06. Compared to the four-factor model, the one-factor model had only a moderate fit, and the chi-square difference test revealed a significant chi-square change, $\Delta\chi^2$ (6, $\underline{n}$ =324) = 158.22, indicating preference for the four-factor model. Another alternative model was a three-factor model, combining loss of interest with negative affect and cognitive dysfunction. This was because an inspection of the four-factor model revealed a high correlation ($\underline{r}$ = .81, $\underline{p}$ < .05) between the two factors. The three-factor model yielded a good fit, χ^2 (227, $\underline{n}$ = 324) = 350.61, $\underline{p}$ < .05, AGFI = .90, NNFI = .93, CFI = .94, RMSEA = .04, SRMR = .04. However, when comparing this three-factor model to the four-factor model, where the three-factor model was nested under the four-factor model, the chi-square difference test revealed a significant chi-square change, $\Delta\chi^2$ (3, $\underline{n}$ = 324) = 10.52, indicating preference for the four-factor model.

Identifying Higher-Order Factor Structure

A higher-order factor analysis was conducted to test that the four factors, Negative Affect and Cognitive Dysfunction, Loss of Interest, Psychosomatic Manifestations as well as Self and Relationship Esteem, are dimensions of one higher-order factor, namely, depression. This higher-order structure yielded a good fit, χ^2 (226, $\underline{n}$ = 324) = 341.50, $\underline{p}$ < .05, AGFI = .90, NNFI = .94, CFI = .94, RMSEA = .04, SRMR = .04.

Cross-Validation of Factor Structure

To test the stability, that is, measurement invariance, of the higher-order factor structure, cross-validation using multiple groups CFA was carried out. This was achieved by applying the structure established with one sample — the development sample to another — the validation sample (Jöreskog & Sörbom, 1993). An invariance hierarchy of increasing restrictive hypotheses was outlined and tested following the recommendations made by Bryne (1998) and Chan and Schmitt (1997). A widely accepted criterion for achieving measurement invariance is to obtain equal factor loadings across groups (Alwin & Jackson, 1981; Sörbom, 1993). A more stringent criterion is to obtain both equal factor loadings and error variances across groups (e.g., see Chan & Schmitt, 1997).

Table 1 presents the fit indices associated with the confirmatory factor analytic models fitted to the 23 x 23 observed variance-covariance matrix of the ACDS. Chi-square difference tests associated with relevant model comparisons were also presented.

Table 1. Model Fit Indices and Nested Model Comparisons in Multiple Group Structure Analysis Across the Development Sample (N = 324) and the Validation Sample (N = 150) for the Asian Children Depression Scale (ACDS)

Model Specification	df	χ^2	Model Comparison	Δdf	$\Delta\chi^2$	AGFI	NNFI	CFI	RMSEA	SRMI
M1	452	698.22*	--	--	--	.90	.91	.92	.03	.07
M2	471	715.21*	M1 vs M2	19	16.99	.90	.91	.92	.03	.08
M3	494	753.50*	M2 vs M3	23	38.29*	.89	.91	.91	.03	.08
M4	497	758.48*	M3 vs M4	3	4.98	.89	.91	.91	.03	.08

M1 : 1st order factor loadings free, indicator error variances free, 2nd order factor loadings free, late factor error variances free, latent factor variance free (fully unconstrained model).

M2 : 1st order factor loadings equal; indicator error variances free, 2nd order factor loadings free, late factor error variances free, latent factor variance free.

M3 : 1st order factor loadings equal, indicator error variances equal, 2nd order factor loadings free; late factor error variances free, latent factor variance free.

M4 : 1st order factor loadings equal, indicator error variances equal, 2nd order factor loadings equa latent factor error variances free, latent factor variance free.

* $p < .05$

Model 1 (M1) represented the fully unconstrained model, where all specification parameters, i.e., factor loadings, error variances and factor variances were set free across the development and validation groups. In subsequent models, increasingly more parameters were constrained to be equal across the two groups, making each subsequent model to be more parsimonious than the previous one. A non-significant chi-square difference value was obtained when comparing Model 2 (M2) to Model 1 (M1), suggesting that M2 was the preferred model; this indicated that the first-order factor loadings were equal between the two groups.

A significant chi-square difference value was found when comparing Model 3 (M3) to Model 2 (M2), indicating that the first-order (i.e., indicator) error variances between the two groups were significantly different. A check of the indicator error variances found that 14 of the 23 items had minute differences of less than or equal to 0.11 between the two groups. For the remaining 9 items, they had error variances with a difference ranging from 0.16 to 0.26 between the groups. These differences were considered to be trivial. Furthermore, as the chi-square statistic is highly sensitive to sample size, the statistical significant difference could be due to the large sample size.

Non-significant chi-square difference value was obtained when comparing Model 4 (M4) to Model 3 (M3), suggesting that M4 was the preferred model; this indicated that that the second-order factor loadings were equal between the groups. In higher-order structures, second-order (i.e., latent factor) error variances are widely accepted to be unequal, hence no further models were tested.

Though the samples differ in the first-order errors, the first-order factor loadings and second-order factor loadings were found to be equal between the two groups. Therefore, the basic structure was invariant across the two samples.

Figure 1 presents the higher-order factor structure and the common metric completely standardized factor loadings of the ACDS. The common metric completely standardized solution is the factor loading solution after taking into account of both samples. The second-order factor loadings were high with .92, .89, .79 and .85 for Negative Affect and Cognitive Dysfunction, Loss of Interest, Psychosomatic Manifestations and Self and Relationship Esteem respectively, all significant at $t > 1.96$. The first-order loadings of the latent variables on the 23 indicators ranged from .36 to .77.

Internal Consistency

The Cronbach alpha, calculated on the basis of the four factors, for the ACDS was high at .80. High Cronbach alphas were obtained as well with each of the sub-samples, with .76 for the Primary (6-7 years old), .80 for the Primary Three (8-10 years old) and .83 for the Primary Six students (11-12 years old).

Construct Validity (I): Correlation

The ACDS was correlated with the CDI with a coefficient of .68. It had lower correlations with state anxiety and trait anxiety, with coefficients of .39 and .38 respectively. The correlations provided evidence for construct validity of the scale (see Table 2).

Construct Validity (II): Exploratory Factor Analysis

A principal components analysis with Varimax rotation on the items in the ACDS, CDI and STAIC was performed to further assess construct validity of the ACDS. It was found that when the items in the ACDS, CDI and STAIC were forced into a two- factor solution, items in the ACDS and CDI loaded onto one factor — depression, while items in the STAIC loaded onto a separate second factor — anxiety (see Table 3). This indicated that the items in the ACDS measured depression, a construct different from that of anxiety.

Table 2.   Mean, Standard Deviations, and Inter-Correlations of Study Variables (N = 474)

Variable	ACDS	CDI	STAIC-S	STAIC-T
1. ACDS	---			
2. CDI	.68**	---		
3. STAIC-S	.39**	.49**	---	
4. STAIC-T	.38**	.32**	.51**	---
Mean	2.28	1.5	1.66	1.75
Standard Deviation	.61	.33	.39	.39

ACDS = Asian Children Depression Scale
CDI = Children Depression Inventory
STAIC-S = State Trait Anxiety Inventory for Children – State subscale
STAIC – T = State Trait Anxiety Inventory for Children – Trait subscale

** p< .01

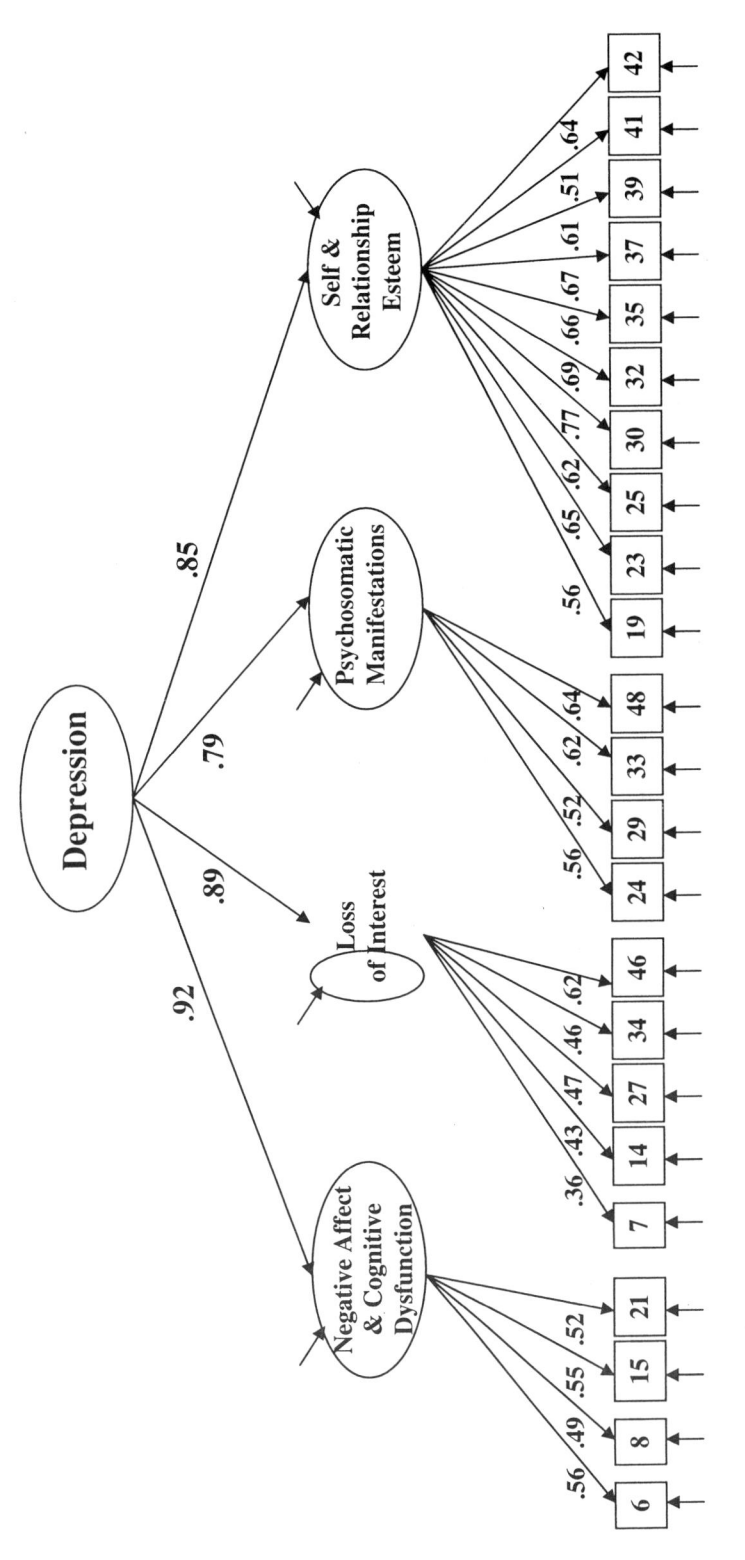

Figure 1.   Common Factor structure and Factor Loading of the Asian Children Depression Scale between groups ($\underline{N}$ = 474)

Table 3. Factor Analysis of the ACDS, CDI and STAIC (N = 474)

Item	F1	F2	Item	F1	F2	Item	F1	F2
ACDS 6	.44	.18	CDI 8	.44	.13	STAIC-S 11	.25	.34
ACDS 7	.35	.09	CDI 9	.52	.08	STAIC-S 12	.15	.45
ACDS 8	.42	.17	CDI 10	.50	.13	STAIC-S 13	.19	.40
ACDS 14	.38	.09	CDI 11	.39	.06	STAIC-S 14	.22	.44
ACDS 15	.42	.20	CDI 12	.32	.02	STAIC-S 15	.23	.46
ACDS 19	.47	.19	CDI 13	.36	.23	STAIC-S 16	.24	.35
ACDS 21	.39	.21	CDI 14	.52	.19	STAIC-S 17	.19	.50
ACDS 23	.55	.21	CDI 15	.37	.08	STAIC-S 18	.17	.34
ACDS 24	.38	.12	CDI 16	.39	.19	STAIC-S 19	.28	.37
ACDS 25	.63	.14	CDI 17	.36	.05	STAIC-S 20	.18	.50
ACDS 27	.49	.04	CDI 18	.38	.13	STAIC-T 1	.00	.51
ACDS 29	.33	.15	CDI 19	.27	.18	STAIC-T 2	.11	.50
ACDS 30	.67	.14	CDI 20	.43	.13	STAIC-T 3	.05	.59
ACDS 32	.64	.10	CDI 21	.40	.09	STAIC-T 4	.04	.49
ACDS 33	.44	.12	CDI 22	.35	.22	STAIC-T 5	.14	.55
ACDS 34	.38	.07	CDI 23	.48	.09	STAIC-T 6	-.02	.67
ACDS 35	.57	.17	CDI 24	.50	.13	STAIC-T 7	.10	.54
ACDS 37	.58	.12	CDI 25	.61	.09	STAIC-T 8	.04	.44
ACDS 39	.58	.03	CDI 26	.41	.04	STAIC-T 9	.08	.58
ACDS 41	.48	.12	CDI 27	.47	.08	STAIC-T 10	.11	.55
ACDS 42	.49	.14	STAIC-S 1	.15	.31	STAIC-T 11	.04	.56
ACDS 46	.54	.10	STAIC-S 2	.25	.43	STAIC-T 12	.06	.51
ACDS 48	.49	.11	STAIC-S 3	.18	.40	STAIC-T 13	-.00	.41
CDI 1	.43	.12	STAIC-S 4	.23	.43	STAIC-T 14	.11	.55
CDI 2	.36	.14	STAIC-S 5	.19	.28	STAIC-T 15	.01	.38
CDI 3	.40	.11	STAIC-S 6	.05	.33	STAIC-T 16	.07	.36
CDI 4	.45	.07	STAIC-S 7	.20	.48	STAIC-T 17	.16	.55
CDI 5	.53	.04	STAIC-S 8	.13	.49	STAIC-T 18	.09	.43
CDI 6	.31	.01	STAIC-S 9	.23	.45	STAIC-T 19	.12	.41
CDI 7	.62	.10	STAIC-S 10	.11	.40	STAIC-T 20	.06	.55

Note:
F1 = Factor 1
F2 = Factor 2
ACDS = Items in the Asian Children Depression Scale
CDI = Items in the Children Depression Inventory
STAIC-S = Items in the State-Trait Anxiety Inventory for Children-State subscale
STAIC-T = Items in the State-Trait Anxiety Inventory for Children-Trait subscale

DISCUSSION

The newly constructed scale, ACDS, was found to have satisfactory psychometric properties, and it measured both the core symptoms of depression found in established measures and the culture-specific symptoms. The ACDS consisted of three dimensions of core symptoms commonly found in Western literature: Negative Affect and Cognitive Dysfunction, Loss of Interest, and Psychosomatic Manifestations. Culture-specific symptoms were found in a separate interpersonal dimension of Self and Relationship Esteem. Notably, the results were found to be highly supportive of the newly postulated interpersonal dimension to be part of the symptomatology of depression for Asian children. This was evidenced by the high factor loading of .85 for the Self and Relationship Esteem dimension in the ACDS.

Construct validation provided support for the ACDS to be a measure of depression. This was supported by the finding of the mutually exclusive loading of the ACDS and CDI items into one factor, and the STAIC items into a second, separate factor. Further, the ACDS was found to have a higher correlation with the CDI, compared to its lower correlations with state and trait anxiety respectively. Many studies have reported correlation coefficients ranging from .45 to .75 between depression and anxiety (Clark & Watson, 1991). As a point to note, the ACDS correlated with state and trait anxiety with correlation coefficients of .39 and .38, respectively. ACDS may have a higher differentiating function from anxiety, compared to other, established measures of depression.

The finding that depression for these Asian children was expressed in interpersonal concerns did not come as a surprise as social others are a highly salient aspect of the children's life. Quality of relationships with others, particularly those with authority figures has been noted to have an impact on one's mental health (Lim, 2000). Compared to established Western measures, such as the CDI (Kovacs, 1980/1981), the existential concern factor was not found as a dimension in the ACDS, again, reflecting cultural differences in the experiences of depression (Chang, 1985).

One interesting finding from this study is the merging of affective manifestations and cognitive dysfunctioning into a single factor. Lutz's (1985) ethnographic study on the Ifaluk, people living on a South Pacific island, reported that the "thought" of these people are not seen as separated from their "emotion". Lutz further asserted that the distinction of the two psychological domains could be a reflection of Western conceptualization of the human mind. In our data, the cognitive dysfunctioning and the affective manifestations were so closely inter-correlated that for practical purposes and the parsimony of the structure, they could be treated as one factor.

In summary, preliminary data supported the interpersonal dimension, namely Self and Relationship Esteem, to be an essential part of Asian children's expression of depression. Existentialist concerns, a common experience associated with depression was not associated with affective distraught indicating such concerns might be specific to contemporary Western cultures (Chang, 1985). Further, dimensions such as Negative Affective and Cognitive Dysfunction, Loss of Interest and Psychosomatic Manifestations were found to be integral parts of Asian children's depressive experiences. With the sampling of both core and culture-specific symptoms in the ACDS, accuracy of assessing depression in Asian children may be enhanced. Nonetheless, being in its preliminary stage of development, the full potential of the ACDS and its ability to function as a screening tool for assessment of depression needs to be further validated.

REFERENCES

Al-Issa, I. (1995). Culture and mental illness in international perspectives. In I. Al-Issa (Ed.), *Handbook of culture and mental illness: An international perspective* (pp. 3-49). Madison, CT: International Universities Press.

Alwin, D. F., & Jackson, D. J. (1981). Application of simultaneous factor analysis to issues of factor invariance. In D. J. Jacksaon, & E. F. Borgatta (Eds.), *Factor analysis and measurement in sociological research* (pp. 249-279). Beverly Hills, CA: Sage.

Angold, A., Costello, E. J., & Pickles, A. (1987). *The development of a questionnaire for use in epidemiological studies of depression in children and adolescents.* Unpublished manuscript, London University.

Beck, A. T., Rush, A. J., Shaw, B. F., & Emery, G. (1979). *Cognitive therapy of depression.* New York: The Guilford Press.

Bentler, P. M. (1990). Comparative fit indexes in structural models. *Psychological Bulletin, 107,* 238-246.

Bentler, P. M., & Bonett, D. G. (1980). Significance tests and goodness of fit in the analysis if covariance structures. *Psychological Bulletin, 88,* 588-606.

Brown, M. W., & Cudeck, R. (1993). Alternative ways of assessing model fit. In K. A. Bollen, & J. S. Long (Eds.), *Testing structural equation models* (pp. 136-162). Newbury Park, CA: Sage.

Bryne, B. M. (1998). *Structural equation modelling with LISREL, PRELIS, and SIMPLIS: Basic concepts, applications, and programming.* New Jersey: Lawrence Erlbaum Associates.

Chan, D. C., & Schmitt, N. (1997). Video-based versus paper-and-pencil method of assessment in situational judgement tests: Subgroup differences in test performance and face validity perceptions. *Journal of Applied Psychology, 82,* 143-159.

Chang, W. C. (1985). A cross-cultural study of depressive symptomatology. *Culture, Medicine and Psychiatry, 9,* 295-317.

Chang, W. C., Chua, W. L., & Toh, Y. (1996). The concept of psychological control in the Asian context. In K. Leung, U. Kim, S. Yamaguchi, & Y. Kashima (Eds.), *Progress in Asian social psychology* (pp. 95-117). New York & Singapore: John Wiley & Sons.

Chang, W. C., Lee, L., & Koh, S. (1996). A model of the Chinese concept of self. In U. Kim, H. Kim, & K. Kwak (Eds.), *Mind, machine and environment: Facing the challenges of the 21st century* (pp. 43-59). Korea: Hak Mun Publishing, Inc.

Cole, M. (1996). *Cultural psychology: A once and future discipline.* Cambridge: Harvard University Press.

Clark, L. A., & Watson, D. (1991). Tripartite model of anxiety and depression: Psychometric evidence and taxonomic implications. *Journal of Abnormal Psychology, 100,* 316-336.

Geertz, C. (1973). *Interpretation of culture.* Cambridge, MA: Harvard University Press.

Jenkins, J. H. (1994). The psychocultural study of emotion and mental disorder. In P. K. Bock (Ed.), *Handbook of psychological anthropology* (pp. 97-120). Westport, Connecticut: Greenwood Press.

Jöreskog, K. G., & Sörbom, D. (1986). *LISREL 6: Analysis of linear structural relationships by maximum likelihood and least square methods.* Mooresville, IN: Scientific Software.

Jöreskog, K. G., & Sörbom, D. (1989). *LISREL 7: A guide to the program and applications* (2nd ed.). Chicago: SPSS.

Jöreskog, K. G., & Sörbom, D. (1993). *LISREL 8: Structural equation modelling with the SIMPLIS command language.* Mooresville, IN: Scientific Software.

Kitayama, S., & Markus, R. (1994). Introduction to cultural psychology and emotion research. In S. Kitayama, & R. Markus (Eds.), *Emotion and culture: Empirical studies of mutual influence* (pp.1-19). Washington: American Psychological Association.

Kleinman, A. (1977). Depression, somatization, and the "new cross-cultural psychiatry". *Social Science and Medicine, 11,* 3-9.

Kleinman, A., & Good, B. (1985). *Culture and depression: Studies in the anthropology and cross-cultural psychiatry of affect and disorder.* Berkeley: University of California Press.

Kovacs, M. (1980/1981). Rating scales to access depression in school-aged children. *Acta Paedopsychiatry, 46,* 305-315.

Kraepelin, E. (1904). Verglechende psychiatrie. *Zentralblatt für Nervenheilkunde, 15,* 433-437.

Lewis-Fernandez, R. & Kleinman, A. (1994). *Culture, personality, and psychopathology. Journal of Abnormal Psychology, 103,* 67-71.

Lim, W. S. L. (2000). *A developmental study of secondary control coping in the context of Singapore.* Unpublished Fourth Year Honors Thesis, Department of Social Work and Psychology, The National University of Singapore.

Lutz, C. (1985). Depression and the translation of emotional worlds. In A. Kleinman, & B. Good (Eds.), *Culture and depression: Studies in the anthropology and cross-cultural psychiatry of affect and disorder* (pp. 63-100). Berkeley: University of California Press.

Markus, H. R., & Kitayama, S. (1991). Culture and the self: Implications for cognition, emotion, and motivation. *Psychological Review, 98,* 224-253.

Marsella, A. (1980). Depressive affect and disorder across cultures. In H. Triandis & J. Draguns (Eds.), *Handbook of cross-cultural psychology, vol 5, Psychopathology.* Boston: Allyn & Bacon.

Mason S. M., Shore, J. H., & Bloom, J. D. (1985). The depressive experience in American Indian communities: A challenge for psychiatric theory and diagnosis. In A. Kleinman, & B. Good (Eds.), *Culture and depression: Studies in the anthropology and cross-cultural psychiatry of affect and disorder* (pp. 331-368). Berkeley: University of California Press.

Matsumoto, D., (2000). Culture and mental health. In D. Matsumoto (Ed.), *Culture and psychology: People around the world* (pp. 251-270). Pacific Grove, CA: Wadsworth/Thomson Learning.

Pfeiffer, W., (1967). Psychiatrische Besonderheiten in Indonesien. *Aktuelle Fragen der Psychiatrie und Neurologie, 5,* 102-142.

Radloff, L. S. (1977). The CES-D Scale. *Applied Psychological Measurement, 1,* 385-401.

Shinfuku, N., Karasawa, A., Yamada, O., Tuasaki, S., Kanai, A., & Kawashima, K. (1973). Changing clinical pictures of depression. *Psychological Medicine, 15,* 955-965.

Sörbom, D. (1993). A general model for studying differences in factor means and factor structures between groups. *British Journal of Mathematical and Statistical Psychology, 27,* 229-239.

Spielberger, C. D. (1973). *State-Trait Anxiety Inventory for Children. Professional manual.* Redwood City, CA: Mind Garden, Inc.

Steiger, J. H. (1990). Structural model equation and modification: An interval estimation approach. *Multivariate Behavioral Research, 25,* 173-180.

Tanaka, M. J., & Draguns, J. G. (1997). Culture and psychopathology. In J. W. Berry, M. H. Segall, & C. Kagitçibasi (Eds.), *Handbook of Cross-cultural psychology, vol. 3* (pp. 449-491). Boston: Allyn & Bacon.

Weiss, M. G., & Kleinman, A. (1988). Depression in cross-cultural perspective: Developing a culturally informed model. In P. R. Dason, J. W. Berry, & J. W. Sartorius (Eds.), *Health and cross cultural psychology: Towards applications, vol. 10: Cross cultural research and methodology series* (pp. 179-206). Newbury Park, CA: Sage.

World Health Organization, (1983). *Depressive disorders in different cultures: Report of the WHO collaborative study of standardized assessment of depressive disorders.* Geneva: WHO.

Zung, W. W. K. (1977). *Operational diagnosis and diagnostic categories of depressive disorder. Phenomenology and treatment of depression.* New York: Spectrum Publishing, Inc.

APPENDIX 1

Sample items of ACDS [2 & 3]

Factor 1: Negative affect and cognitive dysfunction

        1.   I feel sad
        2.   I cannot think well

Factor 2: Loss of interest

        1.   I feel that nothing is fun
        2.   I do not feel like doing anything

Factor 3: Psychosomatic manifestations

        1.   I often have headaches
        2.   My body feels painful

Factor 4: Self and relationship esteem

        1.   I feel that I am not a good son/daughter
        2.   I feel that my teachers do not like me anymore
        3.   I feel that my friends are good and I am bad

---

[2] Items were taken from children's daily expressions of unhappiness

[3] Items were taken from children's spoken expressions, majority of the children in the Singapore Chinese sample are bilingual, hence there is a Chinese version of the scale. Sample items of the Chinese version can be provided with request from the authors.

12

Assessment of Family Functioning in Chinese Adolescents: The Chinese Family Assessment Instrument

Daniel T. L. Shek
The Chinese University of Hong Kong

Daniel T. L. Shek · The Chinese University of Hong Kong · Department of Social Work · Chatin, New Territories · Hong Kong.

International Perspectives on Child and Adolescent Mental Health. Volume 2: Proceedings of the Second International Conference, edited by N. N. Singh, T. H. Ollendick, and A. N. Singh. © 2002 Elsevier Science Ltd. All rights reserved.

With growing emphasis on family intervention and the rising demand for family assessment tools in different helping professions (e.g., Halvorsen, 1991; Reichertz & Frankel, 1993), there is a strong need to develop objective assessment tools on family functioning in different cultures. However, a survey of the literature shows that there is a severe lack of objective measures of family functioning in different Chinese contexts (Shek, 1998). Phillips, West, Shen, and Zheng (1998) explicitly warned that the lack of family assessment measures has hindered the development of appropriate family interventions for mental patients in China.

Two basic approaches can be adopted when one attempts to develop family assessment tools in the Chinese culture. First, existing Western scales can be translated and adapted. While some attempts have been carried out to validate Western measures in the Chinese culture (e.g., Phillips, et al., 1998) and there is support for the translated measures (e.g., Phillips, et al., 1998; Shek, 1998, in press - a, in press - b), this approach has been criticized. The basic criticism is that the translated Western measures may not be relevant to non-Western people and they may not be universally applicable. The second approach that can be adopted is to develop indigenous measures of family assessment by constructing culturally sensitive measures. The adoption of this approach requires the researchers to have a thorough understanding of family processes and related cultural emphases in that particular culture. It also demands that the indigenous measures developed possess acceptable psychometric properties.

The purpose of this chapter is to report the psychometric properties of a locally constructed measure of family assessment – the Chinese Family Assessment Instrument (C-FAI). There were three steps in the development of this scale. In the first step, a literature review was carried out to identify the basic elements of optimal families and the related assessment tools. The literature review showed that different components on optimal families have been proposed in the Western literature. For example, Walsh (1992) suggested several important processes for healthy family functioning; connectedness, respect for individual family members, positive couple relationship, caretaking and nurturance, family stability, adaptability, open communication, effective problem solving processes, a shared belief system, and adequate resources. Fisher, Giblin, and Hoopes (1982) examined the views of 208 nonclinical members regarding their views of a healthy family and compared them with those held by therapists. They found that healthy families were perceived by both groups as having the following characteristics: an attitude of comradery and mutuality (reciprocally accepting, supporting and caring one another), honoring agreement, respect for differences, open and direct communication, encouragement of expression of feelings, and feelings of security, trust, and being positive. Similarly, Quatman (1997) found that emotional bondedness, mutuality, expressive communication, time together and love are important attributes of high functioning families. This review showed that several basic components, including connectedness, mutuality, and open and direct communication, are intrinsic to healthy family functioning at least from a Western perspective. The review also showed that there were few adolescent family assessment tools and scales that assess both dyadic relationship (e.g., parent-child relationship) and systemic functioning (e.g., global family climate) are rare.

The second step in the scale development process was to examine how Chinese people view healthy families. Based on data collected previously (Shek, 1998), the views of 416 Chinese parents and their adolescent children on the attributes of a happy family, collected via individual interviews, were examined. Results showed that Chinese parents and their children regarded the absence of conflict, interpersonal harmony, mutuality, connectedness, and positive parent-adolescent relationship as important attributes of a happy family. They were less likely to mention emotional expressiveness and communication as attributes of a happy family (Shek, & Chan, 1998).

The final step was to generate items by integrating the information collected via the above two steps. Initially, items based on those attributes that were commonly proposed in the West (e.g., Walsh, 1993) and emerged from the qualitative study (Shek & Chan, 1998) as attributes of healthy families were developed. In addition, items based on those attributes frequently mentioned by Chinese people as characteristics of a happy family (Shek & Chan, 1998) were also constructed. These initial items were subsequently discussed by a team of researchers comprising two psychologists and one social worker. Eventually, 33 items on adolescents' assessment of family functioning were developed. For each item, the respondent is asked to decide whether his/her family resembles the situation described in the item on a five-point scale. The content of the 33 items can be seen in Table 3. The 33 items in the C-FAI can be categorized into four areas: (a) Mutuality (e.g., mutual support among family members); (b) Communication and Connectedness (e.g., family members talk to each other, few barriers among family members); (c) Conflict and harmony (e.g., frequent fighting among family members); and (d) Parent-child subsystem quality (e.g., parents love their children, parental control too harsh) There are 11, 5, 7, and 10 items in each of these areas, respectively.

To evaluate the psychometric properties of the Family Assessment Instrument (C-FAI), three studies were conducted. In Study 1, the test-retest reliability, internal consistency, concurrent validity and construct validity of the C-FAI were studied. In Study 2, the reliability and validity of the C-FAI were examined in a clinical group and a nonclinical group. In Study 3, the reliability and validity of the C-FAI in a community sample were investigated.

METHOD

Study 1
Sample and Procedures

The study is based upon the responses of 361 secondary school students (240 boys and 121 girls; mean age = 14, $\underline{SD}$ = 1.26). All were Secondary 1 and Secondary 2 students in a Band 5 school. In Hong Kong, a Band 5 school is a school with students whose academic performance is in the lowest range in the Secondary School Placement Allocation exercise. The purpose of the study was provided and confidentiality of the data collected was emphasized repeatedly to all students in attendance on the day of testing. The students were asked to indicate their wish if they did not want to participate in the study (i.e., "passive" informed consent was obtained from the students). All participants responded to all the instrument scales in the questionnaire in a self-administration format. Adequate time was provided for the participants to complete the questionnaire. A trained research assistant was present throughout the test administration session. The respondents were requested to respond to the same questionnaire after two weeks to assess the test-retest reliability of the measure.

Instruments
Measures of Family Functioning

Besides the Chinese Family Assessment Instrument (C-FAI), the following measures of family assessment tools were employed.

Chinese Self-Report Family Inventory (C-SFI): This instrument is a 36-item scale which was found to be able to distinguish competent families from dysfunctional ones (Beavers, & Hampson, 1990). Research findings supporting the reliability, validity, and factor structure of the C-SFI have been reported elsewhere (Shek, 1998; Shek, & Lai, in press).

Chinese Family Awareness Scale. This scale is a 14-item scale designed to measure family competence as outlined in the Beavers-Timberlawn Model of Family Competence. Research findings on its internal consistency, concurrent validity, and construct validity have been reported (Green, 1987). The Chinese version of the scale was translated by the author. Shek (in press - a) reported that the C-FAS scores possessed adequate reliability and validity status.

Chinese Family Assessment Device (C-FAD). This device is a 60-item measure assessing family functioning based on the McMaster model (Epstein, Baldwin, & Bishop, 1983). According to Kabacoff, Miller, Bishop, Epstein, and Keitner (1990), the General Functioning subscale of the FAD (GENF scale) can be used as an indicator reflecting global family functioning. The Chinese version of the FAD (C-FAD) was translated by the author. Shek (in press - b) reported that the GENF scale is a global measure of family competence that has excellent psychometric properties.

Measures of Psychological Well-Being

Trait Anxiety Scale of the Chinese State-Trait Anxiety Inventory (A-TRAIT). This scale was constructed to measure trait anxiety (Spielberger, Gorsuch, & Lushene, 1970). It was translated by Tsoi, Ho and Mak (1986) who found that A-Trait scores were able to discriminate groups of women with different pregnancy histories. Additional research findings show that the A-Trait possesses acceptable psychometric properties (Shek, 1988, 1991, 1993a).

Existential Well-Being Scale (EXIST). This scale was constructed by Paloutzian and Ellison (1982) to assess life direction and satisfaction. Shek (1992) showed that the EXIST was internally consistent and valid.

Life Satisfaction Scale (LIFE). This scale was designed by Diener, Emmons, Larsen, and Griffin (1985) to assess an individual's own global judgment of his or her quality of life. Shek (1992) showed that this scale was internally consistent and there was support for the concurrent validity of the test.

Mastery Scale (MAS). Modeled after the Mastery Scale of Pearlin and Schooler (1978), this 7-item scale was constructed by the author to measure a person's sense of control of his or her life. Shek (1992) showed that this scale was internally consistent and valid.

RESULTS AND DISCUSSION

Results showed that the C-FAI was internally consistent at Time 1 and Time 2 (see Table 1). The C-FAI was also found to be temporally stable (test-retest reliability coefficient = .84, p < .0001). These findings suggest that the C-FAI possesses acceptable reliability status.

In view of the large number of correlations between the CFAI total scores and other measures of family functioning and adolescent adjustment, the multistage Bonferroni procedure was carried out to determine those significant correlations that are not attributable to Type 1 error. All correlations (i.e., 14 correlations for both test and retest sessions) were initially included in the evaluation and the analysis stopped when there were no more significant correlations at a particular step (Larzelere & Mulaik, 1977). The findings showed that the C-FAT had substantial correlation with other measures of family functioning. This observation supports the convergent validity of the C-FAT. Regarding the link between the C-FAT and measures of adolescent adjustment, results showed that the C-FAT scores were significantly correlated with measures of trait anxiety, existential well being, life satisfaction and sense of mastery at Time 1 and Time 2. These findings give support for the construct validity of the test.

METHOD

Study 2

To test the discriminant validity of the C-FAI, the test was administered to a clinical group (160 boys and 121 girls, mean age = 5, $\underline{SD}$ = 1.5) and a non-clinical group (269 boys and 182 girls, mean age = 15, $\underline{SD}$ = 1.6).

Sample and Procedures

A "clinical" group (with individuals from families presenting for clinical services) and a "nonclinical" group (with individuals from families who are not dysfunctional) are usually employed in a typical study that intends to validate family functioning instruments and there are different ways by which participants could be recruited. For the clinical subjects, researchers have recruited psychiatric patients (e.g., Green, 1987, 1989) and members from families receiving family therapy (e.g., Hampson, Beavers, & Hulgus, 1989) as subjects. In contrast, families that are not currently receiving any counseling service (e.g., Hampson, Beavers, & Hulgus, 1989) and ordinary college students (e.g., Epstein, Baldwin, & Bishop, 1983) have been employed to represent non-clinical participants.

Four different samples of clinical subjects were included in the present study. The first sample consisted of 114 children (98 boys and 16 girls) attending schools admitting adolescents with behavioral and emotional problems. The second sample consisted of 123 children (51 boys and 72 girls) whose families were currently receiving family counseling from family service centers because of family problems such as marital problems, relationship problems among the family members, and/or adjustment problems of the children. The third sample consisted of 22 female students who were receiving counseling service from school social workers because of family problems. The final sample consisted of 22 female adolescents who were outpatient psychiatric patients suffering from non-psychotic disturbances. The combination of subjects in these four samples forms the Clinical Group (N = 281). In terms of external behavioral criterion, all the subjects were currently receiving counseling service because of family problems, which included marital problems of the parents, relationship problems among the family members, and/or behavioral and emotional problems of adolescent members in the family.

In contrast, 451 participants from 2 schools (269 boys and 182 girls) were recruited to form the Non-Clinical Group. For each participant, the participant and his or her family had not sought professional help because of family problems. In terms of external behavioral criterion, subjects in this group have not received counseling because of family problems.

All participants responded en masse to all the instrument scales in the questionnaire in a self-administration format. Adequate time was provided for the subjects to complete the questionnaire. Informed consent was obtained for all participants. Except for those questionnaires collected via family service centers, a trained research assistant was present throughout the test administration session.

Instruments

The participants responded to the same measures of family functioning and individual adjustment used in Study 1.

RESULTS AND DISCUSSION

The Clinical Group ($\underline{M}$ = 90.7, $\underline{SD}$ = 25.2) and Non-Clinical Group ($\underline{M}$ = 83.4, $\underline{SD}$ = 24.9) differed significantly in C-FAI scores, t (677) = 3.7, p < .0001; effect size = .29. Similar differences between the two groups were found for the male sample ($\underline{M}$ = 89.9, $\underline{SD}$ = 24.8 for the Clinical Group; $\underline{M}$ = 84.1, $\underline{SD}$ = 25.5 for the Non-Clinical Group; t (400) = 2.2, p < .05; effect size = .23, and female sample ($\underline{M}$ = 91.8, $\underline{SD}$ = 25.8 for the Clinical Group; $\underline{M}$ = 82.2, $\underline{SD}$ = 23.9 for the Non-Clinical Group; t (274) = 3.2, p < .01; effect size = .39. The findings further showed that the two groups did not differ in background demographic and socio-economic characteristics, including age, educational attainment, sex ratio, family income, and number of persons in the household. Taken as a whole, the findings suggest that the C-FAI possesses acceptable discriminant validity.

Results also showed that the C-FAI scale was internally consistent in both groups (see Table 1). Based on the multi-stage Bonferroni correction procedure, it was found that C-FAI scores were significantly correlated with measures of family functioning and individual psychological well-being. These findings suggest that the C-FAI has acceptable convergent and construct validities in clinical and non-clinical samples.

Study 3

One of the limitations of the previous validation studies of the C-FAI is that convenient samples have been commonly employed. To overcome this problem, a community survey based on adolescent students was conducted.

Participants and Procedures

The participants were 3,649 adolescents in Hong Kong. The participants were Secondary 1 (N = 880), Secondary 2 (N = 898), Secondary 3 (N = 930,) and Secondary 4 (N = 941) students. They were selected from secondary schools in Hong Kong by the multiple stage stratified random sampling method, with school banding (i.e., ability of the students) as the stratifying factor (Moser, & Kalton, 1980). A total of 26 schools from different parts of Hong Kong participated in this study. The participants could be considered as heterogeneous because they came from different areas and socio-economic classes in Hong Kong. The mean age of the participants was 14 years ($\underline{SD}$ = 1.4).

During the data collection process, the purpose of the study was provided and confidentiality of the data collected was emphasized repeatedly to students in attendance on the day of testing. The students were asked to indicate their wish if they did not want to participate in the study. All participants responded en masse to all instrument scales in the questionnaire in a self-administration format. Adequate time was provided for the subjects to complete the questionnaire. A trained research assistant was present throughout the administration procedure.

Instruments

The C-FAI, C-FAD, and C-SFI used in Study 1 and Study 2 were employed to assess family functioning. In addition, each participant was also requested to indicate his or her global assessment of the pleasantness of family life. The respondents were asked to rate this item as "Very Pleasant", "Pleasant", "Unpleasant", or "Very Unpleasant."

To assess adolescent adjustment, the Existential Well-Being Scale, Mastery Scale and Life Satisfaction Scale used in Study 1 and Study 2 were employed. In addition, the Chinese version of the 30-item General Health Questionnaire was employed. The General Health Questionnaire has been developed to measure current non-psychotic disturbances (Goldberg, 1972). Chan (1985) found that the Chinese GHQ compared favorably with the English version at the scale level. Data from other studies have also shown that the Chinese GHQ possesses acceptable psychometric properties (Shek, 1987, 1989, 1993b)

RESULTS AND DISCUSSION

The findings showed that the C-FAI scale is internally consistent in different adolescent samples (see Table 1). Regarding the relationship between the C-FM and other measures of family functioning, results based on the multi-stage Bonferroni procedure showed that the C-FAI had substantial correlation with other measures of family functioning. In addition, the findings also showed that the C-FAI scores were correlated with the participant's global perception of the degree of pleasantness of family life (see Table 2). These findings provide support for the convergent validity of the test. With respect to the link between the C-FAI and measures of adolescent adjustment, the C-FAI scores were significantly correlated with measures of general psychological symptoms, existential well-being, life satisfaction, and sense of mastery. The significant results were not due to inflated Type 1 error (see Table 2). These findings provide support for the construct validity of the test.

A principal components analysis was performed on the participants' responses to the C-FAI, yielding five factors with eigenvalues exceeding unity, explaining 61.7% of the variance. To avoid overfactoring, further analyses using the screen test (e.g., Shek, 1998) showed that five factors could be meaningfully extracted. The five-factor solution, which could be considered as a relatively adequate representation of the data, was rotated to varimax criterion for interpretation. The first factor, which could be labeled as Mutuality, includes items 1, 2, 4, 5, 6, 15, 17, 18, 19, 20, 21, and 32. These items are basically concerned with mutual behavior of family members; this factor explained 45.6% of the variance.

Factor II, which included Items 7, 8, 9, 10, 11, 25, 26, 27, and 28, explained 5% of the total variance. These items are concerned with communication and cohesiveness; therefore, this factor was labeled as the Communication factor. The third factor, which included Items 3, 12, 13, 14, 16, and 33, could be labeled Conflict and Harmony, accounting for 4.2% of the variance. Factor IV explained 3.8% of the total variance; this included Items 22, 23, and 24. These items are concerned with parental concern and love; therefore, this factor was labeled as the Parental Concern factor. The final factor, which included items 29, 30 and 31, could be labeled Parental Control, explaining 3.1% of the variance. Table 3 shows the varimax rotated factor structure of the C-FAI.

Based on the factor analysis, the following subscales of the C-FAI were formed; the Mutuality Subscale (Items 1, 2, 4, 5, 6, 15, 17, 18, 19, 20, 21, and 32), Communication Subscale (Items 7, 8, 9, 10, 11, 25, 26, 27, and 28), Conflict and Harmony Subscale (Items 3, 12, 13, 14, 16, and 33), Parental Concern Subscale (Items 22, 23, and 24), and Parental Control Subscale

(Items 29, 30 and 31). Reliability analyses showed that these subscales were internally consistent (see Table 4).

Table 1. Internal consistency of the Family Assessment Instrument (C-FAI) in different adolescent samples

		C-FAI Total Scale	Mean Item-total Correlation
Study 1			
Test		.96	.65
Retest		.96	.66
Study 2			
Total		.96	.64
Clinical		.96	.63
Non-clinical		.96	.64
Study 3			
Total		.96	.65
Random 1		.96	.65
Random 2		.96	.64
Male		.96	.63
Female		.96	.66
Secondary	1	.96	.66
Secondary	2	.96	.63
Secondary	3	.96	.65
Secondary	4	.96	.63

Note. Study 1: Test = test session; Retest = retest session. Study 2: Total = total sample; Clinical = clinical sample; Non Clinical = non-clinical Sample. Study 3: Total = total sample; Random 1 = random subsample 1; Random 2 = random subsample 2; Male = male sample; Female = female sample; Secondary 1 = Secondary 1 students sample; Secondary 2 = Secondary 2 students sample; Secondary 3 = secondary 3 students sample; Secondary 4 = Secondary 4 students sample.

Table 2. Correlation coefficients on the relationships between the C-FAI scores and other measures of family functioning and indicators of individual psychological well-being.

		C-SFI	C-FAS	GENF	GA
Study 1					
	Test	.91*	-.77*	79*	--
	Retest	.93*	-.81*	.82*	--
Study 2					
	Total	.89*	-.78*	.82*	--
	Clinical	.86*	-.79*	.83*	--
	Non-clinical	.91*	-.77*	.80*	--
Study 3					
	Total	.91*	--	.84*	-.63*
	Male	.90*	--	.82*	-.60*
	Female	.92*	--	.85*	-.66*
	Secondary 1	.91*	--	.84*	-.61*
	Secondary 2	90*	--	.83*	-.62*
	Secondary 3	.91*	--	.83*	-.65*
	Secondary 4	.91*	--	.85*	-.64*

		A-TRAIT	EXIST	LIFE	MAS	GHQ
Study 1						
	Test	.35*	-.50*	-.42*	-.27*	--
	Retest	.52*	-.61*	-.39*	-.41*	--
Study 2						
	Total	.43*	-.52*	- .46*	-.39*	--
	Clinical	.38*	-.54*	-.47*	-.41*	--
	Non-clinical	.44*	-.50*	-.44*	-.37*	--
Study 3						
	Total	--	-.58*	-.54*	-.46*	.39*
	Male	--	-.55*	-.50*	-.42*	.38*
	Female	--	-.61*	-.58*	- 49*	.40*
	Secondary 1	--	-.57*	-.53*	-.52*	.45*
	Secondary 2	--	-.63*	-.56*	-.44*	.46*
	Secondary 3	--	-.55*	-.53*	-.42*	.30*
	Secondary 4	--	-.55*	-.52*	- .44*	.32*

Note. A two-tailed multistage Bonferroni procedure was used to evaluate the correlations between the C-FAI and other family functioning measures and indicators of adolescent adjustment for inflated Type 1 error in each study. *pFW* is based on the familywise Type 1 error rate. GENF = General Functioning Scale of the Chinese Family Assessment Device. C-FAS = Chinese Family Awareness Scale. GA = Participant's global assessment of the degree of pleasantness of family life. A-Trait = Trait Anxiety Scale of the State-Trait anxiety Scale. EXIST = Existential Well-Being Scale. MAS = Mastery Scale. LIFE = Life Satisfaction Scale. GHQ = General Health Questionnaire.

Table 3. Five-factor solution of the Chinese Family Assessment Instrument based on the total sample.

			Fl	F2	F3	F4	F5
Item	1	(family members support each other)	.56	.35	.37	.28	.09
Item	2	(family members love each other)	.54	.34	.45	.29	.09
Item	3	(no mutual concern)	.24	.17	.58	.36	.14
Item	4	(family members care each other)	.52	.26	.35	.39	.02
Item	5	(mutual consideration)	.60	.36	.29	.26	.12
Item	6	(family members understand each other)	.52	.36	.24	.20	.12
Item	7	(family members talk to each other)	.28	.64	.31	.14	.04
Item	8	(arranging family activities)	.23	.64	.25	-.03	-.02
Item	9	(family members are cohesive)	.44	.47	.39	.18	.05
Item	10	(family members enjoy getting together)	.29	.56	.41	.15	.01
Item	11	(not much barrier among family members)	.30	.49	.40	.14	.10
Item	12	(much friction among family members)	.27	.26	.57	.06	.31
Item	13	(frequent fighting among family members)	.27	- .06	.54	.10	.32
Item	14	(not much quarrel among family members)	.32	.14	.42	.04	.14
Item	15	(family members get along well)	.51	.36	.49	.25	.16
Item	16	(lack of harmony among family members)	.30	.24	.61	.27	.23
Item	17	(good family relationship)	.51	.38	.44	.26	.16
Item	18	(family members tolerate each other)	.80	.24	.17	.10	.17
Item	19	(family members forebear each other)	.82	.22	.14	.10	.17
Item	20	(family members accommodate each other)	.76	.29	.20	.14	.15
Item	21	(family member trust each other)	.60	.36	.28	.21	.17
Item	22	(parents love their children)	.24	.21	.21	.77	.13
Item	23	(parents do not concern their children)	.12	.09	.30	.72	.20
Item	24	(parents take care of their children)	.25	.31	.16	.71	.13
Item	25	(parents know children's need)	.28	.61	.03	.35	.31
Item	26	(parents understand children's mind)	.29	.68	.03	.27	.33
Item	27	(parents often talk to children)	.23	.75	.16	.20	.21
Item	28	(parents share children's concern)	.27	.65	.06	.20	.21
Item	29	(parents scold and beat children)	.21	.09	.24	.20	.68
Item	30	(parents force children to do things)	.16	.19	.18	.12	.73
Item	31	(parental control too harsh)	.06	.14	.13	.08	.77
Item	32	(children are filial)	.38	.30	.06	.31	.14
Item	33	(poor marital relationship of parents)	.01	.17	.57	.20	.06

Note. The highest loading obtained by a variable among the factors is underlined. Fl = Factor 1 (Mutuality) . F2 = Factor 2 (communication) . F3 = Factor 3 (conflict and Harmony) . F4 = Factor 4 (Parental concern) . FS = Factor 5 (Parental control).

To understand the stability of the factors extracted, the total sample was randomly split into two subsamples and identical factor analytic procedures were then carried out to assess the stability of the factor structure (Shek, 1998). Analyses based on coefficients of congruence showed that the degree of similarity amongst the corresponding factors derived from the two random subsamples was high (see Table 4).

Further analyses were performed separately on the responses of adolescent boys and girls. Results showed that the solutions derived from the male and female samples resembled those factors based on the total sample and the related factor structures yielded high coefficients of congruence amongst the corresponding factors in the male and female samples (see Table 4).

Table 4.   Coefficients of congruence among the factors derived from the different samples

| | Sample | | | | |
	1	2	3	4	5
Factor 1					
1. Total	.94 (.74)				
2. Random 1	.99	.95 (.75)			
3. Random 2	.99	.99	.94 (.73)		
4. Male	.99	.99	.99	.94 (.72)	
5. Female	.99	.99	.99	.99	.95 (.76)
Factor 2					
1. Total	.91 (.68)				
2. Random 1	.99	.91 (.69)			
3. Random 2	.99	.99	.90 (.67)		
4. Male	.99	.99	.99	.89 (.64)	
5. Female	.99	.99	.99	.99	.92 (.70)
Factor 3					
1. Total	.78 (.53)				
2. Random 1	.99	.80 (.56)			
3. Random 2	.99	.99	.77 (.52)		
4. Male	.99	.99	.99	.76 (.51)	
5. Female	.99	.99	.99	.99	.80 (.56)

310

Table 4 continued.

	Sample				
	1	2	3	4	5

Factor 4					
1. Total	.83 (.69)				
2. Random 1	.99	.84 (.70)			
3. Random 2	.99	.99	.83 (.68)		
4. Male	.99	.99	.99	.82 (.68)	
5. Female	.99	.99	.99	.99	.83 (.70)
Factor 5					
1. Total	.75 (.58)				
2. Random 1	.99	.75 (.58)			
3. Random 2	.99	.99	.73 (.55)		
4. Male	.99	.99	.99	.74 (.57)	
5. Female	.99	.99	.99	.99	.76 (.59)

Note. Total = total sample. Random 1 = Random Subsample 1. Random 2 = Random Subsample 2. Male = Male Sample. Female = Female Sample. Cronbach's alpha associated with each subscale for each factor in different samples are presented in the diagonal. The mean item-total correlation for a subscale is presented in parenthesis.

GENERAL DISCUSSION

The overall conclusion that can be drawn from the findings of these three studies is that the C-FAI possesses excellent psychometric properties. With regards the internal consistency of the scale, the C-FAI was found to be internally consistent (alpha greater than .9 and mean item-total correlation greater than .6 in all samples). The C-FAI was also found to be stable across time (test-retest reliability = .84). With respect to the validity of the scale, several sources of data suggest that the scale is valid. Significant relationships were found between the C-FAI and other measures of family functioning (convergent validity) and between the C-FAI and measures that are theoretically related to family functioning (construct validity), and the C-FAI scores were able to discriminate the clinical group from the non-clinical group (divergent validity).

Results from the factor structure and subscales of the measure suggest that there are five stable dimensions intrinsic to the C-FAI, and the C-FAI subscales were found to be internally consistent. Thus, the present study shows that the psychometric properties of the C-FAI are acceptable.

However, in view of the high correlation between the C-FAI scores and other measures of family assessment, one might ask why this is the case. There are several possible explanations for this finding. One, the results may be due to spuriousness. One possible source of spurious relationships is common method variance because all the measures that were used are self-report rating scales. Two, because Chinese people in Hong Kong are quite Westernized, their views on the attributes of a happy family in the qualitative study might have already reflected some elements that are emphasized in the western culture, for example, mutuality and connectedness. As a result, the items on the C-FAI might measure things that are also assessed by Western family assessment tools, which may account for the observed high correlation between the C-FAI and other measures of family functioning. Three, the ingredients that contribute to a well-functioning family are basically the same across cultures. This universalist view hypothesizes that because the core emphases on healthy families are relatively the same across cultures, there should be a substantial overlap in the scores derived from measures of family functioning developed in different cultures. In the area of personality assessment, for example, Yik and Bond (1993) reported that the findings based on imported and indigenous measures of personality perception for Hong Kong Chinese did not differ much. They argued that "imported measures may cut the phenomenal world differently from the indigenous measures, but still enable scientists to predict behavior just as effectively, the present results would challenge the investment required to develop local instrumentation on scientific grounds" (p.75). Obviously, the present study constitutes an interesting addition to the literature pertinent to the debate on whether there is a need to develop indigenous measures of family assessment. It is suggested that a wide range of Western measures of family functioning should be employed in future to further examine this issue.

The present study is based on adolescents in Hong Kong, therefore, there is a need to replicate the study and examine the extent to which the findings are generalizable to adolescent samples in different Chinese communities (e.g., mainland China) and Chinese adolescents living in non-Chinese contexts (e.g., Chinese Americans). Further work to examine the clinical utility of the C-FAI, particularly its cutoff scores, would also be helpful to establish its clinical usefulness.

Another limitation of the present study is that the effect sizes related to the t-tests in

Study 2 were not high. This finding suggests that the ability of the C-FAI to discriminate clinical and nonclinical participants may not be strong. According to Akister and Stevenson-Hinde (1991), problems associated with dysfunctional families are not uncommon in nonclinical families. Therefore, the small effect size observed in the present study may be acceptable.

Despite the above limitations, these studies clearly demonstrate that the C-FAI possesses acceptable psychometric properties that can be used objectively in Chinese adolescent samples. Essentially, the three studies reported in this paper can be regarded as a constructive response to the warning from Phillips, West, Shen, and Zheng (1998) that the absence of family assessment devices in the Chinese culture has adversely affected the development of family intervention work in Chinese communities. The C-FAI shows promise in filling this void.

ACKNOWLEDGMENTS

The preparation of this chapter was financially supported by the Research Grants Council of the UGC (Grant CUHK4O12/97H), The Chinese University of Hong Kong and Madam Tan Jen Chiu Fund. The author wishes to thank Chan Lai-kwan and Danny Yam for their assistance in collecting the data

REFERENCES

Akister, J., & Stevenson-Hinde, J. (1991). Identifying families at risk: Exploring the potential of the McMaster Family Assessment Device. *Journal of Family Therapy, 13,* 411-421.

Beavers, W. R., & Hampson, R. B. (1990). *Successful families: Assessment and intervention.* New York: Norton.

Chan, D.W. (1985). The Chinese version of the General Health Questionnaire: Does language make a difference? *Psychological Medicine, 15,* 147-155.

Diener, E., Emmons, R. A., Larsen, R. J., & Griffin, S. (1985). The Satisfaction with Life Scale. *Journal of Assessment, 49,* 71-75.

Epstein, N. B., Baldwin, L. M., & Bishop, D. 5. (1983). The McMaster Family Assessment Device. *Journal of Marital and Family Therapy, 9,* 171-180.

Fisher, B. L., Giblin, P. R., & Hoopes, M. H. (1982, July). Healthy family functioning: What therapists say and what families want. *Journal of Marital and Family Therapy,* 273-284.

Goldberg, D. P. (1972). *The detection of psychiatric illness by questionnaire.* Oxford: Oxford University Press.

Green, R. G. (1987). Self-report measures of family competence. *American Journal of Family Therapy, 15,* 163-168.

Green, R. O. (1989). Choosing family measurement devices for practice and research: SF1 and FACES III. *Social Service Review, 63,* 304-320.

Halvorsen, J. O. (1991). Self-report family assessment instruments: An evaluative review. *Family Practice Research Journal, 11,* 21-55.

Hampson, R. B., Beavers, W. R., & Hulgus, Y. F. (1989). Insiders' and outsiders' views of family: The assessment of family competence and style. *Journal of Family Psychology, 3,* 118-136.

Kabacoff, R., Miller, I., Bishop, D., Epstein, N., & Keitner, G. (1990). A psychometric study of the McMaster Family Assessment Device in psychiatric, medical, and nonclinical samples. *Journal of Family Psychology, 3,* 431-439.

Larzelere, R. E., & Mulaik, S. A. (1977). Single-sample tests for many correlations. *Psychological Bulletin, 84,* 557-569.

Moser, C. A., & Kalton, G. (1980). *Survey methods in social investigation.* London: Heinemann Educational Books.

Paloutzian, R. F., & Ellison, C. W. (1982). Loneliness, spiritual well-being and the quality of life. In L.A. Peplau & D. Perlman (Eds.), *Loneliness: A sourcebook of current theory, research and therapy.* New York: Wiley.

Pearlin, L. I., & Schooler, C. (1978). The structure of coping. *Journal of Health and Social Behavior, 22,* 337-356.

Phillips, M. R., West, C. L., Shen, Q., & Zheng, Y. P. (1998). Comparison of schizophrenic patients' families and normal families in China, using Chinese version of FACES-II and the Family Environment Scales. *Family Process, 37,* 95-106.

Quatman, T. (1997). High functioning families: Developing a prototype. *Family Therapy, 24,* 143-165.

Reichertz, D., & Frankel, H. (1993). Integrating family assessment into social work practice. *Research on Social Work Practice, 3,* 243-257.

Shek, D. T. L. (1987). Reliability and factorial structure of the Chinese version of the General Health Questionnaire. *Journal of Clinical Psychology, 57,* 683-691.

Shek, D. T. L. (1988). Reliability and factorial structure of the Chinese version of the State-Trait Anxiety Inventory. *Journal of Psychopathology and Behavioral Assessment, 10,* 303-317.

Shek, D. T. L. (1989). Validity of the Chinese version of the General Health Questionnaire. *Journal of Clinical Psychology, 45,* 890-897.

Shek, D. T. L. (1991). The factorial structure of the Chinese version of the State-Trait Anxiety Inventory: A confirmatory factor analysis. *Educational and Psychological Measurement, 51,* 985-997.

Shek, D. T. L. (1992). "Actual-ideal" discrepancies in the representation of self and significant-others and psychological well-being in Chinese adolescents. *International Journal of Psychology, 27,* 229.

Shek, D.T.L. (1993a). The Chinese version of the State-Trait Anxiety Inventory: Its relationship to different measures of psychological well-being. *Journal of Clinical Psychology, 49,* 349-358.

Shek, D. T. L. (1993b). The factor structure of the Chinese version of the General Health Questionnaire (GHQ-30): A confirmatory factor analysis. *Journal of Clinical Psychology, 49,* 678-684.

Shek, D. T. L. (1998). The Chinese version of the Self-Report Family Inventory: Does culture make a difference? *Research on Social Work Practice, 8,* 315-329.

Shek, D. T. L. (in press-a). Psychometric properties of the Chinese version of the Family Awareness Scale. *Journal of Social Psychology.*

Shek, D. T. L. (in press-b). The General Functioning subscale of the FAD: Does it work in the

Chinese culture? *Journal of Clinical Psychology*.

Shek, D. T. L., & Chan, L. K. (1998). Perceptions of the happy family in a Chinese context. *Journal of Youth Studies, 1*, 178-189.

Shek, D. T. L., & Lai, K. Y. C. (in press). The Chinese version of the Self-report Family Inventory: Reliability and validity. *American Journal of Family Therapy*.

Spielberger, C. D., Gorsuch, R. C., & Lushene, R. F. (1970). *Manual for the State-Trait Anxiety Inventory*. Palo Alto, CA: Consulting Psychologists Press.

Tsoi, M. M., Ho, E., & Mak, K. C. (1986). Becoming pregnant again after stillbirth or the birth of a handicapped child. In L. Dennerstein & I. Fraser (Eds.), *Hormone and behavior (pp. 310-316)*. Holland: Elsevier Science Publisher.

Walsh, F. (1993). *Normal family processes*. New York: Guilford Press.

Yik, M. S. M., & Bond, M. H. (1993). Exploring the dimensions of Chinese person perception with indigenous and imported constructs: Creating a culturally balanced scale. *International Journal of Psychology, 28*, 75-95.

13

Problem Behavior in Adolescence: Differential Manifestations, Developmental Trends, and Risk Factors

Maja Dekovic
University of Amsterdam

Ellen Reitz
University of Amsterdam

Anne-Marie Miejer
University of Amsterdam

Maja Dekovic · University of Amsterdam · Department of Special Education · Wibautstraat 4 Amsterdam 1091 GM · Netherlands.

International Perspectives on Child and Adolescent Mental Health. Volume 2: Proceedings of the Second International Conference, edited by N. N. Singh, T. H. Ollendick, and A. N. Singh.

The period of adolescence, often called a "critical developmental transition", appears to be particularly important for the development of healthy status versus problems and pathology. The multiple changes occurring simultaneously both within and outside of the individual, seem to make adolescents especially vulnerable as indicated by an increase in prevalence of a variety of clinical disorders and behavior problems in this period (Jessor, 1991; McCord, 1990; Moffit, 1993). According to the research findings, almost 80% of adolescents get involved in some kind of problem behavior in the course of adolescence: school- and authority problems, substance use, aggression, and minor delinquent acts (Kazdin, 1993, 1997; Loeber, 1990; Resnick & Burt, 1996). Given the direct negative consequences of such behavior for both the individual and the community, there is a clear need for more information regarding the occurrence, the meaning and the determinants of these problems.

Adolescent problem behavior is characterized by its heterotypical expression. In addition, there is often a co-occurrence of different types of problem behavior in the same individual (Wenar & Kerig, 2000). There is no broad agreement about interpreting the interrelationship among various forms of problem behavior. The question whether various manifestations of problem behavior should be considered in terms of a single underlying tendency ("a deviant adolescent life-style") or whether different types of problem behavior represent diverse underlying difficulties, has been subject to much debate (Donovan & Jessor, 1985; Farrell, Kung, White, & Valois, 2000; Gillmore, Hawkins, Catalano, Day, Moore, & Abbott, 1991; Jessor &Jessor, 1977).

In the present study we examine the usefulness of differentiating among four types of problem behaviors that occur often in adolescence: disobeying parents, school misconduct, substance use, and antisocial behavior. These four types of problems are often studied together under the term "externalizing problems." It has been shown that externalizing problems are one of the most frequent causes for clinical referral in child and adolescent treatment services and have quite substantial stability and poor long term prognosis (Kazdin, 1997). However, some of these behaviors, such as disobedience to parental rules, might be seen as developmentally normative during adolescence and to some extent even constructive for adolescent development (Maggs, Almeida, & Galambos, 1995), whereas other behaviors, such as aggressive antisocial acts might mark advancing risk for chronic and serious problems. Therefore, the aims were first, to examine the relationship between these four types of problem behavior, and second, to examine whether different types of problem behavior show specific gender and age patterns.

Next we examine whether these four types of problem behaviors have different determinants. In accordance with the notion that all types of problem behavior are complexly determined, we consider multiple sources of risk that might contribute to the development of these problems. Risk factors are defined as those conditions that are associated with a higher likelihood of negative outcome (Luthar, 1993; Rutter, 1987). The presence of risk factors does not guarantee that a negative outcome will occur, but simply increases the probability of its occurrence (Small & Lester, 1994). As a framework for organizing these factors an ecological perspective (Bronfenbrenner, 1986, 1989) was used, in which a child is viewed as being nested within a complex network of interconnected systems. We focus on factors at an individual level —adolescents themselves—and factors within their principal interpersonal environments: family, peer group, and school. Based on the results of previous research, we assessed the most consistently identified risk factors in these four domains.

At the level of the individual, risk factors consistently found across studies that relate to externalizing behaviors include low self-esteem and high levels of impulsiveness (Jessor, Bos, Vanderryn, Costa, & Turbin, 1995; White, et al., 1994). It has been suggested that engaging in problem behavior might be a way to cope with a low sense of self-worth, dissatisfaction and low confidence in one's own abilities (Jessor, Bos, Vanderryn, Costa, & Turbin, 1995). Empirical findings show that low self-esteem is negatively related to various psychological problems, including anxiety and depression (Robertson & Simons, 1989), and drug use and delinquent behavior (Stacy, Sussman, Dent Burton, & Flay, 1992). On the other hand high self-esteem has been found to relate positively to several domains of adolescent development, including academics and social activities (Chung & Elias, 1996). Researchers have posited that impulsivity may be viewed as a personality characteristic that predisposes individuals to develop long-term antisocial behavior (Moffitt, 1993; Tremblay, Pihi, Vitaro, & Dobkin, 1994). It has been found that high levels of impulsivity relate to high levels of delinquent behavior (White, et al., 1994). This may suggest that children with poor self-control may be more likely to be antisocial because they are unable to control or monitor their behavior.

With regard to the level of the family, many studies have identified family variables that covary with problem behaviors. One of the most important factors that relates to the behavior and well being of adolescents is the quality of the relationship within the family: the presence of a warm, nurturing, and supporting relationship with at least one parent (Deković, 1999; Steinberg, Elmen, & Mounts, 1989). Research demonstrates that a low level of parental support and involvement increases the possibility of problem behavior (McCord, 1990). Another aspect consistently found as important in predicting problem behavior is parental monitoring (Jacobson & Crockett, 2000; Patterson, Reid, & Dishion, 1992). Higher levels of parental monitoring have been associated with lower levels of antisocial behaviors (Patterson & Stouthamer-Loeber,

1984), substance use (Brown, Mounts, Lamborn, & Steinberg, 1993), and with better school functioning (Brown, et al., 1993). Parental monitoring decreases unsupervised time and narrows the range of negative social influences (Stacy, et al., 1992).

When the adolescent enters high school, the peer group becomes increasingly important The nature and quality of peer affiliations in adolescence is an important determinant of antisocial behavior and substance use (Fergusson & Horwood, 1996). Association with deviant peers is often found as a predictor of several kinds of problem behavior (Patterson, et al., 1992). For instance, adolescents with deviant friends exhibit more norm-breaking behavior (Brendgen, Vitaro, & Bukowski, 2000), more substance use (Aseltine, 1995), and more school problems (Berndt & Keefe, 1995) than adolescents with conventional friends. Exposure to deviant friends may foster problem behaviors through positive reinforcement and through modeling of new types of problem behavior. Peer pressure to conform to friends' deviant behavior may also increase the likelihood of adolescents' exhibiting antisocial acts. Indeed, Santor, Messervey, and Kusumakar (2000) have shown that peer pressure and peer conformity are strong predictors of behaviors like substance use, school performance, and sexual behaviors.

Not only are adolescents' family and friends important in predicting problem behavior, so too are school related factors. Success in school as measured by academic achievement and participation has been reported as a protective factor among some at-risk populations (Rutter, 1985). This may imply that good grades and achievement motivation buffer the adolescent against negative social behavior. Several studies have found negative correlations among problem behaviors and school performance (Donovan & Jessor, 1985; Donovan, Jessor, & Costa, 1988; McGee & Newcomb, 1992). O'Donnell, Hawkins and Abbott (1995) have demonstrated that adolescent boys involved in serious delinquent behavior and substance use have lower levels of school bonding and achievement when compared with boys who do not show delinquent behavior.

In addition to examining the effect of a particular risk factor, we employ a cumulative risk approach that focuses on variation in the number of different risk factors involved. An underlying assumption of this approach is that different risk factors potentate each other and therefore, a particular risk factor, in isolation, is of little importance - it is the overall amount of risk that should be a key parameter (Flannery, Vazsonyi, Torquati, Fridrich, 1994; Hawkins, Catalano, & Miller, 1992; Jessor, Bos, Vanderryn, Costa, & Turbin, 1995; Rutter, 1987). To that end, one cumulative risk score is typically computed and treated as a single predictor variable of risk. Studies that employed this approach showed that there is a significant relationship between the number of risks and a variety of outcomes, but the nature of this association is unclear

(Rutter, 1980; Sameroff, Seifer, Baldwin, & Baldwin, 1993; Small & Luster, 1994). Whereas in some studies a linear relationship is reported (that is, the severity of problem behavior increases proportionally with the number of risk factors present), other studies found an exponential increase of problems as a function of the number of risks (Coie, 1993; Rutter, 1980). In the present study, we examined the association between the amount of risk factors and four types of problem behavior in more detail. We test the hypothesis that the probability of an adolescent being involved in problem behavior is an increasing function of the number of risk factors he/she is exposed to, and we try to determine whether a certain number of risks could be considered as a cut-off point for development of problems.

The present study extends previous research on risk factors for development of problem behavior in adolescence in several ways. First, by assessing four types of problems, we move away from a focus on single outcome to a more detailed examination of the ways risk factors may contribute to development of different types of problem behavior during adolescence (Small & Luster, 1994). Second, we employ a multivariate framework and consider simultaneously possible risks in various domains, covering both personal and environmental (family, peers, school) factors. This provides the opportunity to examine the relative importance of a specific domain for the development of problem behavior and determine whether some of these domains can be identified as a more central influence than others. Third, it has been suggested that the importance of a given risk factor might vary depending on the aspect of adjustment studied, i.e. the same factor might play a different functional role to different domains of functioning (Gest, Nemann, Hubbard, Masten, & Tellegen, 1993). By simultaneously considering multiple outcomes and multiple risk factors we are able to examine whether these risk factors have a differential importance for different types of problem behavior. Finally, in addition to examining the role of a particular risk factor, we also focus on the amount of risk that is present in adolescents' lives and explore the relationship between the number of risk factors and problem behavior.

METHOD

Sample and Procedure

The sample consisted of 508 families with adolescents (254 females and 254 males). Three age groups were represented: early adolescence (between 12 and 13 years old, 86 females and 84 males), middle adolescence (between 14 and 15, 73 females and 76 males), and late adolescence (between 16 and 18, 95 females and 94 males). Seven percent of the children were the only child in the family, 35% were the oldest child, and 41% the youngest child. Most of the families (91%) were intact families, 7% of the parents were divorced or separated and 2% were widowed. The sample represented a wide range of socioeconomic and educational backgrounds: unskilled workers (12% of the mothers and 3% of the fathers); semi-skilled workers (20% of the mothers and 3% of the fathers); clerical and sales workers, or semi-professionals (45% of the mothers and 34% of the fathers); small business owners (8% of the mothers and 10% of the fathers); professionals (9% of the mothers and 23% of the fathers); and higher executives (6% of the mothers and 16% of the fathers). Two percent of the mothers and 6% of the fathers had a university degree. The percentage of parents currently employed was 54% of the mothers and 94% of the fathers. Socioeconomic status of the families, based on education and occupation of both parents, was as follows: 29% low class, 62% middle class, and 9% high class.

The data for this study were collected as part of a national program of research on children/adolescents and their parents, "Child-rearing in the Netherlands in the 1990s". The families were selected from a larger sample of 10.000 families representative of Dutch population and were first contacted by phone. In the phone interview the general purpose of the research was explained and the criterion for participation (e.g., having an adolescent child) was checked. From all contacted families with adolescent children, 53% agreed to participate. No information is available regarding the demographic variables of non-participants. The most frequent reason of refusal was the father's lack of time. Data collection took place at the subjects' homes, where a battery of questionnaires was administered individually to adolescents, mothers and fathers. All three family members filled the questionnaire independently of each other in the presence of the interviewer. The central concepts in the present study (problem behavior and risk factors) were all assessed from the perspective of adolescents themselves.

MEASURES

Problem Behavior

The frequency of problem behavior in the last 12 months was measured by an 18-item scale. Adolescents rated "how many times in the last year" they had engaged in these 18 behaviors on a 5-point scale ranging from 0 = never to 4 = more than 10 times. The four types of problem behavior were defined: Disobeying Parents (e.g., missed curfew), School Misconduct (e.g., cheated on a test), Substance Use (e.g., drinking alcohol), and Antisocial Behavior (e.g., shoplifting, fighting).

Risk Factors

Two risk factors represented the individual attributes of adolescents: low self-esteem and high impulsiveness.

Self-Esteem. Rosenberg's Self-Esteem Scale (Rosenberg, 1965) assesses the value and sense of worth that adolescents perceive about themselves. Adolescents rated themselves on 10 items (alpha = .85) using four response categories (1 = highly undescriptive of me to 4 = highly descriptive of me).

Impulsiveness. The Adolescent Temperament Questionnaire (ATL) (Feij & Kuiper, 1984) measures several behavioral traits that are assumed to be inherited and relatively stable aspects of personality. Two scales were selected as being most likely to affect the level of problem behavior: Impulse control (9 items; e.g., "I don't lose my self-control ever" – reverse coded); and Disinhibition (8 items; e.g., "When I do something, I almost never stop to think whether it is allowed or not"). The items were rated on a dichotomous scale: true/untrue. Because of the similarities in content of the items of these two scales and high interrelation (.58), it was decided to construct a more robust measure by summing up the score of 17 items (alpha .67). Higher score indicate low level of behavioral control, impatience, tendency to react impulsively and to seek new exciting experiences.

The following two measures constitute risk factors within the family: low level of attachment and low monitoring. These variables were assessed separately for mothers and for fathers, but given the strength of associations between maternal and paternal scores (correlation varied between .57 and .71) in the further analysis their scores were averaged to provide a parental score.

Attachment to Parents. This construct was measured with a short version of the Inventory of Parent and Peer Attachment (IPPA) (Armsden & Greenberg, 1987; Nada Raja, McGee, & Stanton, 1992). The scale consists of 12 items for each parent (alpha for mother = .78 and for father .81) tapping the quality of communication, and the degree of trust and alienation in parent-adolescent relationships (e.g., "I tell my mother/father about my problems and troubles"). A 4-point Likert scale was used with categories of 1 = almost never, 2 = sometimes, 3 = often, and 4 = almost always.

Monitoring. The 6-item scale assesses the parent's supervision of the child and monitoring of the child's daily activities. The adolescents were asked to indicate on a 4-point scale (1 = almost nothing to 4 = almost everything) how much their mother and father know about the adolescent's whereabouts after school, in leisure time, when the adolescent goes out in the evenings and during weekend. The alphas for this scale were .84 for mothers and .78 for fathers.

The assessment of risk factors within the peer relations included: association with deviant peer and peer conformity.

Association with Deviant Peers. Adolescents were asked to indicate the extent to which their friends approve of deviant behavior. The same 18 items were used as for their self-report (see above). The responses range from 1 = none of my friends approve of such behavior to 5 = all of my friends approve of such behavior. The internal consistency was .80.

Peer Conformity. The degree to which adolescents place importance on their relationship with peers and their readiness to sacrifice developmentally positive aspects of their lives in order to maintain these relationships (Fuligni & Eccles, 1993) was assessed with 4 items (e.g., "It's okay to let your schoolwork slip or get a lower grade in order to be popular with your friends") (alpha=.61).

The risk factors in school consisted of a low grade point average and a low achievement motivation.

Grade Point Average. Adolescents reported their grade point average in terms of the average overall grade they usually get in the four major courses (mathematics, Dutch, history and biology). The score ranges, according to the Dutch school system, from 1 = very poor to 10 = excellent. The alpha was .70.

Achievement Motivation. A negative orientation toward school, low value of academic achievement and low expectations of success were assessed with a 6 items questionnaire (Hermanns, 1980). The items (e.g., "Good grades are important to me") could be answered on a 4-point scale (1 = completely disagree to 4 = completely agree). The internal consistency was .67.

All variables representing risk factors were coded in the manner that a higher score indicated a higher level of risk.

Risk Factor Index

The score on each risk measure was dichotomized to represent the presence of a risk factor (roughly the extreme 20% of score on that measure). The Risk Factor Index (RFI) was computed by adding the dichotomized scores on 8 risk measures. The RFI therefore ranged from 0 (no risk) to 8 (high risk on each variable measured).

RESULTS

Intercorrelations Among Problem Behavior Measures

Table 1 presents the bivariate relations among four problem behavior measures. All correlations are significant at p<.00l, but the magnitude of coefficients is moderate, which seems to support the notion that these four types of problem behavior are empirically distinct constructs.

Table 1.   Interrelationship Between Types of Problem Behavior

	1	2	3
1. Disobeying Parents	--		
2. School Misconduct	.41	--	
3. Substance Use	.38	.36	--
4. Antisocial Behavior	.52	.42	.42

Developmental Trends and Gender Differences in Problem Behavior

In order to examine age and gender differences in adolescent problem behaviors, a 3 (early, middle and late adolescence) x 2 (adolescent's gender) analysis of variance (ANOVA) was conducted for each of four types of problems.

A significant main effect of age was found for all types of problems: disobeying parents, $F(2, 503) = 7.99$, $p<.001$, school misconduct, $F(2, 507) = 25.85$, $p<.001$, substance use, $F(2, 507) = 32.08$, $p<.001$, and antisocial behavior, $F(2, 502) = 10.89$, $p<.001$. The developmental trends were, however, not the same for all of the problems. Whereas disobeying parents, school misconduct, and antisocial behavior show typical inverted U-shaped curve—the highest level of problems are reported by middle adolescents—substance use shows steady increase in the period from early to late adolescence.

A significant gender effect was found for disobeying parents, $F(1, 503) = 10.71$, $p<.001$, and antisocial behavior, $F(1, 502) = 14.50$, $p<.001$, with girls reporting lower levels of such behavior than boys.

A significant age x gender interaction was found only for disobedience, $F(2, 503) = 5.01$, $p<.01$. Boys tend to be more disobedient than girls during early adolescence. In the period of middle adolescence these gender differences disappear, due to a sharp increase of girls' disobedience. In late adolescence, however, girls' disobedience decreases, whereas boys' disobedience increases, leading to gender differences similar to those in early adolescence.

These developmental trends are shown in Figure 1, separately for boys and girls.

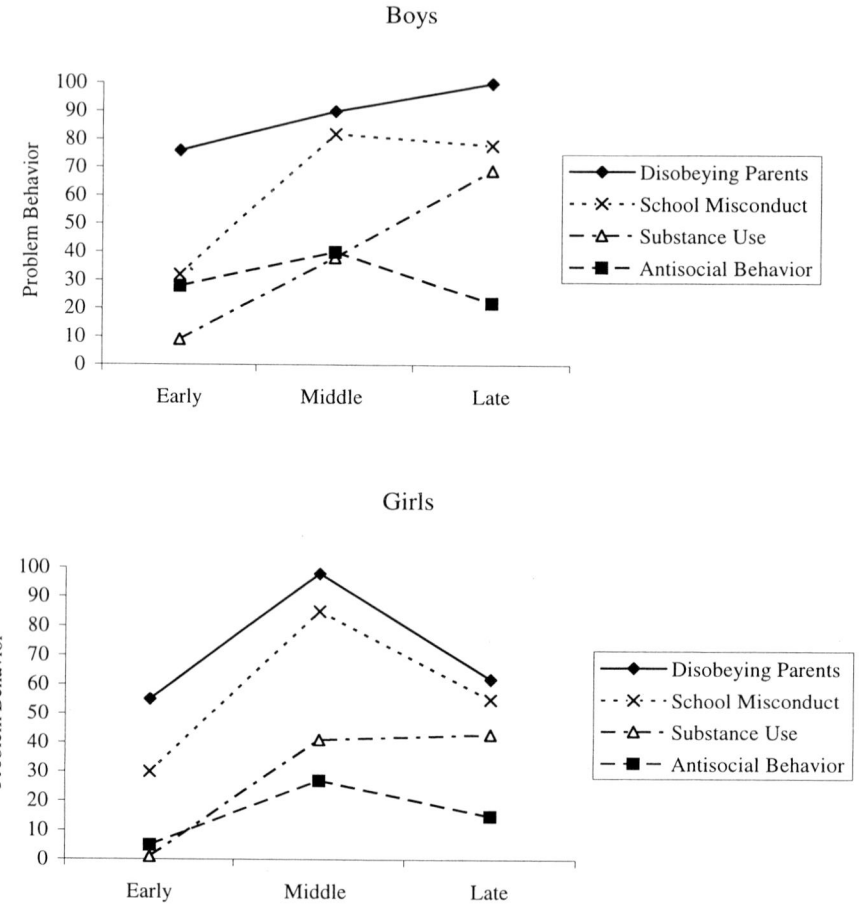

Figure 1. Age Differences in Frequency of Different Types of Problem Behavior

For the total group of adolescents the highest frequency of occurrence of problem behaviors was found for the disobedience. Only 23% of adolescents reported that they followed all parents' rules in the last 12 months. Substance use was least frequently reported: 38% of adolescents had used alcohol and/or drugs at least once in the last year. Finally, 49% reported school misconduct and 56% engagement in antisocial behaviors.

Disobedience and school misconduct remain the most frequently reported problems during the whole period of adolescence. Substance use occurs least frequently of all problems in the early adolescence, but in middle and late adolescence substance use is reported more often than antisocial behavior.

Predicting Problem Behavior from Separate Risk Factors

To examine the relative importance of separate risk factors from four domains (individual attributes, family, peer and school factors) for different types of problems, a hierarchical multiple regression was conducted for each of the four problem behaviors as a separate criterion measure (see Table 2). Age and gender were entered first, followed by risk factors at the level of individual, risk factors within the family, within the peer group, and in the last step, risk factors at school.

The entry of demographic control variables explained a significant percentage of variance in all four outcomes. This was mostly due to the effect of age. Gender appears to be a significant predictor only for antisocial behavior. When entered in the next step, individual factors added a significant increment in the explained variance in problem behaviors. Low self-esteem significantly predicted substance use, whereas low level of impulse control appeared a significant predictor of disobedience, school misconduct and antisocial behavior. In the third step family risk factors were entered. These factors made an independent contribution to all types of problems, as indicated by the significant increase in R square, although none of the separate predictors reached significance for substance use. Lack of attachment to parents and low level of parental monitoring appear to be especially important for disobedience and antisocial behavior. In addition, parental monitoring also predicted problems at school. When the peer risk factors were added in Step 4, the R squares of change were also statistically significant. Association with deviant peers emerged as the most potent predictor for all types of problems. Adolescents with friends who show high tolerance of deviant behavior report the highest level of disobedience, school problems, substance use and antisocial behavior. Adolescents' readiness to conform to peer pressure also significantly predicted engagement in antisocial behavior. Finally, risk factors at school were related to disobedience and school misconduct, but not to substance use and antisocial behavior. Grade point average seems to be less important than adolescents' motivation to do well at school. Adolescents with negative orientation toward school tend to report more problems at home and at school.

To summarize, for all types of problem behaviors support was found for the notion regarding the "multideterminism of problems". In other words, risk factors are not confined to only one domain, but exist at all levels: individual, family, peers and school. The pattern of findings with regard to the relative importance of the different risk factors is quite similar across four types of problems. For all four problem behaviors association with deviant peers is consistently the most influential predictor, followed by two risk factors at the level of the family: low level of attachment to parents and lack of monitoring. There are, however, also some dissimilarities. Demographic variables seem to be somewhat more important for substance use, family factors for disobedience, and peer factors for antisocial behavior. There are also differences among the different problems in the number of significant predictors. Contrary to other problems, when predicting the adolescents' substance use, only three predictors emerged as significant: age, low self-esteem, and deviant peers.

Cumulative Risk Analysis

In the preceding analysis focus was on the effects of separate risk factors. In the following analysis, we concentrate on the amount of risk present, that is, risk factor index (RFI). An examination of the distribution of the RFI showed that there were very few adolescents with seven or eight risk factors. Consequently, adolescents with seven or eight risk factors were grouped together with those with six risk factors.

In order to examine predictability of problem behavior from the RFI, we conducted hierarchical multiple regression analyses separately for each problem behavior measure as a criterion. A set of two demographic variables — age and gender — was again entered in the first step, followed by the RFI in the second step. The demographic control measures accounted for a significant proportion of the variance in adolescent problem behaviors. The entry of the RFI in the second step yielded a significant increment in the amount of variance explained. The beta coefficients were: for disobedience .42, for school misconduct .31, for substance use .29, and for antisocial behavior .24, all significant at $p<.001$. It is worth pointing out that using the RFI in regression analyses (while controlling for demographic variables) yielded a final R square of .21, .14, .20, and .24 for disobedience, school misconduct, substance use and antisocial behavior, respectively. This single predictor therefore explained quite a substantial proportion of variance in problem behavior.

The results of regression analyses suggest a strong linear relationship between the number of risk factors present and the level of problem behavior that adolescents experience. In order to examine this relationship in more detail, analysis of variance (ANOVA) was conducted

Table 2.   Regression Analysis Predicting Different Types of Problem Behavior From Individual-, Family-, Peer-, and School-Risk Factors

Step/Predictor	Disobeying Parents		School Misconduct		Substance Use		Antisocial behavior	
	Beta	R² Change	Beta	R² Change	Beta	R² Change	Beta	R² Change
1. Control variables		.04**		.06***		.13***		.05***
Age								
Gender[a]			.16***		.30***		-.10*	
2. Individual Factors		.09***		.06***		.06***		.07***
Self-Esteem								
Impulsiveness	.13**		.11*		.15**		.10**	
3. Family factors		.11***		.04***		.02*		.08***
Attachment to Parents	.12*						.10*	
Monitoring	.17***		.11*				.15**	
4. Peer Factors		.05***		.05***		.09***		.16***
Association with Deviant Peers	.20***		.19***		.30***		.40***	
Peer Conformity							.12**	
5. School Factors		.01*		.04***				
Grade Point Average	.13*		.22***					
Achievement Motivation								
Total R²		.30***		.25***		.30***		.35***

Note. [a] 1=male; 2=female. *p<.05; **p<.01; ***p<.001. Only significant coefficients are reported.

for each type of problem behavior using the RFI as an independent variable. Figure 2 shows the relationship between the frequency of four types of problem behavior and the RFI.

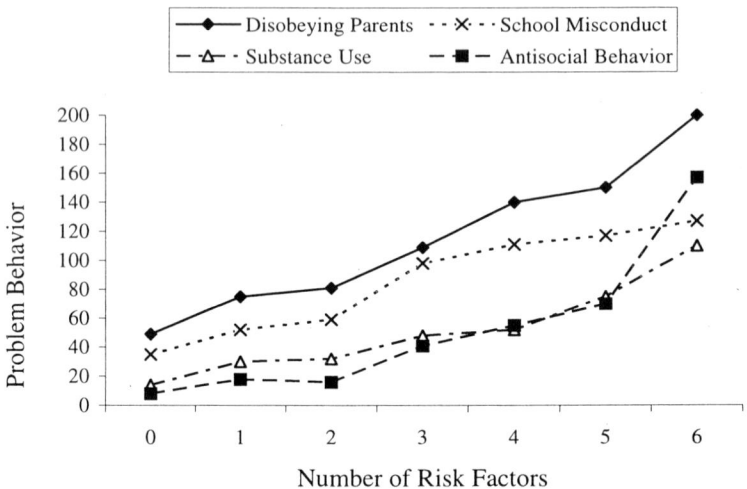

Figure 2. Frequency of problem Behavior as a Function of Number of Risk Factors

Not surprisingly, given the above reported results of the regression analyses, a significant effect of the number of risk factors was found for each type of problem behavior: disobedience, $F(6, 503) = 19.51$, p<.001; school misconduct, $F(6, 507) = 10.17$, p<.001; substance use, $F(6, 507) = 8.47$, p<.001; and antisocial behavior, $F(6, 502)=33.32$, p<.001. More interesting are the results of post hoc analyses. We used Scheffe test to examine whether adolescents with none, with one, two, three, etc. risk factors significantly differ from each other in the level of problem behavior. The results were consistent for each type of problem behavior: adolescents with no risk factors present, with only one and with two risk factors did not significantly differ in the level of problem behavior. A significant increase in problem behavior starts with three risk factors and it is especially sharp in case of disobedience and antisocial behavior. Compared to adolescents with no risk present, those with six risk factors are about four times more likely to show such behaviors.

DISCUSSION

In the present study we first examined the relationship between four types of externalizing problem behavior that occur with increasing frequency from early through late adolescence: disobedience, school misconduct, substance use and antisocial behavior. Researchers differ in the extent to which they have considered these to be distinct problems or a functionally similar social behavior that share common etiology. Our findings seem to provide more support for the notion of differentiated problems. Similar to the results of several other studies (Farrell, et al., 2000; Gillmore at al., 1991), different types of problem behavior appear to be only moderately correlated, and seem to have distinct developmental trajectories. Some types of the problem behavior, as for example school misconduct, show a curvilinear relationship with age, that is, the level of problem behavior tends to increase in the period of early to middle adolescence and afterwards tends to decrease. Other types, however, show a steady increase during this whole period of adolescence. Although there are gender differences in occurrence of problem behavior, developmental curves of boys and girls appear to be quite similar, with the exception of disobedience to parents.

Disobedience to parents and antisocial behavior show the highest interrelation, a similar developmental trend and a similar pattern of predictors. Though former types of problems occur more often and could be seen as less serious, it has been suggested that parental disobedience is often precursor of more serious antisocial behavior (Dishion, French, & Patterson, 1995; Loeber, 1990). Our results indeed show a lot of similarity between these two types of problem behavior.

This evidence indicates that the notion of "overall" problem behavior is of questionable utility. Problem behavior may be best described and studied as a multidimensional construct. In future research it would be more useful if discussions were presented in terms of specific domains of problem behavior.

Next we examined the relative importance of several risk factors that cover four conceptual domains: individual attributes, family factors, peer factors and school factors for these four types of problem behavior. The findings clearly indicate that risk factors exist at all levels of the adolescent personal and social world.

Individual attributes explain a significant percentage of variance in each of the four types of behavior. Not surprisingly impulsiveness was a significant predictor of externalizing problem behavior, with the exception of problems related to substance use that are better predicted by low self-esteem. In other words, low self-esteem appears to be one of the reasons for using drugs and alcohol in adolescence. Similar findings have been reported in other studies as well (Stacy, et al.,

1992). This seems to suggest that this type of problem behavior is somewhat different from the other three. Substance use is of course more directly self-destructive than the other assessed problems that are more overtly destructive (Frick, et al., 1993). On the other hand, adolescent age was also a strong predictor of substance use. In other words, an increasing age, regardless of other factors, predicted more frequent substance use. This might be especially true for alcohol use: a relatively large proportion of adolescents find alcohol consumption socially acceptable behavior in middle and late adolescence (Hawkins, Catalano, & Miller, 1992).

Family attributes significantly predicted all four types of problem behavior, although the contribution of a particular parental behavior measure did not reach significance in all equations. Adolescents who disobey their parents' rules and behave antisocially tend to have parents who are not well informed about their adolescents' whereabouts. Their relationship with parents is characterized by emotional distance and lack of intimacy and trust. Parental monitoring predicted, in addition to disobedience and antisocial behavior, also adolescents' school misconduct. In general, parental monitoring seems to be a stronger predictor of involvement in various types of problem behavior than the quality of parent-adolescent relationship.

Our findings point out the highly significant influence of peers on each type of problem behavior and especially on substance use and antisocial behavior. This is consistent with a number of previous studies that show that peer relations become increasingly important as children grow older and spend relatively more unsupervised time with peers outside home (Dishion, et al., 1995; Kim, Hetherington, & Reiss, 1999; Patterson, Reid, & Dishion, 1992). Deviant peers provide opportunities to engage in problem behavior, provide considerable social pressure and positive reinforcement for deviant behavior, and supply the adolescent with attitudes, motivation, and rationalization to support such behavior (Dishion, Andrews, & Crosby, 1995; Patterson, Reid, & Dishion, 1992).

Risk factors at school (low academic achievement and lack of motivation to succeed in school) appear to be important for less serious problem behavior, that is, disobedience to parents and school misconduct, but they seem to be of no importance for the development of more serious problems such as substance use and antisocial behavior, which are both better explained by individual attributes of adolescents' and the quality of their relationship with parents and peers.

The amount of risk, as indicated by the number of risk factors present, has a strong relation to variation in all four types of problem behavior. The frequency of problem behavior increases with the number of risk factors present. The significant cut-off point for all four types of problem behavior appear to be at three risk factors. That is, adolescents with no risk, with one or two risk factors did not differ significantly in the frequency of problem behavior, but they differed significantly from adolescents who are exposed to three or more risk factors.

Although the number of risk factors as a single predictor explained a substantial proportion of variance in problem behavior, it should be pointed out that the use of such index results in treating risk factors as equally weighted and interchangeable (Jessor at al., 1995). The risk factor index may be useful for conceptual purposes and in clinical practices for quick screening and selecting adolescents at risk, but the information that this index provides is limited, as it obscures the differential importance of particular risk factors and therefore also offers too little directions for interventions.

Several limitations of this study should be noted. First, cross-sectional nature of the data prevents us from making any claims regarding the causal relations between risk factors and the predicted outcome. In the present study, for example, deviant peers are seen as risk factors for development of various types of problem behavior, but it is just as possible that adolescents who engage in problem behavior select friends who are similar to them (Quinton, Pickles, Mughan, & Rutter, 1993). Similarly, parental attachment and monitoring are seen here as risk factors, but it has been pointed out that, as children grow older, they play an increasingly powerful role in shaping parental behavior and that this is particularly true with respect to externalizing problems (Lytton, 1990). Second, the data were collected using adolescents' self-reports, which could lead to method variance bias. Third, the environmental risk factors did not include factors in a broader environment, such as neighborhood characteristics or socio-economic status of the family that have been shown to affect adolescents' problem behaviors (McCord, 1990; Small & Luster, 1994). Finally, the focus of this study was on risk factors, but in order to fully understand occurrence, development and determinants of problem behavior during adolescence, it is necessary to study also the factors that foster competence, promote successful development and thus, decrease the likelihood of engaging in problem behavior (Deković, 1999). As Jessor (1991, p.604) aptly put it: "Two adolescents characterized by the same pattern of risk factors may be at very different degrees of risk, depending on the protective factors that affect their lives."

Notwithstanding these limitations, the present findings have several implications for prevention and/or interventions with adolescents who experience problems and their families. The implication of the finding that for all types of problems risk factors are not confined to a single domain, is that a single approach to prevent problem behavior is not likely to be effective. Instead of dealing with separate risk factors, it is necessary to design more complex interventions characterized by more comprehensive and simultaneous efforts to alter multiple domains of functioning and to intervene in each of the relevant settings (Tolan, Guerra, & Kendall, 1995). The results regarding parental monitoring suggest that parents need to be key players in these efforts. In addition, the results of the present study point clearly to the importance of peers for the development of various types of problem behavior. Intervention efforts for dealing with adolescent problem behavior should therefore include also strategies for dealing effectively with pressure from peers to engage in socially undesirable behavior (Flannery, Vazsonyi, Torquati, Fridrich, 1994). Powerful influence of peers during this developmental period could be harnesses in a positive direction. There is, however, reason to be cautious when using interventions delivered in peer group. Research findings show that aggregating high-risk adolescents into intervention groups often results in increase, rather than decrease of adolescent problem behavior (i.e. iatrogenic effects) (Dishion, McCord, & Poulin, 1999). The optimal strategy to reduce problem behavior seems to involve both the family and peer focus interventions, but these peer-training groups should be designed to include a mix of prosocial and deviant adolescents, in order to avoid danger of inadvertently reinforcing problem behavior.

REFERENCES

Armsden, G. C., & Greenberg, M. T. (1987). The Inventory of Parent and Peer Attachment: Individual differences and their relationship to psychological well-being in adolescence. *Journal of Youth and Adolescence, 16*, 427-453.

Aseltine, R. H. (1995). A reconsideration of parental and peer influences on adolescent deviance. *Journal of Health and Social Behavior, 36*, 103-121.

Berndt, T. J., & Keefe, K. (1995). Friends' influence on adolescents' adjustment to school. *Child Development, 66*, 1312-1329.

Brendgren, M., Vitaro, F., & Bukowski, W. M. (2000). Deviant friends and early adolescents' emotional and behavioral adjustment. *Journal of Research on Adolescence, 10*, 173-1 89.

Bronfenbrenner, U. (1986). Ecology of the family as a context for human development. *Developmental Psychology, 22*, 521-530.

Bronfenbrenner, U. (1989). Ecological systems theory. *Annals of Child Development, 6*. 187-249.

Brown, B. B., Mounts, N., Lamborn, S. D., & Steinberg, L. (1993). Parenting practices and peer group affiliation in adolescence. *Child Development, 64*, 467-482.

Chung, H., Elias, M. (1996). Patterns of adolescent involvement in problem behaviors: Relationship to self-efficacy, social competence, and life events. *American Journal of Community Psychology. 24*, 771-784.

Coie, J. D., Watt, N. F., West, S. G., Hawkins, D., Asarnow, J. R., Markman, H. J., Ramey, S. L., Shure, M. B., & Long, B. (1993). The science of prevention: A conceptual framework and some directions for a national research program. *American Psychologist, 48*, 1013—1022.

Deković, M. (1999). Risk and protective factors in the development of problem behavior during adolescence. *Journal of Youth and Adolescence, 28*, 667-685.

Dishion, T. J., Andrews, D. W., & Crosby, L. (1995). Antisocial boys and their friends in early adolescence: relationship characteristics, quality, and interactional process. *Child Development, 66*, 139-151.

Dishion, T. J., French, D. C., & Patterson, G. P. (1995). The development and ecology of antisocial behavior. In D. Ciccetti & D. C. Cohen (Eds.), *Developmental psychopathology. Vol. 2: Risk, disorder, and adaptation* (pp. 421-471). New York: Wiley.

Dishion, T. J., McCord, J., & Poulin, F. (1999). When interventions harm: peer group and problem behavior. *American Psychologist, 54,* 775-764.

Donovan, J. E., & Jessor, R. (1985). Structure of problem behavior in adolescence and young adulthood. *Journal of Consulting and Clinical Psychology. 53,* 890-904.

Donovan, J. E., Jessor, R., & Costa, F. M. (1988). Syndrome of problem behavior in adolescence: A replication. *Journal of Consulting and Clinical Psychology, 56,* 762-765.

Farrell, A. D., Kung, B. M., White, K. S., & Valois, R. F. (2000). The structure of self-reported aggression, drug use, and delinquent behaviors during early adolescence. *Journal of Clinical Child Psychology, 29,* 282-292.

Feij & Kuiper, (1984). *Adolescent Tempetament List (ATL) [Adolescent temperament questionnaire].* Lisse, The Netherlands: Swets & Zeitlinger.

Fergusson, D. M., & Horwood, L. J. (1999). Prospective childhood predictors of deviant peer affiliations in adolescence. *Journal of Child Psychology and Psychiatry, 40,* 581 -592.

Flannery, D. J., Vazsonyi, A. T., Torquati, J., & Fridrich, A. (1994). Ethnic and gender differences in risk for early adolescent substance use. *Journal of Youth and Adolescence, 23,* 195-213.

Fuligni, A. J., & Ecdes, J. S. (1993). Perceived parent-child relationships and early adolescents' orientation toward peers. *Developmental Psychology, 29,* 622-632.

Frick, P. J., Lahey, B. B., Loeber, R., Tannenbaum, L., Van Horn, M. A., Christ, M. A., Hart, B. L., & Hanson, K. (1993). Oppositional defiant disorder and conduct disorder. A meta-analytic review of factor analyses and cross-validation in a clinic sample. *Clinical Psychology Review, 13,* 19-340.

Hanson, K., Nemanin, J., Hubbard, J. J., Masten, A. S., & Tellegen, A. (1993). Parenting quality, adversity, and conduct problems in adolescence: testing process-oriented models of resilience. *Development and Psychology, 5,* 663-682.

Gillmore, M. R., Hawkins, J. D., Catalano, R. F., Day, L. B., Moore, M., & Abbott, R. (1991). Structure of problem behavior in preadolescence. *Journal of Consulting and Clinical Psychology, 59,* 499-506.

Hawkins, J. D., Catalano, R. F., & Miller, J. Y. (1992). Risk and protective factors for alcohol and other drug problems in adolescence and early adulthood: Implications for substance abuse prevention. *Psychological Bulletin, 112,* 64-1 05.

Hermanins, H. J. M. (1980). *Prestatiemotief en faalangst in gezin en onderwijs [Achievement motivation and fear of failure in family and education].* Lisse, The Netherlands: Swets en Zeitlinger.

Jacobson, K. C., & Crockett, L. J. (2000). Parental monitoring and adolescent adjustment An ecological perspective. *Journal of Research on Adolescence, 10,* 65-97.

Jessor, R. (1991). Risk behavior in adolescence: A Psychological framework for understanding and action. *Journal of Adolescent Health, 12,* 597-605.

Jessor, R., Bos, J. van den, Vanderryn, J., Costa, F. M., & Turbin, M. S. (1995). Protective factors in adolescent problem behavior: Moderator effects and developmental change. *Developmental Psychology, 31,* 923-933.

Jessor, R., & Jessor, S. I. (1977). *Problem behavior and psychosocial development. A longitudinal study of youth.* New York: Academic Press.

Kazdin, A. E. (1993). Adolescent mental health: Prevention and treatment programs. *American Psychologist, 48,* 127-123.

Kazdin, A. E. (1997). Psychosocial treatments for conduct disorder in children. *Journal of Child Psychology and Psychiatry, 38,* 161-178.

Kim, J. E., Hetherington, E. M., & Reiss, D. (1999). Associations among family relationships, antisocial peers, and adolescents' externalizing behaviors: Gender and family type differences. *Child Development, 70,* 1209-1230.

Loeber, R. (1990). Development and risk factors of juvenile antisocial behavior and delinquency. *Clinical Psychology Review, 10,* 1-41.

Luthar, S. S. (1993). Methodological and conceptual issues on research on childhood resilience. *Journal of Child Psychology and Psychiatry, 34,* 441-454.

Lytton, H. (1990). Child and parent effects in boys' conduct disorder: A reinterpretation. *Developmental Psychology, 26,* 683-697.

Maggs, J. L., Almeida, D. M., & Galambos, N. L. (1995). Risky business: The paradoxical meaning of problem behavior for young adolescents. *Journal of Early Adolescence, 15,* 344-362.

McCord, J. (1990). Problem behaviors. In S. S. Feldman & G. R. Elliott (Eds.), *At the threshold: The developing adolescent* (pp. 414-430). Cambridge, MA: Harvard University Press.

McGee, L., & Newcomb, M. D. (1992). General deviance syndrome: Expanded hierarchical evaluations at four ages from early adolescence to adulthood. *Journal of Consulting and Clinical Psychology, 60,* 766-776.

Moffit, T. (1993). Adolescence-limited and life-course-persistent antisocial behavior: A Developmental taxonomy. *Psychological Review, 100,* 674-701.

Naja Raja, S., McGee, R., & Stanton, W. R. (1992). Perceived attachments to parents and peers and psychological well-being in adolescence. *Journal of Youth and Adolescence, 21,* 471-485.

O'Donnell, J., Hawkins, J. D., & Abbott, R. D. (1995). Predicting serious delinquency and substance use among aggressive boys. *Journal of Consulting and Clinical Psychology, 63,* 529-537.

Patterson, G. R., Reid, J., & Dishion, T. (1992). *Antisocial boys.* Eugene, OR: Castaglia.

Patterson, G. R., & Stouthamer-Loeber, M. S. (1984). The correlation of family management practices and delinquency. *Child Development, 55,* 1299-1307.

Quinton, D., Pickles, A., Maughan, B., & Rutter, M. (1993). Partners, peers, and pathways: Assortative pairing and continuities in conduct disorder. *Development and Psychopathology, 5,* 763-783.

Resnick, G., & Burt, M. R. (1996). Youth at risk: Definitions and implications for service delivery. *American Journal of Orthopsychiatry, 66,* 172-1 88.

Robertson, J. F., & Simons, R. L. (1989). Family factors, self-esteem, and adolescent depression. *Journal of Marriage and the Family, 51,* 125-138.

Rosenberg, M. (1965). *Society and adolescent self-image.* Princeton: Princeton University Press.

Rutter, M. (1980) *Changing youth in a changing society.* Cambridge, MA: Harvard University Press.

Rutter, M. (1985). Resilience in the face of adversity: Protective factors and resistance to psychiatric disorder. *British Journal of Psychiatry, 147,* 598-611.

Rutter, M. (1987). Psychosocial resilience and protective mechanisms. *American Journal of Orthopsychiatry, 57,* 316-331.

Sameroff, A. J., Seifer, R., Baldwin, A., & Baldwin, C. (1993). Stability of intelligence from preschool to adolescence: the influence of social and family risk factors. *Child Development, 64,* 80-97.

Santor, D. A., Messervey, D., & Kusumakar, V. (2000). Measuring peer pressure, popularity, and conformity in adolescent boys and girls: Predicting school performance, sexual attitudes, and substance abuse. *Journal of Youth and Adolescence, 29,* 163-182.

Small, S. A., & Luster, T. (1994). Adolescent sexual activity: An ecological, risk-factor approach. *Journal of Marriage and the Family, 56,* 181-192.

Stacy, A. W., Sussman, S., Dent, C. W., Burton, D., & Flay, B. R. (1992). Moderators of peer social influence in adolescent smoking. *Personality and Social Psychology Bulletin, 18,* 163-172.

Steinberg, L., Elmen, J. D., & Mounts, N. (1989). Authoritative parenting, psychosocial maturity, and academic success among adolescents. *Child Development, 60,* 1424- 1436.

Tolan, P. H., Guerra, N. G., & Kendall, P. C. (1995). A developmental-ecological perspective on antisocial behavior in children and adolescents: Toward a unified risk and intervention framework. *Journal of Consulting and Clinical Psychology, 63,* 579-584.

Tremblay, R. E., Pihl, R. 0., Vitaro, F., & Dobkin, P. L. (1994). Predicting early onset of male antisocial behavior from preschool behavior. *Archives of Genetic Psychiatry, 51,* 732-739.

Wenar, C., & Kerig, P. (2000). *Developmental psychopathology: From infancy through adolescence.* New York: McGraw Hill.

White, J. L., Moffitt, T. E., Caspi, A., Bartusch, D. J., Needles, D. J., & Stouthamer-Loeber, M. (1994). Measuring impulsivity and examining its relationship to delinquency. *Journal of Abnormal Psychology, 103,* 192-205.

14

Adolescents at Risk of School Exclusion: The Identification of Key Risk Factors to Guide Intervention

Richard Cains
West Sussex County Council for Educational Psychology Service

Richard Cains · West Sussex County Council Educational Psychology Service · Crawley · West Sussex RH10 2GP · United Kingdom.

International Perspectives on Child and Adolescent Mental Health. Volume 2: Proceedings of the Second International Conference, edited by N. N. Singh, T. H. Ollendick, and A. N. Singh. © 2002 Elsevier Science Ltd. All rights reserved.

The risk factors that may be hypothesised as bringing about increased chance regarding the onset of problem behavior or causing a move to a more serious maintained state may encompass individual and environmental conditions. The complexity of the nature of such factors and their interactions inevitably suggest that the relationship between risk and protective factors in terms of resultant resilience or protection is not clear-cut. Kirby and Fraser (1997) cited different models when attempting to explain such complexities.

The "additive" models of risk and protection presume that the presence of risk factors inevitably increases the risk of negative outcomes for the child, and positive outcomes occur when risk is lower (Luthar 1991; Pellegrini 1990). Thus, competence in managing a situation declines as stress levels in the child increase. Risk and protection are seen to both influence and moderate one another.

"Interactive" theory suggests that protective factors have less impact on behavior when stress is low, but influence more as stress increases (Rutter 1983). Protective factors such as good social support serve to cushion the effects of other risk factors – the "buffer" effect. Interventions that reduce family conflict interrupt the cascade of events associating family environment with negative peer pressure, and other social risk factors – the "risk interruption" effect. Positive psychological characteristics such as accepting praise and reassurance, or being friendly and good-natured bring out positive responses in significant adults who would otherwise seek to punish – the "preventive" effect.

Interactions among risk and protective factors of course operate also at many different levels of the child's ecosystem. An interesting theory is that factors that are closer to the child within its ecosystem will have the greatest influence. This makes common sense. However, what seems a distant factor to the child (e.g., poverty and it's implications) may in fact "kick off" a reaction that results in much "closer" influences (e.g., parent stress) that impinge on the child more directly.

Kirby and Fraser (1997) suggested that generally both additive and interactive effects occur – effects that are best understood within an ecological framework. Thus the identification/assessment of factors that influence risk and resilience can be approached via such a framework. Kirby and Fraser (1997) summarised the important common protective factors as:

(a) Opportunity. Good educational and employment opportunities reduce frustration and anger. If the child expects to succeed antisocial values are more likely to be rejected.

(b) <u>Social Support</u>. Social support for children and families identified as high-risk promote positive outcomes and mitigate the effects of stressful events for children. Schools have a key role in providing social support.

(c) <u>Supportive Families</u>. Supportive families provide models of skills such as problem solving, motivation and valuing school achievement.

(d) <u>A Caring, Supportive Adult</u>. A caring, supportive adult – parent, extended relative, teacher – can also model prosocial behavior and help to build self-esteem.

(e) <u>Positive Parent-Child Relationship</u>. A good relationship with at least one parent reduces the risk effect of inter-parent conflict, and protects against more generalised life stress (e.g., poverty, bereavement etc.). Feelings of security are enhanced and both cognitive and social development can be helped.

(f) <u>Effective Parenting</u>. Effective parenting promotes more secure attachments and may persuade children of their own feelings of self-efficacy.

(g) <u>Good Temperament</u>. Accepting help, having a balanced attitude to stress can elicit positive responses from significant adults who might otherwise seek to punish or penalise.

(h) <u>Social Competence</u>. Leads to awareness of personal effectiveness in a social world and thus promotes adaptation, coping, and achievement across the ecosystem.

(i) <u>Self Esteem</u>. Determines perceived competence and self worth, and thus supports the notion of learning from both success and failure. An increase in the pursuit of protective factors such as positive use of leisure time is a further indirect outcome of good self-esteem.

(j) <u>Intelligence</u>. Low intelligence is often correlated with aggressive, antisocial behaviors and a reduced capacity to problem solve at a social or academic level. Good intelligence increases the likelihood of more effective responses to stress.

Indicators of school failure inevitably overlap. Richman and Bowen (1997) pointed to the need to continually evaluate progress, suggesting that a measuring instrument can be useful in the planning and intervention process. Germain and Gitterman (1995) highlighted the ecological-interactional-developmental perspective as a useful framework in the evaluation of risk and resilience. The "needs-supplies" relationship emphasises individual needs in the context of opportunities, supplies, and resources in the environment. Children find it hard to develop resilience in situations where chaos and unpredictability render even the basic needs (e.g., safety and security) unlikely to be met.

The degree of congruency between demands and requirements from an environment such as school and the child's competencies and skills for meeting demands is also central to resilience (Germain & Gitterman, 1995). School's can of course be both over- and under-demanding in terms of the child's abilities. If the child cannot meet environmental demands, lowered self-esteem, hopelessness and despair may ensue. Further, it is important to note that demands increase in school with age rather than with maturity. On the other hand, inadequate challenge can result in the need to seek out experiences with negative implications in terms of well-being and social performance. As Richman and Bowen (1997) observed, children respond to their own subjective perceptions of their reality, and those perceptions form the basis for the development of resilience.

With these issues in mind, this research is aimed at investigating the psychosocial factors that are perceived by teachers as having influence on pupil behavior. From this research it was planned to derive a general-purpose inventory of such factors that may be relevant to or have an influence on the behavior of pupils in secondary schools, wherein such behavior may lead to permanent or fixed term exclusion from school. The purpose of the instrument is to help teachers and other significant adults who work in secondary schools to formulate a risk profile relating to these influential factors and, thus, understand the nature of the problems and challenges young people are up against as they progress through school. From such a profile appropriate intervention can be considered and implemented.

METHOD

Questionnaire Construction

On the basis of the ecological framework and associated previous research a questionnaire containing 60 items was devised and circulated to all secondary schools in West Sussex (see Appendix 1). The items were drawn from current research and literature, educational psychology case files, and teacher comments. Each school was asked to complete a questionnaire on individual pupils who had been excluded either permanently or for a fixed term, and schools were also asked to complete an identical questionnaire for individual pupils who had experienced behavioral problems warranting intervention but who had not been excluded. The number of questionnaires sent to each school was calculated on the basis of a proportion of their excluded pupil population. All schools were sent five questionnaires to be completed for non-excluded pupils. Teachers (who best knew the pupils) were asked to rate the 60 psychosocial items in terms of their influence on the pupil's behavior on a scale of 0 to 3 (0 = not an issue, 1 = a slight influence, 2 = an important influence, and 3 = a considerable influence).

Excluded Pupil Population

The excluded pupil population identified in the questionnaires returned, by age and gender, was:

	Male	Female	Total
Year 7	17	3	20
Year 8	34	4	38
Year 9	46	14	60
Year 10	22	22	44
Year 11	18	8	26

Selection of Items for Inclusion in the Risk Profile

Forty-three items were selected from the responses and comments obtained from schools. In order to select the final items, 3 "zones of influence" relating to the excluded population were conceptualised on the basis of the notion "strength of influence" of each item. "Strength of influence" was calculated as a percentage, wherein each item's total rating score was compared to the maximum rating score possible. The three zones were: (a) the important/considerable influence zone; (b) the slight/important influence zone, and (c) the no issues/slight influence zone.

The final items were selected on the following basis:

- All items whose influence was in the important/considerable zone.
- Items that were high in the slight/important influence zone.
- Items that were lower in the slight/important influence zone but were nonetheless significantly more influential (statistically) than the non-excluded pupil group.
- "Low occurrence – high impact" items - those influencing items that may not have had an overall high occurrence in terms of the entire population but whose influence was associated closely with the influence of other key items that were in themselves having an important/considerable influence.

Exploratory factor analysis was undertaken in order that the 43 individual items could be clustered into a number of "risk sets". The derivation of these risk sets was not, however, entirely dependent upon factor analysis. Factor analysis played a role in confirming the validity of the sets but the overriding importance in terms of clustering the items was in order that the risk sets were psychologically meaningful and not merely a product of statistical analysis.

The 43 items were grouped together into psychologically meaningful sets relating to the excluded population. These are presented as below, with Risk Set title abbreviations in brackets.

General Attitude and Coping (Att/Cop)

- Tends to blame others for his/her actions.
- Generally resents authority
- Finds it hard to accept praise
- Is poorly motivated
- Does not readily accept help with learning
- Handles criticism badly
- Praise has little positive impact on behavior
- Seldom takes responsibility for actions

General Behavior Pattern (GenBeh)

- Has an impulsive nature.
- Can be somewhat aggressive
- Has an established behavior reputation from earlier years
- There is some history of truancy
- Tends to react aggressively when admonished
- Completing homework is a problem
- Has problems with a few, particular teachers

Family and Parenting Issues (FamPar)

- Parental control of behavior seems to be a problem.
- There is a lot of stress in the family
- Lives in a socially disadvantaged family
- Lives in a re-constituted family (step-parent)
- Parents don't co-operate well with school

General Learning Issues (Learn)

- Low literacy levels
- Verbal abilities are low
- Curriculum access is a problem because of learning difficulties
- Number skills weak
- Has problems with personal organisation
- Keeping up in many lessons is a problem
- Has attention problems in class

Psychological and Well-being Factors (Psych)

- Often seems to be tired
- Low self esteem
- Seems somewhat depressed
- Seems somewhat anxious
- Has very few friends
- Is in the midst of adolescent development
- Is or has been bullied
- Keeps feelings very much to self
- Has a pessimistic outlook for self (resigned to the problems)

Social Skills and Social Performance (Social)

- Does not get on well with peers
- Is easily led by more dominant peers
- Is subject to undesirable peer influence
- Has many problems at unstructured times (breaks etc.)
- Social communication skills poor
- Has few if any leisure interests
- Has been in trouble with police

Risk Profile Data Findings

Comparison of the Excluded and Non-Excluded Populations

Tables 1 to 6 provide details of responses for the two populations – excluded and non-excluded pupils for each of the six Risk Sets. The data are presented according to:

- The percentage of pupils for whom items are rated 2 or 3 (important/considerable influence),
- The percentage of pupils for whom items are rated 0 (not an issue), and
- Significant differences in item ratings (t test). between the two populations.

Each table is followed by a brief comment that relates to risk set item correlation data for the excluded population, and individual item rating.

Table 1.   Excluded and Non-Excluded Populations: Risk Set "Attitude and Coping"

	blames others	poor motivation	resents authority	not accepting praise	not accepting help	handles criticism badly	praise not effective	won't take responsibility
Excluded Pupils								
rated 2/3	72%	74%	80%	56%	39%	83%	65%	79%
not an issue	11%	5%	4%	18%	27%	5%	9%	5%
Non-excluded Pupils								
rated 2/3	68%	74%	64%	38%	38%	66%	47%	65%
not an issue	16%	9%	11%	33%	34%	11%	23%	17%
t-test			**	**		**	**	

** p<.005

      Particular associations emerge. For example those who refuse to take responsibility for their actions frequently appear to blame others, and those who strongly resent authority handle criticism badly. Poor motivation relates to not wanting help and therefore praise is not in itself effective. Ratings of 2/3 are fewer for all items in the non-excluded population other than for "poor motivation."

Table 2. Excluded and Non-excluded Populations: Risk Set "General Behavior Pattern"

	impulsive	somewhat aggressive	behavior reputation	completing homework a problem	history of truancy	aggressive if told off	problems with particular teachers
Excluded Pupils							
rated 2/3	89%	84%	70%	79%	38%	81%	62%
not an issue	3%	6%	14%	5%	37%	4%	19%
Non-excluded Pupils							
rated 2/3	81%	74%	61%	69%	28%	65%	52%
not an issue	5%	16%	22%	8%	52%	18%	33%
t-test		**	**		*	**	

** $p<.005$ * $p<.01$

Inevitably this risk set is the most influential in terms of the profile of the excluded population. Impulsiveness combines with aggressive behavior patterns, whilst truancy relates strongly to homework problems. Although truancy occurs in a minority of the excluded population, it does not appear to relate to problems with particular teachers, but rather to much broader issues. Ratings of 2/3 are fewer for all items in the non-excluded population.

Table 3. Excluded and Non-Excluded Populations: Risk Set "Family/Parenting Issues"

	parental control poor	family stress	parents not co-operative with school	socially disadvantaged family	re-constituted family
Excluded Pupils					
rated 2/3	79%	82%	35%	40%	37%
not an issue	8%	2%	39%	41%	56%
Non-excluded Pupils					
rated 2/3	75%	63%	26%	39%	31%
not an issue	8%	8%	44%	48%	64%
t test		**			

** $p<.005$

There is a notable link between family stress, parental control, and social disadvantage. The latter also seems to impact on the level of co-operation between home and school. Ratings of 2/3 are fewer for all items in the non-excluded population.

Table 4.   Excluded and Non-excluded Populations: Risk Set "General Learning Issues"

	low literacy	low verbal skills	curriculum access a problem	low number	poor attention	poorly organised	can't keep up
Excluded Pupils							
rated 2/3	44%	42%	40%	35%	84%	52%	51%
not an issue	31%	38%	39%	38%	4%	20%	23%
Non-excluded Pupils							
rated 2/3	35%	33%	39%	32%	70%	59%	41%
not an issue	49%	52%	48%	50%	6%	22%	20%
t test	*						

* p<.01

At the heart of the learning issues set is the influence of poor attention. Indeed this item dominates the entire risk set. Ratings of 2/3 are fewer for all items in the non-excluded population.

Table 5   Excluded and Non-excluded Populations: Risk Set "Psychological and Well-being Factors"

	often tired	low self esteem	seems depressed	seems anxious	in midst of adolescent development	bullied	few friends	keeps feelings inside	pessimistic
Excluded Pupils									
rated 2/3	45%	68%	47%	49%	68%	23%	42%	53%	65%
not an issue	24%	13%	20%	23%	6%	55%	32%	20%	15%
Non-excluded Pupils									
rated 2/3	43%	52%	36%	25%	73%	14%	26%	49%	53%
not an issue	32%	31%	38%	48%	9%	76%	52%	30%	22%
t-test		**	*	**		*	**		*

** p<.005 * p<.01

There is strong correlation between nearly all items. Self-esteem associates particularly strongly with all items except issues concerning adolescence. Though influential in its own way, the influence of adolescent development does not relate strongly to any other issues here. Depression and anxiety seem to be inevitably intertwined, and also very much link with pessimism and keeping feelings to oneself.

Table 6   Excluded and Non-excluded Populations: Risk Set "Social Skills and Social Performance"

	poor peer relationships	easily led	trouble with police	undesirable peer influence	break time problems	social communication poor	few leisure interests
Excluded Pupils							
rated 2/3	61%	46%	41%	64%	74%	51%	45%
not an issue	17%	37%	38%	16%	8%	26%	29%
Non-excluded Pupils							
rated 2/3	45%	35%	18%	55%	47%	35%	39%
not an issue	35%	38%	56%	20%	16%	36%	39%
t-test	**		**		**	*	

** p<.005 * p<.01

As can be expected, those who are easily led are subject to undesirable peer influence. This influence is particularly at work at unstructured times of the school day. On the other hand, those who are not getting on with peers also have significant problems at unstructured times, and they seem to lack adequate social skills to extricate themselves. Ratings of 2/3 are fewer for all items in the non-excluded population.

Comparing the Excluded Population by Age Groups

Comparative data for the two populations – years 7, 8, 9 and years 10 and 11 – for the excluded pupil population, according to the percentage of ratings at 2/3 and 0 reveals that significant differences in ratings between the two populations are few. Within the behavioral risk set, ratings for "somewhat aggressive" and "aggressive when told off" are significantly different (p<.005), with the older population having more 2/3 ratings.

Within the psychological well being risk set ratings for "seems anxious" are significantly different (p<.05). Significantly more of the younger population receive 2/3 ratings. That population also receive significantly more 2/3 ratings for "few leisure interests" (p<.05) within the "Social Skills and Social Performance" risk set.

Comparing the Excluded Population by Gender

Comparative data for the two gender groups for the excluded pupil population were analysed and, in terms of the percentage of ratings at 2/3 and 0, there were few significant differences in ratings between the two populations. The risk set "General Learning Issues" produce the following item ratings that are significantly different, wherein boys receive higher 2/3 ratings: Low literacy (p<.05) Curriculum access (p<.05) Poor attention (p<.025) Poorly organised (p<.01).

Low-Occurrence and High-Influence Factors

An analysis of all items included in the original 60-item questionnaire suggests that it is important to look at the influence of particular item influences. These influences may be somewhat less common, but they are interesting because when they do occur as important influences they bring with them associated items that assume a higher degree of influence than for the remainder of the population. Five such pupil groups associated with these "special" items of influence are: bullied pupils (n = 43); pupils who truant (n=69); pupils with low literacy (n=83); looked-after pupils (n=31); and pupils with a history of abuse (n=33).

It is possible to assess the impact of these factors when one looks at the key associated risk items as compared to the excluded population as a whole. To do so, one can conceptualise each item as having a strength of influence based on the percentage of ratings at 2 or 3.

In order to compare the profiles of these five populations, we can first look at key items in the whole population which have the highest influence (important/considerable). These items are presented in Table 7 in order of strength of influence.

Table 7.   Key items found to be important/considerable

Item	rated 2/3 (%)
Impulsiveness	89
Somewhat aggressive	84
Poor attention	84
Handles critisism badly	83

Table 7 continued.

Item	rated 2/3 (%)
Family stress	82
Aggressive if told off	81
Resents authority	80
Won't take responsibility	79
Completing homework a problem	79
Parental poor control	79
Break time problems	74
Poor motivation	74
Blames others	72
Behavior reputation	70
In midst of adolescent develompent	68
Low self esteem	68
Pessimistic	65
Praise not effective	65
Bad peer influence	64
Problems with particular teachers	62
Poor peer relationships	61

These twenty-one items form approximately 50% of the final risk profile schedule items. They provide a useful baseline for facilitating comparisons with the five special populations.

Tables 8 to 12 show the most influential items associated with the pupils of the five special populations. The data refer to percentages rated 2/3 for each associated item, and are compared with similar percentage ratings for the rest of the excluded population. Comments after each table refer to statistically significant differences in item ratings.

Risk Profile of Bullied Pupils

Table 8. Comparison of Bullied Pupils with the Rest of the Excluded Population

Item	bullied (%)	rest (%)
Somewhat aggressive	95	81
Impulsive	91	89
Family stress	91	79
Won't take responsibility	86	77
Break time problems	86	71
Handels critisism badly	84	83
Behavior reputation	79	68
Aggressive if told off	79	82
Parental control poor	79	79
Poor attention	79	85
Low self esteem	77	65
Poor peer relationships	77	57
Blames others	74	71
Pessimistic	74	63
Resents authority	72	82
Completing homework a problem	72	81
Few friends	70	34
Praise not effective	67	64
Poor motivation	65	77
In midst of adolescent development	65	69
Seems anxious	63	46

There is significantly more family stress in the bullied population, and anxiety is significantly higher. Self-esteem is lower. Peer relationships are markedly poorer, and these pupils have fewer friends. They also have more problems at break times. Interestingly, they are better motivated than the rest of the excluded population.

Risk Profile of Pupils who Truant

Table 9.   Comparison of Pupils who Truant with the Rest of the Excluded Population

Item	truancy (%)	rest (%)
Impulsive	92	96
Completing homework a problem	90	79
Parental control poor	89	79
Resents authority	87	82
Poor motivation	85	74
Family stress	83	89
Handles critisism badly	82	92
Poor attention	82	93
Won't take responsibility	80	86
Somewhat aggressive	80	94
Aggressive if told off	76	93
Break time problems	76	80
Undesirable peer influences	75	64
In midst of adolescent development	72	72
Trouble with police	70	26
Behavior reputation	69	78
Pessimistic	69	69
Blames others	68	81
Praise not effective	65	71
Often tired	62	38
Low self esteem	61	79

These pupils are far more often in trouble with the police, and generally tend to resent authority more. Homework causes greater problems, though no learning issues appear other than relating to attention problems in class. Parental control is poorer, as is motivation. The population also appears to be significantly more tired.

Risk Profile of Pupils with Low Literacy

Table 10. Comparison of Pupils with Low Literacy with the Rest of the Excluded Population

Item	low literacy (%)	rest (%)
Impulsive	95	85
Poor attention	94	75
Completing homework a problem	93	68
Won't take responsibility	92	70
Handles criticism badly	90	77
Family stress	88	77
Parental control poor	87	72
Blames others	86	61
Aggressive if told off	86	78
Break time problems	86	66
Curriculum acces a problem	84	6
Poor motivation	83	67
Resents authority	83	77
Can't keep up	83	25
Somewhat aggressive	82	86
Low verbal skills	81	11
Poorly organized	81	30
Behavior reputation	78	64
Low self esteem	76	61
Social communication poor	76	30
Undesirable peer influence	75	56
Praise not effective	72	59
Poor peer relationships	70	54
Low number	67	10
Pessimistic	66	65
Not accepting praise	64	50
Problems with particular teachers	63	62
Easily led	61	33

Table 10 shows the pervasive impact of low literacy on the school performance of this population of excluded pupils. As well as the predictable influence of other learning issues, attitude and coping influences listed above (other than for "resents authority") are all significantly stronger. This is also the case for social skills and social performance items. Self-esteem is also significantly lower than for the population for whom low literacy is not an important issue.

Risk Profile of Looked-after Pupils

Table 11. Comparing the Looked-after Pupils with the Rest of the Excluded Population

Item	looked after (%)	rest (%)
Somewhat aggressive	94	81
Aggressive if told off	90	79
Impulsive	87	89
Completing homework a problem	84	77
Family stress	84	81
Poor attention	84	82
Pessimistic	84	61
Handles criticism badly	81	82
Parental control poor	81	77
Resents authority	77	79
Poor motivation	74	73
Behavior reputation	74	69
Low self esteem	74	65
Won't take responsibility	68	81
In midst of adolescent development	68	67
Often tired	65	41
Seems depressed	65	43
Break time problems	65	75
Blames others	61	73
Praise not effective	61	65
Poor peer relationships	61	60

The two psychological/well-being items "seems tired" and "pessimistic" are significantly stronger influences, and the item "seems depressed" is also approaching a significant difference.

Risk Profile of Pupils with an Abusive History

Table 12. Comparison of Pupils with an Abusive History with the Rest of the Excluded
Population

Item	abused (%)	rest (%)
Impulsive	91	89
Family stress	88	81
Somewhat aggressive	85	84
Aggressive if told off	85	81
Parental control poor	82	78
Won't take responsibility	79	79
Behavior reputation	79	68
Completing homework a problem	79	79
Blames others	76	71
Handels criticism badly	76	85
Poor attention	76	85
Low self esteem	76	66
Break time problems	76	74
Resents authority	73	81
Seems anxious	73	45
Poor peer relationships	73	59
Pessimistic	64	66
Poor motivation	61	77
Praise not effective	58	66
Poorly organized	58	51
Seems depressed	58	45

Within the items listed in Table 12 only "seems anxious" and "seems depressed" have
significantly higher influence ratings. "Family stress" is approaching significance. This
population shows significantly stronger influence ratings also for items "socially disadvantaged
family" and bullying.

DISCUSSION

Germain (1991) observed that it is the interaction of individual characteristics and
contextual influences that generally explains human behavior. But whether ecological or system
theory are used as the frame of reference for providing more specific information about children
at risk, one needs detail and explicit information in order to examine and plan on a case-by-case

basis. The aim of this research was to examine in detail adolescents who have to all intents and purposes been subject to failure in their school lives. To this end the findings from the original questionnaire have been applied in the construction of a risk profile schedule for use in schools.

The profile is intended to help teachers to devise support plans both from school resources and hopefully by harnessing support and involvement from other agencies (e.g., the pastoral support programme approach may provide a vehicle for such support and intervention).

Of course, although the schedule presents a means of devising a profile for pupils at risk of exclusion in terms of psychosocial factors, it must be remembered that the children are functioning within an education/school system. As such systemic factors relevant to the child's performance in school must always be taken into account. It is essential that the derived profile should generate thought and consideration as to how the system can best or better support the individual pupil.

The schedule should not be seen as a test or a cut and dried measuring instrument. Indeed to do so would lend weight to arguments that schedules and checklists like this can represent naïve attempts to measure or quantify extremely complex and invariably interacting issues out there in the real world.

The schedule is a tool offered to help clarify thinking. It is intended to give teachers and other adults working with troubled pupils in secondary schools a guide and framework for considering what might be happening in the pupil's world – within and without – in order that planning and discussion can be facilitated.

A schedule such as this is dependent for usefulness on those who complete it being as objective as possible in their evaluations of what is influencing pupils' behavior. Objectivity is not easy, as we all bring our own values and personal meaning systems into play when trying to figure out our fellow man. Thus we need a sense of balance and perspective.

The schedule helps achieve perspective by providing data which compares excluded pupils with pupils who have behavioral problems in school but who have not been excluded. The pupil thought to be at risk of exclusion needs to be compared against these two population groups when rating perceived behavior influences is undertaken.

The schedule needs to be completed collaboratively among those adults who really know the child, and possibly with a "referee" who can challenge and question beliefs and assumptions. If such collaboration is not undertaken, the quality of the information obtained from the schedule will inevitably be compromised. Ideally the referee needs to be a neutral professional – someone with consultation skills and experience.

Bringing the actual pupil and parents into the debate is also sensible. In such circumstances, the schedule can be employed as a structured interview. Using the six risk sets as a framework and an aid to discussion, without of course involving direct questioning on individual items if particular sensitivities are apparent, could be a useful means of getting valuable input on how the situation might be helped or changed. Confidentiality should always be stressed.

By carefully rating the items in the schedule, the numbers derived (i.e., raw scores) can be converted into percentiles. The percentile for each of the six risk sets provides a means of placing the pupil on a continuum that can be compared with the population of pupils who have been excluded. But is important to note that the raw scores or percentiles do not in themselves represent amounts of anything. If a pupil's raw score on a risk set is equivalent to the 60th percentile, it merely suggests that this raw score would only be exceeded by 40% of the excluded population, based on the data available within this project.

Of course it must also be noted that time can change the profile. Problems and circumstances come and go. The derived scores are best viewed as a reflection of the current situation. But if intervention follows on from the completion of the schedule and associated planning, the schedule can be re-used to evaluate and review.

The idiosyncrasies of the individual must also never be lost, and the schedule should not be used in isolation. To get an effective and clear focus on what might be driving the situation, other relevant information and data needs to be taken into account. The diversity of influence the risk profile might expose inevitably means processes that are likely to bring about positive change must involve many different systems. This is the major challenge, though importantly the need for schools, social services, and health services to expand and enhance knowledge of risk/resilience theory is vital in order to guide policy. Such multisystemic intervention strategies are emphasised by Henggeler and Borduin (1990). Further, Garmezy (1993) observed in relation to this that the influence of risk factors is tempered, if not removed, by protective factors such as personal strengths, family strengths and environmental resources (e.g., school and community).

REFERENCES

Garmezy, N. (1993). Children in poverty: Resilience despite risk. *Psychiatry, 56*, 127-136.

Germain, C.B.(1991). *Human behavior in the social environment: An ecological view*. New York: Columbia University Press.

Germain, C.B. & Gitterman, A. (1995). Person-in-environment. In R.L. Edwards (Ed.), *Encyclopoedia of social work* (19th ed., Vol. 2, pp. 1818 –1827) Washington DC: NASW Press.

Henggeler, S.W.& Borduin C.M. (1990). *Family therapy and beyond: A mulitisystemic approach to treating the behavior problems of children and adolescents*. Pacific Grove, CA: Brooks/Cole.

Kirby, L.D. & Fraser, M.W. (1997). Risk and resilience in childhood. In M.W. Fraser (Ed.), *Risk and resilience in childhood: An ecological perspective* (pp. 10-33). Washington DC: NASW Press.

Luthar, S.S. (1991). Vulnerability and resilience: A study of high risk adolescents. *Child Development, 62*, 600-616.

Pelligrini, D.S. (1990). Psychosocial risk and protective factors in childhood. *Developmental and Behavioral Pediatrics, 11*, 201-209.

Richman, J.M. & Bowen. G.L. (1997). School failure: An ecological-interactional-developmental perspective. In M.W. Fraser (Ed.), *Risk and resilience in childhood: An ecological perspective* (pp. 95-116). Washington DC: NASW Press.

Rutter, M. (1983). Statistical and personal interactions: Facets and perspectives. In D Magnussen & V.L.Allen (Eds.), *Human development: An interactional perspective* (pp. 295-320). New York, NY: Academic Press.

15

Relationship Between Child Psychopathology and Parental Alcoholism

R. C. Jiloha
Maulana Azad Medical College

R. C. Jiloha · Maulana Azad Medical College and G. B. Pant Hospital · Department of Psychiatry · New Dehli 1100 02 · India.

International Perspectives on Child and Adolescent Mental Health. Volume 2: Proceedings of the Second International Conference, edited by N. N. Singh, T. H. Ollendick, and A. N. Singh. © 2002 Elsevier Science Ltd. All rights reserved.

The child who is a product of bio-psycho-social milieu comes into the world with biologically based capacity for the perception of and empathic responsiveness to, the bodily expressed feelings and attitudes of other people (Hobson, 1997). The first and probably the most important relationship begins in the family where parents play a major role in socializing and conditioning the child. Parents also help the child to achieve a sense of reality, a sense of identity, and in meeting his needs of affection. Home environment and the manner in which family members interact contribute to shaping the child's behavior.

Families of alcoholics have lower levels of family cohesion, a restricted range of emotional expressiveness, limited independence and inadequate intellectual orientation (Jiloha & Smita, 1994). These families have high levels of conflict compared with non-alcoholic families. Research findings suggest that some children from these families suffer negative consequences due to parental alcoholism. The family environment way also affects transmission of alcoholism to the children of alcoholic parents. Therefore, they are in a particularly vulnerable position as they grow up in an environment disrupted by alcoholic behavior (Chafetz, Blaine, & Hill, 1971). Frequent arguments, separation, divorce, financial difficulties and emotional disturbances are the usual characteristics among the families of alcoholics (Chafetz, et al., 1971; Nylander, 1960). Further, children from such families feel insecure and anxious due to rejection, isolation, punishment, and the unpredictable behavior of the alcoholic parent. All these might lead the child to react to frustration through grossly maladjusted behavior.

An estimated 6.6 million American children under the age of 18 years live in households with at least one alcoholic parent. With almost similar situations elsewhere in the world, these children, besides being at the risk of genetic vulnerability for alcoholism, are also exposed to the risk of a wide range of cognitive, emotional, and behavioral problems. For example, many researchers have examined cognitive functioning because it is an important element needed for adaptation at all stages of development. Studies comparing children of alcoholic and non-alcoholic parents suggest that the observed differences in cognitive performance can be attributed to alcoholism in parents.

Research studies have found that performance on intelligence tests was lower among children raised by alcoholic fathers than among children raised by non-alcoholic fathers. Many other researchers have reported similar results for verbal and full scale I.Q. but not for performance tests (Chafetz, et al., 1971). Conolly, Casswell, Stewart, Silva, and O'Brien (1993) found that children from families of alcoholics had a lower I.Q. and lower arithmetic, reading and verbal scores. Johnson, O'Malley, and Bachman (1995) compared the academic ability and cognitive functioning of the children of alcoholics and non-alcoholics and found no differences between the groups. The investigators noted, however, that the children with alcoholic parents underestimated their own competence. In addition, their mothers underrated their children's ability. School-aged children of alcoholic parents often have academic problems such as repeating grades, and failing to graduate from high school. Although cognitive deficits may account, in part, for poor academic performance, motivational difficulties or a stressful home environment also contribute to their problems in school. Divorce, parental anxiety, affective disorders, undesirable changes in the family or in life situations add to the negative effect of parental alcoholism on children's emotional functioning.

Parental alcoholism is linked to a number of psychological disorders. The results of several studies have shown that children from families of alcoholics report higher levels of depression and anxiety and exhibit more symptoms of generalized stress (i.e., lower self esteem) than do children from non-alcoholic families. These children also express a lack of control over their environment. It was noted that children of alcoholics show more depressive affect than children of non-alcoholics. Roosa, Sandler, Beals, and Short (1988) and Tubman (1993) stated that children of alcoholics have more anxiety and symptoms related to depression than children whose parents are not alcoholic.

Children from alcoholic parents often demonstrate behavioral problems such as lying, stealing, fighting, truancy, and problems at school. Also, they are often diagnosed to be suffering from Conduct Disorder (CD). Teachers have rated them as significantly more overactive and impulsive than children from non-alcoholic families. West and Prinz (1987) reported an increased frequency of delinquency, truancy, social inadequacy, and somatic problems in children of alcoholic parents, and Fergusson, Lynsky and Horwood (1994) reported that these children begin drinking early in life.

Early studies found increases in the rate of Attention Deficit Hyperactivity Disorder (ADHD) (Earls, Reich, Jung, & Cloninger, 1988; Goodwin, 1985; Goodwin, Schulsinger, Hermansen, Guze, & Winokur, 1975; Stewart, DeBlois, & Cummings, 1980), Conduct Disorder (CD) and Oppositional Defiant Disorder (ODD) (Earl, et al., 1988; Merikangas, Weissman, Prusoff, Pauls, & Leckman, 1985; Steinhausen, Globel, & Nestler, 1984), among children of alcoholic parents but more recent studies have not confirmed these findings. Hill and Hruska (1992) in their study did not find differences among children who had family history of alcoholism and those who did not have such a history. Reich, Earls, Frankel, and Shyka (1993) found that the rates of ODD, CD, Overanxious Disorder (OAD), and drug-abuse increased significantly as the number of patients with alcohol dependence increased from 0 to 2 in a study of 123 children. Finally, Hill and Muka (1996) found that 36 adolescents who came from families where multiple family members suffered from alcoholism were more likely to have a psychiatric diagnosis than 38 matched adolescents from families without a history of alcoholism in first-and second-degree relatives.

While research findings suggest that some children suffer negative consequences due to parental alcoholism, a large proportion of children of alcoholic parents function well and do not develop serious problems. Some investigators report that many children from alcoholic homes do not develop either psychopathology or alcoholism. Therefore, the relationship between parental alcoholism and rates of psychiatric disorders among children of alcoholic parents is not clear. MaGaha (1993) showed that persons raised in alcoholic homes are more likely to exhibit anger and a variety of acting out behaviors and are more likely to have contact with the criminal justice system than those not raised in non-alcoholic homes. Barrera, Chassin, and Rogosch (1993) found no correlation between the alcoholic status of the parents and the level of self-esteem of the children. However, Swartzenberg and Swartzenberg (1990) found that the children of alcoholics had low self-esteem, and Churchill, Broida, and Nicholson, (1990) in their work on locus of control and self-esteem in children of alcoholic parents found that girls have lower levels of self-esteem than boys. Bush, Ballard, and Fremouw (1995) also found lower self-esteem and depression among children of alcoholics.

Why do the children from the same environment and gene pool experience such different developmental outcomes? The differences have been attributed to various factors: firstly, because of increased rate of parental separation, divorce, marital discord, dysfunctional parenting and family income; secondly, because only few studies have examined the possibility that the increased rate of childhood psychiatric disorders in children of alcoholics is because of co-morbid psychiatric diagnosis in alcoholic parents. This factor has been ignored in most of the studies. Another important factor is that smaller samples have been used for comparison in most of the studies (Garmezy & Masten, 1994). The composition of the sample chosen for the studies also has a significant effect on the results. In addition, studies are often conducted without the benefit of matched groups. The absence of control groups makes it difficult to generalize the results. All these limitations can affect the outcome of the study.

Alcoholism is a major public health problem in India (Mohan, Sethi, & Tongue, 1995) and alcohol is widely used in both rural and urban areas. However, there are no studies investigating the relationship between child psychopathology and parental alcoholism in a culture where family ties are described as being strong and where marriages are ranged by elders in many instances (Jiloha & Smita, 1994). A marriage in India is considered to be a sacrament and not a contract. Therefore, the divorce rate in India is relatively low and married life generally continues despite many difficulties including a husband's alcohol problem. In traditional India society, women, by and large, do not consume alcohol and they silently suffer their alcoholic husbands. The extended family system still prevails in India to a large extent and this provides social and emotional support to a family member who may be suffering. Children are generally not ignored and their needs are may be met by their grand parents living in the same house or the non-alcoholic mother who has more contact with the child. The extended family also takes care of financial difficulties occurring in the family even when the alcoholic member does not contribute to the family income. In a society where a child's needs are taken care of by other members of the family, it can be presumed that child is not impacted negatively by having an alcoholic parent. This study examines the impact of alcoholic fathers on Indian children.

METHOD

Fifty married male alcohol-dependent patients who were attending the de-addiction clinic of GB Pant Hospital New Delhi, India participated in the study. Their ages ranged from 30 to 50 years, and the mean number of years they had been consuming alcohol was eight years. They were diagnosed as alcoholics according to the DSM-IV criteria. None of the patients participating in the study had associated psychiatric co-morbidity, marital discord due to reasons other than alcohol dependence, and/or suffered from a major physical illness. All 50 alcoholics came from extended families that included either the parents or brother(s). They had children between the ages of 7-18 years. In total, there were 108 children all of whom were students.

Thirty married non-alcoholics males were drawn from the general medical clinic undergoing treatment for minor physical ailments such as headache, fever, and upset stomachs. They were comparable with their alcoholic counterparts in terms of age, family type, and socio-economic status. Their children were also students within the same age range. In the non-alcoholic group there were a total of 62 children. No one in these 30 families had a history of alcohol abuse.

The nature of the study was explained to all family members of both groups and an informed consent was obtained to express their willingness to participate in the study. All 170 children were administered a semi-structured questionnaire to collect data on socio-demographic variables. In addition to the children, other significant family members such as mothers, grandparents, and uncles were interviewed to obtain maximum information on socio-demographic variables. For identification of a case, Rutter's (1966) definition was used, "a condition in which there is abnormality of behavior, emotion or relationship which is sufficiently marked and sufficiently prolonged to cause the child to be impaired in his social functioning and/or to lead to distress or disturbances in the family and community."

The screening and identification of psychiatric problems in these children was determined by administering the Reporting Questionnaire for Children (RQC), a questionnaire designed to identify problem cases in Indian children (Jiloha & Murthy, 1981). Administration of the RQC was followed by detailed psychiatric evaluation of potential cases. The mothers of these children were also interviewed in detail. No specific psychological tests were administered. Two experienced psychiatrists evaluated all positive cases and diagnostic labels were given according to the DSM-IV criteria.

RESULTS

In the 50 families in which the father was receiving treatment for alcohol dependence, there were a total of 108 children. Of these, 30 families had no other elder member living in the extended family abusing alcohol. In this group (Group 1) there were a total of 68 children, 35 boys and 33 girls (see Table 1). In the other 20 families there was an elder member of the extended family abusing alcohol but was not receiving treatment in the de-addiction clinic. This group, Group II, had 40 children, 20 boys and 20 girls. The control group (Group III) of 30 non-alcoholic families had 62 children, 30 boys and 32 girls.

Table 1.   Subject Sample

	Families	Children		
		Male	Female	Total
Group 1	30	35	33	68
Group II	20	20	20	40
Group III	30	30	32	62
Total	80	85	85	170

Assessments of the problem children indicated that some of them fell within one of the following six diagnostic categories: Attention Deficit Hyperactivity Disorder (ADHD), Oppositional Defiant Disorder (ODD), Separation Anxiety Disorder (SAD), Over-Anxious Disorder (QAD) and Drug/Alcohol Abuse (DA). Table 2 shows the frequency of the various disorders within the three groups of children.

Table 2.   Frequency of Psychiatric Disorders

Diagnosis	Group I (n=68)	Group II (n=40)	Group III (n=62)
ADHD	8(11.8)	8(20)	4(6.5)
ODD	4(5.9)	4(10)	2(3.2)
CD	4(5.9)	4(10)	2(3.2)
SAD	8(11.8)	5(12.5)	2(3.2)
OAD	4(5.9)	4(10)	2(3.2)
DA	1(1.8)	3(7.5)	1(1.6)

The frequency of childhood disorders was highest in families where an elder member of the extended was also consuming alcohol (Group II). Twenty percent of the children from this group were diagnosed as having ADHD. In the control group (Group III), the frequency of ADHD among the children was comparatively lower. Only four children (6.5%) out of 62 were diagnosed as having ADHD. Thus the incidence of ADHD was found to be almost three times higher in the families where more than one member abused alcohol than in families where there was no consumption of alcohol. The incidence of ODD in the two groups of families with alcoholics was 5.9% and 10%, respectively; in control group families, it was 3.2 %. The same pattern of occurrence was found for CD and OAD. The percentage of children diagnosed with SAD was only slightly higher in Group II than Group I but lower in the group of non-alcoholic families. The percentage of children diagnosed with DA was almost the same for Groups I and III but almost four times higher among children in Group II.

Table 3 presents the psychiatric diagnoses in relation to gender. ADHD was three times higher among the boys (p<.0000 1) and ODD was four times higher (p<.0[1]). None of the girls in our sample was diagnosed with CD. SAD was 1.5 times higher among girls than boys and it was observed that it was higher among younger girls. The incidence of OAD was the same for both boys and girls. There was no incidence of DA among the girls. Other findings reveal (not depicted in the table) that SAD and ODD were comparatively more common in younger subjects; all substance users were boys who were either 17 or 18 years old; and CD was more common in older males.

Table 3.   Psychiatric Diagnosis by Gender.

Diagnosis	Total	Males	Females
ADHD	20	15(75)	5(25)
ODD	10	8 (80)	2(20)
CD	10	10(100)	0
SAD	15	6(40)	9(60)
OAD)	10	5(50)	5(50)
DA	5	5(100)	0

DISCUSSION

The results of this study are similar to those of other studies. For example, Szatmari (1992) also found a higher incidence of ADHD among boys. Children with ODD were more likely to be younger boys whereas CD occurred in older males. In our study, SAD was more frequent in girls and these findings are similar to the results seen all over the world. It has been found that the girls of alcoholic parents have low self-esteem and higher rates of depression than their male counterparts. While SAD was often found in younger girls, OAD was more common in older girls (Bell-Dolan & Brazeal, 1993). These observations match our findings. The incidence of SA among children in families where more than one family member was abusing alcohol was much higher than among those in families where only the father was abusing alcohol. This suggests that there may be a genetic predisposition towards alcoholism.

All substance users were adolescent males. The finding of a higher incidence of childhood psychopathology among children where the father and other elder members of the family abuse alcohol is not unique to this study as it has been documented in the western literature (Hill & Hruska, 1992; Hill & Muka, 1996). In the Indian context, despite strong family ties and the extended family system, alcohol abuse leaves its impact on the children.

CONCLUSION

Children from families with alcohol dependent fathers and from families in which another elder member was abusing alcohol in addition to alcoholic father, were at increased risk for several psychiatric diagnoses including ADHD, ODD, CD, OAD, and SAD. This risk was much more higher in the second group. Risk of substance abuse was three times higher in the children from the families where father and some other member consumed alcohol as compared to children from families where no one was abusing alcohol. This indicates the potential risk of genetic predisposition as well as the possibility of other environmental interactions that were not measured in this study.

The study raises several treatment issues: Will the successful treatment of parental alcoholism low the risk of psychiatric disorder in the children? Will the successful treatment of a child with a psychiatric disorder who has an alcoholic father and other elders in the family abusing alcohol lower the risk of psychiatric disorder and dependence on alcohol and other drugs.

REFERENCES

American Psychiatric Association. (1994). *Diagnostic and Statistical Manual of Mental Disorders* (4th Ed.). Washington D.C.: Author.

Barrera, M., Chassin, L., & Rogosch, F. (1993). Effects of social support and conflict on adolescent children of alcoholic and non-alcoholic fathers. *Journal of Personality and Social Psychology, 64,* 602-612.

Bell-Dolan, D., & Brazeal, T.J. (1993). Separation anxiety disorder, and school refusal In H.L. Leonard (Ed.), *Anxiety disorders* (pp. 563-578). Philadelphia: Saunders.

Bush, S.I., Ballard, M.E., & Fremouw, W. (1995). Attribution style, depressive features and self-esteem. *Journal of Youth and Adolescence, 24,* 177-185.

Chafetz, M.E., Blaine, H.T., & Hill, M.J. (1971). Children of alcoholics: Observation in a child guidance clinic. *Quarterly Journal of Studies on Alcoholism, 32,* 687-698.

Churchill, J.C., Broida, J.P., & Nicholson, N.L. (1990). Locus of control and self-esteem of adult children of alcoholics. *Journal of Study of Alcohol. 51,* 373-376.

Conolly, G.M., Casswell, S., Stewart, J., Silva, P.A., & O'Brien, M.K. (1993). The effect of parents' alcohol problem on children's behavior as reported by parents and by teachers. *Addiction, 88,* 1383-1390

Earls, F., Reich, W., Jung, K.G., Cloninger, C.R. (1988). Psychopathology in children of alcoholic and antisocial parents. *Alcohol Clinics and Experimentation, 12,* 281-287.

Fergusson, D.M., Lynsky, M.T., Horwood, U. (1994). Childhood exposure to alcohol and adolescent drinking patterns. *Addiction, 89,* 1007-1010.

Garmezy, N., & Masten, A.S. (1994). Chronic adversities. In M. Rutter, E. Taylor, & l. Hersov (Eds.), : *Child and adolescent psychiatry: Modern approaches* (pp. 191-208). London: Blackwell Scientific Publications.

Goodwin, D. W. (1985). *Alcoholism and genetics: The sins of the fathers. Archives of General Psychiatry, 42,*171-174.

Goodwin, D.W., Schulsinger, F., Hermansen, L., Guze, S.B., & Winokur, G. (1975). Alcoholism and the hyperactive child syndrome. *Journal of Nervous and Mental Disorders, 160,* 349-383.

Hill, S.Y., & Hruska, D.R. (1992). Childhood psychopathology in families with multigenerational alcoholism. *Journal of the American Academy of Child and Adolescent Psychiatry, 31,* 1024-1030.

Hill, S.Y., & Muka, D. (1996). Childhood psychopathology in children from families alcoholic

female probands. *Journal of the American Academy of Child and Adolescent Psychiatry*
35, 725-73

Hobson, P. (1997). Understanding persons: The role of affect. In C.S. Baron, F.H. Tager, &
D.J. Cohen (Eds.), *Understanding other minds: Perspective from autism* (pp. 204-227).
New York Oxford Medical Publications.

Jiloha, R.C., & Murthy, R.S. (1981). An epidemiological study of psychiatric problems in
primary school children. *Child Psychiatry Quarterly.*

Jiloha, R.C., & Smita, S. (1994). Influence of family and marital relationship in alcoholism. *10*,
77-82.

Johnston, L.D., O'Malley, P.M., & Bacbman, J.G. (1995). *National survey results on drug use*
from monitoring the future study, 1975-1992. Vol I: Secondary school students.

MaGaha, J.E. (1993). Alcohol and chemically dependent family. *Journal of Offender*
Rehabilitation., 19, 57-69

Merikangas, K.R., Weissman, M.M., Prusoff, B.A., Pauls, D.L., & Leckman, J.F. (1985).
Depressives with secondary alcoholism: Psychiatric disorders in offsprings. *Journal of*
Study of Alcohol, 46, 199-204.

Mohan, D., Sethi, H.S. & Tongue, E. (1995). *Drug abuse in India, Series II.* New Delhi, India:
Jaypee Brothers

Nylander, I. (1960). Children of alcoholic fathers. *Acta Paediatrica, 49,* 5-13.

Reich, W., Earls, F., Frankel, O., & Shyka, J.J. (1993). Psychopathology in children of
alcoholics. *Journal of American Academy of Child and Adolescent Psychiatry, 32,* 995-
1002.

Roosa, M.W., Sandler, I.N., Beals, J., & Short, J.L. (1988). Risk status of adolescent children of
problem - drinking parents. *American Journal of Community Psychology, 16,* 225-241.

Rutter, M. (1966). An epidemiological study of childhood mental disorders. *Psychological*
Medicine, 1, 38-53.

Steinhausen, H.C., Globel, D., & Nestler, V. (1984). Psychopathology in the offspring of
alcoholic parents, *Journal of the American Academy of Child and Adolescent Psychiatry,*
23, 465-471.

Stewart, M.A., DeBlois, C.S., & Cummings, C. (1980). Psychiatric disorders in the parents of
hyperactive boys and those with conduct disorder. *Journal of Child Psychology and*
Psychiatry, 21, 283-292.

Swartzberg, A.Z., & Swartzberg, K.W. (1990). Short-term group psychotherapy with adult
children of alcoholics. *Psychiatric Annals, 2,* 391-394.

Szatmari, P. (1992). The epidemiology of Attention -Deficit Hyperactivity Disorder. In G. Weiss (Ed.), *Attention-Deficit Hyperactivity Disorder* (pp. 361-384). Philadelphia: Saunders.

Tubman, J.O. (1993). A pilot study of school-age children of men with moderate to severe alcohol dependence: Maternal distress and child outcome. *Journal of Child Psychology and Psychiatry, 34,* 729-741.

West, M.O., & Prinz R. (1987). Parental alcoholism and childhood psychopathology. *Psychological Bulletin, 102,* 204-218

16

Psychiatric Comorbidity with Anxiety Disorders in Adolescents: Frequency and Clinical Consequences

Cecilia Essau
Westfaliche Wilhelms-Universitat Munster

Cecelia Essau · Westfalische Wilhelms-Universitat Munster · Psychologisches Institute I · Fliednerstr. 21 · 48149 Munster · Germany.

International Perspectives on Child and Adolescent Mental Health. Volume 2: Proceedings of the Second International Conference, edited by N. N. Singh, T. H. Ollendick, and A. N. Singh. © 2002 Elsevier Science Ltd. All rights reserved.

The term comorbidity was introduced into the medical literature by Feinstein (1970, pp. 456-457) to mean "any distinct additional clinical entity that has existed or that may occur during the clinical course of a patient who has the index disease under study." At a more general level, comorbidity has been defined as the presence of more than one specific disorder in a person in a defined period of time, which can be either cross-sectional (4 weeks, 6 months) or lifetime (Wittchen & Essau, 1993). This approach makes it possible to determine the occurrence and clustering of disorders over the whole life span of a proband. Patterns of comorbidity can be very different in different persons. For example, some individuals have an onset of anxiety prior to another psychiatric disorders and vice versa; others have these disorders at the same time.

Although the concept of comorbidity has been described as far back as the Hippocratic times (Akiskal, 1990), an interest in comorbidity has been associated with the shifts towards the "neo-Kraepelinian" paradigm during the 1970s (Klerman, 1990), and with the advent of the third edition of the Diagnostic and Statistical Manual of Mental Disorders (DSM-III; APA, 1980). DSM provides explicit diagnostic and operationalized diagnoses, which lead to the development of structured interviews and diagnostic algorithms that permit the systematic and reliable assessment of psychiatric disorders. In DSM-IV, there is an increase in the number of specific diagnostic categories instead of the broadly defined classes of disorders (Wittchen & Essau, 1993). Another feature of DSM, which facilitates the study of comorbidity, is the reduction of diagnostic hierarchies, and the provision of separate and multiple axes. The latter permits the possibility of comorbidity between disorders in different axes. These principles have an impact on clinical and research strategies and findings; namely, patients are frequently assigned to more than one diagnostic category.

Current literature on psychiatric disorders (including anxiety disorders) seems to suggest comorbidity as the rule rather than the exception. The degree of comorbidity in adolescents is even more pervasive than in adults (Rohde, et al., 1991). The comorbidity rates, however, vary across studies, possibly due to differences in informants, assessment procedure (e.g., clinical judgment, diagnostic instruments), sample size, diagnostic criteria, age range, gender composition, and developmental processes (Nottelmann & Jensen, 1999).

Despite the pervasiveness of comorbidity between anxiety and other psychiatric disorders, the meaning of comorbidity for psychopathology and classification issues remains unclear. At least three explanations have been suggested to explain for an association between two or more disorders: methodological bias, assessment bias, and etiological issues.

1. Methodological biases include treatment or sampling bias (also known as "Berkson's bias") in which persons with two or more disorders have a greater chance to be hospitalized or treated. As such, the clinic samples generally comprised of individuals with comorbid disorders. This phenomenon arises because the chances of being referred to mental health services are higher for adolescents with a comorbid disorder than for those with only anxiety disorder. Data from clinical samples may also be problematic due to factors affecting referral process such as the presence of parental psychopathology or externalizing disorders (Verhulst & van der Ende, 1993).

2. Assessment bias, which may include the lack of discrete diagnostic definitions in which a large degree of symptoms overlap (e.g., depressed mood, poor appetite, and sleep disturbance may be present in several other disorders) between different diagnostic categories, or the application of diagnostic hierarchies, which may mask an association between disorders (Widiger & Ford-Black, 1994).

3. Another explanation is related to the etiology of disorders. As argued by Merikangas (1989), the co-occurrence of disorders could be etiologic in that one disorder causes the second disorder (i.e., causal association), or that the two disorders are manifestations of the same underlying etiologic factors (i.e., common etiology), or that it may reflect different stages of the same disease.

According to some authors there are some indicators to support the presence of "true" comorbidity. Rutter (1994) argued that the core of every disorder is a struggle for adaptation, but the way in which the phenotype is expressed depends on environmental conditions and person-environment interactions. The former suggest that an index disorder causes or predisposes the development of the subsequent disorders. In order words, the presence of one disorder is the prerequisite condition for the development of the other. Others claimed that developmental processes might contribute to diagnoses of multiple disorders in children and adolescents (Angold & Costello, 1993; Caron & Rutter, 1991; Nottelmann & Jensen, 1995). For example, underlying psychopathology may manifest differently at successive stages of development, but during transition from one to the next developmental stage may show the existence of comorbidity. Nonspecificity in symptom pictures also may contribute to diagnostic comorbidity.

Until this controversy is resolved, the implications of comorbidity need to be examined. Some authors have argued that comorbidity may change the clinical course of the disorder by affecting the time of detection, prognosis, and treatment selection (Regier, et al., 1992).

Assessment and diagnostic procedures may be complicated by the presence of comorbidity. In addition to these clinical implications, studying comorbidity could have implication for nosology and etiological mechanism (Lewinsohn, et al., 1995).

In this chapter, findings on the comorbidity of anxiety disorders (including comorbidity rates, patterns, and sequencing of disorders) and its clinical implication in terms of the psychosocial impairment and mental health services utilization will be summarized. However, before doing so, community studies and the frequency of anxiety disorders will be discussed first.

EPIDEMIOLOGICAL STUDIES

As presented in several review articles, a number of community studies of children and adolescents have been conducted in various countries in the past 15 years (Essau & Dobson, 1999). These studies include: the Isle of Wight Studies (Graham & Rutter, 1973), the New Jersey County Study (Whitaker, et al., 1990), the Midwest Study (Kashani, et al., 1987), the Ontario Child Health Study (Boyle, et al., 1993), the Puerto Rican Child Psychiatry Epidemiologic Study (Bird, et al., 1993), the Dunedin Multidisciplinary Health and Developmental Study (McGee, et al., 1990), the Christchurch Health and Developmental Study (Fergusson, et al., 1993), the Northeastern Study (Reinherz, et al., 1993), the New York Child Longitudinal Study (Cohen, et al., 1993), the Great Smoky Mountains Study (Costello, et al., 1996), the Oregon Adolescent Depression Project (OADP; Lewinsohn, et al., 1994), the Cambridgeshire Study (Cooper & Goodyer, 1993), the Methods for the Epidemiology of Child and Adolescent Mental Disorders Study (Lahey, et al., 1996), and the Bremen Adolescent Study (Essau, 1999). Although these studies have contributed to our understanding of the prevalence and nature (e.g., risk factors) of anxiety and psychiatric disorders in youths, only a few of them have data on the comorbidity of anxiety disorders. Since most of the data in this chapter come from the OADP and the Bremen Adolescent Study, the design of these two studies will be reviewed.

The Oregon Adolescent Depression Project

A total of 1710 high school students (mean age = 16.6 years) in three cohorts (1987, 1988, 1989) were recruited for the Oregon Adolescent Depression Project (OADP; Lewinsohn, et al., 1993, 1994). The schools were located in two urban communities with a population of about 200,000, and three rural communities in West Central Oregon. The schools were chosen because of their locations, all being within 100 miles from the project center. Sampling was designed based on parental consent and proportional stratification according to gender, grade, and school size.

Participants were interviewed once (T1), between the ages of 14 and 18, and again approximately one year later (T2). Demographic characteristics of the sample at T1 were as follows: the average age of the participants was 16.6 (SD = 1.2), approximately half the participants were female (53%), and most participants were white (91%). A third wave of assessments (T3) has been completed at age 24. Adolescent reports on the Schedule for Affective Disorders and Schizophrenia for School-Age Children (K-SADS; Puig-Antich & Chambers, 1983) were used at T1 to make diagnoses of current and past DSM-III-R disorders. The Longitudinal Interval Follow-Up Evaluation (LIFE; Shapiro & Keller, 1979) was used to obtain diagnostic information at T2 and T3. The assessment at T3 provides information on rates of psychopathology and psychosocial impairments in a community sample of adolescents followed into adulthood.

The Bremen Adolescent Study

The Bremen Adolescent Study is a longitudinal study of the epidemiology of psychiatric disorders among 12-17 year olds (Essau, 1999; Essau, Conradt, & Petermann, 2000). The specific aims of the study are to estimate the prevalence, risks, course and outcome of psychiatric disorders, to determine their age of onset and severity, to examine the comorbidity patterns of disorders, and associated psychosocial impairment, as well as service utilization patterns.

A model of health and functioning, proposed by Boyle, et al. (1996), was used to help guide the selection of concepts for measurement (see Figure 1) included in the study. The term "determinants" refers to risk or protective factors that may include characteristics of individuals or their environments that contribute to changes in health status. The assessment of "determinants" was restricted to some important characteristics of the adolescent's family of origin. "Health status" refers to the presence of psychiatric disorder, whereas "correlates" are associated features of disorders. The "correlates" selected focus on the adolescent's sociodemographic and psychological characteristics. The "psychiatric disorders" examined included in addition to anxiety disorders are depressive, somatoform, and substance use disorders; they have been chosen because of their features that include their high prevalence, early onset, severity, and chronicity. "Consequences" are byproducts of changes to health status that focus on impairment and utilization of mental health services. "Impairment" focuses on interference of functioning in important life areas relative to usual standards of attainment and performance. "Utilization of services" refers to the use of inpatient and outpatient services due to mental health and/or alcohol or drug problems. The main concepts included in the Bremen Adolescent Study are presented in Table 1.

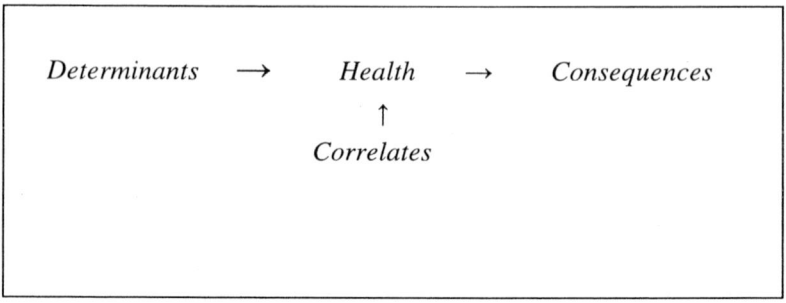

Figure 1.   Model of health and functioning

In order to provide a well-differentiated picture of the adolescents, multiple sources of information were used:

a) A structured diagnostic interview (computerized Munich version of the Composite International Diagnostic Interview; CAPI; Wittchen & Pfister, 1997) to assess anxiety and other psychiatric disorders according to DSM-IV (APA, 1994) and ICD-10 (World Health Organization; WHO, 1993). The interview, which was supplemented by a separate respondent's booklet, comprised of several scales (Bremer Interview Schedule for Adolescents, Bremer Life Event and Problem Solving Alternative Scale, and Premenstrual Syndrome Questionnaire [Essau, 1999]) was conducted individually with each adolescent.

b) Self-administered questionnaires (Perceived Control Scale [Weisz, et al., 1993], Self-perception Profile for Adolescents [Harter, 1988], SCL-90-R [Derogatis, et al., 1977], and Parent and Peer Attachment scale [Armsden & Greenberg, 1987]) evaluating current functioning and psychosocial constructs. These questionnaires were administered to the adolescents at an average of three days after the interview;

Table 1.   Concepts included in the Bremen Adolescent Study

Constructs		Operationalization
Determinants	Parental psychopathology	CAPI
	Parental conflict leading to divorce	CAPI; Household Questionnaire; Family Dysfunction scale
	Early childhood experience	CAPI
Correlates	Sociodemographic features	CAPI
	Psychological characteristics	
	- control orientation	Perceived Control Scale
	- perceived competence	Self-perception Profile for Adolescents
	- parent-peer attachment	Parent and Peer Attachment scale
	Life events and coping	Bremen Life Event; Problem Solving Alternative Scale
Psychiatric disorders/ Symptoms	Anxiety disorders, Depressive disorders,	CAPI
	Substance use and Somatoform disorders,	CAPI
	Conduct and oppositional defiant disorder,	Bremer Interview Schedule for Adolescents
	Attention-Deficit/Hyperactivity Disorder	Bremer Interview Schedule for Adolescents
	Premenstrual Syndrome	Premenstrual Syndrome Questionnaire
	Psychological distress	SCL-90-R
Impairment	Interference of functioning with daily activities	CAPI, Columbia Impairment Scale
Utilization of mental health services	Inpatient and outpatient utilization	CAPI

Note: CAPI = computer-assisted personal interview of the Munich version of the Composite International Diagnostic Interview

c) Information from parents about themselves (e.g., education, occupation, health status), their family and the child via a set of questionnaire, which they completed at their home. These questionnaires comprised the Problem Checklist for Parents and Household Questionnaire (Essau, 1999), the Revised Dimensions of Temperament Survey (Windel & Lerner, 1986), and the McMaster Family Assessment Device - Family Dysfunction scale (Epstein, Baldwin, & Bishop, 1983).

Adolescents were administered the computerized Munich version of the Composite International Diagnostic Interview (Wittchen & Pfister, 1997) to make diagnosis of current and past disorders according to DSM-IV. Participants were randomly recruited from 36 schools in Bremen, Germany. Data collection for the first wave of the study took place between 1996 and 1997, and for the second wave, about 15 months later, between 1997 and 1998 (see Table 2). The first wave of the study was comprised of 1,035 adolescents (421 males and 614 females), and the second wave consisted of 523 adolescents (195 males and 328 females).

Table 2.   Sociodemographic characteristics of the adolescent in the Bremen Adolescent Study

	T1 Interview N	T1 Interview (%)	T2 Interview N	T2 Interview (%)
X Gender				
boys	421	(40.7)	195	(37.3)
girls	614	(59.3)	328	(62.7)
X Age (years)				
12	223	(21.5)	-	
13	157	(15.2)	97	(18.5)
14	161	(15.6)	110	(21.0)
15	189	(18.3)	102	(19.5)
16	166	(16.0)	92	(17.5)
17	139	(13.4)	54	(10.3)
18	-		52	(9.9)
19	-		16	(3.0)

Table 2 continued.

	T1 Interview		T2 Interview	
	N	(%)	N	(%)
X Type of education				
"Orientierungsstufe"*	226	(21.8)	01	(0.2)
"Hauptschule"**	116	(11.2)	46	(11.5)
"Realschule"***	195	(18.8)	86	(21.5)
"Gymnasium"****	299	(28.9)	177	(44.3)
"Others"*****	199	(19.2)	89	(22.3)

Note: *primary school; **=mandatory basic school; ***=an intermediate type of advanced school between "Gymnasium" and "Hauptschule"; ****=secondary education between ages 10 and 19 which prepares students for entrance to university; *****=Various types of professional schools.

RESEARCH FINDINGS

Frequency of Anxiety Disorders

Recent epidemiological studies have shown anxiety disorders to be one of the most common disorders in adolescents. As shown in our Bremen Adolescent Study (Essau, et al., 2000), 18.6% of the adolescents met the lifetime diagnosis of any anxiety disorders. In Wittchen, et al.'s (1998) study, a lifetime prevalence of anxiety disorders was 14.4%. Much lower rates have been reported by Lewinsohn, et al. (1993) and Fergusson, et al. (1993); the values being 8.8% and 10.8%, respectively. The 6-month rates of anxiety disorders reported by Verhulst, et al. (1997) was 23.5% and by Wittchen, et al. (1998) 9.3%. The current rates have been reported to range from 2.7% to 10.8% (Canals, et al., 1997; Fergusson, et al., 1993). Differences in sampling procedures, age and gender composition, assessment instruments, and the number of anxiety disorders included in the analysis could account for the differences in the prevalence of anxiety disorders.

Comorbid Patterns in Anxiety Disorders

The co-occurrence of anxiety with other disorders in adolescents is a new area of investigation. However, existing studies seem to indicate the comorbidity of anxiety and other psychiatric disorders is a rather common phenomenon (see reviews by Emmelkamp & Scholing, 1997; Nottelman & Jensen, 1999). Anxiety disorders occur frequently in adolescents with depressive disorders, conduct disorder, oppositional defiant disorder, attention-deficit/hyperactivity disorder, and alcohol abuse or dependence (Bird, Gould, & Staghezza, 1993; Cohen, Cohen, Kasen, et al., 1993; Lewinsohn, Zinbarg, Seeley, Lewinsohn, & Sack, 1997; Rohde, Lewinsohn, & Seeley, 1991). In Lewinsohn, et al.'s (1997) study, 70.1% of the anxiety cases also met diagnosis of other psychiatric disorders. Among adolescents with comorbid disorders, most of them met the diagnosis of major depression (53.7%) and alcohol abuse/dependence (11.9%). Indeed, anxiety disorders are even more likely to be comorbid with depression than with another anxiety disorders.

In the Bremen Adolescent Study (Essau, et al., 2000), 48.9% of the adolescents with anxiety disorders met criteria for any anxiety disorder only (i.e., pure anxiety cases), 36.4% had one additional disorder, and 14.5% had at least two other disorders. 30.2% of the anxious adolescents with comorbid disorders met the lifetime diagnosis of depressive disorders and 26.6% the lifetime diagnosis of somatoform disorders; the comorbidity rates between anxiety and substance use disorders was much lower, being 11.5% (see Table 3). The odds ratios were significant between anxiety and depressive disorders, as well as between anxiety and somatoform disorders. However, when boys and girls were analyzed separately, the most common pattern in boys was that of anxiety and substance use disorders, and in girls between anxiety and depression.

Table 3. Comorbidity of Anxiety Disorders (N = 192) and Other Psychiatric Disorders[1]

	N	Any Anxiety Disorders (%)	OR	95% CI
Depressive Disorders	58	(30.21)	2.44***	1.69 - 3.50
Major Depression	47	(24.48)	2.46***	1.67 - 3.64
Dysthymic Disorder	15	(7.81)	1.57	0.86 - 2.90
Somatoform Disorders	51	(26.56)	3.22***	2.18 - 4.77
Undifferentiated Disorder	42	(21.88)	2.99***	1.97 - 4.56
Conversion Disorder	4	(2.08)	1.78	0.55 - 5.71
Pain Disorder	6	(3.13)	2.23	0.83 - 6.02
Substance Use Disorders	22	(11.46)	0.91	0.56 - 1.48
Alcohol Use Disorders	17	(8.85)	0.94	0.54 - 1.63
Cannabis Use Disorders	16	(8.33)	1.44	0.80 - 2.59
Amphetamine Use Disorders	2	(1.04)	4.43	0.62 - 31.62
Halluzinogen Use Disorders	2	(1.04)	2.21	0.40 - 12.14

[1]Comorbidity rates were presented without taking into account the hierarchical rules; * $p < 0.05$; ** $p < 0.01$; *** $p < 0.001$

Compared to a rather high degree of comorbidity between anxiety and other disorders, the comorbidity rates among the anxiety disorders were relatively low. In the Bremen Adolescent Study (Essau, 1999), the level of comorbidity among the anxiety disorders was relatively low in that the majority (85.9%) of the anxiety cases had only one type of anxiety disorder. The most frequent comorbid patterns within the anxiety disorders were that of panic and posttraumatic stress disorder, and panic and generalized anxiety disorder, as well as between obsessive-compulsive disorder and specific phobia. The low comorbidity rate within the anxiety disorders can be interpreted as lending support for the different subtypes of anxiety disorders as appeared in DSM. Similar results have been reported by Lewinsohn, et al. (1997). In that study, 81.3% adolescents with a lifetime anxiety disorder were diagnosed as having only one anxiety disorder, 15.7% had 2 and 4.3% had 3 subtypes of anxiety disorders. Angold and Costello (1995) found no association between phobic and panic disorders. Costello, et al. (1993) even showed a negative association between phobic disorder and overanxious anxiety disorder/generalized anxiety disorder and separation anxiety disorder. However, in some clinical studies (Francis, et al., 1992; Last, et al., 1992; Strauss & Last, 1993), high comorbidity rates were found between avoidant disorder and social phobia. This finding has been interpreted as suggesting these disorders as not being separate disorders and therefore justifies the changes made in DSM-IV where avoidant disorder is being subsumed under social phobia.

Temporal Sequencing of Disorders

Studying the temporal order of disorders is important. As Lewinsohn, et al. (1991) put it "comorbid disorders may constitute an etiological trigger, a prodromal manifestation, or a residual stage for the other disorders" (pp. 205). Furthermore, knowledge about the temporal sequence of disorders may have nosologic implication. As mentioned earlier, the most common comorbid conditions are that of anxiety and depression. Similar to those found in adult studies, anxiety disorders were more likely to precede rather than to follow depression. For example, in the Bremen Adolescent Study, 72% of the adolescents with both these disorders had anxiety before that of depression (Essau, 1999); only 12% had depression before anxiety, and 16% had anxiety and depression within the same year. Considering the subtypes of anxiety disorders, half of those with agoraphobia and generalized anxiety disorder first had these disorders before that of major depression. All of those with social and specific phobia had these two subtypes of anxiety disorders before that of depression. About half of those with panic disorder and depression experienced the onset of these disorders within the same year.

In the OADP (Rohde, et al., 1991) study, 85% of comorbid cases with anxiety and depression had an anxiety disorder before that of depression. The anxiety disorders that precede depression are simple phobia, separation anxiety, overanxious disorder, and social phobia (Lewinsohn, et al., 1997). Their data also indicated that 42% of the anxiety disorder cases at the index investigation met the diagnosis of a depressive disorder at a follow-up interview (Orvaschel, et al., 1995). By contrast, only 6.5% of the depressed cases at the index interview had an anxiety disorder at a follow-up interview.

Clinical Impact of Comorbidity

Although several authors have argued that comorbidity may have important clinical implications, hardly any studies have gone beyond investigating the frequency of comorbidity of anxiety disorders. While the meaning of comorbidity remains unclear, the presence of comorbid disorders in anxiety disorders seems to have negative consequences on functioning, especially with impaired role functioning, and academic problems. In our study (Essau, 1999), the impact of comorbidity with regards to psychological distress (measured using the SCL-90-R) and the use of mental health services were examined. As shown in Table 4, the non-disordered group had the lowest means on almost all the subscales, and the anxiety cases with at least 2 comorbid disorders the highest. The findings also showed the mean scores of SCL-90-R to increase with the number of comorbid disorders. A closer look at the result showed no significant difference between the non-disordered and only anxiety group, except for phobic anxiety. Anxiety cases with at least 2 comorbid disorders had significantly higher scores than those with pure anxiety, and those with anxiety and one disorder in all the SCL-90-R subscales, except for phobic anxiety and psychoticism.

Table 4. Psychological Distress and Anxiety Disorders

	No Disorders (N=512) M (SD)	Only Anxiety (N=78) M (SD)	Anxiety + 1 Disorder (N=60) M (SD)	Anxiety + 2 Disorders (N=23) M (SD)
Somatization	5.68 (4.9)[a]	6.85 (4.6)[ab]	8.68 (7.1)[b]	13.39 (8.8)[c] ***
Obsessive-compulsive behavior	5.39 (4.5)[a]	6.63 (5.0)[ab]	8.27 (6.6)[b]	11.04 (5.8)[c] ***
Interpersonal sensitivity	4.93 (4.7)[a]	5.96 (4.5)[a]	8.22 (6.3)[b]	10.96 (6.4)[c] ***

Table 4 continued.

	No Disorders (N=512) M (SD)	Only Anxiety (N=78) M (SD)	Anxiety + 1 Disorder (N=60) M (SD)	Anxiety + 2 Disorders (N=23) M (SD)
Depression	6.16 (5.8)[a]	7.29 (5.5)[a]	9.97 (8.4)[b]	16.43 (9.8)[c] ***
Anxiety	4.48 (4.3)[a]	5.28 (4.1)[a]	7.57 (6.2)[b]	11.26 (7.2)[c] ***
Hostility	3.17 (3.3)[a]	3.77 (3.3)[a]	5.89 (5.1)[b]	9.47 (4.9)[c] ***
Phobic Anxiety	1.38 (2.2)[a]	2.47 (3.2)[b]	2.73 (3.2)[b]	3.26 (2.4)[b] ***
Paranoid ideation	3.28 (3.3)[a]	3.83 (3.2)[a]	5.47 (4.3)[b]	6.83 (3.4)[c] ***
Psychoticism	3.49 (5.3)[a]	3.27 (5.1)[a]	6.75 (7.7)[b]	8.48 (5.6)[b] **

Note: Means having different subscripts significantly differed on the ANOVA;
      *** p < 0.001

Which comorbid pattern was associated with the highest level of psychological distress? For this purpose, three groups of adolescents were formed: anxiety and depression, anxiety and substance use disorders, and anxiety and somatoform disorders. Our finding showed no significant group differences on any of the SCL-90-R scales. However, there were trends showing cases with anxiety and somatoform disorders to have higher scores on obsessive-compulsive behavior, interpersonal sensitivity, depression, hostility, and paranoid ideation. Scales related to somatization, anxiety, phobic anxiety, psychoticism were higher in the anxiety and depression group.

The next question of interest was related to the impact of the temporal sequence of disorders and impairment level. When concentrating on those with anxiety and depression, our result showed that the cases that reported the onset of depression first before that of anxiety were the most distressed compared to those who had anxiety first before depression or those who had these two disorders at the same year. These cases had the highest scores on all the SCL-90-R.

Although a high number of those with an anxiety disorder were highly impaired in various life domains, only a small portion of the anxiety cases did receive professional help (Essau, et al., 1999). The extent to which help was sought tended to be affected by the presence of comorbid disorders. As shown in Figure 2, the frequency of using any mental health services increased with the number of comorbid disorders. 10.6% (N=10) of the pure anxiety cases reported having sought professional help due to emotional or psychiatric problems, compared to 22.9% (N=16) of anxious cases with one comorbid disorder, and to 32.1% (N=9) of those with at least two

388

comorbid disorders. The association between comorbid disorders and mental health services utilization was stronger in males than in females. That is, only one male in the pure anxiety group, compared to 22 of those with one comorbid disorder, and to 8 with at least 2 comorbid disorders. Among females, 9 with pure anxiety disorder, and 12 with one comorbid disorder, and 6 with at least 2 comorbid disorders did seek professional help for emotional or psychiatric problems.

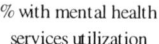

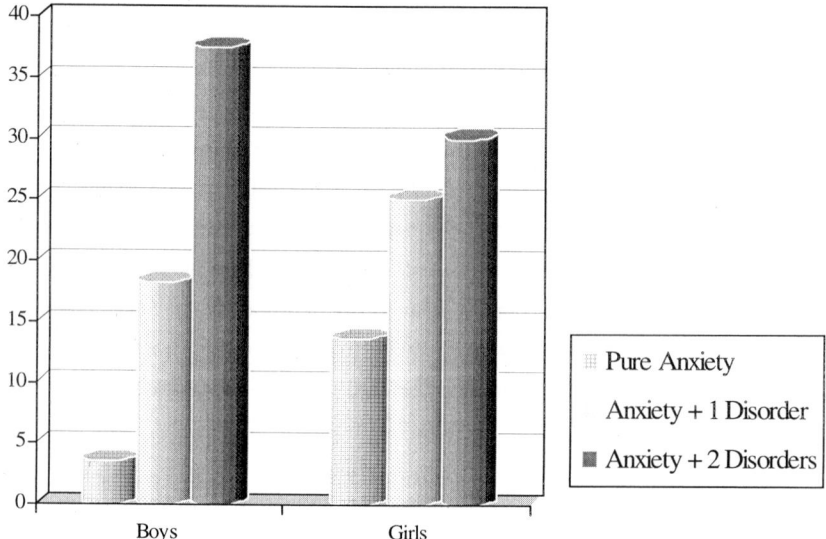

Figure 2   Anxiety disorders and mental health service utilization

Among the different comorbidity patterns, mental health services utilization was the highest among those with anxiety and depression (26.5%), followed by those with anxiety and somatoform disorders (20%). This is interesting given the finding that anxious adolescents with somatoform disorders were most impaired.

In the OADP study, although the rate of treatment utilization increased with the number of comorbid disorders, treatment seeking was not related to comorbid pattern (Lewinsohn, et al., 1995). This means that the adolescent's tendency to receive treatment was not affected by the presence of any specific combination of disorders, but by the number of disorders. Adolescents with anxiety disorders with a comorbid substance use disorders (66.7%) and those with a comorbid disruptive behavior (66.7%) were most frequently associated with treatment utilization. Only 18.4% of the pure cases of anxiety disorders received treatment. The greatest impact of comorbidity was found for academic problems, use of mental health services, and previous suicide attempts. Poor global role functioning and conflicts with parents were moderately influenced by comorbidity.

Comorbidity and Course and Outcome of Anxiety Disorders

Of interest was the impact of comorbidity in the course and outcome of anxiety disorders at follow-up investigation. In our study (Essau, 1999), adolescents who had anxiety disorders during the index interview were divided into those who had comorbid disorders (n = 48) and those who did not (n = 56). As shown in Figure 3, adolescents with comorbid anxiety disorders were more likely than those with pure anxiety to develop anxiety, depressive and somatoform disorders at a follow-up investigation, conducted at an average of 15 months later.

The comorbid group was also the least likely to recover from their anxiety during the 15-month assessment period. Further analysis also showed the presence of comorbid somatoform and substance use disorders as significant predictors for the stability of anxiety disorders.

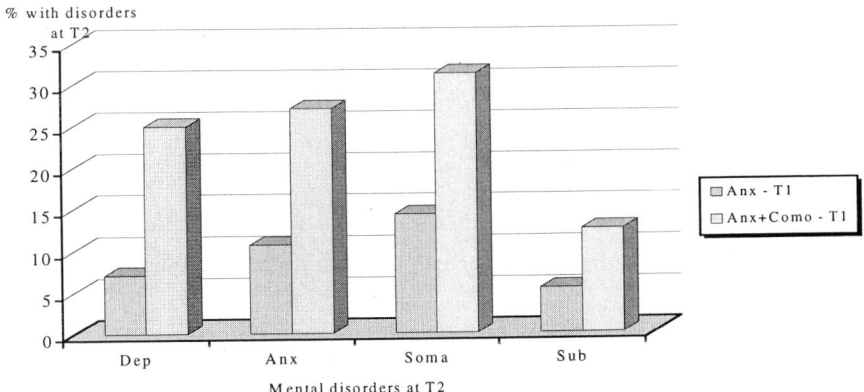

Figure 3. Mental disorders (at T2) among T1-anxiety cases (pure or with comorbid disorders)

CONCLUSIONS

The main aim of this chapter has been to present findings on the frequency and patterns of comorbidity of anxiety disorders and its clinical consequences. The degree of comorbidity of anxiety disorders and other psychiatric disorders, especially with depression, was a frequent phenomenon. Given the finding on the strong and frequent association between anxiety and depression, some models have been proposed to explain for the relationship between these two disorders. For example, Clark and Watson's (1991) tripartite model suggested that anxiety and depressive disorders share a nonspecific component of generalized affective distress or negative affect. Features related to "anhedonia or diminished positive affect" are specific to depression, whereas those related to "physiological symptoms of hyperarousal" are specific to anxiety.

Among adolescents with both anxiety and depression, anxiety most often developed first before that of depression. Alloy, et al. (1990) suggested that the temporal sequence of disorders might correspond to the manner in which individuals respond to life stress. That is, the experiences of uncertainty about the ability to control outcomes (i.e., uncertain helplessness), generally lead to the feeling of "aroused anxiety." If this lack of control increases (i.e., certain helplessness), a state of mixed "anxiety-depression" is experienced. Finally, when an individual's sense of control is diminished (i.e., hopelessness) and there is certainty of a negative outcome, a depressive state is experienced.

The meaning of comorbidity for psychopathology and classification issues remains unanswered. However, our findings seem to indicate that the presence of comorbid disorders in anxiety may have important clinical impact. First, both the impairment level and the use of mental health services by the anxiety cases increased with the number of comorbid disorders, especially in males more so than in females. The fact that treatment utilization was highly associated with the number of comorbid disorders may suggest that adolescents with multiple disorders are overpresented in clinical settings. This finding stresses the importance of conducting a comprehensive assessment, not only for the disorder for which they have been referred for but also other disorders. Second, the high degree of comorbidity also suggests the need to use intervention to deal with cases with multiple disorders.

REFERENCES

Alloy, L.B., Kelly, K.A., Mineka, S., & Clements, C.M. (1990). Comorbidity in anxiety and depressive disorders: A helplessness-hopelessness perspective. In J.D. Maser & C.R. Cloninger (Eds.), *Comorbidity of mood and anxiety disorders* (pp. 499-544). Washington, DC: American Psychiatric Press.

American Psychiatric Association. (1980). *Diagnostic and statistical manual of mentaldDisorders* (3rd ed.). Washington, DC: Author

American Psychiatric Association. (1994). *Diagnostic and statistical manual of mental disorders* (4th ed.). Washington, DC: Author.

Angold, A., & Costello, E.J. (1993). Depressive comorbidity in children and adolescents: Empirical, theoretical, and methodological issues. *American Journal Psychiatry, 150,* 1779-1791.

Akiskal, H.S. (1990). Toward a clinical understanding of the relationship of anxiety and depressive disorders. In J.D. Maser & C.R. Cloninger (Eds.), *Comorbidity of mood and anxiety disorders* (pp. 597-610). Washington, DC: American Psychiatric Press.

Armsden, G.C., & Greenberg, M.T. (1987). The inventory of parent and peer attachment: Individual differences and their relationship to psychological well-being in adolescence. *Journal of Youth and Adolescence, 16,* 427-453.

Bird, H.R., Gould, M.S., & Staghezza, B.M. (1993). Patterns of diagnostic comorbidity in a community sample of children aged 9 through 16 years. *Journal of the American Academy of Child and Adolescent Psychiatry, 32,* 361-368.

Boyle, M.H., Offord, D.R., Campbell, D., Catlin, G., Goering, P., Lin, E., & Racine, Y.A. (1996). Mental health supplement to the Ontario Health Survey: Methodology. *Canadian Journal of Psychiatry, 41,* 549-558.

Boyle, M.H., Offord, D.R., Racine, Y., Fleming, J.E., Szatmari, P., & Sanford, M. (1993). Evaluation of the revised Ontario Child Health Study scales. *Journal of Child Psychology and Psychiatry, 34,* 189-213.

Canals, J., Domenech, E., Carbajo, G., & Blade, J. (1997). Prevalence of DSM-III-R and ICD-10 psychiatric disorders in a Spanish population of 18-year-olds. *Acta Psychiatrica Scandinavica, 96,* 287-294.

Caron, C., & Rutter, M. (1991). Comorbidity in child psychopathology: Concepts, issues, and research strategies. *Journal Child Psychology and Psychiatry, 32,* 1063-1080.

Clark, L.A., & Watson, D. (1991). Tripartite model of anxiety and depression: Psychometric evidence and taxonomic implications. *Journal of Abnormal Psychology, 100,* 316-336.

Cohen, P., Cohen, J., Kasen, S., Velez, C.N., Hartmark, C., Johnson, J., Rojas, M., Brook, J., & Streuning, E.L. (1993). An epidemiological study of disorders in late childhood and adolescence - I: Age- and gender-specific prevalence. *Journal of Child Psychology and Psychiatry, 34,* 851-866.

Cooper, P.J., & Goodyer, I.M. (1993). A community study of depression in adolescent girls. I. Estimates of symptom and syndrome prevalence. *British Journal of Psychiatry, 163,* 369-374.

Derogatis, L.R. (1977). *SCL-90-R, administration, scoring & procedures manual für die (Revised) version.* Baltimore, MD: Johns Hopkins University School of Medicine.

Emmelkamp, P.M.G., & Scholing, A. (1997). Anxiety disorders. In C.A. Essau & F. Petermann (Eds.), *Developmental psychopathology: Epidemiology, diagnostics and treatment* (pp. 219-263). London: Harwood.

Epstein, N.B., Baldwin, L.M., & Bishop, D.S. (1983). The McMaster Family Assessment Device. *Journal of Marital and Family Therapy, 9,* 171-180.

Essau, C.A., Conradt, J., & Petermann, F. (2000). Frequency, comorbidity, and psychosocial impairment of anxiety disorders in adolescents. *Journal of Anxiety Disorders, 14,* 263-279.

Essau, C.A., & Dobson, K.S. (1999). Epidemiology of depressive disorders. In C.A. Essau & F. Petermann (Eds.), *Depressive disorders in children and adolescents: Epidemiology, risk factors, and treatment* (pp. 69-103). New Jersey: Jason Aronson, Inc. Publishers.

Fergusson, D.M., Horwood, L.J., & Lynskeyl, M.T. (1993). Prevalence and comorbidity of DSM-III-R diagnoses in a birth cohort of 15 year olds. *Journal of the American Academy of Child and Adolescent Psychiatry, 32,* 1127-1134.

Francis, G., Last, C.G., & Strauss, C.C. (1992). Avoidant disorder and social phobia in children and adolescents. *Journal of the American Academy of Child and Adolescent Psychiatry, 31,* 1086-1089.

Harter, S. (1988). *Manual: Self-Perception Profile for Adolescents.* Denver, CO: Universty of Denver.

Kashani, J.H., Carlson, G.A., Beck, N.C., Hoeper, E.W., Corcoran, C.M., McAllister, J.A., Fallahi, C., Rosenberg, T.K., & Reid, J.C. (1987). Depression, depressive symptoms, and depressed mood among a community sample of adolescents. *American Journal of Psychiatry, 144,* 931-934.

Klerman, G.L. (1990). Approaches to the phenomena of comorbidity. In J.D. Maser & C.R.

Cloninger (Eds.), *Comorbidity of mood and anxiety disorders* (pp. 13-40). Washington, DC: American Psychiatric Press.

Last, C.G., Perrin, S., Hersen, M., & Kazdin, A.E. (1992). DSM-III-R anxiety disorders in children: Sociodemographic and clinical characteristics. *Journal of the American Academy of Child and Adolescent Psychiatry, 29,* 31-35.

Lewinsohn, P.M., Hops, H., Roberts, R.E., Seeley, J.R., & Andrews, J.A. (1993). Adolescent psychopathology: I. Prevalence and incidence of depression and other DSM-III-R disorders in high school students. *Journal of Abnormal Psychology, 102,* 133-144.

Lewinsohn, P.M., Clarke, G.N., Seeley, J.R., & Rohde, P. (1994). Major depression in community adolescents: Age of onset, episode duration, and time to recurrence. *Journal of the American Academy of Child and Adolescent Psychiatry, 33,* 809-819.

Lewinsohn, P.M., Zinbarg, R., Seeley, J.R., Lewinsohn, M., & Sack, W.H. (1997). Lifetime comorbidity among anxiety disorders and between anxiety disorders and other mental disorders in adolescents. *Journal of Anxiety Disorders, 11,* 377-394.

Lewinsohn, P.M., Rohde, P., & Seeley, J.R. (1995). Adolescent psychopathology: III. The clinical consequences ob comorbidity. *Journal of the American Academy of Child and Adolescent Psychiatry, 34,* 510-519.

McGee, R., Feehan, M., Williams, S., Partridge, F., Silva, P.A., & Kelly, J. (1990). DSM-III disorders in a large sample of adolescents. *Journal of the American Academy of Child and Adolescent Psychiatry, 29,* 611-619.

Merikangas, K. R. (1989). Comorbidity for anxiety and depression: Review of family and genetic studies. In J.D. Maser & C.R. Cloninger (Eds.), *Comorbidity of mood and anxiety disorders* (pp. 331-348). Washington, DC: American Psychiatric Press, Inc.

Nottelmann, E.D., & Jensen, P.S. (1999). Comorbidity of depressive disorders in children and adolescents: Rates, temporal sequencing, course and outcome. In C.A. Essau & F. Petermann (Eds.), *Depressive disorders in children and adolescents: Epidemiology, risk factors, and treatment.* Northvale, NJ: Jason Aronson.

Orvaschel, H., Lewinsohn, P.M., & Seeley, J.R. (1995). Continuity of psychopathology in a community sample of adolescents. *Journal of the American Academy of Child and Adolescent Psychiatry, 34,* 1525-1535.

Puig-Antich, J., & Chambers, W. (1983). *The Schedule for Affective Disorders and Schizophrenia for School-aged Children (6-18).* New York: State Psychiatric Institute, New York.

Reinherz, H.Z., Giaconia, R.M., Lefkowitz, E.S., Pakiz, B., & Frost, A.K. (1993). Prevalence of psychiatric disorders in a community population of older adolescents. *Journal of the American Academy of Child and Adolescent Psychiatry, 32,* 369-377.

Rohde, P., Lewinsohn, P.M., & Seeley, J.R. (1991). Comorbidity of unipolar depression: II. Comorbidity with other mental disorders in adolescents and adults. *Journal of Abnormal Psychology, 100,* 214-222.

Rutter, M. (1994). Comorbidity: Meanings and mechanisms. *Clinical Psychology: Science and Practice, 1,* 100-103.

Shapiro, R., & Keller, M. (1979). *Longitudinal Interval Follow-up Evaluation (LIFE).* Unpublished manuscript.

Strauss, C.C. & Last, C.G. (1993). Social and simple phobias in children. *Journal of Anxiety Disorders, 7,* 141-152.

Verhulst, F.C., & van der Ende, J. (1997). Factors associated with child mental health service use in the community. *Journal of the American Academy of Child and Adolescent Psychiatry, 36,* 901-909.

Weisz, J.R., Sweeny, L., Proffitt,V., & Carr, T. (1993). Control-related beliefs and self-reported depressive symptoms in late childhood. *Journal of Abnormal Psychology, 102,* 411-418.

Whitaker, A., Johnson, J., Shaffer, D., Rapoport, J.L., Kalikow, K., Walsh, B.T., Davies, M., Braiman, S., & Dolinsky, A. (1990). Uncommon troubles in young people: Prevalence estimates of selected psychiatric disorders in a nonreferred population. *Archives of General Psychiatry, 47,* 487-496.

Widiger, T.A., & Ford-Black, M.M. (1994). Diagnoses and disorders. *Clinical Psychology: Science Practice, 1,* 84-87.

Windle, M., & Lerner, R.M. (1986). Reassessing the dimensions of temperamental individuality across the life span: The Revised Dimensions of Temperament Survey (DOTS-R). *Journal of Adolescent Research, 1,* 213-230.

Wittchen, H.-U., & Essau, C.A. (1993). Mixed anxiety-depressive disorders: Is there an epidemiological evidence? *Journal of Clinical Psychiatry,* 54, 9-15.

Wittchen, H.U., Nelson, C.B., & Lachner, G. (1998). Prevalence of mental disorders and psychosocial impairments in adolescents and young adults. *Psychological Medicine, 28,* 109-126.

Wittchen, H.U., & Pfister, H. (1997). *DIA-X-Manual: Instrumentsmanual zur Durchführung von DIA-X-Interviews.* Frankfurt: Swets & Zeitlinger.

17

Symptom Patterns of Children and Adolescents with Chronic Fatigue Syndrome

Katherine S. Rowe
Royal Children's Hospital

Kenneth J. Rowe
The University of Melbourne

Katherine S. Rowe · Department of General Pediatrics · Royal Children's Hospital · Flemington Road
Parkville · Victoria 3052 · Australia.

*International Perspectives on Child and Adolescent Mental Health. Volume 2: Proceedings of the Second International
Conference*, edited by N. N. Singh, T. H. Ollendick, and A. N. Singh. © 2002 Elsevier Science Ltd. All rights reserved.

Chronic Fatigue Syndrome (CFS) is a condition of unknown etiology, characterized by extreme fatigue exacerbated by minimal physical activity. In addition, symptoms such as difficulty with concentration, headache and sleep disturbance, muscle aches and pains and recurrent sore throat are common (Fukuda, et al., 1994; Holmes, et al., 1988; Lloyd, Wakefield, Boughton, & Dwyer, 1988). CFS is predominantly an illness of young adults. Although it has been reported in adolescents and children (Bell, 1995, 1997; Bell, Bell, & Cheney, 1994; Carter, Edwards, Kronenberger, Michalczyk, & Marshall, 1995; de Jong, et al., 1997; Feder, Dworkin, & Orkin, 1994; Franklin, 1998; Krilov, Fisher, Friedman, Reitman, & Mandel, 1998; Lask & Dillon, 1990; Marshal, 1999; Rowe, 1997a; Rowe & Rowe, 1999a, 1999b; Smith, et al., 1991), most research related to CFS (including diagnostic criteria and definition of the syndrome) has been undertaken with adults (Demitrack, 1998a, 1998b; Demitrack, et al. 1991; Fukuda, et al., 1994; Holmes, et al. 1988; Hickie, et al., 1995; Komaroff & Buchwald, 1991, 1998; Lloyd, Hickie, Boughton, Spencer & Wakefield, 1990; Lloyd, Hickie, Dwyer & Wakefield, 1992; Lloyd, Wakefield, Boughton & Dwyer, 1988; Natelson, et al., (1998); Vercoulen, et al., 1994).

Although the differentiation of CFS from a somatization disorder has been debated, (Hadler, 1997; Johnson, DeLuca & Natelson, 1996; Manu, Lane & Matthews, 1993; Robbins, Kirmayer & Hemami, 1997; Sharpe, 1997; Wessely, 1997) and the role of psychological factors in "perpetuating" the illness has been discussed (Abbey, 1993; Sharpe, Chalder, Palmer & Wessely, 1997), it is generally agreed that the symptom complex is consistently reported by patients and that it does differ from depression and other common fatiguing conditions (Hickie, Kirk & Martin, 1999; Koschera, Hickie, Hadzi-Pavlovic, Wilson & Lloyd, 1999; Lloyd, et al., 1992; van der Linden, et al., 1999; Wessely, Chalder, Hirsch, Wallace & Wright, 1996).

Concerns have been expressed, however, that the illness in children and adolescents may be a psychological disorder such as depression or abnormal illness behavior (Pilowsky, 1991). Indeed, suggestions have been offered that a diagnosis of CFS may be counterproductive in young people (Harris & Taitz, 1989) and even that it should not be diagnosed in children (Plioplys, 1997, 1999). Whereas several studies have identified symptoms and outcomes in children and adolescents with chronic fatigue (Bell, 1997; Carter, et al., 1995; Feder, Dworkin & Orkin, 1994; Krilov, et al., 1998), many of the children in these studies did not fit the Center for Disease Control definition (Holmes, et al., 1988; Fukuda, et al., 1994) at the initial presentation, since their symptoms were of less than 6 months duration. Nevertheless, as the outcomes appear to be better for young people (Rowe, 1997b, 2001; Feder, Dworkin & Orkin, 1994), it is important to establish whether the symptom clusters are similar to those identified in adults and to formally characterize the reported symptoms from a sufficiently large sample.

To date, there is little evidence that appropriate measurement models have been fitted to CFS symptom data to determine their underlying structure and explanatory adequacy. Possible exceptions to this include the work of Hickie, et al. (1995) and Levine (1999). Despite inherent methodological limitations in the procedures employed (as noted by the authors), Hickey, et al. (1995) used Latent Class Analysis (Green 1951, 1952; McCutcheon, 1987) to identify two clinical sub-groups of subjects with CFS in an attempt to define the distinct clinical features of the illness in adults.

The present study documents the symptoms reported, in terms of presence and severity, by 189 young people presenting for assessment of chronic fatigue, and compares them with responses from a matched sample of 68 normal, healthy controls. The key objectives of the study were fourfold: (1) to identify the salient symptoms reported by adolescents with chronic fatigue, (2) to determine the symptom content and measurement properties of the latent factors underlying these symptoms, (3) to establish whether these factors can be adequately accounted for by a single syndrome factor, and (4) to estimate the direction and magnitude of the interdependent effects among the identified factors.

METHOD

Study Population

Between 1989 and 1997, the first author collected clinical data on 189 subjects referred for assessment of chronic fatigue to a large tertiary pediatric referral center at the Royal Children's Hospital (Melbourne, Victoria, Australia). The mean age for this clinical group was 15 years (SD = 2.1; range: 10.6-18.6 years) and the ratio of males to females was 1:3.3. Subjects from all socioeconomic background categories (based on parental occupation) were represented, although the proportion of subjects with parents classified as "unskilled workers" were under-represented compared with their known proportion from census data for Victoria (Australian Bureau of Statistics, 1993). The distribution for parental country of birth also approximated the census data. Three subjects had at least one parent from South East Asian origins; the remainder was Caucasian. Eighty-six subjects had participated in a clinical trial of gammaglobulin (Rowe, 1997a), and all 189 subjects met the following criteria for inclusion in the study:

(1) an identifiable time of onset of symptoms and a subsequent course marked by chronic, persisting or relapsing fatigue of a generalized nature exacerbated by minor exercise, giving rise to significant disruption of normal daily activities including schooling, and being present for more than 6 months;

(2) neurocognitive dysfunction including impairment of concentration evidenced by difficulty in completing mental tasks that were easily accomplished prior to onset of the illness, and/or new onset of short term memory impairment; and

(3) the persistence or recurrence of at least 3 of the following symptoms and signs with no other cause found on investigation: myalgia, arthralgia, headaches, sleep disturbance, abdominal pain, dizziness, nausea, pharyngitis and lymphadenopathy.

A careful history was taken and examination was performed, paying particular attention to Crohn's disease, coeliac disease, thyroid disease, autoimmune diseases such as systemic lupus erythematosis, and evidence of clinical depression or other major psychosocial problems. Haemoglobin and differential white cell count, liver and thyroid function tests, erythrocyte sedimentation rate, urea and electrolytes, blood glucose, antinuclear antibody and serology for cytomegalovirus and Epstein Barr virus, were routinely measured.

The control group consisted of 68 young people attending a youth activities program with similar, age, gender and socioeconomic background characteristics to the clinical group. The mean age for control group was 14.6 years (SD = 1.4; range 12.7-18.0 years). Approval to conduct the study was sought and obtained from the Ethics Committee of the Royal Children's Hospital Research Foundation, and informed consent was obtained for all subjects

History Record

A history record for Chronic Fatigue Syndrome developed by Lloyd and colleagues (Lloyd, et al., 1992) was used to identify the presence and severity of symptoms in the month prior to the hospital visit. This record consists of 38 symptom items, some of which are characteristic indicators of CFS. Since these items were the ones used by Hickey, et al. (Hickie, et al., 1995) to classify the syndrome in adults, for comparative purposes the wording was not altered for subjects in the present study. The control group completed the same 38-item record.

Each symptom item required a response on a multiple-category, Likert-type, ordinal scale (Likert, 1932) coded: '0' (Never suffered from it), '1' (Mild or rare symptoms during the last month, causing minor disruption to usual daily activities), '2' (Moderate or frequent symptoms during the last month, causing major disruption to usual daily activities), and '3' (Severe or very frequent symptoms during the last month, making you unable to perform your usual daily activities).

Additional self-report data were obtained that related to factors affecting ability to do tasks, pattern of illness, activity levels, past and present 'treatment' and level of functioning. Standard instruments measuring depression, (Beck Depression Inventory; Beck, et al., 1961), anxiety (State-Trait Anxiety Inventory; Spielberger, 1977), general well-being, the 12 item General Health Questionnaire (Goldberg & Williams, 1988), and parent-child relationship, Parental Bonding Instrument (Parker, et al. 1979) were used. The Parental Bonding Instrument is a 25 item 4 point Likert scale scoring from 'very unlike', to 'very like' describing various attitudes and behaviors of parents. It was scored describing the qualities most like their mother. The Beck Depression Inventory was scored in the standard way but comparisons among items were made between the clinical group and the control group due to the 6 items concerning somatic complaints that overlap with the symptoms of CFS. The General Health Questionnaire was scored in 2 ways: 0 to 3 for the four categories and also as a dichotomous score 0 or 1, collapsing the 4 categories into 2. For the dichotomous score a rating of 5 or more was considered significant.

Data Analyses and Statistical Modeling

Using STATISTICA, (Statsoft, 1999) a frequencies analysis of subjects' responses on the ordinal scale for each of the 38 symptom items was conducted for both groups separately. To identify the underlying structure of the items, a second-order, confirmatory factor-analytic measurement model (CFA) was fitted to the item data from the clinical group, followed by a recursive structural equation regression model to estimate the magnitude and direction of the interdependent effects among the identified factors.

It is important to note that these analyses were conducted on a scaled covariance matrix of the polychoric correlations among the 38 observed item scores computed from PRELIS, (Jöreskog & Sörbom, 1999a) and fitted via LISREL, (Jöreskog & Sörbom, 1999b) under a maximum likelihood method of parameter estimation. Since the special measurement and distributional properties of ordinal-scaled data of the present kind, and the dangers of not accounting for these properties in statistical analysis, are well documented (Bollen, Scott Long, 1993; Carroll, 1961; Jöreskog, 1994; Jöreskog, Sörbom, du Toit, du Toit, 1999; Marsh, Balla, & Hau 1996; Marsh, Balla, & McDonald, 1988; Morris, Bergan, & Fulginiti, 1991; Poon, & Lee, 1987), they need not be reiterated here. Similarly, for interested readers, detailed accounts of the relevant specifications for the models fitted, including model goodness-of-fit indices, are provided elsewhere, (Bollen, Scott Long, 1993; Jöreskog, Sörbom, du Toit, du Toit, 1999; Marsh, Balla, & Hau 1996; Marsh, Balla & McDonald, 1988) and presented in several publications by the present authors (Rowe, 1991; Rowe & Rowe 1992a, 1992b, 1997, 1999).

Using well established procedures designed to minimize the effects of measurement error variance in composite scores derived from ordinal-scaled indicators (Brown, 1989; Fleishman & Benson, 1987; Jöreskog, 1971) factor scores for each composite were computed by multiplying the observed item scores by their proportionally-weighted factor score regression coefficients, such that each factor score was a continuous variable ranging in value from a minimum of 0 to a maximum of 3. This meant that the composite factor scores thus computed had the advantage of each being measured on a common metric, regardless of the number of constituent items, and preserved the metric of the original response categories (i.e., 0-3). To estimate the magnitude of the differences between the clinical and control groups on the means of all composite factor scores, a multiple analysis of variance (MANOVA) was undertaken using STATISTICA (Statsoft, 1999).

RESULTS

Salience of Symptoms

Results of the frequencies analysis for the 38 symptom items for both the clinical and the control group are summarized in Figure 1. For the clinical group, prolonged fatigue following minor activity, headache, the need for excessive sleep, loss of ability to concentrate, disturbed sleep, excessive muscle fatigue, and myalgia following minor activity, were each experienced by more than 87% of the subjects during the previous month and were rated as 'severe' or 'moderately severe' by more than 60% of the subjects. Sore throat without coryzal symptoms, tender cervical lymph nodes, feeling of disturbed balance, abdominal pain, shortness of breath, and nausea were also rated as 'severe' or 'moderately severe' in more than 50% of the clinical group.

Fourteen symptom items (given in the lower part of Fig. 1) had low response frequencies in terms of both presence and severity, and were not considered to be characteristic of CFS. For example, symptoms such as loss of bowel and bladder control, redness and swelling around joints, episodic loss of vision in one or both eyes, were either absent or experienced by less than 10% of subjects. Moreover, when analyzed with the data on the 24 items listed as "key symptoms" in Figure 1, the estimated squared multiple correlation coefficients (R^2) for these 14 items were not significantly different from zero.

Thus, these items were not included in subsequent analyses employed to determine the factor structure of CFS on three grounds, namely: (1) non-significant relationship with the underlying scale described by the 24 salient items, (2) low occurrence and severity response frequencies, and (3) marginal relevance to CFS symptomatology in the clinical experience of the

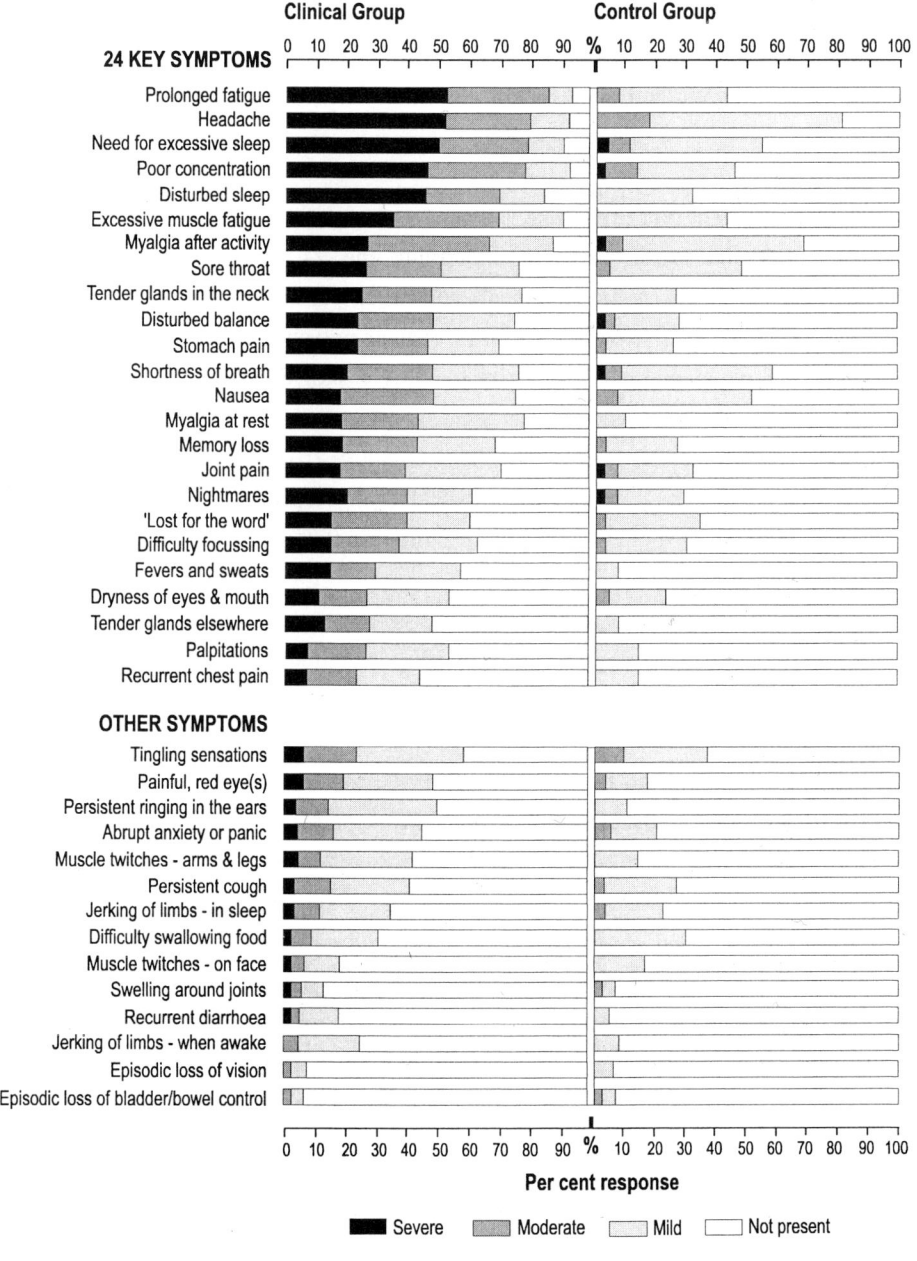

Figure 1.   Stacked histograms showing percentage frequencies in four response categories on 38 symptom items for clinical group (n = 189) and control group (n = 68)

first author (Rowe 1997a; Rowe & Fitzgerald, 1999; Rowe & Rowe 1999a, 1999b). Nonetheless, in the interest of completeness, and for comparison with the findings reported by Hickey, et al. (1995) from their adult cohort, the factor underlying structure of these items was determined independently, as reported below.

Syndrome Measurement and Structure

To identify the factor structure underlying the 24 salient items, a second-order, confirmatory, factor-analytic measurement model (CFA) was fitted to the relevant data for the clinical group, from a scaled covariance matrix of their polychoric inter-correlations. Using a recommended iterative, model-generating procedure, (Jöreskog & Sörbom, 1999) the best-fitting solution (Fig. 2a) yielded one second-order syndrome factor (ξ_1) and five correlated first-order factors, labeled: muscle pain & fatigue (η_1); neurocognitive (η_2); abdominal, head & chest pain (η_3); neurophysiological (η_4); and immunological (η_5), respectively. As indicated by the goodness-of-fit indices, the model accounted for more than 97% of the variances and covariances in the observed item data.

To assist interpretation of Figure 2a, the five first-order factors (bounded by ellipses) have been ordered from top-to-bottom by decreasing magnitude of their factor means, ranging from Muscle pain and fatigue (Mean: 1.58) to Immunological (Mean: 1.28). Similarly, the item descriptions (bounded by rectangles) within each first-order factor have been ordered by the magnitude of their standardized factor loadings. For example, loadings of the constituent item indicators for the Immunological factor (η_5) ranged from 0.907 for 'Tender glands in the neck', to 0.534 for 'Repeated fevers and sweats'.

Whereas the 14 symptom items considered to be of marginal relevance to CFS symptomatology (mentioned above) had low response frequencies in terms of presence and severity, a separate CFA model fitted their data for the clinical group yielded 3 highly correlated factors, labeled: Somatic 1, Involuntary muscle sensations, and Somatic 2 (Fig 2b). Although this model was not a good fit to the data (accounting for < 79% of variances and covariances in the data), the solution yielded stable factor score regression estimates that facilitated calculation of composite scores for these two factors, using the same approach as described above.

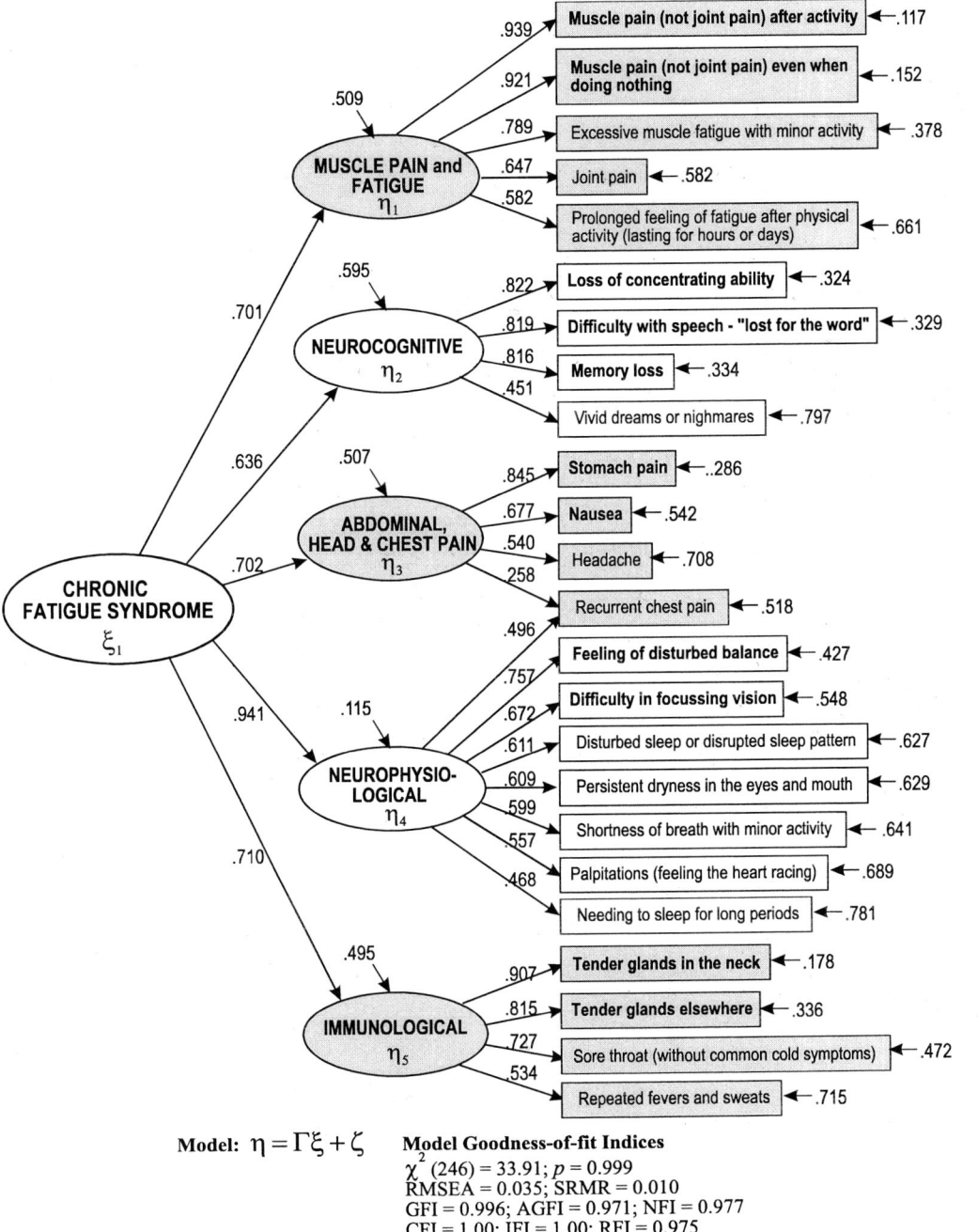

Model: $\eta = \Gamma\xi + \zeta$

Model Goodness-of-fit Indices
$\chi^2 (246) = 33.91; p = 0.999$
RMSEA = 0.035; SRMR = 0.010
GFI = 0.996; AGFI = 0.971; NFI = 0.977
CFI = 1.00; IFI = 1.00; RFI = 0.975

Figure 2a. Completely standardized solution to second-order confirmatory factor analysis, showing 'loadings' and error variances for 24 CFS indicators, five underlying latent factors, and a single syndrome factor

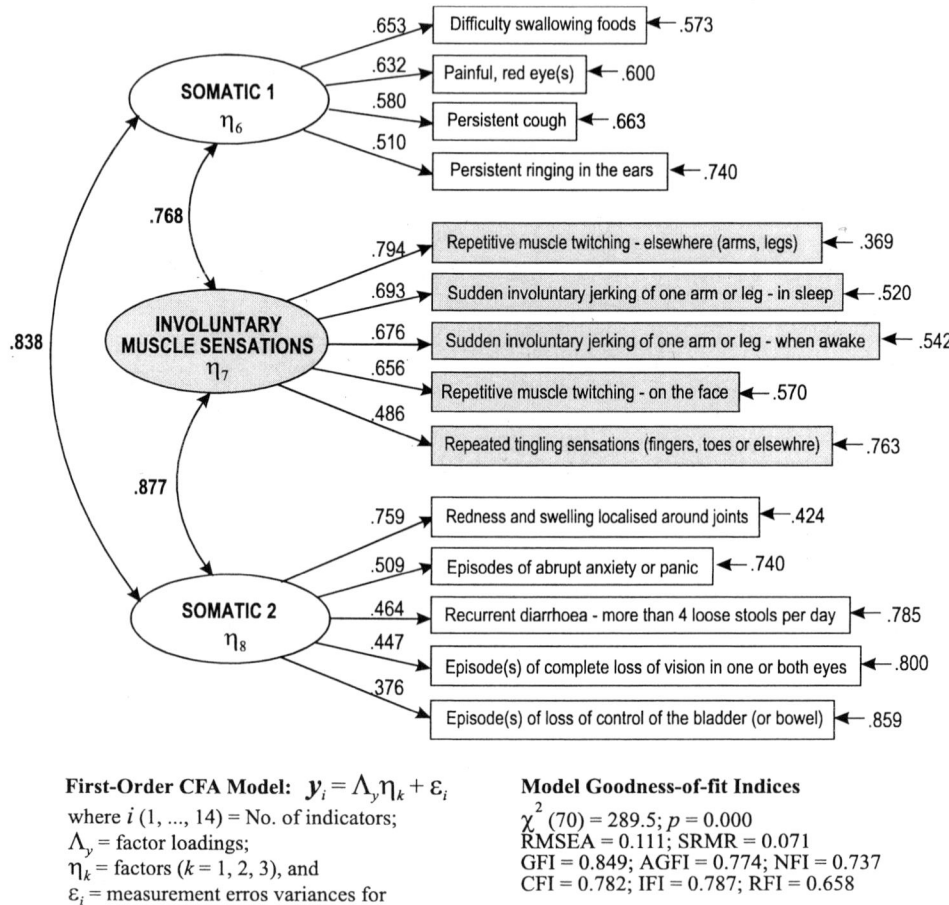

First-Order CFA Model: $y_i = \Lambda_y \eta_k + \varepsilon_i$

where i (1, ..., 14) = No. of indicators;
Λ_y = factor loadings;
η_k = factors (k = 1, 2, 3), and
ε_i = measurement erros variances for
    the 14 indicators

Model Goodness-of-fit Indices

χ^2 (70) = 289.5; p = 0.000
RMSEA = 0.111; SRMR = 0.071
GFI = 0.849; AGFI = 0.774; NFI = 0.737
CFI = 0.782; IFI = 0.787; RFI = 0.658

Figure 2b. Completely standardized solution to first-order, confirmatory 3-factor model, showing factor inter-correlations, 'loadings' and error variances for 14 low response frequency symptom indicators

Comparison of Factor Score Means for Clinical and Control Groups

Figure 3 summarizes the results from a multiple analysis of variance (MANOVA) designed to estimate the magnitude of differences between the clinical and control group on their means for all 8 composite factor scores. The method used to compute these scores has been outlined in the Data analyses and statistical modeling section above. The plots for the two groups show the mean point-estimates bounded by their 95% confidence intervals for the 8 factors, indicating that the clinical group had significantly higher mean scores on all 8 factors than the control group [multivariate Wilk's $\lambda = 0.566$; Rao's R (8, 248) = 23.74; p < 0.000001]. Moreover, the univariate F-ratios for each of the 8 factors (with 1 and 255 degrees of freedom, respectively) ranged from a low of 26.7 (for Involuntary muscle sensations) to a high of 152.5 (for the Neurophysiological factor). All related univariate p-values were < 0.000001.

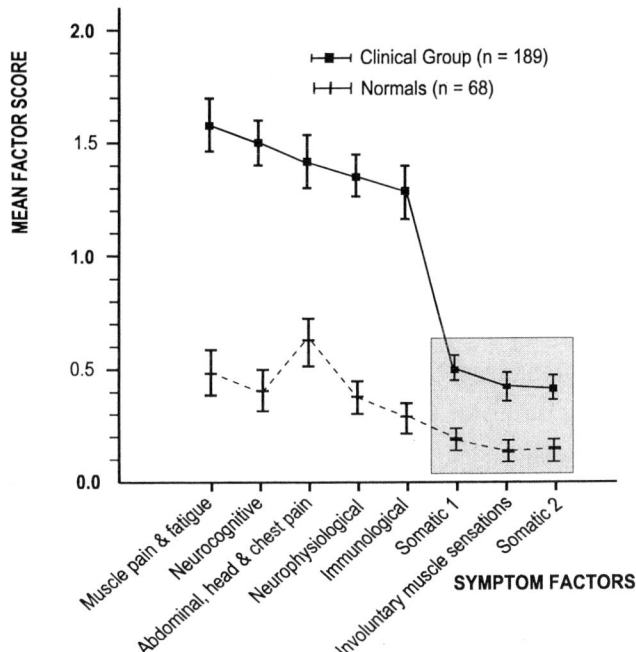

Figure 3.   Plot of CFS symptom factor means for clinical group and normal controls, showing point-estimates bounded by their 95% confidence intervals.

Estimating the Direction and Magnitude of the Interdependent Effects Among Factors

To estimate the direction and magnitude of the interdependent effects among the five key CFS factors identified, a recursive structural equation regression model was fitted to the computed factor score data for the clinical group. Using a recommended model-generating procedure, (Jöreskog, et al., 1999) and the modification indices derived from fitting earlier models, the final, best-fitting solution is illustrated by the path diagram given in Figure 4. The path coefficients proximal to the unidirectional arrows (from ellipse to ellipse) shown in Figure 4 are standardized estimates of the direct effects of one factor score on another. Typically, these effects are interpreted as standardized regression coefficients. For example, the solution illustrated in Figure 4 indicates that one standard deviation increase in the immunological factor score (η_5) leads to a corresponding increase of 0.73 standard deviation units in the neurophysiological factor score (η_4). Similarly, the coefficients proximal to the double-headed arrows are standardized covariances (correlations) among the relevant factor scores, indicating, for example, that the correlation between the abdominal, head/chest pain (η_2) and neurocognitive factor scores (η_2) is 0.488. Further, the R^2 values for structural equations given in Figure 4 indicate, for example, that 56% of the variance in the abdominal, head/chest pain factor score (η_3) is accounted for simultaneously by the direct effects of the immunological (η_5) and neurophysiological (η_4) factor scores, as well as the indirect effect of the immunological factor score, mediated by the neurophysiological factor score. In brief, a substantive interpretation of the results summarized in Figure 4 suggests that immunological symptoms are primary, having significant direct and indirect effects on the other four key symptom factors. The excellent model-data-fit indices, indicating that in excess of 99% of the relative variances and covariances in the data were accounted for by the fitted model (i.e., AGFI = 0.991), should be noted, since they underscore the importance of this finding.

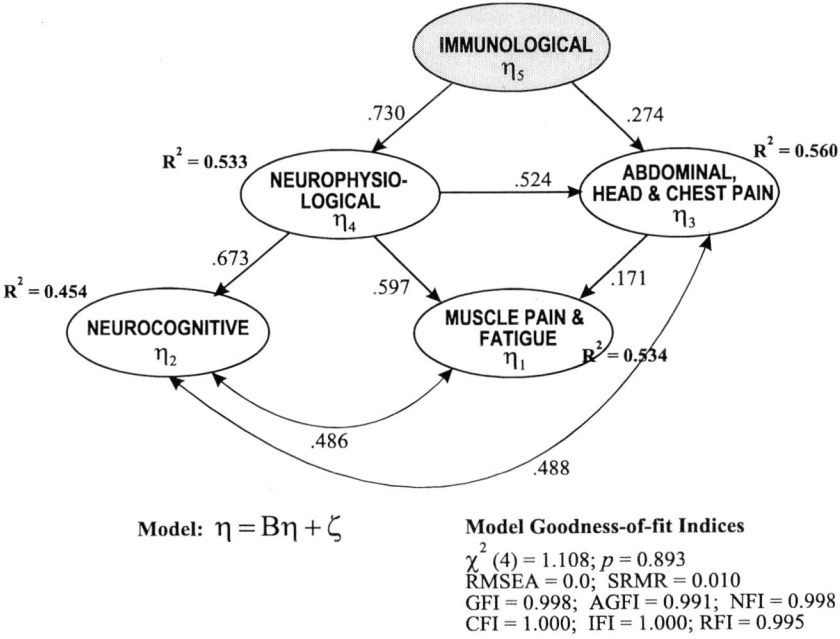

Model: $\eta = B\eta + \zeta$

Model Goodness-of-fit Indices

$\chi^2 (4) = 1.108; p = 0.893$
RMSEA = 0.0; SRMR = 0.010
GFI = 0.998; AGFI = 0.991; NFI = 0.998
CFI = 1.000; IFI = 1.000; RFI = 0.995

Figure 4.   Solution to recursive structural equation regression model, showing standardized direct effects and covariances

Note: All recorded path coefficients are significant beyond the $p < 0.05$ level, by univariate 2-tailed tests; R^2 values refer to squared multiple correlation coefficients for structural equations

Clinical Features: Identified Onset Factors

The was a seasonal variation in the onset of the illness with a steady rate all year but peaks in April (mid autumn) and June (early winter) and lower frequency at the end of the school year (November, December) (Figure 5) (Chi square 25.24, df=11, p<0.008). Sixty two per cent reported an onset associated with a viral or 'flu-like' illness and a further 20% reported that a specific infection was diagnosed usually with serology. The majority was EBV infection but CMV, viral menigitis, varicella, mycoplasma, Ross River Virus, Toxoplasmosis, Parvo virus, and enteroviruses were all documented. Three percent associated the onset with an operation for appendicitis, cholecystitis or chronic sinusitis. One per cent associated the onset with immunization and 15% could not identify a trigger although 4% had a sibling with documented EBV infection around the time of onset of their illness and they were also noted to have positive IgG for EBV several months later. Sixteen percent reported a family history of CFS.

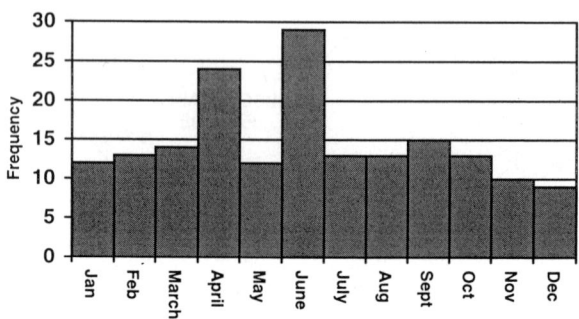

Figure 5. Reported month of onset of illness with peaks in mid-autumn and early winter (n=177) (Chi-square=25.24, df=11, p<0.008)

Clinical Features: Impact of Illness on Activities

The majority (75%) reported a continuous illness with fluctuating severity or with a relapsing and remitting pattern with some days better than others. Fatigue, concentration problems, muscle and joint pain and to some extent lack of motivation, were attributed to limiting their ability to perform tasks that they would have completed easily prior to becoming ill. Seventy three percent reported that depression limited their ability to perform moderately frequently with 7% reporting that the impact was very frequent or severe in its effect (Figure 6).

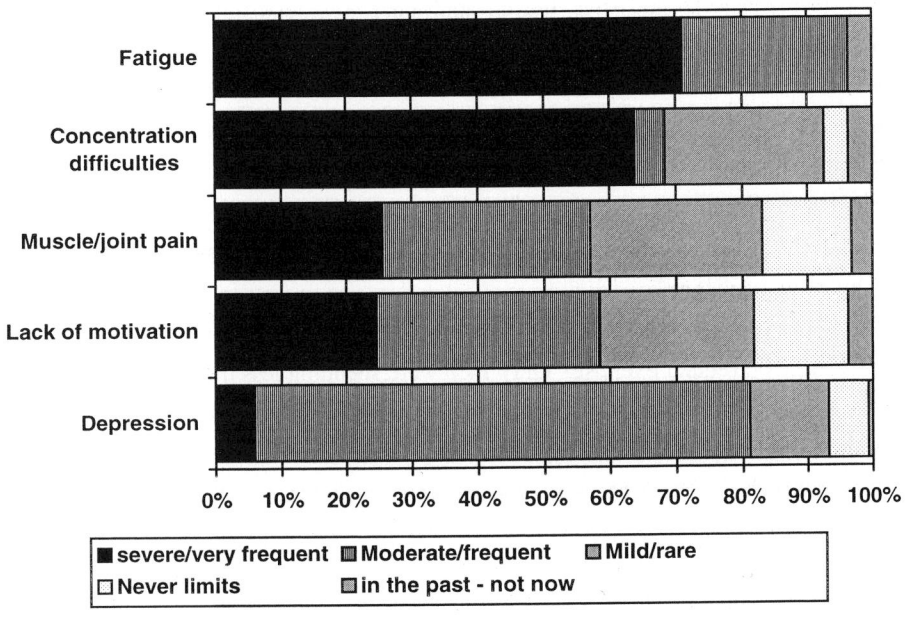

Figure 6. Symptoms occurring during the previous month that limit the ability to perform tasks that would easily have been completed prior to the onset of this illness

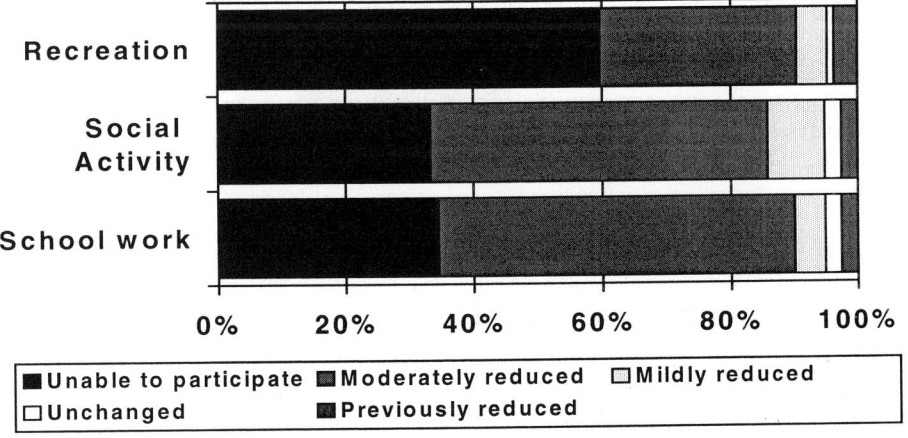

Figure 7. Impact of illness on school, social and recreational activities (n=189)

The illness had a marked impact on their life with 60% reporting that they were unable to participate in recreational activities and an additional 40% reporting a moderate reduction in such activities. Ninety one per cent reported that they had a moderate reduction in their schoolwork or were unable to do any. (Figure 7) One third was not able to participate in social activities and 35% were unable to attend school with a further 40% able to attend part-time only. Twenty two per cent used the services of a Visiting Teacher provided by the Education Department who visited at least once per week and assisted with liaison with school (Rowe & Fitzgerald, 1999). Sixteen per cent used Distance Education that enabled them to study some subjects by correspondence.

Sixty per cent reported being only able to walk for short distances or only in the house with 42% having no regular exercise. Only 14% were spending less than 4 hours lying down per day, while 40% were spending 8-16 hours lying down during the day. This is contrasted with their reported level of physical activity prior to the illness, which indicated that 54% participated in at least 1 hour per day of vigorous activity or exercise (Figure 8).

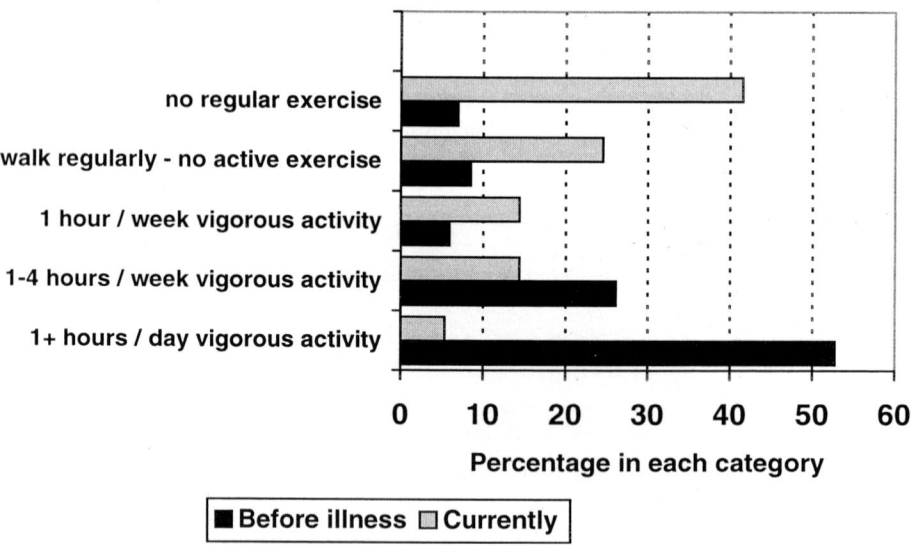

Figure 8. Participation in physical activity prior to illness compared with current participation (n=189

Sixty two per cent reported that the illness had damaged their relationship with their family with 22% reporting an ongoing severe or moderately severe effect. Twenty seven per cent reported that for some of the time at least they thought that others would be better off if they were dead. Of these, 7% thought about it for a 'good part or most of the time'. Sixty five percent reported feeling like crying or actually having crying spells (Figure 9).

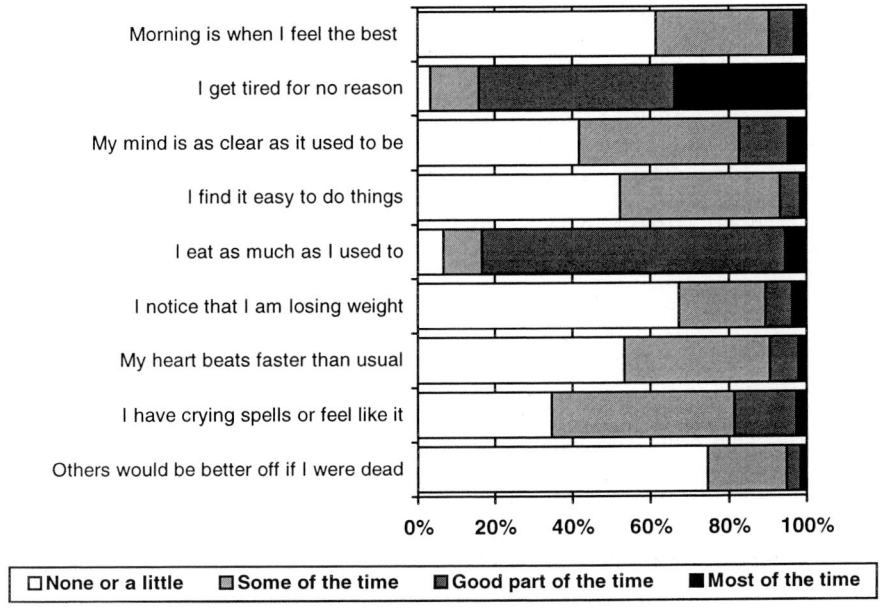

Figure 9. Symptom pattern for the previous month of illness (n=189)

Psychological Measures

The total scores for the Beck Depression Inventory, State-Trait Anxiety Inventory, and the General Health Questionnaire (GHQ) were all significantly different from the control group (Table 1). Eleven per cent of the control group and 51% of the clinical group scored above 5 on the General Health Questionnaire indicating significant emotional distress. The Parental Bonding Instrument was not scored significantly different from the control group apart from the items 'Tends to baby me' and 'Tries to make me dependent on her' and 'intrudes on my privacy'. The control group scored the latter item as a problem, whereas the clinical group rated the first two as a problem. All other items relating to control, overprotection, wanting the child to grow up, independence, appropriate emotional support, awareness of needs, were not significantly different from the control group.

Table 1.   Questionnaire scores for the clinical group and the control group for the Beck Depression Inventory, Spielberger State Trait Anxiety Inventory and the General Health Questionnaire

	Clinical group CFS				Control Group					
	n	Mean	sd	se	n	Mean	sd	se	t value	p value
Beck	159	12.47	6.96	0.55	65	5.33	5.69	0.71	7.97	<.0005
Spielberger	118	85.4	22.4	2.06	65	69.6	17.7	2.19	5.28	<.0005
GHQ	171	16.6	6.95	0.53	66	10.06	5.34	0.66	7.8	<.0005

When the item responses on the Beck Depression Inventory were compared between the control and the clinical groups, there was no significant difference between the groups for the items measuring anhedonia (feeling a failure, feeling guilty or unworthy, feeling as though they were being punished, loss of interest in other people, feeling ugly or unattractive, dislike of self). There was a marked difference (p < .0005) for fatigue, sleep disturbance, concentration difficulties, ability to work, ability to make decisions, sadness, crying and pessimism. Eighteen per cent of the control group had considered harming themselves compared with 20% of the CFS group, but 7% of the CFS group had thought they "would be better off dead" or that their "family would be better off if I were dead". This was consistent with the scoring of other items in the history questionnaire (Figure 9). The CFS group were sad and felt like crying frequently apart from a small but significant percentage did not have features of anhedonia. Higher scores on the Beck Depression Inventory were associated with severity of illness and also with duration until diagnosis. The mean duration until diagnosis was 14 months for the severe group compared with 7 months for the other 2 groups.

DISCUSSION

Comparison between the CFS symptomatology experienced by adolescents and adult patients (Hickie, et al., 1995; Komaroff & Buckwald, 1991) highlights similarities in the proportion of subjects who experienced various symptoms. In the present study, all clinical group subjects presented with a defined onset over one or several days, with 85% describing an apparent infective illness at the outset – similar to that reported by Komaroff and Buckwald (1991). There was also evidence of seasonal variation in onset of illness with an increase over autumn (fall) and winter, and a decrease in incidence towards the end of the school year when many young people report being under extra stress with examinations. These findings lend support for the anecdotal evidence that the illness in adolescents more commonly follows an infective episode and more commonly has a 'defined onset'.

The adolescents in the present study had a shorter duration of illness (18 months) when reporting symptoms, compared with either group in Hickey, et al.'s (1995) study (5.9 and 8.3 years). The pattern of symptoms in adolescents was comparable to that for the adults in latent class I of Hickey, et al.'s study, except that nausea, abdominal pain, fevers and sweats and sore throat without coryza, tender cervical glands and 'tender glands elsewhere', were more common among the adolescents.

For those symptoms present in the clinical group, the patterns of severity were closer to those adults identified in latent class II of Hickey, et al.'s study (1995), but the adolescents reported less severe and fewer instances of 'panic attacks' than those reported by the adults in either of the latent class groups of Hickey at al.'s study. Shortness of breath following exercise was experienced by 82% of the adolescents and was considered 'severe' by 23%. However, this may be indicative of physical de-conditioning due to the illness rather than another medical condition, or 'atypical symptom' as suggested by Hickie, et al. Nevertheless, 'recurrent fevers and sweats' – also considered an 'atypical symptom' – was common and experienced by 66% of the adolescents at presentation, but this was rarely reported as 'high fever'. Rather, it was a low grade fever associated with feeling 'hot and flushed' or feeling 'cold and shivery'. The symptom pattern was similar to that described by Smith, et al. (1991), but the number of subjects in that study was small (n = 15).

Feeling sad was common, and high scores on the Beck Depression Inventory reflected the somatic symptoms identified as consistent with CFS and not anhedonia. There was a high level of consideration of suicide among the control group and this was not significantly different from the clinical group. Nonetheless, 7% of the clinical group were considered depressed. There was no evidence in this group that the relationship with their mother contributed to 'illness behavior' in that there was no difference between the clinical group and the controls in their relationship with their mother. Depression was related to severity of illness and to delay in receiving a diagnosis. This lends support for the view that the illness contributes to the reported sadness.

Historical data were consistent within the clinical group, with 'prolonged fatigue after physical exercise' being present in all subjects. The features of CFS reported by adolescents, were similar to those reported by adults, with headache, difficulty concentrating, disturbed sleep, abdominal pain, and myalgia being especially salient. The excellent fit of the second-order CFA measurement model to the key 24-item symptom data for the clinical group, yielding one underlying syndrome factor, indicated that the symptom complex can be legitimately designated as a syndrome, and provided evidence for consistent reporting of CFS symptoms by adolescents. Evidence for the presence of somatization disorder, however, was negligible. Indeed, reports by adolescents of symptoms unrelated to CFS were inconsistent and had low response frequencies. Nonetheless, compared with normal controls, the clinical group had significantly higher scores on all 8 identified factors. The finding that 'immunological' symptoms (rather than pain and fatigue symptoms) had significant direct and indirect effects on the other four key symptom factors has important implications for understanding the etiology of CFS, and supports the prevailing view that CFS has an immunological basis.

The adolescents reported high levels of distress (GHQ), anxiety and sadness compared with the control group but the relationship with their mother as measured by the Parental Bonding Instrument was not significantly different from the control group. This was despite nearly two thirds of the clinical group reporting that they felt the illness had damaged their relationship with family members. The levels of sadness are not surprising when the severity of the impact of the illness on all aspects of their life such as their ability to participate in education, recreational, social and physical activities apart from constant presence of physical symptoms. There is evidence for seasonal variation, reported and documented association with infectious agents in the majority of cases, and consistency in reporting of symptomatology. The young person's distress at not being believed, not taken seriously or not receiving a diagnosis for many months, highlights the need for recognition and acknowledgement of the syndrome, and the need for early and appropriate management strategies to be implemented.

ACKNOWLEDGMENTS

The willingness of the young people with chronic fatigue to participate in our studies, and to teach us so much is greatly appreciated. The study was supported financially by the ME/CFS Society of Victoria.

REFERENCES

Abbey, S.E. (1993). Somatization, illness attribution and the sociocultural psychiatry of chronic fatigue syndrome. *Ciba Foundation Symposium, 173,* 238-261.

Australian Bureau of Statistics. (1993). *1991 Census data for Victoria.* Canberra: Australian Government Printing Service.

Beck, A.T., Ward, C.H., Mendelson, M., Mock, J., & Erbaugh, J.K. (1961). An inventory for measuring depression. *Archives of General Psychiatry, 41,* 561-71.

Bell, D.S., Bell, K.M., Cheney, P.R. (1994). Primary juvenile fibromyalgia syndrome and chronic fatigue syndrome in adolescents. *Clinical. Infectious. Diseases, 18,* Suppl 1, S21-3.

Bell, D.S. (1995). Diagnosis of chronic fatigue syndrome in children and adolescents: Special considerations. *Journal of Chronic Fatigue Syndrome, 1,* 9-33.

Bell, D.S. (1997). Illness onset characteristics in children with CFS and idiopathic chronic fatigue. *Journal of Chronic Fatigue Syndrome, 3,* 43-51.

Bollen, K.A., Scott, L. J. (1993). *Testing structural equation models.* Newbury Park, CA: Sage Publications.

Brown, R.L. (1989). Using covariance modeling for estimating reliability on scales with ordered polytomous variables. *Educational and Psychological Measurement, 49,* 385-398.

Carroll, J.B. (1961). The nature of data, or how to choose a correlation coefficient. *Psychometrika, 26,* 347-372.

Carter, B.D., Edwards, J.F., Kronenberger, W.G., Michalczyk, L., & Marshall, G.S. (1995). Case control study of chronic fatigue in pediatric patients. *Pediatrics, 95,* 179-86.

de Jong, L.W., Prins, J.B., Fiselier, T.J., Weemaes, C.M., Meijer-van den Bergh, E.M, & Bleijenberg, G. (1997). [Chronic fatigue syndrome in young persons]. [Dutch]. *Nederlands Tijdschrift voor Geneeskunde, 141,* 1513-1516.

Demitrack, M.A., Dale, J.K., & Strauss, S.E., (1991). Evidence for impaired activation of hypothalamic-pituitary-adrenal axis in patients with Chronic Fatigue Syndrome. *Journal of Clinical Endocrinology and Metabolism.,73,* 1224-34.

Demitrack, M.A. (1998a). Chronic fatigue syndrome and fibromyalgia: Dilemmas in diagnosis and clinical management. *Psychiatric Clinics of North America, 21,* 671-92.

Demitrack, M.A.(1998b). Neuroendocrine aspects of chronic fatigue syndrome: A commentary. *American Journal of Medicine, 105,* 11S-14S.

Feder, H.M., Dworkin, P.H., & Orkin C. (1994). Outcome of 48 pediatric patients with chronic fatigue. *Archives of Family Medicine, 3,* 1049-55.

Fleishman. J., & Benson, J. (1987). Using LISREL to evaluate measurement models and scale reliability. *Educational and Psychological Measurement, 47,* 925-939.

Franklin, A. (1998). How I manage Chronic Fatigue Syndrome. *Archives of Disease in Childhood, 79,* 375-378.

Fukuda, K., Straus, S.E., Hickie, I., Sharpe, M.C., & Dobbins, J.G., & Komaroff, A. (1994). The chronic fatigue syndrome: A comprehensive approach to its definition and study. International Chronic Fatigue Syndrome Study Group. *Annals of Internal Medicine, 121,* 953-9.

Goldberg, D.P., & Williams. P. (1988). *A users guide to the General Health Questionnaire.* Windsor: NFER-Nelson.

Green, B.F. (1951). A general solution for the latent class model of latent structure analysis. *Psychometrika, 16,* 151-166.

Green, B.F. (1952). Latent structure analysis and its relation to factor analysis. *Journal of the American Statistical Association, 47,* 71-76.

Hadler, N.M. (1997). Fibromyalgia, chronic fatigue, and other iatrogenic diagnostic algorithms: Do some labels escalate illness in vulnerable patients? *Postgraduate Medicine, 102,* 161-2, 165-166, 171-172.

Harris, F., & Taitz, L.S. (1989). Damaging diagnosis of myalgic encephalomyelitis in children. *British Medical Journal, 299,* 790.

Hickie, I., Kirk, K., & Martin, N. (1999). Unique genetic and environmental determinants of prolonged fatigue: A twin study. *Psychological Medicine, 29,* 259-68.

Hickie, I., Lloyd, A., Hadzi-Pavlovic, D., Parker, G., Bird, K., & Wakefield, D. (1995). Can the chronic fatigue syndrome be defined by distinct clinical features? *Psychological Medicine, 25,* 925-935.

Holmes, G.P., Kaplan, J.E. Gantz, K.A.L., Schonberger, L.B., Straus, S.E., Jones, J.F., Dubois, R.E., Cunningham-Rundles, C., Pahwa, S., Tosato, G., Zegans, L.S., Purtilo, D.T., Brown, N., Schooley, R.T., & Brus, I. (1988). Chronic Fatigue Syndrome: A working case definition. *Annals of Internal Medicine, 108,* 387-389.

Johnson, S.K., DeLuca. J., & Natelson, B.H. (1996). Assessing somatization disorder in the chronic fatigue syndrome. *Psychosomatic Medicine, 58,* 50-57.

Jöreskog. K.G. (1971). Statistical analysis of sets of congeneric tests. *Psychometrika, 36,* 109-133.

Jöreskog, K.G. (1994). On the estimation of polychoric correlations and their asymptotic covariance matrix. *Psychometrika, 59*, 381-389.

Jöreskog, K.G., Sörbom, D., du Toit, S., du Toit, M. (1999). *LISREL 8: New statistical features.* Chicago: Scientific Software International, Inc.

Jöreskog, K.G., & Sörbom, D. (1999a). *Interactive LISREL: PRELIS 2.3 for Windows '95 and Windows NT.* Chicago: Scientific Software International, Inc.

Jöreskog, K.G, & Sörbom, D. (1999b). *Interactive LISREL: LISREL 8.3 for Windows '95 and Windows NT.* Chicago: Scientific Software International, Inc.

Komaroff, A.L., & Buchwald, D. (1991). Symptoms and signs of Chronic Fatigue Syndrome. *Reviews of Infectious Diseases, 13,* (Suppl.).

Komaroff, A.L., & Buchwald, D.S. (1998). Chronic fatigue syndrome: an update. *Annual Review of Medicine, 49,* 1-13.

Koschera, A., Hickie, I., Hadzi-Pavlovic, D., Wilson, A., & Lloyd, A. (1999). Prolonged fatigue, anxiety and depression: exploring relationships in a primary care sample. *Australian & New Zealand Journal of Psychiatry, 33,* 545-552.

Krilov, L.R., Fisher M., Friedman, S.B., Reitman, D., & Mandel, F.S. (1998). Course and outcomes of chronic fatigue in children and adolescents. *Pediatrics, 102,* 360-366.

Lask, B., & Dillon, M.J. (1990). Postviral fatigue syndrome. *Archives of Disease in Childhood, 65,* 1198.

Levin, P. (1999). *Evidence for an environmental-related Gulf war syndrome by factor analysis.* Paper presented at the Second World Congress on Chronic Fatigue Syndrome and Related Disorders: Towards Effective Diagnosis and Treatment in the 21st Century. Brussels, Belgium, September 9-12, 1999.

Likert, R.A. (1932). A technique for the measurement of attitudes. *Archives of Psychology, 140,* 5-53.

Lloyd, A., Hickie, I., Hickie, C., Dwyer, J., & Wakefield, D. (1992). Cell-mediated immunity in patients with chronic fatigue syndrome, healthy control subjects and patients with major depression. *Clinical Experimental Immunology, 87,* 76-9.

Lloyd, A.R., Hickie, I., Boughton, C.R., Spencer, O., & Wakefield, D. (1990). Prevalence of chronic fatigue syndrome in an Australian population. *Medical Journal of Australia, 153,* 522-8.

Lloyd, A.R., Wakefield, D, Boughton, C., & Dwyer, J. (1988). What is myalgic encephalomyelitis? *Lancet, i,* 1286-7.

Manu, P., Lane, T.J., & Matthews, D.A. (1993). Chronic fatigue and chronic fatigue syndrome: Clinical epidemiology and aetiological classification. *Ciba Foundation Symposium, 173,* 23-42.

Marsh, H.W., Balla, J.R., & Hau, K.T. (1996). An evaluation of incremental fit indices: A clarification of mathematical and empirical properties. In G.A. Marcoulides & R.E. Schumacker (Eds.), *Advanced structural equation modeling: Issues and techniques* (pp. 315-353). Mahwah, NJ: Lawrence Erlbaum.

Marsh, H.W., Balla, J.R., & McDonald, R.P. (1988). Goodness-of-fit in confirmatory factor analysis: The effect of sample size. *Psychological Bulletin, 102,* 391-410.

Marshal, G.S. (1999). Report of a workshop on the epidemiology, natural history, and pathogenesis of chronic fatigue syndrome in adolescents. *Journal of Pediatrics, 134,* 395-405.

McCutcheon, A.L. (1987). *Latent class analysis: Quantitative applications in the social sciences.* London: Sage.

Morris, R.J., Bergan, J.R., & Fulginiti, J.V. (1991). Structural equation modeling in clinical assessment research with children. *Journal of Consulting and Clinical Psychology, 59,* 371-379.

Natelson, B.H., LaManca, J.J., Denny, T.N., Vladutiu, A., Oleske, J., Hill, N., Bergen, M.T., Korn, L., & Hay, J. (1998). Immunologic parameters in chronic fatigue syndrome, major depression, and multiple sclerosis. *American Journal of Medicine, 105,* 43S-49S.

Pilowsky I. (1991). Somatic symptoms and other related disorders. *Current Opinion in Psychiatry, 4,* 220-224.

Plioplys, A.V. (1997). Chronic fatigue syndrome should not be diagnosed in children. *Pediatrics, 100,* 270-1.

Plioplys, A.V. (1999). Chronic Fatigue Syndrome? *Pediatrics, 104,* 130-2.

Poon, W-Y, & Lee, S-Y. (1987). Maximum likelihood estimation of multivariate polychoric correlation coefficients. *Psychometrika, 52,* 409-430.

Robbins, J.M., Kirmayer, L.J., & Hemami, S. (1997). Latent variable models of functional somatic distress. *Journal of Nervous & Mental Disease, 185,* 606-15.

Rowe, K.J. (1991). The influence of reading activity at home on students' attitudes towards reading, classroom attentiveness and reading achievement: An application of structural equation modeling. *British Journal of Educational Psychology, 61,* 19-35.

Rowe, K.J., & Rowe K.S. (1992a). The relationship between inattentiveness in the classroom and reading achievement (Part A): Methodological Issues. *Journal of the American*

Academy of Child and Adolescent Psychiatry, 31, 349-356.

Rowe, K.J., & Rowe, K.S. (1992b). The relationship between inattentiveness in the classroom and reading achievement (Part B): An explanatory study. *Journal of the American Academy of Child and Adolescent Psychiatry, 31,* 357-368.

Rowe, K.J., & Rowe, K.S. (1999). Investigating the relationship between students' attentive-inattentive behaviors in the classroom and their literacy progress. *International Journal of Educational Research, 31,* 1-138 (Whole Issue).

Rowe, K.S. (1997a). Double-blind placebo-controlled trial to assess the efficacy of intravenous gammaglobulin for the management of Chronic Fatigue Syndrome in adolescents. *Journal of Psychiatric Research, 31,* 133-147.

Rowe, K.S. (1997b). Follow-up of young people with Chronic Fatigue Syndrome. *Journal of Paediatrics & Child Health, 33,* A42, P34.

Rowe, K.S. (2001, January). *Follow up of 200 young people with CFS: Functional outcomes and relationship to symptom patterns and psychological features.* Paper presented at the fifth Conference of the American Association for Chronic Fatigue Syndrome, Seattle.

Rowe, K.S., & Fitzgerald, P. (1999). Educational strategies for chronically ill students: Chronic Fatigue Syndrome. *The Australian Educational and Developmental Psychologist,16(2),* 5-21.

Rowe, K.S., & Rowe, K.J. (1997). Norms for parental ratings on Conners' Abbreviated Parent-Teacher Questionnaire: Implications for the design of behavioral rating inventories and analyses of data derived from them. *Journal of Abnormal Child Psychology, 25,* 425-451.

Rowe, K.S., & Rowe, K.J. (1999a, May). *Symptom patterns of adolescents with chronic fatigue syndrome.* Paper presented at the 44th Annual Scientific Meeting of the Australian College of Paediatrics, Perth, Western Australia.

Rowe, K.S., & Rowe, K.J. (1999b, September). *Does the symptom complex of chronic fatigue syndrome occur in adolescents?* Paper presented at the Second World Congress on Chronic Fatigue Syndrome and Related Disorders: Towards Effective Diagnosis and Treatment in the 21st Century. Brussels, Belgium.

Sharpe, M., Chalder, T., Palmer, I., & Wessely, S. (1997). Chronic fatigue syndrome. A practical guide to assessment and management. *General Hospital Psychiatry, 19,* 185-99.

Sharpe M. (1997). Cognitive behavior therapy for functional somatic complaints: The example of chronic fatigue syndrome. *Psychosomatics, 38,* 356-362.

Smith, M.S., Mitchell, J., Corey, L., Gold, D., McCauley, E.A., Glover, D., & Tenover, F.C. (1991). Chronic fatigue in adolescents. *Pediatrics, 88,* 195-202.

Spielberger, C.D. (1977). *Self-evaluation questionnaire State-Trait Anxiety Inventory.* Palo Alto, California: Consulting Psychologists Press.

StatSoft. (1999). *STATISTICA for Windows 95/98/NT (Version 5.5).* Tulsa, OK: StatSoft Inc.

van der Linden, G., Chalder, T., Hickie, I., Koschera, A., Sham, P., & Wessely, S. (1999). Fatigue and psychiatric disorder: Different or the same?. *Psychological Medicine, 29,* 863-868.

Vercoulen, J.H.M.M., Swanink, C.M.A., Fennis, J.F.M., Galama, J.M.D., van der Meer, J.W.M., & Bleijenberg, G. (1994). Dimensional assessment of chronic fatigue syndrome. *Journal of Psychosomatic Research, 38,* 383-392.

Wessely, S., Chalder, T., Hirsch, S., Wallace, P., & Wright, D. (1996). Psychological symptoms, somatic symptoms, and psychiatric disorder in chronic fatigue and chronic fatigue syndrome: A prospective study in the primary care setting. *American Journal of Psychiatry, 153, 1050-*1059.

Wessely, S. (1997). Chronic fatigue syndrome: A 20th century illness?. *Scandinavian Journal of Work, Environment & Health, 23* Suppl 3,17-34.

18

A Multidimensional Evaluation of Adolescent Drug Abusers: Preliminary Results of a Longitudinal Study

Monique Bolognini
Psychiatric University Clinic for Children and Adolescents

Bernard Plancherel
Psychiatric University Clinic for Children and Adolescents

Jacques Laget
Psychiatric University Clinic for Children and Adolescents

Olivier Halfon
Psychiatric University Clinic for Children and Adolescents

Monique Bolognini · Psychiatric University Clinic for Children and Adolescents · SUPEA Research Unit · Bugnon 25A · Lausanne CH-1005 · Switzerland.

International Perspectives on Child and Adolescent Mental Health. Volume 2: Proceedings of the Second International Conference, edited by N. N. Singh, T. H. Ollendick, and A. N. Singh. © 2002 Elsevier Science Ltd. All rights reserved.

Adolescent drug abuse has become a very serious public-health issue in most European countries. Whereas a large range of treatment facilities have been developed no standardised evaluation instruments are available, either in the field of research or in the field of clinical activities. There is an obvious need for diagnostic tools adapted for adolescent drug abusers, particularly those that would enable the assignment of adolescents to appropriate therapeutic programs and the evaluation of treatment options. There has been little European research in this area despite the fact that it is a very important problem. This can be partially explained by the lack of a specific instrument.

In the United States, several instruments have been created in the last decade to evaluate adolescent substance use. Some provide diagnosis of substance abuse or dependence and others enable a wider evaluation, including biographical, psychological and social aspects. The former category includes the ADI (Adolescent Diagnostic Interview; Winters & Henly, 1993), a structured questionnaire for the diagnosis of 13-17-year-old adolescents; the MMPI-A (Weed, Butcher, & Williams, 1994), a self-report measure describing the attitudes of 14-18-year-old adolescents towards drugs and alcohol; the PESQ (Personal Experience Screening Questionnaire, Winters, 1992), a six-item questionnaire modelled on the CAGE, which investigates adult alcohol use. In the latter category, there are evaluation instruments such as the T-ASI (Teen-Addiction Severity Index, Kaminer, Bukstein, & Tarter, 1991), a structured interview investigating seven areas (drug use, school status, employment status, family relationships, legal status, social relations, and psychiatric status); the POSIT (Problem Oriented Screening Instrument for Teenagers, Hall, Richardson, Spears, & Rembert, 1998), a 139-item self-report covering 10 different areas (drug use, medical status, psychological status, peer relations, family relations, school status, employment status, social skills, spare-time activities, and aggressive/delinquent behaviour); the APSI (Adolescent Problem Severity Index, Metzger, Kushner & McLellan, 1991), and the PEI (Personal Experience Inventory, Winters & Henly, 1989), structured interviews identifying attitudes towards drug use and psycho-social factors and, finally, the ADAD (Adolescent Drug Abuse Diagnosis, Friedman & Utada, 1989), a 150-item structured interview investigating nine life problem areas (medical status, school history and status, employment status, social and peer relationships, family background and relationships, psychological status, illegal and delinquent behaviours, drug use, and alcohol use).

A follow-up study on adolescent drug or alcohol users was started in October 1998, supported by the Swiss Federal Office of Public Health. It was planned as the continuation of previous research on dependency behaviour and will last for three years. The main objective is to obtain a better understanding of addictive behaviour during adolescence, to draw individual profiles in different areas, and to evaluate life trajectories (care follow up, life events).

METHOD

Several evaluation instruments were included in the protocol in order to achieve the objectives.

(a) The MINI (Mini International Neuropsychiatric Interview; Sheehan, et al., 1992): an interview schedule, which gives a psychiatric diagnosis in different areas. In this research project only diagnoses referring to drug and alcohol abuse and dependence were investigated.

(b) A life events inventory (SUPEA, 1998), an evaluation covering major life events on a lifetime scale. Questions were asked in an interview which made it possible to control information and get details on when the event happened and how many times it happened.

(c) The Adolescent Drug Abuse Diagnosis, which provides a comprehensive evaluation of the subjects and enables measurement of their evolution over time. The SUPEA research team developed a French version of the instrument in agreement and with the collaboration of Alfred Friedman, the instrument's author (Friedman & Utada, 1989). It was adapted from the Addiction Severity Index (ASI; McLellan, et al., 1980), an investigation instrument that was developed for adults. It is a 150-item instrument for structured interview administration. The investigation relates to nine life problem areas. It gives a comprehensive evaluation of the adolescent and a severity rating for each of the life problem areas investigated (see Appendix I and II).

Some of the questions refer to a 30-day period while others investigate aspects over a lifetime scale. The adolescent is asked to report on facts of his/her life, behaviour, feelings, perceptions of problems or social relations, and apply ratings to both the frequency of certain behaviours and the intensity of specific reactions. The interviewer's and subject's opinions are required: at the end of each problem area the interviewer asks the subject how troubled he/she has been by this type of problem over the past 30 days and the degree to which he/she believes he/she needs help or treatment for those problems.

Severity ratings are calculated on the basis of the information collected. These ratings correspond to the subject's need for treatment in each area, taking into account the answers to the objective and factual items, and, to a lesser degree, the subject's own perception of problems and needs. The rating scale varies from "no problem" to "severe disturbances." In order to get more reliable ratings, a systematic calculation method has been developed (composite scores). The ADAD is administered individually and the interviewer must be trained, both for the instrument's use and in order to calculate severity ratings.

Participants

A total of 102 adolescents, aged 13 to 20 years, were recruited for the study in the French part of Switzerland. Data were collected between January 1999 and March 2000. All the subjects gave written consent to take part in the study. They agreed to be interviewed three times but were free to discontinue participation at any time if they so wished. Four psychologists were trained to collect the data through an interview lasting between 90 and 150 minutes. Second and third interviews were scheduled after 9 months and 18 months, respectively.

The participants recruited comprised one-third girls ($n = 36$) and two-thirds boys ($n = 66$), which is representative of the gender distribution of drug use in the Swiss population. The youngest participants were 13.5 years old and the oldest were 20 years, with a mean age of 17.0 years. There was an equal distribution between the extreme ages for both boys and girls (see Table 1).

The adolescents were recruited from several different contexts, institutional and non-institutional. The variety of recruitment sources provided a sample that was representative of young adolescent drug users. A significant proportion of the adolescents came from the general population (one-third); around 40 % of them were receiving medical care either in outpatient clinics or in a hospital Psychiatric Unit, and only a few adolescents were from closed residences (see Table 2).

Table 1. Distribution of subjects according to age

Age (years)	Boys		Girls		Total	
	N	%	N	%	N	%
13.5 - 15.5	10	15.2	7	19.4	17	16.7
15.5 - 16.5	11	16.7	8	22.2	19	18.6

Table 1 continued.

Age (years)	Boys		Girls		Total	
	N	%	N	%	N	%
16.5 - 17.5	22	33.3	5	13.9	27	26.5
17.5 - 18.5	11	16.7	11	30.6	22	21.6
18.5 - 20.0	12	18.2	5	13.9	17	16.7
Total	66	100.0	36	100.0	102	100.0

Mean age: 17.0 years

Table 2. Places from Which Subjects were Recruited

	Boys		Girls		Total	
	N	%	N	%	N	%
General population	21	31.8	11	30.6	32	31.4
Out-patient Units	20	30.3	5	13.9	25	24.5
In-patient Units	9	13.6	8	22.2	17	16.7
Residential institution	8	12.1	5	13.9	13	12.7
Detention institution	8	12.1	7	19.4	15	14.7
Total	66	100.0	36	100.0	102	100.0

RESULTS

The results refer only to the first interview. In accordance with the project's perspective, a large variety of substances were used (see Table 3). The criteria for drug use corresponded to minimum use of once a week. Almost all the adolescents were daily smokers. Two-thirds of boys and girls, in the same proportions, were regular alcohol users. The substance most commonly used was cannabis (87.9% of boys and 75% of girls). There was a very low proportion of regular hard drug users, due probably to the young age of the population. However, more girls than boys used ecstasy, amphetamines, heroin, and cocaine.

Table 3. Distribution of the Subjects According to Substances Used*

	Boys		Girls		Total	
	N	%	N	%	N	%
Tobacco	62	93.9	35	97.2	97	95.1
Alcohol	42	63.6	25	69.4	67	65.7
Cannabis	58	87.9	27	75.0	85	83.3
Ecstasy	3	4.5	4	11.1	7	6.9
Amphetamines	2	3.0	4	11.1	6	5.9
Heroin	3	4.5	6	16.7	9	8.8
Opioids	2	3.0	2	5.6	4	3.9
Cocaine	2	3.0	8	22.2	10	9.8
Other drugs (benzodiazepines, crack, hallucinogens)	3	4.5	7	19.4	10	9.8

* At least once a week during the last three months

Referring to the ADAD data, severity ratings were calculated for every area: medical, school, social, family, psychological, legal, alcohol and drug. Results for boys and girls are shown in Table 4. Girls had significantly higher scores in the medical, social, family and psychological areas.

Table 4. Severity Rating: Differences According to Gender

	Boys	Girls	p
Medical	1.9	3.2	<.01
School	4.8	5.0	ns
Social	3.8	4.8	<.05
Family	5.2	6.7	<.01
Psychology	4.5	5.9	<.05
Legal	4.4	3.8	ns
Drug	5.6	6.0	ns
Alcohol	3.5	4.0	ns

The area scores were then correlated (see Table 5). The fact that some areas were not significantly correlated, as was the case for the alcohol area and partially for the psychological area, justifies the need for separate measures to characterise the subjects. Moreover, it shows that those two domains must be investigated specifically due to the denial attitude they induce.

Table 5. Inter-area Correlations

	Medical	Family	Psychology	Legal	Alcohol	Drug	Social
School	-.127	.203	.110	.062	-.119	.131	.106
Medical		.263*	.391**	.006	.120	.119	.030
Family			.343**	.245*	.183	.301**	.283**
Psychology				.063	.110	.074	.229
Legal					.027	.379**	.411**
Alcohol						.134	.163
Drug							.353**

** $p < .01$

* $p < .05$

A cluster analysis for all 102 adolescents gave six sub-groups corresponding to a variety of profiles (see Figure 1). Drug use was found to be important, with high scores for five out of the six groups. There were very few adolescents with high scores except in the area of medical problems ($n = 6$). A group of 26 adolescents had low scores in all the areas, whereas another group of 15 adolescents had high scores only in the areas connected to dependent behaviour (i.e. legal, drug and alcohol). The largest group ($n = 32$) had high scores (except for the medical and legal areas). The two last groups were high in all areas except in the medical area ($n = 14$) and high in all areas except in the social and psychological area ($n = 9$), respectively.

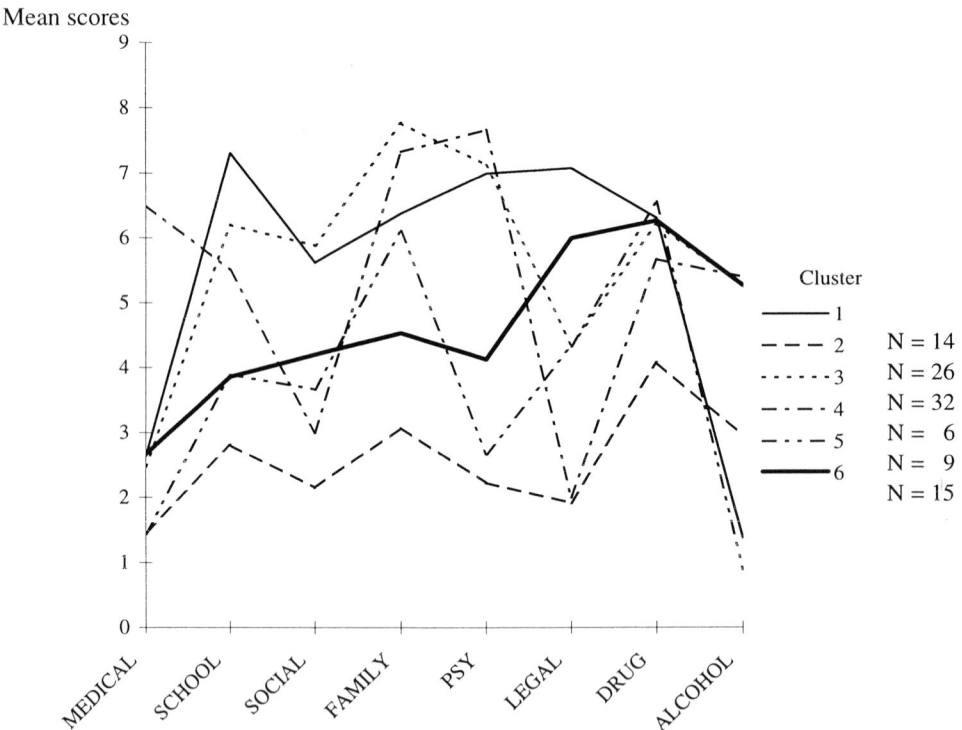

Figure 1. Subjects profiles according to the areas

Life events were evaluated on a lifetime scale. Compared to the data from another recent study that included a control group, it appeared that there were more important family problems (serious illness, alcoholism, suicide attempts) and more adolescents who had been abused or suffered from a serious physical illness in the present study. There was no significant difference for the other events (i.e., separation, divorce, death of a parent). Some questions were not asked in the control population. However, incidence seemed to be particularly high in the case of drug use in the family and for runaways (see Table 6).

Table 6. Life Time Life Events

Type of Event	Drug abuse group (n = 102)	Control group (n = 121)
	%	%
Separation, adoption	31	20
Divorce	46	40
Important family problems	46	30
Drug use in the family	52	*
Death of a parent	67	67
Serious psychological problems	44	*
Rape	10	4
Runaway	43	*

*Question not asked

The correlations between life events and severity ratings are given in Table 7. Most of the events were correlated with severity ratings. The highest correlations were found for psychological problems, rape, and runaway. The family and psychological areas were systematically linked to life events, except for divorce.

Table 7. Correlations between Severity Ratings and Life Events [1]

Severity ratings areas	Separation	Divorce	Family problems	Drug	Death of a parent	Psychological problems	Rape	Runaway
Medical				.30**		.38**	.34**	
School	.44**		.22*			.39**	.41**	.31**
Social	.21*					.28**	.32**	.21*
Family	.30**		.21*	.27**	.23*	.45**	.43**	.27**
Psychological	.30**		.33**	.34**	.21*	.68**	.47**	.26*
Legal	.38**	.25*						
Drug					.23*	.24*		
Alcohol							.30**	

** p < .01
* p < .05

[1] Only significant correlations are mentioned in this table

DISCUSSION

These preliminary results show the importance of a multi-dimensional approach to evaluate drug abuse during adolescence. Young adolescents mostly use soft drugs like cannabis and the majority of the adolescents included in the study had never tried hard drugs. The first evaluation shows that girls seem to use more drugs than boys, notably hard drugs. Moreover, the girls appear to have more problems than boys in the areas of family and psychological adjustment. It also appears that there are important connections between the psychological and family areas and drug use. As predictive factors, some negative life events appear to play an important role and have a direct or indirect effect on drug use. Data from the second and third assessments (9 months and 18 months after the first interview, respectively) will allow us to evaluate whether drug use will be reinforced or will decrease, and what the factors are that determine the observed changes.

ACKNOWLEDGMENTS

We thank all those who collaborated actively with this research project, notably Pablo Cascone, Léonie Chinet, Valérie Rossier, Philippe Stéphan, Grégoire Zimmermann, and Patrice Charpentier.

REFERENCES

Friedman, A.S., & Utada, A. (1989). A method for diagnosing and planning the treatment of adolescent drug abusers: The Adolescent Drug Abuse (ADAD) Instrument. *Journal of Drug Education, 19*, 285-312.

Hall, J.A., Richardson, B., Spears, J., & Rembert, J.K. (1998). Validation of the POSIT: Comparing drug using and abstaining youth, *Journal of Child and Adolescent Substance Abuse, 8 (2)*, 29-61.

Kaminer, Y., Bukstein, O., & Tarter, R.E. (1991). The Teen-Addiction Severity Index: Rationale and Reliability. *The International Journal of the Addictions, 26*, 219-226.

McLellan, A.T., Luborsky, L., Woody, G.E., & O'Brien, C.P. (1980). An improved diagnostic evaluation instrument for substance abuse patients: The Addiction Severity Index. *Journal of Nervous and Mental Diseases, 168*, 26-33.

Metzger, D., Kushner, H., & McLellan, A.T. (1991) *Adolescent Problem Severity Index* Philadelphia PA: University of Pennsylvania.

Sheehan, D., Janavs, J. , Knapp, E., Lecrubier, Y., & Weiler, E. (1992). *M.I.N.I.: Mini International Neuropsychiatric Interview*. Unpublished manuscript.

Weed, N.C., Butcher, J.N., & Williams, C.L. (1994). Development of MMPI-A Alcohol/Drug Problem Scales. *Journal Studies of Alcohol, 55*, 296-302.

Winters, K.C. (1992). Development of an adolescent alcohol and other drug abuse screening scale: Personal Experience Screening Questionnaire. *Addictive Behaviors, 17*, 479-490.

Winters, K.C., & Henly, G.A. (1989). Development of psychosocial scales for the assessment of adolescents involved with alcohol and drugs. *International Journal of the Addictions, 24*, 973-1001.

Winters, K.C., & Henly, G.A. (1993). Measuring alcohol and cannabis use disorders in an adolescent clinical sample. *Psychology of Addictive Behaviors, 7*, 185-196.

Appendix 1. Examples of ADHD Questions

I. MEDICAL STATUS
- Do you worry about your health?
- Have you ever been seriously ill?

II. SCHOOL HISTORY AND STATUS
- How many days in the past 30 have you been absent?
- How many of those absences were due to illness?
- How many of those absences were due to being truant?

III. EMPLOYMENT SECTION
- How many days were you paid for working during the past month?
- What was the longest period of time you held one job?

IV. SOCIAL ACTIVITIES AND PEER RELATIONS
- How much of your free or leisure time do you spend with the following persons?
1) Your family
2) Friends who use drugs
3) Friends who do not use drugs
4) Alone

0 = None/Not at all	2 = A fair amount
1 = A little	3 = A lot

V. FAMILY BACKGROUND AND RELATIONSHIPS
- How close do you feel to your mother?
- How much do you feel you can rely on what your father tells you?

0 = None/Not at all	2 = A fair amount
1 = A little	3 = A lot

VI. PSYCHOLOGICAL STATUS AND PROBLEMS
Have you ever had a significant period of a week or more (that was not a direct result of drug/alcohol use), in which you have
1) experienced serious depression
2) experienced serious anxiety or tension
3) experienced trouble understanding, concentrating, or remembering
4) experienced trouble controlling violent behavior
5) experienced serious thoughts of suicide
6) attempted suicide

VII. DELINQUENT/CRIMINAL BEHAVIOR
- How many times in your life have you been picked up by the police?
- What was the longest single time you were in jail?

0 = Never in jail
1 = Less than 24 hours - overnight
2 = 2 to 14 days
3 = 15 to 30 days
4 = more than 30 days

What for?

VIII. DRUG AND ALCOHOL ABUSE
- did you ever find that you needed larger and larger amounts of a particular drug to get high?
- Have you ever tried to cut down on any drugs but found you could not do it?
- Have you gotten in trouble in school due to alcohol or drugs within the past month?

Appendix II – Examples of ADHD rating scale

Client's Rating Scale

0 = None/Not at all
1 = A little
2 = A fair amount
3 = A lot

- How troubled or bothered have you been in the past 30 days by family problems?
- How important is it to you to get counseling or treatment for family problems?

Interviewing severity rating

- How would you rate the client's need for counseling for family problems?

Confidence ratings

Is the above information significantly distorted by:
- Client's misinterpretation
- Client's inability to understand

19

Incidence of Nonverbal Learning Disability in a High School Anger Management Class

Dee Duncan
The Neurodevelopmental Center

Keren Whiting-Monson
Granite High School

Jackie Kotter-Campbell
Granite High School

Jamie Fargo
University of Utah

David E. Nilsson
The Neurodevelopmental Center

Dee Duncan · Tremonton Psychological Services · 881 North Tremont Street · Tremonton · Utah 84337-1025 · United States.

International Perspectives on Child and Adolescent Mental Health. Volume 2: Proceedings of the Second International Conference, edited by N. N. Singh, T. H. Ollendick, and A. N. Singh. © 2002 Elsevier Science Ltd. All rights reserved.

Nonverbal learning disability (NLD) is a relatively new syndrome that is gaining increased attention in the educational and research literature. Rourke (1989) proposed a neuropsychological model in which NLD was conceptualized as a neurological syndrome believed to result from damage to the white matter connections in the right hemisphere of the brain that is important for intermodal integration. The resulting developmental and clinical characteristics were later described in a study identifying the assets and deficits found in persons with NLD (Harnadek & Rourke, 1994). Deficits have been noted in motor skills, visual-spatial skills, and social skills with accompanying assets in verbal skills and auditory memory with higher Verbal IQ compared to Performance IQ on tests of cognitive abilities (Rourke, Dietrich, & Young, 1973; Thompson, 1997).

Visual spatial deficits can present problems at home and school. Because of these visual-spatial deficits, individuals with NLD may wander away and get lost easily. These individuals may be disorganized and may present with disheveled appearance, misalignment of shirt buttons or a history of trouble learning to tie shoelaces. Poor performance in mathematics may result because of misalignment when calculating long division and double-digit multiplication problems. Difficulties may be noted in other visual-spatial skills, such as map reading or drawing complex figures and designs. The Rey-Osterreith Complex Figure Drawing (see Lezak, 1983) requires the ability to draw a complex, novel stimulus and may be useful in identifying individuals with NLD. Figure 1 is a sample of the Rey-Osterreith Complex Figure Drawing (ROCFD).

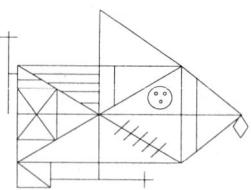

Figure 1. The Rey-Osterreith Complex Figure Drawing

In addition to visual spatial deficits, individuals with NLD have many social skills deficits. Social skills deficits often lead to difficulties at school where high rates of social contact occur. By the time these students get to secondary school, they are at risk for dropping out of the educational system and usually has a history of suspensions, fighting, excessive absences and tardies. In creating classes to address the behavioral excesses and social skills deficits of students with behavior problems, school districts often place students with NLD in these special behavioral intervention classes independent of a diagnosis and completely unaware that the student may have a non-verbal learning disability.

Another possible deficit experienced by students with NLD is the ability to recognize emotional facial expressions. Paul Ekman, an expert in the field of facial emotions, indicated that he was unaware of any studies looking at the ability of students with NLD to recognize facial emotions (personal communication, August 13, 1999). The purpose of this study was to estimate the number of students in a high school anger management class with possible features of NLD by assessing their visual spatial skills using the ROCFD and their ability to recognize facial expressions of emotions.

METHOD

Participants

One hundred high school students, ages 14 to 18 years, enrolled in an anger management class participated in the study. A control group of 32 student volunteers from a community service class also participated in the study.

Task 1

All subjects completed the copy, immediate and 30-minute delay drawings of the Rey-Osterreith Complex Figure Drawing (ROCFD). Samples of the drawings by students from the anger management class are presented in Figure 2. The first row contains the copy, immediate and delayed drawings of a 17-year-old male student. A 17-year-old female completed the second row drawings. Row 3 drawings are from a 16-year-old male. Not all students in the anger management class had difficulties in drawing the ROCFD as indicated by the quality of the drawings in Row 4 from a 16-year-old female.

Task 1 Scoring. Drawings were scored using the Denman system (Denman, 1987) that rated the 24 individual segments of the student's drawing on accuracy, position and angle. Raw scores were obtained by rating each of the 24 segments on a scale of 0 to 3 for a total of 72 possible points. Raw scores were converted to scaled scores with a mean of 10 and a standard deviation of 3.

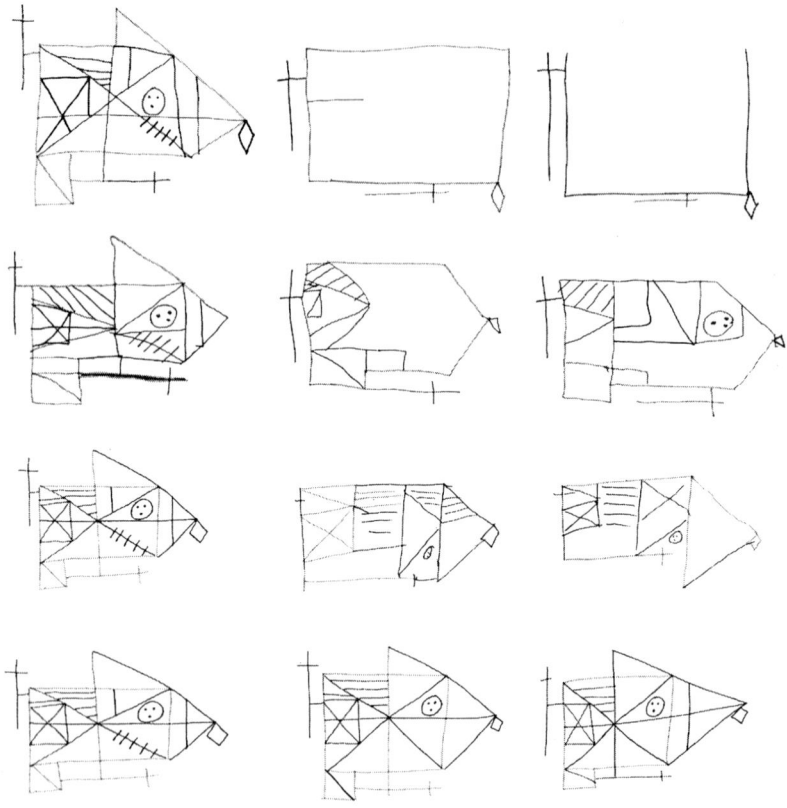

Figure 2.   Drawings of the ROCFD (Copy, Immediate and Delayed) of AMC Students

Qualitative scoring was accomplished using three raters with experience using the ROCFD. Rater 1 had 10 years experience and was the supervisor of the two post doctorate interns who were raters 2 and 3. Rater 2 had four years experience with the ROCFD and Rater 3 had 2 years experience. The drawings were randomly distributed to the three raters. The drawings were rated on a scale of 0 to 5 (0 or 1 = no impairment, 2 = mild, 3 = moderate, 4 = severe, and 5 = profound). The rater reviewed the student's three drawings (copy, immediate and delay) to make a rating that reflected the overall quality of all three drawings. Inter-rater agreement was accomplished by randomly assigning 30% of the drawings to a different rater. For purposes of inter-rater reliability, the ratings were grouped as follows: 0 - 1=no impairment,

2 - 3 mild/moderate, 4 - 5 severe/profound. Inter-rater agreement was calculated by dividing agreements by agreements plus disagreements. The mean inter-rater agreement was 63%. In reviewing the inter-rater agreements, it was noted that a correlation existed between years of experience and severity of rating. As the years of experience increased, the severity of the ratings also increased.

Task 2

Pictures of facial emotions were obtained from Paul Ekman's Human Interaction Laboratory and consisted of 110 pictures displaying the following emotions: happy, sad, anger, fear, surprise, disgust, and neutral (Ekman & Friesen, 1976). The faces were randomly displayed on a computer screen and the students circled their response on an answer sheet. Sixty two students from the anger management class participated. The control group (n = 52) was comprised of students from a community service class and from a pottery class who volunteered to participate.

RESULTS

Table 1 compares the anger management class with controls on the copy, immediate and delayed drawings of the ROCFD. On the copy drawings, 48 students (48%) from the anger management class received scaled scores of 3 or less compared to 6 students (19%) from the control group. The raw scores were converted to percentage scores for ease of comparison.

Table 1.   Percent of Scaled Scores on ROCFD by Group and by Drawing

		1	2	3	4	5	6	7	8	9	10	11	12	13	14	15	16	17
Copy																		
	AMC	31	6	11	9	3	10	5	1	8	2	3	2	4	4	0	1	0
	Ctl	16	0	3	6	0	6	3	0	9	25	9	0	19	3	0	0	0
Immediate																		
	AMC	19	3	6	10	7	14	5	9	10	8	6	3	0	0	0	0	0
	Ctl	3	3	3	3	3	6	13	3	13	9	6	9	13	6	6	0	0
Delay																		
	AMC	18	8	4	8	9	8	11	13	6	6	7	1	0	1	0	0	0
	Ctl	9	3	0	9	0	6	3	6	13	9	3	13	9	3	9	0	0

Note. AMC=Anger Management Class, Ctl=Control Group

Figure 3 presents the data in graphical form for comparing the performance of the AMC and the control group on just the copy version of the drawing. The percent of participants is listed for each of the scaled scores. From the AMC, 31% of the students obtained a scaled score of 1 compared to only 16% from the control group. By way of contrast, only 2% of the students from the anger management class obtained a scaled score of 10 compared to 25% of the students in the control group.

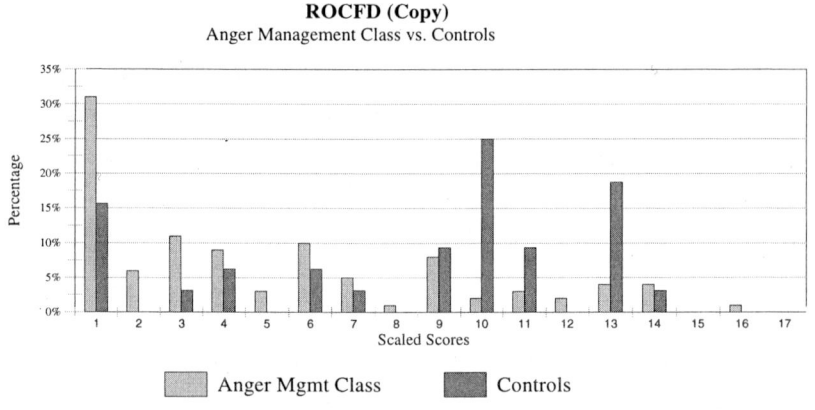

Figure 3.   Percentage of scaled scores on the copy drawing of the ROCFD by group

Table 2 lists the frequency of the impairment scores obtained by the AMC students. On the impairment index, 52 students received an impairment index rating of 4 or higher. Note that the higher the score, the higher the impairment. No qualitative scores were obtained for the control group.

Table 2.   Frequency of Impairment Index Scores of the AMC students

	Impairment Index					
	0	1	2	3	4	5
Frequency	2	6	15	25	29	23

Note. AMC=Anger Management Class.

In rating the facial expressions emotions, there was no significant difference on the mean number of correct answers between the anger management class and the control group. The AMC obtained an average of 81.58 correct answers (S.D. 11.8) and the control group obtained an average of 83.19 correct answers (S.D. 9.6).

DISCUSSION

A significant number of students from the AMC failed to accurately draw the ROCFD compared to the control group.   Both quantitative and qualitative ratings indicated that approximately 50% of the students in the AMC class had visual spatial deficits as measured by the ROCFD.   As indicated above, visual spatial deficits are a feature of NLD. Enrollment in an anger management class as an indicator of social skills deficits suggests that many of the students in this study have at least two of the prominent features known to be associated with NLD: visual-spatial deficits and social skills deficits.

It is not currently known if students with NLD have deficits in recognizing facial expressions of emotions. This study did not find any differences between the AMC and control groups. One possible explanation for the non-significant results is that too many pictures were used and that averaging the number of correct responses across groups may have diluted any differences that may have existed. An inspection of the responses of the top ten students on the ROCFD and the lowest ten students on the ROCFD identified 15 pictures that may be useful in future studies to discriminate between the AMC and control groups.

Poor performance on the ROCF by the AMC group may be accounted for by IQ scores. That is, the level of cognitive ability may be impacting the quantitative scores on the ROCFD. This study did not obtain a measure of cognitive abilities. Future studies may need to investigate the role of cognitive abilities on the ROCFD by treating it as an intervening variable.

Underachievement may be contributing to poor performance on the ROCFD. Underachievement may lead to poor classroom performance and subsequent risk for dropping out of school. Being at risk for dropping out of school was one of the admission criteria to the AMC. Lack of trying to accurately copy the ROCFD would lead to poor scores. Therefore it is possible that a student who was an underachiever might obtain scores similar to those of a student with NLD.

Many students work in the afternoons and evenings after school, sometimes until late at night when the business closes for the night. Many fast food businesses hire students to work the night shift and, as a result, the student is sleepy the next day. Low arousal levels and drowsiness may impact on drawing performance of the ROCFD. Other factors that may lead to poor performance include gang membership, substance abuse or mood disorders. While no concrete numbers were available, many members of area gangs were enrolled in the AMC because of fighting at school, high rates of absences and at risk for dropping out. High academic performance is not generally required by gangs, which may have impacted on the number of students obtaining poor scores on the ROCFD. Students with substance abuse problems are also at risk for dropping out of school, hence their enrollment in the AMC. It is unknown how many, if any, of the students were under the influence of drugs or alcohol during testing which may have impacted the number of students who failed the ROCFD.

Students with NLD are often at risk for depression and anxiety (; Rourke & Fuerst, 1991; Rourke, Young, & Lenars, 1989; Thompson, 1997). Future studies would benefit from assessing for mood disorders in students with possible NLD. In addition, a neurological history to determine the presence of head injury would be useful in better understanding the complex nature of students who get referred to an anger management class. Perhaps a measure of executive function would be useful in identifying students with NLD. Future studies could examine correlations between the ROCFD and test of executive functioning.

This study was useful in pointing out that a high number of students in an anger management class have visual spatial difficulties, a feature of non-verbal learning disability. The possibility exists that a higher than usual number of students with NLD may be unknowingly enrolled in these types of special intervention classes. Accurate assessment and identification of these students with NLD would allow for a more precise and specific curriculum of greater academic and behavioral benefit.

REFERENCES

Ekman, P., & Friesen, W. V. (1976). *Pictures of Facial Affect.* San Francisco: Human Interaction Laboratory, University of California Medical Center.

Harnadek, M. C. S., & Rourke, B. P. (1994). Principal identifying features of the syndrome of nonverbal learning disabilities in children. *Journal of Learning Disabilities, 27,* 144-154.

Lezak, M. (1983). *Neuropsychological assessment* (2nd Ed.). New York: Oxford University Press.

Rourke, B. P. (1989). *Nonverbal learning disabilities: The syndrome and the model.* New York: Guilford Press.

Rourke, B. P., & Fuerst, D. R. (1989). *Learning disabilities and psychosocial functioning: A neuropsychological perspective.* New York: Guilford Press.

Rourke, B. P., Young, G. C., & Leenaars, A. A. (1989). A childhood learning disability that predisposes those afflicted to adolescent and adult depression and suicide risk. *Journal of Learning Disabilities, 22,* 169-175.

Rourke, B. P., Dietrich, D.M., & Young, G. C. (1973). Significance of WISC Verbal-Performance discrepancies for younger children with learning disabilities. *Perceptual and Motor Skills, 36,* 275-282.

Thompson, S. (1997). *The source for nonverbal learning disorders.* East Moline, IL: LinguSystems.

20

Effects of Environmental Factors on Psychological Adjustment in Very Low Birthweight and Higher Birthweight Jamaican Adolescents

Michael C. Lambert
Michigan State University

Maureen E. Sarnms-Vaughan
University of the West Indies

Neal Schmitt
Michigan State University

Beth Kirsch
Michigan State University

Nigel Paneth
Michigan State University

Chad M. Russ
Michigan State University

Michael C. Lambert · Michigan State University · Department of Psychology · Psychology Research Building · East Lansing · Michigan 48824-1117 · United States.

International Perspectives on Child and Adolescent Mental Health. Volume 2: Proceedings of the Second International Conference, edited by N. N. Singh, T. H. Ollendick, and A. N. Singh. © 2002 Elsevier Science Ltd. All rights reserved.

The development of neonatal intensive care units (NICU) throughout the developed world have increased the survival rates of Very Low Birth Weight (VLBW) neonates (i.e., <1,500 grams) (Paneth, 1995). Some authors (e.g., Lorenz, Wooliever, Jetton, & Paneth, 1998; Paneth, 1995) are, however, concerned about the long term sequela of NICU and its effects on biologically based developmental processes, including hearing (Aram, Hack, Hawkins, Weissman, & Borawski-Clark, 1991; Veen, et al., 1993), vision, and cognitive and neurological functioning (Breslau & Chilcoat, 2000; Breslau, Chilcoat, Johnson, Andreski, & Lucia, 2000; Escobar, Littenberg, & Petitti, 1991; Veen, et al., 1991b). Thus, researchers interested in how such outcomes affect VLBW children, have focused primarily on physical disability and mental retardation have documented moderate or severe disabilities in 15-20% of VLBW infants (Escobar, et al., 1991; Veen, et al., 1991a). Some investigations have revealed that despite "normal" intellectual abilities, VLBW children have higher levels of academic underachievement than HBW children (Klebanov, Brooks-Gunn, & McCormick, 1994a, 1994b; Omstein, Ohisson, Edmonds, & Asztalos, 1991) and that their academic underachievement is often associated with high rates behavior and emotional problems (Schraeder, Heverly, & Rappaport, 1990).

Recent research has shown that behavior problems and especially Attention Deficit Hyperactivity Disorder (ADHD) in VLBW children may have a basis in perinatal brain injury (Whitaker, et al., 1997). Many scholars of VLBW children, however, continue to focus primarily on physical disability and only intellectual development (i.e., aptitude for academic functioning). More recently some researchers (e.g., Whitaker, et al., 1997) have begun to focus on behavioral outcomes but few investigators have been began to address the direct, indirect, and mediated effects of intellectual development and behavior problems on adjustment, including academic achievement (i.e., school-based learning) among the VLBW population (Pharoah, Stevenson, Cooke, & Stevenson, 1994).

Behavior and emotional problems can have severe consequences for children who exhibit them, including poor academic outcomes and disturbed interpersonal relationships (Klebanov, et al., 1994a; Ornstein, Ohisson, Edmonds, & Asztalos, 1991). Attention Deficit Hyperactivity Disorder (ADHD) represents one of the most prevalent child behavior problem syndromes in all children (Nigg, Hinshaw, Cane, & Treuting, 1998; Tannock, 1998) and has been repeatedly documented as more prevalent among VLBW children (Hille, et al., 2000; Klebanov, et al., 1994a; McCormick, Gortmaker, & Sobol, 1990; Ornstein, et al., 1991) than controls. High prevalence of ADHD in VLBW children places them at severe risk for other psychological problems because of its high comorbidity with such problems (Shelton, et al., 1998; Tannock, 1998) including conduct and social problems (Hinshaw, 1992) and it also makes them vulnerable to poor adaptive functioning throughout their adolescent and adulthood years (Barkley, 1990; Klein & Mannuzza, 1991).

Although VLBW children are at risk for poor psychological adjustment, the environment in which children reside can mediate such risks (Liaw & Brooks-Gunn, 1994). For example, the effects of sociocultural factors including SES and family functioning, can mediate certain risk factors. Indicators of SES such as maternal education, parental occupation and material resources have been linked not only to physical health, but cognitive abilities, school achievement and emotional outcomes in most children (Brooks Gunn, Duncan, & Britto, 1999; Jimerson, Egeland, & Teo, 1999; Liaw & Brooks-Gunn, 1994; Wills, McNamara, & Vaccaro, 1995). Therefore, some researchers who study VLBW children (Liaw & Brooks-Gunn, 1994) have begun to investigate the effects of sociocultural variables including ethnicity and SES and how such factors influence critical developmental outcomes including scholastic achievement, (e.g., Ross, Lipper, & Auld, 1990), intellectual development (e.g., Liaw & Brooks-Gunn, 1994; Ross, Lipper, & Auld, 1992; Saigal, Szatmari, Rosenbaum, Campbell, & King, 1990) academic achievement (Klebanov, et al., 1994a; Ornstein, et al., 1991) and behavioral and emotional problems (e.g., Liaw & Brooks-Gunn, 1994; Whitaker, et al., 1997).

Family risk factors (e.g., maternal intelligence, teenage parenthood) have been linked to poor intellectual development and severe behavior problems in VLBW children. However, virtually no research addressing how functioning (e.g., cohesiveness among members) within existing families predict outcomes for these children. There is even less research on the effects on family functioning, SES, and other factors on psychological adjustment in VLBW and other Jamaican children. Recent research has indicated higher levels of behavior and emotional problems in VLBW than higher birthweight (HBW) Jamaican children (Lambert, Samms-Vaughan, Bellas, & Russ, 2000), a finding similar to those in other nations including the United States (McCormick at al., 1992). The pathways to such problems and how the problems themselves might influence school achievement and other forms of adjustment remain unexplored.

For normal birthweight (NBW) children, it has been repeatedly documented that a causal relationship exists between child behavioral and emotional problems, especially externalizing (e.g., aggression) problems and academic achievement (see Hinshaw [1992] for review). Family functioning has also been shown to be negatively associated with child behavioral and emotional problems (Carter, Grigorenko, & Pauls, 1995) but data on this factor including its effects on intellectual abilities and academic achievement even in general populations samples of children is sparse (Hinshaw, 1992). Most research addressing risk (e.g., low SES) and protective factors (e.g., material resources) associated with outcomes in VLBW and other children, however, have achieved their goals via traditional methodological designs including general linear models methodology such as analysis of variance and multiple regression (Greenberg, et al., 1999). These studies have furthered our understanding of the outcomes for VLBW and other children, but like most research the methodology used possess limitations. Among drawbacks inherent in such methodology is the limited number of risk and protective factors one may examine in a given analysis and failure to simultaneously account for critical issues such as measurement error in addressing mediation, an issue that is important to most social scientists (Hoyle & Smith, 1994).

Although more powerful, flexible, and comprehensive in addressing such questions, structural equation modeling (SEM), a procedure that simultaneously employs multiple regression, factor analysis, and path analysis simultaneously while accounting for measurement error is seldom used (Fassinger, 1987; Hoyle, 1994; Hoyle & Smith, 1994). Other strengths of SEM include its ability to test not only ones model of interest but to test alternative models and to do so simultaneously in two or more samples of interest. Use of this procedure is increasing in behavioral sciences research (e.g., Wills, et al., 1995). Its complexity and the need for specialized training in its employment makes SEM a rarely employed method in outcomes for children who are at risk for developmentally based problems including VLBW children who are vulnerable to a myriad of risk factors and whose outcomes may be mediated by numerous protective factors. Thus, it is difficult to determine whether the risk and protective factors and the outcome trajectories identified for NBW children are the same for their VLBW peers.

The data analytic issues discussed above are evident for VLBW White youth, but they are salient for VLBW and other children of color, including those of the African Diaspora, especially those living outside industrialized nations of Europe and North America who are usually neglected in most empirical investigations. Lack of focus on Black VLBW children within and across such nations continues despite our knowledge that neonates of African descent are more likely to be born VLBW than their White counterparts (Paneth, 1995). It is uncertain whether Black VLBW infants differ from their higher birthweight (HBW) peers according to the direct effects of specific factors and the variables documented to mediate their effects psychological adjustment. Also unknown is whether the sociocultural context in which Black children reside may influence their psychological adjustment. For example, VLBW neonates in the United States, an industrialized nation are treated more aggressively than their counterparts in a developing nation such as Jamaica, which cannot afford very aggressive intervention. Thus, only the hardiest VLBW infants survive with little or no intervention. Consequences of different types of aggressive intervention on physical disabilities in the VLBW children have recently been documented but this research has not specifically focused on behavioral outcomes of Black VLBW children within and outside the United States. Differences in outcomes by intensiveness of neonatal service provision have recently been documented through a comparison of infants born before 27 weeks in the US and Holland. Little is known of the outcomes of VLBW infants in Jamaica, or in any other setting where circumstances permit only the hardiest of such infants to survive. The United States and Jamaica may well differ considerably in the range of physical disabilities and cognitive and behavioral outcomes found among VLBW survivors. In the United States attempts to provide intensive care to even the most immature and lowest weight newborns is fairly routine, while in Jamaica, health care resources do not permit providing intensive care services to any but a small fraction of VLBW neonates.

Being of African descent and growing up in a predominantly Black society like Jamaica, has its own set of challenges (e.g., economic) and benefits (e.g., less racial discrimination) that may influence the psychological outcomes (Lambert, et al., 1999a) for the VLBW child. Thus, although indirect, direct, and mediating predictors of adjustment may lead to specific outcomes, in different groups of children, the pathways between such predictors and criterion (dependent) variables are virtually unknown for children of color, especially those of African descent living in developing nations. Moreover, no information seems to exist regarding whether such pathways are the same for both VLBW and HBW children within different societies.

The present study begins to disentangle the issues outlined above by focusing on VLBW Jamaican children and their HBW peers. All research participants are Black, eliminating concerns regarding comparisons across different races, and some of the sociocultural confounds of race and SES often emerging from other studies (see Liaw & Brooks-Gunn, 1994). Most hospital care in Jamaica is based on the practice of socialized medicine and because of the need for hospitalization in one of the few centralized institutions in that nation that provide neonatal intensive care, almost all VLBW survivors in Jamaica receive uniform care. Prenatal and perinatal health care services are scarce in contrast to the industrialized nations, but service utilization varies less than in some industrialized nations where the interaction between race, SES, and service utilization is a major issue for researchers (Williams & Rucker, 1996).

Despite the strengths of the present study, a major obstacle for almost all types of behavioral sciences research in Jamaica is finding measures that are culturally relevant for, and even normed on that population. Most measures employed in Jamaican-based research are either used in their current form or slightly modified in language and content for that population. The psychometric properties of such measures are unknown, making SEM techniques discussed above most appropriate as they allow the simultaneous examination of the measurement and structural model (Fassinger, 1987). Flexibility of these techniques for modification and retesting including the removal of nonsignificant paths and retesting whether removal of such paths removes important information from the model (Fassinger, 1987) makes them especially appropriate for research on not only VLBW children but on both VLBW and HBW Jamaican children who are seldom studied. Structural equation modeling also allows the simultaneous testing of direct, indirect, and mediating effects, of factors within a specified theoretical model and can therefore determine the relative contribution of importance of various risk and protective factors for the groups studied (Fassinger, 1987; Hoyle & Smith, 1994). This technique also allows the simultaneous testing of the same theoretical model across two or more groups of research participants and therefore permits one to determine whether the causal pathways are similar for the groups studied. The causal model and the resulting hypotheses that the present study tests are presented next and followed by the methodology employed to assess this model.

Causal Model

The theoretical model tested is presented in Figure 1. We hypothesized that similar causal linkages exist between the hypothesized constructs for VLBW and HBW children. For both samples, hypothesized causal relationships existing between resources available to the family in the form of maternal education and the material resources to which it contributes affect family functioning which in turn determine intellectual development of the child Intellectual ability then influences child behavioral and emotional problems and achievement, with a causal pathway between child behavioral and emotional problems and achievement. Specifically, it depicts positive causal linkages between maternal education and possessions and to family functioning via a positive pathway to cohesion (i.e., closeness between family members) and a negative causal link to distance (separation between family members) wit cohesion and distance being positively and negatively linked respectively to intellectual functioning and academic achievement. Cohesion and distance are also hypothesized to be negatively and positively linked respectively to child behavioral and emotional problems. The model therefore indicates the testing of several direct paths and their possible mediation via other indirect paths, but this chapter focuses only on the direct and mediated paths presented below. Besides the paths described above, the error terms between a measure of nonverbal intelligence and the Arithmetic are covaried to reflect the strength of nonverbal reasoning, constructs shared by both measures (Satler, 1992) and the fact that both measures were administered to each child by the same professional. Each variable and its critical relationship with other variables in the model are described in detail below.

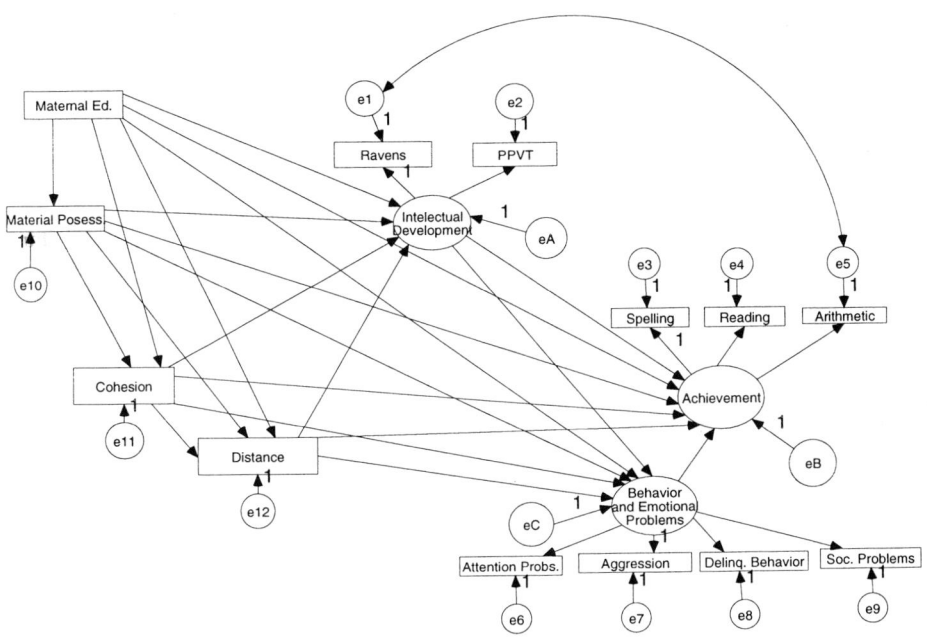

Figure 1. Hypothetical causal model

Maternal Education

The model depicts direct causal links between maternal education and intellectual development, achievement, and behavior and emotional problems. It contributes to income and material possessions (Brooks-Gunn, et al., 1999) but should only be moderately and positively associated with possessions in our sample as many Jamaicans receive unreported material goods and money (e.g., remunerations from relatives overseas), which might be unrelated to their education level (Lambert, et al., 1999b). Maternal education is also positively associated wit intellectual development and achievement (Chen, Lee, & Stevenson, 1996) but negatively associated with behavior and emotional problems (Brooks-Gunn, et al., 1999). Links from this exogenous variable to these two endogenous variables have been identified in North American samples (Brooks-Gunn, et al., 1999; Chen, et al., 1996). However, because of the emphasis most Jamaican adults place on education (Lambert, Knight, Taylor, & Achenbach, 1996), we believed that the effects of maternal education on achievement should be mediated by intellectual ability. Furthermore, we hypothesized a direct path from maternal education to intellectual ability and tat the relationship would also be mediated by material possessions in the home. The material possessions are believed to be indicators of a more enriched environment, which fosters intellectual development (Greenberg, et al., 1999). We also reasoned tat because of greater exposure to the importance of appropriate family functioning among more educated Jamaicans, cohesiveness, a family attribute that is important to most Jamaicans (Brice, 1982) should be positively associated with maternal education, but maternal education should be negatively associated with distance and separation. Similarly we presumed that because of the emphasis that Jamaican place on appropriate child behavior, irrespective of educational level, there should be a nonsignificant relationship between maternal education and behavior.

Material Possessions

Summed material possessions (e.g., telephone, cable television, automobile) have been linked to psychological outcomes for Jamaicans (Lambert, et al., 1999b; Samms-Vaughan, 2000) and to psychological functioning in North American children (Brooks-Gunn, et al., 1999; Wills, et al., 1995). The direct effects of this endogenous variable on family functioning, intellectual development, child behavioral and emotional problems, and achievement were of interest and are included in the model. However, we predicted that because of the emphasis all Jamaicans (regardless of their material wealth) place on appropriate behavior (Lambert, Weisz, & Knight, 1989) the effects of material possessions on these outcomes should be infinitesimal and thus be nonsignificant.

Family Functioning

Understanding family functioning and its effects on children's psychological outcomes is important but literature on this issue is sparse (Hinshaw, 1992) and virtually no literature on the effects of SES on family functioning exists. Nonetheless, theoretical literature suggests that the quality of child and parent relationship vary according to SES (Bronfenbrenner, 1956). Some empirical work indicates that high SES mediates negative family effects at least in single parent family structure (McCandles, Lueptow, & McClendon, 1998). Thus, direct causal pathways from possessions (a proxy for SES) to family functioning as determined by cohesion (i.e., emotional closeness between family members) and distance (avoidance of family members and family activities) are represented in the model. A negative association was hypothesized between distance and both intellectual development and achievement but a positive causal link between distance and behavior problems was predicted. Cohesion was hypothesized to be positively associated with intellectual ability and achievement but negatively associated with behavior.

Intellectual Ability

Intellectual functioning is widely known to be directly and positively associated wit achievement (see Satler 1996) but is also documented to be negatively associated wit child behavioral and emotional problems. Therefore, these relationships were tested. The effects of education, possession, cohesion and distance on intellectual functioning, achievement, and behavior problems were also estimated. In addition, indirect effects of these exogenous variables on achievement and behavior problems were explored (Jimerson, et al., 1999).

METHOD

Sample Descriptions

Two samples of children, one of very low birth weight (i.e., < 1,500 grams or les than 32 weeks gestation) and their higher birthweight peers were compared, both identified from the Jamaican Perinatal Mortality and Morbidity Survey of 1986-87. This survey was originally designed to identify factors contributing to perinatal, neonatal and maternal mortality and morbidity. The maternal mortality and morbidity (cohort) study included all mothers delivering a product of gestation throughout the island of Jamaica, regardless of the outcome of the pregnancy. Some 10,500 mothers were interviewed and their babies examined, representing 94% of all births in the island over a two-month period. The Morbidity (VLBW) Study included all children admitted to the seven neonatal care units throughout the island (i.e., units with a pediatrician), during the six-month period September 1, 1986 to February 28, 1987. There were a total of 1,822 admissions. Only VLBW children (n = 108) and their (n = 1,137) peers with completed measures on all the constructs on which the present study focused were included in the study.

Higher Birthweight Sample

At age 11 years, a geographical sub-sample of the 1720 families of the HBW cohort children were contacted and all children were evaluated. All cohort survivors living or attending school in the Kingston and St. Andrew region, the most urban areas in Jamaica, were included. The normal birth weight sample is drawn from these cohort children, after excluding 19 children who criteria for inclusion in the very low birth weight sample.

Very Low Birthweight Sample (VLBW)

At age 11 years, all VLBW survivors with a birth weight 1 500g and/or less than 32 weeks gestation from the cohort and morbidity studies throughout the entire island were evaluated in a similar manner to the normal birthweight children, although additional assessments of hearing, vision, and neurological status were also assessed (not discussed in this chapter). These children formed the very low birthweight sample. VLBW survivors (N = 213) were identified from the Cohort and Morbidity studies. Contact was made with 154 families (72.3%). Forty-six of these children were unable to be evaluated due to non-response, migration and death occurring after the cohort and morbidity studies were completed. Of the original sample 108 50.7% were evaluated. Forty-three children (39.8%) were born during the cohort months and 65 (60.2%) during the additional four months of the morbidity survey.

Cohort and non-cohort VLBW children were similar at birth with regard to their mean birth weights (1,604.4, 1,559.4g), mean gestational ages (31.1, 30.7 weeks), and mean Apgar scores at one minute (7.2, 6.6) and five minutes after birth (8.7, 8.3). Apgar scores have a value of 0 (worst) to 10 (best) and are used to determine the need for resuscitation of a newborn at birth. Cohort and non-cohort children also had a similar gender distribution (37.3% and 43.9 % male) and a similar proportion of children that were small for their gestational age (20.6%, 17.9%). Some VLBW cohort children (49.9%) were admitted to neonatal care units.

Data Collection Procedures

The parent data were collected via interviews conducted in the participants' homes, schools, or neighborhood clinics according to the participants' preferences. Parents who agreed to participate were handed a copy of a demographic questionnaire that included questions on maternal education and other demographic information and a copy of the FACES. Trained nurse interviewers interviewed each parent and tested each child but to circumvent problems associated with method variance, the nurses who assessed children were different from those who interviewed their parents. Each parent was asked permission for their adolescent to receive individualized intellectual and school achievement testing, which occurred in the child's school or neighborhood clinic.

Measures

SES Parental occupation has been widely used as a proxy for SES in Jamaican and other youth (see Achenbach Lambert, Lyubansky & Achenbach, 1998) but this practice often excludes unemployed Jamaican adults. As documented above maternal education is highly predictive of outcomes in children and families, but household possessions while somewhat associated with maternal education are also linked to children's adjustment (see Samms-Vaughan, 2000). Both maternal education and material possessions were used as proxies for SES in the model. The possessions variable was derived from a group of nine questions addressing the presence or absence of items (i.e., television, refrigerator, living room furniture, telephone, stereo equipment, cable/satellite connection, motor vehicle, washing machine, and freezer) in each household. Weighting each item according to value (i.e., based on the average cost of each item) has been documented to be as predictive of children's outcomes as simple addition how many items were endorsed as present Samms-Vaughan, 2000) and thus the latter was used.

Family Functioning

The Family Adaptability and Cohesion Scales (FACES-II) (Olson, Portner, & Lavee, 1985), a 30-item measure of family functioning was used. Adult or adolescent family members (mothers in this study) rate each item on a five-point Likert scale ranging from 1 (almost never) to 5 (almost always). Items on this scale form two factors, labeled cohesion (e.g., "1. Family members are supportive of each other during difficult times," "7. Our family does things together") and adaptability ("4. Each family member has input in major decisions," "20. Our family tries new ways of dealing problems"). Thus, the 16 items on the cohesion scale reflect bonding family members have toward one another while the 14 items forming the adaptability scale reflect the ability of the family to change in response to situational and developmental stress (Knight, Tein, Shell, & Roosa, 1992). The FACES is widely used internationally and was recently used in research on Jamaican immigrants (Hohn, 1996). Coefficient alphas for the two factors established for this measure were .87 and .80 but for the Jamaican sample they were abysmal at .37 and .48 respectively. Reasoning that the Factor Structure of the FACES was not suitable for Jamaica, we performed a confirmatory factor analysis of this measure on our sample which revealed that the structure was not confirmed (χ^2 404) = 3,448.53, p < 0001; Comparative Fit Index (CFI) = .61 Normed Fit Index (NFI) = .58, Root Mean Square Error of Approximation (RMSEA) = .08. Principal factor analysis was performed on the measure and the screen test suggested the retention and rotation of two factors. The Promax option in SPSS was used to retain and perform oblique rotations for two, three and four factor solutions. On the basis of theoretical meaningfulness and highest set of coefficient alphas (i.e., .90 and .74) the two factor solution was chosen and named as cohesion (e.g., helping other family members emotionally, sharing free time with each other) and distance (e.g., doing one's own thing, feeling closer to others outside one's family).

Intellectual Development

The Peabody Picture Vocabulary Test (PPVT), a measure of verbal comprehension (Dunn, 1997) and the Raven's Color Progressive and Standard Matrices (Raven, Raven, & Court, 1995), a measure of reasoning, were used to assess intellectual abilities. Both measures have been successfully used to evaluate Jamaican children in the past and psychometric properties identified for Jamaica were similar to those for the United States (Simeon, Callender, Wong, Grantham-McGregor, & Ramdath, 1994; Walker, Grantham McGregor, Himes, & Williams, 1994). The measures were chosen because of their ease in administration and the need for little or no language in usage, thus limiting the effects of differences in U.S. versus Jamaican English usage required in administration of other widely used U.S.-normed intelligence tests.

School Achievement

The Wide Range Achievement Test-Revised (WRAT-R), a measure of school achievement in the domains of spelling, reading and arithmetic (Wilkinson, 1994) was used. Like the PPVT, this measure has been successfully used in Jamaica and is documented to have acceptable psychometric properties for this population (Simeon, et al., 1994; Walker, et al., 1994).

Behavior and Emotional Problems

The Jamaican Youth Checklist (NC), patterned after the Child Behavior Checklist (CBCL) was the measure of behavior problems. Parents rate children on each problem item by circling a Q if the item is not true of the child, 1 if it is somewhat or sometimes true, and 2 if it is very true or often true Extensive research using the Jamaican Youth Checklist (Lambert & Lyubansky, 1999; Lambert, Lyubansky, & Achenbach, 1998; Lambert, et al., 1999a) has been done, but no information on the factor structure (i.e., syndromes) for Jamaican youth exists. Like the previous studies on Jamaican youth, we therefore relied on the classification system of the CBCL (Achenbach, 1991a, 1991b, 1991c, 199 ld) to group the behavior of the children surveyed in the present study. Four of the eight cross-informant syndromes were derived from principal components analyses of parent- teacher- and self report forms of the CBCL. The syndromes are labeled Social Problems (e.g., acts too young, clings), Attention Problems (e.g., can't sit still, impulsive), Delinquent Behavior (e.g., swears, steals), and Aggressive Behavior (e.g., mean, attacks others) were the manifest variables used for the latent variable behavior problems as such factors are deemed to have very high comorbidity with one another (Hinshaw, 1992). Moreover as Table 1 indicates they are significantly correlated with each other. The CBCL, on which the Jamaican measure is patterned, is widely used in national and international research and has excellent psychometric properties. Normative research on the Jamaican measures is ongoing, but earlier research has documented that the measures have psychometric properties for Jamaicans that are similar to those for U.S. samples (Lambert, Knight, Taylor, & Achenbach, 1994; Lambert, et al., 1996; Lambert, et al., 1998).

Data Analyses

All structural equation modeling (SEM) analyses were performed using AMOS 4.0 (Arbuckle & Wothke, 1999). SEM is documented to have numerous advantages over more traditional analyses as a single analysis can accommodate multiple potentially dependent predictors and outcomes, it allows the researcher to simultaneously estimate a measurement model, make specifications regarding measured variables and the latent construct they theoretically measure and specify the structural relationships between latent constructs (DeShon, 1998 #967 [Hoyle, 1994]). Using specific statistical programs, the SEM technique provides fit indices, used to assess whether a hypothesized model ft the researcher's data (DeShon, 1998).

Table 1. Correlations Among Variables Used in SEM Modeling

	1	2	3	4	5	6	7	8	9	10	11	12	13
Higher **Birthweight Children**													
1. Maternal Education													
2. Material Possessions	.353****												
3. Ravens Progressive Matrices	.248****	.378****											
4. Peabody Picture Vocab. Test	.339****	.406****	.606****										
5. WRAT-R Spelling	.318****	.359****	.559****	.669****									
6. WRAT Reading	.278****	.312****	.571****	.973****	.87[a]								
7. WRAT-R Arithmetic	.285****	.355****	.636****	.612****	.76[a]	.707****							
8. Social Problems	.02	-.072*	-.103****	-.087**	-.11[a]	-.115****	-.13****						
9. Attention problems	.00	-.1***	-.173****	-.163****	-.26[a]	-.251****	-.287****	.575****					
10. Delinquent Behavior	-.09**	-.121****	-.189****	-.175****	-.26[a]	-.257****	-.249****	.271****	.407****				
11. Aggressive Behavior	-.04	.-.112****	-.165****	-.179****	-.22[a]	-.224****	-.216****	.422****	.517****	.557****			
12. Cohesion	.114****	.14****	.126****	.086**	.10[a]	.109****	.081**	-.123****	-.155****	.-.127****	-.104****		
13. Distance	-.151****	-.153****	-.183****	-.192****	-.20[a]	-.198****	-.199****	.126****	.191****	.251****	.224****	.074*	
Standard Deviation	1.29	2.16	6.92	30.51	8.70	10.56	6.911	1.95	2.70	1.58	5.06	7.13	3.70
Mean	3.23	5.27	27.53	115.96	31.14	37.68	35.611	2.28	3.03	1.74	7.48	27.50	4.20
Very Low Birthweight Children													
1. Maternal Education													
2. Material Possessions	.22*												
3. Ravens Progressive Matrices	.23*	.29**											
4. Peabody Picture Vocab. Test	.28**	.33****	.65****										
5. WRAT-R Spelling	.27**	.16	.59****	.63****									
6. WRAT Reading	.27**	.17	.61****	.64****	.92[a]								
7. WRAT-R Arithmetic	.28**	.16	.58****	.62****	.76[a]	.73****							
8. Social Problems	-.07	-.0	5	-.18	-.16	-.29[c]	-.25**	-.17					
9. Attention problems	-.08	-.1		-.15	-.16	-.32[b]	-.33****	-.24*	.68****				
10. Delinquent Behavior	-.16	-.05	-.25**	-.3**	-.39[a]	-.41**	-.36****	.54****	.48****				
11. Aggressive Behavior	-.11	-.08	-.21*	-.28**	-.26[c]	-.25	-.26**	.6****	.73****	.53****			
12. Cohesion	.08	.02	.02	.2	.17	.12	.19*	-.04	.05	-.02	.13		
13. Distance	-.18	.07	-.14	-.14	-.39	-.15	-.21*	.34****	.25**	.3**	.37****	-.11	
Standard Deviation	1.1	2.2	7.33	28.68	9.21	11.02	7.4	2.65	4	4	6.7	5.89	3.36
Mean	2.79	4.52	21.65	89.44	23.27	26.58	28.86	4.02	5.94	5.94	11	24.44	5.94

Note: [a] p<.0001; [b] p<.001; [c] p<.01; [d] p<.05

For all latent variables (i.e., constructs derived from measures used) such as intellectual development, academic achievement, and behavior and emotional problems shown in the model shown in Figure 1, a confirmatory factor analysis was run to assess the degree to which multiple indicators (e.g., Ravens and PPVT indicating intellectual development) reflected single latent constructs (Newcomb, 1994). As discussed in the Results, the CFA models for the latent variables indicated in Figure 1 fit adequately by several SEM criteria, so we proceeded to test the full model depicted in this figure. The subtractive approach which includes all paths (hypothesized or not) in the model and the subsequent removal of nonsignifcant paths was chosen to capture the "true model" (MacCallum, 1986). Thus, after trimming nonsignificant paths, the SEM analysis is repeated. Next·the original χ^2 and its degrees of freedom (DF) is subtracted from the resulting χ^2 and its DF respectively. The difference in χ^2 values and degrees of freedom (i.e., χ^2 difference test) is then examined for significance where nonsignificant χ^2 indicates that trimming the nonsignificant path resulted in no loss of information from the model. Similar procedures were applied when constrained paths (i.e., testing whether the paths across samples are identical) versus unconstrained paths.

The χ^2 statistic is also used to assess model fit, but it is known to be sensitive to large sample sizes (Schumacker & Lomax, 1996) such as those used in the present study and can result in the commission of Type I error by rejecting model fit. Therefore, the Tucker-Lewis Index (TLI), Comparative Fit Index (CFI), and Root Mean Square Error of Approximation (RMSEA) all of which are insensitive to sample sizes, were used to judge model ft where models with TLI and CFI> .90 and RMSEA < .05 are deemed good fit. RMSEA values between .05 and .08 are considered to be moderate ft (Browne & Cudeck, 1993; Steiger, 1990). It should also be noted that (Hu & Bentler, 1998) stated that slightly higher values of CFI and TLI (i.e., .95) be used as indicators of good fit.

RESULTS

CFA Models

Prior to constructing the path models we verified that all latent constructs for VLBW and HBW cohorts were the same. First a CFA with the latent variables for intellectual ability, academic achievement, and behavioral and emotional problems with the loadings for both groups unconstrained was calculated, yielded χ^2 (48) = 382.43, p < .0001, TLI = .92, CFI = .95, RMSEA = 07 suggesting at least moderate fit. With loadings for both VLBW and HBW constrained the following indices were obtained χ^2 (54) = 386.66, TLI = .92, CFI = .95, RMSEA

= .07 and χ^2 (2) diff. =4, p> .05 indicating no differences between loadings for VLBW versus HBW children. Our conclusion is that the measurement model for the indicators of these constructs fit well and that the same model was appropriate for both the VLBW sample (N = 108) and the HBW sample (N = 1,137).

Structural Models

In the first wave of analyses, data from both VLBW and HBW cohorts as represented in the model in Figure 1 were analyzed simultaneously with all paths across the two samples unconstrained. Various indices χ^2 (94) = 364.79, p < .0001, TLI = .94, CFI = .96, RMSEA = 04) indicated excellent fit. Figures 2 and 3 contain the paths and resulting standardized regression weights for the VLBW and HBW children. This model was subsequently trimmed by removing the following four paths that were nonsignificant across both samples: possessions to behavior; family distance to achievement; cohesion to achievement; and maternal education to achievement and retested. The fit indices were χ^2 (102) = 367.82, p < .0001, TLI = .94, CFI = .96, RMSEA 04 and the χ^2 (6) dif. = 3.03, p> .05 indicating that the model remained virtually the same with the nonsignificant paths removed.

The second set of analyses involved the constraining structural parameters across VLBW and HBW samples in the trimmed model and thus testing whether the paths for both samples were identical. The fit indices were χ^2 (120) = 395.60, p < .0001, TLI = .95, CFI = .96, RMSEA = .04 and the χ^2 (18) dif. = 27.78, p> .05 indicating that the paths for VLBW versus HBW children in the decomposed and constrained models were identical. Because the RMSEA for the CFA model was > .05, we not only constrained the structural parameters in the next set of analyses but the factor loadings for each latent variable and repeated the analyses. The fit indices were χ^2 (126) = 399.48, TLI = .95 CFI = .96 and RMSEA = .04 indicating excellent fit. The χ^2 (24) dif. =31.66, p> .05 indicating no difference between the totally versus partially constrained models. The standardized regression weights for the constrained models are listed in Fig. 4 with the weights for VLBW children in parentheses.

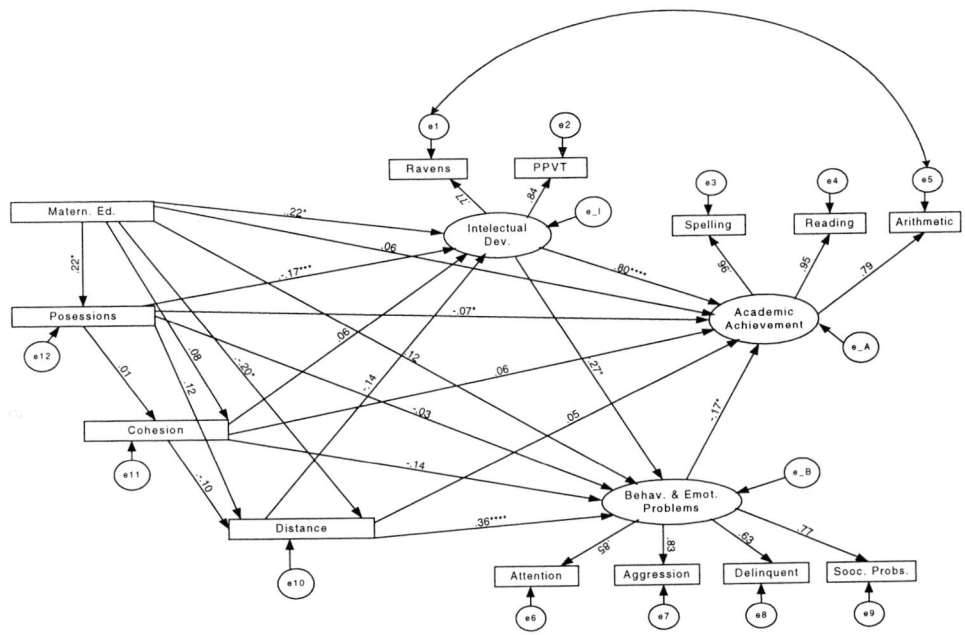

Figure 2.   Very Low Birthweight unconstrained

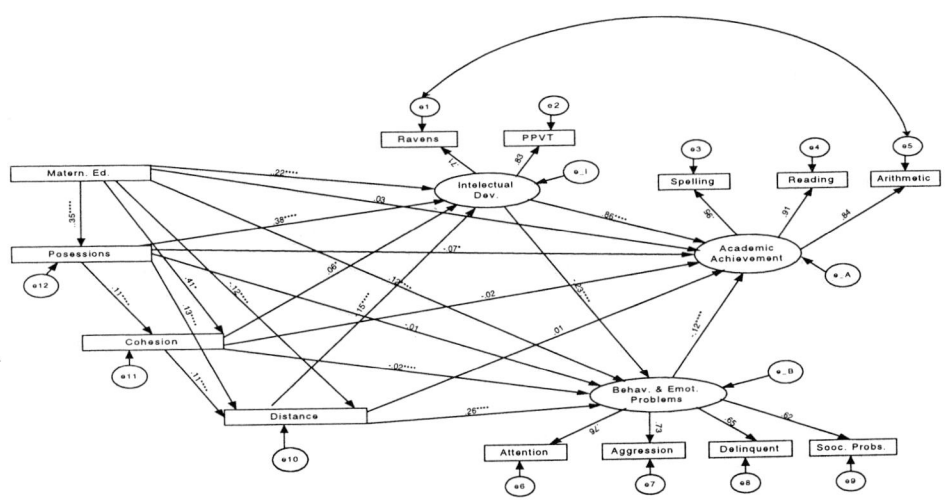

Figure 3.   HBW cohort unconstrained

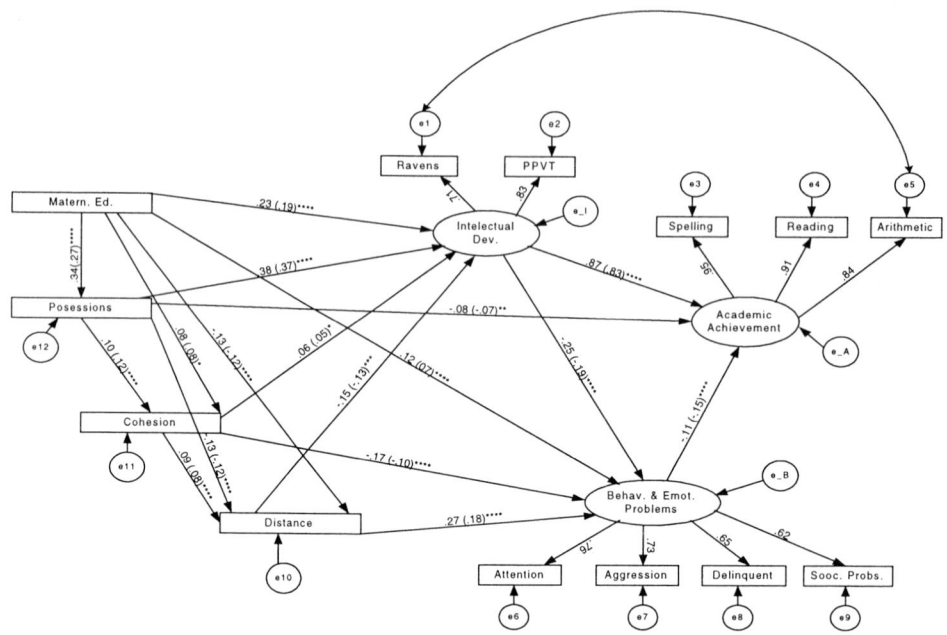

Figure 4.   VLBW and HBW decomposed and constrained model.

Direct. Mediated and Indirect Effects

Of greatest importance is that the analyses revealed that the causal links between the endogenous and exogenous variables described above were the same for VLBW Jamaican adolescents and their HBW peers. Interestingly, in the entire model only one path from maternal education was removed, which indicated that this exogenous variable is directly associated with most types of psychological functioning in Jamaican children and families depicted in the model. The model indicated that maternal education had no significant direct effect on school achievement but indirectly predicted school achievement via several mediational mechanisms. These mediational effects are calculated and summarized in Table 2. As can be seen in that table, maternal education has its greatest impact on intellectual development through family possessions (.13); relatively smaller effects occur through cohesion and distance associations between cohesion and material possessions.   Maternal education was directly and positively associated with problem behavior but this relationship was mediated by a positive association between this variable and distance between family members and also a negative association between it and cohesion.

Material possessions was negatively associated with achievement but was mediated by a positive relationship between this variable and intellectual ability. However, the relationship between material possessions and intellectual development was mediated by a strong positive relationship between this variable and cohesion, which was also positively associated with intellectual ability. Cohesion was negatively associated with behavior but was mediated by its positive association with intellectual development. The opposite was true for the relationships between these variables and distance. Although intellectual ability strongly predicted school achievement, it was negatively associated with problem behavior its mediator, which was in, turn negatively associated with achievement.

Table 2. Summary of Direct and Indirect effects of exogenous variables on intellectual development, academic achievement, and behavior problems [a]

Variables	Effect Size
A. Intellectual Development	
Maternal Education (direct)	.2300
Through Possessions	.1300
Through Cohesion	.0048
Through Distance	.0195
B. Behavior Problems	
Maternal Education (direct)	.1200
Through Cohesion	-.0136
Through Distance	.0351
Possessions	None
Trough Intellectual Development	.0950
Through Cohesion	-.0170
Through Cohesion and Distance	-.0024
Distance (direct)	.2700
Through Intellectual Development	.0375
Cohesion (direct)	-.1700
Through Intellectual Development	.0150
Through Distance	.0243

Table 2 continued.

Variables	Effect Size
C. Academic Achievement	
Maternal Education (direct)	None
Through Intellectual Development	.2001
Through Behavior Problems	-.0132
Possessions (direct)	-.0800
Through Intellectual Development	.3300
Cohesion (direct)	None
Through Intellectual Development	.0522
Through Behavior Problems	.0187
Distance (direct)	None
Through Intellectual Development	-.1305
Through Behavior Problems	-.0297

[a] It is recognized that other mediated effects are presented in Figure 4, but effects are more distal (e.g., maternal education on academic achievement through possessions, cohesion, distance, and behavior problems). As a consequence, the sizes of these effects are relatively small and not included in the table.

DISCUSSION

The confirmation of similar paths for VLBW and HBW children suggests that both groups of children may share the same protective and risk factors as far as their psychological functioning is concerned. The information provided by these models is intriguing especially when viewed in the context of what we know about both VLBW Jamaican children and their HBW peers and our knowledge regarding most Jamaican children and families. Previous research (Lambert, et al., 2000; Samms-Vaughan, 2000) has documented that VLBW Jamaican children's psychological functioning (i.e., intellectual development, achievement and behavior), is significantly compromised when compared with their HBW peers. Nevertheless, the present study revealed that in spite of such global differences in outcomes, the effects of direct, indirect, and intervening variables on the trajectories both groups of children take are the same. This finding may have emerged for Jamaica as only the hardiest VLBW children who can live with or without minimal or major medical treatment survive. The effects of environmental variables on such children may be the same as they are for their HBW peers and may be very different from those of their VLBW peers in other countries who survive with the help of intensive medical intervention.

Nevertheless, confirmation of the model indicates tat as documented in industrialized nations (Brooks-Gunn, et al., 1999), maternal education is pivotal for appropriate psychological adjustment in Jamaican children regardless of the presence or absence of VLBW and its pre- and perinatal risk factors. Maternal education has significant and direct effects with substantial effect sizes (ES) on all outcome variables except academic achievement. The substantial indirect effect of maternal education on achievement through possessions however indicates not only its proximal but distal effects on critical indicators of adjustment in both VLBW children and their HBW peers. The effects of maternal education on psychological outcomes, especially on intellectual development and academic achievement may in part reflect the effects of shared genetic and environmental factors documented to predict intellectual capabilities and academic achievement in children (see Satler [1992] for review). It is, however, important to note that while maternal education seems critical to psychological adjustment in Jamaican children, other factors although related to this exogenous variable are important. For example, although maternal education accounts for some of the variance in material possessions, as indicated in Table 2, the latter mediates the effect of the former by accounting for a substantial percentage of the variance (ES = .13) in intellectual development.

The direct effects of maternal education on behavior and that of material possessions on academic achievement are particularly interesting. Both direct effects are mediated by intellectual development. The former indicates that mothers with higher education levels are more likely to report problem behavior in their children. This relationship might reflect that such mothers are more likely to be more authoritative in their child rearing which may result in more assertiveness on their children's part (Baumrind, 1996). Their low thresholds for such assertive child behavior as the Jamaican culture promotes (Lambert, et al., 1989) may influence their views of such behavior as problematic. Interestingly, this view was mediated by intellectual ability indicating that the higher the children's intellectual abilities the less likely their mothers were to view such behavior as problematic.

Turning to material possessions and achievement, initially we found the negative relationship between these variables surprising. The mediating effects of intellectual abilities, however indicates that children in families with considerable amount of material resources and lowered intellectual abilities may not be as academic achievement oriented as their peers with higher intellectual functioning. That is, given the higher level of effort they must invest to achieve academic success in contrast to their peers with higher intellectual abilities, they may view such exertion as unnecessary, given the resources available to them and their families.

Another intriguing issue is that one of the few a priori hypotheses we made regarding the model was upheld. That is maternal education should not directly influence achievement. While this exogenous variable influences achievement it does so indirectly by its effect upon intellectual development. We believe that the strong emphasis that all Jamaican adults, regardless of their education levels place on academic achievement may contribute to this finding.

Bearing in mind the mediated effects of maternal education via possessions on family functioning as measured by family cohesion and distance between family members, the effects of these endogenous variables on VLBW and HBW children's adjustment are intriguing. First, causal links between maternal education and these variables and the fact that its effects on such variables are mediated by material possessions indicate that high maternal education and material possessions may positively influence cohesion in the family but is negatively associated with distance. Cohesion in turn positively but indirectly influences achievement via its effect on intellectual development but the converse might be said for distance. The effects of both family variables on behavioral outcomes are also important as family cohesion, an attribute highly valued by Jamaicans seems to decrease behavioral and emotional problems in both VLBW and HBW children but are both mediated by the intellectual abilities the child possesses. This finding suggests that the child with poor intellectual strengths may be vulnerable to the negative effects of poor family functioning on their behavioral and emotional adjustment, but that higher intellectual abilities may buffer the effect on this outcome.

Most intriguing is the mediating effect of behavior problems between intellectual ability and achievement. Jamaican adults and especially teachers have almost always held that child behavior problems negatively influences children's achievement. A typical statement that such teachers make to parents and others is that "the child has the ability for good school work but his/her misbehavior (e.g., attention problems, aggressiveness) gets in the way of his/her performance." Evidence for this stance was evident in a recent national call by the Jamaica Teacher's Association to their Ministry of Education to assist them in addressing behavior problems in the classroom as they viewed this as inhibiting their pupils' academic achievement. Findings from the model for both sets of children indicate that this assumption might be true and is especially meaningful since parent and not teacher ratings measured problem behavior.

The findings from the present study are intriguing, but they must be interpreted within the context of the study's shortcomings. Foremost, is the use of measures designed for, and normed on U.S. populations to measure the constructs of interest in Jamaica. While such measures have been "successfully" used in earlier research in Jamaica (Samms-Vaughan, 2000), their psychometric properties have hardly been addressed for that nation. The NC, our measure of behavior and emotional problems, for example, is currently undergoing substantial empirical investigation to determine its psychometric properties for that nation yet we have no information on whether its items cluster to form the U.S.-based syndromes we used to represent behavior and emotional problems in the present study (Lambert, et al., 1999a). We do know that Jamaican children present several problems that do not match the CBCL on which many of the NC items are patterned but we have no information on whether and how these items cluster to form syndromes for this population. If the FACES, our measure of family functioning is an example of how the measures might behave when subjected to confirmatory factor analytic procedures on data from Jamaicans, the factor structures established on these measures may not show mathematical equivalence and may even lack appropriate content validity for Jamaican children and families.

Another problem is that related to method variance, as the measures of family functioning and child behavior were both completed by parents of VLBW and HBW children. If either or both measures were completed by the children themselves or by teachers, the findings presented may differ from those observed in the present study. Equally important is the cross-sectional nature of the study, which makes it difficult to infer causality in the relationships of the variables in the model. Also, the research project focused primarily on problems derived from the externalizing groupings of problems and not also on internalizing problems. The latter may lead to very different relationships between the variables in the model. It is also noteworthy that while the VLBW cohort was sampled nationwide, the HBW cohort was sampled from the most urbanized areas of Jamaica. Earlier research has (Lambert & Lyubansky, 1999) indicated that children from urban and rural areas do not differ in rates of behavior and emotional problems, but we cannot be sure that this finding holds for other constructs assessed in the present study. The attrition in the VLBW sample is also problematic. While we lost potential participants to death, some had migrated to other nations.

Further research on the measures used in the present study is needed to establish appropriate psychometric properties for participants in Jamaica. Such research may use the existing measures to obtain data from large numbers of Jamaican participants and where appropriate CFAs may be used to assess the mathematical equivalence of these measures. Further research may also pattern our own research on the measurement of behavioral and emotional problems in Jamaican children (Lambert, et al., 1998) where steps are taken to ensure that the measures are modified to reflect content that is relevant for Jamaicans while including information that is appropriate across Jamaica and other nations. Future research should also include family and behavioral data from both parents and children themselves and thus determine whether the findings reported here might be replicated. Such research should also focus on internalizing problems as a latent and endogenous variable. Also important is that the research projects suggested above sample both VLBW and HBW children nationwide and address issues of causality via longitudinal studies. It may also be valuable to obtain information from as may informants as possible, and to include fathers or father figures in ratings of behavior and family functioning. Children's perspectives on family functioning might also be important to examine in future studies. Finally, information from samples in an industrialized nation such as the United States may also allow the determination of whether causal modeling might predict the same outcomes for such children who are recipients of intensive medical intervention versus their Jamaican peers who survive virtually without such treatment.

Despite its drawbacks, the present study is the only effort we know to use complex causal modeling to determine whether environmental pathways are the same for VLBW children and their HBW peers. It suggests that in spite of risk factors associated with being VLBW, environmental factors such as maternal education and material possessions as well the factors that mediate them may be as important in determining their psychological adjustment as such variables are for their peers who are higher in birthweight.

AUTHOR NOTES

We gratefully acknowledge the support from the National Institute of Health to Nigel Paneth and a Minority Supplement to the same grant that supported the work of Michael C. Lambert. Further support for the project was obtained from an International Development Bank Grant to Maureen Samms-Vaughan and administered by the Planning Institute of Jamaica, which we also thankfully acknowledge. We are indebted to Maria Jackson, for their help with data collection and data reduction. To Karlene Aliwood, Karen Jones, Cheryl Morison, Jasneth Mullings, Hazel Naysmith, Andrea Sinclair, Denielle Smith, Desrene Walters, and Margaret Whyte, the research nurses who collected the data, we owe much gratitude. Also, we are grateful to Meginton Brown, Ann-Marie Graham and Aniph Nicholson for their assistance with data management and reduction and Kevin Brooks for his systems analytic contributions. Finally, we thank the many participating youth, family members, school principals, teachers, and other staff members who made the project possible.

REFERENCES

Achenbach, T. M. (1991a). *Integrative guide for the 1991 CBCL/4-18 YSR and TRF profiles.* Burlington: University of Vermont, Department of Psychiatry.

Achenbach, T. M. (199lb). *Manual for the Child Behavior Checklist and 1991 profile.* Burlington: University of Vermont Department of Psychiatry.

Achenbach, T. M. (1991c). *Manual for the Teacher's Report Form and 1991 profile.* Burlington: University of Vermont, Department of Psychiatry.

Achenbach, T. M. (1991d). *Manual for the Youth Self-Report and 1991 profile.* Burlington: University of Vermont, Department of Psychiatry.

Aram, D. M., Hack, M., Hawkins, S., Weissman, B. M., & Borawski Clark, E. (1991). Very-low-birthweight children and speech and language development. *Journal of Speech and Hearing Research, 34,* 1169-1179.

Arbuckle, J. L. (1999). *Amos users guide.* Chicago, IL: Smallwaters Corporation.

Barkley, R. A. (1990). *Attention-Deficit Hyperactivity Disorder: A handbook for diagnosis and treatment.* New York: Guilford.

Baumrind, D. (1996). The discipline controversy revisited. *Family Relations: Journal of Applied Family and Child Studies, 45,* 405-414.

Brice. (1982). West Indian families. In M. McGoldrick, J. Pearce, & G. J (Eds.), *Ethnicity and family therapy* (pp. 123-133). New York: Guilford.

Bronfenbrenner, U. (1956). Socialization and social class through time and space. In E. Maccoby, T. Newcomb, & E. Hartley (Eds.), *Readings in social psychology* (pp. 400-425). New York: Rinehart & Wilson.

Brooks-Gunn, J., Duncan, G. J., & Britto, P. (1999). Are socioeconomic gradients for children similar to those of adults? In D. P. Keating & C. Hertzman (Eds.), *Developmental health and the wealth of nations: Social. biological, and educational dynamics* (pp. 94-123). New York: Guilford.

Carter, A. S., Grigorenko, E. L., & Pauls, D. L. (1995). A Russian adaptation of the child behavior checklist: Psychometric properties and associations with child and maternal affective symptomatology and family functioning. *Journal of Abnormal Child Psychology, 23,* 66 1-684.

Chen, C., Lee, S. Y., & Stevenson, H. W. (1996). Long-term prediction of academic achievement of American, Chinese, and Japanese adolescents. *Journal of Educational Psychology, 88,* 750-759.

Dunn, L. M. (1997). *Examiner's manual for the Peabody Picture Vocabulary Test-Third Edition.* Circle Pines, MN: American Guidance Service.

Escobar, G. J., Littenberg, B., & Petitti, D. B. (1991). Outcome among surviving very low birthweight infants: a meta-analysis. *Archives of Diseases of Childhood, 66,* 204-11.

Fassinger, R. E. (1987). Use of structural equation modeling in counseling psychology research. *Journal of Counseling Psychology, 34,* 425-436.

Greenberg, M. T., Lengua, L. J., Coie, J. D., Pinderhughes, E. E., Bierman, K., Dodge, K. A., Locbman, J. E., & McMahon, R. J. (1999). Predicting developmental outcomes at school entry using a multiple risk model: Four American communities. *Developmental Psychology, 35,* 403-417.

Hille, E. T. M., den Ouden, A. L., Saigal, S., Wolke, D., Meyer, R., Lambert, M. C., & Paneth, N. (2000). *Behavior in very and extremely low birthweight infants at school age: Is outcome different in different countries.* Unpublished Manuscript.

Hinshaw, S. P. (1992). Externalizing behavior problems and academic underachievement in childhood and adolescence: Causal relationships and underlying mechanisms. *Psychological Bulletin, 111,* 127-155.

Hobn. G. (1996). *Effects of family functioning on the psychological and social adjustment of Jamaican immigrant children.* Unpublished Doctoral Dissertation, Columbia University, New York.

Hoyle, R. H. (1994). Structural equation modeling in clinical research. *Journal of Consulting and Clinical Psychology*, 62, 427-428.

Hoyle, R. H., & Smith, G. T. (1994). Formulating clinical research hypotheses as structural equation models: A conceptual overview. *Journal of Consulting and Clinical Psychology, 62,* 429-440.

Jimerson, S., Egeland, B., & Teo, A. (1999). A longitudinal study of achievement trajectories: Factors associated with change. *Journal of Educational Psychology, 91,* 116-126.

Klebanov, P. K., Brooks-Gunn, J., & McCormick, M. C. (1994). Classroom behavior of very low birth weight elementary school children. *Pediatrics, 95,* 700-708.

Klein, R. G., & Mannuzza, S. (1991). Long-term outcome of hyperactive children: A review. *Journal of the American Academy of Child and Adolescent Psychiatry, 30,* 383-387.

Lambert, M. C.(1992). Jamaican and American adult perspectives on child psychopathology: Further exploration of the threshold model. *Journal of Consulting and Clinical Psychology, 60,* 146-49.

Lambert, M. C., Knight, F., Taylor, R., & Achenbach, T. M. (1994). Epidemiology of behavioral and emotional problems among children of Jamaica and the United States: Parent reports for ages 6-11. *Journal of Abnormal Child Psychology, 22,* 113-128.

Lambert, M. C., Knight, F., Taylor, R., & Achenbach, T. M. (1996). Comparisons of behavioral and emotional problems among children of Jamaica and the United States: Teacher Reports for Ages 6-11. *Journal of Cross Cultural Psychology, 27,* 82-97.

Lambert, M. C., & Lyubansky, M. (1999). Behavior and emotional problems of children and adolescents in urban and rural Jamaica: Parent-, teacher-, and self -reports for ages 6-18. *International Journal of Intercultural Relations, 56,* 727-751.

Lambert, M. C., Lyubansky, M., & Achenbach, T. M. (1998). Behavioral and emotional problems among adolescents of Jamaica and the United States: Parent-, teacher- and self reports for ages 12 to 18. *Journal of Emotional and Behavioral Disorders, 6,* 180-87.

Lambert, M. C., Samms Vaughan, M. E., Lyubansky, M., Podolski, C. L., Hannah, S. D., McCaslin, S. E., & Rowan, G. T. (1999). Behavior and emotional problems of clinic-referred children of the African Diaspora: A cross-national study of African American and Jamaican children ages 4 to 18. *Journal of Black Psychology*, 25, 504-523.

Lambert, M. C., Samms-Vaughan, M. E., Bellas, V. F., & Russ, C. M. (2000). *Problems in very low birthweight Jamaican children.* Paper presented at the Second International Conference on Child and Adolescent Mental Health, Kuala Lumpur, Malaysia.

Lambert, M. C., Samms-Vaughan, M. E., Lyubansky, M., Rose, D., Hannah, S. D., Grandison, T., Holness, A., Podolski, C. L., Rowan, G. T., & Durst, J. (1999b). Identification of emotions and emotional confusion in Jamaican adults: Do they predict severity and types of psychopathology. *West Indian Medical Journal, 48,* 203-207.

Lambert, M. C., Weisz, J. R., & Knight, F. (1989). Over- and under-controlled clinic referral problems of Jamaican and American children and adolescents: The culture general and the culture specific. *Journal of Consulting and Clinical Psychology, 57,* 467-472.

Liaw, F. R., & Brooks-Gunn, J. (1994). Cumulative familial risks and low-birthweight children s cognitive and behavioral development. *Journal of Clinical Child Psychology.*

Lorenz, J. M., Wooliever, D. E., Jetton, J. R., & Paneth, N. (1998). A quantitative review of mortality and developmental disability in extremely premature newborns. *Archives of Pediatric Adolescent Medicine, 152,* 425-435.

Luster, T., & McAdoo, H. (1996). Family and child influences on educational attainment: A secondary analysis of the high/scope Perry Preschool data. *Developmental Psychology, 32,* 26-39.

MacCallum, R. (1986). Specification searches in covariance structure modeling. *Psychological*

Bulletin, 100, 107-120.

McCandles, N. J., Lueptow, L. B., & McClendon, M. (1998). Family socioeconomic status and adolescent sextyping. *Journal of Marriage and Family, 51*, 627-635.

McCormick, M. C., Gortmaker, S. L., & Sobol, A. M. (1990). Very low birth weight children: Behavior problems and school difficulty in a national sample. *Journal of Pediatrics, 117*, 687-693.

Newcomb, M. D. (1994). Drug use and intimate relationships among women and men: Separating specific from general effects in prospective data using structural equation models. *Journal of Consulting and Clinical Psychology, 62*, 463-476.

Nigg, J. T., Hinshaw, S. P., Carte, E. T., & Treuting, J. J. (1998). Neuropsychological correlates of childhood attention-def cit/hyperactivity disorder: Explainable by comorbid disruptive behavior or reading problems? *Journal of Abnormal Psychology, 107*, 468-480.

Olson, D. H., Portner, J., & Lavee, Y. (1985). *Family adaptability and cohesion evaluation scales: III.* St. Paul, MN: University of Minnesota, Department of Family Social Science.

Ornstein, M., Ohisson, A., Edmonds, J., & Asztalos, E. (1991). Neonatal follow-up of very low birthweight and extremely low birthweight infants to school age: a critical overview. *Acta Paediatrica Scandinavia, 80*, 741-748.

Paneth, N. S. (1995). The problem of low birth weight. *The Future of Children, 5*, 19-34.

Pharoah, P. O., Stevenson, C. J., Cooke, R. W., & Stevenson, R. C. (1994). Prevalence of behavior disorders in low birthweight infants. *Archives of Diseases of Childhood, 70*, 1-4.

Raven, J., Raven, J. C., & Court, J. H. (1995). *Manual for Raven's Progressive Matrices and Vocabulary Scales.* New York: Oxford Psychologists Press.

Ross, G., Lipper, E., & Auld, P. A. (1992). Hand preference, prematurity and developmental outcome at school age. *Neuropsychologia, 30*, 483-94.

Ross, G., Lipper, E. O., & Auld, P. A. (1990). Growth achievement of very low birth weight premature children at school age. *Journal of Pediatrics,* 117, 307-309.

Saigal, S., Szatmari, P., Rosenbaum, P., Campbell, D., & King, S. (1990). Intellectual and functional status at school entry of children who weighed 1000 grams or less at birth: a regional perspective of births in the 1980s. *Journal of Pediatrics, 116*, 409-416.

Samms-Vaughan, M. E. (2000). *Cognition. educational attainment and behavior in a cohort of Jamaican children: A comprehensive look at the development of eleven year olds.* Kingston, Jamaica: University of the West Indies.

478

Satler, J. M. (1992). *Assessment of children* (3rd ed). San Diego: Author.

Shelton, T. L., Barkley, R. A., Crosswait, C., Moorehouse, M., Fletcher, K., Barrett, S., Jenkins, L., & Metevia, L. (1998). Psychiatric and psychological morbidity as a function of adaptive disability in preschool children with aggressive and hyperactive-impulsive-inattentive behavior. *Journal of Abnormal Child Psychology*, 26, 475-494.

Simeon, A., Callender, l., Wong, M., Grantham-McGregor, S. M., & Ramdath, D. (1994). School performance, nutritional status, and trichuriasis in Jamaican school children. *Acta Petitirca, 83*, 1188-1193.

Tannock, R. (1998). Attention deficit hyperactivity disorder: Advances in cognitive, neurobiological, and genetic research. *Journal of Child Psychology and Psychiatry, 39*, 65-99.

Veen, S., Ens Dokkum, M. H., Scbreuder, A. M., Brand, R., Verloove Vanhorick, S. P., & Ruys, J. H. (1991a). Impairments, disabilities, and handicaps in low-birthweight babies. *Lancet, 338*, 1011-10112.

Veen, S., Ens Dokkum, M. H., Schreuder, A. M., Verloove Vanhorick, S. P., Brand, R., & Ruys, J. H. (1991b). Impairments, disabilities, and handicaps of very preterm and very-low-birthweight infants at five years of age: The Collaborative Project on Preterm and Small for Gestational Age Infants (POPS) in The Netherlands. *Lancet, 338*, 33-36.

Veen, S., Sassen, M. L., Schreuder, A. M., Ens Dokkum, M. H., Verloove Vanhorick, S. P., Brand, R., Grote, J. J., & Ruys, J. H. (1993). Hearing loss in very preterm and very low birthweight infants at the age of 5 years m a nationwide cohort . *International Journal of Pediatric Otorhiolaryngology, 26*, 11-28.

Walker, S., Grantham McGregor, S., Himes, J., & Williams, S. (1994). *Nutritional and health determinants of school failure and dropout in adolescent girls in Kingston. Jamaica (USAID 1)*. Kingston, Jamaica: International Center for Research on Women.

Whitaker, A. H., Van Rossem, R., Feldman, J. F., Schonfeld, I. S., Pinto Martin, J. A., Tore, C., Shaffer, D., & Paneth, N. (1997). Psychiatric outcomes in low-birth-weight children at age 6 years: relation to neonatal cranial ultrasound abnormalities. *Archives of General Psychiatry, 54*, 847-56.

Wilkinson, G. 5. (1994). *The Wide Range Achievement Test administration manual*. Seattle, WA: Jastak & Jastak.

Williams, D. R., & Rucker, T. (1996). Socioeconomic status and the health of racial minority populations. In P. Kato & T. Mann (Eds.), *Handbook of diversity issues in health psychology* (pp. 407-423). New York: Plenum.

Wills, T. A., McNamara, G., & Vaccaro, D. (1995). Parental education related to adolescent stress coping and substance use: Development of a mediational model. *Health Psychology, 14*, 464-478.

21

Cross-Cultural Differences in Suicidal Ideation Between Children in Nigeria and Botswana

Emmanuel A. Akinade
University of Botswana

Emmanuel A. Akinade · University of Botswana · Faculty of Social Sciences · Private Bag UB0705 · Gaborone, Botswana.

International Perspectives on Child and Adolescent Mental Health. Volume 2: Proceedings of the Second International Conference, edited by N. N. Singh, T. H. Ollendick, and A. N. Singh. © 2002 Elsevier Science Ltd. All rights reserved.

Nigeria is a West African country with an estimated population of about 115 million people. Botswana is a southern African country with an estimated population of only 1.5 million people. Both countries are blessed with natural resources that yield a lot of income. However, the per capita income in both countries is very low and many people are quite poor. For instance, in Nigeria, the average income was $310 in 1999. In both countries, individuals whose age ranges from 0 to 18 years are legally regarded as children.

People in both countries exhibit suicidal behavior. However, unlike several countries in which empirical studies have been carried out, there is little literature on Nigerian and Batswana (as people of Botswana are called) children. This is despite the fact that suicide is now reported more frequently in the electronic and print media than ever before, especially so in Botswana. Suicidal behavior in African society has a long history that was passed down through several generations via oral tradition. But it had always been rarely reported until quite recently.

There is some universal agreement that suicidal behavior (thought, plan, or action) is a multi-causal, multidimensional, and complex behavior that is associated with several risk factors (Brent & Perper, 1988; Lewinsohn, 1996). It seems to follow this pattern:

suicidal ideation → suicidal attempt → completed suicide.

In other words, suicidal ideation is a precursor of suicide and that suicide is the terminal step in the suicidal process. Several studies show that entertaining suicidal ideation is no respecter of age, gender, color, class, creed or geographical boundaries as revealed by current clinical literature on suicide from several countries, such as USA, UK, Canada, France, Australia, New Zealand, Switzerland, Russia, Japan, Finland, and Germany.

Researchers have asserted that for every completed suicide across the world, there are about eight suicidal attempts, and that for every attempt; there could be at least eight suicidal ideations (Leenars & Wenkstern, 1991). When it is recognized that suicidal ideation is a covert behavior, then one can speculate that the above is a conservative estimate. Epidemiological surveys around the world indicate the widespread dramatic increases in suicidal behavior, particularly among young people as the sample below shows.

The trend towards suicide at younger age in American society is alarming. Between 1980 and 1992, the suicide rate among adolescents ages 10 to 14 rose by 120% and was especially high among black males in this age group, an increase of 300% (Leary, 1995). The rate of suicide increased more than 600% since 1950. Suicide is now the third leading cause of death among adolescents (Centre for Disease Control and Prevention, 1999; Kochnek 7 Murphy,

1999). This age group has been found to commit more suicides in recent decades than all the years before. The increase is largely related to the accessibility and use of firearms as a method (Boyo & Moscicki, 1986; Kachur, et al., 1995). The world leaders in suicide have more scary stories to tell. More than 30 suicides are recorded among 1,000 young people annually in the Russian Federation, Finland, Lithuania, and New Zealand. In Japan, suicide is described as a natural affliction and a problem of epidemic scale. In 1998, a record 32,863 suicides were reported, three times the number of traffic fatalities. In France, 12,000 people committed suicide in 1998. There are 160,000 attempted suicides every 40 minutes. One out of every three French persons has experienced the trauma of having someone close to them commit suicide. Australia has an unenviable recognition of having one of the highest rates of suicide in the world, 16 per 100,000 and it exceeds accidents as the primary cause of death in males and females of age 15-24 years. More than three out of every 10 deaths due to violent causes, including accidents in Switzerland, are attributed to suicide. Experts say that in United Kingdom, the suicide rate has doubled amongst men aged 15 to 24 years in the last 25 years. In 1999,1,500 men under 35 years killed themselves in England and Wales (Makinwa, 2000).

Currently there is no available comparable empirical research report on suicidal behavior of Nigerian and Batswana children. Also, there appears to be no university or research institute involved in suicidology as a discipline in either country. In the past, it was even a taboo in the traditional African societies to discuss suicide. For instance in Nigeria, individuals identified as planning to kill themselves were banished from their villages. Even when individuals completed suicide, they were often denied a decent funeral—the corpses were buried far away from the villages, in the bush or forests. A few exceptions existed however. For instance, oral tradition stated that long ago, some tribal kings committed suicide so as to avoid the disgrace of being captured during tribal wars in their kingdoms. Apart from that, the traditional system of controlling behavior was quite efficient, effective, and helpful to family members. It served as a reliable and very supportive social network and psychological shock absorber for those experiencing great emotional problems.

Nowadays, however, the rate of suicidal behavior among young children below age 18 seems to be increasing. The youngsters are exposed to several environmental factors that have impinged adversely on their psychic durability. This has eroded seriously the positive and helpful services of the extended family. A disturbing trend is emerging in some African societies as a result of this. The 'so-called big men' in the societies who became bankrupt or were exposed for carrying out dubious or nefarious activities such as engaging in culturally unacceptable behavior or fouled a taboo such as sleeping with one's daughter (i.e., committing incest) or a close relative used to attempt or complete suicide. This was in order to avoid the shame of public ridicule. There is a popular saying among the Yoruba (i.e., people of the south western part of Nigeria). "Iku ya ju esin"—death is preferable to shame. This explains why some people exhibit suicidal behavior that children observe and are affected by.

In Nigeria, suicidal ideation is rife among those who are freshly bereaved. Such individuals often include young people who express the wish to kill themselves. Some of the affected children actually attempt to enter the graves as the corpses are being lowered into them. As the culture demands on such occasions, the individuals are given rich doses of social, religious, financial and emotional support. Eventually they do not kill themselves. However, those who do not enjoy such cultural support eventually become very depressed and might engage in suicidal behavior.

Tembo, et al. (1989) conducted a study on suicide in Botswana. They found that the main factors associated with suicide and suicidal attempts were mental illness (32%) and alcohol (68%). Out of the cases they examined, 78% were males and 22% were females. 55% were completers and 45% were attempters. They used only data collected from police sources and found that suicide rates per 100, 000 people from 1978 to 1988 in Botswana ranged from 23 in 1982 to 61 in 1983 with an annual average of 45/100,000 There has been no empirical follow up on this pioneer study. Recently, Botswana Police Research Unit released official statistics on suicide rates in Botswana. It stated that "between January and August 2,000,112 Batswana (104 men and eight women) committed suicide. That means an average of 10 individuals killed themselves in one week as suicide rates increases." The report stated that the age of victims ranged from 10 to 88 years, but the majority were in their 20s and 30s (Annealing, 2,000) Another report stated that six people, five men and one woman committed suicide during a recent week (16th to 23rd October 2000). They were aged between 20 and 83 years. The 83-year-old man was a mental patient who hanged himself on a tree. According to a survey conducted in America, 8% of high school students (adolescents) had made at least one suicidal attempt (King, 1997) while 27% reported that they had thought seriously about killing themselves. Sixteen per cent had made specific plans for killing themselves. One quarter of the attempts were serious enough to require medical attention (Centre for Diseases Control, 1991).

Observational studies among Nigerians and Batswana reveal that methods contemplated or used for suicide differ from those of their counterparts in developed countries, such as UK and USA. The commonest method of choice are hanging, using pesticides, swallowing caustic soda, jumping across moving trains, into swift rivers, deep wells or soak-away pits, and setting fire to their huts and themselves after bathing in paraffin or petrol. Use of firearms is the most common method of suicide by American youth, younger and older adolescents of all races (Kachur, et al., 1995). The use of firearms is not a familiar method to Nigerian and Batswana children. This is probably because they do not access to guns. The use of firearms is under very strict government control in these two countries.

Several studies have revealed that no single factor may precipitate suicidal behavior; it is usually a combination of risk factors (Alan, et al., 1998). The behavior may have cultural undertones such as underlying influences related to community expectations of young people. It may develop out of family dysfunction or poor parenting. They may result from educational or work failure leading to poor self esteem, a feeling of loss of control over personal decisions, and pessimism about the future. A recent loss of any kind, failure to gain attention or help, or a rejection may lead to a belief that life is not worth living or cannot be changed, or that relatives and friends will be punished if the young person dies and they believe it to be their fault.

Psychosocial and environmental factors seem to instigate suicidal behavior among the children in Nigeria and Botswana. Individuals who are high-risk candidates for suicidal behavior tend to have a combination of overlapping risk factors, such as: physical or sexual abuse, a family history of or exposure to suicidal behavior, or mental illness. Other related factors are parental or caregiver loss [as in the case of HIV/AIDS orphans], decreased familial or social support, chronic physical or terminal illness, pregnancy in adolescent females or being recently jilted. A humiliating negative life event is frequently the trigger to suicide in many cases. In Nigeria, common losses as a result of inability to achieve good grades in external examinations (e.g., secondary school certificate) often-precipitate suicidal ideation among students, especially in girls (Akinade, 1998).

Age is a significant factor in suicidal behavior. Suicide is uncommon in 8 to 14 year olds and early adolescence. It occurs almost as often among females and males. Childhood suicidal ideation seems to be catalyzed and sustained predominantly by depression, hopelessness, and anxiety. Children with suicidal ideations may report that they experience more negative life events and tremendous stress due to negative perceptions of routine events (Alan, et al., 1998). They may experience problematic parent-child relationships such as discordant, hostile family interactions, development of feelings of worthlessness, and a desire to die (Kosky, Silburn, & Subrick, 1990). So also are dysfunctional family relations and non-punitive environments that may result from parental psychopathology such as depression (Kashani, Allan, Dalkmeir, Rezvani, & Reids, 1995). Other factors that may mediate suicidal ideation are poor role models, feelings of isolation, and pessimistic outlook. Children with co-morbid anxiety and suicide ideation tend to be more active and display more intense reactions than those with low anxiety

(Allan, et al., 1998). Some of these behavioral characteristics are present in some Nigerian and Batswana children too.

Gender is one of the most reliable predictors of suicidal ideation and behavior among adolescents in USA. Adolescent females are twice as likely than males to report suicidal ideation and engage in non-fatal suicidal act (Canetto, 1995). However, mortality is a low frequency event during adolescence and it is typically a male behavior (King, 1997). Gender differences in the rates of nonfatal suicidal behavior are not apparent in childhood and early adolescence (Lewinsohn, et al., 1996; Shaffer, 1996). However, as they become older adolescents, and are in the process of identity definition, they may take cultural messages about "appropriate" gender suicidal behavior more seriously than adults (Hill & Lynch, 1983).

Gender specific differences in the risk factors for suicide may help explain these differences. Males are more likely than females to present with illegal substance abuse syndromes, conditions that are associated with suicidal behavior (Canetto, 1991). Studies have shown that individuals who exhibit suicidal tendencies because of losing a personal relationship are perceived as more feminine than those who become suicidal as a result of achievement failure (Dahlen & Canetto, 1996). Females are thought to be more likely than males to show this behavior (De Rose & Page, 1985). Surviving a suicidal act is perceived as culturally unacceptable for males in USA. Nonfatal suicidal behavior is frequently interpreted as feminine and a cry for help. It is most acceptable and most common in younger males (Canetto, 1995).

From the above literature review, one can note that while several studies have been reported on (completed) suicide per se, only scanty research recognition had been accorded to its genesis—suicidal ideation. Also, insufficient research had been done on it among children in both Nigeria and Botswana.

Bearing in mind the paucity of empirical data about suicidal behavior among children in Nigeria and Botswana, this study examined the status of suicidal ideation in these countries. It was designed to provide basic data about why children in Nigeria and Botswana show suicidal ideation, the methods they contemplate, and the type of supports they are familiar with. It was envisaged that this would motivate further research studies to be conducted on African children and that appropriate intervention would be formulated to curb the growing incidence of suicidal behavior. Specifically, answers were sought for the following questions: What are the age and gender characteristics of child suicidal ideators? Is suicidal ideation more prevalent in rural or urban areas? What factors sustain the suicidal ideation of children in Nigeria and Botswana? What suggestions could be made to help curb the spread of suicidal ideation in the children in Nigeria and Botswana?

METHOD

The descriptive research design using the survey method was used. In this study, suicidal ideation was regarded as at least a communication of suicidal thoughts, plans, or interested discussion of suicide within the preceding 12 months. Informed consent was requested and obtained prior to administration of the study instruments.

Participants

The sample consisted of 197 non-institutionalized children aged between 9 and 18 years. In Botswana, the sample was from locations on the southeastern and central parts of the country—areas with a relatively high density of population. In Nigeria, participants were from the south-western part of the country—areas with very heavy population. To qualify for participation in this study, subjects had to meet part or all of the following requirements. A prominent criterion was that they had given at least a hint about suicide to other people within 12 months before the study. The participants were to be identified and recommended by teachers, religious leaders, social workers, friends, counselors, neighbors or schoolmates. The sample comprised of children whose childhood history revealed that they were unhappy, at great risk of having grown up in a family environment characterized by a combination of socio-economic adversity, additive effects of depressogenic family discord or violence, or disruption, separation or divorce, exposure to negative life events, and parental/caretaker death.

Instrument

A self constructed 28-item questionnaire and a corresponding interview protocol were used to collect data. The researcher and two university colleagues cross-validated the questionnaire, named African Suicidal Behavior Rating Scale (ASBRS). It was tested and retested on a pilot study group of 37 children at an interval of four weeks. Its test-retest reliability was found to be .79. It was able to discriminate suicidal ideators from non-suicidal ideators. The response was in a bipolar mode.

Data Collection

Three hundred copies of ASBRS were made available for the study but only 197 were completely filled and regarded as scientifically useful for analysis. The researcher and three of his counseling students in Nigeira administered the questionnaire. In Botswana, four of his undergraduate students helped to administer the test. They also assisted in interpreting some of the items on the questionnaire to some Batswana children. In both countries, the researcher and his students took part in the interview sessions with a sample of the participants. On all occasions, the participants were informed that the exercise was for research purposes and it was designed to help formulate policies that would curb the increase in suicidal behavior in the society. On average, each consenting respondent spent about 15 minutes taking the test and 15 minutes doing the interview.

RESULTS

Table 1 shows that male and female participants in both countries reported suicidal ideations. Those in the 12- to 15-year-old age group indicated it most, followed by the 16- to 18-year-olds, and least by the 9- to 11-year-olds. Females in all groups in both countries indicated suicidal ideation more than their male counterparts.

Table 1. Prevalence of Suicidal Ideation by Gender and Age Among Children in Nigeria and Botswana.

Gender	Nigeria				Botswana			
	No.	Yes	No	% Yes	No.	Yes	No	% Yes
Male	25	7	18	28.0	33	16	17	48.8
9-11 yrs	4	1	3	25.0	6	2	4	33.3
12-15 yrs	8	3	5	37.5	12	7	5	58.4
16-18 yrs	13	4	9	30.8	15	7	8	46.7
Female	54	21	33	38.8	85	45	40	52.9
9-11 yrs	9	4	5	33.3	15	6	9	40.0
12-15 yrs	20	8	12	40.0	28	17	11	60.7
16-18 yrs	25	10	15	36.0	42	22	20	52.5

Table 2 shows that suicidal ideation is engaged in by more children in the urban areas than those in the rural areas in Nigeria and Botswana. The gap is closer between the rural and urban samples in Botswana, especially with the female participants.

Table 2.   Suicidal Ideation between Children in Both Rural and Urban Areas of Nigeria and Botswana.

Dwelling	Nigeria				Botswana			
	No.	Yes	No	% Yes	No.	Yes	No	% Yes
Rural	31	9	22	29.0	55	32	22	58.2
Male	11	2	9	22.2	17	9	8	52.9
Female	20	7	13	35.0	38	23	15	60.5
Urban	48	24	24	50.0	63	37	26	59.6
Male	16	6	10	37.5	16	9	7	56.3
Female	32	18	14	56.5	47	28	19	59.6

Table 3 shows that thoughts predominate suicidal ideation while plans and efforts to take suicidal actions follow in that order among the children in Nigeria and Botswana.

Table 3. Factors Responsible for Suicidal Ideation Among Children in Nigeria and Botswana

	Nigeria		Botswana			
	Male	Female	Male	Female	Total	Rank
I come from a poor family background	21	47	28	67	162	1
I know I am unhappy in my life	21	29	39	48	128	2
I have sometimes felt like taking my life	10	23	13	35	81	3
I have a sense of no further hope in life'	12	11	31	19	77	4
I do not enjoy the social support of close family members or friends	17	36	18	35	76	5

Table 3 continued.

| | Nigeria | | Botswana | | | |
	Male	Female	Male	Female	Total	Rank
A dear family member e.g. a parent died of suicide	3	3	14	7	64	6
I am personally ashamed of my bad behavior	14	20	14	13	61	7
My problems are caused by others in the society	12	8	22	27	59	8
*I think I am being bewitched	4	7	8	19	58	9
I experience a great deal of anxiety	18	12	11	16	57	10
*I know people who died of suicide	3	4	24	22	53	11
*I use alcohol to solve my problems	16	3	22	10	51	12
*I feel ashamed that I fail my examinations	14	23	6	6	49	13
*I use drugs to solve my problems	17	2	19	5	43	14
I fear what people will say about my unwanted pregnancy	0	39	0	24	43	15
People around me often talk about suicide	10	7	8	14	39	16
I am disappointed that I cannot get a job	8	5	9	9	31	17
My parents /caregivers criticize me too much	7	9	8	6	30	18
I feel a serious loss of a dear boy/girl friend	2	10	7	8	27	19
I have been physically abused for a long time	3	3	4	7	17	20
I want to kill myself to spite my parents /partner	7	3	4	3	17	21
I like listening to sorrowful music or story or both	4	2	3	1	11	22
I want to give away my precious possessions	2	2	3	3	10	23

Table 3 contiuned.

| | Nigeria | | Botswana | | | |
	Male	Female	Male	Female	Total	Rank
I want to die because I am HIV positive	0	1	1	5	7	24
I have attempted suicide before	1	1	1	3	6	25
I had been raped/forced to have sexual intercourse	0	1	0	4	5	26
I feel a severe loss of a much wanted opportunity	2	1	1	0	4	27
I want to change to a radically new personality	1	1	1	0	3	28

Table 4 shows that participants in Botswana tend to have more ideas about how to commit suicide than those in Nigeria.

Table 4.　Common Methods Often Thought of by Children Who were Involved in Suicidal Ideation.

| | Nigeria Number/Percent | | Botswana Number/Percent | |
Methods	Male (n = 25)	Female (n = 54)	Male (n = 33)	Female (n = 85)
Hanging (on tree/ceiling/rafter)	1/4%	0/0%	17/51.2%	24/28.2%
Drinking poisons (paraffin, chemicals/pesticides)	3/12%	12/48%	1/3%	7/5.9%
Swallowing caustic soda, dangerous tablets	4/16%	8/32%	1/3%	4/3.4%
Jumping into deep wells/soak away pits/fast rivers	5/20%	0/0%	0/0%	0/0%
Setting self (and huts/building) on fire	3/12%	0/0%	14/42.4%	25/21.2%
Lying on railway lines	1/4%	1/4%	3/9.1%	17/14.4%
Use of guns/inhaling exhaust pipe gases	1/4%	0/0%	3/9.1%	0/0%

Table 5 shows that participants in Botswana appear to be better informed about strategies to be used to curb suicidal ideation.

Table 5.   Suggestions Made to Curb Suicidal Ideation among Participants

	Nigeria	Botswana
Suggestions	Yes (%)	Yes (%)
Strengthening the extended family system	41	69
Encouraging reasonable communication in families	24	63
Encouraging people to embrace counseling	03	31
Removal of stigmatization in communities	34	46
Expand mental health facilities	09	38
Establishing suicide Aid or crisis centers	02	27

DISCUSSION

Results in Table 1 show that. 6.6% of those aged 9-11 years of the total respondents, who were mainly females, indicated suicidal ideation. The prepubescent children (who indicated the least suicidal ideation) were probably still being cared for by members of their nuclear or extended families. They probably had not experienced prolonged trauma that could instigate suicidal ideation among many of them. This is particularly so in the traditional settings as were available in the two countries. Here, extended family ties were relatively strong and they provided strong psychological support for such children.

On the other hand, the older adolescents might entertain suicidal ideations but the severity of its shock might have been absorbed by the more relatively diverse experiences of life they had undergone. For instance, they could share their fears, plans and thoughts with close friends in school, at work (where applicable) and among their neighbors. However, those in the 12 to 15 age range that showed the highest degree of suicidal ideation could be undergoing psychological dissonance as they might be experiencing "no-man's land syndrome." It is a time when it seems to them that no one is concerned with them. This is also a period when significant physiological changes are bothering them. If they do not have adequate attention and information from loving parents or relatives on the various problems they could be battling with, suicidal ideation might find a place in their minds. The findings show that female participants indicate suicidal ideation more than their male counterparts just as Canetto (1995) had earlier found among children and adolescents in USA.

Table 2 shows that suicidal ideation was more prevalent among urban dwellers than those in the rural areas in both countries. The Nigerian male rural group and the Botswana female urban group indicated the least and highest percentage of suicidal ideation, respectively. The latter could be so because of the effect of loss of one's relationship with the family ties and the anonymity that urban life tends to generate. If individuals are unable to obtain adequate social support (as may happen in the urban areas), they may feel hopeless and ultimately entertain suicidal ideation. However, the variation in the difference in suicidal ideation among children in urban and rural areas in Botswana is very close, closer than that among Nigerians. This may be explained by the fact that the concept of urbanity and rurality is not the same in both countries. Many of the so-called rural areas in Botswana have facilities similar to those found in the urban areas. Good roads service several suburban areas effectively and this makes it possible for Batswana to move frequently in and out of their various homes. Most Batswana are said to have four homes—one in the urban areas, one in the 'cattle posts,' another in the lands where crops are planted, and one in the villages. All these contribute to the fact that what happens in the urban areas can also happen in the rural areas almost at the same time or with similar effects. Hence many Batswana in the areas sampled have comparable experiences.

The gap between suicidal ideation between female and male respondents in Botswana is also close because both genders seem to experience the same type and degree of environmental stressors in the rural and urban areas. Nigerian males had the lowest percentage of suicidal ideation probably because such behavior was regarded as feminine and unacceptable by the society. The relatively lower percent recorded for Nigerian samples may be due to the fact the population is large and dense; and that social support is more readily available than in Botswana.

Table 3 shows the ranking of several factors the respondents indicated as being responsible for suicidal ideation in both countries. Debilitating thoughts tantamount to depression and feeling of hopelessness and helplessness seem to top the list. This seems to tally with the belief the world over (see Allan, et al., 1998). Statements such as: "I come from a poor family; I know I am unhappy in life; I have no sense of further hope in life; I do not enjoy the social support of close family members or friends" were highly rated by many of the respondents. Many of them seem to demonstrate that their locus of control is external. This view is supported by the relatively high endorsement of the following statements: 'I think I am being bewitched; A dear family member died of suicide; My problems are caused by others in the society; I fear what people will say about my unwanted pregnancy." The respondents revealed that their suicidal ideation followed the trend of: "thought → plan → action".

This may explain why statements such as: "I want to kill myself to spite my parents or partner; I want to give away my possessions; I want to die because I am HIV positive; I have attempted suicide before and I want to change to a radically new person" were picked by relatively few respondents. Poverty that was checked by most respondents in both countries could be explained by the fact that 47% Batswana live below poverty level (Botswana, Ministry of Finance, 1997) and that poor single mothers head 50% of Botswana households. The situation of poverty may be similar in Nigeria too but relevant data were not available to support this. However, single parenthood has definitely not reached that level. In Nigeria, a few people are extremely rich while the masses are extremely poor.

Table 4 shows the responses to the question: What are common methods often thought about by child suicidal ideators in Nigeria and Botswana? The two commonest methods indicated by Nigerian females were drinking of poisonous chemicals such as kerosene and liquid insecticides and pesticides (48%) and swallowing of caustic soda and taking overdose of dangerous (sleeping) tablets (32%). Among their male counterparts, it seems taking fatal jumps such as diving into deep wells; soak-away pits or fast moving rivers was attractive (20%). Others of nearly equal interest to them were swallowing deadly poisons such as corrosive materials like caustic soda and acid (battery water)—16%; drinking paraffin and setting self on fire (12%). The three most common methods indicated by male Botswana participants were hanging on a tree, ceiling, or rafter (51.2%), setting self (and huts or buildings) on fire (42.4%), and the use of guns (9.1%). The three most commonly mentioned methods by female Botswana participants were hanging (28.2%), setting self on fire (21.2%,) and lying on railway line (14.4%). Among the least common methods mentioned by the female Nigerian participants was lying on the railway lines (4%); hanging, drinking or ingesting poisonous substances, setting self on fire, or using firearms scored zero. Their Botswana counterparts did not pick use of gun or the taking fatal jumps (0). Taking of poison deliberately did not appeal to them (5.9% and 3.4%). The male Batswana participants did not pick jumping into fast or deep rivers or soak-away pits (0). Also, drinking or swallowing poisonous substances were the other less common methods indicated (3%).

One may suggest that males had been traditionally conditioned to take drastic and quick actions in their upbringing. This could explain their recourse to thinking of using fast or masculine methods of committing suicide as indicated above. Jumping into floods, swift rivers, or soak-away pits would ensure immediate completion of their suicidal plans. Incidentally, most rivers flow perennially in the south west of Nigeria and as such the subjects were aware that it was a possible suicidal method. Falling into them would make it unattractive for nonsuicidal ideators to rescue them if there were people around when such acts were committed. While these methods could be attractive to Nigerian males, it was not so to their female counterparts and the Batswana respondents. In addition, the sample in Botswana was taken at a time when there were no rains. Most rivers were predominantly dry and seasonal, and they hardly flooded. It was therefore possible for them not to think of using that means.

Hanging and setting self (and huts) on fire seemed to be popular methods of choice for both male and female participants from Botswana while they were not as popular in Nigeria. This is probably because they are very easy, cheap and convenient methods and the commonest ones the participants had observed being used by completers. They might be methods beyond the immediate imagination of their Nigerian counterparts. On the contrary, Nigerian male and female participants endorsed the use of drinking poisonous chemical preparations in various forms while their Botswana counterparts did not. Some Nigerian female students who failed their examinations or who fell pregnant while still at school had been overheard threatening to adopt these methods to kill themselves. This was because of shame and fear of rejection by the Nigerian society. However, it seems the Botswana society is more understanding and supportive if such fate befalls the adolescent girls. Very limited stigma or rejection follows the pregnant girl and such a girl could resume schooling after delivering the baby. There are even YWCA schools for teen-mothers in Botswana.

Lying on railway lines seemed to be popular among both male and female Batswana. Trains run frequently in Botswana and it could be an effective way of actualizing suicide. It could also be an ostentatious way of crying for help. However, it is not popular in Nigeria. This is most probably because the trains have virtually stopped running throughout the length and breadth of Nigeria. Unlike their foreign counterparts, use of firearms did not appeal to the participants except to some Batswana males (see Kachur, et al., 1995). Those who made the choice probably read in newspaper reports about guns being used by members of the armed forces. Its unpopularity could be explained thus: in both countries, use of firearms is seriously prohibited for civilians. Inhaling poisonous gases is becoming popular among the elite people in the cities.

Table 5 reveals responses indicated in order to curb suicidal ideation by the participants from Nigeria and Botswana. The Batswana were more forthcoming with ideas and programs that could reduce the incidence of suicidal ideation. This could be because they seem to have more suicide awareness and supportive services than those in Nigeria. The latter is a larger country but it has less of such information. Although both countries highly subscribed to strengthening the extended family system, removal of stigmatization in the community, and encouraging reasonable communication in families, the Batswana participants indicated this more than the Nigerians. This may be because the latter realize the need for them more than their Nigerian counterparts. The Nigerian group responded minimally to encouraging people to embrace suicide counseling, expansion of mental health services, and establishing Suicide Aid or Crisis Centre, but their Botswana counterparts indicated greater wish for such services. This could be because the Batswana recognized that if not provided this could lead to further depletion of the country's sparse population and that would not augur well for the future of the country. It could also mean that the Batswana are more anxious to curb the spread of suicidal behavior in the society than their Nigerian counterparts.

In sum, among the suicidal ideators in both countries, those in age group 12-15 years indicated the highest percent; the 9-11 years old indicated the lowest while those in 16-18 years old bracket were intermediate. Those who live in the urban areas indicated suicidal ideation more than those in the rural areas in both countries, but the gap was narrower in Botswana than Nigeria. Several factors could instigate suicidal ideation among respondents in both countries. Batswana participants seem to be more sensitive or aware of suicide in the society than their Nigerian counterparts. They also proffered more information about how to curb the spread of suicidal ideation.

In terms of limitations of the study, the sample used was relatively small and the sample consisted of only non-psychiatric participants. The low number might be due to under-identification of suicidal ideators or stigmatization that volunteers might face in their communities. Concern about the release of such highly sensitive information about suicide might have contributed to the unwillingness of some individuals to participate in the study. There was no control over non-school variables that might encourage suicidal behavior such as child or sexual abuse, bereavement and pre-existing child, or family psychopathology. The translation of some items might have impacted on the responses of some of the participants from Botswana. Therefore, the findings in this study cannot be generalized to the population of children in both countries as such.

Since suicide is avertable, all efforts should be made to prevent its onset. Information, education, and communication of empirically derived facts should be used to dispel myths about suicide. Adequate and prompt counseling should be given to those at risk. In addition, the following steps should be taken:

- Establish primary suicide prevention educational programs, to empathize, make people more understanding, and have less prejudicial attitude towards suicidal persons.
- Introduce a suicide prevention curriculum in schools.
- Establish suicide crisis centers and equip them adequately with relevant resources such as personnel, books, video and articles.
- Compile or procure a suicide crisis training or management handbook.
- There should be toll free lines dedicated to dealing with suicidal behavior in urban areas; a toll free line was installed in Botswana in 2000.
- Organize standby and long-term mental health referral system and personnel who can provide quick, intensive and coordinated services to schools and the community.
- Keep careful and adequate records of suicidal behavior of individuals (especially school-going ones). This will help in the process of monitoring at risk-children.
- Encourage at risk-children to open up, actively seek medical or professional attention on their emotional or psychological problems early enough.
- There should be dedicated suicide counselors. These would receive calls, provide appropriate support, identify at risk children, note warning signs, and treat suicidal individuals and present suicide prevention information to students, staff and parents. They would also be responsible for the development of communication abilities, coping strategies or problem-solving skills and help in reducing the stigma of surviving a suicidal act in the community.
- Let health workers and others in the helping profession be educated in suicide prevention, intervention and post-intervention.

REFERENCES

Akinade, E.A. (1998). *Suicidal thoughts and plans among Nigerian secondary school students.* An unpublished paper. Faculty of Education, Lagos State University, Lagos, Nigeria

Allan, W.D., Kashani J.H., Dahlmeier, J.M., Beck. N., & Reid C. (1998). 'Anxious suicidology': Anew subtype of childhood suicide ideation? *Suicide and Life Threatening Behavior, 28,* 251-260.

Anneleng, O. (2000, October). *Police report says suicide is on the increase.* Botswana Gazette.

Brent, D., Perper, J.A., Goldstein, C.E., Allan, M.J., Allman, C.J., & Zellnak, J.P (1988). Risk factors for adolescent suicide. *Archives of General Pschiatry, 45,* 581-588.

Canetto, S.S (1991). Gender roles, suicidal attempts, and substance abuse. *Journal of Psychology, 125,* 605-620.

Canetto, S.S. (1997). Meaning of gender and suicidal behavior during adolescence. *Suicide and Life Threatening Behavior, 27,* 339-351.

Centre for Diseases Control (1991). Attempted suicide among high school students in United States. *Journal of American Medical Association, 266,* 1911

Centre for Diseases Control and Prevention (1999). *Suicide deaths and rate per 100,000. On-line.* Available.http://www.cdc.gov/ncipc/data/us9794/suic.htm.

Dahlen E.R., & Canetto, S.S. (1996, April). *The role of gender and context in attitudes towards nonfatal suicidal behavior.* Paper presented at the meeting of American Association of Suicidology, St Louis, MO.

De Rose, N., & Page, S. (1985). Attitudes of professional and community groups towards male and female suicide. *Canadian Journal of Mental Health, 4,* 51-64.

Hill, J. P., & Lynch, M.E. (1983). The intensification of gender-related role expectations during adolescence. In J. Brooks-Gunn & A.C. Petersen (Eds.), *Girls at puberty* (pp. 221-228). New York: Plenum Press.

Kachur, S.P., Potter, L.B., James, S.P., & Powell, K.E. (1995). *Suicide in United States 1980-1992.* Violence Surveillance Summary Series, No.1.

Kashani, J., Allan, W. D., Dahlmeier, J.M., Rezvani, M. & Reid, J.C. (1989). An examination of family functioning utilizing the circumflex model in psychiatrically hospitalized children with depression. *Journal of Affective Disorders, 35,* 65-73.

King, C.A. (1997). Suicidal behavior in adolescence. In R.W. Marries, M.M. Silverman, & S.S. Canetto (Eds.), *Review of suicidology* (pp. 61-95). New York: Guilford Press.

Kosky, R., Silburn, S., & Zubrick, S.R. (1990). Are children and adolescents who have suicidal thoughts different from those who attempt suicide? *Journal of Nervous and Mental Disease, 178,* 38-43.

Leary, W.E. (1995,April 21). Young people who try suicide may succeed more often. *New York Times.*

Leenars, A. A., & Wenckstern, S (1990). Suicide prevention in schools: An introduction. *Death Studies, 14,* 297-302.

Lewinsohn, P.M., Rhode, P., & Seeley, J. R. (1996). Adolescent suicidal ideation and attempts: Prevalence, risk factors, and clinical implications. *Clinical Psychology: Science and Practice, 3,* 25-46.

Makinwa, B. (2000,Sept.4). *Who knows why rich people prefer to die.* The Guardian Online-http://www.ngrguardiannews.com.

Moscicki, E.K. (1995). Epidemiology of suicidal behavior. *Suicide and Life Threatening Behavior, 25,*22-35.

Shafter, D., Gould, M.S., Fisher, P., Truatman, P., Moreau, D., Kleinman, M., & Florry, M. (1996). Psychiatric diagnosis in child and adolescent suicide. *Archives of General Psychiatry, 53,* 339-348.

Tembo, P., Taziba, S., Rantwa, M., Masuge, P. & Mahkwade, K. (1989). *A study to determine factors associated with suicide and suicide attempts in selected areas of Botswana.* Botswana: Health Research Unit, Ministry of Health.

22

Exploring the Associations Between Social Class, Binge Drinking, and Other Risk Behaviors Among Brazilian Young People

Roberta Uchoa
Federal University of Pernambuco

Kim Wolff
National Addiction Centre

Vikram Patel
Sangath Centre

Sophia Rabe-Hesketh
National Addiction Centre

John Strang
National Addiciton Centre

Roberta Uchoa · Rua Prof. Gondim Filho, 71/31 · Boa Viagem, Recife, PE · 51111-120 · Brazil.

International Perspectives on Child and Adolescent Mental Health. Volume 2: Proceedings of the Second International Conference, edited by N. N. Singh, T. H. Ollendick, and A. N. Singh. © 2002 Elsevier Science Ltd. All rights reserved.

Public interest in young people's health is immense. Particular interest and concern surrounds issues related to young people's alcohol misuse, e.g. binge drinking (getting drunk) and engaging in risk behaviours such as use of other drugs, unprotected sex and involvement in criminal activities (Foxcroft, 1997). At one level, alcohol use among young people might be viewed as just for fun or pleasure. Nevertheless, whilst most young people will lower their alcohol intake as they grow up (Pappe and Hammer, 1996), many will experience social harm and serious physical alcohol-related problems (British Paediatric Association, 1995; Paton, 1999).

There is not a general consensus with regard to the relationship between alcohol use and social class. Some authors have reported few class-based differences and that differences are age-dependent (Peck & Plant, 1986; Martin & Pritchard, 1991; British Paediatric Association, 1995; Shucksmith, et al., 1997), whilst others have suggested a clear pattern of social class differences among young people (Romelsjo, 1989; Green, et al., 1991; Perez, et al., 1995; Romelsjo & Lundberg, 1996).

Young people (late teens and early twenties) are more likely to experience binge drinking rather than alcohol dependence, as they do not have a sufficient duration of drinking history. In addition, alcohol intoxication might be seen as an escape from adolescent conflicts (e.g. seeing themselves as adolescent rather than adult and not having made the social transition to an adult). Lacking the self-image as an adolescent or not having resolved the balance between dependence on others and independence are conflicts that could generate frustrations and painful confusion of feelings (Edwards, et al, 1997).

The choices young people make regarding leisure activities to satisfy their needs depend on their present social contexts. Leisure as an activity carried out for the person's own sake and satisfaction provides an arena for young people's experimentation with the challenges that will face them as adults, including issues related to friendship, sexuality, aggression and the use of alcohol or other drugs. Leisure includes pleasurable activities such as sports and reading, and also consists of engaging in risky behaviours, for instance binge drinking, sexual relationships, use of other drugs and involvement in criminal activities (Raymore, et al., 1999).

Data on alcohol use among young people are extensive within developed countries (e.g. UK, USA, Australasia and Scandinavia). But, despite massive research in this field, there is still a lot to learn, as data often vary according to social class, age, gender, location and field researched (Lowe, et al., 1993; Fossey, 1994; Ellickson, et al., 1996; Miller & Plant, 1996).

In developing countries such as Brazil there is still very little information about alcohol use among young people, and its causes and consequences. Data on alcohol history, prevalence, tendencies, prevention, services and forms of treatment are deficient in some parts of the country and in others, virtually non-existent. Data on alcohol use among young people in Brazil predominantly relate to the South and Southeast regions of the country (Pechansky & Barros, 1995; Muza, et al 1997; Araújo & Gomes, 1998). In addition, there is a lack of research attempting to understand this topic from the perspective of young people's social-economic background. In Brazil, young people's drinking behaviour needs to be understood more fully in the context of environmental influences in order to develop local and national policies on alcohol consumption. Recommendations (e.g. sensible drinking) for tackling alcohol-related problems among young people ought to be evidence-based and different populations will need different messages. Therefore, the purpose of this study is to contribute to the fuller understanding of alcohol use among young people in Recife, Northeast Brazil.

Background to the design and conduct of the study

Setting

Recife is located in the Northeast coast of Brazil and has a population of 1.3 million. The city was built as a port city and got its name from the coral reefs that line the coast. Recife is famous for its 16th and 17th-century colonial buildings, tropical white-sand beaches with coconut trees, mangrove swamps, rivers, channels and bridges (EMBRATUR, 2000). The private (fee paying) schools selected were in one of the town centre's best locations where middle class families have been resident for more than 100 years; and the public (state) schools were in the city boundaries where poor class families have taken up residence in more recent years.

Sampling procedures and subjects

Quantitative cross-sectional design was chosen for the study (Hennekens & Buring, 1987). Respectively, middle and poor class young people were recruited within private (fee paying) and public (state) schools. Four hundred and twenty young people registered among the second half of the first degree (basic education) and the second degree (complementary education) of the Brazilian educational system from the selected schools were randomly chosen based upon year of birth and gender.

Measurements

Young people were approached and those who consented to participate were interviewed while they were at school, using a structured questionnaire. The questionnaire was inittially composed at the National Addiction Centre in London and then tested through a pilot study conducted in 1997 with young people in Recife, Brazil. There was no direct translation from existing questionnaires and a structured interview schedule developed by CEBRID (1997) was used to collect data on alcohol and other drugs. Data analyses were based on results obtained from a selection of 7 social variables potentially associated with binge drinking, which consisted of: social class (poor and middle class); age (10 – 15 and 16 – 19 years); gender (male and female); ever smoked cigarettes; ever used other drugs (illegal or legal); ever had unprotected sex (sexual relationships without using a condom); and ever involved in criminal activities (violence against a person or a property, shoplifting, fraud, selling drugs, using a gun or a knife).

Statistical analyses

The analyses were carried out with Stata6 statistical package (version 6). Data were analysed using cross-tabulation, with chi-square tests for categorical data, and using logistic regression. Simple and multiple logistic regression were carried out for each of the social variables for the entire sample. The likelihood-ratio test was used to test the evidence for effect modification (interaction) between the effects of confounding variables (social class, age and gender) and the explanatory variables included in the models (Clayton & Hills, 1998; LSHTM, 1999). In the final stages of the analyses, stepwise regression was employed using backward elimination for inclusion of regressors in the model. All tests used a significance level of 0.05 (Kirkwood, 1988; Everitt, 1998).

The findings from the Recife sample

Characteristic of subjects

From the original sample an overall response rate of 80% (336 of 420) was achieved. Eighty-four young people were not recruited of these, of whom 52 could not be contacted at all. Absenteeism (8), dropout (18), changing school (8), pregnancy (3), being in a fellowship exchange students programme in the United States (3) and incorrect class registers (12) explained those not contacted. Thirty-two young people explicitly did not want to be interviewed and gave no explanations for non-participation. A total of 336 subjects took part in the study, mean age 14 years (range 10 - 19 years, SD 2.7), comprising 153 males and 183 females, who fell into 3 distinct age groups: 10 – 12 years (n=121), 13 – 15 years (n=105) and 16 – 19 years (n=110).

From the total of 336 subjects, 183 (55%) from the middle class (80 males and 103 females) and 153 (45%) were from the poor class (73 males and 80 females) with approximate equal number of subjects in each age group and similar mean age (14 years). Most (84%) non-responders among the poor class group (n=57) were not at schools when the interviews were conducted. In contrast, the majority (85%) of non-responders among the middle class group (n=27) were at school, but declined the invitation to participate in the study.

Prevalence of binge drinking and other risk behaviours

The majority (79%) of young people reported lifetime alcohol use (i.e. use of alcohol at least once in their lifetime). Almost a quarter (23%) of young people had engaged in binge drinking at least once with percentages increasing with increased age: 12% (10 – 12 years) vs. 22% (13 – 15 years) vs. 66% (16 – 19 years) (p<0.001). The mean age of the first binge drinking was 14 years (SD 2.8). Male subjects were more likely to have engaged in binge drinking than females (57% vs. 43%, p<0.05).

Twenty three per cent (n=77) of the 336 subjects had used tobacco on one occasion. A small number (13%; n=43) of the whole group used illegal drugs (e.g. cannabis and inhalants) and 18% (n=59) used legal drugs (e.g. prescription-only1 and over-the-counter medications). The most common drugs that had been used among young people were inhalants (12%; n=41), tranquillisers (11%; n=35) and cannabis (3%; n=9). Prescription-only medications most used were tranquillisers (11%; n=35), amphetamine (2%; n=8) and barbiturates (2%; n=7), and the most frequently used over-the-counter medication was appetite stimulants (5%; n=15). More than half (54%) of the 59 subjects who had used prescription-only medication had bought it from the pharmacies without a prescription.

Twenty four per cent (n=79) of subjects had had sexual relationships at least once, of which 24% (n=19) had had unprotected sex. Male and older young people (16 – 19 years) were more likely to engage in sexual relationships (77% male vs. 23% female, p<0.001; 73% aged 16 – 19 vs. 27% aged 10 – 15, p<0.001). All young people reported being heterosexual. Almost one third (31%) engaged in sexual relationships after consumption of alcohol and 3% after taking other drugs.

Seven per cent (n=23) of the sample had been involved in criminal activities. These offences varied from violence against a person or a property to shoplifting, selling drugs and using a gun or a knife. The incidence of criminal activities was significantly more common among those aged 16 and above (78% aged 16 – 19 vs. 22% aged 10 – 15, p<0.001) and was also more common among male subjects (74% male vs. 26% female, p<0.005). Two young people (1%) reported drinking alcohol or using another drug before being involved in criminal activities, both were males from the older age group (16 – 19 years).

Associations between social class, binge drinking and other risk behaviours

Young people from the poor class group were more likely to engage in binge drinking (Table 1). Social class differences were also observed among the under-aged (10 – 15 years) binge drinkers (69% poor class vs. 31% middle class, p<0.01), and female binge drinkers (64% poor class vs. 36% middle class, p<0.05).

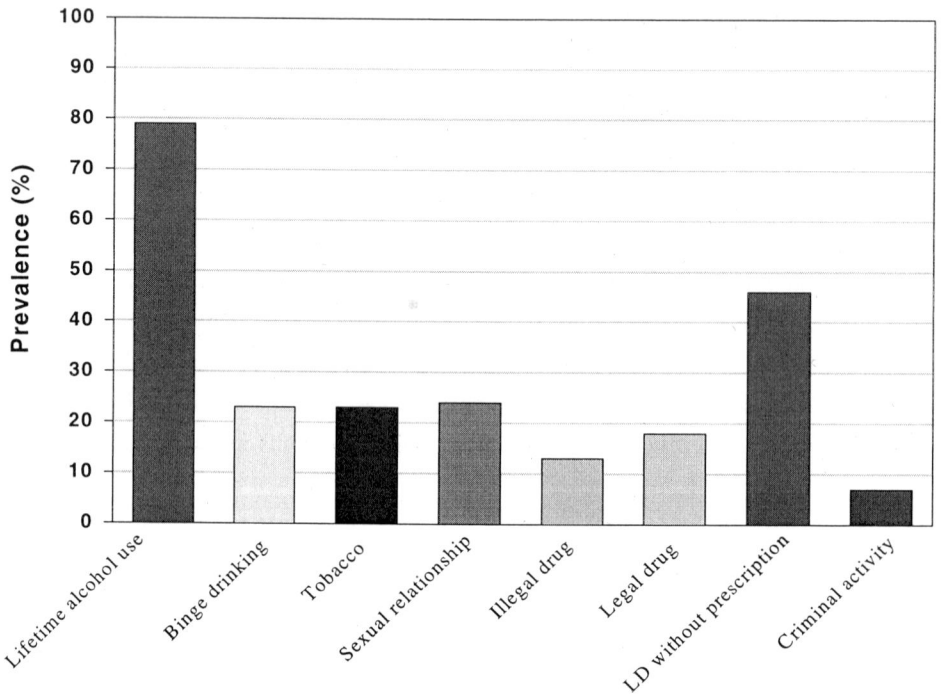

Figure 1. Prevalence of binge drinking and other risk behaviours among Brazilian young people

There were no social class differences for smoking and using other drugs. However, among the middle class group, "lança-perfume"2 was the drug of preference. Only one young person from the middle class inhaled glue. In the poor class group the drugs of preference were cannabis and inhalants (e.g. "loló"3 and glue). Poor class young people were significantly more likely to have engaged in unprotected sex and to be involved in criminal activities (Table 1).

Table 1. Characteristics of binge drinking and other risk behaviours according to social class (%)

	Poor class (n = 153)	Middle Class (n = 183)	x^2
Binge drinking	61	39	0.005
Smoked	47	53	NS
Used other drugs[1]	40	60	NS
Unprotected sex	79	21	0.005
Involved in criminal activities	65	35	0.05

[1] Illegal or legal drugs.

Using simple logistic regression, overall binge drinking was associated with being from a poor class background, male and from an older age group (16 – 19 years). Engaging in other risk behaviours (e.g. smoking cigarettes, use of illegal or legal drugs, unprotected sex and involvement in criminal activities) also increased the likelihood of binge drinking (Table 2).

Table 2. Simple logistic regression of binge drinking by social variables

Binge Drinking	OR	95%Cl		P
Poor class	2.1	1.30	3.69	0.005
Older age[1]	6.4	3.68	11.16	<0.001
Males	1.7	1.06	2.97	0.05
Smoked	11.3	6.25	20.50	<0.001
Used other drugs[2]	8.4	4.76	14.91	<0.001
Unprotected sex	8.7	3.19	23.88	<0.001
Involved in criminal activities	9.6	3.79	24.46	<0.001

[1] Age groups: 10 – 15 and 16 – 19 years. 2 Illegal or legal drugs.

Using multiple logistic regression for the entire sample together (Table 3), the effect of all social variables on the likelihood of binge drinking remained significant. Poor class group and older age group (16 – 19 years) were more likely to engage in binge drinking and other risk behaviours. Apart from involvement in criminal activities, the remaining outcomes were more likely among male subjects. There was not evidence of interactions between the effects of confounding variables (social class, age and gender) and the explanatory variables included in the model.

Table 3. Multiple logistic regression of binge drinking by social variables controlled for social class, age and gender

Binge Drinking	OR	95%Cl		P
Smoked	10.5	5.29	20.98	<0.001
Used other drugs[1]	7.6	3.91	15.09	<0.001
Unprotected sex	5.3	1.80	15.62	0.005
Involved in criminal activities	4.1	1.48	11.76	0.01

[1] Illegal or legal drugs.

In the final analysis using stepwise regression (Table 5), binge drinking was explored with alll explanatory variables together, controlling for the potential confounders (social class, age and gender).

Table 4. Stepwise logistic regression of binge drinking by social variables controlled for social class, age and gender

Binge Drinking	OR	95%Cl		P
Poor class	4.0	1.97	8.44	<0.001
Older age[1]	3.4	1.73	6.73	<0.001
Males	2.8	1.44	5.80	0.005
Smoked	7.2	3.46	15.11	<0.001
Used other drugs[2]	4.7	2.23	9.991	<0.001

[1] Age groups: 10 – 15 and 16 – 19 years. [2] Illegal or legal drugs.

The data provide evidence, that in this subject population, binge drinking was more common in the older (16 – 19 years) poorer class males who also smoked cigarettes and used other drugs (illegal or legal). Social class differences were significant for binge drinking with the poor class group more likely to engage in this pattern of drinking than their middle class peers. Furthermore the social class differences for binge drinking were found significant throughout all stages of the analyses (cross-tabulation, and simple, multiple and stepwise logistic regression), showing a consistent distinction between poor and middle class young people.

Considering the implications of the findings

This study has explored binge drinking in a sample of young people (10 – 19 years) in Recife, Brazil. Data collection focused on a range of social factors potentially associated with this risky pattern of alcohol use such as social class, age, gender, use of other drugs, sexual relationships and involvement in criminal activities. Within this sample (n=336), 23% had had at least one episode of binge drinking, 23% had smoked cigarettes and 26% had tried other drugs (illegal or legal). In addition, 24% had had sexual relationships, of which 24% had had unprotectes sex, and 7% had been involved in criminal activities.

Social class emerged as significantly related to binge drinking, with greater likelihood of this event among poor class older adolescents, after adjusting for gender, age and social variables. One could argue that reverse causality could explain the association between binge drinking and poor class. However, reverse causality is unlikely since social mobility as a consequence of personal behaviour could not be considered with subjects at such a young age. On the contrary, one could speculate that the effects of this risky pattern of alcohol use are not yet apparent at a young age. In addition, these effects could be manifested later playing against a chance of upward social mobility, as there are greater chances of risk of health hazards. Life chances themselves could be determined by health (Karvonen, et al., 1999; Marmot & Wilkinson, 1999).

The overall percentage of binge drinking (23%) was far from figures from the USA and the UK (44% and 55%, respectively) (Bell, et al., 1997; Wechsler, et al., 1995). When comparing figures by age and gender between the UK and Recife, differences were even greater. According to the British Paediatric Association (1995), among British 13 year olds, 28% of boys and 15% of girls had already been drunk at least once; and at 15 year olds the figures were 55% for boys and 48% for girls. In contrast, among 10 – 13 year olds in Recife, the percentages were 3% for both boys and for girls; and at 15 year olds, 13% for boys and 10% for girls.

The results confirm previous data showing a tendency for young people in Recife to use solvents, cannabis and psychoactive medication, because these were easiest drugs for young people attending school in the Northeast of Brazil to obtain. Cocaine and crack were not used among these subjects from the Northeast region and possibly the use of these drugs is more common among young people from the Southeast region of the country (Noto, et al., 1997). Additionally, the results corroborate previous findings of a substantial use of prescription-only medication in Brazil as a greater amount of young people used prescription-only medication (18%) compared to illicit drugs (13%) (Mari, et al., 1993; CEBRID, 1997). A high percentage (54%) of prescription-only medications was obtained without prescription from community pharmacies, a common practice among young people and adults in Brazil. This finding suggests that there is no effective surveillance from the health authorities of this practice, and that for young people there is easy availability of medicine from the pharmacies in the area.

Drinking alcohol was highly correlated with engaging in sexual behaviour. Among those who had episodes of binge drinking, 79% had sexual relationships on one or more occasions without using a condom and 84% had more than one partner. As shown in the literature, sex under the influence of alcohol is associated with risky behaviour such as failure to use contraception and casual partners rather than a regular partner (Traeen & Kvalem, 1999). One of the implications of these results is that there is a pressing need for sex education campaigns targeting young people, drinking and sexual behaviours.

There were significant associations between binge drinking and criminal behaviour. However, despite the observed linkages between risky patterns of drinking and offending behaviour, the data do not necessarily reflect a direct cause-effect association, with one increasing the risk of the other, or the existence of a common main tendency to problematic behaviours among these subjects (Fergusson, et al., 1996). Ideally, further studies with a longitudinal design should be carried out to determine the pathways, which causally link risky patterns of alcohol use and criminal activities.

A cross-sectional design was chosen for this study because this was the most appropriate method available. A crucial question in a cross-sectional study is how accurate and consistent are the data in surveys of this kind, as methodological problems are commonly acknowledged in the literature (Midanik, 1988; Oppenheim, 1996). In order to increase the probability of representativeness of the study, we chose to select a convenience sample (Dunn & Ferri, 1999) which was drawn from public (state) and private (fee paying) schools and then to use a random sampling method to assign a representative sample within the schools. Bearing in mind the non-response rate (20%), we are satisfied that the sample can be considered representative of young people in Recife attending school, with regard to gender and age distribution (Oppenheim, 1996). It needs to be acknowledged that different characteristics exist between those who participate in such a study and those who refused. If the reason for non-participation is associated with the outcome of interest (e.g. risky patterns of alcohol use) or exposure variables (e.g. problems at school, working experience, family environment), then the risk of selection bias increases. Since poor class young people were more likely not to be at school, there is the possibility that selection bias might have occurred. The fact that higher percentages of poor class young people (28% vs. 13%) were not recruited poses a limitation as these non-recruited (e.g. dropouts, truants) are more likely to be a higher-risk behaviour group (Crowley, 1991; Carlini-Cotrim, 1995; Powis, et al., 1998). Therefore, the findings are limited to young people attending school and cannot be generalised to young people out of school. However, even taking into account sample loss or possible response bias (e.g. over or under-reporting), the percentages are still likely to be valid for young people in Recife when compared with other studies carried out in the city and in other regions of Brazil (CEBRID, 1997; Noto, et al., 1997).

Putting it all together

This study aimed to investigate the relationships between social class, binge drinking and other risk behaviours among young people in Recife, Brazil. Data are representative of poor and middle class young people attending school and do not characterise those who dropped-out of school and the various sub-groups of the so-called "street children" that exist in Brazil.

Results on alcohol use and risk behaviours obtained in the present study should certainly be a matter of concern. Education programmes in Brazil need to take these results into account without a moral, criminal, religious or panic appeal. In many developing countries (e.g. UK, Holland, Australia, New Zealand and Canada), the target outcome on alcohol and other drug prevention programmes has moved towards health promotion (e.g. sensible drinking and harm reduction) rather than absolute and control-dominated policies (e.g. abstinence, scare techniques, locking up and charging illicit drug use). Educational efforts in Brazil should perhaps investigate a wider range of possible approaches and consider providing young people, parents, schools and health professionals with information on alcohol and other drug prevention on the basis of the health promotion approach (Carlini-Cotrim, 1994; Edwards, et al., 1995; Foxcroft, et al., 1997).

Intervations need to be focused on the particular drugs that young people are exposed to or to which they may become exposed. In the particular case of the young in Recife, these actions should mainly address alcohol, tobacco, inhalants, tranquillisers and cannabis. Interventions should be planned at a local level (e.g. community or school) so that they can reflect properly the needs of the targeted population (Wagemar, et al., 2000). Possibly initiatives should aim at social class background, age and gender groups in order to deliver more socially adequate actions.

Notes

In Brazil, prescription-only medication such as amphetamines, tranquillisers, anticholinergics and barbiturates are easily obtained from the pharmacies without prescription.

A small metal container filled with ether or ethyl chloride made clandestinely and sold illegally exclusively for the purpose of drug abuse.

A homemade version of "lança-perfume".

ACKNOWLEDGMENTS

This research was entirely sponsored by Fundação Coordenação de Aperfeiçoamento de Pessoal de Nível Superior - CAPES (Post-Graduate Federal Agency from the Brazilian Government). The Wellcome Trust supported the presentation of this work at the Second International Conference on Child and Adolescent Mental Health, in Kuala Lumpur.

REFERENCES

Araújo, L.B., & Gomes, W.B. (1998). Adolescência e expectativas em relação aos efeitos do alcool (Adolescence and expectancies related to alcohol effects). In W.B. Gomes (Ed.), *Fenomenologia e Pesquisa em Psicologia*. Rio Grande do Sul, Porto Alegre: Editora da Universidade Federal do.

Bell, R., Wechsler, H., & Johnston, S. (1997). Correlates of college student marijuana use: Results of a U.S. national survey. *Addiction, 92*, 571-578.

British Paediatric Association and the Royal College of Physicians. (1995). *Alcohol and the young*. Suffolk: The Lavenham Press.

Carlini-Cotrin, B. (1994). An overview on drug abuse prevention in Brazilian schools. *Drugs: Education, Prevention and Policy, 3*, 275-288.

Carlini-Cotrin, B. (1995). Inhalant use among Brazilian youth. *NIDA Research Monograph Series, 148*, 64-78.

CEBRID (1997). *IV Levantamento sobre o Uso de Drogas entre Estudantes de 1º e 2º Graus em 10 Capitais Brasileiras* (IV Survey on the Use of Drugs among 1st and 2nd Grade Students in 10 Brazilian Cities), CONFEN, Brasília.

Clayton. D., & Hills. M. (1998). *Statistical models in epidemiology*. Oxford: Oxford Science Press.

Crowley, J.E. (1991). Educational status and drinking patterns: How representative are college students? *Journal Studies on Alcohol, 52*, 10-16.

Dunn, J., & Ferri, C. (1999). Epidemiological methods for research with drug misusers: Review of methods for studying prevalence and morbidity. *Revista de Saúde Pública, 33*, 206-215.

Edwards, G., Anderson, P., & Babor, T.F. (1995). *Alcohol policy and the public good*. Oxford: Oxford University Press.

Edwards, G., Marshall, E.J., & Cook, C. (1997). *The treatment of drinking problems: A guide for the helping professions*. Cambridge: Cambridge University Press.

Ellickson, P.L., McGrigan, K.A., Adams, V., Bell, R.M., & Hays, R.D. (1996). Teenagers and alcohol misuse in the United States: By any definition, it's a big problem. *Addiction, 91*, 1489-1503.

EMBRATUR – Instituto Brasileiro de Turismo (2000) Internet site: http:\\www.embratur.gov.br (date of consultation: 31.03.2000).

Everitt, B.S. (1998). *The Cambridge dictionary of statistics.* Cambridge: Cambridge University Press.

Fergusson, D.M., Lynskey, M.T., & Horwood, L.J. (1994). Childhood exposure to alcohol and adolescent drinking patterns. *Addiction, 89,* 1007-1016.

Fossey, E. (1994). *Growing up with alcohol.* London: Routledge.

Foxcroft, D.R. (1997). Editorial – Special issue on adolescent health. *Journal of Adolescence, 20,* 3-7.

Green, G., Macintyre, S., West, P., & Ecob, R. (1991). Like parent like child? Associations between drinking and smoking behavior of parents and their children. *British Journal of Addiction, 86,* 745-758.

Hennekens, C.H., & Buring, J.E. (1987). *Epidemiology in medicine.* Boston: Little Brown and Company.

Karvonen, S., Rimpela, A.H., & Rimpela, M.K. (1999). Social mobility and health related behaviors in young people. *Journal of Epidemiology & Community Health, 53,* 211-217.

Kirkwood, B.R. (1988). *Essentials of medical statistics.* Oxford: Blackwell Science Ltd.

Lowe, G., Foxcroft, D.R., & Sibley, D. (1993). *Adolescent drinking and family life.* Chur: Harwood Academic Publishers.

LSHTM (1999). *Statistical methods in epidemiology – Study Unit 1999.* London: London School of Hygiene and Tropical Medicine.

Mari, J.J., Almeida-Filho, N., Coutinho, E., Andreoli, S.B., Miranda, C.T., & Streiner, D. (1993). The epidemiology of psychotropic use in the city of São Paulo. *Psychological Medicine, 23,* 467-474.

Marmot, M., & Wilkinson, R.G. (Eds.) (1999). *Social determinants of health.* Oxford: Oxford University Press.

Martin, M.J., & Pritchard, M.E. (1991). Factors associated with alcohol use in later adolescence. *Journal Studies on Alcohol, 52,* 5-9.

Midanik, L.T., & Clark, W.B. (1994). The demographic distribution of U.S. drinking Patterns in 1990: Description and trends from 1984. *American Journal of Public Health, 84,* 1218-1222.

Miller, P., & Plant, M. (1996). Drinking, smoking and illicit drug use among 15 and 16 year old in the United Kingdom. *British Medical Journal, 313,* 394-397.

Murgraff, V., Parrot, A., & Bennett, P. (1999). Risky single-occasion drinking amongst young people: Definition, correlates policy and intervention: A broad overview of research findings. *Alcohol & Alcoholism, 34,* 3-14.

Muza, G.M., Bettiol, H., Mucillo, G., & Barbieri, M.A. (1997). Consumo de substâncias psicoativas por adolescentes escolares de Ribeirão Preto, Brasil: Distribuição do consumo por classes sociais (The intake of psychoative substances by school-age adolescents in an urban area of southeastern region of Brazil: Distribution of consumption by social levels. *Revista de Saúde Pública, 31*, 163-170.

Noto, A.R., Nappo, S.A., Galduroz, J.C., Mattei, R., & Carlini, E.A. (1997). Use of drugs among street children in Brazil. *Journal of Psychoactive Drugs, 29*, 185-192.

Oppenheim, A.N. (1996). Questionnaire design, interviewing and attitude measurement. London: Pitter Publishers.

Pape, H., & Hammer, T. (1996). How does young people's alcohol consumption change during the transition to early adulthood? A longitudinal study of changes at aggregate and individual levels. *Addiction, 91*, 1345-1357.

Paton, A. (1999). Reflections on alcohol and the young. *Alcohol &Alcoholism, 34*, 502-505.

Pechansky, F., & Barros, F.C. (1995). Problems related to alcohol consumption by adolescents living in the city of Porto Alegre, Brazil. *The Journal of Drug Issues, 25*, 735-750.

Peck, D., & Plant, P. (1986). Unemployment and illegal drug use: Concordant evidence from a prospective study and national trends. *British Journal of Medicine, 293*, 929-932.

Perez, A.M.G., Manrique, J.F.D., Martin, C.P., & Usieto, E.G. (1995) Problemas relacionados con el alcohol en cantabria (Problems associated with alcohol in cantabria). *Actas Luso-Españolas de Neurologia Psiquiatrica Y Ciencias Afines, 23*, 20-24.

Powis, B., Griffiths, P., Gossop, M., Lloyde, C., & Strang, J. (1998). Drug use and offending behavior among young people excluded from school. *Drugs: Education, Prevention and Policy, 5*, 245-256.

Raymore, L.A., Barber, B.L., Eccles, J.S., & Godbey, G.C. (1999). Leisure behavior pattern stability during the transition from adolescence to young adulthood. *Journal of Youth and Adolescence, 28*, 79-103.

Romelsjo, A. (1989). The relationship between consumption and social status in Stockholm: Has the social pattern of alcohol consumption changed? *International Journal of Epidemiology, 18*, 842-851.

Romelsjo, A. & Lundberg, M. (1996). The changes in the social class distribution of moderate and high alcohol consumption and alcohol-related disabilities over time in Stockholm county and in Sweden. *Addiction, 91*, 1307-1323.

Shucksmith, J., Glendining, A., & Hendy, L. (1997). Adolescent drinking behavior and the role of family life: A Scottish perspective. *Journal of Adolescence, 20*, 85-101.

Traeen, B., & Kvalem, I.L. (1996).   Sex under the influence of alcohol among Norwegian adolescents. *Addiction*, *91*, 995-1006.

Wagemar, A.C., Murray, D.M., & Toomey, T.L. (2000). Communities mobilizing for change on alcohol (CMCA): Effects of a randomized trial on arrests and traffic crashes. *Addiction*, *95*, 209-217.

Wechsler, H., Dowdall, G.W., Davenport, A., & Catillo, S. (1995).   Correlates of college students binge drinking. *American Journal of Public Health*, *85*, 921-926.

23

The Psychological and Sociocultural Adaptation of Chinese and Vietnamese Immigrant Adolescents in Australia

Cynthia Leung
Victoria University

Wally Karnilowicz
Victoria University

Cynthia Leung · Victoria University · P.O. Box 14428 · Melbourne Central Mail Center · Victoria 8001 · Australia.

International Perspectives on Child and Adolescent Mental Health. Volume 2: Proceedings of the Second International Conference, edited by N. N. Singh, T. H. Ollendick, and A. N. Singh. © 2002 Elsevier Science Ltd. All rights reserved.

Australia is a multicultural society with immigrants coming from many different countries. With the abolition of the White Australian policy in 1973, increasing numbers of Asian immigrants came to scale in Australia and the two largest groups were the Chinese (the second largest non-English language group in Australia) and the Vietnamese (the fourth largest non-English language group in Australia) (Australian Bureau of Statistics, 1997). According to the 1996 census, there were 323,955 Chinese-speaking people and 134,011 Vietnamese-speaking people living in Australia (Australian Bureau of Statistics, 1997). Research into the adaptation of these two groups in Australia will help to provide a better understanding of their needs and better service provision.

The present study examines the adaptation experience of Chinese and Vietnamese immigrant adolescents in Australia, in comparison to a group of Anglo-Australian adolescents. Adolescents were chosen as the focus of this study because adolescence is a period of psychological and physical changes, and a period for search of personal identity. Migration necessitates many changes and a search for ethnic identity in the society of settlement. Information on how immigrant adolescents deal with the changes resultant from puberty and migration would provide useful guidelines for service providers such as teachers, youth workers, and school welfare workers.

Adaptation is related to changes that individuals or groups make as a response to demands in the environment (Berry, 1997). Searle and Ward (1990) argue that adaptation can be divided into two domains: the internal psychological (affective and emotional) domain and the external sociocultural (behavioral) domain. The two are thought to be related to each other but predicted by different variables. Adaptation, whether psychological or sociocultural, can be measured in both positive and negative ways. Psychological adaptation can be measured through measures of psychological well-being such as life satisfaction, self esteem and satisfactory functioning, or measures of psychopathology such as presence of psychological symptoms. Sociocultural adaptation can again be measured through adaptive functioning such as the ability to perform everyday activities in school and home or maladaptive functioning such as presence of social and behavior problems. In the present study, adaptation is measured through various measures of psychological well-being and psychopathology, adaptive and maladaptive functioning including self esteem, life satisfaction, academic achievement, school adjustment, psychological distress, and behavior problems.

Berry (1997) presented a conceptual framework to illustrate the main issues related to migrant adaptation. In this framework, both group or societal variables and individual variables are considered. Acculturation begins wit cultural groups in contact, resulting in changes in the groups' collective features such as political, economic and social structures. These changes in turn affect the individual who is experiencing acculturation, leading to various psychological experiences and changes. According to Berry (1997), individuals may experience various levels of difficulties during this acculturation experience. For some, the experience might be quite easy, involving learning new social skills or rules, but for others, the experience might be more difficult, and individuals may experience various levels of stress, or even psychopathology. Searle and Ward (1990) point out that as life changes are associated with physical and psychological problems, the life changes associated with migration could possibly lead to psychological problems among immigrants. Similarly, Schwarzer, Hahn, and Schroder (1994) suggest that migration can be considered as a critical life event and critical life events have been found to be associated with psychopathology. These ideas lead to the migration-morbidity hypothesis (Klimidis, Stuart, Minas, & Ata, 1994) where immigrant status is hypothesized to be associated with greater psychological morbidity.

The nature of a person's adaptation or the severity of the psychological problems experienced are dependent on both group level variables and individual variables (Berry, 1997). Some of the individual variables are related to the adaptation of all adolescents, immigrants and non-immigrants, while others are specific to immigrant adolescents only. Below is a discussion of some of the important variables that appear to play an important role in a number of studies related to immigrant adaptation and adolescent psychological well-being.

One of the factors relevant to the psychological and sociocultural adaptation of all adolescents is locus of control or sense of personal mastery. Research has shown that academic achievement is related to the concept of locus of control. Walden and Ramey (1983) and Willig, Harnisch, Hill, and Maehr (1983) found that an internal locus of control, or attribution of success to internal controllable factors such as effort was correlated with relatively high academic achievement. Locus of control has also been found to be related to psychopathology. For example, Ralph, Merralls, Hart, Porter, and Tan (1995) reported that external locus of control was positively related to anxiety and negatively related to self esteem among Australian high school students. Ward and Kennedy (1992) found that sojourner students with an internal locus of control reported high levels of psychological well-being. Hountrus and Scharf (1970) found that males with external locus of control were less confident of themselves. Deboer (1985) found that women with lower self esteem explained their success by external factors. Low self esteem is frequently implicated in the linkage between poor academic performance and behavior problems, including delinquency (Maughan, 1994).

Apart from a sense of personal competence, relationship with parents is another important variable related to the psychological and sociocultural adaptation of adolescents. For example, Lu (1995) found that among Chinese adolescents, social support was negatively related to psychological symptoms. Scheier and Botvin (1997) reported that adult functional support was related to levels of psychological distress. Conflicts between generations in values, particularly in areas of family life, such as parental authority arid children's rights (Georgas, Shaw & Berry, 1996) could be a potential cause of psychological distress among adolescents. Parent-child relationship and family values were also thought to be related to academic achievement. Rosenthal and Feldman (1991a) found that a demanding family environment, in the context of control without conflict, was related to positive academic achievement among Chinese, Australian and American students. For immigrant adolescents, conflicts between cultures of the society of settlement and the family culture could cause potential stress (Feldman, Monte-Regnaud & Rosenthal, 1992). On the other hand, immigrant adolescents who respected and endorsed their parent's values were likely to experience lower levels of conflicts wit their parents (Fan, 1995).

Another variable related to the adaptation of adolescents is age. It is recognized that older youths, particularly adolescents, experience more psychological problems, probably because the conflicts between parent authority and individual independence are maximal during this period (Berry, 1997, Sam & Berry, 1995). It is also during adolescence that one has to search and establish one's own identity and deal with the transition between childhood and adulthood. For immigrant adolescents, the task is more difficult as they have to deal with these issues in the context of cultural transition and questions of ethnic identity.

Gender is another variable related to adaptation. Crystal, et al. (1994) found that high school girls from USA, Japan, and Taiwan reported more maladjustment, including stress and depression, than their male peers. Rosenthal (1984) also found that adolescent girls reported more parent-child conflict than boys. This issue of gender might have special relevance for immigrant girls, especially the situation when there are differences in sex role expectations between the original culture and the culture of the society of settlement. Sam and Berry (1995) found that immigrant girls reported more depressive tendencies and psychological symptoms.

The above variables are related to the psychological and sociocultural adaptation of all adolescents, immigrant or non-immigrants. There are, however, some variables that are specific to immigrant adolescents. One of the individual variables that result from intercultural contact is the acculturation strategy (Berry, Kim, Power, Young, & Bujaki, 1989) being pursued. These strategies take into account an individual's preferences with respect to two issues: cultural maintenance (to what extent individuals strive for the maintenance of their cultural identity); and contact and participation (to what extent individuals want to become involved with other cultural groups, particularly the host cultural group). When these two central issues are considered simultaneously, four possible acculturation strategies result. The assimilation strategy is the case where individuals do not wish to maintain their cultural identity and seek daily interaction with other cultures. In contrast, when non-dominant persons emphasize holding onto their original culture, and at the same time wish to avoid interaction with others, then the separation alternative is defined. When there is an interest in both maintaining one's original culture, and in daily interactions with other groups, integration is the option. Finally, marginalization is the case when there is little possibility or interest in cultural maintenance, and lift le interest in relations with others. Attitudes towards these four alternatives, and actual behaviors exhibiting them, together constitute an individual's acculturation strategy. Research evidence suggests that individuals who pursue the integration strategy have the most positive adaptation, while those who are marginalized by the process of acculturation are least well adapted (Berry & Sam, 1997). Chan (1987) found that among Chinese students in Australia, endorsement of Chinese values was positively correlated with academic achievement. Fan (1996) also found that degree of Chinese identification was positively correlated with academic achievement among Chinese-Australian students.

Of increasing importance in Australia's diverse society is an individual's experience of ethnic or racial discrimination. Both internationally (e.g., Fernando, 1993) and in Australia (Chan, 1987) the experience of being a victim of prejudice and discrimination is predictive of poorer adaptation.

Length of time in the receiving society is also thought to be relevant to immigrant adaptation. It is now recognized that the relationship between length of time in the receiving society and adaptation is variable (Berry, 1997) and it depends on the specific nature of experience and problem, and the personal resources of the individual. In general, academic performance improves with time (Fan, 1996) but the relationship between length of time in the receiving society and psychopathology is variable (Ward, 1996).

For group or societal level factors, one of the relevant factors here is society of origin. It is thought that the political, economic and demographic situation in the society of origin might determine the motivation for migration or the degree of voluntariness of migration. In this respect, refugees are often regarded as involuntary immigrants (Berry, 1997). In the present study, the majority of the parents of the Vietnamese-Australian adolescents came to Australia as refugees. In relation to psychopathology, refugees, or immigrants whose motivation for migration are mostly reactive, have been found to have more psychological problems than voluntary immigrants, or those whose motivation for migration is mostly proactive, seeking a better future (Wong-Rieger & Quintana, 1987). Furthermore, many of the Vietnamese immigrants who came to Australia are from a rural background, especially those who arrived after 1975 (Sue & Sue, 1990) and they may face additional adaptation difficulties in adjusting to life in urban cities. Chiu and Ring (1998) found that Vietnamese-American adolescents reported more negative life events and rated them as more stressful than Chinese-American adolescents. Fan (1996) and Luckey and Jupp (1990) found that immigrant students from a proactive migration background performed better in school and were more satisfied wit school than those from a reactive migration background.

Finally, as mentioned above, immigrant status is hypothesized to be associated with greater psychological morbidity (Klimidis, et al., 1994). Chang (1996) found that Asian-Americans reported more psychological symptoms than Caucasian-Americans. Huang, Leong and Wagner (1994) also reported that Asian-Americans exhibited more psychological distress than their Anglo-American counterparts. Klimidis, et al. (1994) found that immigrant adolescents in Australia reported lower self concept than Anglo-Australian adolescents.

The aims of this study are twofold. First, this study aims to examine factors related to the psychological and sociocultural adaptation of adolescents in general. Second, this study aims to examine factors related to the psychological and sociocultural adaptation of immigrant adolescents in particular. Third, this study aims to examine possible differences in patterns of adaptation between immigrant and non-immigrant adolescents. The hypotheses are:

1. Among adolescents, psychological and sociocultural adaptation are related to sense of personal control, family values, age and gender.

2. Among immigrant adolescents, psychological and sociocultural adaptation are related to sense of personal control, family values, age, gender, ethnic identity, acculturation strategies, length of time in receiving society, perceived discrimination, country of origin and motivation for migration.

3. Immigrant adolescents report more problems wit psychological and sociocultural adaptation than non-immigrant adolescents.

METHOD

Participants

There were 334 participants, with 174 Anglo-Australian adolescents (106 females, 68 males), 65 Vietnamese-Australian adolescents (46 females, 18 males, 1 unidentified) and 95 Chinese-Australian adolescents (46 females, 49 males). The classification was based on the participant's report of their ethnic backgrounds and that of their parents' ethnic backgrounds. Among the Vietnamese-Australian adolescents, the majority of them were born in Australia (n=40) or in Vietnam (n = 20) and among the Chinese-Australian adolescents, the majority were born in Australia (11=38) or Hong Kong (n=37). Among those born outside Australia, the mean length of residence in Australia for Chinese-Australians was 7.59 years ($\underline{SD}$ = 3.27 n = 57) and that for Vietnamese-Australians was 9.10 years ($\underline{SD}$ = 4 00 n = 21).

The participants were recruited through community groups such as churches, schools and through research method students, as part of their course requirement. Participants recruited through the schools were younger than those recruited through other means. This was because in some schools, only students from lower grades participated, due to administrative reasons. The mean age of Anglo-Australian participants was 14.71 ($\underline{SD}$ = 1.69) (female: 14.61, males: 14.87); the mean age of Vietnamese-Australian participants was 14.22 ($\underline{SD}$ = 1.57) (females: 14.33, males: 13.94) and the mean age of Chinese-Australian participants was 14.85 ($\underline{SD}$ = 1.69) (females: 14.54, males: 15.14).

For socio-economic status, in terms of father's occupation, the fathers of the Anglo-Australian participants were mainly skilled workers (25.6%) or professionals (25.0%), whereas the fathers of the Vietnamese-Australian participants were mainly unskilled (27%) or skilled workers (20.6%) and the fathers of the Chinese-Australian participants were mainly professionals (29.3%) or white collar workers (21.7%). The concentration of the Chinese-Australians in the professionals category and the Vietnamese-Australians in the unskilled or skilled workers categories is consistent with the general occupational profiles of the Hong Kong-born Chinese and Vietnamese-born in Australia (Coughian, 1998; Thomas, 1997).

Materials

The materials consisted of a questionnaire with 11 sections:

Demographic information. Participants were requested to indicate their age, gender, grade, place of birth, age of arrival in Australia (if born outside Australia), their own ethnicity, ethnicity of their parents and places of birth of their parents.

Family values. This was measured by a 14-item scale based on Nguyen and Williams (1989), Georgas (1989) and Georgas, Berry, Shaw, Christakopoulou, and Mylonas (1996). This scale was sub-divided into two scales, one with 10 items on parental authority (e.g., parents always knows what is best) and children's obligations (children should obey their parents) and the other with 4 items on children's rights (e.g., when a girls reaches the age of 16, it is all right for her to decide whom to go out with and when to go out). The participants indicated their degrees of agreement with each statement on a five-point scale. The reliability for children's obligation was .74 (.79 for Anglo-Australians, .78 for Vietnamese-Australians and .56 for Chinese-Australians). The reliability for children's fights was .84 (.83 for Anglo-Australians and Vietnamese-Australians, .76 for Chinese-Australians).

Acculturation strategy. The scale measuring acculturation strategy was based on the model of Berry, Kim, Power, Young and Bujaki (1989), measuring four acculturation attitudes (assimilation, integration, separation and marginalization) with regard to three domains, cultural traditions, marriage and language. This scale consisted of 20 items and participants rated their degrees of agreement with each statement on a five-point scale. The Anglo-Australian participants only answered a shortened version of 4 items on this scale, with one item per attitude. The reliability for assimilation was .54 (.55 for Vietnamese-Australians and .55 for Chinese-Australians). The reliability for separation was .55 (.64 for Vietnamese-Australians and .47 for Chinese-Australians). The reliability for integration was .23 (.18 for Vietnamese-Australians and .43 for Chinese-Australians). The reliability for marginalization was .63 (.65 for Vietnamese-Australians and .59 for Chinese-Australians).

Identity. Two forms of identity were measured, namely ethnic identity and Australian identity. Ethnic identity was measured by a 7-item scale based on Phinney (1992). An example is "I feel part of Chinese/Vietnamese culture". Australian identity was measured by a 3-item scale based on Phinney and Navarro (1997). An example is " I am proud of being Australian". Participants indicated their degrees of agreement wit these statements on a 5-point scale. The reliability for majority identification was .82 (.82 for Anglo-Australians, .66 for Vietnamese-Australians and .84 for Chinese-Australians). The reliability for ethnic identification was .87 (.84 for Vietnamese-Australians and .89 for Chinese-Australians).

School adjustment. This was measured by a 5-point scale made up of nine items (7 of which dealt with satisfaction with school; and two looking at school performance: average grade, and perception of teacher's evaluation), and was based on the work of Andersen (1982), Moss (1989), Wold (1995), Olweus (1989) and Sam (1994). The reliability was .62 (.63 for Anglo-Australians, .59 for Vietnamese-Australians and .52 for Chinese-Australians).

Behavior problems. These were measured by a 10-item scale that was an adaptation of Qiweus' (1989, 1994) and Bendixen & Olweus' (1999) anti-social behavior scale. A-5 point response category ranging from "Never" to "Several times in the course of a 12 month period" was used. The scale measured frequencies of behavior including bullying, sanctions, and other anti-social behaviors. The reliability was .82 (.81 for Anglo-Australians, .86 for Vietnamese-Australians and .67 for Chinese-Australians).

Self esteem. This was measured by the 10-item Rosenberg self esteem scale (Rosenberg, 1965). The items in the scale require respondents to report feelings about the self directly. In this study, a 5-point response category was used. The reliability was .77 (.78 for Anglo-Australians, .64 for Vietnamese-Australians and .79 for Chinese-Australians).

Perceived discrimination. This was measured by a 5-point scale consisting of seven items that measured perceived frequency of unfair treatment or non-acceptance due to one's ethnic background. The reliability was .86 (.86 for Vietnamese-Australians and .87 for Chinese-Australians). The Anglo-Australian participants did not have to answer this section. They only answered a shortened scale on acculturation attitudes.

Sense of personal control. This was measured by a 6-item scale that assessed the degree to which people felt a sense of mastery and personal control of their lives and was based on Connel (1985), Levenson (1981), Paulus (1983) and Pearlin and Schooler (1978). Participants rated their degree of agreement with each of the statements on a 5-point scale. The reliability was .76 (.72 for Anglo-Australians, .77 for Vietnamese-Australians and .76 for Chinese-Australians).

Life satisfaction. This was measured by a 5-item scale which is based on Diener, Emmons, Larsen, and Griffin's (1985) Satisfaction With Life Scale and was designed to measure global life satisfaction. A 5-point response category ranging from "strongly disagree" to "strongly agree" was used. The reliability was .82 (.82 for Anglo-Australians, .81 for Vietnamese-Australians and .83 for Chinese-Australians).

Psychological symptoms. This was measured by a 5-point scale with 15 items, with five items measuring each of the following three areas: depression, anxiety and psychosomatic symptoms. The scale was based on Beiser and Flemming (1986), Kinze, Manson, Vinh, Tolam, Anh, and Pho (1982), Kovacs (1980/1981), Mollica, Wyshak, deMarneffe, Khuon, and Lavelle (1987), Reynolds and Richmond (1985) and Robsinson, Shaver, and Wrightsman (1991). The overall reliability was .88 (.87 for Anglo-Australians, .89 for Vietnamese-Australians and .91 for Chinese-Australians). The reliability for the depression subscale was .82 (.80 for Anglo-Australians, .82 for Vietnamese-Australians and .86 for Chinese-Australians). The reliability for the anxiety subscale was .72 (.65 for Anglo-Australians, .74 for Vietnamese-Australians and .85 for Chinese-Australians). The reliability for the psychosomatic symptoms subscale was .77 (.78 for Anglo-Australians, .78 for Vietnamese-Australians and .76 for Chinese-Australians).

Procedures

Upon obtaining parental consent and permission from school authorities, participants were given the questionnaires. They could either complete the questionnaire individually at home or in small groups in schools. The questionnaires were then returned to the researchers directly or via various community groups.

RESULTS

There were five measures of psychological and sociocultural adaptation, including academic achievement (average grade in school), school adjustment, behavior problems, self esteem, life satisfaction and psychological symptoms (a combination of the summated values for anxiety, psychosomatic symptoms and depression). Regression analyses were used to determine significant predictors for adaptation. First, variables common to all adolescents were examined. They were age, gender, immigrant status, children's obligations towards parents, children's fights and sense of personal control.

Children's obligations toward parents ($\beta = .31$, $p < .001$), sense of personal control $\beta = .22$, $p < .00$ 1) and immigrant status ($\beta = .22$, $p < .00$ 1) were predictive of life satisfaction ($\underline{F}(6,325) = 10.45$, $p < .001$). Life satisfaction was positively related to the endorsement of children's obligations toward their parents, their sense of personal control and being a non-immigrant.

Gender ($\beta = -.12$, $p < .005$), sense of personal control ($\beta = -.16$, $p < .005$) and age ($\beta = .11$, $p < .05$) were predictive of psychological symptoms ($\underline{F}(6,325) = 3.62$, $p < .05$). Participants with a low sense of personal control reported more psychological symptoms while females and older participants reported more psychological symptoms.

Children's obligations toward their parents ($\beta = .15$ $p < .05$), age ($\beta = -.12$, $p < .05$) and immigrant status ($\beta = -.14$, $p < .05$) were predictive of school adjustment ($\underline{F}(6, 325) = 4.37$, $p < .00$ 1). Better school adjustment was predicted by a higher endorsement of children's obligations toward their parents as well as being younger and of immigrant status. The regression on academic achievement (average grade in school) was not significant.

Children's rights ($\beta = .14$, $p < .05$), gender ($\beta = .12$, $p < .05$), immigrant status ($\beta = .20$, p

< .001) and children's obligations toward their parents (β = - .15, p < .01) predicted behavioral problems ($\underline{F}$(6,325) = 8.83, p < .001). Males and non-immigrants and those who endorsed children's rights reported more behavior problems while those who endorsed children's obligations toward their parents reported fewer behavior problems.

Sense of personal control (β = .28, p < .001) and immigrant status (β = .18, p < .005) were predictive of self esteem ($\underline{F}$(6,325) = 8.62, p < .00 1). Higher levels of self esteem were predicted by a higher sense of personal control and being a non-immigrant.

The psychological and sociocultural adaptation variables were significantly correlated with one another, except for academic achievement and psychological symptoms, as well as behavior problems and self esteem. The highest correlation was between life satisfaction and self- esteem ($\underline{r}$ = .59, p < .001).

In the second stage of the analysis, predictors of psychological and sociocultural adaptation among immigrant and non-immigrant adolescents were separately examined. Among non-immigrant adolescent, the dependent variables included academic achievement, school adjustment, behavior problems, life satisfaction, self-esteem and psychological symptoms (determined through a combined value summing levels of anxiety, psychosomatic symptoms and depression). The independent variables were age, gender, children's obligations, children's fights, and sense of personal control.

Children's obligations toward parents (β = .29,2< .001), and sense of personal control (β = .34, p < .001) were predictive of life satisfaction ($\underline{F}$(5,167) = 9.05, p < .001). Life satisfaction was positively related to the endorsement of children's obligations toward their parents, and sense of personal control.

Children's obligations toward parents (β = -.20, p < .05), was predictive of psychological symptoms ($\underline{F}$(5,167) = 4.03, p < .01). Psychological symptoms were negatively related to children's obligation towards parents.

Gender (β =-.28 p < .001) was predictive of academic achievement (average grade in school), ($\underline{F}$(5,167) = 3.16, p < .01). Females performed better than males academically. The regression equation for school adjustment was not significant.

Though the regression for behavior problems was significant, ($\underline{F}$(5,167) = 2.50, p < .05), there was no variable which significantly predicted behavior problems.

Sense of personal control (β = .28, p < .001) was predictive of self esteem ($\underline{F}$(6,325) = 8.62, p < .001). Higher levels of self esteem was predicted by a higher sense of personal control.

For immigrant adolescents, the dependent variables included academic achievement, school adjustment, behavior problems, life satisfaction, self-esteem and psychological symptoms (determined through a combined value summing levels of anxiety, psychosomatic symptoms and depression). Predictors included age, children's obligations, children's fights, sense of personal control, and those specific to immigrant adolescents including ethnic identification, acculturation strategies and perceived discrimination.

Children's obligations toward their parents ($\beta = .27$, $p < .001$), perceived discrimination ($\beta = -.23$, $p < .005$) and length of time in receiving society ($\beta = -.20$, $p < .05$) predicted life satisfaction ($F(8,141) = 4.23$, $p < .001$). Among immigrant adolescents, higher life satisfaction was predicted by those who endorsed children's obligations toward their parents, who perceived less discrimination and had been in Australia for a shorter period of time.

Assimilation strategy ($\beta = -.23$, $p < .05$) and children's obligations toward their parents ($\beta = .18$, $p < .05$) predicted psychological symptoms ($F(8,141) = 2.36$, $p < .05$). Immigrant adolescents who endorsed the assimilation strategy reported fewer psychological symptoms whereas those who endorsed children's obligations towards parents reported more symptoms.

Children's obligations toward their parents ($\beta = .18$, $p < .05$) and marginalization strategy ($\beta = -.26$, $p < .01$) predicted school adjustment ($F(8,141) = 3.79$, $p < .001$). Immigrant adolescents who endorsed children's obligations toward their parents and a lesser marginalization strategy reported better school adjustment. Ethnic identification ($\beta = .21$, $p < .05$), assimilation ($\beta = .35$, $p < .001$) and marginalization strategies ($\beta = -.29$, $p < .005$) predicted academic achievement ($F(8,141) = 3.07$, $p < .005$). Immigrant adolescents who endorsed ethnic identification and assimilation strategy reported higher academic achievement whereas those that endorsed marginalization strategy reported poorer academic achievement.

Children's obligations toward their parents ($\beta = -.18$, $p < .05$), assimilation strategy ($\beta = -.24$, $p < .05$), children's fights ($\beta = .23$, $p < .005$), marginalization strategy ($\beta = .22$, $p < .05$) and perceived discrimination ($\beta = .26$, $p = .00\,1$) were predictive of behavioral problems ($F(8,141) = 5.27$, $p < .001$). Immigrant adolescents who endorsed children's obligations toward their parents and the assimilation strategy reported fewer behavior problems. Immigrant adolescents who endorsed children's fights, who adopted the marginalization strategy and who perceived more discrimination reported more behavior problems.

Sense of personal control ($\beta = .24$, $p < .005$) and perceived discrimination ($\beta = .18$, $p < .05$) predicted self esteem ($F(8,141) = 2.63$, $p = .01$). Immigrant adolescents who perceived a higher sense of personal control and little discrimination reported higher self esteem.

To examine differences in psychological and sociocultural adaptation, and the related measures, due to different countries of origin, a series of independent t tests were performed. Due to the problem of inflated alpha, Bonferroni adjustment was calculated and the new alpha level was .003. Chinese-Australians reported higher levels of school adjustment (mean = 39.31, $\underline{SD}$ =3 46) than Vietnamese-Australians (mean = 36 85, $\underline{SD}$ = 4.51). Chinese-Australians also reported higher academic achievement (mean = 457, $\underline{SD}$ = .52) than Vietnamese-Australians (mean = 3.97, $\underline{SD}$ = .85).

DISCUSSION

With regard to factors related to psychological and sociocultural adaptation, whether among immigrant or non-immigrant adolescents, family values and a sense of personal control appear to be the most important common predictors. High endorsement of children's obligations towards parents was positively related to the two psychological well-being outcome measures, school adjustment and life satisfaction, and negatively related to the maladaptive functioning outcome measure of behavior problems. Sense of personal control was also positively related to two of the psychological well-being measures, life satisfaction and self-esteem, and negatively related to the psychopathology measure of psychological symptoms. Endorsement of children's obligations towards parents can be interpreted as implying a respect for authority, and a sense of duty towards the family and this has been found to be important to the psychological well-being of adolescents.

Respect for authority and sense of personal control are related to different measures of adaptive and maladaptive functioning, and psychopathology and psychological well-being though they are both related to life satisfaction. Respect for authority is related to school adjustment and behavior problems and they are both related to the adolescent's functioning within the society, in relation to social rules and institutions. Sense of personal control is related to self-esteem and psychological symptoms, which are related to the individual's subjective internal psychological functioning. The results of the present findings are supportive of Searle and Ward's (1990) distinction of psychological and sociocultural adaptation distinction. Some respect for authority and sense of duty seem to be necessary for satisfactory functioning within social institutions but a sense of personal control is related to subjective well-being. Both, however, are related to overall life satisfaction.

Among non-immigrant adolescents, endorsement of children's obligations towards parents and sense of personal control were predictive of measures of internal psychological adaptation, namely, life satisfaction, psychological symptoms and self-esteem. Sense of personal control was related to measures of adaptive functioning such as life satisfaction and self esteem. However, these variables failed to predict external sociocultural adaptation such as school adjustment, academic achievement and behavior problems.

Among immigrant adolescents, endorsement of children's obligations to parents, acculturation strategies and perceived discrimination were found to be related to psychopathology and well-being. Specifically, marginalization strategy was related to the external sociocultural (behavioral) measures of school adjustment, academic achievement and behavior problems, and marginalization was consistently related to poorer or less adaptive outcomes. The relationship between marginalization and poor adaptation outcomes is consistent with other findings (e.g., Berry & Sam, 1997). Assimilation strategy was related to the reduction of psychopathology and maladaptive measures such as psychological symptoms and behavior problems, but was, in most cases, not related to improvement of well-being outcomes, except for academic achievement. Similar to marginalization strategy, perceived discrimination was related to poorer adaptation outcomes, in the sense that it was negatively related to measures of psychological well-being, life satisfaction and self esteem, but positively related to the maladaptive measure of behavior problems. Endorsement of children's obligation to parents, or some form of respect for authority and sense of duty, was positively related to well-being and adaptive measures of life satisfaction and school adjustment, and negatively related to the maladaptive measure of behavior problems. However, it was positively related to psychological symptoms.

On the whole, among immigrant adolescents, a sense of alienation seems to be related to increased psychopathology, poorer psychological well-being and maladaptive functioning. This can be reflected in the case of marginalization strategy where the adolescent does not feel attached to either culture. Perceived discrimination also reflects a sense of alienation from the society of settlement. On the other hand, a sense of connectedness with the family and the society of settlement, as reflected by an acceptance of parents' authority and sense of duty towards the family, and the intention to maintain contact with the society of settlement, is related to positive adaptation outcomes.

In examining the different factors related to adaptation among immigrant and non-immigrant adolescents, it is clear that a sense of connectedness with the family and a sense of personal control are related to the adaptation of non-immigrants. However, among immigrant adolescents, a sense of connectedness with the family and the receiving society, is related to most measures of adaptation, but a sense of personal control is only related to self-esteem. It seems that among immigrant adolescents who are cut off from their extended families and former social ties (if any), a sense of social connectedness is particularly important.

In terms of the migration-morbidity hypothesis, the results of the present study are mixed. Non-immigrant status was related to higher life satisfaction and self esteem scores, both being measures of internal psychological adaptation. Immigrant status, however, was related to better school adjustment and fewer behavior problems, both being measures of external sociocultural adaptation. It must, however, be pointed out that among immigrant adolescents, the Chinese-Australians reported significantly higher school adjustment scores than the Vietnamese-Australians.

For successful adaptation among adolescents, both immigrants and non-immigrants, the present results indicated tat a sense of control and a sense of connectedness to one's family and the larger society, are conducive to positive adaptation. A sense of alienation from the family and from the larger society is detrimental to adaptation. In other words, a sense of social connectedness is important for adaptation. This sense of social connectedness is especially important for immigrant adolescents.

In terms of service provision, counseling programs should be directed towards increasing the sense of personal control among adolescents, whether immigrants or non-immigrants. Furthermore, programs should also aim at maintaining a sense of connectedness with the family. For immigrant adolescents, services should focus at developing a sense of connectedness with the society of settlement.

534

ACKNOWLEDGMENTS

The data for the present study are part of the Australian research derived from the project of the International Comparative Study of Ethnocultural Youth (ICSEY). Questionnaire scales for ICSEY were developed by the research team of John W. Berry and Kyunghwa Kwak (Canada), Karmela Liebkind (Finland), Colette Sabatier (France), David L. Sam (Norway), Erkki Virta and Charles Westin (Sweden), and Jean Phinney (U.S.A). Members of the ICSEY project group are (in alphabetical order): J. W. Berry and K. Kwak (Canada), G Horenczyk (Israel), K. Liebkind (Finland), F. Neto (Portugal), C. Parra (Chile), J. Phinney (U.S.A.), C. Sabatier (France), D. L. Sam (Norway), D. Sang, C. Fan and R. Pe-pua (Australia), P. Schmitz (Germany), C. Westin and E. Virta (Sweden), P. Vedder and F. Van deVijver (The Netherlands).

REFERENCES

Anderson, C. (1982). The search for school climate: A review of the research. *Review of Educational Research, 53*, 368-420.

Australian Bureau of Statistics (1997). *1996 census of population and housing: Basic community profile catalogue.* Canberra: Commonwealth of Australia.

Australian Bureau of Statistics (2000, February). *Net overseas migration at record level in 1998-99.* Author.

Beiser, M. (1990). Mental health of refugees in resettlement countries. In W.H. Holtzman, & T.H. Bournemann (Eds.), *Mental health of immigrants and refugees* (pp. 50-65). Austin: Hogg Foundation.

Bendixen, M., & Olweus, D. (1999). Measurement of antisocial behavior in early adolescence and adolescence: Psychometric properties and substantive findings. *Criminal behavior and Mental Health, 9*, 323-354.

Berry, J.W. (1997). Immigration, acculturation, and adaptation. *Applied Psychology: An International Review, 46*, 5-68.

Berry, J.W., Kim, U., Power, S., Young, M., & Bujaki, M. (1989). Acculturation attitudes in plural societies. *Applied Psychology: An International Review, 38*, 185-206.

Berry, J.W., & Sam, D. (1997). Acculturation and adaptation. In J.W. Berry, M. Segall, & C. Kagiticibasi (Eds.), *Handbook of cross-cultural psychology, vol. 3 social behavior and applications.* Boston: Allyn & Bacon.

Chan, H. (1987). *The adaptation and achievement of Chinese students in Victoria.* Unpublished doctoral dissertation, Monash University, Melbourne.

Chang, B.C. (1996). Cultural differences in optimism, pessimism, and coping: Predictors of subsequent adjustment in Asian American and Caucasian American college students. *Journal of Counseling Psychology, 43*, 113-123.

Connell, J. (1985). A new multidimensional measure of children's perception of control. *Child Development, 56*, 941-1018.

Coma, L., & Mandinach, E.B. (1983). Using existing classroom data to explore relationships in a theoretical model of academic motivation. *Journal of Educational Research, 77*, 33-42.

Coughlan, J.E. (1998). The changing characteristics of Chinese migrants to Australia. In B. Sinn (Ed.), *The last half century of Chinese overseas.* Hong Kong: Hong Kong University Press.

Crittenden, K.S. (1996). Causal attribution processes among the Chinese. In M.H. Bond (Ed.),

The handbook of Chinese psychology. Hong Kong: Oxford University Press.

Crystal, D.S., Chen, C., Fuligni, A.J., & Stevenson, H.W. (1994). Psychological maladjustment and academic achievement: A cross-cultural study of Japanese, Chinese and American high school students. *Child Development, 65*, 738-753.

Deboer, G.E. (1985). Characteristics of male and female students who experienced success or failure in the first college science course. *Journal of Research in Science Teaching, 22*, 153-162.

Diener, B., Emmons, R. A., Larsen, R. J., & Griffin, A. (1985). The satisfaction with life scale. *Journal of Personality Assessment, 49*, 71-75.

Fan, C. (1995). The academic, psychological and social adjustment of Chinese immigrant girls in Australia. Unpublished doctoral dissertation, Monash University, Melbourne.

Fan, C. (1996). Family relationship, stress level and academic achievement of Chinese immigrant girls in Australia. *Australian Educational and Developmental Psychologist, 13(2)*, 63-73.

Feldman, S., Monte-Regnaud, R., & Rosenthal, D. (1992). When east moves west: the acculturation of values of Chinese adolescents in the U.S. and Australia. *Journal of Research on Adolescence, 2*, 147-173.

Fernando, S. (1993). Racism and xenophobia. *Innovations in Social Science Research, 6*, 9-19.

Georgas, J. (1989). Changing family values in Greece: From collectivist to individualist. *Journal of Cross-Cultural Psychology, 20*, 80-91.

Georgas, J., Berry, J., Shaw, A., Christopoulou, S., & Mylonas, K. (1996). Acculturation of Greek family values. *Journal of Cross-Cultural Psychology, 27*, 329-338.

Hountrus, P.T., & Scharf, M.C. (1970). Manifest anxiety and locus of control of low-achieving college males. *Journal of Psychology, 74*, 95-100.

Huang, K., Leong, F.T.L., & Wagner, N. (1994). Coping with peer stressors and associated dysphoria: Acculturation differences among Chinese-American children. *Counseling Psychology Quarterly, 7*, 53-68.

Kinze, J.D., Manson, S.M., Vinh, D.T., Tolan, N.T., Anh, B., & Pho, T.N. (1982). Development and validation of a Vietnamese-language depression rating scale. *American Journal of Psychiatry, 139*, 1276-1281.

Klimidis, S., Minas, I.H., Stuart, G., & Ata, A.W. (1994). Immigrant status and gender effects of psychopathology and self concept in adolescents: A test of the migrant-morbidity hypothesis. *Comprehensive Psychiatry, 35*, 393-404.

Kovacs, M. (1980/81). Rating scales to assess depression in school-aged children. *Acta*

Paedopsychaitry, 46, 305-315.

Levenson, H. (1981). Differentiating among internality, powerful others and chance. In H.M. Lefcourt (Ed.), *Research with locus of control construct* (pp.15-63). New York: Academic Press.

Lu, L. (1995). The relationship between subjective well-being and psychological variables in Taiwan. *The Journal of Social Psychology, 135*, 351-357.

Luckey, J., & Jupp, J.J. (1990). A survey of educational experiences in Australia of a representative sample of Indo-Chinese refugee high school students. *Australian Counseling Psychologist, 6*, 37-46.

Maughan, B. (1994). School influences. In M. Rutter & D. Hay (Eds.), *Development through life: A handbook for clinicians*. Oxford: Blackwell Science.

Mizokawa, D.T., & Ryckman, D.B. (1990). ,Attributions of academic success and failure: a comparison of six Asian-American ethnic groups. *Journal of Cross-Cultural Psychology, 21*, 434-451.

Mollica, R.F., Wyshak, G., deMameffe, D., Khuon, F., & Lavelle, J. (1987). Indochinese versions of the Hopkins symptom checklist-25: A screening instrument for the psychiatric care of refugees. *American Journal of Psychiatry, 44*, 496-500.

Moss, R. (1989): *Evaluating educational environments*. San Francisco: Jossey-Bass.

Nguyen, N., & Williams, H. (1989). Transition from east to west: Vietnamese adolescents and their parents. *Journal of the American Academy of Child and Adolescent Psychiatry, 28*, 505-515.

Olwcus, D. (1989). The prevalence and incidence in the study of antisocial behavior: Definition and measurement. In M. Mien (Ed.), *Cross-national research in self-reported crime and delinquency* (pp. 187-201). Dordrecht, Holland: Kluver Academic.

Olweus, D. (1994). *The revised Olweus Bully/Victim Questionnaire*. Bergen: Research Center for Health Promotion: University of Bergen.

Paulus, D.L. (1983). Sphere-specific measures of perceived control. *Journal of Personality and Social Psychology, 44*, 1253-65.

Pearlin, J. & Schooler, C. (1978). The structure of coping. *Journal of Health and Social Behavior, 19*, 2-21.

Phinney, J.S. (1992). The multi-group ethnic identity measure: A new scale for use with adolescents and young adults from diverse groups. *Journal of Adolescent Research, 7*, 156-176.

Phinney, J.S., & Devich-Navarro, M. (1997). Variations in bicultural identification among

African American and Mexican American adolescents. *Journal of Research in Adolescence, 7*, 3-32.

Ralph, A., Merralls, L., Hart, L., Porter, J.S., & Tan, A. (1995). Peer interactions, self concepts, locus of control, and avoidance of social situations of early adolescents. *Australian Journal of Psychology, 47*, 110-118.

Reynolds, C.R., & Richmond, B.O. (1985). *Revised Children's Manifest Anxiety Scale Manual.* Los Angeles: Western Psychological Services.

Robinson, J.P., Shaver, P.R., & Wrightsman, L.S. (Eds.). (1991). *Measures of personality and social psychological attitudes.* San Diego: Academic Press.

Rosenberg, M. (1965). *Society and the adolescent self-image.* Princeton: Princeton University Press.

Rosenthal, D. (1984). Intergenerational conflict and culture: A study of immigrant and non-immigrant adolescents and their parents. *Genetic Psychology Monographs, 109*, 53-75.

Rosenthal, D., & Feldman, S.S. (1991a). The influence of perceived family and personal factors on self reported school performance of Chinese and western high school students. *Journal of Research in Adolescence, 1*, 135-154.

Rosenthal, D., & Feldman, S.S. (1991b). The acculturation of Chinese immigrants: perceived effects on family functioning of length of residence in two cultural contexts. *Journal of Genetic Psychology, 27*, 19-31.

Sabatier, C., & Berry, J.W. (1997) *Adaptation sociale, estime de soi, et attitudes d'acculturation des adolescents de seconde generation.* Report to Social Sciences and Humanities Research Council of Canada.

Sam, D. L. (1994). School adaptation of young Vietnamese refugees in Norway. *Migration: European Journal of International Migration and Ethnic Relations.*

Sam, D., & Berry, J.W. (1995). Acculturative stress among young immigrants in Norway. *Scandinavian Journal of Psychology, 36*, 10-24.

Schcier, L.M., & Botvin, G.J. (1997). Psychosocial correlates of affective distress: Latent-variable models of male and female adolescents in a community sample. *Journal of Youth and Adolescence, 26*, 89-115.

Schwarzer, R., Hahn, A., & Schroder, H. (1994). Social integration and social support in a life crisis: effects of macrosocial change in East Germany. *American Journal of Community Psychology, 22*, 685-706.

Thomas, M. (1997). The Vietnamese in Australia. In J.B. Coughlan, & D.J. McNamara (Eds.), *Asians in Australia: Patterns of migration and settlement.* Melbourne: MacMillan

Education Australia Pty Ltd.

Walden, T.A., & Ramey, C.T. (1983). Locus of control and academic achievement: results from a preschool intervention program. *Journal of Educational Psychology, 75*, 347-358.

Willig, A.C., Harnisch, D.L., Hill, K., & Mach, M.L. (1983). Sociocultural and educational correlates of success-failure attributions and evaluation anxiety in the school setting for Black, Hispanic and Anglo children. *American Educational Research Journal, 20*, 385-410.

Ward, C. (1996). Acculturation. In D. Landis, & R. Bhagot (Eds.), *Handbook of intercultural training*. Thousand Oaks, CA: Sage.

Ward, C., & Kennedy, A. (1992). Locus of control, mood disturbance and social difficulty during cross-cultural transitions. *International Journal of Intercultural Relations, 16*, 175-194.

Wold, B. (1995). *Health behavior in school-aged children: A WHO cross-national survey (HSCB)*. Bergen: Research Center for Health Promotion, University of Bergen.

Wong-Rieger, D., & Quintana, D. (1987). Comparative acculturation of southeast Asian and Hispanic immigrants and sojourners. *International Journal of Intercultural Relations, 8*, 153-184.

AUTHOR AND SUBJECT INDEX

552

554